MEMORIAL AND GENEALOGICAL

RECORD

OF

TEXAS
(EAST)

CONTAINING BIOGRAPHICAL HISTORIES AND GE-
NEALOGICAL RECORDS OF MANY LEADING
MEN AND PROMINENT FAMILIES.

ILLUSTRATED.

Southern Historical Press
Greenville, South Carolina

This volume was reproduced from
An 1895 edition located in the
Publisher's private Library

Please direct all correspondence and orders to:

www.southernhistoricalpress.com
or
**SOUTHERN HISTORICAL PRESS, Inc.
PO BOX 1267
Greenville, SC   29601
southernhistoricalpress@gmail.com**

Originally published: Chicago, IL. 1895
New Material Copyright 1982
       By: The Silas Emmett Lucas, Jr.
ISBN #0-89308-300-3
All rights Reserved.
Printed in the United States of America

PREFACE.

THE publishers, with much pleasure, present this beautiful and interesting volume to their friends and patrons, for whom it is prepared. It will be found full of thrilling personal and historical reminiscences of the days when Texas was gaining her independence and her proud position among the sisterhood of states. The detailed family records will also be found of great present interest and future value. All sketches, after having been typewritten, were submitted by mail to the subject for correction or revision; still, no doubt, a few mistakes will be found which the publishers, as is their custom, stand ready to correct by special errata sheet to be sent to each purchaser, to be pasted in the book. We are satisfied our work will bear the closest scrutiny and sustain our well-known reputation for accuracy and fidelity.

THE PUBLISHERS.

TABLE OF CONTENTS.

Page.

De Soto and La Salle............. 17
Origin of the Name "Texas"...... 17
Location and Boundaries of the
 State........................... 17
Area of Land and Water.......... 17
Timber and Watercourses.......17,18
Elevation Above the Gulf........ 18
Mineral Resources...............18,19
Precious Stones, etc............. 19
First Catholic Missions.......... 19
Subsequent Missions.............19,20
Texas as a Mexican Province...... 20
Colonization of Texas by the
 French....................... 20
Advent of the Americans......... 20
The Austin Colony............... 21
Character of Government......... 22
Cruelty of the Indians..........22,23
Nolan, the Adventurer........... 23
Insurrection of Hidalgo.......... 23
Perry's Invasion of Texas........23,24
Long's Proclamation............. 24
Other Grants of Lands...........24,25
Flourishing Settlements.......... 25
Colonization Laws Infringed...... 25
Acts of Congress................. 25
Three Colonies Only............. 25
Lawlessness and Rebellion....... 26
Proceedings of Santa Anna....... 26
Attempts to Subdue the Colonists. 26
Texas Separated from Coahuila... 27
Santa Anna's Dictatorship....... 27
Beneficial Measures............. 28
Mexican Outrages............... 28
The Indians Aroused............. 29
Companies Organized and Drilled. 29
Open War...................... 29
Convention of 1835.............. 29
The Revolution Begun...........29,30
Troops Called for............... 30
Commission to the United States.. 30
Capture of San Antonio..........30,31
Conflict of State Authorities....... 31
Convention of March, 1836........ 31
Legal Plundering................ 45
Texas Republic Recognized by the
 United States................. 45

Page.

Laws and Internal Improvements. 45
"Lone Star State"—how Named... 46
Capital of Texas................. 46
List of Texan Executives........46,47
Constitution of 1868.............47,48
Texan School System 47,48
Normal Schools.................48,49
Agricultural College and Stations.. 49
Independence Declared.......... 31
Mexican Army Enters Texas...... 32
Americans Declared Outlaws...... 32
The Alamo Described...........32,33
Siege of the Alamo.............. 33
Fall of the Alamo............... 33
Heroism of the Texans........... 35
Battle of Colita................. 36
The Affair of San Jacinto.........36,37
Norris and Others............... 38
Defeat of the Comanches......... 38
Lamar's Scheme of Territorial Ex-
 pansion.......................38,39
Capture of His Command......... 39
Annexation to the United States
 proposed..................... 39
Opposition of the Mexicans....... 39
Declaration of Santa Anna....... 39
Letter of Houston............... 39
The Archive War................ 40
Troubles Over the "Neutral
 Ground"..................... 40
Independent Military Expeditions. 40
Battle of Mier.................. 40
Seventeen Ordered Executed...... 41
Annexation to the United States... 41
War Between Mexico and the
 United States................. 41
Texas in this War............... 41
Treaty of 1848................. 41
Territory Relinquished by Mexico. 41
Acts of Violence upon Mexicans.. 41
The Cart War.................. 42
Ordinance of Secession by Texas.. 42
Revolution of Cortina............ 42
Incidents of the Civil War........42,43
Texas Under Various Governments. 43
Early Officers of the State........ 43
Executives, etc.................. 44

	Page.		Page.
Financial Affairs	44	Newspapers	53
Counties Established	44	Railroad Systems	53,54
Towns Incorporated	44	Miles of Railroads	55
Sale of Lands	44	Population of Texas	55
State Asylums, etc	49,50	Names of Counties	55,58
Reformatories and Penitentiaries	50,51	Counties,—When Organized	55,58
Church Extension	53	Statistics	55,58

BIOGRAPHY AND MISCELLANY.

	Page.		Page.
Gen. Sam Houston, portrait, facing	61	Stephen W. Blount, biography	115
Gen. Sam Houston, biography	61	Neill McLennan, biography	116
Davy Crockett Burleson, biography	64	Adam Wangeman, biography	119
James H. Culberson, biography	66	Adam Wangeman, portrait, facing	119
Judge Bennett Blake, biography	69	Dr. Robert E. Rowell, biography	121
Judge Bennett Blake, portrait, facing	69	F. D. Futrell, biography	122
Mrs. Bennett Blake, portrait, facing	72	Capt. C. G. Graham, biography	124
Rev. W. H. McClelland, biography	75	Gen. Ben McCulloch, biography	125
Hon. John Adriance, biography	77	Popularity of Gen. McCulloch with the soldiery	127
Capt. Z. B. Garrison, biography	80	F. C. Ford, M. D., biography	128
Capt. J. H. Garrison, biography	83	Hon. James A. Wilkins, biography	129
Col. C. B. Kilgore, biography	85	Dr. Thomas H. Taylor, biography	131
Political career of Col. Kilgore	87	Judge W. H. Ford, biography	133
Col. James B. Hawkins, biography	88	James F. Crow, biography	135
Judge J. L. M. Pirtle, biography	89	R. G. Brown, biography	136
Ellis P. Bean, biography	91	Stephen Fuller Austin, biography	138
Bean's Adventure with a Serpent	92	Stephen Fuller Austin, portrait, facing	138
E. Reichardt, portrait, facing	94	J. H. Barham, M. D., biography	139
E. Reichardt, biography	94	Col. G. W. L. Dawson, biography	141
State Capitol, view	100	Hon. S. B. Maxey, biography	142
Dr. Robert Leake, biography	101	Dr. St. Cloud Cooper, biography	143
Hon. William Clark, portrait, facing	105	Julius B. Van Ness, biography	144
Hon. William Clark, biography	105	Gen. T. J. Rusk, biography	147
William T. Atkins, biography	107	Elisha Anglin, biography	147
John McConnell, biography	109	Escape of Mr. Anglin from the Indians	148
James Bowie, biography	110	Capt. George Thomas Todd, biography	149
Lorenzo De Gavala, biography	111	James W. Power, biography	153
David Crockett, biography	111	Henry Hodde, biography	154
Dr. J. H. Taylor, biography	113	Dr. H. I. Hilliard, biography	156
A. J. Roberson, biography	114	Wilson E. Hail, biography	157
Mr. and Mrs. A. J. Roberson, portraits, facing each other between pages	114,115	Col. S. C. Robertson, biography	158
		Judge Jeff Chaison, biography	162

Page.

Walter Boyd, Sr., biography.... 164
Jose Antonio Navarro, biography. 166
Hon. Joseph D. Sayers, biography.......................... 169
Scene on the Nueces River...... 169
W. W. Heartsill, biography..... 170
Hon. Marion DeKalb Taylor, biography................... 172
M. B. Lamar, biography......... 173
Capt. V. H. Claiborne, biography. 174
Dr. E. B. Blocker, biography.... 176
Capt. G. W. O'Brien, biography.. 177
Gen. Albert Sidney Johnston, biography................... 180
Battle Map of Shiloh........... 183
Samuel M. Ward, biography.... 184
Hon. Albert C. Horton, biography.......................... 186
William F. Jones, biography.... 191
William Umbdenstock, biography.......................... 192
Gen. H. E. McCulloch, biography. 193
James Graham Lowdon, biography.......................... 195
Capt. B. F. Houston, biography. 196
Benjamin R. Milam, biography.. 201
Dr. Thomas M. Marks, biography 201
Thomas N. Lockett, biography.. 203
David G. Burnett, biography.... 205
Capt. Milton Mast, biography... 205
Dr. Stephen T. Beasley, biography.......................... 207
William E. Singleton, biography. 209
Thomas Henry Mathis, biography.......................... 211
Thomas Henry Mathis, portrait, facing...................... 211
John J. Hayter, biography...... 217
Col. J. D. Buie, biography....... 218
Solomon A. Spellings, biography. 219
Hon. Herman Knittle, biography. 221
Gen. Webster Flanaghan, biography.......................... 223
A. S. Field, biography.......... 226
Major Elijah Pennington, biography.......................... 228
C. G. Burnett, biography........ 230
Albert H. Rowell, biography..... 232
Charles Cobb, Jr., biography.... 233
James L. Ford, biography...... 234
William McFadden, biography.. 235

Page.

Dr. Thomas H. Stallcup, biography.......................... 238
Hon. Nathan E. Dever, biography.......................... 239
William Watson, biography...... 241
Louis Webster, biography....... 243
Rison D. Gribble, biography.... 244
Dr. T. O. Hynes, biography..... 245
Dr. W. D. Northcutt, biography.......................... 247
Judge James M. Maxey, biography.......................... 248
Capt. Bolling Eldridge, biography.......................... 250
Dr. A. D. Strond, biography..... 252
Rev. Samuel M. Russell, biography.......................... 254
George W. Pettey, biography.... 256
John W. Addis, biography...... 257
Mrs. Kate Wood, biography..... 259
Judge James T. Maroney, biography.......................... 260
John J. Hoffman, biography..... 261
A. M. Clay, biography.......... 263
Thomas H. Langham, biography. 265
J. M. Marshall, biography....... 267
Theodore A. Low, Sr., biography. 269
Dr. H. F. Ford, biography....... 271
Major W. H. Pitts, biography... 272
Elmore D. Mayes, biography.... 275
Dr. C. B. Phillips, biography.... 276
Thomas J. Peel, biography...... 277
Rev. Father L. Wyer, biography. 278
Hon. Thomas C. Greenwood, biography...................... 279
Judge R. H. Coleman, biography. 282
J. D. Anderson, biography....... 283
Major Samuel B. Bales, biography.......................... 284
Jack Sutherland, biography..... 286
Judge Ed R. Kone, biography.. 288
George W. Watson, biography.. 291
Capt. R. D. Chapman, biography.......................... 292
Judge Leroy W. Cooper, biography.......................... 295
Judge Leroy W. Cooper, portrait, facing...................... 295
Frederick A. Piper, portrait, facing.......................... 211
Frederick A. Piper, biography... 297

Page.

Henry Exall, biography......... 300
Henry Exall, portrait, facing.... 211
Joseph Crockett Hart, biography 303
S. P. Simpson, biography....... 304
Erastus Smith, biography..... 306
Gen. Thomas N. Waul, biogra-
　phy........................ 306
Josiah Wilbarger, biography.... 307
Gen. James Hamilton, biography 309
John C. Hays, biography....... 310
Adventures of Col. Jack Hays.. 311
Capt. James W. Swisher, biogra-
　phy........................ 313
John L. Wilbarger, biography... 313
Col. George G. Alvord, biogra-
　phy........................ 314
Hon. Charles Stewart, biography. 315
Dr. J. F. Rosborough, biography. 317
Samuel Thurman, biography.... 319
A. H. Schluter, biography....... 321
John A. Fiedler, biography..... 323
Earle Adams, biography........ 324
W. B. Ward, biography......... 326
George Lord, biography........ 327
George Lord, portrait, facing... 327
Charles A. Leuschner, biography. 334
Dr. Robert T. Knox, biography.. 335
James W. Dickey, biography... 338
Judge Basley G. Neighbors, biog-
　raphy...................... 341
David S. H. Darst, biography.... 343
Capt. W. L. Foster, biography.. 345
James H. Moore, biography.... 347
Dr. Peter C. Woods, biography.. 350
John Hallet, biography........ 351
Judge John O'Neill, biography.. 354
Major Israel B. Donelson, biogra-
　phy........................ 355
Letter from Mrs. Logan........ 356
Carnot Bellinger, biography.... 358
Richard J. Burgess, biography... 361
Judge Felix J. Hart, biography. 363
Frank R. Pridham, biography... 365
Joseph M. Bickford, biography.. 367
Capt. John L. Lane, biography.. 368

Page.

Walter Little, biography........ 370
Virgil S. Robb, biography....... 372
Louis Turner, biography....... 376
James C. Odom, biography..... 378
Major Edward Burleson, biogra-
　phy........................ 381
Crawford Burnett, biography... 385
John Williams, biography...... 387
Judge Joseph O'Connor, biogra-
　phy........................ 388
Capt. Ferg. Kyle, biography..... 391
Hon. Edward H. Ragan, biogra-
　phy........................ 395
Rev. William J. Joyce, biography. 398
Mrs. Sarah Ann Braches, biogra-
　phy........................ 400
Joel W. Robison, biography..... 407
Mrs. Tobitha Killough, biogra-
　phy........................ 410
Col. John J. Myers, biography.. 413
"Hunters of Kentucky"......... 414
Judge John P. Bell, biography.. 415
William Armstrong, biography.. 418
Jacob Hill, biography.......... 420
Thomas Sterne, biography...... 421
Judge Charles Riley, biography. 423
Judge Don E. R. Braman, biogra-
　phy 425
Bishop Alexander Gregg, biogra-
　phy 427
Isaac H. Julian, biography...... 431
Robert W. Pierce, biography... 433
Gen. W. H. Young, biography... 438
Jesse J. Harrison, biography.... 440
E. Mullen, biography.......... 441
E. Mullen, portrait, facing...... 441
Clarence W. McNeil, biography.. 443
Judge W. J. Phillips, biogra-
　phy........................ 445
William H. Wheeler, biography. 447
Abnus B. Kerr, biography...... 449
Hon. James H. McLeary, biogra-
　phy 454
Col. F. M. Hicks, biography..... 461
Col. S. M. Blount, biography.... 465

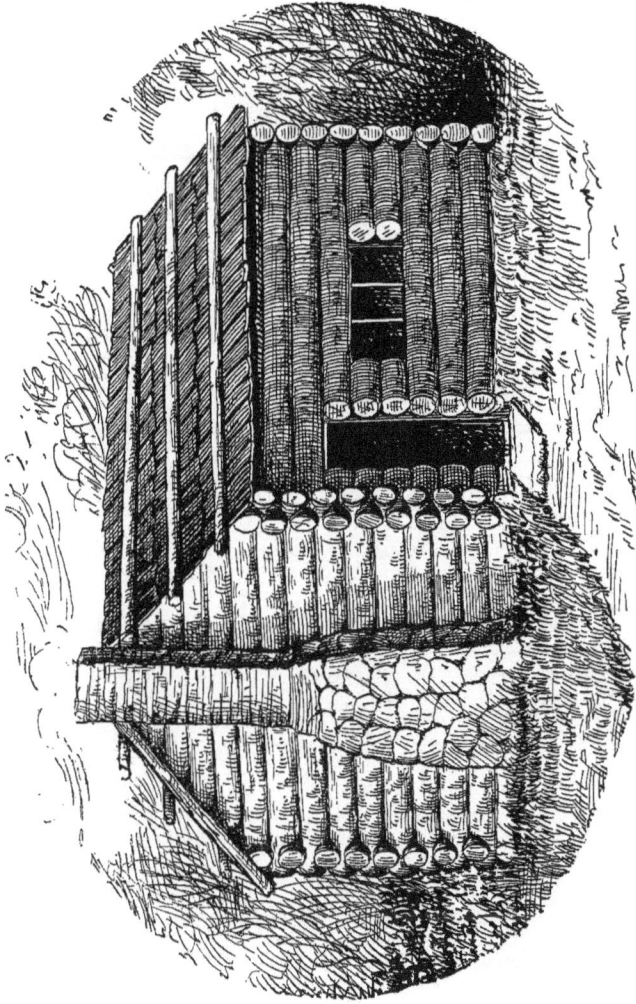

TYPICAL LOG CABIN.

HISTORY OF TEXAS.

THE history of Texas, like the State herself, interests the student and political economist, as it does the ordinary reader. Within its boundaries, the first great explorer of the Gulf region, De Soto,* turned from his westward course toward the Mississippi in 1542, and there also, the chivalrous Robert Cavalier de La Salle, a French traveler, laid down his life March 19, 1687, after having explored the Mississippi to its mouth and the Gulf Coast beyond the mouth of the Trinity.

According to the various authorities, there are several derivations of the name Texas: 1, Spanish, tejas (roof-tiles), because the inhabitants had roofed houses; 2, old Spanish or Celtiberian, denoting a plain; 3, an Indian word signifying friend; 4, another Indian word meaning paradise, or a beautiful land; 5, a common termination of several tribal names in Indian, as Tlaxcaltecas, Chlolutecas, Cuitlachtecas, and Zacatecas.

It is located in the extreme southern part of the United States, between the 26th and 36th parallels of north latitude and the 17th and 32nd meridians of longitude. The distance between the extreme northern and southern points is nearly 740 miles, and about 825 miles from east to west. Custom has divided the State geographically into five parts, namely: Central, northern, southern, eastern and western Texas, though the dividing lines are not well defined. The country lying east of the 19th degree of longitude and north of the 30th parallel of latitude, and known as "East Texas," is characterized by a long range of hills running in an irregular line from northeast to southwest, and containing large deposits of brown hematite iron ore. It is also marked by a heavy growth of timber, consisting principally of forests of pine, oak and hickory.

Texas has an area of 271,856 square miles of land, and 2,510 square miles of water surface, the latter consisting of lakes and bays, making a total of 274,366 square miles, equal to about 8.7 per cent. of the entire area of the United States and Territories. It is much the largest State in the Union, being six times larger than New York, seven times as large as Ohio, and 100,000 square miles larger than all the Eastern and Middle States, including Delaware and Maryland.

The Gulf Coast is thus described by Prof. Loughridge, of the United States Census Bureau: "The coast of Texas presents features different from those of any other State, for while in many other States the mainland coast is greatly cut up into large bays, extending many miles inland, it is here bordered by an almost continuous chain of islands and peninsulas (the latter

---

*In Caddo parish, Louisiana, and in the neighborhood of Marshall, Texas, evidences of De Soto's travels have been unearthed, though history does not state positively that the explorer was ever within her present boundaries.

2   17

having the same trend as the islands). The Gulf border of this chain is a very regular line southwest from the mouth of the Sabine River or lake to near Corpus Christi, which occupies the highest point on the entire coast, and thence turns with a regular curve south and slightly southeast to Mexico."

The territory east of the timber region and north of the Gulf, as above outlined, is a vast open plain composed of gently rolling prairies and gradual elevations. It is covered with a luxuriant growth of native grasses and dotted by an occasional mott of timber, and extends to the Red River on the north and the mountain ranges of the west and northwest. The water-courses and ravines are usually fringed with a growth of hackberry, ash, elm, cottonwood, pecan, walnut and the various oaks. West and northwest lie the hills and mountain ranges of the State, which are continuations of the mountains of Mexico, New Mexico and Colorado. In the extreme northwest, bordering Kansas on the south and New Mexico on the west, is the elevated table land formerly known as the Llano Estacado, or Staked Plains. It is now designated as the Panhandle of Texas, and is destined to be one of the best agricultural and stock-raising sections of the State. On a line north of Austin and San Antonio, and running in a southwesterly direction, there is a low range of hills that marks a change in the topography of the country. Westward it is more broken and the elevations more abrupt. The valleys are broad and the lands very fertile.

The water surface of Texas is estimated at 2,510 square miles. Of this number, 800 square miles are accredited to the rivers and smaller streams which drain the State. The balance consists of bays which lie along the coast of the Gulf of Mexico, and small inland lakes. The principal rivers are the Brazos, which drains 35,000 square miles; the Red River, 29,000 square miles in Texas; the Colorado, 25,000 square miles; the Trinity, 17,000; the Neuces, 16,000; the San Antonio, the Guadalupe, the Rio Grande, the Pecos, the Neches, the Sulphur Fork, the Sabine, San Marcos, Canadian, and Caney, with their feeders.

The figures below denote the elevation above sea level, in feet, of points named:

Galveston 40, Indianola 26, Brownsville 43, Palestine 495, Corsicana 448, Denison 767, Austin 513, San Antonio 676, Fort Ewell 200, Fort Chadbourne 2,120, Jacksboro 1,133, Henrietta 915, Fort Concho 1,888, Fort Stockton 3,050, El Paso 3,370, Fort Davis 4,918, Eagle Pass 800, Fort Elliott 2,500, Silver Falls 3,800, Midland 2,779.

The elevation of the land above the water dates to the middle of the cretaceous time, and is contemporary with the movements that created the Rocky Mountains. The strata, excepting the paleozoic groups, yield easily to disintegration. Eruptive masses are found in the trans-Pecos country and granitic masses in the Central and trans-Pecos paleozoic deposits.

The mineral resources of the State received very little attention until recent years. Silver and lead ores exist in the trans-Pecos region. In Llano and Mason counties silver and gold quartz were mined; copper ores exist in the drift of the gypsum country, and iron in the tertiary formations of Eastern Texas. Wood for fuel abounds in Eastern Texas, but becomes scarcer toward the west, until the mesquite root or Mexican dagger are welcome to the fire-builders. A lignite bed exists from the Sabine River, in Sabine County, west to the Red River, being found in fifty-four counties.

Coke and gas are produced from this deposit. The bituminous coal fields are known as the Brazos or Northern, and the Colorado or Southern. The linear extent of the outcrops of seams No. 1 and No. 7 is 250 miles, and the area 2,500 square miles. Asphaltum is found in Hardin and Liberty counties, as well as throughout the tertiary and cretaceous formations; tar springs are numerous, while oil is found in the Nacogdoches district, associated with natural gas. A phosphate of lime, called apatate, bat guano, gypsum, greensand marl and calcareous marls are counted among the natural fertilizers found throughout the State. Fictile materials, such as glass and porcelain sands, pottery clays, and kaolin are abundant, while granite, porphyry, marble, limestone, sandstone, slate, lithographic stone and cement materials may be quarried in the State. From the Louisiana line, 150 miles southwest, iron ore is found, of various values. The laminated ores are dark brown, ranging to black; the nodular, or geode ores, range from buff to brown in color, and the conglomerate, found in the sand, of a sandy color. Hematite ironstone, hematite and magnetite, abound near the Wolf crossing of the Colorado River; between the Packsaddle and Riley mountains, and in the Iron Mountain belt. Copper ores are found in Hardeman, Archer, Haskell, Throckmorton and other counties in that section of the State. Lead and zinc ores are found in the Riley Mountains, Burnett and adjoining counties. Gold has been panned in the Colorado River, while the quartz of the Quitman Mountains contain the yellow metal. In Presidio County silver ore has been profitably worked. In Burnett and Mason counties tin ore has been mined, as well as mercury, manganese and bismuth. Precious stones, such as the garnet, chalcedony, carnelian, amethyst and agate, as well as the pearls of the Llano, Concha and Colorado rivers show Texas to be rich in these valuable little things. Salt, sulphur, graphite, ochers, alkalies, niter, alum, epsomite and strontia are found in abundance, so that, were the mineral deposits developed, Texas would not only be independent of the outside world for their supply, but might also supply that outside world.

The recorded history of the Caucasian in Texas may be said to begin in 1580, when Catholic missionaries from Mexico City established churches at El Paso and Santa Fé, and ventured eastward toward the Mississippi, preaching to the various Indian tribes and founding missions among them. The early Spanish (Catholic) missions, within the present boundaries of Texas, were established by Franciscan monks, under the auspices of the Spanish government, and were called presidios. They consisted of a chapel for worship, the cells for the monks, the dwellings for the inhabitants, and a fort for defense. The mission was, of course, under the control of the ecclesiastical power, and the military force was under an officer of the army, who, in most matters, was under the control of the priest. A list of the principal missions is as follows: In 1690 the mission of San Francisco was established on the Lavaca River, at Fort St. Louis, by the Spanish fathers, under Captain Alonzo de Leon. In the same year the mission of San Juan Bautista was founded on the Rio Grande River. In 1714 the priests, accompanying Captain Ramon, established the mission of San Bernard, also the mission of Adayes, among the Indians of that name, fifteen miles west of Natchitoches. In 1715 was established the mission of Dolores, west of the Sabine, among the Orquisaco Indians. In the same year, one among the Nacogdoches Indians, near the site of the present town of that name; also another among the Aes

Indians, near the site of the present town of San Augustine. The mission and fortress of San Antonio de Valero was soon after this established on the San Pedro River, near the site of the present city of San Antonio. In 1721 a post and mission were established at the crossing of the Neches, and another on the bay of San Bernard, called Our Lady of the Loretto. In the same year the mission of La Bahia (the bay) was established at the lower crossing of the San Antonio River. In 1730 the church of San Fernando, in the present city of San Antonio, was founded. In 1731 was established, not far from the same place, the mission La Purisima Concepcion de Acuna. All the buildings are yet standing.

Under the old Mexican regime Texas was a province controlled by a "commandant," who resided at Chihuahua, and whose powers in this control were independent of the viceroy. Each province was ruled by a military and political governor, who, by his delegated powers, had cognizance of all causes, being dependent as regards military matters upon the commandant-general. In financial affairs he was subject to the intendant at San Luis Potosi, with recourse to the supreme council of finance at the City of Mexico.

The colonization of Texas by the French was commenced on New Year's Day, 1685, when the merchantmen and frigates of De Beaujeau's fleet anchored near the entrance to Matagorda Bay, Lavaca, and disembarked stores and colonists. Subsequently De Beaujeau acted independently of La Salle and sailed for home on the King's frigate, leaving a ship at the disposal of the colonists to escape from such a dreary land. On that ship La Salle set out for the mouth of the Mississippi, so that he could proceed northward to Fort St. Louis, where Lieutenant Tonti was in command, procure provisions for the colonists and give them hope until the soil would yield its fruits. The vessel was wrecked in the Gulf, but the explorer, escaping, returned to Matagorda to apprise his friends of the wreck and to prepare for an overland expedition to Fort St. Louis. In March, 1687, he with Père Anastace and nineteen men set out on the long journey, but on the 19th of the month, a mutiny took place in which La Salle's nephew, a few of his trusted lieutenants and himself were killed. Shortly after, Spanish troops captured the survivors of the mutiny and the colonists, condemned all the guilty parties to the mines, sent the priests to France, adopted the colonists and summarily closed French designs on Texas until 1817, when St. Denis the commander of Natchitoches in Louisiana attempted to reintroduce French traders beyond the Sabine.

When the purchase of Louisiana was proclaimed in 1803, adventurers and fugitives from justice flocked into Texas, believing that any crimes or conspiracies, against the residents of that part of Mexico, which they might commit, would escape punishment. The great majority of them were unprincipled desperadoes, like Nolan or his Mexican associates—men who would at all times rather rob than earn a livelihood honestly. When Mexico cast off the Spanish viceroys, English-speaking colonists came to cultivate the rich lands. The principal Anglo-Saxon settlements at the beginning of the present century were San Antonio de Bejar, with about 2,000 inhabitants; La Bahia del Espiritu Santo, now Goliad, about 1,400; and Nacogdoches, with 500.

Nacogdoches was first settled by Anglo-Americans in 1822–23, when many of the emigrants who left the United States with the view of joining Austin's colony stopped at this place. The little trade carried on was effected with Mexico, by way of Monterey and Monclova, and with New Orleans through

Natchitoches; the latter, however, was contraband. In 1806 Texas was allowed a port, namely, at Bahia de San Bernardo. The exchange for merchandise consisted in specie, horses and mules.

After the fall of Napoleon, two refugees from France, Generals Lallemand and Rigault, concluded to try Texas as a place of residence, although they received no reply to their request for a permission to do so from the Spanish court. In March, 1818, Lallemand, with 120 settlers, sailed from New Orleans, landed at Galveston Bay and selected a spot on the Trinity River about twelve miles above its mouth, and began to fortify the post. These colonists issued a proclamation that they had settled there to remain, earning their livelihood by the peaceable pursuits of agriculture and the chase, and would defend their settlement, but, after the drought of 1818 and the destruction of the crops, several families left the place, and the Mexicans showed the remaining few that the laws of the territory had to be observed and taxes paid to regularly constituted officers.

The treaty of amity of February 22, 1819, having confirmed her in the possession of Texas, Spain felt herself in a position to remove the exclusion of Anglo-Americans as colonists in her territory, which hitherto had been insisted on in all colonization schemes. Moses Austin saw in this too liberal policy an opportunity to enrich himself. He was a native of Durham, Conn., but in 1797 resided in Missouri, whence he moved to Northern Louisiana in 1799. His son, Stephen Fuller Austin, of New Orleans, received a grant of land on the Brazos from the Mexican authorities, the condition being the settlement thereon of 300 families, who were to receive 640 acres for the father, 320 for the mother, and 100 acres for each child. The price, 12½ cents an acre, to be paid in installments, was levied to pay expenses of transfer and review.

The first immigrants of the Austin colony arrived in December, 1821, settling on the Brazos River at the Bahia crossing, mainly in what is now Austin County; but many difficulties and hardships were encountered. Shipments of supplies from New Orleans failed to reach them, and they had to subsist too much on the products of the chase; and this was dangerous on account of the hostile Indians. During the spring of 1822 Austin went to San Antonio to report progress, and there learned for the first time that under the change in political affairs he would have to obtain from the Mexican congress a confirmation of the grant conceded to his father by the Spanish government, and receive special instructions relative to the distribution of land and other details connected with the grant. This was a sore disappointment. He would have to travel 1,200 miles by land on roads infested by banditti and deserters, and he was ill prepared for such a journey. Nevertheless, in ragged clothes and a blanket, he disguised himself as a poor traveler going to Mexico to petition for compensation for services in the revolution, and unflinchingly started out on the long and perilous journey.

While on his way to the City of Mexico, with but two persons in company, arriving at San Antonio, he (Austin) was told that it was dangerous to proceed without an escort, for a war party of Comanches was abroad. The savages did intercept him and robbed him, but on representations to the chief, his property was restored and permit given to proceed. On April 19, 1822, Austin arrived in Mexico City, but, owing to the delays of the administration, was kept there for about three months. Returning to the Brazos, he found only a few of his colonists there, yet by 1824 he had the 300 families well established and the colony in a prosperous condition. Himself being administrator of civil and military affairs, he ruled like a feudal lord—kind to his friends, hostile to his enemies. Although Austin was exact in his administration of justice and extravagantly benevolent to the needy, there were many in the colony disposed to complain and make trouble. In the United States and Europe the impression began to prevail that Austin's early colonists were in great part fugitives from justice; but he maintained, with every show of fact and reason, that his colony was as moral as any community in the States.

The limits of the county were undefined by the law, and the immigrants were allowed to settle at various distances from the center according to their own free will. In response to Austin's petition, the government allowed him to introduce 500 more families to locate upon the unoccupied lands lying between the tracts already occupied by his colonists. Straggling settlements were made between the Brazos and the Sabine, but not until 1833 was there an appreciable influx of these spirits, who will obtain money or property justly or otherwise.

Two causes seem to have operated to prevent the earlier settlement of the province of Texas and to retard the development of its resources. In the first place the jealous policy of the old Spanish government uniformly discouraged all attempts to penetrate into the country. It was the policy of the government that completely locked up Texas and all the Spanish-American possessions, and excluded even visitors and travelers. It was a favorite saying of the Spanish Captain-general of the internal provinces, Don Nemisio Salcedo, that he would stop the birds from flying over the boundary line between Texas and the United States if it were in his power! This rigid policy prevented any one from attempting to explore the country by land, for perpetual imprisonment was the inevitable result of detection and capture. In the second place, the Carancahua Indians, who inhabited the coast, were represented to be of a character uncommonly ferocious. They were popularly believed to be cannibals; and many tales of most frightful import were told of them—such as, if true, it must be acknowledged, were sufficiently appalling to check the enterprise and damp the ardor of the most eager adventurer. These representations of the character of the Carancahuas, though in a measure true, were greatly exaggerated.

Prior to 1833, fully 20,000 English speaking persons inhabited Texas between the Sabine and Colorado rivers. Though the heads of families had conformed to the articles of citizenship, there is scarcely an instance where the oath was observed in any particular, for every adventurer who preached sedition in secret was safe in the homes of the very people to whom the Mexican Republic gave fertile lands and many rare privileges. The pages devoted to military and political affairs speak very plainly of the relations of the new inhabitants to Mexico, of their wars and of their repeated efforts to establish an independent republic. The last decade brought many advantages to the State. Great numbers of industrious Northern agriculturists settled there; villages were transformed into beautiful cities; railroad lines were constructed in all directions, and Texas became truly a State in population and wealth, as it was in name, organization and area.

THE CHURCH OF THE ALAMO. SAN ANTONIO, TEXAS.

JACOBS, SC.
S. A.

From 1801 to 1864, the story of military affairs in this extreme south-western State of the Union is one of romance, full of startling realities and altogether interesting in their number, personnel, desperation, machiavelianism and disregard for human life on the part of ruler and rebel. It was a territory indeed where, when treason succeeded, no one dared to call it treason, until a superior power rose above the ruin of its predecessor. Life was a bagatelle, given to the adventurers to be frittered away in petty insurrections and piracies, or, when opportunities in these directions failed, in attacks upon the Kiowa or Comanche. Beginning with Nolan, in 1801, and ending with Palo Alto, May 13, 1864, the story of Texas in its military bearing is one where gallantry, deviltry, heroism, patriotism and machiavelianism are so mixed that no one can tell where the one begins and the other ends.

Philip Nolan, whose name is associated with the first English speaking adventurers in Texas, was raised in the wild atmosphere of Natchez, by a resident of that town. He it was who made the first map of Texas other than the charts of Spanish and French travelers. He was versed in astron-omy, was a student of geography, a surveyor, soldier, horse dealer and stealer and as unprincipled as Aaron Burr, who fashioned his public life after that of Nolan. In July, 1797, he procured a passport to visit Texas for the purpose of buying horses. To do so he swore falsely. At the close of that month he had 1,297 head of horses in the Trinity River pastures, which he drove to Natchez during the fall. In 1800 his plans for the conquest of Texas were matured, and early in 1801 put in practice. On March 21, 1801, Lieutenant Muzquiz, with sixty-eight Spanish regulars and thirty-two volunteers, attacked the entrenched camp of Nolan's army. At nine o'clock Nolan was killed, and his fourteen American, one Creole and seven Mexican fol-lowers, with two slaves, made prisoners. Three of them were wounded, one died, one—Ephraim Blackburn—was hanged at Chihuahua, November 11, 1807, and the others were sent to the mines, where all died save Ellis Bean, who returned to Mississippi.

The Louisiana boundary troubles next engaged the attention of the Texan authorities, but the question was settled amicably by making the Sabine River the Western line of United States territory.

The attempt of Aaron Burr to conquer not only Texas but also Mexico, and proclaim himself emperor and successor to the Montezumas, irritated the Mexican authorities. The plans of Burr were so patent that the United States troops had to break up his flotilla and order the arrest of the disturber.

The insurrection of Hidalgo, followed in 1810. This was intensified in January, 1811, when Juan Bautista Casas, captured the governor and officials of Texas. On March 1, following, Zambrano and a *posse* captured Casas and his officers, and restored the vice-regal authority. In 1812, Bernardo Gutierrez de Lara, and Augustus Magee, of Natchitoches, organized the out-laws of Mississippi and the border, and with 800 of those desperadoes entered Texas. On April 1, 1813, Magee's force captured San Antonio, the seat of government, had a council of thirteen members elected, and appointed Gutierrez, governor. The new rulers reveled in blood for a few weeks, butch-ering their opponents in a wholesale manner, and this continued on a smaller scale until 1814, when the Spaniards restored law and order.

In 1815, shortly after the defeat of the British at New Orleans, an adven-turer named Perry really advertised his intention to invade Texas, and, with the connivance of Jose Manuel de Herrera, did establish a State government in 1816, making Matagorda the capital. This adventure ended with the suicide of Perry and the execution of many of his followers; though Commodore Aury continued his piratical doings in the Gulf of Mexico for some time after. Among the troops of Perry, and the marines of Aury, were almost 1,000 of Lafitte's pirates. Indeed, Lafitte, himself, built a residence at Campeachy, near Galveston, where he resided until his second pirate colony was broken up by the United States officers on Mexican territory.

In March, 1818, the Lallemand colonists, 120 in all, came from New Orleans to a point twelve miles above the mouth of the Trinity, and proclaimed their intention of protecting themselves against all comers, while attending to their own affairs. Failure of the first season's crops left the colony in a feeble condition, and the Mexican authorities had little trouble in establishing their authority over it.

The treaty of February 22, 1819, negotiated by the Spanish Minister at Washington, defined the present eastern boundary of Texas; but the Spanish king failed to ratify it, and other disagreements resulted; but on February 28, 1821, the treaty was accepted by the contracting parties. Natchez was then a hotbed of antipathy to French and Spanish authority in North America, as it was from the time that Ellicott and his followers appeared first on the bluff.

In June, 1819 or 1820, James Long and seventy-five men set out for Nacogdoches, Texas, where the old rebel Gutierrez and one Samuel Davenport joined him. Long organized a supreme council, appointed himself President, and on June 23, these self appointed statesmen proclaimed Texas a free and independent Republic.

Long sought the aid of Lafitte at Galveston, but the arch pirate told him it was useless to oppose Mexico without an overwhelming force. *En route* to Lafitte's home, President Long learned that 700 Mexicans, under Colonel Perez, were advancing to destroy his citadel; and sent a dispatch to Cook, his military agent, to drive them back while he himself waited developments at a safe distance. His dupes were killed or captured, while President Long retired to New Orleans. There he met two foolhardy Mexicans—Milam and Trespalacios, and with them organized another expedition early in 1821; entered Texas, were driven off and returned to Orleans to squander their lives away in debauchery. Long was killed there in 1822, and the other leaders died unknown. The doings of Long created tribulations for the legitimate English and French speaking colonists of Eastern Mexico, and brought ruin to the greater number who could in any way be connected with their revolutionary propaganda.

The final revolution may be said to have been born in October, 1825, when Hayden Edwards, returned to Texas to fill his contract with the Texan Governor. It appears that he received a grant of lands, surrounding Nacogdoches, provided he would settle thereon 800 families; but on the date stated found many claimants on such lands and a population unfriendly to his personality and his claims. The election of an álcalde in December, led to the rejection of Chaplin, the son-in-law of Edwards, and to a number of petty acts contrary to the spirit of justice. The annulment of the grant was based on right, as Edwards did not fulfill his part of the contract; so that its subsequent division between David G. Burnett and Joseph Vehlein, was considered equitable, and the action of the new grantees won many immigrants or settlers.

Dewitt, although his first settlers were temporarily driven off by Indians, had laid out the town of Gonzalez in 1825, naming it after Rafael Gonzalez, a temporary governor of the State, and during 1827–'28 he succeeded in introducing considerable numbers of colonists. In De Leon's grant the town of Victoria was founded, and La Bahia del Espiritu Santo had developed into a town of such appreciable dimensions that in 1829 it was raised to the rank of a villa, and the high sounding title of Goliad given to it. Filisola, in an endeavor to wrench an anagram out of Hidalgo's name, spelled the name Golhiad. On the Brazos a flourishing settlement called Brazoria had also sprung up. However, the experience which the Mexican government had with the Fredonians (Edwards' colonists) caused them to be more watchful of the movements of American immigrants. Under the liberal and non-aggressive policy of Guerrero the colonists were left pretty much to themselves, and he even aided them in the abolition of slavery. But when he was overthrown, in December, 1829, and Bustamante seized the helm of government, the sleeping tiger of Mexican suspicion and belligerency arose and showed its teeth.

Lucas Alaman, the Minister of Relations, memorialized Congress, Feb. 8, 1830, showing the carelessness of the State of Coahuila and Texas in carrying out the colonization laws;—that the orders providing that no more than the number of families designated in a contract should settle on the corresponding grant, and that colonies near the boundary line should be composed of settlers, not natives of the United States, had been without effect; and he expatiated on the fact that a large number of intruders had taken possession of lands, especially near the frontier, without any pretension of satisfying the formalities of the colonization laws. To preserve Texas to Mexico, he insisted that the Mexican population in Texas should be increased by making that country a penal settlement, the criminals transported thither to be employed in the cultivation of the soil; that foreign colonists differing from American interests, habits and language should be introduced; that a coasting trade be established between Texas and other parts of the republic, which would tend to nationalize the department; that the colonization law of August, 1824, be suspended as far as concerns Texas, and the settlement of that department be placed under the direction of the general government; and that a commissioner be appointed to examine and report upon the condition of affairs in the Texas colonies, etc. The Congress passed an Act in accordance with the memorial and the exemption from taxes promised hitherto to settlers from the United States was annulled. Also, along with the execution of this odious law the government sent a large military force into Texas, under the command of Manuel Mier y Teran, commandant-general of the eastern provinces, and he was also authorized to establish inland and maritime custom-houses. A military despotism was naturally inaugurated at an early period. The only colonies recognized were those of Austin, Dewitt and Martin de Leon; all other concessions were suspended until their contracts could be examined and their fulfillment verified. Titles were denied to a great number of settlers already domiciled, and new immigrants from the United States were ordered to quit the country immediately upon their arrival. Several large military posts were established, manned by convicts and other bad charac-

ters. A series of outrages was directly begun. Military jurisdiction was
substituted for that of the local authorities in many places; settlers were dis-
possessed of their lands and property, many of them were imprisoned, and no
redress could be obtained for thefts and robberies committed by the troops.

During the year 1831 the local authorities and also the frequently changing administration were at odds with each other, one party almost constantly
colliding with another, and these in so rapid succession that the true interests
of the masses were lost sight of. Outrages increased as the military officers
were angered by resistance or lack of respect, until even the settlers in the
Austin colony began to rise in arms. A spirit of rebellion began to spread
like a prairie fire before a wind. One John Austin, not a relative of Stephen
F., was an alcalde at Brazoria and a brave and influential citizen. On June
10, 1832, he joined the insurgents, and with about a hundred men demanded
the release of certain prisoners at Anahuac, was refused, and some shots were
fired. Bradburn, the Mexican officer, agreed to release the men if Austin
with his force would retire six miles away. Austin did this, but Bradburn
broke faith, opened fire upon the insurgents remaining in Anahuac and drove
them from the place. In January, this year (1832), Santa Anna at Vera Cruz
pronounced against the government of Bustamante, and the usual war followed,
a la Mexican. The colonists, being enraged by the latter's administration, a
number of them met at Turtle Bayou, drew up a list of their grievances,
June 13, and passed resolutions adopting Santa Anna's plan and pledged their
support to the constitution and the leaders who were then fighting in defense
of civil liberty.

The first skirmish, June 13, 1832, resulted in the insurgents taking
the fort at Velasco from the brave Ugartechea. Meanwhile, John Austin's
men around Anahuac successfully cut off supplies and communication.
Piedras, commanding at Nacogdoches, hastened hitherward to aid the Mexicans, but before arriving fell into the hands of the insurgents, and was converted to their cause. By his assistance, Travis and other prisoners, were
released. Piedras appointed another man to succeed Bradburn at Anahuac,
and started back to Nacogdoches; but as soon as he turned his back, the garrison at Anahuac mutinied in favor of Santa Anna. Bradburn was persuaded
by some of the officers to re-assume command, but he immediately found so
many of the men committed to Santa Anna that he quit in disgust and went to
New Orleans.

In the Southern United States the opinion began to prevail that the colonists in Texas were attempting to separate from Mexico and annex themselves
to the Union. On this account, Montezuma, commanding at Tampico, and
having declared in favor of Santa Anna, sent a force into Texas to reduce
the insurgents. His colonel, Mejia, on entering Texas, first had an amicable
conference with the leader of the Bustamante party, so as to prevent interruption, and proceeded to the mouth of the Brazos, taking with him
Stephen F. Austin, who was on his return from the State Legislature.
Consulting John Austin, the latter professed perfect loyalty and said that
the insurgents had no intention to separate from Mexico; they were only
rebelling against certain tyrannical acts of some of the officers. Mejia went
on to Galveston, where he was similarly received, and he returned to Tampico.
He actually advocated the cause of the insurgents, and the seed he had sown
in Texas, in so doing, bore rapidly. Piedras, at Nacogdoches, being opposed

to Santa Anna, was ousted by the Mexicans. By the end of August not a Mexican soldier remained in the Texan colonies, the victory over the Bradburn party was so complete. A troop of about seventy men were stationed at San Antonio, scarcely a sufficient number to keep the Indians in check in that vicinity. Peace was restored. This victory of the Texan colonists would have been far more costly, if not indeed impossible of attainment, had there been no revolution going on beyond the Rio Grande.

The separation of Texas from Coahuila forms an important event in the history of the State. In October, 1832, a convention of delegates from different municipalities was held at San Felipe, and some discussion took place concerning the formation of a State constitution; but as sufficient notice had not been given, and the attendance was slim, the convention adjourned without taking action. Their discussion, however, brought the matter seriously before the public, and when the second convention assembled, April 1, 1833, it was prepared to accomplish the work assigned to it. At this convention were Stephen F. Austin, Branch T. Archer, David G. Burnett, Sam Houston, J. B. Miller and William H. Wharton, the last mentioned being the president of that body. A committee was appointed to draft a form of State constitution, and another committee was appointed to draw up a memorial petitioning the general government to grant a separation of Texas from Coahuila. Sam Houston was appointed chairman of the first, and David G. Burnett of the second. The constitution drafted was thoroughly republican in form, modeled on that of the United States. After much discussion it was concluded that banking should not be provided for by that constitution, and that the document should maintain absolute silence with reference to religious liberty, such was the blighting power of Catholic influence. The commissioners appointed to convey the petition for separation to the City of Mexico were Stephen F. Austin, William H. Wharton and J. B. Miller; but Austin was the only member who actually went there, and on arriving he found that city the scene of virulent party faction and political confusion. Affairs in Mexico had been undergoing the customary vicissitudes and revulsions. No more stability of principle was observable in Santa Anna than in Bustamante. Both used the constitution of 1824 to push themselves into power, and then both cast it to the winds. By the end of 1832, these two generals, after much bloodshed, came to terms, and agreed to unite in support of the said constitution.

On March 30, 1833, Santa Anna was declared duly elected president of the Republic of Mexico, and Gomez Farias, vice president; and from this time on Santa Anna's course was remarkable for subtle intrigue for selfish purposes. He never appeared, however, as the principal actor, but always used other parties as cat's-paws for his own advancement. Dictatorial power was his highest ambition. Farias was the known champion of reform, and Santa Anna absented himself from the capital to intrigue with bishops and religious orders, leaving his colleague at the seat of power to inaugurate his new measures, which he (Santa Anna) knew would foment discord and redound to the discomfiture of the instigator and ultimately to his own advancement. Three weeks later Santa Anna resigned the presidency to lead the army against the rebels of Halpani, while Austin, not understanding the delay in carrying out promises, repaired to Mexico City in October. Austin, seeing the prospective delay, wrote to the city council of San Antonio, recommending that it obtain the concurrence of all other corporations in Texas in a scheme for separation from Coahuila, with the hope that, under the provision of the general law of May 7, 1824, a local government could be successfully organized, even though the general government should refuse its consent.

The result of Austin's visit, after the war had been closed, was a respectful and honest effort to improve the legal facilities of the Texans, but it was believed by the convention assembled for the purpose that the time had not yet arrived for the erection of Texas into an independent State. But Austin, on his return trip to San Antonio, was arrested at Saltillo, by order of Farias, on account of the letter he had written to the San Antonio council, and on account of the hasty language used at the interview at the same time. He was sent back to Mexico, and was in prison eight months, awaiting trial, with no opportunity, much of this time, of communicating with the outside world. He was not finally liberated until the expiration of nineteen months. Much has been said *pro et contra* by Austin's friends and enemies concerning his actions at this period; but the Texans generally believe him to have been sincere and competent, and probably as judicious as any other man they could have commissioned for that errand. Santa Anna seemed to be a friend of Austin and the Texans, but those knowing his character entertained doubts as to his sincerity. The legislature of January, 1834, passed various measures beneficial to Texas. The municipalities of Matagorda and San Augustin were created; Texas was divided into three departments, the new one of Brazos, with San Felipe as its capital, being organized; the English language was permitted to be used in public affairs, and an additional representative at the State congress allowed; the privilege of purchasing vacant lands was granted to foreigners; laws were passed for the protection of the persons and property of all settlers whatever might be their religion, and freedom from molestation for political and religious opinions was guaranteed provided public tranquillity was not disturbed; a supreme court for Texas provided for, and a system of trial by jury.

In 1834, Santa Anna's Centralist party won everywhere, save in Texas, Coahuila and Zacatecas. Hence these States must be punished. Zacatecas was scandalously plundered. Santa Anna, in the meantime, was preparing, under cover of collecting revenue in Texas, for the military occupation of the province. He landed 500 men at Lavaca Bay, and forwarded them under General Ugartechea to San Antonio. The custom-house at Anahuac was taken in charge and enormous dues were demanded. So excessive were they that W. B. Travis raised a company and captured Captain Tenorio and the soldiers at the custom house. They were shortly after released, as the act of Travis was thought by his friends to be too hasty. When Tenorio reported these proceedings to his superior officer, he was sent on a still more uncalled-for errand. A Mexican Republican, Lorenzo de Zavala, had taken refuge in Texas, and Santa Anna, fearing his influence, ordered his arrest; but no one would undertake the task. Another order was sent from headquarters to arrest R. M. Williamson, W. B. Travis, Samuel M. Williams, Moseley Baker, F. W. Johnson and John H. Moore, and a subsequent order included the names of J. M. Carravahal and Juan Zambrano. The two last, being Mexican citizens, were carried off; but the job of arresting the first six persons was considered so dangerous that no officer had the temerity to attempt it. In addition to these Mexican outrages on the Texans, the Indians were becoming troublesome. Merchants and traders were intercepted and killed, and their goods carried off. But these Indian outrages served one important purpose; they gave the Texans an excuse for forming companies, procuring arms and drilling ostensibly for operations against the savages, but really to resist the encroachments of the despotic Mexican government. The companies were called "committees of safety," and their business was to disseminate information, secure arms, ammunition, etc. A central committee was also formed, which met at San Felipe, and an administrative council was organized. The council sent Messrs. Barrett and Gritton to San Antonio on a mission of peace to General Ugartechea, but nothing was accomplished. Stephen F. Austin, in the meantime, was returning, when he was made chairman of the council at San Felipe. He expressed regret at the action of his friends, and stated that he had hoped to find everything peaceful. Santa Anna still professed to have the kindest feelings toward the Texans, and he authorized Austin to tell his people that he was their friend, and that he desired their prosperity; that he would do all he could to promote it, and that in the new constitution he would use his influence to have conditions therein to give Texas a special organization, suited to their education and habits. But Santa Anna could be nothing but treacherous, as the treatment of the people in that portion of the State occupied by his troops but ill accorded with his professions of good will. Citizens were arrested, money forced from those who fell into the hands of the despot's minions, and communities stripped of their arms, the soldiers compelling families to support them, the attempt to disarm all citizens being a principal feature of the plan of subjugation. Captain Castenado was sent to Gonzales to seize a small cannon which had been given to the corporation for protection against Indians. The citizens were unwilling to part with their gun, and prepared to resist the demand of Castenado, who had 150 soldiers to back him. A company was organized, which charged the Mexicans and put them to flight in disorder. The news of this conflict roused a warlike spirit in the Texans. A company was raised to capture the Mexican garrison at Goliad. Captain George Collingsworth led the party, and almost without firing a gun the exultant Texans made prisoners of the whole force, about twenty-five, including Colonel Sandoval, besides obtaining 300 stand of arms and military stores to the amount of $10,000. The Mexican fort at Lipantitlan was also captured shortly after.

Not only had Austin returned, but the noted Benjamin R. Milam had escaped from Monterey and returned and joined the patriot forces. Austin, who was a born commander, was put in immediate command of the Texan forces on his arrival at Gonzales, which was on the 11th of October. The convention met October 16, 1835, but there being only thirty-one members present an adjournment was made until November 1. November 5th a preamble and set of resolutions were adopted, in which the declaration was made that although they repudiated Santa Anna and his despotic government, they yet clung to the Constitution of Mexico of 1824. On November 12th an ordinance was passed for the creation of a provisional government, with an executive council, to be composed of one member from each municipality. Henry Smith was made Governor, and James W. Robinson Lieutenant-Governor. Sam Houston, who, it will be noticed, had figured somewhat in Texas history since 1832, was selected to command the army to be raised.

General Cos, with 500 soldiers, landed at Pass Cavallo, in September, 1835, and marched immediately to San Antonio, when he superseded General

Ugartechea. Austin, after reaching Gonzales, and effecting a reorganization of the volunteers, started for San Antonio. He reached the Mission La Espada, nine miles below the city, on the 20th. On the 27th, after resting his men, he detached the companies of Fannin and Bowie, ninety-two men, to ascend the river and if practicable select a more suitable camping ground. Fannin spent that night in a bend of the San Antonio River, near the Conception Mission. The point was well chosen, but the Mexicans looked upon it as simply a trap to secure their game from, which was all they had to do. It was a natural fortification, but General Cos thought he had a sure thing of it; so he marched out in the morning and made an attack. The Mexicans surrounded their supposed prey, and the battle began. The Texans, with their deadly rifles, plucked off all the gunners from the enemy's battery, as they came within range. A charge was made, or attempted, three separate times, but they were hurled back in confusion by the Texans, who remained masters of the field. Sixteen dead bodies were found near the abandoned cannon, which had been discharged but five times; so true was the aim of the riflemen that the Mexican gunners were shot before they could fire, in most cases. This was the first battle of the Revolution, and the loss of the Texans was one man—Richard Andrews. The Mexican loss was about sixty, as every one of the patriots who fired took aim and usually brought down his man. Austin, in October, moved up about half a mile, on the Alamo ditch, near the old mill, and next day to within one mile east of the city. He had nearly 1,000 men, but they were ill provided with arms and ammunition of war and without cannon. He was poorly prepared to attack a larger force than his own in a strongly fortified city. He, however, sent to Gonzales for the cannon at that place. Then came a number of skirmishes with the enemy and the capture of 300 horses by Bowie. The executive or general council, in view of the lack of funds wherewith to provide the supplies, etc., so much needed at that time, sent Messrs. Austin, Archer and Wharton as Commissioners to the United States, in order to negotiate a loan of $1,000,000 in bonds of $1,000 each, and the commander-in-chief was authorized to accept the services of 5,000 volunteers and 1,200 regulars. Provision was also made for a navy.

The army encamped before San Antonio was under General Edward Burleson. Many of the men had gone home, although others were arriving daily; still, only about half the original force remained. There had been about 1,400 men in the camps at one time; 600 was the number on the 1st of December, while Cos had a much larger force in the city, and was expecting 500 more. Those additional troops arrived in time to take part in the defense of the city. The defenses had been put in order and the old fortress of the Alamo on the east side of the river had been repaired and fortified with cannon. The main plaza had been fortified and the streets barricaded, while the adobe houses in the narrow streets afforded shelter for the Mexican soldiers. Many of Burleson's officers, in consideration of these facts, were in favor of abandoning the siege. On the 2d of December it was decided to make the attack. The force was paraded and a strong address was made by Colonel William H. Jack. A call was then made for volunteers, and 450 men, including the New Orleans Grays, responded, the latter under the command of Major R. C. Norris. It was decided to make the attack next morning, although many considered the project as a hopeless one. But three

CONCEPCION

SANTIAGO

citizens arrived in camp from the city and gave such encouraging news that the next morning Colonel Milam suggested to Burleson to make the attempt while the enthusiasm was at its height. He agreed, and Milam stepped in front of Burleson's tent and gave a loud and ringing *huzzah*, which, together with his magnetism, aroused the whole camp. He said he was going into San Antonio, and wanted volunteers to follow him. A ready response was made, and the little band, forming into two sections and accompanied by two field pieces, entered the town by different directions. A description of this famous battle has so often been given that its details are almost like household words to all Texans. The result was sufficient almost to place it in the category of one of the "decisive battles of the world," for the *result* of a battle is what makes it great. Hundreds of battles have been fought where thousands on each side have been slain, and yet the result has been *nil*. This siege and capture of the strongly protected city of San Antonio de Bexar was all important to Texas. It gave the Mexicans to understand that not in numbers alone consists the strength of an army. Here was a force of undisciplined frontiersmen, poorly armed and equipped, only a few hundred in number, attacking a well organized army of regular soldiers, advancing into their very midst and forcing them to surrender. The difference in apparent strength of the two forces and the result would appear ridiculous were it not so serious a matter. The spectacle of a general such as Cos seemed to be, surrendering to a few Texans, was a scene to be remembered by those who took part in the siege. But it is the old story of the Anglo-Saxon against the field. He is rarely ever the under dog in the fight at the finish.

During the time the fighting men were doing such splendid work, the politicians were quarreling; nor were they lacking in a more "modern instance" or two, on both sides of Mason and Dixon's line. Governor Smith vetoed some matters that the council had voted, and the council promptly deposed him and placed Lieutenant-Governor Robinson in the executive chair. Smith held the archives and claimed to be Governor still, and there were consequently two governors at once; but that state of affairs is not uncommon in these days. Much other legislative matter of some interest at the time was transacted, but it is not now of supreme importance. The main historic facts are what the compiler wishes to emphasize in these pages. Several declarations of independence were adopted in different sections of the embryo State, but an election was held for delegates to a convention which met on the 1st of March, 1836, and on the second day a committee was appointed to draft a declaration of independence, which was done, and it was unanimously passed, Sam Houston offering the resolution that the report of the committee be adopted. Richard Ellis, for whom Ellis county was named, was president of the convention. A constitution was also framed which was adopted March 17, and a government *ad interim* inaugurated: David G. Burnett, President; Lorenzo de Zavala, Vice-president, and Sam Houston, Commander-in-Chief of the army in the field. Zacatecas, and the district over which Governor Garcia still had nominal sway, the remaining portion of old Mexico wherein the Republicans held out the longest, at last fell, Santa Anna having gained a complete victory over the forces of the Governor. This swept away the last vestige of the Republican party in Mexico. Yet Texas was not only holding her own, but gaining strength with every day; so Santa Anna determined to subjugate this State. He proposed to send two columns into the province, Gen-

eral Urrea being ordered to Matamoras to take one division along the coast to
Goliad and Victoria, while the President himself, with the main division,
would take the province by way of Presidio, thence to San Antonio and San
Felipe.

In January, 1836, Santa Anna reached Saltillo, and Guerrero by the 15th
of February. From the latter place he wrote to Señor Tornel, Minister of
War, giving that official an outline of his plans in reference to Texas, which
were "to drive from the province all who had taken part in the revolution,
together with all the foreigners who lived near the sea-coast, or the borders
of the United States; to remove far into the interior those who had not taken
part in the revolution; to vacate all lands and grants of lands owned by
non-residents; to remove from Texas all who had come to the province and
were not entered as colonists under Mexican rules; to divide among the officers
and soldiers of the army the best lands, provided they would occupy them; to
permit no Anglo-American to settle in Texas; to sell the remaining vacant
lands at $1 per acre, allowing those speaking the French language to pur-
chase 5,000,000 acres, those speaking English the same, and those speaking
Spanish without limit; to satisfy the claims of civilized Indians; to make the
Texans pay the expense of the war; and to liberate and to declare free the
negroes introduced into the colony." And further, to cut off from Texas the
hope of aid from the United States, the Minister of War, Tornel, issued a general
order to all commanders to treat all foreigners (volunteers from the United
States) as outlaws, to show no quarter, and slay them when taken as prisoners—in short, to take no prisoners alive. Colonel Travis, with 145 men, who
was in the vicinity of San Antonio, on the approach of the invading army,
retired to the fortress of the Alamo, on the east side of the river. And just
here a description of this famous fortress, the Alamo, and its armament, will
be in place; and although it has often been described, yet the memories surrounding it, glorious though sad, cannot be kept too fresh in the minds of all
who love supreme heroism—the Spartan heroism as shown by Travis and his
little band. "The main chapel is 75 x 62 feet, walls of solid masonry, four
feet thick and twenty-two and a half feet high, roofless at the time of the
siege. It fronts to the west toward the city, one-half mile distant. From
the northwest corner a wall extended fifty feet to the convent building.
The convent was a two-story building, with a flat roof, 186 x 18 feet. From
the northeast corner of the chapel a wall extended 186 feet north, thence 102
feet west to the convent, inclosing the convent yard. From the southwest
corner of the chapel a strongly built stockade extended seventy-five feet to a
building called the prison. The prison was one-story, 115 x 17 feet, and
joined a part of the south wall of the main Alamo plaza, of which the convent
formed a part of the east wall; and some low buildings, used as a barracks,
formed a part of the west wall. The main plaza, inclosed with walls, was
154 x 54 yards. The different inclosures occupied between two and three
acres—ample accommodations for 1,000 men. The outer walls were two and
a half feet thick and eight feet high, though as they were planned against the
Indians the fortress was destitute of salient and dominant points in case of a
bombardment. A ditch, used for irrigation, passed immediately in the rear
of the church; another touched the northwest angle of the main square. The
armament was as follows: three heavy guns, planted upon the walls of the
church—one pointing north, toward the old mill; one west, toward the city;

and one south, toward the village of Lavalleta. Two guns protected the stockade between the church and the prison; two protected the prison, and an eighteen-pounder was planted at the southwest angle of the main square; a twelve-pound cannon protected the center of the west wall, and an eight-pounder was planted on the northwest angle; two guns were planted on the north wall of the plaza—in all, fourteen in position. Over the church floated the flag of the provisional government of Texas, the Mexican tri-color, with the numerals 1824, in place of the eagle in the white stripe."

The siege began on the 23d of February, and so stubbornly did Travis and his men resist the furious onslaughts of the Mexicans that not until Sunday, March 6, did the fall of the Alamo occur, an account of which, briefly told, will here be given: The Mexicans advanced to the attack at about four o'clock in the morning, but the Texans were ready, and poured upon the advancing columns a shower of grape and musket and rifle balls. Santa Anna was watching the operations from behind a building about 500 yards south of the church. Twice the assailants reeled and fell back in dismay. Rallied again by the brave Costrellon (who fell at San Jacinto), according to Filisola, the columns of the western and eastern attacks meeting with some difficulty in reaching the tops of the small houses forming the wall of the fort, did, by a simultaneous movement to the right and to the left, swing northward until the three columns formed one dense mass, which under the guidance of their officers finally succeeded in effecting an entrance into the inclosed yard. About the same time the column on the south made a breach in the wall and captured one of the guns. This gun, the eighteen-pounder, was immediately turned upon the convent, to which some of the Mexicans had retreated. The cannon on the center of the west wall was still manned by the Texans, and did fearful execution upon the Mexicans who had ventured into the yard. But the feeble garrison could not long hold out against such overwhelming numbers. Travis fell early in the action, shot with a rifle ball in the head. After being shot he had sufficient strength to kill a Mexican who attempted to spear him. The bodies of most of the Texans were found in the buildings, where hand-to-hand fights took place. The body of Crockett, however, was in the yard, with a number of dead Mexicans lying near him. Bowie was slain in his bed, and it is said that he killed three Mexicans with his pistols before they reached him after breaking in the door. The church was the last place entered by the foe. It had been agreed that when resistance seemed useless, and suspecting their fate, any surviving Texan should blow up the magazine. Major Evans, it is said, was performing this sad duty when he was killed in time to prevent the explosion. Several Texans appealed to their inhuman captors for quarters, but they were cut down without mercy. The butchery was complete; not a Texan soldier was spared! Two ladies and a negro servant were the only occupants who remained to tell the tale of the Alamo. Lieutenant Dickinson attempted to escape with a child on his back, but their bodies fell, riddled with bullets. 180 bodies of the Texans were collected and partially buried. The Mexicans lost twice that number.

Santa Anna, in the meantime, had ordered Urrea to proceed along the Texan coast, and that general reached San Patricio on the 28th of February, entirely unknown to the Texans. Some narrow escapes were made by Colonel F. W. Johnson and others, but a party under Major Morris and Dr. Grant

3

were captured and they fell victims to the Mexican murderers,—for they were nothing less. Colonel Fannin had been ordered to prepare for a descent on Matamoras, but hearing of the advance of Urrea, he re-entered Goliad, where he had been in command some time. Having been requested to send some reinforcements to Captain King, his force was thereby depleted by 112 men. King and his men, after a skirmish or two, by some means got separated from another portion of his force, and were captured and killed. Fannin, in Goliad, on the 16th of March, was reinforced by the Twenty-eighth Cavalry. He then prepared for a retreat; but just at nightfall a large force of the enemy was discovered in the neighborhood, when he remounted his cannon and prepared for defense. The following account of the disastrous battle of Colita, which followed, is copied from an able historian of Texas: "The morning of the 17th was foggy, and as no enemy appeared to be in sight Fannin concluded to make good his retreat. After reaching a point about eight miles away from Goliad, they halted to permit the oxen to graze. They then resumed their march, and were within two miles of Colita Creek when a company of Mexican cavalry was discovered in front of them, issuing from a point of timber. Urrea had taken advantage of the fog to get around and in front of Fannin's force. Horton's cavalry had gone in advance to make arrangements for crossing the stream, and could not get back to their companions. Two charges of Urrea's cavalry were gallantly repulsed by Fannin's artillery, which did great damage to the Mexicans. The fight was kept up till nightfall, when the enemy retired out of range and the Texans prepared for a renewal of the fight in the morning. Their condition was indeed critical. Fourteen of their number had been killed, and sixty others, including Fannin, were wounded. Urrea received during the night heavy reinforcements. With no adequate protection, in an open prairie, without water, surrounded by an enemy five times their number, what could they do but surrender as prisoners of war? A white flag was raised and the following terms of surrender agreed upon: That the Texans should be treated as prisoners of war according to the usages of civilized nations; that private property should be respected and restored, but side arms of the officers should be given up; the men should be sent to Copano, and thence in eight days to the United States, or as soon as vessels could be procured to take them; the officers should be paroled and returned to the United States in like manner.

General Houston had been re-elected commander-in-chief of the army, and had gone to Gonzales, with the intention of reorganizing the forces, in which he had great difficulty, for the fate of Travis and Fannin and their men caused a great panic when the news became known. Besides, thirty-two of the citizen soldiers of Gonzales, who had entered the Alamo the night before the battle, were slain, leaving a dozen or more families of that town without a head. A number of desertions also occurred, and the alarm was, indeed, widespread. Then came some movements on the part of General Houston that caused great criticism of his actions. There was not a very considerable cordiality between the commander and the newly inaugurated president, and in an order to the former from the latter these words were added: "The enemy are laughing you to scorn. You must fight them. You must retreat no further. The country expects you to fight. The salvation of the country depends on your doing so." The affair at San Jacinto followed. The marching of April 18, 19 and 20, 1836, led to the battle of April 21.

According to a report signed by Sam Houston, commander-in-chief, the Texan force numbered 783 men, while the government troops under Santa Anna numbered 1,500 men, including General Cos' division. The First Regiment, commanded by Colonel Burleson, was assigned the center. The Second Regiment, under the command of Sherman, formed the left wing of the army. The artillery, under special command of Colonel George W. Hockley, inspector-general, was placed on the right of the First Regiment; and four companies of infantry, under the command of Lieutenant-Colonel Henry Millard, sustained the artillery upon the right. The cavalry, sixty-one in number, commanded by Colonel Mirabeau B. Lamar, placed on the extreme right, completed the line. The cavalry was dispatched to the front of the enemy's left, for the purpose of attracting their notice, while an extensive island of timber afforded an opportunity of concentrating the forces and deploying from that point, agreeably to the previous design of the troops. Every evolution was performed with alacrity, the whole advancing rapidly in line, and through an open prairie, without any protection. The artillery advanced, took station within 200 yards of the enemy's breastwork, and commenced an effective fire with grape and canister. Colonel Sherman, with his regiment, having commenced the action upon the left wing, the whole line, at the center and on the right, advancing in double-quick time, rung the war cry, 'Remember the Alamo!' received the enemy's fire, and advanced within point-blank shot before a piece was discharged, then advanced without a halt until they were in possession of the woodland and the enemy's breastwork, the right wing of Burleson's and the left of Millard's taking possession of the breastwork, the artillery having gallantly charged up within seventy yards of the enemy's cannon, when it was taken. The conflict lasted about eighteen minutes from the time of close action until the Texans were in possession of the enemy's encampment, taking one piece of cannon (loaded), four stands of colors, all their camp equipage, stores and baggage. The cavalry had charged and routed that of the enemy upon the right, and given pursuit to the fugitives, which did not cease until they arrived at the bridge. Captain Karnes commanded the pursuers. The conflict in the breastwork lasted but a few moments; many of the troops encountered hand to hand, and, not having the advantage of bayonets on the Texan side, riflemen used their pieces as war clubs, breaking many of them off at the breech. The rout commenced at half-past four, and the pursuit by the main army continued until twilight. A guard was then left in charge of the enemy's encampment, and the Texans returned with their killed and wounded — or two killed and twenty-three wounded, six of whom mortally. The enemy's loss was 630 killed, among whom were one general officer, four colonels, two lieutenant-colonels, five captains, twelve lieutenants; wounded, 208, of whom five were colonels, three lieutenant-colonels, two second lieutenant-colonels, seven captains, one cadet; prisoners, 730; President-General Santa Anna, General Cos, four colonels (aids to General Santa Anna), and the colonel of the Guerrero Battalion, are included in the number. General Santa Anna was not taken until the 22, nor General Cos until the 24th, very few having escaped. About 600 muskets, 300 sabers and 200 pistols were collected after the action; several hundred mules and horses were taken, and nearly $12,000 in specie.

During the latter part of 1838 the Nacogdoches rebellion occurred, when a considerable number of Mexican settlers assembled on the banks of the

Angelina, with 300 Indians, under the leadership of Nathaniel Norris, Vicente Cordova, and others. Their numbers soon increased. President Houston, who was then at Nacogdoches, received a communication from these leaders, disclaiming allegiance to Texas. The malcontents then directed their march to the Cherokee Nation. President Houston sent out General Rusk, with the main body of the army, to the headquarters of Bowles, the Cherokee chief, while Major Augustin, with 150 men, followed the trail of the malcontents. Rusk presently discovered that the Mexican leaders had gone to the head-waters of the Trinity River, his followers had dispersed and many of them returned to their homes without any blood being shed. The precise object of this attempt at revolution has never been fully explained.

The rout of the Cherokees from their hunting grounds was the introduction to the massacre of the Comanches. In February, 1840, showing a disposition to enter into a treaty of peace, twelve of their principal chiefs met, March 19, the Texan commissioners at Bejar, where General H. D. McLeod was in command. It was known that the Comanches had thirteen white captives in their power, and the release of these was demanded The Indians brought forward only one, a little girl. After a brief discussion, in which the Indians exhibited defiance, an order was sent to Captain Howard, to bring his company into the council room; and as soon as the men had taken their position the chiefs were informed that they would be detained as prisoners until the captives were surrendered. A terrible conflict ensued; the twelve chiefs, armed, were all killed in the council room, while the warriors in the yard outside maintained a desperate fight. All were finally slain, thirty-two in number, while seven women and children were made prisoners. Naturally the Comanches in general were resolved on revenge for what they considered treachery, and in return for the destruction of so many of their chiefs. With a band of 600 they raided Linnville and the vicinity of Victoria, which latter place they made two efforts to capture, and carried off to their homes immense numbers of live stock and large amounts of other property. During August (1840) the whites had several skirmishes with them, under command of General Felix Houston, and drove them away, with considerable loss. Furthermore, on October 5th following, Col. John H. Moore, with ninety Texans and twelve Lipan Indians, was sent up the Colorado in pursuit of the escaped Comanches, and on reaching them he destroyed their village and killed many of the escaping Indians. The rout was complete, and Lamar's system of extermination or extinction was for once thoroughly carried out.

A comparatively long interval of peace with Mexico was occasioned by internal strifes in the latter country. The northern "Federalists" failed to establish their "Republic of the Rio Grande," a scheme wholly ignored by the Texans. The latter, however, as has already been remarked, claimed all the territory east of the Rio Grande to its source, which was indeed much farther into the interior than they were warranted in going. Accordingly, in 1841, they sent out an expedition toward Santa Fe, in order more perfectly to establish their possession to that section of the country. This scheme was a wild one, from the fact that the population of Santa Fe was thoroughly Mexican, and separated from the Texas settlements by an Indian country fully 600 miles in width. Indeed it was not sanctioned by the Texan congress, and the scheme was wholly Lamar's. He proclaimed in advance to the authorities at Santa Fe the object of the expedition. If they in that section were unwilling to submit to Texas, said he, then he wished to establish friendly commercial relations with New Mexico. He instructed his commander not to subjugate the country if the people were unwilling to submit; the military organization of the expedition was only for protection against the savages. The expedition, which consisted of 270 soldiers, left Austin June 20, 1841, met with many disasters, and, after some loss of men, was captured before it reached Santa Fe, and most of the men sent to the City of Mexico, where they were kept in prison for a time. Among them was the commissioner, J. A. Navarro, who, after languishing in prison for fourteen months, finally escaped at Vera Cruz, in January, 1845.

As an argument for annexation to the United States, it was stated that Mexico had for six years failed to reconquer Texas or even to send an army within her borders, and that the war therefore might be considered ended, although no formal recognition of the independence of Texas had been made by the mother country. Her prolonged inactivity might be considered an acknowledgment that reconquest was impossible. Mexico, however, in order to make good her claim, prepared at the close of 1841 to invade Texas. On January 9, 1842, General Arista issued a proclamation from his headquarters at Monterey that the Mexican nation would never consent to the separation of the territory, and that it was owing only to the civil wars in Mexico that no effort had recently been made to subjugate Texas. He declared that his country was determined to recover her rights through the only means left her, namely, persuasion or war; that hostilities would be directed against only those who sustained and fought to maintain the Texan nationality; and he called upon the people to reflect and consider their own interests, and return to their allegiance. On March 5, General Rafael Vasquez appeared before San Antonio de Bejar at the head of 500 men. The Texan force there, being small, evacuated when the surrender of the town was demanded. Vasquez entered the place, hoisted the Mexican flag and departed. About the same time small forces of Mexicans occupied Refugio and Goliad, and also soon retired. Aroused, the Texans bristled up for another engagement, and Houston, on the 10th of March, issued a proclamation calling upon all citizens subject to military duty to hold themselves in readiness to repair to the scene of action in the event of a formidable invasion. On the 21st he addressed a letter to Santa Anna, again in power, which was published far and wide. In it were criticisms incited by injudicious correspondence between him (Santa Anna) and Bernard E. Bee and General Hamilton. Santa Anna declared that Mexico would not cease her efforts until she had planted her standard upon the Sabine. Houston replied promptly and boldly, that Texas would never yield, writing a very eloquent letter to the old treacherous Mexican. He declared blockaded all the Mexican ports on the eastern coast from Tobasco, including the mouth of the Rio Grande and the Brazos Santiago. The Texan navy at this time consisted of four vessels, the other vessels that had been purchased by authority of the congress having been wrecked. These vessels were transferred to the United States the next year, upon annexation.

When Vasquez occupied San Antonio much alarm was felt for the safety of Austin and the government archives. The President removed his cabinet to Houston, where Congress held its special session of June 27, 1842, and this aggravated the indignation of the people of Austin. A vigilance committee was formed, the records were packed in boxes and a guard placed over them.

Besides, a force was sent out to guard the roads, to see that no wagon passed with the archives. December 10, 1842, Houston instructed Captain Thomas I. Smith to raise a company secretly and bring the most necessary books and documents to Washington, where Congress was to convene in regular session that month. Smith avoided the regular patrols by a circuitous route, entered Austin December 30, at night, and succeeded in loading three wagons with records. This act was a surprise to the inhabitants of Austin. Smith hastened back, after having been fired upon without effect by Captain Mark B. Lewis, who, having rallied a volunteer company and procured a cannon from the arsenal, fired at the intruders. Smith encamped at Kinney's Fort on Brushy Creek, and on the following morning discovered that Lewis, with his cannon pointed, had taken a position in front. After some parley, Smith agreed to take the wagons back to Austin. This affair has been called the Archive war. No further attempt was made to remove the records. The Austin people retained them until 1845, when, on occasion of the annexation convention being summoned to meet in July, they delivered them over to the administration of Anson Jones, on condition that the convention should assemble at Austin.

This breeze took place during the second administration of President Houston, in 1842. Early in this century the "neutral ground" became the asylum of adventurers and desperate men. Land commissioners, especially in Shelby County, found a profitable business in issuing "headright" certificates. During this year one Charles W. Jackson, an English-speaking resident of Louisiana, and a fugitive from justice, arrived in Shelby County, and offered himself as a candidate for the Texan Congress. Being defeated, he undertook to expose the land frauds, declaring that his defeat was owing to the opposition of the party connected with them. He notified the general land office of the illegal proceedings had there, and a man named Joseph Goodbread intimated that his life was in danger if he did not desist. Jackson shot him dead on the spot. He was called to trial, the court was thronged by armed men, and the judge failed to appear. The Louisianian then organized his party, under the name of "Regulators." Their operations were somewhat irregular, and doubtless many honest men lost their lands, etc., by their work. The "Moderators" were therefore organized in opposition, and a kind of warfare was carried on for three years, when the two factions drew up in actual battle array in front of each other; but the President had General Smith, with a force of about 500 men, put a stop to the threatening strife. However, many a murder was afterward committed in quarrels growing out of the issues.

The Texan Congress authorized war with Mexico, in 1842, but Houston vetoed the Bill, as the Republic had no means to carry on such a war. Independent parties, however, rushed to arms, and under an adventurer named Davis met the Mexicans at Nueces, in July.

In September, the Mexican general—Woll, occupied Antonio, driving out the Anglo-Texan element. Then Matthew Caldwell, with 220 Texans, and Nicholas Dawson, with fifty-three men came forward, met the Mexicans, and were killed, except two who escaped and fifteen who were made prisoners.

In September, 1,200 men answered Houston's call to arms. The expedition may be said to have ended at Mier, where 250 Texans surrendered to Gen. Ampudia. Very few of the members ever returned, for after their

SANTA ANNA BEFORE GENERAL HOUSTON.

1. Gen. Sam Houston.
2. Gen. Lopez de Santa Anna.
3. Thomas J. Rusk.
4. Mirabeau B. Lamar.
5. Ben McCulloch.
6. —— Chaddock.
7. R. S. McManus.
8. Col. Almonte.

9. Gen. Ed. Burleson.
10. Col. John A. Wharton.
11. Gen. Sidney Sherman.
12. Joel. W. Robison.
13. Walter P. Lane.
14. J. A. Sylvester.
15. Jesse Billingsby.
16. Tom. J. Green.
33. —— Hobson.

17. Gen. George G. Alford.
18. Bailey Hardiman.
19. Silas Bostic.
20. —— McFadden.
21. Col. Ed. Burleson.
22. Washington Anderson.
23. James M. Hill.
24. John W. Buntin.
34. Moses Austin Bryan.

25. M. G. Whitiker.
26. —— Clemens.
27. John Milton Swisher.
28. Deaf Smith.
29. Sterling C. Robertson.
30. Surgeon.
31. Geo. Nall.
32. Dr. S. Perry.

escape from the Hacienda del Salado, they suffered untold hardships, many died, others were recaptured, and seventeen of the leaders executed. Of the total, 107 were liberated in 1844 by Santa Anna.

Of course, this act of annexation of Texas to the United States meant war with Mexico on a larger scale than ever. In Texas, at this time, there were probably about 75,000 inhabitants, about 4,000 of whom were Mexicans. The nationality of the new State was very composite. As to the criminal element, there was no more of that, than in any frontier settlement, which generally have a class of ruffians that disappear on the approach of more settled civilization.

When the resolution of Congress in favor of annexation was published, March 7, 1845, General Almonte, the Mexican minister at Washington, demanded his passports. War with Mexico, indeed, the Government had been preparing for, and General Zachary Taylor was ordered to move from the Sabine with a strong force to Corpus Christi, at the mouth of the Nueces, at the end of June, 1845. In the meantime, the Mexicans, too, had been preparing for the contest, establishing their first base at Matamoras. The Texas legislature appointed Governor Henderson to take command of the Texans who might be mustered into the service of the United States. On May 2, 1846, a requisition for two regiments of infantry and two of cavalry was made on Texas. Henderson reached the army of General Taylor at Comargo, after the war had begun. The limited means of transportation, and uncertainty with regard to supplies, induced Taylor, while on his march against Monterey, to leave a large number of volunteers on garrison duty in towns on the Rio Grande, and only the first and second regiments of the Texan division accompanied the main army on that memorable campaign. In the attack upon Monterey, the first regiment of mounted volunteers under Colonel John C. Hays, familiarly known as " Jack," was detached and sent with General Worth west of the town, while Shield's, under Taylor, assaulted the East side, leading to the capitulation on the 24th.

The treaty of Guadalupe Hidalgo, negotiated February 22, 1848, surrendered Texas, New Mexico, Utah, Nevada, Arizona and California to the United States.

In 1857, Texan wagoners committed many acts of violence upon Mexican cartmen in the transportation of goods from San Antonio. The freight rates were so low as to drive the Texan wagoners from the field. The latter, moreover, were not quite so faithful as the Mexicans. Outrages became so numerous and high-handed that General Twiggs, the United States commander at San Antonio, was compelled to furnish a military escort to trains transporting Government supplies. In October, the Mexican minister at Washington addressed the United States Government on the matter, stating that he had been assured that the number of men thus murdered was no less than seventy-five and that many Mexicans had been compelled to fly to Mexico in a state of destitution. In November, Governor Pease addressed special messages to the Legislature on the matter, stating that Mexican citizens engaged in the business of teaming were not safe without a military escort. As the counties in which the deeds of violence were committed did nothing to stop them, he suggested the propriety of legislative interference. The Senate referred the matter to a committee, who reported in favor of inflicting a penalty upon those counties, but introduced no bill to that effect, and so the matter ended. The Legislature, however, approved the action of the Governor in calling out a company of troops, which, by the way, was ineffectual in regulating a large section of country with the criminals scattered over it. When the road was abandoned by the Mexican cartmen and booty became scarce, they began to commit depredations on the property of the citizens. The latter, though so indifferent to the rights of the Mexicans previously, were now enraged and resorted to lynching; and in the neighborhood of Goliad, the traveler would see many a corpse suspended from the boughs of the black oaks. The " Cart War," was thus brought to an end.

The Knights of the Golden Circle, organized originally to establish a slave empire in the Antilles, called a convention at Austin for January 28, 1861. That convention, on February 1, 1861 passed the Ordinance of Secession, the vote being 107 pro and 7 contra; which ordinance was to be submitted to a popular vote on February 23. Meantime the delegates elected representatives to the Confederate convention at Montgomery, Ala., and appointed three commissioners to accept the surrender of General Twiggs, with that of the soldiers and property of the United States in Texas. Houston opposed secession in a logical, prophetic speech, but went with the State, "right or wrong." On February 23, there were 39,415 votes cast for secession and 13,841 against it. The revolution of Cortina was an incident of the time, for it caused the devastation of the Rio Grande valley for 120 miles of its length. The civil war was inaugurated at Valverde, February 21, 1862, when the Confederate Sibley with 1,750 men, repulsed the Federal Canby with 3,810 men. Colonel Slough subsequently defeated Sibley, who lost 500 men in the expedition. In May, 1862, the United States vessels appeared before Galveston, but not until October 4, did the United States soldiers retake possession of the town; but the Confederate Magruder ultimately repossessed it.

After the recovery of Galveston Island, no other operation of importance occurred until September, 1863, when the Federals attempted to effect a lodgment at Sabine City, the terminus of a railroad. The blockade of Sabine Pass was temporarily broken by the capture of two United States gunboats, outside the bar. Afterward the Confederates erected a fort at Sabine City, defended by a formidable battery of eight heavy guns, three of which were rifled. A detachment of 4,000 men, with gunboats, from Banks' army, made an attempt in September, 1863, to take Sabine City, but met with ignominious defeat, losing two gunboats, 100 men killed and wounded, and 250 prisoners. The garrison of the fort consisted of only 200 Texans, of whom only forty-two took part in the action. These were presented by President Davis with a silver medal, the only honor of the kind known to have been bestowed by the Confederate government. Late in October, 1863, supported by a naval squadron under Commander Strong, Banks sailed with 6,000 troops from New Orleans for the Rio Grande. The immediate command, however, was given to General Napoleon Dana. By November 2 the force reached Brazos Santiago, and on the 6th took Brownsville, and soon afterward Corpus Christi, Aransas Pass, Cavillo Pass and the mouth of Matagorda Bay. Indianola and the Matagorda peninsula were soon in the hands of the Federals, but early in 1864 all were evacuated, save Brazos Santiago, left in charge of the U. S. Navy, which captured several boats belonging to the Confederacy. Banks' Red River campaign was undertaken with the object of possessing all the country west and south of Red River. The Louisianians and Texans defeated him at all points and drove him ignominiously away.

During the month of September, Brownsville was captured by her old enemy, Cortina, under peculiar circumstances. A French force of about 5,000 took Bagdad, at the mouth of the Rio Grande, with the object of taking possession of Matamoras, where Cortina was then in command. Brownsville was at that time occupied by Colonel Ford with a considerable force of Texan cavalry, and Brazos Santiago was still held by the Federals. On the 6th the French began to move up the right bank of the river, and their advance became engaged with Cortina, who had marched with 3,000 Mexicans and sixteen pieces of artillery from Matamoras to meet them. There seems to have been some understanding between Ford and the French commander, for during the engagement the former appeared on the other side of the Rio Grande with a large herd of cattle for the use of the invading army, and, immediately crossing the river, took part in the conflict by attacking the rear of Cortina's army. The Mexican commander, however, succeeded in repulsing both Ford and the French, who retreated to Bagdad. Cortina next turned his attention to Ford. On the 9th he passed with his whole force and drove the Texans from Brownsville, and took possession of the town for the United States. The tactics of Kirby Smith prolonged the war in Texas until May 26, 1864, when he surrendered to General Canby, the last battle being fought at Palo Alto on May 13—the scene of Austin's defeat in the war with Mexico. The history of the Reconstruction period, would be the reciting of shocking cruelties and injustices, more methodical than during the war, but none the less brutal. Cortina was a mild, just soldier and statesman, compared with the leaders of the conquerors and conquered in Texas, from 1865 to 1871 and, perhaps, until 1879.

Under the rule of Spanish viceroys, Texas was governed by a commandant, who made his headquarters at Chihuahua. Later the commandancy merged into a governorship, which obtained until 1821, when Mexico became a Republic, and Texas with Coahuila became one of her States. In 1830, civil rulers gave place to military government in the joint State, which continued until April 21, 1836, when Santa Anna, the Mexican Republican was defeated at San Jacinto, and the Republic of Texas was master of the situation. The story of the troubles leading up to the formation of the Republic is best told in the pages devoted to military affairs. Here is given a brief sketch of its political life from November, 1835, to February, 1846, when officers were elected to administer Texas as a State of the United States.

By authority of a resolution adopted December 10, 1835, by the provisional government of Texas, which existed from November, 1835, to March, 1836, delegates, clothed with plenary powers, were elected February 1, 1836, to meet in convention at Washington, on the Brazos, March 1. The provisional government was composed of Henry Smith, Governor; James W. Robinson, vice-Governor; and a council. At the period of the meeting of the convention, the council had quarreled with and deposed the Governor, and Mr. Robinson was Acting Governor. A series of resolutions, known as the Declaration of Independence was signed by fifty-eight delegates on March 2, 1836. The executive ordinance was adopted March 16, and the Constitution of the Republic of Texas on the night of March 17, that year. On the 18th of March, the convention assembled for the last time, and elected David G. Burnett President *ad interim* of the Republic, and Lorenzo de Zavala, a patriot Mexican exile, vice-President. They also elected the members of the

Cabinet, namely: Samuel P. Carson, Secretary of State; Bailey Hardeman, Secretary of the Treasury; Thomas J. Rusk, Secretary of War; Robert Potter, Secretary of the Navy; and David Thomas, Attorney General.

In October, 1836, a regular election was held, when Houston was chosen President and Mirabeau B. Lamar, vice-President. Burnett and Zavala retired so as to permit the prompt inauguration of the new president. President Houston appointed as members of his cabinet eminent men from the principal parties. Stephen F. Austin was made Secretary of State; Henry Smith, Secretary of the Treasury; Thomas J. Rusk, of War; S. Rhodes Fisher, of the Navy; Robert Burr, Postmaster General; and J. Pinckney Henderson, Attorney General. General Felix Houston was given command of the Army.

On November 16, Congress empowered the President to appoint a minister to the United States, to negotiate with this government for the recognition of the independence of Texas and her annexation to this Republic. A bond issue for $5,000,000, bearing ten per centum interest was authorized; a twenty-four-gun sloop of war, two armed steamers and two eleven-gun schooners were purchased; the Texas Railroad, Navigation and Banking Company was chartered; the boundaries of the Republic defined and other legislation, just and otherwise, enacted. The recognition of Texas by the United States dates to March 1, 1837. Subsequently Alcee La Branche was appointed United States Chargé d'affaires in Texas, and Mexico lost all hope of ever resuming authority over that great State, which she had so long treated with contempt.

The Congress which assembled May 1, 1837, devoted attention particularly to the intricate land question, to the establishment of county boundaries and the incorporation of towns. The towns of Shelbyville, Brazoria, Richmond, San Felipe de Austin, Lagrange, San Antonio, Victoria, Gonzalez, Matagorda, Mina, Houston, Washington, Crockett, Refugio, Columbia, Clarksville, Lexington, Milam, Goliad, San Patricio and Jonesborough were all incorporated during this session; and the new counties of Montgomery, Fayette, Fannin, Robertson and Fort Bender were created. Some of the above mentioned towns, however, had been incorporated once before.

From the reports of the State officers, it is seen that 10,890 certificates of land title had been issued by the different county boards up to November 1, 1838, representing 26,242,199 acres; that up to October 15, 2,990,000 acres had been distributed to soldiers as land bounties; that the issues of land scrip amounted to 2,193,000 acres, of which scrip to the amount of 870,000 acres had been returned by the agents, and a portion, representing 60,800 acres, had been funded. But financially, the outlook was bad. The public debt had been increased, and the credit of the Republic was nearly exhausted. Considerable legislation was enacted with reference to the public finances, with the prospect that immigration and the increased interest taken in Texan securities by persons in the United States, the way out of their difficulties would be found in due time. By the constitution the term of office of the President was limited to two years, without his being eligible for re-election; succeeding Presidents were to hold their office for three years. Consequently Houston's term expired on the first Monday in December, 1838. The election was held in September, the candidates being Mirabeau B. Lamar, Peter W. Grayson, James Collingsworth and Robert Wilson; but before the election Grayson and Collingsworth both committed suicide. Lamar was chosen President almost unanimously, and David G. Burnett, vice-President. One historian says that during the three years of Lamar's administration the public debt increased from $1,887,526 to $7,300,000, and that the securities decreased from sixty-five and eighty-five to fifteen and twenty cents; but, according to ex-President Houston's subsequent report, matters were not quite as bad as that. It may be said, however, that the officials had as little regard for the purses or property of the people as the carpet baggers of *post-bellum* days had. Legal plundering ruled.

The establishment of the Republic was so well received in the United States that President Jackson sent an agent into Texas to report on the political and military state of the little Republic. This agent found a population of 58,500, and a debt of $1,250,000; reported favorably to President Jackson, and this report led to American recognition in 1837.

During the first presidency of Mr. Houston, General J. P. Henderson was sent to London and Paris to obtain an acknowledgment from those countries of Texan independence, and from the first the British government was favorably disposed, on account of Texas being an agricultural country and the people inclined to free trade, thus opening new channels for English commerce. France, indeed, recognized the independence of Texas in 1839, but this friendly relation was soon interrupted by a ridiculous affair until some time in 1842. Holland and Belgium recognized it in 1840, and England in 1841. But all the efforts made to obtain a like recognition from Mexico failed.

The Texas presidential election of September, 1844, resulted in a victory for the anti-annexationists, being a choice of Anson Jones for President, who was known to be opposed to annexation. Kenneth L. Anderson was chosen vice-President. Edward Burleson was the defeated candidate for the presidency. Houston, in his farewell message, gave a very cheerful view of political affairs. But, being yet weak, Texas was in fact only a shuttlecock for the stronger powers. Houston, by his pacific policy, had brought the Indians to terms of peace, and by his economical administration had improved the financial condition of the Republic, while in agricultural and commercial respects Texas began to thrive. In his inaugural address President Jones said that his policy would be the maintenance of the public credit, the reduction of the expenses of government, the abolishment of paper issues, the revision of the tariff law, the establishment of public schools, the speedy attainment of peace with Mexico and just and friendly relations with the Indians, the introduction of the penitentiary system, and the encouragement of internal improvements. Not a word did he say with reference to annexation. But annexation loomed up so rapidly that Jones' administration was destined to be short. February 28, 1845, only three months after his inauguration, the United States Congress passed a joint resolution in favor of admitting Texas into the Union. May 5th, President Jones proclaimed an election of delegates to a convention to consider the adoption of the proposition of the United States, and, meeting at Austin, July 4, they recommended annexation, and submitted to a popular vote the proposition of the United States Congress, along with a proposed State constitution, which, on October 13, were ratified by a vote almost unanimous. February 19, 1846, President Jones surrendered the executive authority to the newly elected Governor, J. Pinckney Henderson, who was inaugurated February 16, 1846. Thus the lone star of Texas became one of a glorious constellation.

It was once generally believed in Georgia that the Lone Star flag was the workmanship of a Miss Troutman, of Crawford County, that State, who afterward married a Mr. Pope, of Alabama; and that she presented the same to a Georgia battalion commanded by Lieutenant-Colonel Ward. It was of plain white silk, bearing an azure star of five points on either side. On one side was the inscription, " Liberty or Death," and on the other side the appropriate Latin motto, " *Ubi Libertas Habitat, ibi Nostra Patria est.*" This flag was unfurled at Velasco January 8, 1836, and proudly floated on the breeze from the same liberty pole with the first flag of independence, which had just been brought from Goliad by the valiant Captain William Brown, who subsequently did such daring service in the Texas navy. On the meeting of the first Congress the flag of the Lone Star was adopted as the national flag of the young Republic. But another authority denies the Georgian belief, and insists that the first Lone Star flag ever unfurled in Texas was presented by Mrs. Sarah R. Dawson to a company of volunteers raised in Harrisburg, Texas, in 1835, and commanded by Captain Andrew Robinson. The flag was a tri-color of red, white and blue, the star being white, five-pointed and set in a ground of red.

January 14, 1839, Congress appointed five commissioners to select a site for the capital of the Republic. The commissioners were Albert C. Horton, Lewis P. Cook, Isaac W. Burton, William Menifee and J. Campbell, who made choice of the location where Austin now stands. Although at that date the new town, which was immediately laid out, was situated on the extreme frontier of the settlements, the commissioners showed their wisdom in their selection. They aimed at establishing a permanent capital, which would occupy a central position when Texas had become a thickly populated country; and though the government would be near the Indians, Austin as the seat would draw settlers more rapidly westward.

During the month of November, 1840, the Congress assembled there, surrounded by the wilderness. The seat of government for the Republic of Texas, like that of most other new governments, was subject to frequent change. The following is the order, with the dates: San Felipe, November, 1835; Washington, March, 1836; Harrisburg, same month; Galveston, April 16, 1836; Velasco, May, 1836; Columbia, October, 1836; Houston, May, 1837; Austin, October, 1839; Houston, in 1842, a short time; Washington, November, 1842; Austin, 1845 to the present time. The new State capitol has a length of 566 feet 6 inches, inclusive of porticos; width, 288 feet 10 inches at widest point; height, 311 feet from grade line to top of statue on dome.

The chief executives of Texas from 1691 to 1891 are named as follows: The first were the Spanish, who ruled from 1691 to 1822, or for 131 years. The commandants, or governors, being: Domingo Teran, Don Gaspardo de Anaya, Don Martin de Alarconne, Marquis de Aguayo, Fernando de Almazan, Melchoir de Madiavilia, Juan Antonio Bustillos, Manuel de Sandoval, Carlos de Franquis, Prudencia Basterra, Justo Boneo, Jacinto de Barrios, Antonio de Martos, Juan Maria, Baron de Riperda, Domingo Cabello, Rafael Pacheco, Manuel Muñoz, Juan Bautista el Guazabel, Antonio Cordero, Manuel de Salcedo, Christoval Dominguez, Antonio Martinez.

The Mexican governors ruled from 1822 to 1835, or 13 years. Their names and dates of appointment are given as follows: Trespalacios, 1822;

Don Luciana le Garcia, 1823; Rafael Gonzales (Coahuila and Texas), 1825; Victor Blanco, 1826; Jose Maria Viesca, 1828; Jose Maria Letona, 1831; and Francisco Vidauri, 1834.

Under the rule of the Texan—1835 to 1846—or 11 years, were Henry Smith, Provisional Governor, 1835–36; David G. Burnett, President *ad interim*, 1836; Sam Houston, Constitutional President, 1836; Mirabeau B. Lamar, President, 1838; Sam Houston, President, 1841; and Anson Jones, President, 1844–46.

The State government since annexation—1846 to 1894—48 years—has been presided over by the following named governors: J. Pinckney Henderson, 1846; George T. Wood, 1847; P. H. Bell, 1849–51; P. H, Bell, 1851–53; E. M. Pease, 1853–55; E. M. Pease, 1855–57; H. R. Runnels, 1857–59; Sam Houston, 1859–61; Edward Clark, 1861; F. R. Lubbock, 1861–63; Pendleton Murrah, 1863–65; A. J. Hamilton (Provisional), 1865–66; James W. Throckmorton, 1866–67; E. M. Pease (Provisional), 1867–70; E. J. Davis, 1870–74; Richard Coke, 1874–76; R. B. Hubbard, 1876–79; O. M. Roberts, 1879–83; John Ireland, 1883–87; L. S. Ross, 1887–91; and J. S. Hogg, 1891–94.

In 1868 a new constitution was adopted, and in 1874 the Kiowa and Comanche Indians, who opposed the settlement of the central and plain regions of Texas, were reduced to submission and ultimately driven out. The sale of the original territory of Texas (north and west of her present boundaries), to the United States, for $10,000,000, was a necessary proceeding at that time, and, indeed, a wise one, as was the article which provided for the ownership of all lands within the State boundaries, and the right to divide the territory into five States when such would appear just and profitable. The Legislature consists of thirty-two Senators, elected for four years, and 115 Representatives, chosen for two years, restricted to biennial sessions of ninety days each. There are thirteen congressional and forty judicial districts, embracing 232 counties, of which seventy counties were unorganized in 1880.

As soon as Texas declared her independence of Mexico, she declared in her constitution the necessity of a school system. In 1839 the Congress of the new republic assigned three leagues of land to each organized county, and in the following year an additional league, for the purpose of establishing primary schools. At the same time, fifty leagues were devoted to the establishment of two colleges or universities, to be thereafter created. In February, 1840, a law was passed making the chief justice of each county, with the two associate justices, a board of school commissioners, as an executive body, and under their supervision many schools were organized and conducted.

In 1850 there were 349 public schools, with 360 teachers and 7,746 pupils. By 1860 there were 1,218 schools, with a corresponding increase of teachers and pupils. But even yet the schools were not entirely supported by public tax. Considering the many political revulsions, Indian depredations, etc., to which the State of Texas has been subject, it is remarkable to observe the advance she has made in education, and the refinements of modern civilized life. The last Civil War was, of course, the greatest interruption to her progress in all directions. Under the constitution of 1866, all funds, lands and other property previously set apart for the support of the free-school system were re-dedicated as a perpetual fund.

The constitution of 1868 did not materially alter these provisions, except in one marked particular, namely, the significant omission of the provision appropriating the taxes paid by colored persons for the support of schools for their children. The schools were made free to all. The article in the constitution reads: "It shall be the duty of the legislature of this State to make suitable provisions for the support and maintenance of a system of public free schools, for the gratuitous instruction of all the inhabitants of this State, between the ages of six and eighteen."

Since the adoption of the constitution of 1868, improvements have been constantly made, either by constitutional provision or legislation, until now, when the State has as good a school system as any in the Union.

In seventy-five counties the schools are operated on a peculiar plan called the community system. The community has no geographical boundaries, and enrollment on the community list is a matter of local enterprise. Local taxes can be levied in community counties.

The State endowment of the common schools is large. About $7,427,-808.75 in interest-bearing bonds, more than $14,380,906.37 in interest-bearing land notes, and about 20,000,000 acres of unsold lands constitute the State endowment. Of the unsold school lands a large amount is leased at four cents per acre, and the funds thus derived added to the annual available school fund.

Besides the State endowment fund, each county has been granted by the State four leagues of land, which constitute county endowment. As these lands are sold, the funds received are invested under the authority of the county commissioners' court, and the interest on the investment is annually applied to the support of the schools. A considerable portion of these lands is leased for varying terms of years, and the rental applied as the rental of the State school lands. These lands are under the exclusive control of the county authorities; 3,896,640 acres have been thus granted to counties, and a reservation has been made from the public domain for the unorganized counties.

In 1879 the Normal School was established by the State of Texas, for the purpose of training competent teachers for the public schools. Regarding the Normal School as the heart of the public-school system, it was decided to name the proposed institution the "Sam Houston Normal Institute," in honor of the hero of Texas independence. Houston had spent the evening of his eventful life in Huntsville. Here was his neglected grave. As an everlasting monument to the honored dead the Normal School was located at Huntsville. On the 1st of October, 1879, the institute opened, with Bernard Mallon as principal.

The Prairie View State Normal School is located six miles east of Hempstead, in Waller County. It is a branch of the Agricultural and Mechanical College of Texas, and under the government of the Board of Directors of that school. Originally it was designed for an industrial school, but the lack of education among the colored people of the State, and the pressing need of trained teachers for the colored schools, led to a change of objects, and it was therefore converted into a normal school for training colored teachers. The constant and steadily increasing patronage it has since received, is the best evidence of the wisdom of the change—the session of 1888-1889, having the largest attendance and being the most prosperous in the history of the institution.

The Agricultural and Mechanical College of Texas owes its foundation and endowment to the act of the United States Congress, approved July 2, 1862, amended July 23, 1865, and to a joint resolution of the Legislature of Texas, approved November 1, 1866, and an act of the same body approved April 17, 1871. Under these acts and the special laws of the Legislature growing out of them, the first board of directors met at Austin, July 16, 1875, and proceeded to organize the college. Finally the constitution of 1876, article VII, provided that the Agricultural and Mechanical College of Texas, established by the act of the Legislature passed April 17, 1871, located in the county of Brazos, is "hereby made and constituted a branch of the University of Texas, for the instruction in agriculture, the mechanic arts, and the natural sciences connected therewith." In November, 1866, the Legislature formally accepted from Congress the gift of 180,000 acres of public land for the endowment of an agricultural and mechanical college. This land was sold for $174,000, which sum was invested in 7 per cent. State bonds. As under the act of Congress neither principal nor interest of this money could be used for other purposes than the payment of officers' salaries, at the time of the opening of the college there was an addition to the fund, from accumulated interest, of $35,000. This was invested in 6 per cent. bonds of the State, thus furnishing an annual income of $14,280. The county of Brazos donated to the college 2,416 acres of land lying on each side of the Houston & Texas Central railroad.

The Agricultural Experiment Station of theAgricultural and Mechanical College of Texas, College Station, Texas, authorized by Congress in 1887, was established shortly after.

The University of Texas owes its existence to the wisdom, foresight and statesmanship of the founders of the Republic of Texas, who made the most ample provision for its establishment and maintenance in the legislation of that period. By an act of the Third Congress, fifty leagues of land were offered as an endowment, to which $100,000 were added by the Legislature of February 11, 1858. The constitution of 1876 reappropriated all grants, save the one-tenth section, in lieu of which 1,000,000 acres were set apart of unappropriated lands. In March, 1881, the act for the location and organization of the university was passed, and by vote Austin was selected as the site. On September 15, 1883, the building was open for the reception of students. In that year 1,000,000 acres of the public debt land were added to the permanent university fund, and of all this acreage 2,020,049 acres remained unsold on the last day of December, 1891.

The State Asylum for the Blind was established September 2, 1856, and has for its object the education of blind persons. It is not an asylum where the indigent and helpless are cared for at the public expense, but a school in which the blind receive such general education and training in industrial pursuits as will aid them to become self-supporting as other classes. When the course of study prescribed has been completed the pupils return to their homes, as do the students of other schools, and like them are no longer a charge upon the State.

The State Deaf and Dumb Asylum is situated at the State capital, on a commanding height south of the Colorado River, and is justly regarded as one of the most beautiful and healthful locations in the city.

The Deaf and Dumb and Blind Asylum for colored youth was established by an act of the Twentieth Legislature, which provided for the appointment of a board to select a site near the city of Austin, and appropriated $50,000 for the erection of buildings and the purchase of furniture. An admirable location, about two and a quarter miles northwest of Austin, was selected for the buildings, and the institution first opened for the reception of students October 1, 1887.

The State Lunatic Asylum is situated about two miles north of Austin, on a beautiful plateau of ground adorned and beautified by flowers, plants, summer-houses and forest trees, the latter constituting a splendid park. The estimated value of the buildings and grounds is $505,000.

The North Texas Hospital for the Insane, located at Terrell, in Kaufman County, was opened for the reception of patients July 15, 1885. It was established in obedience to a general demand for increased accommodations for the insane.

The State Orphan Asylum was required to be established by an act of the Twentieth Legislature, approved April 4, 1887. The Governor was required to appoint three commissioners to select a site for the asylum. Competition between the various towns in the State for the location of the institution was invited, which resulted in the selection of Corsicana, in Navarro county. The sum of $5,700 was appropriated out of the available Orphan Asylum fund for the establishment of the institution. Subsequently, at the special session of the Twentieth Legislature, $15,000 and the available fund to the credit of the asylum in the State treasury was appropriated for the erection of the buildings and other improvements. The site on which the asylum is located and the surrounding scenery are unsurpassed by any place in the State for their beauty and adaptability to such an institution. The buildings, which are constructed on the cottage plan, and have a capacity of about 200 inmates, were completed and the institution formally opened July 15, 1889.

Texan benevolence is not solely administered by the State. No less than eight hospitals, with several orphanages and asylums are carried on without State aid.

By act of the Twentieth Legislature, approved March 29, 1887, a State house of correction and reformatory for youthful convicts were authorized, and the Governor required to appoint a commission to locate the same. The institution was located two and one-fourth miles northeast of Gatesville, Coryell county, and the necessary buildings erected there during the summer of 1888. Up to date of the last report of the Superintendent $75,890 had been expended in the purchase of land, erection of buildings, and equipping the institution. The institution has a capacity of about 100, and was opened January 3, 1889.

The law of 1881 for organizing the State penitentiaries provided that the system of labor in the State penitentiaries should be by lease, by contract, by the State, or partly by one system and partly by the other, as shall be in the discretion of the penitentiary board deemed for the best interests of the State. The Eighteenth Legislature in 1883 repealed that portion of the law of 1881 authorizing the lease of the penitentiaries, and consequently the contract and State account systems only are allowed. At Huntsville, Rusk, Harlem and other places the convicts are worked on State and private farms.

Prior to the era of independence about the only efforts, of which there is record, to establish Protestantism in Texas were those of the Baptists, who failed to make their institutions permanent. In 1837 a Baptist church was

organized at Washington, Z. N. Morrell being chosen pastor, and money was subscribed to build a house of worship. The first Protestant Episcopal church was established in 1838, at Matagorda, by Caleb S. Ives, who collected a congregation, established a school and built a church. During the same year R. M. Chapman organized a parish in Houston. The statistics of religious denominations in Texas is estimated as follows; the actual adult members being only recognized. Methodist Episcopal, South, 151,533; Baptist, 127,377; Episcopal,9,982; Methodist Episcopal(North), 25,739; German Lutheran(1877), 2,270; Presbyterian, 2,414; Southern Presbyterian(1877), 13,555; Cumberland Presbyterian, 24,257; Christian, 55,000; Primitive Baptist, 1,000; Seventh-Day Adventists, 300; Universalists, 95; Brethren (Dunkards), 125; Free Methodists, 100; Catholics, 157,000; Hebrew, 300; Methodist Protestant, 6,300; Colored M. E. Church in America, 12,162; African Methodist Episcopal, 12,900; Colored Baptist, 100,681.

The first printing-press in Texas was put into operation at Nacogdoches in 1819, and was brought to that place by General Long, who established a provisional government and a supreme council, and issued a declaration proclaiming Texas an independent republic. The office was placed under the management of Horatio Bigelow, and was used for the publication of various laws enacted and proclamations issued by that short lived government.

The first regular newspaper, however, made its initial appearance about 1829, at San Felipe, bearing the name, *The Cotton Plant.* Godwin B. Cotten was editor and proprietor. In 1832 its name was changed to the *Texas Republican.*

The second paper was the *Texas Gazette* and *Brazoria Advertiser*, published in Brazoria in 1830. In September, 1832, it was merged into the *Constitutional Advocate* and *Texas Public Adverliser*, with D. W. Anthony as owner and editor, who died in 1833, and the paper ceased.

Next was the *Texas Republican* of Brazoria, by F. C. Gray, in December, 1834. This was printed on the old press brought into the realm by Cotten, before mentioned. In January, 1835, this was the only paper published in Texas, and in August, 1836, it was discontinued.

The fourth newspaper was the *Telegraph*, started in August 1836, at San Felipe, by Gail and Thomas H. Borden and Joseph Baker. A Mexican force seized this in April, 1836, and threw the material of the office into a bayou at Harrisburg, to which place it had been moved after the abandonment of San Felipe by the Americans. In August, that year, the Bordens bought a new press and material and revived the *Telegraph* at Columbia, and subsequently moved to Houston, where the paper was published for many years, under the name of the *Houston Telegraph.*

After the establishment of Texan independence the number of newspapers increased rapidly, until now the State has as many newspapers as any other in proportion to population. The first daily paper established in Texas was the *Morning Star* by Cruger & Moore of the *Telegraph* between 1840 and 1844. The Texas Editorial and Press Association was organized September 10, 1873, and afterward incorporated.

During the last fifteen years railroad systems have been established at a comparatively rapid rate. In 1870 there were less than 300 miles in operation; in 1876, 1,600 miles; in 1885, over 7,000 miles; and in 1890, according to the last census, 8,914.

4

In the time of the Republic numerous charters for railroads were granted, but no road was built. It was not until 1852 that the first road was commenced. That year a preliminary survey was made and some work done on what was then called the Buffalo Bayou, Brazos & Colorado Railroad, starting from Harrisburg and going westerly; and within the same year the first locomotive was set to work at Harrisburg, the first in Texas and the fourth west of the Mississippi. The company was organized June 1, 1850, at Boston, Mass., by General Sidney Sherman, who may be regarded as the father of railroads in Texas. The work progressed slowly, and the Colorado was not reached till 1859, when the line was opened to Eagle Lake, sixty-five miles from the place of beginning. By 1866 the line had reached Columbus, the river being bridged at Alleyton. A change in the charter made in 1870 fixed upon San Antonio as the objective point, and since that time it has been known as the Galveston, Harrisburg & San Antonio Railway, or "Sunset route," but is now incorporated in the great Southern Pacific system. January 15, 1877, the road reached San Antonio, the citizens of Bexar county having voted, in January, 1876, $300,000 in county bonds to secure the speedy completion of the line. In the same month the passenger terminus was changed from Harrisburg to Houston by a line from Pierce Junction. The line has since been extended to El Paso, to connect there with the Southern Pacific, going on to the Pacific coast. At that point it also connects with the Mexican Central. The length of the main line is 848 miles, and no railroad in Texas has had more influence in the settlement and development of the country.

The next railroad commenced in Texas was the Houston & Texas Central. The original charter was granted in 1848, by which the company was incorporated under the title of the Galveston & Red River Railroad Company. Their line was to extend from Galveston to the northern boundary of the State. Work was begun in 1853, at Houston, by the first incorporator, Ebenezer Allen, and at that time the name was changed to its present form. The rivalry between Galveston and Houston was satisfied by a compromise, under which arrangement the two cities were connected by the Galveston, Houston & Henderson Road, which was begun at Virginia Point, and completed in 1865, and a junction was made with the Houston & Texas Central. In 1859 a bridge was constructed across the bay by the city of Galveston.

Construction proceeded slowly, only eighty miles having been made by the time of the breaking out of the Civil War, which completely interrupted further building. In March, 1873, it reached Denison, forming there a junction with the Missouri, Kansas & Texas Road, thus opening rail communication with St. Louis. Houston has become the railroad center of the State, having at least ten trunk lines.

The Gulf, Colorado & Santa Fe line was chartered in May, 1873, as a Galveston enterprise. Construction was commenced at Virginia Point in May, 1875, and the road opened for traffic as far as Richmond in 1878. Other important systems of late introduction are the Missouri, Kansas & Texas, Atchison, Topeka & Santa Fe, San Antonio & Aransas Pass, St. Louis, Arkansas & Texas ("Cotton Belt,"), International & Great Northern, Texas & Pacific, and the recent extension of the Chicago, Rock Island & Pacific from the Red River to Fort Worth by an auxiliary corporation, etc.

All the above mentioned trunk lines have of course several branches, so that it can now be said in familiar parlance that the State of Texas is "gridironed " with railroads, and still construction is going on, and many more lines are projected. The following table shows the number of miles of railroad in the State:

Austin & Northwestern 76, East Line & Red River 121.35, Fort Worth & Denver City 467.34, Fort Worth & New Orleans 40.50, Fort Worth & Rio Grande 112.54, Galveston, Harrisburg & San Antonio 926.30, Galveston, Houston & Henderson 50, Houston & Texas Central 510, Gulf, Colorado & Santa Fe 958.25, Gulf, West Texas & Pacific 111.10, Houston, East & West Texas 191.38, International & Great Northern †647, New York, Texas & Mexican 91, Missouri, Kansas & Texas 389.39, *Sherman, Denison & Dallas 9.53, *Dallas & Greenville 52.43, *East Line & Red River 31.76, *Gainesville, Henrietta & Western 70.57, *Dallas & Wichita 37.62, *Dallas & Waco 65.57, *Trinity & Sabine 66.55, *Taylor, Bastrop & Houston 105.89, San Antonio & Aransas Pass 637.20, St. Louis, Arkansas & Texas 554.05, Southern Kansas & Texas 100.41, Sabine & East Texas 103.47, Texas Central 288.80, Texas Mexican 178.61, Texas, Sabine Valley & Northwestern 38, Texas Trunk 51, Texas & Pacific 1,125.95, Tyler Southeastern 89.08, Texas Western 52.25, Texas & New Orleans 105.10, Weatherford, Mineral Wells & Northwestern 20.05, Central Texas & Northwestern 12, Wichita Valley 51.36. Totals, 8,914.13.

The population of Texas, by decades, is shown as follows—1835—50,000; 1845—150,000; 1850—212,592; 1860—604,215; 1870—818,579; 1880—1,591,749, and 1890—2,235,523. Of the total for 1890, 2,082,567 are natives of the United States and 152,956 of other countries. The number of whites in 1890 was 1,745,935, and the number of Africans, 488,171. There were three Japanese and 704 civilized Indians within its boundaries when the last census was taken. Of the native born white population 1,082,533 are males, and 1,000,034 females; of the foreign born whites, 90,020 are males and 62,936 females, while of the colored population 246,517 are males and 243,071 females. There were 402,422 dwellings in the State in 1800, or 5.56 persons to a dwelling, against 27,988 dwellings in 1850 and 287,562 dwellings in 1880, when there were 5.54 persons to each habitable house. The population by counties (as enumerated in 1890) and the date of organization of each county, are given as follows:

COUNTY.	POP. 1890.	ORGANIZED.	COUNTY.	POP. 1890.	ORGANIZED.
Anderson	20,923	1846	Bee	3,720	1858
Andrews	24	....	Bell	33,377	1850
Angelina	6,306	1846	Bexar	49,266	1837
Aransas	1,824	1871	Bexar District	......	....
Archer	2,104	1880	Blanco	4,649	1858
Armstrong	944	1890	Borden	222	1877
Atascosa	6,459	1856	Bosque	14,224	1854
Austin	17,859	1837	Bowie	20,267	1841
Bailey	......	....	Brazoria	11,506	1837
Bandera	3,795	1856	Brazos	16,650	1843
Bastrop	20,736	1837	Brewster	710	1887
Baylor	2,595	1879	Briscoe	......	....

†Only 250.80 miles are taxed.
*Operated by the Missouri, Kansas & Texas.

COUNTY.	POP. 1890.	ORGAN-IZED.	COUNTY.	POP. 1890.	ORGAN-IZED.
Brown	11,421	1857	Encinal	2,744	....
Buchel	298	....	Erath	21,594	1856
Burleson	13,001	1846	Falls	20,706	1850
Burnet	10,747	1854	Fannin	38,709	1838
Caldwell	15,769	1848	Fayette	31,481	1838
Calhoun	815	1846	Fisher	2,996	1886
Callahan	5,457	1877	Floyd	529	1890
Cameron	14,424	1848	Foard	......	1891
Camp	6,624	1874	Foley	25	....
Carson	356	1888	Fort Bend	10,586	1838
Cass	22,554	1846	Franklin	6,481	1875
Castro	9	1891	Freestone	15,987	1850
Chambers	2,241	1858	Frio	3,112	1871
Cherokee	22,975	1846	Gaines	68	....
Childress	1,175	1887	Galveston	31,476	1839
Clay	7,503	1873	Garza	14	....
Cochran	......	....	Gillespie	7,056	1848
Coke	2,059	1889	Glasscock	208	1887
Coleman	6,112	1864	Goliad	5,910	1836
Collin	36,736	1846	Gonzales	18,016	1836
Collingsworth	357	1890	Gray	203	....
Colorado	19,512	1837	Grayson	53,211	1846
Comal	6,398	1846	Gregg	9,402	1873
Comanche	15,608	1856	Greer	......	1886
Concho	1,065	1879	Grimes	21,312	1846
Cooke	24,696	1849	Guadalupe	15,217	1846
Coryell	16,873	1854	Hale	721	1888
Cottle	240	....	Hall	703	1890
Crane	15	....	Hamilton	9,313	1858
Crockett	194	1891	Hansford	133	1889
Crosby	346	1886	Hardeman	3,904	1884
Dallam	112	1891	Hardin	3,956	1858
Dallas	67,042	1846	Harris	37,249	1837
D a w s o n (disap-peared)	......	....	Harrison	26,721	1842
Dawson	29	....	Hartley	252	1891
Deaf Smith	179	1890	Haskell	1,665	1885
Delta	9,117	1870	Hays	11,352	1848
Denton	21,289	1846	Hemphill	519	1887
Dewitt	14,307	1846	Henderson	12,285	1846
Dickens	295	1891	Hidalgo	6,534	1852
Dimmit	1,049	1880	Hill	27,583	1853
Donley	1,056	1882	Hockley	......	....
Duval	7,598	1876	Hood	7,614	1866
Eastland	10,373	1873	Hopkins	20,572	1846
Ector	224	1891	Houston	19,360	1882
Edwards	1,970	1883	Howard	1,210	1837
Ellis	31,774	1850	Hunt	31,885	1846
El Paso	15,678	1871	Hutchinson	58	....
			Irion	870	1889

County.	Pop. 1890.	Organized.	County.	Pop. 1890.	Organized.
Jack	9,740	1857	Morris	6,580	1875
Jackson	3,281	1837	Motley	139	1891
Jasper	5,592	1837	Nacogdoches	15,984	1837
Jeff Davis	1,394	1887	Navarro	26,373	1846
Jefferson	5,857	1837	Newton	4,650	1846
Johnson	22,313	1854	Nolan	1,573	1881
Jones	3,797	1881	Nueces	8,093	1846
Karnes	3,637	1854	Ochiltree	198	1889
Kaufman	21,598	1848	Oldham	270	1891
Kendall	3,826	1862	Orange	4,770	1852
Kent	324	—	Palo Pinto	8,320	1857
Kerr	4,462	1856	Panola	14,328	1846
Kimble	2,243	1876	Parker	21,682	1856
King	173	1891	Parmer	7	—
Kinney	3,781	1874	Pecos	1,326	1872
Knox	1,134	1886	Polk	10,332	1846
Lamar	37,302	1841	Potter	849	1887
Lamb	4	—	Presidio	1,698	1875
Lampasas	7,584	1856	Rains	3,909	1870
La Salle	2,139	1880	Randall	187	1889
Lavaca	21,887	1846	Red River	21,452	1837
Lee	11,952	1874	Reeves	1,247	1884
Leon	18,841	1846	Refugio	1,239	1837
Liberty	4,230	1837	Roberts	326	1889
Limestone	21,678	1846	Robertson	26,506	1838
Lipscomb	632	1887	Rockwall	5,972	1873
Live Oak	2,055	1856	Runnels	3,193	1880
Llano	6,772	1856	Rusk	18,559	1843
Loving	3	—	Sabine	4,969	1837
Lubbock	33	1891	San Augustine	6,688	1837
Lynn	24	—	San Jacinto	7,360	1870
McCulloch	3,217	1876	San Patricio	1,312	1837
McLennan	39,204	1850	San Saba	6,641	1856
McMullen	1,038	1877	Schleicher	155	—
Madison	8,512	1854	Scurry	1,415	1884
Marion	10,862	1860	Shackelford	2,012	1874
Martin	264	1884	Shelby	14,365	1837
Mason	5,180	1856	Sherman	34	1889
Matagorda	3,985	1837	Smith	28,324	1846
Maverick	3,698	1871	Somervell	3,419	1875
Medina	3,730	1848	Starr	10,749	1848
Menard	1,215	1871	Stephens	4,926	1876
Midland	1,033	1885	Sterling	—	1891
Milam	24,773	1837	Stonewall	1,024	1888
Mills	5,493	1887	Sutton	658	1890
Mitchell	2,059	1881	Swisher	100	1890
Montague	18,863	1858	Tarrant	41,142	1850
Montgomery	11,765	1837	Taylor	6,957	1878
Moore	15	—	Terry	21	—

County.	Pop. 1890.	Organized.	County.	Pop. 1890.	Organized.
Throckmorton	902	1879	Washington	29,161	1837
Titus	8,190	1846	Webb	14,842	1848
Tom Green	5,152	1875	Wharton	7,584	1846
Travis	36,322	1843	Wheeler	778	1879
Trinity	7,648	1850	Wichita	4,831	1882
Tyler	10,877	1846	Wilbarger	7,092	1881
Upshur	12,695	1846	Williamson	25,900	1848
Upton	52	——	Wilson	10,655	1860
Uvalde	3,804	1856	Winkler	18	——
Valverde	2,874	1885	Wise	24,134	1856
Van Zandt	16,225	1848	Wood	13,932	1850
Victoria	8,737	1837	Yoakum	4	——
Walker	12,874	1846	Young	5,049	1874
Waller	10,888	1873	Zapata	3,562	1858
Ward	77	——	Zavalla	1,097	1884

The area of the State is 274,366 square miles, or over 70,000 square miles larger than France; about 78,000 larger than Spain; 63,000 larger than the German Empire, in Europe; 73,000 more than the Austro-Hungarian Empire and within 24,000 square miles of Sweden and Norway. In 1890 there were only forty-four inhabitants to every five square miles of its area, while England and Wales, having only an area of 58,320 miles, were credited with 29,001,018 inhabitants in 1891, (of whom 780,457 were registered dependents or paupers) or over 497 inhabitants to each square mile, against eighty-eight in Texas. Were Texas as thickly populated as England, it would contain 136,359,902 inhabitants. With her sea coast, her fertile lands capable of producing cotton and sugar as well as potatoes and wheat, her storehouses of mineral wealth and wealthy neighbors on the West, East and North, Texas to-day holds the key to her destiny. Her development rests in good hands

GEN. SAM HOUSTON.

BIOGRAPHICAL SKETCHES.

GEN. SAMUEL HOUSTON.

In early days there drifted within the borders of Texas men of splendid talents and marked genius, who sought new scenes, far removed from those of earlier days. One of those who bravely fought for the freedom of Texas, and was one of the most striking types of her early men, was General Samuel Houston, whose life is inseparably linked with the early history of the Lone Star State. He came of Virginia stock, and was himself a native of Rockbridge County, that state, his birth occurring March 2, 1793, and from his ancestors he inherited Scotch and Irish blood. After the death of his father the family removed to near the Cherokee Territory, in the State of Tennessee, and there much of his time was spent among the Indians, by one of whom he was adopted. He grew up with but little education, and in 1813 enlisted in the Seventh United States Infantry, and soon attained the rank of sergeant. He took part in the battle of Horseshoe Bend, where his great courage attracted the attention of General Jackson, and he continued fighting, although he was wounded several times. He soon rose to the rank of second lieutenant, and for a time acted as sub-agent for the Cherokees, at Jackson's request. He became first lieutenant in March, 1818, but resigned the following May, owing to criticism which emanated from the War Department, which accused him of complicity in smuggling negroes from Florida into the United States; but he demanded an investigation and was fully exonerated. In June, 1818, he began studying law in Nashville, and in a few months was admitted to the bar, and his first practice

was done in Lebanon. The following year he was elected attorney
of Davidson District, moved to Nashville, and was appointed adjutant-general of the state. In 1821 he was elected major-general, and
within a year resigned the office of district attorney. In 1823 he was
elected to Congress, was re-elected in 1825, and in the last year of his
term he fought a duel with General White, whom he wounded. In
1827 he became a candidate for governor, and so great was his popularity that he was elected by an overwhelming majority. In January, 1829, he married a Miss Allen of Sumner County, Tenn., but
after a few weeks of wedded life Houston suddenly left his wife, without a word of explanation, but always protested that the cause of
separation in no way affected his wife's character. He was very
strongly condemned for his action in this matter, and amid a storm of
vituperation, made his way up Arkansas River to the mouth of the
Illinois River, where for three years he made his home with his Cherokee father by adoption. In 1832 he made a trip to Washington in the
interests of the Indians, wore the Indian garb, and was warmly wel-
comed by President Jackson. While there he was accused by William
Stansberry, an Ohio congressman, of attempting to obtain a fraudu-
lent contract for furnishing Indian supplies, and to retaliate, he attacked Stansberry and gave him a beating. For this he was fined
$500 and mildly reprimanded, but Jackson remitted the fine. He then
made a trip to Texas and became a member of the convention that
met at San Felipe de Austin, April 1, 1833, at which a constitution
was adopted in which Houston inserted a clause prohibiting the establishment of banks; was shortly after elected general of Texas
east of the Trinity River, and was a member of what was called the
"General Consultation," that met in October, 1835, for the purpose of
establishing a provisional government, and successfully opposed a
declaration of independence as premature. At this time he was
elected commander-in-chief of the Army of Texas, but was deprived
of his office through jealousy, before he could perfect a military organization. He was a member of the convention that met at New
Washington, and adopted a declaration of complete independence
March 2, 1836, and he was re-elected commander-in-chief. After the
battles of the Alamo and of Goliad, Houston, with 700 men, met the
main body of the Mexicans, 1,800 men, on the banks of the San Ja-

cinto, during which engagement the American battle-cry was, "Remember the Alamo!" The battle lasted less than an hour, during which time the Mexicans were totally defeated, their loss in killed being 630, and in captured 730, Santa Anna being among the latter. Houston, who was slightly wounded in the ankle, was treated with great injustice by the civil authorities, and retired to New Orleans, but in the autumn of 1836 returned to Nacogdoches. An election for president of the Republic had been announced, and twelve days before the election Houston announced himself as a candidate for the office, and out of 5,104 votes polled, he received 4,374, and became the first president of the Republic of Texas. Upon the expiration of his term, December 12, 1838, he left the country in a healthy condition, at peace with the Indians, on a friendly footing with Mexico, and with its treasury notes at par. For the two terms of 1839-1841 he was a member of the Texas Congress and did effective service for the state. In 1840 he was married to Miss Margaret Moffette, having secured a divorce from his first wife, and his second wife exercised a most wholesome and restraining influence over him. At the close of his second term in Congress he was again elected to the presidency of the Republic, and labored faithfully from December 12, 1841, to December 9, 1844, to remedy the mistakes made by his predecessor, Lamar. Congress in June, 1842, passed a bill making him dictator, and 10,000,000 acres of land were voted to resist the Mexican invasion that threatened. These measures were vetoed by Mr. Houston, and in time the danger passed away. In 1838 he took the first steps toward securing the annexation of Texas to the United States, and in 1845 Texas was admitted to the Union, and in March of the following year Mr. Houston became a United States Senator and served until 1859. He was a stanch Union man, strongly opposed the repeal of the Missouri compromise, and voted for all measures of compromise during the slavery agitation. He also opposed the Kansas and Nebraska bill, refused to sign the Southern address, and, during his entire term of service, he earnestly advocated the cause of the Indians, whom he always maintained had never violated a treaty. He was widely spoken of as a presidential candidate, but Franklin Pierce received the nomination. At Concord, N. H., he was again brought forward by the Democrats in 1854, as the people's candidate, and in the conven-

tion that met in 1856 Millard Fillmore was nominated in his stead.
In the convention that met in Baltimore, in 1860, John Bell of Tennessee received the nomination, although Houston stood next.   In
1857 Mr. Houston had been defeated for Governor of Texas by Harrison B. Runnels, but in 1859 he entered the lists as an independent
candidate and defeated Runnels.   He greatly deplored Lincoln's election to the Presidency in 1860, but maintained that this was no
grounds for secession.   When Texas declared for secession in 1861,
and all State officials were requested to take the oath of allegiance,
Mr. Houston refused to do so, and was deposed on the 18th of
March.   He likewise refused United States troops that were offered
him, and on the 10th of May, 1861, he made a speech at Independence,
Tex., in which he defined the position of the Southern Unionists, but
took no part in public life thereafter.

DAVY CROCKET BURLESON.

He who heads this sketch is the only living child of General Edward and Sarah G. Owen Burleson, who were born in North Carolina and Kentucky, respectively.   In 1848 General Edward Burleson
moved to Hays County, Tex., and located at the head of the San
Marcos River, where he made his home until death closed his early
career, January 1, 1851, at which time he was holding the office of
State Senator.   The subject of this sketch was reared in San Marcos,
and was educated there and at Baylor University.   He began life for
himself as a tiller of the soil, on a farm of his own near San Marcos,
and was following this occupation at the opening of the Civil War.
In March, 1862, he assisted in raising and organizing a company for
the Confederate service at Seguin, of which he was elected to the
office of second lieutenant.   Upon the organization of the regiment
to which it belonged, he was elected first lieutenant of Company B,

Thirty-second Texas Cavalry, and saw the most of his service in Texas and Louisiana. The first battle in which he participated was at Blair's Landing, Louisiana, being in the thickest of the fight, and after that he was in daily service and followed up General Banks on the latter's retreat down Red River to Yellow Bayou, where was fought one of the hardest battles of the war. In the winter of 1864 his command came to Texas, and in the spring of 1865 it was disbanded at Houston. Prior to the Civil War he had seen some military service, for he, in 1855, went out with Captain James H. Callihan, as a ranger, to protect the frontier against the Indians. While they were stationed in Kerr County, the captain suggested the plan to invade Mexico, and at Santa Rosa captured many escaped negro slaves, but this expedition was opposed by Lieutenant Edward Burleson and some others, who withdrew from the service, but Callihan and many others crossed the Rio Grande and had a battle on the San Fernando River and were defeated, losing several men, although the majority of them escaped and made their way back to the United States. In 1856 the brother of the subject of this sketch, Edward Burleson, was commissioned by several to go to Mexico and secure title to lands about San Marcos, and in this expedition he was accompanied by Davy Crocket Burleson and four others. They visited Saltillo, but could come to no satisfactory terms, and it was then proposed that with the funds on hand they should buy stock which they could drive back to Texas. They were captured by a Mexican mob, were imprisoned at Hascienda Potosi and were kept in captivity, in divided parties, for some two weeks. The Alcalde at that place then told them that it had been decided to shoot them, but fortunately for the prisoners the Mexicans afterwards changed their minds, and they were eventually released and returned to Texas. In 1857 the subject of this sketch completed his education in a well-conducted college of the Lone Star State, and in 1858-59 he held the position of sergeant-at-arms in the State Senate at Austin. In 1860 he again entered the service of the state as a member of his brother Ed's rangers, and while thus occupied had some thrilling experiences. In 1861 he led to the altar Miss Louisa Ware, a native of Mississippi, and a daughter of Colonel A. G. Ware, a prominent official of Mississippi at one time, who came to Texas in 1850, settling at Manchaca Springs, where he acquired large land interests and was very prominent in public affairs. He was for some time sheriff of Travis County, and there passed from life in 1859. In 1865 Mr. Burleson removed from San Marcos to the mountains, and took up his residence on a horse ranch, but two years later he moved to the vicinity of the town of Buda, and here his home has since continued to be. He has an excellent farm of 236 acres, of which 140 are under cultivation. In 1893 he lost his estimable wife. She was a worthy member of the Christian Church, and had borne him eight children. The subject of this sketch is a sterling and useful citizen, and is a member of one of the oldest and most highly honored families of Texas. His father, General Burleson, was a conspicuous figure in Texas, and was an active soldier from the firing of the first gun at Gonzales to the battle of San Jacinto, throughout the history of the Republic of Texas and during the Mexican War.

JAMES H. CULBERSON.

Among the prominent and able lawyers of the state, noted for his skill in handling cases, is James H. Culberson, who is possessed of far more than the share of ability with which the average man is endowed. He has won his enviable position in the legal field by the exercise of talent with which nature has endowed him, allied to great application. He comes of a very prominent Texas family, his nephew, Charles Culberson, being the present Governor of Texas, and his brother, David B. Culberson, being one of the oldest politicians in the state, having served in the United States Congress for over twenty years. James H. Culberson is a product of Georgia, born in La Grange, Troup County, and when but a small child went with his parents, David B. and ———— (Wilkinson) Culberson, to Alabama. During his youth he lived in Tallapoosa and Macon

JUDGE BENNETT BLAKE.

counties, Alabama. After reaching mature years he came to Jefferson, studied law with Gen. J. H. Rodgers, and was just admitted to practice when the war broke out. He immediately gave up his practice and enlisted in the Seventeenth Texas Cavalry, Company G. He was captured by the enemy at Arkansas Post and taken to Camp Chase, Columbus, Ohio, where he was held a prisoner for four months. Later he was taken to Fort Delaware, opposite Jersey City, and soon after exchanged at City Point, Va. Following this he was assigned to Bragg's army in Tennessee and ordered west of the river in the Trans-Mississippi department under command of General Dick Taylor. He participated in the battle of Arkansas Post, Mansfield and Yellow Bayou, besides numerous skirmishes. He served faithfully until the close of the war and then, in 1866, returned to Jefferson, where for ten years he followed farming in the vicinity of that city. He then commenced the practice of law in connection with overseeing his plantation and his career at the bar has been one of honor and success. He has been identified with most of the important cases that have been tried since he commenced practice and was for the defense in the celebrated Rothschild murder case, which terminated in his client's acquittal. Mr. Culberson has been twice married, first in 1860 to Miss S. E. Bridges, who died in 1880. Later he wedded her sister, Miss M. E. Bridges, with whom he is now living. They have one living child—S. J. Culberson.

JUDGE BENNETT BLAKE.

If a long life, filled with good deeds and great activity, places a man in the ranks of public benefactors, then surely the name of Bennett Blake will be one long remembered by the residents of the Lone Star State, where he has lived and labored for the good of others as well as for his own and his family's welfare for a period of three-score years. It often transpires in this grand country of ours, where advantages are open alike to rich and poor, that a man will rise from the obscure walks of life and assert his right for a position among the best of his kind, through sheer force of intellect and will, and this is eminently true in the case of Judge Blake, who is essentially self-made. He hails from Vermont, his birth having occurred at Sutton, Caledonia County, in the shadow of the Green Mountains, November 11, 1809. He was one of eight children born to Samuel D. and Abigail (Lee) Blake, natives respectively of New Hampshire and Manchester, Mass. In the state of his birth the father grew to manhood, but in 1792 became a resident of Sutton, Caledonia County, Vt., of which place he was one of the first inhabitants, in the vicinity of which he opened up a farm and reared his family. The mother was a daughter of Ebenezer Lee, a pioneer of Manchester, Mass. As a tiller of the soil Samuel D. Blake was reasonably successful, and after a well-spent life died on the farm which his industry had brought him, about 1852. Of his children but one son and a daughter survive, the latter, Miss Levina, being a resident of Judge Blake's home, whither she came in the fall of 1894. The youthful days of Judge Bennett Blake gave no particular promise of the success which was to attend his efforts in later years, although he was even then wide-awake, active and enterprising. Notwithstanding the fact that his educational advantages were of a very limited description he became a well-informed young man, quick to see and grasp at every opportunity that presented itself, and he soon came to realize that his native county did not offer such advantages as he desired, and when about twenty-six years of age, or in May, 1835, his adventurous spirit led him to the Lone Star State, with the interests of which he immediately identified himself. At the time of his location in Nacogdoches the town contained about 400 people, 300 of whom were Mexicans and the rest Americans, and boasted of a few inferior business houses and residences. At that early day mail was received once a month and so great was the eagerness of the settlers to receive news from the outside world that they flocked to Nacogdoches for many miles around at the time, exchanged gossip and indulged in other mild dissipations. Judge Blake opened a mercantile establishment and in this field of enterprise his energy and activity found full scope and he accordingly prospered. The business was contineud successfully for twenty years, and during this long period he became well known throughout that section and his name became a synonym for all that was honest, upright and reliable. Three years after locating here his sound judgment was recognized by his election to the office of justice of the peace and for a period of ten years he continued to adjust the difficulties of his neighbors in such an impartial and intelligent manner as to win him universal respect. During this time he tried 7,000 civil and 2,000 criminal cases. He was then elected judge of Nacogdoches County, and during the fifteen years he was on the bench he bore the honors of his office with dignity and was no less popular in this capacity than as a justice. So keen was his knowledge of human nature and his insight into the motives of men that he became a terror to evil-doers and for this reason crime became much rarer than it had formerly been. He was a friend and associate of Governor Sam Houston and General Rusk, Nacogdoches being the home of the latter, who spent the active years of his career as a lawyer and statesman here. During the Texas rebellion in 1836 Judge Blake enlisted in the service as a private and was on detached duty the greater part of the time, being one of three detailed to watch and report the movements of the Indians to the commander of the army. He was in a number of engagements with the wily redman, and witnessed the killing of the Cherokee chief— Bowles. Since 1852 Judge Blake has resided on the farm situated about four miles northeast of Nacogdoches, where he now lives, and although he has sold large tracts of land and was at one time quite extensively engaged in the real estate business, he still owns 5,000 acres in this county, besides some 20,000 acres in adjoining counties. He has a very comfortable home and a very fine and valuable farm, but the weight of years has compelled him to retire from the active duties of life, and he has for some time past lived in retirement. He has seen the growth and development of this part of the state during the sixty years of his residence here, and in the improvement of this great commonwealth has also borne the burden and heat of the day with other notable Texas pioneers. Not only has he been thus prominent, but he has also assisted in making the laws of the state, being an active member of the General Assembly of Texas from the time of his first election in 1861 until 1867, thus serving after two re-elections. Here he found full scope for his abundant energy and brilliant mental powers, and during this time he was chairman of two important committees and a member of seven others. He distinguished himself as a legislator during the troublous times of the great civil war and was said to be one of the most sagacious business men of the Lower House. In 1875 he was elected a delegate to the constitutional convention and in this capacity, as in all others which he has filled, he was a faithful and efficient official. Judge Blake is a Democrat of the Jacksonian type, the principles of which party he has ever believed in and supported. He has been married twice, first in Nacogdoches County, in 1849, to Miss Keziah Harrison, a native of Georgia, whose death he was called upon to mourn some three years later. In 1853 the judge took for his second wife Miss Ella Harris, also a native of Georgia, born and reared in Putnam County, who died November 24, 1886, just thirty-three years to the day after her marriage. To them three children were born: Bennett, Jr., who is a prosperous farmer of this county, is married and the father of seven children; Myrta S., wife of Judge James Perkins of Cherokee County, Tex., has six children, and Addie L., widow of W. E. Bowler. Their marriage occurred March 26, 1876. He was born in Virginia, reared in Kentucky and about 1874 came to Texas. He was a traveling man, successful and intelligent, but his promising career was closed November 25, 1886, and being a prominent Mason he was buried with Masonic honors. His widow and five daughters reside with Judge Blake, the names of the latter being Ella A., Lizzie A., Myrta A., Willie May and Carrie L. A son, Samuel A., died at the age of one year. Judge Blake is a Royal Arch Mason and has served as master of his lodge and treasurer of the chapter for a number of years, and on various occasions has represented his lodge in the grand lodge of the state. Judge Blake is about the only survivor of the honored first settlers of the state and his name will always remain inseparably linked with her progress and prosperity.

MRS. BENNETT BLAKE.

REV. W. H. M'CLELLAND.

Rev. W. H. McClelland, for many years a distinguished minister of the Baptist church, is now a resident of Gilmer and classed among the old settlers and pioneers of Upshur County. He is a native of Lee County, Va., born March 28, 1831, and his father, Rev. W. C. McClelland, was a native of the same state and county. The grandfather, Hugh McClelland, was born in Ireland, but at an early date came to America and settled in Lee County. He was a man of education and a teacher by profession. He was also a soldier in the Revolution. W. C. McClelland was reared in Lee County and there married Miss Martha Clardy, a native of Tennessee. He was a minister of the Baptist church and spent his life in this work. He moved with his family to Tennessee and thence to Missouri, settling in Buchanan County, where he died in 1875. He was a soldier in the War of 1812. His wife passed away in Virginia in 1852. W. H. McClelland is one of a family of three sons and four daughters, who grew to mature years, three of whom now survive. One son John McClelland, resides in Greenup County, Ky., and Martha is the wife of W. Parks and makes her home in Troy, Iowa. Our subject was educated in Lee County and at Sneedville, Tenn., but for the most part is self-educated. After completing his studies he went to Missouri in 1851, located in Ray County, teaching one year. Returning to Virginia in 1852 he attended school at White Shoals until 1853, when he came back to Ray County, Mo., and made teaching a profession up to 1859. In 1853 he was married in Ray County to Miss Jane Stanley, a native of Missouri, born and reared in Ray County, and the daughter of Jacob Stanley, who was an early settler of this region from Tennessee. In 1859 Mr. McClelland turned his attention to agricultural pursuits, continued this for two years, and having been ordained a minister in the Baptist church in 1856, began his ministerial work. He has had three and sometimes four country churches in his charge and at the same time was engaged in farming. Previous to this Mr. McClelland had charge of the Bap-

tist church at Kingston, his first charge, and most successfully ministered to the spiritual wants of his fellow-men. He has baptized
1,041 people in Texas, and 283 while a resident of Missouri. In
1863 he was taken prisoner by the Federal soldiers and held in St.
Louis six months, after which he was banished under guard to the
Confederates at Mobile Bay. While a prisoner he preached fifty-
three times to the prisoners. Returning to Lee County he was in the
Confederate government employ until the close of the war. In 1865
he moved to Texas and located in Upshur County, and on the 25th
of November during that year bought a farm seven miles southeast of Gilmer and where, in connection with farming, he continued
his ministerial duties. After farming and preaching for three years
he built a schoolhouse on his place and conducted a private school
for four years; then on account of poor health was obliged to give
up teaching, and he afterward turned his attention to agricultural
pursuits. In 1878 he moved to Harrison County, settled on a farm
there, and in 1883 built a schoolhouse and again gave his attention
to teaching. This he continued for three years, when he was stricken
with paralysis, which so affected his eyes that he was obliged to
abandon that profession. In 1886 he moved to Gilmer and took
charge of the First Gilmer Baptist Church for two years. In 1887
he was permitted by the church to labor for the prohibition cause
over the state. He made over sixty speeches, had seventeen joint
discussions and rendered valiant service for the cause. After this,
in the fall of 1887, he moved on his farm and remained there until
the fall of 1893, when he again returned to Gilmer and erected his
present beautiful and comfortable residence. During all these years
most of his time and attention have been given to his ministerial
duties, having served the churches as pastor at Gilmer, Pittsburg,
Lafayette, Coffeeville and Wood Lawn. The most successful labors
were while missionary in Soda Lake Association in East Texas from
1886 to 1892. This mission field received a part of his most earnest
toil. Mr. McClelland is noted for his love of and success in con-
troversy, having debated with presiding elders, Campbellite editors,
and anti-missionary Baptists. At this time he is pastor of four
churches. Mr. McClelland's first wife died in Missouri in 1858.
Three children were the fruits of this union, two of whom are now

living. He was married in Ray County, Mo., to Miss Margaret Blain, a native of that county. She died in Tennessee in 1863. Of the two children born to this union only one is now living, Dr. R. H. McClelland, a practicing physician in Upshur County, Tex. Mr. McClelland's third union was with Mrs. Martha Scaggs, a native of Lee County, Va., and the daughter of Harvey Davis. Four children were born to this union, two of whom are deceased. The others are: Virginia, wife of T. C. Morris, of this state, and W. H., a graduate of Baylor University, Texas, and a professional teacher. Mr. McClelland lost his wife February 22, 1875, and subsequently married Miss Leela Wilkerson, a native of Texas, who was reared in Upshur County. The seven children born to them were named as follows: Charles Edwin, attending school; Fay, May, Gracie Delou, Bidwell Canfield, and Ruth. Our subject takes quite an active part in politics and is identified with the Prohibition party. He has been a resident of Upshur County for about thirty years and has contributed his share toward its advancement in every way, more especially to the cause of religion.

HON. JOHN ADRIANCE.

The name Adriance has been identified with the growth and progress of this country for many generations, and this family trace their ancestry in America back to the settling of New Amsterdam. The Adriance and Brinkerhoff families were closely connected, and were prominent and influential in the section in which they lived. Among those who are justly entitled to be enrolled among the makers of the great commonwealth of Texas is John Adriance, who has been a resident of the state for nearly sixty years. He was born at Troy, N. Y., November 10, 1818, and when but a child, was left fatherless. His father, George C. Adriance, was a hatter and fur dealer,

and a man of excellent business ability. He resided at Troy, N.
Y., and although heavily insured, lost heavily by the great fire there.
Socially a Mason, he was a very prominent member of that order.
John Adriance secured a good education in his native town, and
later attended a select school at Truxton, N. Y. After the death of
his father he lived with an uncle, Hon. John Miller, who was an emi
nent physician and a member of the United States Congress. In the
stores of Truxton our subject received an excellent business training
and later went to Berlin, Chenango County, N. Y., where he was in
the employ of the Farmers and Mechanics' Cotton Manufacturing
Co. Still later he entered the employ of John Haggerty & Sons,
the largest house in New York City, an auction house dealing in
package goods. At the suggestion of his uncle he made up his mind
to come to Texas for his health, and left there on the 25th day of
October, 1835, on the schooner Julius Caesar and engaged as a
clerk for Townsend & Jones. He did not expect to remain, but settled at Bell's Landing, Tex., subsequently named Marion, and for
many years past known as Columbia, and has since made his home
there. He is truly a Texas veteran, having served in Capt. Jacob
Eberly's volunteer company of thirty-five mounted men, detailed by
Gen. Sam Houston before he crossed the Brazos at Groce's, to remain
at Marion until all the families fleeing before the enemy had crossed
the river. Being cut off from reaching the army across the country,
they thus made their way to San Luis, where they crossed the pass
with the aid of a yawl from the steamer Yellowstone, and by a night
march reached the east end of Galveston Island. The following
morning the steamboat Laura started with provisions and volunteers
with the hope of reaching the army, when Capt. Eberly and fifteen of
his men (including the subject of this sketch) volunteered as part
of the guard on the steamer, and the balance remained as a corps
of observation on the island. At Redfish Bar they met the steamer
Cayuga with Mexican prisoners and the glad tidings of the battle
of San Jacinto. Returning to the island, they embarked for the
battleground on the steamer Yellowstone. When Santa Anna and
his officers were placed aboard the Yellowstone, he was one of the
volunteer guard while lying in the stream, thence to Galveston
Island, where they were transferred to the steamer Laura and accom-

panied them to Velasco. Mr. Adriance is one of the oldest merchants of Texas now living, having commenced business with Mr. C. Beardslee at West Columbia during the first session of Texas Congress in 1836 and 1837, under the firm name of Beardslee & Adriance. This firm was dissolved in the spring of 1839. In the fall of 1839 in connection with Col. Morgan L. Smith, formerly of the city of New York, an ex-alderman of that city, and the first colonel of the celebrated Seventh Regiment of that city, he took the first regular stock of goods to the present capital of Texas, Austin, under the firm name of John Adriance & Co. Disposing of this stock, he returned to Columbia on January 1, 1840, and entered into business with Colonel Smith under the firm name of Smith & Adriance, which continued for several years. Columbia at that period was the trading point for a good portion of the state. At the close of this co-partnership, Mr Adriance continued in mercantile pursuits until the close of the war when he retired. He was the first to volunteer to enter the Confederate service during the Civil War, but on account of his age was not accepted. He built the warehouse here. At one time he owned most of the land on which Columbia now stands and still owns quite extensive interests. Merchandising has been his principal business in life, and as he is a man thoroughly trustworthy and reliable, and possesses a true appreciation of all the requirements of his line, he amassed quite a fortune previous to the war. Mr. Adriance was one of the incorporators of the Galveston & Brazos Canal, and, through his influence, New York merchants contributed many thousands of dollars towards the completion of the enterprise. He and Col. M. L. Smith were the first owners of the Waldeck plantation, where they started the manufacture of sugar, but later he sold out his interest. Mr. Adriance was one of the most earnest workers and contributors in building the Houston Tap & Brazoria Railroad and its extension to Wharton, and for three years was in charge of the immigration department of the International & Great Northern Railway at Palestine. He was a member of the thirteenth Legislature of Texas, nominated at Galveston without his knowledge until two days after it was made, and has often been solicited to run for the same office, which he has declined, preferring the quiet paths of life. He has taken a deep interest in the welfare of the Agricultural and

Mechanical College of Texas since its first establishment, also of the
Prairie View State Normal School, and a member of the board of
directors at this time.   He is a prominent Mason and Past Grand
High Priest of the Grand Royal Arch Chapter of Texas, and well
known throughout the state.   He joined this order in 1851.   For
twenty-five years he was a member of the committee of work, Grand
Chapter.   In the A. & M. College he was a member of the finance
committee for five years, first with L. L. Foster and now J. E. Hollingsworth.   Mr. Adriance was married in Watertown, N. Y., to
Miss Lydia A. Cook, daughter of Dr. Cook, a surgeon in the United
States navy.   She died in 1871, leaving one son, Duncan, who is
associate professor of chemistry in the A. & M. College, and a daughter who is now Mrs. George C. Munson of this county, and an unmarried daughter at his home.   After her death Mr. Adriance married Mrs. D. E. Nash, a sister of his former wife.   He is a member
of the Episcopal church and has been a lay reader many years.   Time
has dealt leniently with him and he bids fair to enjoy many years
more of usefulness.

CAPT. Z. B. GARRISON.

Nothing is truer than the statement that in this country alone, of
all countries upon the face of the earth, a man's family connections
do not assist him to positions of honor and distinction, but he must
win his way by his own exertions or by his own honest merit.   In
the old countries the accident of birth usually determines the preferment of an individual, and if he is not born to a title, or is not
the near relative of one who is, he might as profitably seek a mode
of travel to the moon as to try to gain social or political equality with
the eminent men of his locality.   This government of the people is
no discriminator of persons, but opens wide its doors for the entrance
of all such persons as possess the requisite qualifications for success

in any particular calling, and birth is not one of these by any means. In the particular instance of Capt. Z. B. Garrison, whose name forms the subject for this sketch, he fortunately springs from an honored and respectable ancestry, but his success in life is almost wholly the result of his own efforts. He was born in Carroll County, Ga., April 20, 1829, his parents being the Hon. James F. and Abigail (Bonner) Garrison, both of whom were also natives of Georgia, their nuptials being celebrated in Fayette County of that state. James F Garrison was one of the typical ante-bellum Southern gentlemen, a man whose word was the soul of truth, dignified, courteous in demeanor and a man beloved by his fellow-men. Although born and married in Fayette County, he removed to Carroll County in 1827, where he was engaged in planting and milling for many years. He was a participant in the Seminole War, and died in Carroll County in 1860. His widow moved to Texas, in order to enjoy the companionship of her children, where she passed from life in 1892 at the advanced age of eighty-four years. The statement will not be disputed that to the mothers of our race is mainly due the moral status of our wonderful civilization. To them is confided the training for good or evil of our youth, upon whom the morality of future generations will have to depend, and as the moral condition of humanity shapes its destiny the state itself is guided by the influence of the mothers. The life-work of Mrs. Garrison was well done in this respect, and she lived to see her children honest, honored and God-fearing people before being called to her just reward above. Capt. Z. B. Garrison was the second in the family of six sons and four daughters, one son, John H., having been killed at the battle of Atlanta in 1864, while serving the cause of the Confederate States. Until the age of nineteen years Capt. Garrison resided in his native county, his education being largely acquired under that hard task-master, "Experience." Believing that the great west afforded better opportunities for a young man, he emigrated to Texas in 1850, arriving in Rusk County on the 27th of January, and for a time was employed as a clerk at Caledonia. Later, in partnership with a brother and cousin, he embarked in mercantile pursuits, which he continued for several years; then purchasing a tract of unimproved land he turned his attention to its tillage and improvement. His efforts have been crowned by success, as is proven by his fine tract of about 1,400 acres on which he has a steam gin, although at one time he was the owner of about 5,000 acres. Loyal to the Confederate States, he recruited Company C of the Fourth Texas Cavalry in 1861, and equipped it with seventy head of horses and mules. As first lieutenant of this company he went to the front, but after being dismounted the company returned home; later was ordered to organize into companies and regiments. Then Mr. Z. B. was elected captain and joined the army at Knoxville, Tenn., and soon after disbanded and Captain Garrison was then commissioned quartermaster of the Fourteenth Texas Regiment, in which capacity he served until the close of the war. The devastating effects of war did not diminish the ardor with which Captain Garrison had previously conducted his business affairs. He accepted the results of internicine strife with becoming fortitude and resumed farming, milling and ginning with his accustomed energy in Rusk County until 1886. In that year he moved to Garrison (the town was named after Z. B. and J. H. Garrison) and in partnership with Captain J. H. Garrison erected a large business building and embarked in mercantile pusuits. In addition to this he not only built for himself a beautiful and commodious home, but has erected and owns several other residences in the town, besides being the owner of considerable real estate in the immediate neighborhood. For the past few years Captain Garrison has been retired from active business pursuits, his time being principally occupied in simply looking after the details of his large estate and in spending his later years in comfort and peace. He began life's battle at the lowest rung of life's ladder and from this meager beginning has, unaided, carved his way to wealth and, what is still better, has gained a name that is honored and respected in Eastern Texas. March 20, 1851, occurred his marriage with Miss Elizabeth H. Lacy, a native of Tennessee, and to their union have been born five children, the eldest being Hon. James G. Garrison, a well-known lawyer of Los Angeles, Cal. The other children are: Ruth, the wife of Dr. Barham, of Nacogdoches, a sketch of whom appears elsewhere in this work; John I., a leading merchant of Garrison; Henry D., a commerical traveler for a wholesale house at Houston, and Nora B., who resides at home with her parents. A stanch Democrat in politics, Captain Garrison has never been an aspirant for public office, although he at one time by appointment held one term in the Legislature in order to attend to special business for his county. Captain Garrison and wife are members of the M. E. church. For a period of nearly half a century (forty-five years) he has been a resident of Eastern Texas, identified with its commercial prosperity and advancement, instrumental in promoting industries and contributing liberally from his means for the welfare of its people. The name of Captain Z. B. Garrison will be remembered for the many good deeds he has accomplished years after the present generation has passed away.

CAPTAIN JAMES H. GARRISON.

One of the positive truths taught by modern science is that mental and physical qualities are hereditary in man, and this statement of fact is as old as Moses, who declared that the generations to come should bear the result of the father's actions. No doubt the subject of this sketch inherits much of his vigor of body and his strong mentality from his parents, and his parents' parents, but this can in nowise detract from the splendid success he has achieved, for he began life with but little means, and what he has acquired has been almost wholly through his own unaided efforts. The same will apply to his education. His schooling was limited, but years passed in the school of experience, his keen observation of persons and events, together with desultory reading, have made him one of the well-informed men of the day. Captain James H. Garrison is a native of Polk County, Ga., his birth occurring May 1, 1836. Judge George M. Garrison, his father, was also a native of Georgia, where he grew to manhood, married Miss Mary Ann Cosper and where, for many years, he resided. By occupation Judge Garrison was a merchant, farmer and trader, and for years served as judge of the inferior court of his county, besides holding other positions of local honor and trust. He emigrated to Texas with his family in 1854 and located on a farm near Caledonia, in Rusk County, but later moved to his farm near Mount Enterprise, where he died in 1883 at the age of sixty-two years. His widow yet survives, hale and hearty, at the age of seventy years, and makes her home with her children. The youth of Captain James H. Garrison was passed in his native county in the usual manner of the boys of that day. He came to Texas with his parents in 1854 and assisted in clearing and improving the home farm. In 1862 he enlisted in the Fourteenth Texas Cavalry, was made sergeant and later elected lieutenant of his company. About two months after the reorganization of his regiment at Corinth, he was promoted to captain of his company, in which capacity he served until the close of the war. Perhaps no man in all Texas saw harder service than did Captain Garrison and his devotion to the cause of the Confederacy was heroic and unswerving. Among the more important events of his military career was his participation in the battles of Farmington, Miss.; Richmond and Perryville, Ky.; Murfreesboro, Tenn.; Jackson, Miss., where they were besieged for eight days by the Federals; Chickamauga; the engagements in and immediately surrounding Dalton; Lovejoy's Station, and the siege of Atlanta, including many of the adjoining engagements. After the fall of Atlanta Captain Garrison was detailed to recruit absentees, leaving his command at Lovejoy's Station. He succeeded in securing sixty-three of his command and was trying to transport them across the Mississippi River when he heard of General Lee's surrender at Appomattox to General Grant. With this remnant of his command he returned to Shreveport and there disbanded. With undaunted courage Captain Garrison laid aside his sword for the ploughshare and for years followed farming in Rusk County. By good management he has become one of the largest holders of real estate in the county, now owning about 3,000 acres in Rusk County and 500 acres in Nacogdoches County, and began to improve the village named in honor of his family. He was associated with Captain Z. B. Garrison, his cousin, for a number of years in merchandising, and after the retirement of his cousin from active business pursuits he has continued mercantile pursuits, buying and selling cotton and dealing in real estate. Captain Garrison is one of the progressive and prominent men of Eastern Texas. He has acquired much wealth by good business methods and from his large means he is a liberal contributor to all laudable public enterprises. Although radical in his political views and an outspoken advocate of the principles of the Democratic party, Captain Garrison has invariably discouraged any attempt toward office-holding so far as he was concerned, preferring to confine his attention exclusively to his large business interests. While this is true as to political matters, it does not apply wholly to social matters. In religion he is a member of the Methodist Episcopal church. Socially he is a member of the Masonic fraternity, in which order he was duly entered, passed and raised, and exalted to the sublime degree of Royal Arch Mason. October 27, 1864, occurred his marriage with Miss Mary C. Young, a native of Polk County, Ga., and a daughter of William Young, whose family was prominently connected in that state. This marriage occurred near Henderson, Rusk County, Tex., whither the father had some years previously removed. Two sons have blessed this union: William Young, a successful druggist of Garrison, and George F., who is connected with Dotson Brothers, extensive merchants of Garrison. Captain James H. Garrison is one of the well-known men of Texas and he stands deservedly high for his many sterling qualities of mind and heart.

COLONEL C. B. KILGORE.

Colonel C. B. Kilgore was born in Newnan, Coweta County, Ga., in 1835. His father, a carpenter, was one of the first settlers in Newnan, and in 1846 came to Texas and settled in Rusk County. He opened up a small farm there, which was cultivated by his sons, he

himself continuing to work at his trade as a carpenter, until the
Civil War began, when he volunteered in Third Texas Cavalry, and
was killed at the battle of Oak Hill in 1861. The family were in
humble circumstances. When Colonel Kilgore was about seventeen
years of age he left home by permission of his parents, taking with
him one suit of clothes and six dollars. He contracted with Judge
Miller, who lived near Henderson, Rusk County, to work for him
as a field hand, Miller agreeing to pay for his services in board,
clothing and schooling. Under this arrangement he acquired a fair
education at the Henderson college, then known as the Fowler Institute. After leaving school he secured employment as clerk in a
store owned by Hon. T. Pilsbury, formerly member of Congress from
Texas. During his leisure hours and at odd times he studied law
and was thus preparing himself for the responsible positions to
which he was to be called in after life. Colonel Kilgore was very
much opposed to secession, but when the ordinance was passed, and
the call was made for soldiers, he volunteered and was made orderly
sergeant of his company, which belonged to the Tenth Texas Cavalry. Afterward he was elected first lieutenant and when the regiment was reorganized at Corinth he was chosen captain of Company
G. While on the Kentucky campaign General Ector, then the adjutant-general of the brigade, was elected colonel of the Fourteenth
Cavalry and Capt. Kilgore was appointed adjutant-general of the
brigade by Col. McCray, the commander, which position he continued to fill when Ector was made brigadier-general of the brigade,
until he was wounded in the battle of Chickamauga. Soon after that
battle he was captured and was held a prisoner until March, 1865.
After the war he worked on the farm, but studied law during his
spare moments. In 1869 he was elected justice of the peace in Rusk
County, when the five justices of the county constituted the county
court, and each assessed the taxes of his precinct. His administration was marked by that fearlessness and impartiality which has
characterized his acts in public life since. In 1873 he was nominated
for the State Senate on the Democratic ticket when Rusk and Harrison constituted a senatorial district. He received the nomination,

although not at the convention, and made the race simply in the interest of the Democratic party, the district at that time being largely Republican and no hope of a Democrat being elected. In the race, so thorough was this canvass, that he carried Rusk County by 500 majority, although at the previous election it had gone Republican by 300 majority, though his opponent, Honorable Webb Flannagan, was one of the most prominent and popular Republicans of the state at that time. This race was purely a sacrifice in the interests of the organization of the Democratic party, as there was no hope, as before stated, of his being elected. In 1875 he was elected a member of the constitutional convention that formed the present Constitution of the state. He represented the counties of Gregg, Upshur, Camp, and Smith, in connection with Col. John L. Henry, then of Smith County, and Mr. B. Abernathy of Camp County. He was on some of the most important committees in that body and acquitted himself well. In 1877 he removed from Kilgore, Gregg County, formerly Rusk County, to Wills Point, Van Zandt County, which has been his place of residence until within the past year. In 1880 he was elector on the Hancock and English ticket. In 1884 he was elected to the State Senate from the seventh senatorial district, composed of the counties of Van Zandt, Henderson, Cherokee, and Anderson. He was regarded by his associates as one of the leading men of the State Senate, and was elected president pro tem. of that body. Succeeding this he was elected to Congress from the third district, was re-elected and served in the sessions of the fiftieth, fifty-first, fifty-second and fifty-third Congresses, his last term expiring in March, 1895. His views on national questions have been in strict accord with southern and western democracy; his correct course of life, both public and private, has won him the universal respect of his fellow-men, and his gallant record as a soldier has endeared him to thousands of the brave followers of the stars and bars. He was appointed United States district judge for the southern district of the Indian Territory on March 20, 1895, and is now filling that appointment, with headquarters at Ardmore, where he resides happily with his family.

COLONEL JAMES B. HAWKINS.

Matagorda County, Tex., has still the honor of numbering among its inhabitants the pioneer settler, Col. James B. Hawkins, who is now a venerable and venerated citizen of eighty-one years. It is the lot of but few men to attain the high position of honor and distinction which he has attained; with him success in life has been reached by his sterling qualities of mind and a heart true to every manly principle. To such men as he the people of the present are indebted for the improvements, well cultivated farms and thriving villages which they now enjoy. Colonel Hawkins was born in Franklin County, N. C., in 1813, and now resides on lower Caney, at Hopkinville, which thriving town was named in his honor. His primary education was received in the schools of Raleigh, and when seventeen years of age he was sent to West Point, where he remained two years. His father gave him a plantation in North Carolina, and he carried this on for eight years. In 1834 he was married to Miss Ariella Alston, a native of North Carolina, and daughter of Wellis Alston, a congressman of note. Sometime after his marriage, Colonel Hawkins went to Mississippi, remained there a short time and then in 1845 made his way to this state with a number of negroes. He immediately began clearing his plantation of the heavy timber with which it was covered, planted sugar cane, and was one of the first to commence that kind of planting, meeting with good success. He continued this business on an extensive scale and shipped to New York City, having a line of steamers to carry his produce there. There were 2,400 acres in his first purchase, and he raised enormous cotton crops aside from his other industries. He continued the sugar business for eight years after the war, handling convict labor, but since then the colonel has given much of his time and attention to the stock business. He now owns between 40,000 and 50,000 acres of land, the finest in the world. He and his most estimable wife have passed together sixty years of married life, and now in the sunset of their career are surrounded by every comfort. They reared eight children, but only two now survive, Virginia, Mrs. Brodie, resides in North Carolina, and Frank, who manages the Lake Austin Stock Ranch. The others were: James, who died before the war; Edgar; Willis was all through the war, and died in the Old North State during that distressing period; John D. was all through the war, and died soon afterward; Sallie was the wife of Ferdinand Stitch of Tennessee at the time of her death, and Ella died in childhood. The colonel and his excellent wife are worthy members of the Episcopal church, and liberal contributors to the same. While a resident of North Carolina, our subject was colonel of the militia in Warren County. His father, John D., represented his county in both the House of Representatives and Senate, and was not only a brilliant young lawyer, but an influential and successful planter.

JUDGE J. L. M. PIRTLE.

To a thorough knowledge of the legal science, Judge Pirtle joins the culture derived from a varied and extended course of reading. He takes an enviable position among the more prominent practitioners of East Texas and in his present office, as judge of Nacogdoches County, his dignity and ability stamp him the equal, if not the superior, of any who have held that position. His sense of justice is acute, and he possesses in a remarkable degree what the lawyers term the judicial mind. He was born in the Lone Star State, Shelby County, November 3, 1852, soon after his parents, A. J. and Caroline (Kennedy) Pirtle, had moved from Arkansas to that state. The father was born in Tennessee and remained there till grown, when he went to Polk County, Ark., and there met and married Miss Kennedy, a native of North Carolina, and daughter of J. M. Kennedy, an old settler of Arkansas. After his marriage

Mr. Pirtle resided on a farm in Arkansas until 1852, when he moved with his family to Texas, and settled in Cherokee County, where he opened up a good farm. He met with good success as an agriculturist and passed his last days on this farm, dying about 1888. His wife had died in 1875. On his father's farm Judge Pirtle reached manhood, assisting in the duties necessary and receiving his education in the common schools. When the Civil War broke out he was too young to enlist, but in 1864, when but fourteen years old, he joined the Eighteenth Texas Infantry, Company G, at Mansfield, La., and remained with that regiment and shared its dangers and hardships until the close. Upon his return home he began to realize that his education had been neglected and he sold his Enfield rifle for $45 and with this sum started to school. By diligent study and close application he was able to teach school in a few years and he pursued that avocation in the common schools of the county for several years. During his leisure moments he began the study of law and was admitted to the bar at Lebanon, Tenn., and licensed to practice in the superior courts of that state. In 1880 he came to Nacogdoches, Tex., began practicing law, and soon after formed a law partnership with Honorable William Clark, a well-known attorney of Eastern Texas, and continued with him until his death. Local as well as general politics have interested him greatly and he supports the men and measures of the Democratic party. He was elected judge of the county court in 1888 and after the expiration of his term was re-elected. Again he was a candidate, but suffered defeat by a small majority by the Populist candidate, but in 1894, when he was nominated for that position at the general election, he was triumphantly elected and is now serving his third term to the satisfaction of his constituents and all concerned. Mr. Pirtle was married in Cherokee County, Tex., December 20, 1880, to Miss Ophelia Norman, a native of Texas, reared in Cherokee County, and the daughter of A. B. Norman of that county. They have four children: Claudie, a daughter, fourteen years old, has taken two medals in the public schools for superior scholarship in penmanship and one for recitation, and is a bright young lady; John, Staten and Alwyn are the names of the others. The judge has been a resident of Texas almost his whole life, and is well known in this and adjoining counties. He has served as a delegate to numerous state and county conventions and to whatever position he has been elected he has discharged its duties very efficiently. He is a worthy member of the Baptist church.

ELLIS P. BEAN.

Ellis P. Bean, the successor of Philip Nolan, in the command of his company of filibusters, was a marked character. In 1800, when he was but eighteen years of age and possessing a spirit of adventure, he left his father's home at Bean's Station, Tenn., went to Natchez and enlisted in Nolan's trading company, then consisting of twenty-two men. Reaching Texas, and while at a point between the Trinity and Brazos rivers, they were attacked and beaten by a body of Spanish troops. Bean, with eight others, was taken as a prisoner to San Antonio, and then to Chihuahua, being kept at the latter place three years, when they began to be allowed some liberty and to labor for themselves. Bean had learned the hatter's trade, and he followed it for a year in Chihuahua, when his longing to see his native land induced him, with two comrades, to run away and endeavor to reach the United States. The three were arrested near El Paso, severely lashed and again ironed and imprisoned. Bean's many friends in Chihuahua soon obtained for him again the freedom of the city, and he made a second effort to escape, but was again taken. He was this time sent under a strong guard to the south of the City of Mexico. On their way they came to the city of Guanajuato, where they remained several days, and while there Bean's noble and manly bearing won the heart of a beautiful Mexican senorita of rank, who wrote a letter to him avowing her passion, and promising her influence to obtain his liberation, when she would marry him, but he was hurried away and never permitted again to see her. Poor Bean was next conveyed to Acapulco, one of the most sickly places of the Pacific, and thrown into a filthy dungeon, where no ray of the light of heaven penetrated, and the only air admitted was through an aperture in the base of the massive wall, which was six feet thick. In this foul abode his body was covered with vermin, no one was allowed to see him, and his food was of the coarsest and most unhealthy kind. In his confinement his only companion was a white lizard, which he succeeded in taming, and which became very fond of him. The only air-hole had to be closed at night to prevent ingress of serpents. One night, neglecting to close it, he was awakended by the crawling of a monstrous serpent over his body. His presence of mind enabled him to lie perfectly still until, getting hold of a pocket-knife which he had been able to keep concealed upon his person, he pierced the monster in the head and escaped his fangs. This exploit so astonished the keeper of the prison that by his influence a petition was sent to the governor for a mitigation of his confinement, and that dignitary graciously decreed that he might work in chains and under a guard of soldiers. Even this was a relief. While thus engaged his desire for freedom again overcame his prudence. He succeeded in freeing himself from his shackles, and with a piece of iron killed three of the guard and fled to the mountains. Again he was hunted down and recaptured, nearly starved. His cell now became his only abode, and flogging and other indignities were heaped upon him. Another year passed and he was again allowed the liberty of the prison yard, under strict surveillance. Once more he made a desperate attempt to escape, killing several soldiers and taking the road to California. This time he had traveled 300 miles, when he was once more recaptured and carried back. He was now confined upon his back, and for weeks was almost devoured by vermin. His appeals for mercy were treated with mockery. But his freedom drew nigh. The Mexican Revolution of 1810 broke out. The royalists became alarmed. They had learned to look upon Bean as a chained lion, and now, in the hour of their trouble, they offered him liberty if he would join their standard. He promised, secretly determining that he would desert at the first opportunity. In a few days he was sent out with a scout to reconnoitre the position of General Morelos, the chief of the republicans. When near the camp of that officer Bean proposed to his comrades that they should all join the patriots. His persuasive eloquence was so successful that they all agreed, and at once reported to Morelos. Upon the information Bean was able to give, an attack was planned and executed against the royalists, resulting in a complete victory. For this Bean received a captain's commission, and his fame spread like a prairie fire throughout Mexico. For three years he was the chief reliance of Morelos, and when he fought victory followed. He was soon conducted with flying banners into the town of Acapulco, the scene of his sufferings. The wretches who had persecuted him now on bended knees begged for mercy, expecting nothing but instant death. But Bean scorned to avenge his wrongs upon them, and dismissed them with warnings as to their future conduct. Three years later it was agreed that he should go to New Orleans and obtain aid for the republicans of Mexico. With two companions, he made his way across the country. On the route, while stopping a few days at Jalapa, Mexico, he became suddenly and violently enamored of a beautiful lady and married her, promising that he would return to her after accomplishing his mission. After various adventures he reached New Orleans, two days before the memorable battle of January 8, 1815. He at once volunteered as aid to General Jackson, whom he had known as a boy, and he fought bravely in the decisive action. He afterward returned to Mexico and joined his wife, with whom he lived happily for many years. In 1827, when the Fredonia war broke out in Nacogdoches, Tex., he was colonel commanding the Mexican garrison at that place. In 1835 he returned to Jalapa, Mexico. In 1843 he was still living in Mexico, as an officer on the retired list of the army of that nation. A volume containing an account of his almost fabulous adventures was written by himself in 1817, and published soon afterward.

E. REICHARDT.

It is generally considered, by those in the habit of superficial think-
ing, that the history of so-called great men only is worthy of preservation, and that little merit exists among the masses to call forth the
praise of the historian or the cheers of mankind. This is unquestionably a gross error. No man is great in all things, and very few are
great in many things. Many, by a lucky stroke, achieve lasting fame
who before that had no reputation beyond the limits of their own
immediate neighborhood. It is not a history of the lucky stroke
which benefits humanity most, but the long study and effort which
made the lucky stroke possible. It is the preliminary work—the
method—that serves as a guide to the success of others. Thus it appears that the lives of the masses out of which come the men who
control the world, will furnish the grandest, truest lessons for the
benefit of humanity. The common soldier, who bears the brunt of the
battle and who does his best, is as much entitled to highest praise
for his efforts as is the general who stands back out of rifle shot
directing the struggling troops to victory. The widow, who places
her mite upon the altar, deserves greater praise for her sacrifice than
the prince who places thereon a costly pearl. The widow gives all
she has; the prince will never miss his gift. The history of the
widow's suffering and sacrifice is of much greater pathos and value to
the student of history and human nature, than the dizzy story of the
ostentatious gift of the prince. All writers agree that the quiet lives
are the ones which furnish the best examples of heroism, sacrifice
and merit. After all this is said, the honest man, the man who has
endeavored, to the best of his ability, to follow the precepts of the
Golden Rule, the man who is nearing the allotted period of age and
universally commands the respect of his fellow-men, even though he
has attained no high political or other preferment, is the one whose
life is worthiest of emulation and whose history is most worthy of
preservation. Such a man is Mr. E. Reichardt, who, for a period of
forty years, was one of the best-known and most active business men
in all Eastern Texas.

E. Richards,

Born October 30, 1833, at Coswig, in Anhalt, in Germany, he there passed his youthful days in attending the schools, thus acquiring a much better education than is usually accorded the boys of our own country. Believing that America afforded better opportunities for advancement than his native land, the ambitious youth determined to emigrate to the El Dorado—the Great West. After a long voyage, when but eighteen years old, he landed in the United States and located in Houston, Tex., which was his home for about twenty years. His first chief object was in learning the English language, and this he succeeded in doing by attending school, employing his spare hours in clerking for that old, well-known firm of Bremond & Van Alstine, with whom he acquired an excellent business training. In 1855, in partnership with another gentleman, he operated the old Texas Hotel at Houston for nearly two years, then for a like length of time was profitably engaged in the manufacture of vinegar. Then, together with a brother, he established a bakery, in which line of trade he continued until 1860, and from then until the breaking out of the great Civil War was extensively engaged in the manufacture of lumber. His sympathies being aroused in behalf of the Confederate cause, he and his brother enlisted in the Southern army, and were assigned to the coast rangers under the command of Colonel H. B. Andrews, who, at the present time, is president of the Southern Pacific Railway. Mr. Reichardt faithfully served in his command in and around Virginia Point, until it became necessary for him to return home to look after his business matters, which were being sadly neglected during his absence. However, he employed a substitute at a cost of $800 before so doing. By hard work and close application he was not long in again placing his business affairs on as sound a basis as was possible under the existing circumstances, and January 20, 1864, again entered the service of the Confederate States. About this time he entered into a contract to furnish 2,000 barrels of charcoal per month to the field transportation department at Hempstead, which he continued doing until the close of the war, but so depreciated had the Confederate currency become that he encountered a great loss, which he could illy afford. In October, 1865, he embarked in the grocery trade in Houston, with Mr. Mark as partner, where he conducted a large trade for three years, and then sold his interest to his partner. A longing to see the old home caused him to then return to his native land, which he did in May, 1868, accompanied by his family, remaining there nearly two years. Returning then to the home of his adoption, he again embarked in mercantile pursuits in Houston, in November, 1869, but owing to the confining nature of the business he was compelled to remove to the country on account of ill health. Selling his business, he purchased two farms in Austin County, near Post Oak Point, where he resided nearly three years, improving their impoverished condition, and engaged in agricultural pursuits. His health being then restored, he moved into Brenham and embarked in the hardware business. Unfortunately, about four months thereafter, the store and its contents were consumed by fire, and there being but little insurance, the loss was very great. Phoenix-like, however, he and his partner immediately rebuilt, and Mr. Reichardt continued in the trade about five years longer. Then disposing of his interest, he purchased the L. M. Campbell farm of 600 acres, situated about three miles from town. Here he has recuperated in health, improved his farm, and is now practically retired from active business pursuits. Such, in short, is a brief outline of the career of one of Texas' best men. Mr. Reichardt has served in various local positions of honor and trust, and invariably with credit to himself and satisfaction to all concerned. He was county commissioner four years, has been a delegate to county, congressional and state conventions, has been mayor and alderman of his city, was one of the organizers of the free school system, and also of the old gas company; was the first man to start the first compress of Brenham, of which he was president and superintendent for two years, and was one of the organizers and president of the Real Estate and Building Association. His career has been one of ceaseless activity; and while he has met with many business reverses, his indomitable energy and courage has surmounted all obstacles. Throughout his diversified career no one has ever questioned his integrity or honesty of purpose. His philanthropy in aiding all needy enterprises is proverbial. Beginning life's battle a poor boy, he has made life a success in every sense of the word, and entirely by his own efforts. He has also justly earned an honored name, which he

CAPITOL OF TEXAS.

prizes more highly than his accumulation of this world's goods. Politically he is a Democrat, his first Presidential ballot having been cast for Franklin Pierce.

In 1858, in the city of Houston, occurred his marriage with Miss Bertha Winterfeld, a lady of German nativity, although having been reared and educated in Houston. Three living children are the result of this union: W. E., a prominent merchant of Brenham; Bertha, the wife of F. W. Schuerenberg, a well-known business man of the city, and E. W., who represents his father's interest in the wholesale grocery house of E. Reichardt, Becker & Co. Three children died in infancy and early childhood. Mr. and Mrs. Reichardt, in addition to their own family, reared and adopted one girl, Louise, who is the wife of Adolph Seelhorst of Brenham. The name of Reichardt is well known throughout Texas, particularly the eastern portion, and is one that will live in the memory of thousands long after the present generation has paid the last great debt to nature.

DR. ROBERT LEAK.

This prominent physician, now retired from the active and arduous duties of his profession, was for many years one of the most successful practitioners of the county. In writing a history of Nacogdoches County, it is just that every historical item, relating to her representative citizens, should be collected and placed in that form which is most readable and most accessible. In this volume it is especially proper that the story of Dr. Robert Leak's life be treated at length, for he is not only an eminent physician, but an old settler of this region, coming here in January, 1858. Like others of this county, the Doctor was born in Georgia, Jasper County, July 12, 1824, and he is a son of Garlington and Eliza (Burge) Leak, natives respectively of South Carolina and Newton County, Ga. The grandfather, Samuel Leak, was one of the first settlers of Pike County, Ga., whither he came from South Carolina. Garlington Leak's youthful days were passed in Jasper and Pike Counties, Ga., and he was married in Newton County to Miss Burge, a native of that county. Later, he began merchandising in Pike County, and in connection also carried on agricultural pursuits with much success. For years he served as justice of the peace, and his last days were passed there. With fair educational advantages, Dr. Leak grew to manhood in Pike County, Ga., and he began to study medicine with Dr. James A. McGeehe, one of the leading physicians of that section at that time. He took his first course of lectures at Augusta, Ga., in 1848-'49, and then returned the following winter and graduated in the class of March, 1850. Soon after he was married in Pike County, April 14, 1850, to Miss Mary A. H. Gilder, a native of that county, daughter of Jacob Gilder, and afterwards practiced in the home neighborhood for about a year. Removing to Fort Valley, he resumed the practice, but a desire to go farther west influenced him and he crossed over into Texas, settling first in Tyler County, where he was one of the pioneer physicians. In 1857 he moved to Nacogdoches County and located at Douglas, where he remained until the following year, when he located at Melrose. From that time up to 1888 this earnest and conscientious physician labored for the good of humanity and ministered to the wants of the sick and distressed. His face was a familiar one at the bedside of the afflicted, and his success in his profession made him popular far and wide. Although now practically retired, he still prescribes for some of the old families, but he does not desire, were he able, to undertake the long journeys of twenty or thirty miles, as in former days. When he first came here he bought a small tract of land, and now on this has a neat and substantial residence. He also owns a farm of fifty acres adjoining, and is comfortable and happy. In politics the Doctor upholds the principles of the Democratic party, but is a strong temperance worker and voted for prohibition. His marriage resulted in the birth of two living children: Dr. E. E. Leak, a noted physician of Center, Tex., and Rev. D. A. Leak, a minister of the Church of Christ, located now at Madisonville, Tex. The Doctor lost four children, Dr. R. A. Leak, who was a physician of unusual ability; Dr. M. G., also prominent in his profession, and two infants, Alonzo, who died at the age of fifteen months, and James, who was

Hon. WILLIAM CLARK.

seven years old. Dr. Leak was formerly an active member of the Masonic fraternity, Melrose lodge, and he and wife are earnest workers in the Church of Christ. He was reared a Methodist, but about 1848 united with the Church of Christ. This worthy and honored old citizen has resided in this part of Texas for forty-two years, and has witnessed the marvelous growth and development of the same. The strictest integrity and uprightness have characterized his career through life.

HON. WILLIAM CLARK.
(Deceased.)

Given the ordinary average of education and good judgment, any man may make a success in the avenues of trade, but in the profession of law he must be endowed with superior intelligence and have gone through with years of careful study and training to be able to cope with the brilliant minds which do honor to the bench and bar of to-day. However, the original of this notice was not only an eminent lawyer and statesman, but a most successful business man of Nacogdoches County, where he was identified with the people and institutions for many years. He was well known throughout the state, more particularly in Eastern Texas, and was prominent in the ranks of the brilliant circle of lawyers of the same. Mr. Clark was a product of Georgia, born November 8, 1828, but when a child crossed the Mississippi River with his parents and settled in Sabine County, Tex. After growing to man's estate, and after having received a good practical education, Mr. Clark took up the study of law and soon after was admitted to the bar. Following this he located at San Augustine and, after practicing law there for a number of years, came to Nacogdoches, where he continued to practice his profession. This was previous to the war. He was a delegate from historic old Nacogdoches County to the convention known as the secession convention of 1860, and was one of (afterward known as) "Seven, serious, sober, sensible" men that voted "No" on the proposition to secede. When the Civil War broke out he raised a company here and joined the Confederate army, being commissioned captain of his company. Later he was promoted to the rank of colonel of his regiment and rendered valuable service for the Confederacy until the close of hostilities. He also served in the Texas-Mexican war during his early life, was corporal in Captain Goodlove's company, and was held in reserve with the company at the battle of Monterey. During his service in the Civil War he participated in a number of important engagements, among them being Jenkins' Ferry, April 30, 1864. At this engagement Colonel Clark particularly distinguished himself. The color-bearer having been shot down, Colonel Clark grasped the flag in his own hands, infused new courage in his wavering troops, practically saving the day. For this gallant conduct he was especially commended by his superior, General Kirby Smith. Colonel Clark returned to Nacogdoches after the war, and became one of the leading lawyers in this part of the state. He was also a man of good business acumen and was a silent partner in a general mercantile business in Nacogdoches. At the time of his death, and for several years previous to that, he served as attorney for the Houston East & West Railroad Co. He took an active interest in politics and was identified with the Democratic party. He held a number of positions of trust and honor in the state, served a number of terms in the Texas Legislature, and was a member of many important committees. On the 11th of July, 1867, Colonel Clark wedded Miss Amelia Taylor, who was born, reared and educated in Nacogdoches, and who was the daughter of Charles S. Taylor. Mr. Taylor was really one of the first settlers of Texas, locating in this state in the twenties, and was an Englishman by birth. He was a prominent lawyer of this county, and here died in 1866. Colonel and Mrs. Clark became the parents of ten children: William, Mary, Charles Taylor, Martha, Julia, Anna, Irion, Lawrence, Adolphus, and Leonard. The first six were well educated and the remainder are now attending the home school. Colonel Clark was well known throughout the state as a man of superior legal ability and sterling character, and his death, which occurred January 6, 1884, caused universal sorrow. His wife and children are well respected in the community and all hold membership in the Catholic church. Colonel Clark was also a member of that church.

WILLIAM T. ATKINS.

The century whose evening is upon us and the shadows of whose end are creeping o'er us has been, in America, prolific of the class of men who have been styled, not inaptly, self-made. By this term have been designated men who, without wealth or the advantages of a more than ordinary education, have educated themselves in a practical way and, by sheer force of character, have attained to eminence beside those who gained distinction by easier paths or shorter cuts. One of the most notable of this class is William T. Atkins, the most efficient cashier of the National Bank of Jefferson, Tex. He was born on a farm in Cumberland County, Va., August 20, 1842, and there passed his youth and boyhood. About the year 1853 he moved with his parents to Prince Edward County, Va., but in 1860 he left that state and went to Mobile, Ala., where he clerked in the office of his uncle, a broker of that place. When the tocsin of war sounded in 1861 his sympathies were with the South and he enlisted in Company K, Third Regiment, Alabama Volunteers, which was known as the Mobile Rifles. This was the same organization, but not the same men, that served in the Mexican war. Mr. Atkins' company was commanded by Captain L. T. Woodruff, and he was in many of the most prominent engagements of the war up to 1863. During the battle of Seven Pines he was wounded in the arm and breast, and during the bloody battle of Chancellorsville he received a severe wound in the head, which incapacitated him for further service. He was discharged and after the war went to Pickensville, Ala., where he clerked in a dry goods store for some time. From there he went to Columbus, Miss., in 1869, but left there in the summer of 1870 and came to Jefferson, Tex., where he was engaged as bookkeeper in

Erastus Jones' bank, where he remained for six years. After that he
became bookkeeper in the Citizens' Bank of Jefferson, remained with
the same several years; was then employed in the same capacity in
the National Bank of Jefferson, of which institution he is now cashier.
Several years later he went to Paris, Tex., where be became bookkeeper in the Paris Exchange Bank, and where he remained for
some time. Then returning to Jefferson, he has been a prominent
and honored citizen here since. Mr. Atkins is the author of a well-
written and interesting article on the "Extension of the National
Bank Act," which appeared in the New York Financial Record May
31, 1893, and which caused considerable comment. He takes a prominent part in local affairs and is deeply interested in all enterprises
that pertain to the welfare of his town. For the past four years he
has been alderman of the town, and during the time was chairman of
the finance committee of the City Council. He is one of the directors
of the Sherman, Shreveport & Southern Railway Company, and vice-
president of the Jefferson Cotton and Refining Company, as well as
president of the Jefferson Iron Company, which is one of the most
extensive smelting plants in Texas. Mr. Atkins is very enthusiastic
over the great resources of Texas, and especially of Marion County.
He says: "Texas has all the material, if manufactories were established, to live exclusively at home. It is evident that this great and
growing state is to-day receiving her proportion of the attention of
capitalists, who desire a safe and steady-paying investment. These
men understand and know that he who establishes his factory where
the material to be manufactured is at hand, has decidedly the advantage. Such is the history of Southern manufactories. Jefferson
has all that can be asked—timber of all kinds, iron ore of the best
quality, a never-failing cotton crop, an inexhaustible supply of the
finest timber, with both water and rail transportation. Lands are
cheap, living cheap, society good, city healthy; and, in fact, no point
in the state is better adapted for manufacturing purposes than Jefferson."

Mr. Atkins has been twice married, first to Miss S. Crawford,
who died shortly afterward, and then to Miss Mattie A. Murphy, who
bore him four children, as follows: Mary Anderson, William T., Jr.,
Samuel J., and a baby girl, named Mattie Ward. In private life Mr.

Atkins is known as a most estimable, refined and companionable gentleman, a man of advanced ideas, dominated by no thought but his own, and one who is prominent in all good work.

JOHN M'CONNELL.

The career of the gentleman whose name heads this sketch is but another evidence of what can be accomplished by those of foreign birth who seek a home and fortune on the free soil of America. He possesses the push, energy and enterprise for which his countrymen are noted, and as a natural consequence he has been successful in the accumulation of means, and has won a reputation for honesty and fair dealing that is in every respect justly merited. Mr. McConnell was born in Ireland in 1818, of which country his parents, Patrick and Bridget (Lynch) McConnell, were natives also. He remained in his native country until almost grown, and then went to Scotland, where he remained two years. From there he went to England, remained there four years, and on the 1st of January, 1839, came to New York. From there he went to New Orleans, thence up the Mississippi River to St. Louis, then to Shreveport, La., and from there to Nacogdoches County, Tex., where he followed the trade of blacksmith. In 1847 he came to Crockett and soon after started in the blacksmith business, which he continued for years. In 1882 he abandoned the blacksmith business and embarked in the hardware business, which he has carried on very successfully since. In 1891 he erected his block, and now carries a fine stock of doors, sash, windows, woodenware, crockery, etc. He has the faculty of making his business associates, as well as all his neighbors, his friends. Mr. McConnell was first married in 1848 to Miss Dickerson, who died in 1863, after bearing five children, two now living: William, a merchant, and John, also a merchant. Those deceased were named Lizzie, Ruth and Jeff. Mr. McConnell's second marriage occurred in

1865 with Mrs. Martha Lovelady, daughter of Cyrus Lovelady, who was an early settler of Texas from Mississippi. Five children were born to this marriage: Henry, a lawyer; Robert E., in business with his father; Phillip (dead), Esther, and Daniel. In 1872 Mr. McConnell was elected county treasurer, holding the office twelve years, to the entire satisfaction of all concerned. He held the office of alderman. He has ever been active in political matters. In 1849 he joined the Masonic fraternity and has been Master and High Priest; also a member of Palestine Commandery No. 3, Knights Templar. He is also a member of the Baptist church. Mr. McConnell is a self-made man and his present enviable position is the result of his own exertions.

JAMES BOWIE.

James Bowie, born in Georgia about the year 1790, settled in Catahoula Parish, La., in 1802, with his parents, and in the twenties became notorious in connection with a duel, fought on the sand-bar opposite Natchez by Dr. Maddox and Samuel Wells, which resulted in the wounding of fifteen and the death of six of the persons interested. Bowie's knife, made from a blacksmith's rasp by his brother Rezin, and used by him in the killing of Major Norris Wright, was sent to Philadelphia, fashioned into the form of a knife and named after the desperate character who used the steel first with such deadly effect. At Galveston, James, Rezin P. and John Bowie engaged in buying negroes from Lafitte's pirates and conducting them through the swamps of Louisiana; in 1819, James was attached to Long's expedition; in 1830 he became a naturalized citizen of Saltillo and by specious promises and exact life won the love of Senorita Veramendi of San Antonio de Bejar. November 2, 1831, with nine other Americans and two negroes, he defeated 164 Tehuacan and Caddo Indians, with the loss of one killed and three wounded, while eighty at least of the Indians lost their lives. In 1835 he broke away from all marital engagements, and in the battles of Nacogdoches and Conception, fought in 1835, opposed Mexican interests and continued so to do until killed at the Alamo, March 6, 1836.

LORENZO DE GAVALA.

Lorenzo De Gavala, born at Merida, Yucatan, in 1781, was a physician of his native place down to 1820, when he was elected deputy to the Spanish Cortes. On returning from Spain, he was elected deputy and subsequently chosen Senator in the Mexican Congress. From 1827 to the outbreak of the Jalapa revolution in 1830, he was Governor of the State of Mexico; but then had to relinquish the office. In 1833, however, he was re-elected deputy and commissioned Governor of the old state; a joint resolution of Congress permitting him to hold both offices. In 1834 he was appointed Minister to France, but resigned the portfolio and was appointed one of the commissioners from Texas and Coahuila in 1834; was one of the signers of the Texan Declaration that year and the second Vice-President of the Texan Republic. He hoped, with the aid of his English-speaking friends and the natives of the Republic, to establish a dictatorship, not only over Texas, but also over Mexico, and might have carried out his plans had not death claimed him on November 15, 1836—eight months and nine days after his friends perished at the Alamo.

DAVID CROCKETT.

David Crockett, born on the banks of the Nola Chucky River, Tennessee, August 17, 1786, was the son of John Crockett, one of the Irish

soldiers of the American Revolution. His grandparents were massacred by the Indians, one uncle was wounded by them, and another
captured. In 1798 his father apprenticed him to a Dutchman, who
had settled in Virginia, but the youth did not appreciate his new
position and soon set out for his distant home at the mouth of Limestone Creek, in Tennessee. A little later he started for Baltimore,
with the object of becoming a sailor; but the man, on whose wagon
he traveled, held his clothing and seven dollars in money, and may be
said to have returned the prodigal to his parents. For some years he
worked on the farm, when not engaged in hunting or making love to
the two girls who jilted him. About the age of nineteen, he met a
girl who did marry him, and moved with him to Lincoln County,
Tenn. In 1813 he enlisted in Captain Jones' company for the Creek
war, and subsequently was commissioned Colonel in Jackson's army
during the campaign in Florida. The death of his wife shortly after
his return made the way clear for his marriage with a soldier's
widow, and with her he moved to Shoal Creek, where he served as
justice of the peace, and in which district he was elected to the
Legislature. Then he removed further into the wilderness, settling
at Obion, Tenn., where he made hunting a profession. Re-elected to
the State Legislature, he opposed General Jackson for United States
Senator, and offered himself as a candidate. Of course, the state
would not spoil an uneducated, unpolished hunter by sending him to
the Senate; so that after adjournment he is found getting out a raft
of lumber for the New Orleans market. In driving the Mississippi
the lumber was lost, and Crockett returned to Obion to re-establish
himself as a statesman. In 1827 he was elected a member of Congress
and re-elected in 1829. In 1831 he was defeated; in 1833 was re-
elected, and in 1835 defeated. Vexed with Tennessee, he directed his
steps toward Texas, where he enlisted a few adventurers like himself; beat a party of fifteen Texans who opposed him, and chased
them to the Alamo, then commanded by Colonel W. B. Travis. On
March 6, 1836, he died within that fortress, pierced by the swords of
the victors.

DR. J. H. TAYLOR.

The medical man is held in the highest esteem by savage, as well as civilized people, and deservedly so, because in his hands are the issues of life and death. All honor is due to the profession of medicine, and to such practitioners as Dr. J. H. Taylor, who deserves more than a passing notice. He was born in Marshall, Tex., in 1851, and was there reared and educated. His father, Hon. James F. Taylor, was a native of Mississippi, in which state and Louisiana he was reared and educated. About the year 1840 the elder Taylor moved to Texas, settled on a large tract of land near Marshall, and became one of the foremost planters of his section. Being a man of much learning and more than ordinary good judgment, he was selected by his numerous friends to represent them in the State Legislature. Later he took a seat in the Senate, in which he served with credit to himself and his constituents. For many years he was prominent in Masonic circles, being Grand Master and Grand High Priest of the Chapter, and he was also an earnest and faithful member of the Methodist church. In his death, which occurred March 6, 1889, the county lost one of its most highly esteemed citizens. When a young man Mr. Taylor had married Miss Mary B. Holman, a native of Massachusetts, and nine children were born to them, of whom our subject was fourth in order of birth. In the year 1869 the latter commenced the study of medicine in Marshall, attended lectures in New Orleans, but graduate from Bellevue College, New York, in 1871. He at once began practicing in Harrison County and in 1881 moved to Marshall, where he has a flourishing practice at the present time. His nuptials with Miss Mollie A. Howard, a native of Harrison County, Tex., occurred in 1873, and their three children are named as follows: Holman, Mabel, and Christine. Mrs. Taylor's father, A. Howard, came from Alabama to Texas at an early date and was one of the pioneers of this section. Socially, the Doctor is a Mason, Chapter and Commandery, and has been District Deputy Grand Master for twelve

years. He has been presiding officer in all the branches. He is
Grand Medical Examiner of the A. O. U. W. of the grand district of
Texas, embracing Texas, Arkansas and Louisiana.

A. J. ROBERSON.

Retired from active pursuits and living the evening of his life in
peace, surrounded by those who love and respect him, the subject of
this sketch looks back on a life of industry, honesty and usefulness.
His home, in the city of Brenham, will probably see the close of a
career marked by activity in all the lines of good citizenship. He
came here to reside permanently on the 18th of December, 1847, but
is a native of Lincoln County, Tenn., where he was born October 24,
1815. His father was Ludwich Roberson, a native of Tennessee,
who there married Miss Anna Holcomb, a native of the same state.
They moved to Alabama, and later to Mississippi, in which state
they followed the occupation of farming, or planting. In the states
of Alabama and Mississippi his children were reared. The father
passed away in Newton County about the year 1847, his wife having
died in Tennessee several years previously. Late in life he married a
second time, and his widow survived him. He served in the war of
1812, and was with General Jackson at the famous battle on the
Plains of Chalmette, near New Orleans. A. J. Roberson was reared
in Pickens County, Ala., and Noxubee County, Miss., and received, in
youth, meager educational advantages, but later in life improved
himself much in this regard by self-imposed study. After marriage
he lived for six or seven years in Noxubee County, but in December,
1848, as above stated, located near Brenham, in Washington County,
Tex. He first opened a large farm near Chapel Hill, but several
years later bought a plantation of about 700 acres within four miles
of Brenham. He owned a number of slaves prior to the war, and was
highly successful in his farming operations. In time, his plantation

A. J. Robertson

Mrs A. J. Roberson.

became one of the best improved and finest in this portion of the state. In 1891 he sold 400 acres, including the residence tract, and bought property in Brenham, upon which to pass his declining years. He began life a poor boy, empty-handed, with little education, but a sound constitution, good sense, industrious and steady habits, and an ambition to live a useful and honorable life. His efforts were crowned with success, as is shown by his ample possessions and his good name. His wife, to whom he was married February 26, 1846, was Miss J. E. Ball, a native of South Carolina, but reared and educated in Alabama. She was a daughter of George Ball, a native of the Palmetto State, but long a resident of Alabama. To the marriage of Mr. Roberson and Miss Ball ten children were born, eight of whom are living: Eugene, a contractor and builder of Brenham; Josephine, widow of Mr. Dysart; Julia, T. J., George (deceased), Louisa, wife of Joseph Ralston; Alice, wife of J. Lockett; Katie, wife of Archibald Watson; Ella (died when she was but twelve years old), and George, moved to Dallas, went to California and there died. In 1863 Mr. Roberson enlisted in the Confederate service, becoming a member of Colonel Barnes' regiment. He entered as a private, but was promoted for merit to a lieutenancy, and served out his period of enlistment. He has always been a Democrat, and himself, wife and daughter are members of the Methodist Episcopal church. For nearly half a century he has lived in Washington County, coming here among the pioneers and seeing the country steadily improve under the hand of industry. With this improvement he can assert with pride that he had much to do. Well advanced in years, he is passing away, but will leave behind him an untarnished name for the satisfaction of his descendants.

STEPHEN M. BLOUNT.

Stephen M. Blount, who was, in 1888, the oldest living survivor of the signers of the declaration of Texas independence, was a native of Georgia, born February 13, 1808, and moved to Texas in July, 1835, settling in San Augustine. In 1836 he was elected a member of the convention that declared the independence of Texas, and nominated General Houston for commander-in-chief of the Texan forces. Blount was a close personal friend of Houston, whom he always afterward regarded as a grand man. In 1837 Blount was elected clerk of San Augustine County, and held that position four years. His whole life was one of activity. Prior to his emigration to Texas he served in several official capacities in his native state. He was colonel of the Eighth Regiment of Georgia militia, and was aid-de-camp to military generals in 1832-'34.

NEILL M'LENNAN.

Neill McLennan, in honor of whom McLennan County is named, was born in the highlands of Scotland in 1777, and emigrated, with two brothers and other relatives, to the State of North Carolina in 1801, where he resided as a farmer until 1816. With a brave and adventurous spirit, and with one companion, he explored the wilds of Florida, and, becoming satisfied with the country, remained there until 1834. He had heard of Texas and, with his two brothers and a few other friends, purchased a schooner at Pensacola, loaded her with their goods and families, navigated her themselves, and landed safely at the mouth of the Brazos River early in 1835. They proceeded up the river and settled on Pond Creek, near its mouth, in what is now Falls County. While there his two brothers were killed by the Indians, Laughlin, one of the brothers, being shot full of arrows. The family of the latter, consisting of a wife and three small children, were captured and taken away. The mother, who was living with them, was killed, the house was burned, and the wife and youngest child died in captivity. The next boy was bought, and the eldest remained with the Indians until grown, when, by a treaty, his uncle, Neil (not Neill) McLennan, brought him to McLennan County.

Adam Baugemann

It was difficult to reconcile him to stay away from his tribe. He finally married and raised six children. His death occurred in 1866. John, the other brother, was ambushed and shot, near Nashville. During the winter of 1839 and spring of 1840 Neill McLennan, accompanied by Captain George B. Erath, went on a surveying tour to the Bosque country, and being impressed with the advantages there for farming and grazing, determined to locate there. Accordingly, he commenced improvements there in 1845, and made it his home during the remainder of his life. At the old homestead still stands the old double log house, where many a wayfaring man has received refreshments and rest without money or charge. Mr. McLennan had six children, namely: John, who died in Milam County in 1887; Christina, wife of Eli Jones of McLennan County; Catherine, wife of L. E. R. Davis; Neil, a resident of McLennan County; Duncan, also of McLennan County; Laughlin, deceased in 1860. Mr. McLennan died in the month of November, aged eighty-one years.

ADAM WANGEMAN.

A fact not generally known concerning the State of Texas is, that to no class is its present prosperity more indebted than to the men and women of the "Fatherland," who are noted the world over for their honesty and industry. Among those who have pushed their way to the front, and who are a credit to their native land, is Adam Wangeman, who, although now living a retired life in the city of Brenham, was, for years, one of the active, enterprising and public-spirited business men of Austin County, Tex. He was born August 5, 1829, in the Kingdom of Saxony, Germany, and there remained until the age of fifteen, receiving good educational advantages from the excellent schools of that country. In 1844, when yet a lad, he emigrated with his parents to America and settled in Austin County, Tex., thus being among the early pioneers of the Lone Star State. Here the father purchased a quarter of a league of land, on which he located, and began improving it, and here, after a well-spent life, both he and wife died. Three sons and two daughters were born to their marriage, only one son and one daughter now living. Since his fifteenth year, Adam Wangeman has been a resident of Texas, and his knowledge of English has been wholly self-acquired. Although a foreigner by birth, Mr. Wangeman's love for his adopted country led to his enlistment for the war against Mexico, in 1847, as a member of Colonel Jack Hays' regiment of cavalry, and as such he participated in numerous skirmishes and engagements, was in pursuit of guerillas a considerable time, and was at Vera Cruz, Pueblo, and Old Mexico. Returning home at the close of the war, he was not allowed to long remain inactive. In 1849 he went overland to California with the first Government expedition sent out to establish forts along the Rio Grande River, but after seventeen months thus spent he returned overland to Texas via El Paso. While in Austin County he wedded Miss F. Kling, a daughter of Dr. Kling, who was a well-known physician of New Orleans, and of German nativity. After this event he settled on the old homestead and engaged in farming until 1858, when he sold out. The spring of 1859 he embarked in mercantile pursuits, which he continued until 1862, when he enlisted in the Confederate cause and became identified with Waul's Legion as private. Seven months later he was transferred to an engineering corps, but in order to look after private matters he hired a substitute and returned home. Still later he was induced to again enlist, and during the remainder of the war served in Louisiana and Texas. Returning to his home, he resumed business with his characteristic energy, which resulted in substantial returns. In 1872 he built the second cotton-seed oil mill in Texas, which he conducted with success for five years, when the mill burned, and there being no insurance, he sustained a loss approximating $25,000. Nothing daunted, he returned to mercantile pursuits, in conjunction with farming, which he continued with gratifying results until 1887. He then sold his store and farm, moved to Brenham, where he purchased property, and built a comfortable home. This has since been his place of residence. While practically retired from the active duties of life, Mr. Wangeman finds plenty of time to look after his many farms, scattered in various counties of the state. He is a stock-owner in the First National Bank, of which he is vice president, and is properly recognized as one of Washington County's foremost citizens. While a Democrat in politics, he has never aspired to official position, preferring, during his busy career, to confine his attention wholly to matters of business. He and wife are the parents of one son and four daughters and the grandparents of eighteen. Their son, Arthur, is one of the prominent business men of Brenham. Mr. Wangeman has been a resident of Texas one year over the half century mark, and his well-known character for honesty and integrity makes him universally respected. While giving him his just dues in this brief sketch, it is not inappropriate to mention that to Mrs. Wangeman he is much indebted for his success in life, for a loving wife, a wise counsellor and a helpmate in every way worthy of the husband.

DR. ROBERT E. ROWELL.

This prominent old medical practitioner is well known for his genial personality, his ready and kindly sympathy with those who come to him as invalids, and for this reason his clientele is perhaps even larger than would have been attracted by his recognized ability and the success which has attended his efforts. Such a man must bring to bear upon the duties of the profession he has chosen a most comprehensive apprehension of its obligations and its possibilities and a broad mind and liberal view of its relations to society and the part it must perform in his hands in the improvement and elevation of mankind; for the physician has had deputed to him a mission no less high than that of the preacher, no less potent upon human affairs than that of the jurist. Dr. Robert E. Rowell, like many of the best men of the county, is a native of Alabama, born in Lowndes County, August 11, 1824, and his youthful days were passed on a farm. In 1838 he moved, with his father, to Tallapoosa County, Ala., and resided there until 1846. He then entered the Louisville Medical

College of Kentucky, and after completing a two-years' course and, graduating, settled down to practice at Notasuga, Ala., where he remained three years. Returning to Tallapoosa County, he formed a partnership with Dr. Allen Kimball, whose daughter, Augusta Kimball, he married in 1852. Four years later he came to Texas, located on a farm eight miles from Jefferson, but subsequently moved to that city, where he has resided since. During the civil war he served as surgeon of Ochiltree's Regiment (Nineteenth Texas) and later was surgeon of a brigade. On account of ill health, he was obliged to abandon the work. The Doctor has not practiced his profession regularly since 1867, and when Jefferson was "booming" he was engaged in the real estate business. For about fifteen years he has been Treasurer of Marion County, being first appointed to that position to fill a vacancy, and he has been regularly elected every two years since, and that, too, in a Republican county, while he is a staunch Democrat. He is one of the largest farmers in Marion County; he owns also much property in the City of Jefferson, and is a man who has considerable influence in his section. His wife died about 1868. Their family consisted of five children, Lizzie, Mollie, Charles A., Zula, and Gussie.

F. D. FUTRELL.

Among the younger element of our prominent, energetic and influential business men, none are better known than F. D. Futrell, who richly deserves the success which he has wrought through a highly honorable business policy. He has been a resident of Gilmer since 1879, and from the first has been engaged in merchandising. Mr. Futrell came originally from the Old North State, born in Rich Square, Northampton County, June 14, 1854, and his father, Berry Futrell, was a native of the same state and county. The latter grew to manhood there and was married in Halifax County to Virginia Camp, a native of North Carolina. Mr. Futrell was a merchant and was thus engaged at the time of his death in 1860. His wife survives him, and resides on the old home place. Four children were born to this union, of whom our subject is the oldest. The others are: J. A., single, resides on the home place; C. D., a business man of Gilmer, and Lucy B., widow of W. A. Lambertson, resides at Rich Square, N. C. The mother of these children was married to Anderson Futrell, a brother of her first husband, and they have these children: Lillie, wife of William Vann, makes her home in Rich Square, and Nellie, is the wife of Mr. Boon of Briant Town, N. C. During his youth our subject received fair educational advantages in Rich Square, N. C., and later began clerking in that place, thus laying the foundation for a thorough business training. As time passed away he decided to venture in business for himself, and at first started in a very small way. He met with fair success, continuing the enterprise for about two years, when he decided to move to the Lone Star state. In December, 1879, he came to Texas and located at Big Sandy, where he clerked for about five months. In the spring of 1880 he made his way to Gilmer and engaged in clerking at this point for about five years, after which he formed a business partnership with J. M. Marshall, the same continuing up to 1892. At that date Mr. Futrell bought out his partner and has since conducted the business on his own responsibility. He now owns his own business house, a large brick building, and carries a large and select stock of dry goods and general merchandise. He is a gentleman with whom the law of commercial integrity is first, and upon this rule he bases his extensive dealings. Mr. Futrell was married in this flourishing town February 4, 1885, to Mrs. Anna Hoyler, a widow, and the daughter of W. Boyd, whose sketch appears elsewhere in these pages. Two children have been born to them, Berry and Frankey. Our subject supports the men and measures of the Democratic party, but does not care to hold office, as his extensive business keeps him fully employed. He and Mrs. Futrell are members of the Baptist Church and active workers in the same. Mr. Futrell is a member of the Legion of Honor and Knights of Honor. Mrs. Futrell is also a member of the Legion of Honor. He commenced life for himself with limited means and by his energy and perseverance has become one of the substantial men of the county.

CAPTAIN C. G. GRAHAM.

Among the honored soldiers of Marion County, Tex., stands the name of Captain C. G. Graham, a liberal, generous, high-minded gentleman, whose correct mode of living has gathered around a large circle of friends. He is a native of Tennessee, born fifty miles from Memphis, on the Tennessee River, in Perryville, Perry County, April 30, 1833. His father, General Charles Graham, was born in the "Old North State" January 29, 1792, and was a man possessed of more than ordinary ability. He participated in the war of 1812-'14 and in the Creek Indian war under General Jackson. During the year 1843 he came to Cass County, Tex., from North Carolina, and surveyed and established the first lines all over this part of the state. He died full of years, respected and esteemed by all, in Cass County in 1876. His wife, whose maiden name was Jennie Rayburn, was a native of Virginia. Until ten years of age, our subject remained in Tennessee, but at that date he moved with his parents to what is now Cass County (then Red River County), and remained there on a farm with his parents until 1847. After that he came to Jefferson County and engaged with his brother in mercantile pursuits, continuing the same until the breaking out of the Civil war, when he enlisted in Company A, First Texas Regiment, Confederate Volunteers, and was attached to Hood's Brigade. In 1862 he was transferred to Ochiltree's command, known as the Eighteenth Texas Infantry, west of the Mississippi River, and was first commanded here by Colonel David B. Culberson and later by Colonel W. H. King. Our subject remained with the Confederate army until it surrendered in 1865, a period of four years, and was holding the rank of captain when the war closed. Since that time, with the exception of four years, when he served as district clerk, Mr. Graham has been engaged in merchandising. In the year 1868 he was married to Miss Texie Harris and has four children, three sons and a daughter. The eldest son, Karl Graham, is a graduate of the A. and M. College at Bryan, Tex., and is now with an engineering corps. For services in the late war, the State of Texas has granted Colonel Graham a land certificate. He has seen Jefferson grow to prominence and go down to ruins, for he came here when there were but three stores in the place, and he has been one of the prominent factors in this section for many years.

GENERAL BEN M'CULLOCH.

The family from which General McCulloch sprung was doubtless of Scotch-Irish origin, and in the distinguished general above named were the best qualities of both races. His great-grandfather came to this country prior to the Revolution, and in direct descent from him is Ben, Alexander and Ben, the latter being the subject of this sketch. His father married a Miss Frances Le Noir, and settled in Nashville, Tenn., from which state he served with General Jackson in the war of 1812. He was a graduate of Yale College, of decided character and of generous disposition. He died in Dyer County, Tenn., August 4, 1846, at nearly sixty-nine years of age, his birth having occurred in Virginia. He was a member of the Methodist Episcopal Church. His son Ben was born in Rutherford County, Tenn., November 11, 1811, and at home he received a fair knowledge of the rudiments, but through much reading in later years he became an educated gentleman. During his youth he was engaged in farm work and found much diversion in hunting, for deer, turkey, bear and other game abounded. He was for a time engaged in flat-boating and rafting, and in 1820 moved to Alabama with his parents. To follow his career through boyhood would be of the utmost interest. Suffice it to say that he was an industrious youth, faithful to all his duties, and the promise he gave of rising to eminence was amply fulfilled. He was an intimate friend, notwithstanding the difference in their years, of the famous Davy Crockett and his son "Bill." About 1835 his career in Tennessee drew to a close and Texas became the scene of his activity, and his love for her grew and strengthened with the number of blows he gave and received in her service. He took an active part in the Texas rebellion and commanded a piece of artillery at the battle of San Jacinto, and for bravery, of which General Sam Houston was a witness, he was promoted to a first lieutenancy. In 1836 he raised a company in Tennessee, but was not called into action, and in 1837 he returned to the state of his birth and fitted himself for surveying, and in February, 1838, began his work there, and at the same time participated in many engagements with the Indians after the battle of San Jacinto, the number of which will never be known. In 1839 he was influenced to become a candidate for Congress and was elected. About three weeks after this the Indians went on the warpath and Mr. McCulloch again took the trail, and off and on for a number of years thereafter he was on the warpath, the engagements with the Comanches being especially bloody and trying. He was chosen as Representative of the first Texas Legislature, served faithfully in that capacity, and showed his interest in the land of his adoption to be as deep and earnest as he had while fighting for her liberty with the Mexicans, during which he distinguished himself for bravery and had won a national reputation as a skillful and daring soldier. In 1849 he was seized with the "gold fever," and made the overland trip through Mexico to the port of Mazatpan, and thence by ship to San Francisco, and was afterward elected sheriff of Sacramento, and it is needless to say made an efficient officer. He returned to his Texas home in 1852, and the following year was appointed by President Pierce as Marshal for the District of Texas, a position he filled for eight years, during which period he spent much time in the libraries of the National Capital, studying the text books upon the art of war. During the Mormon troubles he accepted the post of Commissioner, and through his wise and prudent measures a collision was averted and the trouble with that turbulent people composed. At the opening of the Civil war he was tendered a colonel's commission by Jefferson Davis, with authority to raise a Texas regiment for the Confederate service, but declined for good reason, and in May of the same year was commissioned a brigadier-general in the service of the Confederate States and assigned to the command of the military district embracing the Indian Territory west of Arkansas, and discharged his duties with distinguished military ability. He afterward took conspicuous part in numerous battles in Missouri, and in various hotly-contested engagements brought order out of confusion, when the chief commander was uncertain what to do, and so calm, cool and collected was he at all times that he inspired all with confidence, and wherever he appeared, Louisianans, Arkansans, Texans and Missourians greeted him with enthusiastic cheers that spoke, in a manner impossible to be misunderstood, the confidence the men had in their general. In that field in the West General McCulloch was one of the towers of Southern strength, and it was to his individual efforts on various occasions and his powers of generalship that resulted in Confederate victories. Very few men acquitted themselves of a more delicate trust, imposing the very weightiest responsibilities, with greater credit to themselves than General McCulloch did on the field of Oak Hills, with which victory his name and fame are indissolubly wedded. His reports of the battle were modest and manly, and on all other occasions he showed himself to be straightforward and accurate. After the evacuation of Springfield the Texas regiment entered the place and was comfortably established for the winter, through the good management and forethought of their gallant commander. Although he was often maligned and had many enemies, it cannot be denied that he possessed executive ability of the highest order and was loved and respected by his men, who hesitated not to follow where he led, and that was always in the hottest part of the engagement, although he wisely did not uselessly expose his men to danger. At the battle of Pea Ridge he commanded a corps of Arkansas, Louisiana and Texas troops, and while riding forward to reconnoitre was killed by the bullet of a sharpshooter. Thus closed a gallant and useful career, in the prime of manhood. Perhaps the character of no public man was more misunderstood than that of General McCulloch, for although he was called a ruffian, desperado, unpolished backwoodsman, etc., he was, on the contrary, genial and kindly in disposition, the idol of his men, a bold, graceful rider, a desperate fighter, a reckless charger, and a courageous ranger, and Indian fighter of the highest type. Had he lived in the days of chivalry he would have been a knight of the superior class, but having lived in the present day he was what may be truly termed a great civilian and a distinguished soldier.

F. C. FORD, M. D.

The general practitioner, as distinguished from the specialist, like the pastor contrasted with the evangelist, is the main personage of the medical profession. He will always be with us. We will always know him when we may never have occasion to seek the more unusual services of his specialist companion in medicine. Like the pastor, the family physician becomes in another realm a mentor to whom we turn in hours of physical trial and a friend in whom we repose the utmost confidence. Personal character thus enters into the general practitioner's greatest successes along with his professional ability. It is to this class in the medical calling that Dr. F. C. Ford of Nacogdoches, Tex., belongs and has met with pronounced success. He is well known in Nacogdoches and adjoining counties and is an eminent physician of this part of the state. For thirteen years he has practiced here and his face is a familiar one at the bedside of the afflicted and helpless. The doctor is a native son of the Lone Star State, born in what is now Newton County, September 17, 1849. His father, Rev. David Ford, was born in South Carolina, and moved with his parents to Mississippi when young. There he grew to manhood and became a minister of the M. E church, devoting the remainder of his days to that holy cause. In 1840 he moved to Texas and took up his residence in what is now Newton County, being a pioneer minister of this section. Here the closing scenes of his life were passed. Dr. F. C. Ford was reared in his native county with good educational advantages and early in life manifested a strong desire for the study of medicine. He took his first course of lectures at Mobile, Ala., in the winter of 1871 and 1872, and returned the following winter and completed the course, graduating with the class of 1873. Afterward he returned to Newton County, located at Burkeville and practiced his profession there for six years. In 1879 he went to New Orleans and took a supplemental course in the medical department of the Louisiana University, now known as the Tulane University, graduating in the spring of 1880.

Following this Dr. Ford resumed practice at Jasper, Tex., and there remained for two years, when he came to Nacogdoches. Here he immediately entered upon an extensive practice, extending through this and adjoining counties, and is classed among the most successful physicians in this part of the state. He keeps thoroughly abreast of the times in his profession and is a member of both the State Medical Association and the American Medical Association. On January 25, 1876, he was married to Miss Fannie Cates, a native of Louisiana, and their nuptials were celebrated in Shreveport, that state. Mrs. Ford was reared in Shreveport, La., educated in Marshall, Tex., and died in Newton County in 1879. The one son born to this union, F. C. Ford, is a young man of good habits and character, and will attend the Vanderbilt University this coming year (1896). Dr. Ford is an active worker for the Democratic party, with which he has long been in harmony, but has never cared to hold office, caring more to give his whole attention to his profession. However, he has served as a delegate to numerous state and county conventions. The doctor is a Royal Arch Mason, has served through all the chairs in both orders and at present is Past Master of the Blue Lodge, Past High Priest of the chapter, and has represented both lodges in the grand lodge of the state. He is also a member of the Knights of Pythias, being a Past Chancellor of this order. Dr. Ford has been a resident of this great state during his whole life, and is thoroughly identified with its people and institutions. For nearly a quarter of a century he has been engaged in his practice and has won an enviable reputation, holding many medical positions of honor and trust under state and corporation.

HON. JAMES A. WILKINS.

The gentleman whose name forms the subject for this sketch is the present efficient mayor of the city of Brenham, and for many years has been identified with its commercial and political history. He is a native of Lowndes County, Ala., his birth occurring February 5, 1831. His father, J. B. Wilkins, was born in North Carolina, there grew to man's estate, moved to Benton, Ala., when a young man, there embarked in mercantile pursuits and there met and married Miss Elizabeth Allen. In the year 1844 Mr. Wilkins, with his family, moved to the young republic of Texas and located at Brenham, which was named the seat of justice for the county the same year of Mr. Wilkins' settlement. He opened the second store in the place and embarked in mercantile pursuits. At this time Brenham contained but three dwellings, and consequently, the history of the city began about the time of Mr. Wilkins' advent. For years he was intimately connected with the commercial history of the place, but later assisted in the location of Hempstead, which he helped survey, plat and to which point he moved. He there died in 1861, an honored and respected citizen. James A. Wilkins is one in a family of five sons and four daughters, all of whom grew to maturity, two sons and three daughters of whom are living at the present writing (1895). Although a native of Alabama Mr. Wilkins has passed almost his entire life in Brenham. He here obtained his early education, and later a careful business training in his father's store. In 1862 his love for his native South led to his enlistment in the Confederate army and he became a member of the company commanded by Captain I. N. Owen, Colonel George Giddings' battery. Mr. Wilkins was appointed quartermaster of the battalion, in which capacity he served until the war ended. When peace was declared he accepted the results of the war in good faith and immediately commenced building up a profitable mercantile trade in Brenham, which he conducted until 1882. He was then elected mayor of the city, and so satisfactorily did he fill the position that he was re-elected. Under his administration of affairs reforms were inaugurated, manufacturing and commercial enterprises were encouraged, municipal affairs were placed on a business basis and a reign of prosperity enjoyed. Mr. Wilkins has since been re-elected chief executive official of Brenham without intermission, and is now serving his thirteenth term. Upon his inauguration he found the streets in a deplorable condition, various monopolies in control of several departments, city script worth but sixty cents on the dollar and a general feeling of unrest and dissatisfaction pervading the official and commercial life of the city. With his characteristic ability and energy Mr. Wilkins soon brought order out of chaos, streets were repaired, the city secured ownership of the electric lighting and water works plant, scrip was soon brought to par and has never since depreciated. Various other reforms were instituted until at the present time the city of Brenham is known as the best-governed municipality of its size in all Texas. This is almost wholly due to the sagacity and integrity of Mr. Wilkins. Aside from his present position he has served as deputy sheriff and deputy clerk of the county, alderman of the city several years, delegate to numerous conventions and various other positions of trust, in all of which he acquitted himself creditably. In 1852 he married Miss Beersheba Lusk, a daughter of Samuel Lusk, who was a native of Tennessee, and who came from Alabama to Texas in 1835, when the country was yet practically in a primitive condition. Samuel Lusk became prominent in Texas and was a delegate from Washington County to the convention that declared the independence of Texas. Three sons and one daughter have been born to Mr. and Mrs. Wilkins, all being dead except one son, Wallace, who at the present time is honorably connected with Giddings & Giddings, bankers. Mr. Wilkins has been a resident of Brenham for fifty-one years and is highly esteemed for his moral character and private worth. Socially he is an Odd Fellow and a Royal Arch Mason. There is no man better or more favorably known in Washington County than Honorable James A. Wilkins.

DR. THOMAS H. TAYLOR.

Nothing strange or singular clings about the fact that health is the paramount topic of interest in all parts of the world. Health is capital, comfort, happiness, life, everything. One of the noblest professions, one of the most beneficial to mankind, the profession of all professions, which, while it is prosecuted for gain, is in its very

nature nearest to beneficent charity, is that of medicine. At the
same time it is one of the most exacting upon its devotees. Longview is fortunate in the number and character of its physicians and
surgeons, and one of the most prominent of them all is Dr. Thomas
H. Taylor, who is now the oldest physician in Gregg County, Tex.
His birth occurred in Copiah County, Miss, and he was the second
in a family of eight children born to his parents, Dr. Job and Matilda G. (Cotton) Taylor, natives respectively of South Carolina and
North Carolina. The first representatives of the Taylor family in
America were three brothers who came from Scotland in colonial
times. One settled in Virginia, one in Kentucky and the other in
South Carolina. Our subject is descended from the South Carolina
branch. His paternal grandfather, Moses Taylor, was born in that
state and there became a large tobacco planter and farmer. He
was a soldier in the Revolution. He remained a Tory and during the
war returned to England. After reaching mature years the father
of our subject went to Georgia, from there to Alabama and thence
to Mississippi, where he followed the practice of medicine fully
twenty years. In December, 1848, he came to Texas, located in Harrison County, and resumed the practice of medicine, continuing this
for about a score of years. He was also an ordained minister in
the M. E. church and preached locally for a long time. His wife
was seventy-two and he eighty-one years old at the time of their
deaths. Dr. Thomas H. Taylor was educated in Mississippi and when
twenty-one years old came with his parents to Texas. He at once
began reading medicine and after taking a thorough course of studies began immediately afterward to practice in Jefferson. Later
he was located at Coffeeville, and in Pittsburg. He then moved to
Gregg (then Upshur) County, but still later made a location near
Baton Rouge, La. In 1861 he entered the Confederate army, Company A, Third Texas Regiment, as a private soldier and first participated in the battle of Wilson Creek. Owing to his medical knowledge he was then taken from the ranks and placed in hospital service.
Soon after he was appointed surgeon and assumed charge of the
hospital at Springfield. After a few months passed east of the Mississippi and in the battles around Corinth, he was placed in charge
of a hospital established in Holmes County, and was also detailed

to other hospitals. On account of illness he was discharged in 1864. In 1885 he came to Longview, where he resides at the present time. He has but just practically retired from his profession, which he carried on successfully for forty-four years. Dr. Taylor was first married in 1853 to Miss Margaret Ann Talkington, a native of Mississippi, who died in 1859, leaving two daughters, both now deceased. In December, 1862, the doctor married Mrs. Cook (nee Coleman), a native of Georgia, and they have two children: Thomas H. and Mittie, who died in Longview. The doctor has held the office of justice of the peace and other local positions and is well-liked in the community. He is a member and an active worker of the M. E. church. Dr. Taylor has now nearly reached the allotted period of man's age—three score and ten years. His life has been brimful of activity and usefulness, and his career in life has met with an excellent degree of success. His chief aim has been to lead an upright, honorable and correct life, such a one that future generations could copy with benefit to mankind, and one that would reflect credit upon himself when Time, the destroyer of all things material, had effaced his name from among the living. That this object has been attained is evidenced by the high esteem in which he is universally held, particularly by those who know him best.

JUDGE W. H. FORD.

There is not among men a position of greater honor than that of judge, nor one involving higher responsibilities nor demanding truer manhood in its incumbents. This truth holds good of the judge, whether of the United States Supreme Court or of courts of lower degree. It is the judge of a district, where all classes are found, who holds in his hands the key to human destiny more truly than the judge who confines his labors to large estates, or the affairs of wealthy corporations. The latter has usually to deal with financial values, while the former deals with the woes and idiosyncrasies of human hearts. One of the best known jurists of Texas, particularly of the eastern portion, is Judge W. H. Ford, of Beaumont, who, although not now on the bench, gained eminence and renown by his impartial rulings for twelve years as judge of the first judicial district. He was born August 13, 1843, in Newton County, Tex., and was one of six sons and six daughters, five of the former and three of the latter arriving to years of maturity, that were born to the marriage of Rev. David Ford and Maria V. Hamilton. The father was a native of South Carolina and was there reared and educated. He went to Mississippi at an early day and for years was known as a pioneer Methodist preacher of that state. While in Madison County, Miss., he met and married the lady who so faithfully and lovingly proved his helpmeet. About the year 1840 he moved to Texas, opened a farm in Newton County and passed the remainder of his days in agricultural pursuits and in preaching the gospel. His strict adherence to Christianity, his many benevolent acts and his noble character made him universally loved and respected. His death occurred in 1873, at the age of sixty-eight years. His widow was a native of New Jersey, although reared and educated in Mississippi. She survived her husband a number of years and finally passed from life at the residence of her son, Dr. F. C. Ford, at Nacogdoches, July 7, 1893. Judge Ford passed his youth in his native county, supplementing his early scholastic training with a course at McKenzie's Institute. March 5, 1863, when nineteen years of age, he joined Whitfield's Legion, which became a part of Ross' brigade of Texas cavalry, and was a gallant participant in the battles of Elkhorn, Iuka, Corinth, Thompson's Station and eighty-three days of active engagements and 112 days out from Dalton, including the evacuation of Atlanta. In December, 1864, he was granted a furlough because of ill health and was at home at the time of the close of the war. With little or no means at his command Judge Ford began to farm and continued this with varying results for seven years. In 1872 he was appointed by Governor Davis to fill an unexpired term as sheriff of Newton County, in which capacity he served with credit and honor to himself and satisfaction to the county. In 1874 he went to Lebanon, Tenn., took a thorough course in law, where he proved his strength of intellect and purpose and then returned to his native county and embarked in legal pursuits. In 1875 he moved to Jasper County, resumed the practice of his profession and early in 1879, so popular and prominent had he become, he was appointed attorney for the First Judicial District, a signal recognition of his ability and character. In November of the succeeding year he was elected judge of the district and by re-election served twelve years on the bench, a fitting tribute to his worth as a man and his purity as a jurist. In 1890 he located at Beaumont, where he is recognized as one of the foremost legal practitioners. He has the general reputation of being among the ablest lawyers and most upright judges in the state. In 1865 Judge Ford wedded Miss Octavine Coleman, to whose sympathy and help he attributes much of his success. This lady, after a lingering illness, died in 1893. Miss Evelyn Thompson became his second wife and a bright little daughter (Jean) is the result of this union. Politically Judge Ford is a Democrat, and has contributed in no small degree to the success of his party throughout the state. He is a man of strong personality, an eloquent speaker, an accurate reader of the methods and hearts of men and a substantial citizen of the great commonwealth of Texas. As a member of the Masonic fraternity he was entered, passed and raised, and was exalted to the sublime degree of the Royal Arch. He is also a Knight of Pythias. He is a member of the Methodist Episcopal Church South. A native of Texas, Judge Ford is a Texan in all the word implies, and is an enthusiastic believer in a glorious future for the Lone Star State.

JAMES F. CROW.

Chemistry, which is the science of the properties of the different forms of matter and their mutual reactions, was developed from the alchemy of the Middle Ages. Another form of the dispenser of medicines is the apothecary, an outcome of the early days, licentiate of the Association's Society, having been incorporated June 6, 1617. The apothecary, or pharmacist, is to-day one of the most essential of all the men of trade. The drug store is a necessity which no community can ignore, and it is but necessary to glance over the array of labels that adorn the bottles behind the counters and in the prescription department of a well-conducted drug shop to get at the truth of the vast amount of knowledge that a person must possess in order to be able to successfully handle the necessities of a chemist's establishment. One of the old and reliable drug establishments of Jefferson is that carried on by James F. Crow, who is one of the honorable business men of the place and thoroughly familiar with every detail of his business. He was born near Linden, Cass County, Tex., August 12, 1857, and made his home in that county until eighteen years of age. His parents were W. H. and Martha (Wadsworth) Crow. In June, 1879, our subject came to Jefferson and began clerking for the drug firm of Dr. P. Thomas. This store he purchased in May, 1886, and has since conducted it in a very successful manner. Being a thorough master of his profession he has the confidence of all and merits it. He has been engaged in his present business for fifteen years and employs two clerks in his large store. Mr. Crow was married July 28, 1886, to Miss Louise Terry and to them have been given three interesting children: Lewis. F., Mary and Phelps Terry.

R. G. BROWN.

Longview, Tex., can well be proud of the amount of brains and energy possessed by her representative business men, for, taken as a whole, there are none brighter, more intelligent, or with more ability and push in any direction, and among the number is R. G. Brown. He is a mill-owner, merchant and lumberman, and those who deal with him find him a very pleasant gentleman, courteous and affable, and in every respect of the term, a true man of busi-

SCENE ON THE NEUCES RIVER.

ness, a man whose experience and thorough knowledge of his different occupations have placed him among the leading business men of this thriving city. His birth occurred on a farm in Rusk County, Tex., February 2, 1852, to the union of John G. and Fannie (Rodes) Brown, and he is of English origin. The father was a native Virginian, born in Buckingham County, was educated at the University of Virginia and a man possessed of much more than ordinary ability and learning. He was a farmer all his life and the old family homestead is in the shadow of the Blue Ridge Mountains, eight miles from Charlottsville. In 1850 Mr. Brown moved with his family to Rusk County, Tex., and later in that county raised a company of soldiers for the Confederate army. He was an active Democrat and in the days of reconstruction was elected to the State Senate by a large majority over his opponent, J. W. Flanigan. Mr. Brown was the father of a large, old-fashioned family of children, twelve in number, as follows: John W., A. Victoria, Mary E., Sidney (daughter), Sarah E., Virginia J., Della G., Lula Frances, Benjamin B., Frank B., Charles T. and our subject. The last-named attended the common schools and Morehouse College at Bastrop, La. From school he went to New Orleans, where he found employment in a large cotton house. When twenty-three years old he accepted a position as clerk with a grocery firm and showed a great aptitude for commercial pursuits. In 1879, being very anxious and ambitious to embark in business for himself, he associated himself with J. J. Flewellen, under the firm name of Brown & Flewellen, handling groceries. This venture prospered and today the firm controls the largest business interest in Longview and the surrounding country. Among other interests a large saw-mill and planer, which represents an investment of over $100,00 and which gives employment to a large force of workmen, is carried on by this firm. The firm also owns several thousand acres of timber land and a logging road eight miles long, fully equipped. Aside from this Mr. Brown has an interest in an oil mill and in the Longview Ice and Bottling Company. In 1874 he was married to Miss Nettie Flewellen and by this marriage they have one daughter, Miss Ada. Mrs. Brown's death occurred the following year. In 1881 Mr. Brown wedded Miss Flora Crutcher, daughter of Mr. and Mrs. J. G. Crutcher of Frankfort, Ky.

His wife, like himself, is a member of the Cumberland Presbyterian Church and active in church work. They have had born to their marriage six children, namely: Robert G., Jr., Hallie, Annie, John C., Flora and Maggie L. In politics he advocates the principles of the Democratic party, is active and influential in his support of that party, but is not an office-seeker. Socially he is a Mason and an Odd Fellow.

STEPHEN FULLER AUSTIN.

Stephen Fuller Austin, born at Austinville, Wythe County, Va., November 3, 1793, entered the Colchester Academy in Connecticut in 1804, the academy at New London in 1805 and the Transylvania University in Kentucky in 1808. At the age of twenty-one years he was chosen a member of the Missouri Legislature and served in that body until 1819, when he moved to Little Rock, Ark., where he was appointed circuit judge. Shortly after he became a resident of New Orleans, where he was to co-operate with his father, Moses Austin, in the colonization of Texas. In the pages devoted to the history of the English-speaking colonies and the wars of Texas his name occurs often. As a military commander he had no ambition. As to his temper, he himself published that he was hasty and impetuous, and that he had forced upon himself a stringent discipline to prevent a fit of passion that might destroy his influence. In his disposition he was open-hearted, unsuspecting and accommodating almost to a fault. He was therefore often imposed upon, especially in the minor demands of benevolence and justice in social life. He excelled in a sense of equity, constancy, perseverance, fortitude, sagacity, prudence, patience under persecution, benevolence and forgiveness. He was never married. During the first years of his residence in Texas his home was at the house of S. Castleman, on the Colorado. Later, when his brother-in-law, James F. Perry, re-

STEPHEN F. AUSTIN.

moved to the colony, he lived, when in Texas, with his sister at Peach Point plantation, in Brazoria County. Besides this sister he had a younger brother named James Brown Austin, who was well-known in Texas.

J. H. BARHAM, M. D.

In none of the various avocations of life are there stronger incentives to persistent study and untiring activity than in the medical profession. Few even among the experienced fully appreciate the important fact that when a young man obtains his degree, has graduated from some well-known medical college, he has just begun his labor, though not his anxiety, and that to keep abreast with the swift progress being made in the science of medicine he must practice constant watchfulness. Not only this, but it is true that to become a highly successful practitioner he must extend his studies to all the collateral sciences and must be possessed of a vast fund of general information bearing upon everything affecting life. Dr. J. H. Barham is a native Tennesseean, born near Savannah, on the Tennessee River, April 27, 1847. His father, John Barham, was born in the Old North State and moved to Tennessee with his father, Newsom Barham, when a child. The latter was a pioneer of Tennessee and settled eight miles from Nashville, where he reared his family and spent the remaining years of his life. Farming was his life's pursuit. He was of English ancestry, his forefathers coming here at an early date. John Barham, father of our subject, upon reaching mature years, turned his attention to merchandising with his brother, R. J. Barham, at Coffee Landing on the Tennessee River. These brothers were the founders of that town and there for many years were thrifty, wide-awake business men. Mr. Barham was twice married, his second wife, Emily F. Hamlett, being the mother of our subject. She was born in Virginia, as was her father, Stephen Hamlett, who subsequently became one of the pioneers of Ten-

nessee. In 1854 John Barham crossed the Mississippi River to
Texas and located in Rusk County, where he bought a large tract
of land and became one of the most successful agriculturists in this
section.   There he reared his family and there passed away in 1876.
His wife is now living and resides with a daughter near the old home
in Rusk County. Time has covered her head with his frosts, but
her mind is still vigorous and active and she is now enjoying a quiet
and contented old age, being in her seventy-seventh year. The four
children born to her marriage, two sons and two daughters, grew
to mature years. The eldest, S. H. Barham, a successful physician,
resides on the old homestead in Rusk County; Mrs. D. A. Langston of
Rusk County; J. H. (our subject), and Virginia, wife of John Arnold,
a lawyer of Henderson, Tex.   During his youth Dr. J. H. Barham secured a good practical education in the common schools and then by
close application in subsequent years and his wonderful ability to
thoroughly master everything he undertook, he became one of the
best educated men of his vicinity.   He began the study of medicine
under the tutelage of Dr. Attaway, and after that gentleman's death
under Dr. Matthews of Rusk County.   Following that he took a
course of lectures at the medical department of the University of
Louisville, Ky. This was in 1874 and 1875, and the following winter
he returned and completed his course, graduating with the class of
1876.   Returning to Rusk County he practiced his profession there
up to 1879, and at the same time was engaged in agricultural pursuits.   At that date he went to New Orleans and took a supplemental
course in the University of Louisiana, now known as Tulane University, graduating with the class of 1880, and in the same class as
Dr. Ford, now a successful physician of Nacogdoches (see sketch).
Upon his return to Rusk County Dr. Barham practiced medicine
there for three years, and then on August 16, 1883, moved to Nacogdoches, where he immediately entered upon a large and successful
practice.   Well read and well posted on all matters relating to
his profession, with a flattering practice, he is in truth a physician
of thorough learning and experience.   His ambition is not for any
one line of special practice, but to be a superior general practitioner,
and his great success thus far places him in the front ranks of the
leading physicians.   In 1892 he took a polyclinic or post-graduate

course at St. Louis Post-Graduate School, and is thoroughly up with the times in all that relates to his profession. All the latest medical journals are found in his office and his library is an extensive and select one. The doctor is a member of the State Medical Association and other societies as well, and is a member of the Knights of Pythias. On April 3, 1878, he was married to Miss Ruth Garrison, a native of Rusk County and the daughter of Capt. Z. B. and Elizabeth Garrison, pioneers of Rusk County from Georgia and Tennessee. Mrs. Barham is a lady of superior attainments and received her education mainly in Athens, Ala., and Carrollton, Ga. Dr. and Mrs. Barham have an interesting family of five children: George, Emmett, Virdian, Joel H., Jr., and Ruth. Mrs. Barham is an active Methodist, but the doctor holds membership in the Baptist church.

COLONEL G. W. L. DAWSON.

This gentleman, a descendant of a prominent Kentucky family, was born near Harrodsburg, Mercer County, that state, March 31, 1837. When young he moved to Missouri with his parents, James and Lucy (Hammond) Dawson, the former a native of Kentucky and the latter of Virginia. Subsequently our subject was sent back to Harrodsburg, Ky., to attend school and later entered the state university of Fulton, Mo. He was residing at Weston, Mo., when the war broke out, and he there raised a company of his own and was made captain of the same. Six months later he was elected colonel of the regiment, the First Missouri, which was an independent one under control of General Price. Colonel Dawson served in the war from May 12, 1861, until 1862, when he was wounded at Elkhorn. He was twice wounded, the last time so seriously that he was compelled to go on crutches for four years. He boasts that he never took the oath of allegiance, never was discharged and says he considers that he has never quit the Confederate service. On account of wounds he was exempt from service a_d now holds an unlimited furlough, which is a document never issued to any one else. On leaving Missouri our subject came first to Marshall, Tex., in 1862, and took charge of what was known as the Atkins House, but he at once remodeled it and renamed it the Capital Hotel. He resided in Marshall until 1870, and then came to Jefferson, Tex., where he opened the Haywood House, which was one of the first buildings to be erected there after the war. He conducted this house for two years and then embarked in the railroad supply business. He held a contract with the Texas & Pacific people for furnishing railroad ties and supplied what were used in the road construction from Jefferson to De Kalb on the Trans-Continental line. He sold this contract out at the end of twelve months and embarked in the grocery business, from which he has recently retired. He is one of the prominent military men and politicians of the state and is well-known over its length and breadth. He has been chairman of the county Democratic executive committee for six years and he was the principal organizer and chairman of the Anti-Prohibition League. His work was most effective. For the past twenty years the colonel has been a delegate to every state convention and was a delegate to the national Democratic convention which met in St. Louis in 1888 and which nominated Cleveland and Thurman. Colonel Dawson selected his wife in the person of Miss Annie Flint of Harrison County, Tex., and their union was celebrated in 1863. Her parents were Thomas and Eliza Flint. The one child born to our subject and wife is deceased. When the colonel came to Jefferson it was a flourishing town of 20,000 people and he has seen as many as seventeen steamboats at the Cypress bayou wharf, where they were being loaded with cotton, which was piled up in hundreds of bales.

HON. SAMUEL BELL MAXEY.

This distinguished soldier and statesman was born March 30, 1825, at Tompkinsville, Ky., and was of Huguenot ancestry. His education was acquired in the public and select schools of his native state, and after being appointed to a cadetship at West Point was graduated from that institution with honor in 1846. He was assigned to the Seventh Infantry for the Mexican War and participated in the battles of Monterey, Tampico, Vera Cruz, Cerro Gordo, Contreras, Churubusco, Molino del Rey and the capture of the City of Mexico. For gallant conduct on the battlefield he was brevetted first lieutenant. For a time after the war he was stationed at Jefferson Barracks, but resigned in 1849 and began practicing law at Albany, Ky. In 1857 he moved to Paris, Tex., and in 1860 was elected to the State Senate, although never taking his seat. He was instrumental in raising the Ninth Texas Infantry, was made a brigade commander and in 1863 was assigned to the command of the Indian Territory. For conspicuous and valiant services he was made a major-general. After the war he resumed the practice of law at Paris, Tex. In 1874 he was elected to the United States Senate and in 1880 was re-elected to a second term of six years. As a citizen, soldier and statesman General Maxey was among the first men of the nation. He was happily married to Miss Matilda Denton. General Maxey died August 16, 1895, at his home in Paris.

DR. ST. CLOUD COOPER.

Jefferson has always been fortunate in its physicians, and it is especially so in recent years, in its younger generation of practitioners, who have contributed so much to the advancement of the city's reputation as a center of medical knowledge. Conspicuous among these is Dr. St. Cloud Cooper, who is a native of this city, born in 1861, and the eldest of five children born to the marriage of J. C. and Lucy (Harris) Cooper, the former a native of Pennsylvania and the latter of Alabama. The paternal grandfather, who was of English origin, was also a native of the Keystone State. The maternal grandfather was born in Alabama, but came to Texas at an early day and was among the pioneers of Harrison County. The father of our subject, J. C. Cooper, who was also a physician of considerable prominence, was reared in Washington, Pa. He selected medicine as his calling in life and in 1857 graduated from the University of Pennsylvania. Following this he went to Mexico for a short time, and then to Nacogdoches, Tex., where he remained two years, or until 1859, when he came to Jefferson. This city pleased him and he here married Miss Harris in 1860. During the Civil War he became surgeon of Lane's regiment, and served in that capacity until cessation of hostilities. In 1866 he went to Carrollton, Mo., and there he resides at the present time, engaged in a successful practice. Dr. St. Cloud Cooper grew to manhood in Missouri, received his education in the high schools of Carrollton, and when grown began the study of medicine at the Missouri Medical College, from which institution he was graduated in 1882. In the following year he came to Tilden, Tex., practiced his profession there for three years, and then went to New York, where he took a post-graduate course. Returning to Texas he located in Jefferson, where he has since had a large and steadily increasing practice. Dr. Cooper is a member of the Texas State Medical Association, also the National Association of Railroad Surgeons and Northeastern Texas Medical Association. He was married in 1888 to Miss Dora Hudson of Carrollton, Mo., and they have three interesting children: Charles Hudson, Lucy Catharine and Dora. Mrs. Cooper is a member of the Christian church. The doctor is one of the oldest physicians in practice in Jefferson and has the entire confidence of all, for he is well-educated and keeps thoroughly abreast of the times. Socially he is a Mason, in which he holds office in the Royal Arch Chapter, and he also belongs to the Knights of Pythias.

JULIUS B. VAN NESS.

The gentleman whose name forms the subject for this sketch is now living a retired life in Brenham, but for a number of years was one of the active and successful business men of Washington County,

Tex. He is a native of New York, his birth occurring in the city of Albany July 19, 1813, and he is a son of Benjamin Van Ness, a grandson of Isaac Van Ness and the great-grandson of John Van Ness. Originally the family came from Holland and were among the early Dutch pioneers to settle the Empire State. Benjamin and Isaac Van Ness were born at Chatham, N. Y. (the former a carpenter and contractor by occupation), and were among the first to settle in and around Clever Rock. John Van Ness made a home at Kinderhook when the country was an unbroken forest. The name of Van Ness is one familiar to all readers of early colonial history, particularly the pioneer history of "York State." In his capacity of skilled mechanic, Benjamin Van Ness was a heavy contractor of the government for years, furnishing immense quantities of timber for the navy department. He moved to the city of Washington, D. C., and became intimately associated with many of the most prominent men of the nation, and his home was situated on the ground where afterward Ford's Theater, in which President Lincoln was assassinated, was built. Owing to reverses of a business nature he moved to Westmoreland County, Va., and began farming on the "Monroe Place," a farm previously owned by President Monroe, and still later moved to Richmond County, Va., where he passed from life in 1863, after an eventful and useful career. When but seventeen years of age he was married to Miss Delia Bishop, a New York lady, who bore him a family of four sons and four daughters, all of whom lived to years of maturity and reared families, but only two of whom are now living. One sister, Emeline Carver, resides in Washington, D. C. Julius B. Van Ness was the second in order of birth in this family. Now past the meridian of life, he has lived to see some of the most important events in the history of our republic. While in Washington he witnessed the arrival of General La Fayette and the magnificent ovation given that great and powerful friend of the American colonies. Until thirteen years of age he lived with his parents in Washington, and with them resided at their two homes in Virginia. In 1837 Miss Ann Palmer became his wife, after which event he engaged in agricultural pursuits, which he continued for a period of six years and succeeding which he was engaged in merchandising for some time. During his career as merchant in Virginia he moved to Richmond County and was appointed a postmaster by the President. His wife died in 1854, having borne him three children: Theodore E. and James A., both gallant soldiers for the Confederacy, and both dying at Belton, Tex., and Laura L., who first married Joseph Linscom, and after his death, Mr. Campbell. In 1855 Mr. Van Ness wedded Miss M. M. Porter, who died in 1867, leaving two children: Llewellyn, married and is a prominent business man of Tyler, Tex., and Henrietta, unmarried, a lady of high accomplishment, who is keeping house for her father. Miss Frances Amanda Porter, to whom he was married in 1868, died in 1889, leaving one son—Olin, a young man of excellent business qualifications, now holding a responsible position with the Brenham Compress Company. In 1857 Mr. Van Ness moved to Belton, Tex., and embarked in mercantile pursuits, but owing to ill health in his family he returned to Virginia. For several years his time was passed in alternating between Virginia and Texas, during which time he crossed the Gulf of Mexico eleven times. In 1860 he located at Sabine Pass, resided there one year, moved to Beaumont, where he followed merchandising one year, then came to Brenham where, for the succeeding four years, he conducted an extensive mercantile trade. During his diversified career Mr. Van Ness has accumulated considerable property, and while he is not actively identified in business at the present time, he superintends the management of his varied interests. An old-fashioned Jacksonian Democrat, he supports the doctrines of his party, but has never asked for, or received official favor. For thirty-eight years he has practically been a resident of Washington County, Tex. Together with his family, in 1887, he visited the east, spending five months at his old home (Washington) and in Baltimore, Richmond, New York and other places of historical note. While the trip was thoroughly enjoyed, Mr. Van Ness was pleased to again return to his home where, surrounded by his friends and neighbors, those who know and love him best for his many sterling qualities of mind and heart, he expects to pass the remaining years of his career in the peace and quietude which follows a well-spent life.

GENERAL T. J. RUSK.

This unfortunate Texan soldier and statesman was born in South Carolina December 5, 1808, and died by his own hand in Texas in 1857. His father was an immigrant from Ireland, and was by trade a stone-mason. It is possible that but for the fact that the Rusks lived on the land of the Honorable John C. Calhoun, the general might have followed in his father's footsteps. Mr. Calhoun, impressed by the boy's brightness and intellectual promise, secured him a place in the law office of William Grisham, clerk of Pendleton District, where he made himself familiar with the law. In due time he was admitted to the bar, and soon afterward located at Clarksville, Ga., where he married the daughter of Colonel Cleveland and acquired a lucrative practice. He was swindled, however, in a mining speculation by which he lost his entire savings, and followed the men who had wronged him to Texas, only to find that they had spent or put beyond his reach all his money. Locating at Nacogdoches he practiced law, and afterward became conspicuous as a Texan patriot. He distinguished himself in the War of Independence, and subsequently commanded various expeditions against the Indians. In 1839 he was appointed chief justice of the republic, but soon resigned and retired to practice law at Nacogdoches. In 1845 he was president of the annexation convention, and was one of the first two Senators to the United States Congress, and this position he held until his suicide in 1857, brought about by a fit of mental aberration induced by a malignant disease and the loss of his wife. He was a man of rare qualities, and held in the highest esteem by all who knew him. On account of his death Congress wore the usual badge of mourning for thirty days.

ELISHA ANGLIN.

Elisha Anglin, a prominent early settler of Central Texas, was born in Powell Valley, Virginia, where he was reared and married; moved to Kentucky, afterward to Clay, Edgar and Cole counties,

Ill., and finally, in 1833, to Texas. He reached what is now Grimes
Prairie, Grimes County, in the fall of 1833, where Austin's colony
still remains. In the summer of 1834, in company with James and
Silas Parker, he visited Limestone County, in Robertson's colony,
and located a claim where the present town of Groesbeck is situated. Silas Parker located his claim north of Anglin's and James
Parker went still further north. They then returned to Grimes
Prairie, each buying a load of corn, preparatory to bringing their
families, which they did in the summer of 1834. Mr. Anglin settled
on his claim February 1, 1835, and Fort Parker was built in the
summer of the same year. When the Parkers and Mr. Anglin settled in the county the Indians were friendly and peaceable, those
in the locality being the Tehuacanas, at Tehuacana Hills; the
Keechies on Keechies Creek, and the Wacoes, who were then occupying their village at Waco. The first trouble was brought about
by raids being made upon them by bands of marauding white
men. The raids were made in the summer of 1835, and the
following spring news reached the fort of the advance of
the Mexicans under Santa Anna. Mr. Anglin, believing that the
fort and all the inmates would fall victims to Mexican foes and hostile Indians, tried to induce the Parkers to abandon it and retire to
the settlements beyond the Trinity. But this they refused to do.
Taking his family, Mr. Anglin, in company with Mr. Faulkenberry
and family and Mr. Bates and family, sought safety at old Fort
Houston, near Palestine. He did not return to Limestone County
until the spring of 1838, when Springfield, afterward the county
seat, was laid out, he being present and assisting in this labor. For
four or five years following this date he resided principally in the
settlements in Grimes County, but in January, 1844, took up his
permanent residence on his claim, where he lived until his last
marriage and until his death, near Mount Calm, in January, 1874,
aged seventy-six. He assisted in the organization of the county,
held a number of minor local positions at an earlier day, was an
unlettered man, but possessed considerable force of character, the
elements of the pioneer strongly predominating. Mr. Anglin was
five times married, and the father of a number of children. His
first wife was Rachel Wilson, a native of Virginia, who died in

Edgar County, Ill., leaving five children: Abram, William, John, Mary, afterward the wife of Silas H. Bates, and Margaret, now Mrs. John Moody. He was then married in Cole County, Ill., to Catherine Duty, who bore him three children, only one of whom reached maturity, Rebecca Catherine, now the wife of Franklin Coates of Utah Territory. His second wife died at Old Fort Houston, near Palestine, this state, and he married the third time, at Tinner's Fort, Robertson County, Mrs. Orpha James. They had eight children, only one of whom is now living: Adeline, wife of Daniel Parker, of Anderson County, Tex. His fourth marriage occurred in Limestone County, to Mrs. Nancy Faulkenberry, widow of David Faulkenberry. His fifth wife was Mrs. Sarah Chaffin (nee Crist), but by the last two unions there were no children.

CAPTAIN GEORGE THOMAS TODD.

The old saying that "a prophet is not without honor save in his own country," which has come to be applied not only to prophets, but to men in nearly every profession, trade and walk of life, is most completely controverted in every community in the country by the manifestations of high esteem on the part of the people for the able and honorable members of the legal profession. Notably is it so with Captain George T. Todd, whose diversified talents rendered it easy for him to select a congenial pursuit, and his perception and intelligence guaranteed that success would reward effort. It is an unwritten law that the secret of success in life in all individual cases is the common property or heritage of all unfortunates of the human race. There are more followers than leaders; more imitators than originators; more of mediocre talents than transcendent gifts, and it is but natural that people, unable to grasp success by their own efforts, should seek the ascent by which others have climbed to fame and fortune. It is therefore eminently proper for the historian to review the lives and characters of those men who have conferred so large a sum of joy upon mankind. Captain George Thomas Todd is a product of Virginia and the son of Judge William S. Todd who, in his day, was one of the most eminent men in the history of Texas. Judge Todd organized the Eighth District of Texas and from 1850 to 1862 presided in the first courts held in Cook, Collin, Grayson and Hunt counties. He was judge of this district twelve years. In 1861 he was a member of the secession convention and signed the ordinance of secession. A native of Virginia, he came to Texas in 1843 and settled at Boston in Bowie County, then the center of civilization in Northern Texas. From there he moved to Clarksville and thence to Jefferson, where he died in 1864, aged fifty-six years. While a resident of Virginia he was a member of the State Legislature and his readiness in debate, his keen, analytical mind and his wonderful ability made him one of the foremost men of that body and enhanced his popularity as a national character. He married Miss Eliza A. Hudgins, a native of Virginia, and eight children were the result of this union. Judge Todd's father, George T. Todd, was a man of great energy and force of character, and was one of the wealthiest men of his day in Caroline County, Va. He died in that county when ninety years old. His father was a Scotch physician who came from Scotland with several brothers and settled in this country. One settled in Kentucky, some in Mississippi, and others in Missouri. To one branch of this family belonged Mrs. Abraham Lincoln. Mrs. Eliza A. (Hudgins) Todd was a woman of more than ordinary attainments, natural and acquired, and a noted educator, conducting a large female school at Boston, and later at Clarksville. She was thus employed from 1846 until her death in 1854, and was one of the best known instructors in the state. Many of the best educated ladies of Texas look back with pride and affection to her as their educational guide and friend. She was deemed by Colonel Charles De Morse, editor of the "Northern Standard" (one of the leading papers in North Texas), as one of the best contributors to the same. Her father, Thomas D. Hudgins, was born in Matthews County, Va., and was a large planter and at one time a large ship-owner. He died at Richmond about 1862. Our subject, the second of eight children born to his parents, was born in the year 1839, and was therefore four years old when he came with his parents to Texas. He received his early scholastic training at the hands of his mother at Boston and Clarksville, then was under the tutelage of Rev. J. W. P. McKenzie for two years, and after that spent some time at Hampton Academy in Virginia. Following this he taught school in Petersburg, Va., until nineteen years old, when in 1858-59 he attended the University of Virginia, where he obtained distinction in several branches of study. In 1860 he returned to Texas and began the study of law under the able teachings of his father. He was admitted to the bar when twenty-one years old, practiced until the Civil War broke out, when he enlisted as a private in Black's Company A, First Texas Regiment Infantry, and was mustered in at New Orleans for twelve months. This company was subsequently organized with other companies into the First Texas regiment, under Colonel Lewis T. Wigfall, and immediately went into active service, reaching the scene of action the day after the battle of Manassas Junction. This regiment was afterward commanded by Hugh McLeod of Galveston, who was succeeded by Colonel (afterward lieutenant-general) John B. Hood, who organized this and two others, Fourth and Fifth regiments from Texas, as well as one Arkansas and one Georgia regiment, into Hood's famous brigade. Mr. Todd's twelve months' service, with others, expiring, the regiment was reorganized by electing new officers, and he was made captain of Company A. Immediately afterward the company participated in all the battles around Richmond from Seven Pines to Malvern Hill. It was subsequently engaged in the second battle of Manassas, then at Antietam, and in December of that year in the battle of Fredericksburg, the battle of the Wilderness, Gettysburg, and still later in the battle of Chickamauga. After the last-mentioned engagement Company A, never having been recruited from home, was reduced to five men and two commanding officers, including Captain Todd. Several of the commands were then consolidated by general order, and upon the application of Captain Todd he was transferred and made adjutant of the cavalry regiment of Colonel (afterward general) Walter P. Lane, with which he remained until close of hostilities. This command had never surrendered and brought all its arms and camp equipage, wagons

and teams home and distributed them among the men.   On reaching
home Captain Todd found that his father had been dead more than
a year and he and his brother had the family to support.   They
worked on the farm left by the father for a year and then our subject
resumed the practice of law at Jefferson, where he has since been
in active practice.   At the first state election prior to reconstruction he was elected state attorney in his father's old district, and
held that office until removed as an impediment to reconstruction, as
were all other state officers at that time.   Our subject's grandfather
was a strong Whig in politics, his father was a Jeffersonian Democrat and he himself has been a lifelong Democrat, with progressive
and liberal views.   Captain Todd was an alternate delegate to the
Greeley convention at Baltimore in 1872, and the same year a member of the state convention.   From 1880 to 1883 he was a member of
the State Legislature, serving on various committees, and was chairman of the committee on education, which committee originated the
bill to establish the University of Texas.   He has served specially
as judge of the District Court bench and also as judge of the Supreme
Court of Texas.   The captain was first married in 1868 to Miss
Eddie Van Dyke, a daughter of L. D. Van Dyke, who came from his
native state, Pennsylvania, to Texas at an early day, and for some
time was a steamboat captain, but later became a noted planter.
He is still living on his plantation in Red River County, and is now
ninety years old.   Mrs. Todd died in 1871, leaving one child, Van
Dyke, who graduated from the law department of the University
of Texas and in 1894 was elected prosecuting attorney of Marion
County.   Captain Todd selected his second wife in the person of Mrs.
Marion B. Miller, their marriage taking place in Rankin County in
1873.   Her father, A. P. Miller, was an old settler of Mississippi.
Captain and Mrs. Todd have six children by this union: Alexander
Miller, a graduate of the A. and M. College, is now employed by the
government in the levee engineering department on the Mississippi
River; Charles C. is a student at the A. and M. College; William
H., May, Eva and Lula.   Socially Judge Todd is a thirty-second
degree Mason, Scottish rite, and has been presiding officer of blue
lodge and commandery, York rite.   He has often been a member
of the grand lodge and is a past grand orator of the grand chapter

of Texas; also a member of the K. of H., he is past grand dictator of the state and ex-member of the supreme lodge of the United States. For thirty years he has held membership in the Baptist church and has been a deacon nearly all the time. For ten years he was regent of the State University, apointed first by Governor Ireland, then by Governor Ross, and afterward by Governor Hogg.

JAMES W. POWER.

Activity and enterprise is in no direction more lucidly marked in a community than in agricultural pursuits. This industry is the pulse of a city's enterprise and vim, for when crops fail, hard times are sure to follow. Numbered among the honored and successful farmers of Nacogdoches County is James W. Power, whose fine farm of 600 acres attests by its fertility and productiveness the enterprise and good management of its owner. He is one of the old settlers of this section, having moved here in 1849, and by his thrift and industry has accumulated an estate which places him among the list of "forehanded." Mr. Power was born in Alabama, Madison County, July 9, 1826. His father, Rev. H. L. Power, was a native of Kentucky, but when young moved with his father to Alabama, where they were among the pioneers. In that state Rev. H. L. Power grew up and was educated. Later he started out for himself as an agriculturist there, and was married in Madison County. In 1850 he crossed the Mississippi River and purchased 1,100 acres of wild Texas land north of Nacogdoches, immediately afterward entering actively upon his career as a tiller of the soil. He was possessed of an unlimited amount of energy and perseverance and stood well in the estimation of all acquainted with him. For many years he was a member of the Baptist church and although he never cared for political honors, he was appointed chaplain in the State Legislature, but declined to serve. His death occurred in October, 1867. His wife survives him and resides with a daughter in this county. She is a well-preserved old lady of eighty-eight. J. W. Power, our subject, grew to manhood in his native state and county, and was married there in October, 1846, to Miss Julia Ann Tindall, a native of Alabama. For three years after this union Mr. Power followed farming in that state, but he then crossed to Texas and bought 300 acres, which he began to improve and cultivate. He was actively engaged in improving this farm when civil war broke out, and in 1862 he joined a Nacogdoches company, with which he remained until it was disbanded. He then joined Polyack's brigade and was on detach duty until the close of the war. Upon his return home he resumed agricultural pursuits and in 1867 settled upon his present farm, 250 acres of which he has improved and fertilized. He is one of the largest and most successful agriculturists in the county, is wide-awake and intelligent, and has ever been up with the times in farming methods and appliances. He was formerly also quite actively engaged in the manufacture of lumber and owned a good mill in the county. For thirty years he has ginned cotton in this county, being the owner of a good steam gin, and it is said that he has handled more cotton in the same than any other man in the county. Mr. Power lost his first wife in 1857. Two daughters were born to them: Sarah, wife of James McChristian of Nacogdoches, and Mary L., wife of Strickland Power. Mr. Power's marriage with Miss Catherine Willingham occurred in December, 1858. She was born in Georgia, but reared in Alabama, and was the daughter of William and Nancy Willingham. Mr. and Mrs. Power became the parents of four daughters: Martha, wife of W. R. Falkner; Belle J., wife of William Weatherly; Eudora, wife of Dr. E. Y. Blount, and Catherine, wife of James Samuels, a druggist of Nacogdoches. This family is one of the best in the county and is foremost in all good work.

HENRY HODDE.

This worthy gentleman, now retired from active duties of life, was for many years prominent in local business affairs in Brenham and is still highly respected for his sincerity of purpose and unblemished character. He is enjoying the fruits of a well-spent life at Brenham, to which city he came November 18, 1859, at the age of twenty years. He was born in Germany (Prussia) November 25, 1839, and there grew to the age of eighteen years, enjoying good educational advantages, and then crossed the strait to London, England, and was there engaged in clerking for about two years, in the meantime studying and becoming familiar with the English language. He then (1859) crossed the Atlantic Ocean, taking shipping at London, and in due time, in the summer of 1859, landed in New York. There he resided about six months, when he started West and, as above stated, stopped at Brenham in November of the same year, where a younger brother (now deceased) had preceded him several years. Mr. Hodde first engaged in agricultural pursuits and so continued until 1862, when he enlisted in the Confederate service in General Thomas N. Waul's Legion of Infantry, was sent to the field and in six months' time was taken prisoner, at Oxford, Miss., but two weeks later managed to make his escape. He then went north to St. Louis and engaged in business, and so continued until the fall of 1865, when he returned to Brenham and clerked for four years, or until 1869, when he formed the business partnership of Hodde & Werner and engaged in general merchandising. The business, owing to their method of courtesy and good management, grew to large proportions and yielded handsome profits. In 1880 Mr. Werner retired from the partnership and moved to Europe, where he now resides. Mr. Hodde still further expanded the business and built up a trade of good profit and a reputation for honesty and integrity that will live long after he has turned to dust. In the fall of 1889 he retired from active business pursuits and is now passing his declining years in peace and security. During his active career at Brenham he was of great utility to local industrial enterprises and to all other objects contributing to the betterment of the city, county and state. He was one of the original stockholders of the First National Bank and one of its first directors. He was also connected with the oil mill and held a portion of its stock. He was one of the first stockholders, and for a time president, of the Brenham Compress Company, and was identified with other similar commercial enterprises. He has seen the city grow from a straggling village to one of compact business houses, and has aided materially in the transformation. He is a Republican in politics, and served four years as county commissioner, and he has represented his party in many county and state conventions. In all these trusts he served his party faithfully and broadened his reputation as an honest man and a useful citizen. He was married in Brenham in August, 1870, to Miss Louisa Kramer, a native of Hanover, Germany, who was brought by her father, Frederick Kramer, to America when a child. To this union ten children have been born, as follows: Katie, wife of William Winkleman; August, in business in Brenham; Amelia, Matilda, Henry, William, Louisa, Fred, Albert, and one, as yet, unnamed. The family attend the Lutheran Church.

DR. H. I. HILLIARD.

He whose name heads this sketch is a successful practicing physician, who has no pet theories to demonstrate at the risk of his patients' lives, and who is prouder of the confidence of the numerous first-class families whom he counts among his patrons than he could possibly be of any fame that could come to him through the following of any fancy calculated to move him. He is a product of Harrison County, Tex., born in 1851, and is of English-Welsh origin. His parents, J—— and Amelia Ann (Toole) Hilliard, were natives of North Carolina, and his paternal grandfather of Virginia, and a Revolutionary soldier. The Tooles were of English descent and came to America in colonial times. The parents of our subject were married in North Carolina, and the father was a successful lawyer by profession. He moved from Oxford, Granville County, N. C., to Harrison County, Tex., in 1848, and engaged quite extensively in farming. He died in 1880 when seventy-six years old. The mother still survives. Like most boys reared on farms, our subject received his primary education in the country schools, but subsequently attended the State University of Louisiana, at Alexandria. In 1869 he began

the study of medicine at the medical department of the University of
Louisiana, at New Orleans, and was graduated in 1872. Immediately
after this he began practicing in the country in Harrison County,
Tex., but in 1883 he moved to Marshall, where he has since been located. He has a good practice and the confidence of all his patrons.
The same year that he graduated (1872) he married Miss Mildred F.
Baldwin, daughter of Dr. F. Baldwin, who came to Texas from Alabama at an early day. Dr. Baldwin is a well-known physician and an
honored citizen. Dr. Hilliard and wife are the parents of ten children,
as follows: Irwin, Annie, Emma, Etta, Vernon, Walter, Henry,
Myrtle and Myra (twins), and Eugene. The Doctor is well and favorably known for his many sterling qualities of mind and heart. Mrs.
Hilliard is a member of the Methodist Episcopal Church.

WILSON E. HAIL.

This prominent old settler of Crockett came originally from Madison County, Tenn., his birth occurring in 1825, to the union of Jonas
and Amanda Melvina (Ewing) Hail. His paternal grandfather was a
native of North Carolina and died in that state in early life. He was
of English origin. The maternal grandfather, Edley Ewing, was born
in Tennessee, near Nashville. He was the first sheriff of Davidson
County and a man of considerable prominence in that section. From
there he removed to Missouri, but returned to Tennessee, and in 1833
came to Texas, locating near San Augustine, where his death occurred in 1846. He was of English descent, and the family was a
prominent one in Tennessee. Jonas Hail was born in the Old North
State, but moved from there to Tennessee, where he met and married Miss Ewing. In 1833 he came to Texas with quite a colony and
located a league of land in Houston County. He also bought large
tracts in other sections of the state. In 1836 he entered the Texas

army in Captain Kimbrough's company, and was in the battle of San Jacinto. He was injured in the battle of San Felipe, and on his return home resumed his large farming interest. He died in the town of San Augustine in 1869, and his wife died in 1872. Our subject was but eight years old when he came with his parents to Texas and, as a consequence, most of his recollections are of this state. He has witnessed its marvelous growth and has contributed his share toward its advancement and progress. In 1844 he was married to Miss Mary H. Smith, a native of Tennessee, and daughter of James Smith, who came to Texas January 1, 1840, and settled at San Augustine. In 1854 Mr. Hail came to Houston County and located on his father's head right, three miles from Crockett, and was residing there at the outbreak of the Civil War. In 1862 he enlisted in Captain Smith's Company B, Thirteenth Texas Infantry. Returning home he turned his attention to farming, and is now the owner of 8,000 acres in this county. For fifteen years he conducted an hotel, "The Hail House," and in 1884 moved to his present home, two miles from Crockett, where he has since been engaged in stock raising in connection with farming. Since 1862 he has not bought a pound of bacon nor a bushel of corn. Mr. Hail has always been active in politics, and from 1859 to 1860 he served as sheriff and was twice county commissioner. To his marriage were born these children: Benjamin Ewing, Edward E., James Wilson, and Taylor J., the last named deceased. Mr. Hail is a member of the Methodist Episcopal Church, and since the year 1847 he has been a Mason.

COLONEL STERLING C. ROBERTSON.

Colonel Sterling C. Robertson, empressario of Robertson's colony, was born in Nashville, Tenn., about 1785. He served as major of the Tennessee troops in the war of 1812, received a good education, and was trained up as a planter, and engaged in agricultural pursuits in Giles County, that state. Enterprising and adventurous, and having considerable means, he formed a company in Nashville in 1823 to explore the "wild province" of Texas. Coming as far as the Brazos, he formed a permanent camp at the mouth of Little River. All the party returned to Tennessee, however, except Robertson. He visited the settlements that had been made, and while there conceived the idea of planting a colony in Texas. Filled with enthusiasm over this plan, he went to his home in Tennessee, where he purchased a contract, which the Mexican government had made with Robert Leftwick, for the settlement of 800 families. The colony embraced a large tract of land, and Robertson was to receive forty leagues and forty labors for his services. In 1829, at his own expense, he introduced 100 families, who were driven out by the militia in consequence of false representations made to the government. The matter was finally adjusted, and in the spring of 1834 the colony was restored. In the summer of the same year he laid out the town of Sarahville de Viesca. A land office was opened about October 1 and the settlements were rapidly made. In the summer of 1835 he made a tour of Tennessee, Mississippi, Louisiana, and Kentucky, making known the inducements to immigration. He had been authorized by the Mexican government to offer to settlers who were heads of families, one league and one labor of land, and lesser proportions to others. Colonel Robertson was a delegate to the general convention of 1836, was one of the signers of the declaration of independence and of the constitution of the Republic of Texas. In the spring of 1836 he commanded a military company, and received therefor a donation of 640 acres of land, having participated in the battle of San Jacinto. He was a member of the Senate of the first Congress of the Republic of Texas. He died in Robertson County March 4, 1842, in the fifty-seventh year of his age. Bold, daring, and patriotic, he had many opportunities for the exhibition of these traits. From the campaigns of the war of 1812 down to 1842, he was a participant in every struggle of his countrymen. When the Revolution broke out in 1835, he had introduced more than 600 families into the colonies, fully one-half of the whole number at his own expense.

JUDGE JEFF CHAISON.

In this state of marvelous growth, both in wealth and population, we have no hesitancy in saying, that of our representative men, four-fifths are our country neighbors. Physical development, power of endurance, indomitable courage, together with intellectual vigor, business instinct, and inventive genius, gather into this great center from country homes. Judge Jeff. Chaison was born on his father's farm in Jefferson County, Tex., March 5, 1839, and his capital in life's start consisted only of robust health, great energy, indomitable perseverance and sterling honesty. With this capital and a limited education received in the district schools, he started in life. The family which he represents is an old and prominent one in the history of Texas, and especially of Jefferson County, his Grandfather Chaison coming here with his family when the settlers were few and far between. Here he passed the remainder of his days, dying in 1844 or '45 at the great age of 110 years. His son, McGuire Chaison, father of our subject, was a native of Louisiana, and in that state grew to mature years. He came to Texas when a young man, in 1833, and settled in what is now Jefferson County, where he bought land and opened up a farm near the present flourishing city of Beaumont. Here he met and married Miss Eliza McFadden, a daughter of James McFadden and a sister of William McFadden (see sketch). Farming and stock-raising continued to be his calling through life and he was well posted on all pertaining to the same. For two or three terms he held the office of county commissioner and discharged the duties of that position in a very satisfactory manner. He died in 1849, when still a comparatively young man. His wife survived him until 1864, and now lies beside her husband in Jirou Cemetery. A man of more than ordinary force of character, and of strong conviction, he still made many friends and was universally respected. The youth of our subject was spent in active duties on the farm, and, as a consequence, his educational advantages were limited. Possessing an excellent memory and an inquiring mind, he devoted his spare moments dili-

gently to study in later years and succeeded in making up for the
loss of a more liberal education in early life. During the Civil War
his sympathies were with the Confederate states and in 1861 he enlisted in the Confederate army, Company F, Fifth Texas Infantry,
Hood's Brigade, serving until the close. Most of the time he was on
detached duty in the adjutant's office, but he participated with his
brigade in all the battles fought by Hood's Brigade, and the battle of
the Wilderness, and there received two wounds, one through the
hand and the other through the groin. At the fight below Richmond,
Va., he was again wounded and there taken prisoner, being held at
Point Lookout for about two months. He was then one of the first
exchanged, and at the close of the war was home on a furlough.
Following this, he engaged in the stock business and became one of
the most active and successful men in this business in the county,
following it up to 1887. In May, 1861, the Judge was married in Jefferson County to Miss Clara Baldwin, a native of the grand old state
of Virginia, where she was reared and educated, and the daughter
of Dr. Charles Baldwin. In 1870 he bought his present fine farm,
just south of the corporation limits of Beaumont, and for twenty-five
years has made his home on this. He continued the stock business
here up to 1887, and since then has carried on farming and fruit-
growing, at which he has made a success. He has an excellent
orchard of 100 peach and 1,600 pear trees, which is just beginning
to bear, and he also raises a variety of small fruit, such as figs, plums,
etc. In 1890 Judge Chaison was elected judge of Jefferson County
and held the position two years. He has a clear, well-balanced mind,
an accurate sense of right and justice, and good judgment, and without wasting words, he carries his hearers direct to the point with his
ready command of well-chosen, classical English. He was the principal mover in securing the new court house, which is one of the best
in the state and a credit to Jefferson County. Politically, Judge
Chaison has ever been identified with the Democratic party, and has
served as a delegate to numerous county, congressional and state
conventions. He is one of the county's most highly honored citizens;
his private character is one to be admired and loved; his public
record is without a blemish. Throughout his life he has been actuated by pure motives and manly principles, and by following a fixed

purpose to make the most and best of himself, he has overcome many difficulties and risen step by step to a place of influence and honor among public-spirited and high-minded men. All his life he has been a resident of Jefferson County and has witnessed and aided in the marvelous growth of this section and of the state. Socially, the Judge is a Royal Arch Mason, served as District Deputy Grand Master and at present is Past Master. He is a member of Beaumont Blue Lodge and Chapter, and is also a member of the Knights of Honor, being Past Dictator of the lodge. To Judge and Mrs. Chaison have been born six children: Charles, a business man of Lake Charles, La.; William, a young man at home; Brandon, who is taking a course in the law department of the University of Texas; Harriet, wife of A. W. Russell of Dallas, Tex.; Elizabeth, a young lady at home, and Jennie. Mrs. Chaison is a member of the Beaumont Presbyterian Church.

WALTER BOYD, SR.

It is a pleasure and privilege to record the character and enterprise of men of business, who, on account of their long tenure and extensive operations, comprise almost a history of the business in which they are engaged. Of such men it is unnecessary to speak in words of colored praise. "By their acts ye shall know them." Their very existence is emphatic evidence of the honorable position they occupy and the long course of just dealing that they have pursued. A gentleman in mind is Walter Boyd, Sr., retired merchant, and capitalist, and president of the Gilmer Bank of Gilmer, Tex. For many years he was one of the active, enterprising and leading business men of Gilmer, and his sterling character has won him many warm friends. He is a native of Alabama, born in Montgomery County November 1, 1827, and is a son of Walter and Lititia (Bussey) Boyd, both natives of South Carolina. After marriage, the parents removed to Montgomery County, Ala., and there the father was engaged in agricultural pursuits for many years. He was a man of prominence in that county, served as a magistrate and held other positions. There his death occurred in 1844, when in the prime of life. His wife survived him twenty years, dying in 1864. Walter Boyd, Sr., is one of four children now living of the sixteen born to the above worthy couple. The eldest, Dempsey, resides on part of the old homestead in Alabama. After our subject is Lititia, widow of Alfred Pool, and a resident of Montgomery County; then Sarah L., wife of M. O. G. Ekwurzel, who is now residing on the old homestead. Mr. Boyd, our subject, received limited educational advantages in his youth and is mainly self-educated since growing up. He came West to Texas in the spring of 1848, when in his twenty-first year, and located in Upshur County when that county was almost a wilderness, and when Upshur, Camp and Gregg Counties had only about 200 voters. Mr. Boyd first turned his attention to agricultural pursuits, but only resided in Upshur County one year, when he moved to Smith County and continued his former occupation for four years. In 1854 he came to Gilmer, and, purchasing a business house, turned his attention to merchandising, which, by his good business management and acumen, brought him in good returns. He has erected numerous business houses and residences in the town, more than any other one man, and was active in promoting every interest tending to the advancement of the same. In 1892 he organized the Gilmer Bank and was made president of the same. This is the first and only bank in Upshur County and it is firmly established. Mr. Boyd was married in this county August 19, 1848, to Miss Margaret E. Mosley, a native of Montgomery County, Ala., who was born, reared and educated in the same neighborhood with her husband. Her parents were Mason and Levina Mosley. The father came to Texas and settled in Upshur County about 1845. Here both passed away. Mr. and Mrs. Boyd became the parents of nine children, as follows: Levina P., wife of J. M. Marshall, a prominent merchant of Gilmer; Lititia, widow of W. A. Boyd, is a resident of Gilmer; Mary V., wife of W. H. Saunders, a prominent physician of Gilmer; J. W., resides at McGregor and is a farmer; Anna T., wife of F. D. Futrell, a leading merchant of Gilmer; Margaret, wife of J. W. Bussey; Walter, a business man of Gilmer; Mattie, wife of W. E. Crosby, a groceryman of Gilmer, and Bes-

sie, a young lady at home. Politically, Mr. Boyd is a Democrat. He
has never cared for office, but has given nearly all his time and attention to business. He and Mrs. Boyd and all the children, with
one exception, are members of the Baptist Church. Mr. Boyd was
made a Mason in 1851 or '52, and is also a member of the Knights and
Legion of Honor. Mr. Boyd has been a resident of the "Lone Star
State" for forty-seven years, and is now classed among the honored
first settlers of the town and county. He is also well and favorably
known over adjoining counties as well, and many will be pleased to
read the life of this most excellent citizen. During the Civil War he
joined the Twenty-second Texas Infantry, under Colonel R. B. Hubbard, Confederate army, and was subsequently promoted to the rank
of first lieutenant, holding that position until the war closed. He
participated in the fight at Jenkins' Ferry, Ark., and was there
wounded in the knee and disabled from service for several months.
He then returned to active service and afterwards came back to his
home and business interests in this county.

JOSE ANTONIO NAVARRO.

Jose Antonio Navarro, in whose honor Navarro County was named,
was born in San Antonio de Bejar, February 27, 1795, his father having been a native of Corsica and an officer in the Spanish army. He
was a staunch Federalist and a foe to military despotism. In 1834-35
Navarro was a land commissioner for Bejar District; a member of the
convention in 1836, and a member of Congress in 1838-39. He was condemned by Santa Anna to imprisonment for life, though during his
captivity he was several times offered pardon, liberty and high office
if he would abjure his native country, Texas, forever. These proposi-
tions were rejected with scorn. In December, 1844, just before the
fall of Santa Anna, he was removed from San Juan de Uloa and allowed to remain a prisoner at large in Vera Cruz, whence he escaped.

January 2, arriving at Galveston February 3, 1845, after an absence of more than three years and a half. On his return he was elected delegate to the convention held that year to decide upon the question of annexation, and was afterward Senator from Bejar District in the State Congress. He died in his native city in 1870.

HON. JOSEPH D. SAYERS.

Hon. Joseph D. Sayers of Bastrop, Tex., was born at Grenada, Miss., September 23, 1841. He removed with his father to Bastrop, Tex., in 1851, was educated at the Bastrop Military Institute, entered the Confederate army early in 1861, and was, October 11, 1861, promoted to the adjutancy of the Fifth Texas Regiment of Mounted Volunteers, commanded by Colonel Thomas Green. He served as such in the New Mexican campaign, was promoted for gallantry in the battle of Val Verde, N. M., on the 30th day of April, 1862, to the captaincy of the battery captured in that engagement, afterward known as the "Val Verde" Battery, and while in command of that battery was severely wounded in the battle of Camp Bisland, La., in April, 1863. He was promoted to a majorate, and, returning to the army on crutches, was assigned to duty with General Thomas Green as chief of staff, and at the battle of Mansfield, La., in April, 1864, was again wounded. Returning to the army on crutches, he was assigned to duty on the staff of Lieutenant General Richard Taylor, General Green having been killed, and with General Taylor served east of the Mississippi River until April, 1865, when the surrender took place. He returned home and taught school, and at the same time studied law under Hon. George W. Jones, and when admitted to the bar was a member of the firm of Jones & Sayers. He was elected to the State Senate in 1872 and served as Senator in the Thirteenth Legislature. He was elected Grand Master of Masons in 1875; was chairman of the Democratic state executive committee during the years 1875-1878; was Lieutenant Governor of Texas in 1879 and 1880;

was defeated for the nomination for Governor by the Democratic party in 1880; was permanent chairman of the Democratic state convention in 1884; was elected to Congress in 1884, and has been re-elected five times. He was chairman of the committee on appropriations, House of Representatives, Fifty-third Congress, and is a member of the present Fifty-fourth Congress. Such, in brief, is a sketch of a well known and favored son of Texas.

W. W. HEARTSILL.

The prosperity of any locality depends almost wholly upon the character of the people who inhabit it, and if the citizens are pushing, energetic and intelligent, the country will prosper accordingly. Tennessee has given to Texas many of her most progressive and prominent citizens, among whom may be mentioned W. W. Heartsill, whose birth occurred in 1839. His parents, Abram and Louisa (Rankin) Heartsill, were natives of Tennessee. The parental grandfather, Abraham Heartsill, was born in North Carolina, but in 1810 moved to Tennessee, settling in the town of Jonesborough, Washington County. Later he moved to Anderson County and there died when eighty-eight years old. He was of German descent and his ancestors were among the colonial settlers. Farming was his principal occupation in life. Our subject's maternal grandfather, John Rankin, was a native of Pennsylvania, and of Scotch ancestry. He was a soldier under Washington. At an early date he moved to Blount County, Tenn., and farmed there until his death. Abram Heartsill, father of subject, was reared in Tennessee, amid rude surroundings, and is still a resident of that state. His wife died when our subject was but a boy. Their family consisted of nine children. of whom our subject was fourth in order of birth. He was fairly educated in his native state and when thirteen years old began clerking in a store at Maryville, Tenn. Three years later he went to Nashville and was in a wholesale boot and shoe house for four years. Then, in 1859, he came to Marshall, Tex., and clerked here until the war. On the 19th of April, 1861, he enlisted in Company F, Second Regiment, Texas Cavalry, under Captain Richardson, went to Austin and was mustered into state service. On the 8th of May he was sworn into the Confederate service and sent to the Rio Grande, where he remained one year. After re-enlisting he was sent eastward and participated in the battle of Arkansas Post. Being captured, he was sent to Camp Butler, Ill., and exchanged at City Point, Va., in May, 1863. Following his release, he was sent to Richmond and later to Bragg's army in Tennessee. He was in almost daily conflicts on the retreat to Chattanooga and soon after participated in the battle of Chickamauga. Being then sent to his old command, he was placed in the Trans-Mississippi department, but later was in Morgan's Regiment, Parson's Brigade, near Bayou Bartholomew. He was next sent to Arkansas, and thence to Texas, where he remained until the war closed. Mr. Heartsill took notes daily of the events that transpired while in service and since the war wrote a history of his company from these notes. This daily journal is very interesting reading and is filled with valuable historical matter. Returning to Marshall, Mr. Heartsill began clerking, followed this for one year, and then engaged in the dry goods business under the firm name of Hill, Hawley & Co. This he continued for nine years and then withdrew. In 1876 he was elected mayor of Marshall and filled that position acceptably for two years. He has been quite active in local politics. Mr. Heartsill was one of the organizers of the Marshall, Paris & N. W. R. R. Co., and for many years was its president. He married Miss Eliza Stevens, a native of Alabama, in 1868, and their children are named as follows: Charles E., a physician of Marshall, graduated from Tulane University, New Orleans, in 1893; Mattie, Maud, wife of C. C. Friend of Marshall; Minnie, Willie, and Katie. Mr. Heartsill is a Mason, a member of Lodge, Chapter and Commandery, and has been Secretary of Marshall Lodge for twenty-six years. He is Recorder of Commandery No. 16 and Scribe of the Chapter. Our subject is also an Odd Fellow, I. O. R. M., K. of P., and a member of the A. O. U. W. He is a member of the Methodist Church and is trustee and steward of the same.

HON. MARION DEKALB TAYLOR.

Although nearly four-score years have passed over the head of this
venerable and venerated citizen, his mind is as keen and as active as
in the days of his early manhood, and it is only so far as his physical
being is concerned that Father Time has left his tràces.   His walk
through life has been characterized by a sturdy independence, un-
compromising honesty, great energy, and he is richer, nobler and
grander for the experience which each successive decade has brought
him. Although one of the old settlers of Marion County, Tex., he was
born in James County, Ga., October 13, 1818, the second in order of
birth of eight children born to Ward and Ann (Mathews) Taylor, the
former a native of South Carolina and the latter of Georgia.   The
Taylor family is of English origin and the first member to settle on
this side of the Atlantic came here prior to the Revolution.   The
paternal grandfather of our subject, Job Taylor, was a product of
Virginia and a Revolutionary soldier.   After the war he settled in
South Carolina.   The maternal grandfather, Abraham Mathews, was
born in the Palmetto State.   Ward Taylor was one of six sons, all of
whom followed the occupation of the father—blacksmithing.   He was
married in Georgia and moved from there to Alabama in 1818, settling in Butler County, where, in connection with his trade, he followed farming.   Later he became a mail contractor and continued in
this until 1845, when he came to Texas, Cass County, where the remainder of his days were passed in farming.   He died in 1866.   While
a resident of Alabama he made a large fortune, but lost it all during
the panic of 1837 (security debts).   He also accumulated considerable
property after moving to Texas and at the time of his death was
quite wealthy.   He was a Mason and a prominent member of the
Methodist church.   The boyhood days of our subject were passed in
Alabama, where he received but a limited education, and when but a
small boy he began riding on the stage and mail routes for his father.
When fifteen years of age he was the practical manager of his
father's business, the latter being at that time the largest mail contractor in the United States, and he was thus employed until 1838,

when he married Miss Sarah Elizabeth McDaniel, a native of Alabama. The same year he bought a farm and began tilling the soil, but ill-health caused him to abandon this, and in 1845 he began the study of medicine under Dr. Hilery Hubbard. In 1847 he came to Texas and began practicing in Cass County, now seven miles east of Jefferson, where he became well known and where he carried on a successful practice for forty years. While a resident of Alabama he served in the State Legislature two terms, and after moving to Texas, as soon as eligible (1849), was elected to the State Legislature of Texas. He was re-elected to that position each succeeding term until 1879, except two sessions, and four times he was elected over his protest. Part of this time he was in the Senate. Mr. Taylor served as Speaker of the House three sessions, President of the Senate one term, and President pro tem. for about ten years. He was holding the first mentioned position when the Civil War broke out. For many years Mr. Taylor was a member of state conventions and one of the best known men in Texas. To our subject's marriage were born eight children: E. W., H. L. of Yazoo City, Miss., F. M. of this county, R. R., a lawyer of Jefferson, and John B., a physician of Mississippi. Three are deceased. Frank died while serving in the Confederate army in Arkansas, Matt died when seventeen years old, and another, Mary, is also deceased. Mr. Taylor's first wife died about 1864, and he was married a second time. He has been a Mason for forty years.

MIRABEAU BUONAPARTE LAMAR.

Mirabeau Buonaparte Lamar, President of Texas, was born August 16, 1798, at Louisville, Ga., of Huguenot ancestry. The first thirty years of his life were passed in securing an education and engaged in agricultural and mercantile pursuits. Having a strong liking for politics, he embarked in journalism in 1828 and founded the Columbus "Independent," in which he strongly advocated state sovereignty. In 1835 he emigrated to Texas, became an active member of the Revolutionary party and commanded a company of horse at the battle of San Jacinto. He was commissioned a major-general, was later made Attorney-General in the cabinet of Governor Smith and yet later was appointed Secretary of War. In 1836 he was elected first Vice-President of the Republic, and two years later was chosen President, which office he held until 1841, and during his incumbency succeeded in having the independence of Texas recognized by the leading countries of Europe. In 1846 he joined General Zachary Taylor's command in the war against Mexico, was in the battle of Monterey and was appointed division inspector, with the rank of lieutenant-colonel. In October he assumed command of an independent company of Texan rangers, with headquarters at Laredo, where for two years he was checking the depredations of the Indians. In July, 1857, he was appointed Minister to the Argentine Republic, but did not qualify. In December of the same year he was commissioned Minister, and the following January, Minister-resident to Nicarauga and Costa Rica, from which posts he retired in May, 1859. He was an author of some note, his "Verse Memorials" being the best known. He died at Richmond, Tex., December 19, 1859. Mr. Lamar was an uncle of Lucius Quintus Cincinnatus Lamar, a recent member of the United States Supreme Court.

CAPTAIN V. H. CLAIBORNE.

The Claiborne family is one of the honored old American families, members of which have been prominent in about every important period of our civilization. The name has made itself honored in war and in peace, in church work, and in every worthy movement. One of its representatives in this section is Captain V. H. Claiborne, who is a product of Richmond, Va., his birth occurring in 1833, and the son of Herbert A. and Delia (Hayes) Claiborne, both natives of the "Old Dominion." The paternal grandfather, Herbert A. Claiborne, was a Virginian and a soldier in the Revolutionary war. He was of English origin, his ancestors settling in this country in early colonial times. Our subject's maternal grandfather, John Hayes, was a native of Fredericksburg, Va., and a physician of note. He was also of English descent. The father of Captain Claiborne was a prominent lawyer of Richmond, Va., but died in the forties. The mother died still earlier. Captain V. H. Claiborne was reared by his brothers, as he was the youngest of ten children, and secured a fair education in Richmond and Alexandria. When starting out to fight life's battles for himself he first engaged in merchandising, which he continued until 1858. Then, seized with the gold fever, he went to California, via the Isthmus, and followed trading and mining there until 1860, when the mutterings of the Civil War caused him to hurry back to. Virginia. In 1861 he was given a captain's commission and assigned to duty under General Van Dorn at Jackson Port, Ark. From there his command went to Corinth, Miss., and was in that retreat. Some time after this he was ordered to Little Rock, Ark., to report to General Holmes and thence to Fayetteville, Ark., to report to General Hindman. After an engagement at Prairie Grove, Captain Claiborne returned to Little Rock and was ordered to Jefferson, Tex., to erect a large packing establishment for supplying the Confederate army with beef, bacon, etc., prior to the battles of Mansfield and Pleasant Hill, La. The captain continued in charge here until the close of the war. Afterward he engaged in the drug business in Jefferson, continued this for a few years and then engaged in farming. He is now in the insurance business and represents the Royal of England, Scottish Union and National of Edinburg, Fire Association of Philadelphia, Orient of Hartford, Conn., Hartford of Hartford and New York Underwriters, and is doing a good business. The year 1864 witnessed his marriage with Miss Lucy Perry, a native of Jefferson, and daughter of William Perry, who came originally from New Hampshire. Mr. Perry first came to the Lone Star State in 1852 and settled in Jefferson, and secured the contract to open navigation from Caddo Lake to Cypress Bayou. He accomplished this work and had the satisfaction of sailing through the bayou to Jefferson on the first steamer that ever reached that point. Later he ran steamboats through the bayou himself. During the war he was an earnest sympathizer with the Southern cause and did all he could to further the cause. He married a Miss Smith of Texas, became a large land owner, and was carrying on his large interest when, on the 2d of January, 1869, he was shot down in the streets of Jefferson by Federal soldiers. He was a man of great force of character and determination, and during his residence in Texas had come in contact with many of the leading men, all of whom admired and liked him. To our subject and wife have been born the following children: Perry, now of Dallas; Howard, also of Dallas; Fannie, Lucy Lee, and four who died in early youth. Captain and Mrs. Claiborne are members of the Episcopal Church and he is vestryman in the same.

DR. E. B. BLOCKER.

Marshall, Tex., is known as a progressive city and contains many able and brainy professional men, among whom our subject takes a prominent place. He was born in Alabama in 1837, and no doubt inherits his energy and perseverance from his German ancestors, his great-grandfather, John Blocker, being a native of Prussia. This worthy gentleman came to America with his father, Michael, who came with a colony, and settled near Edgefield, S. C. Michael was the founder of this family in America. General Jesse Blocker, our subject's grandfather, was born in South Carolina, and during the war of 1812 he was commander of the militia of that state. He was a prominent planter and an influential citizen. His son, William J. Blocker, was born in South Carolina and there attained his growth and received his education. He was married in that state to Miss Mary Butler, a native of Virginia, whose father, Jesse Butler, was also a native of that state, and of English origin. After marriage, or in 1839, Mr. Blocker moved to Texas and, settling in the eastern part of Harrison County, became an extensive planter. There his death occurred in 1859. His wife is still living and finds a pleasant home with a son in this county. Of the fourteen children born to them, our subject was second in order of birth. He supplemented a good common school education by attending Strawberry Plains College, from which institution he was graduated in 1858. Soon after he began the study of medicine in Harrison County, Tex., under Dr. H. B. Perry, a successful physician, and then attended lectures in New Orleans, graduating in 1861. The same year he married Miss Frances A. Ware, a native of Alabama, and daughter of Henry Ware, who was a prominent settler of this section, and who is now residing in Mississippi. In 1862 he enlisted in Company A, Third Texas Cavalry, and went to Arkansas, thence to Mississippi, and participated in the battle of Corinth. He was then made assistant surgeon of that regiment and served through the war in that capacity. He participated in the battle of Iuka and then went to Northern Mississippi and Alabama under Van Dorn. After that he was in Tennessee and Georgia under Johnson and Hood, and was in the battle of Nashville. After the retreat from that place our subject obtained leave of absence and in March, 1865, came home. The war soon ended and Dr. Blocker at once began practicing in Harrison County. During the winter of 1866-'67 he went to New Orleans, engaged in merchandising and remained there until 1874, when he returned to Harrison County and resumed his practice, in connection with farming. In 1884 he moved to Marshall, where he practiced medicine, but at the same time carried on his farm. He is a member of the K. of P. and St. John of Malta. Dr. and Mrs. Blocker are the parents of nine children: William Frank, Eugene E., James Henry, Mary, Mattie, Fannie, ——, John W. and Eads T. The Doctor and wife are members of the Methodist Episcopal Church, and he is a Democrat in politics.

CAPTAIN G. W. O'BRIEN.

The profession of law is one which has ever had a charm for the literary student and the student of men and measures. The courts constitute a vast dramatic representation of human life and human

aims in which, as in human life, the same scene is never repeated
and the same actors are never twice grouped together. To the be-
wildered onlooker it would seem like an awful, ever changing kaleido-
scope of human enterprise, interest, love, passion, virtue and depravity. To the trained lawyer it is a refuge of safety to the inno-
cent and oppressed, an engine of punishment to the vicious and the
criminal, the one strong arm which stands eternally between liberty
and anarchy. It is prolific of pathos, of tragedy, of melodrama, and of
comedy. It is an unraveler of mysteries and a searchlight penetrat-
ing the dark corners in the shadow-land of life. No man has experienced this in Jefferson County better or more fully than Captain G.
W. O'Brien, the subject of this all too brief biography, who, for the
past thirty years, has been one of the leading lawyers in Jefferson
County, as well as in Eastern Texas. He is a native of what is now
Vermillion Parish, La., his birth occurring May 28, 1833. His father,
George O'Brien, more generally known as George Bryan, was born in
the Blue Grass State, went to Louisiana early in the present century,
was a soldier in the war of 1812, and was twice married, his second
wife, formerly Miss Eliza A. Bryan, being mother of the subject of
this sketch. In company with two brothers, he first settled near
Berwick's Bay, in Louisiana, but later moved to La Fayette (now
Vermillion) Parish, married, and there became a prosperous planter
and slave owner. In 1839 he moved to Beaumont, Tex., where for
three years he was engaged in mercantile pursuits, and from there
moved to Galveston County, where he passed the remainder of his
days, his death occurring in Galveston city in 1856.

Captain G. W. O'Brien became a resident of Texas in the year 1849
and for several years resided in the city of Galveston, a large part of
the time being employed in the Government postoffice. In 1852 he
came to Beaumont, which has since been his home. Taking an active
interest in public affairs, he was elected clerk of the District Court in
1854, in which capacity he served two years, and during which time
he began the study of law; but having been in 1856 elected county
clerk, filled that office six years. Although strongly opposing secession, his ardent love for the South led him to espouse the cause of the
Confederacy, and August 28, 1861, he became a member of Company
F, Captain K. Bryan, afterward part of the Fifth Texas Regiment In

December of the same year he was discharged for disability, returned to Beaumont and, after recovery, recruited a company, of which he was elected and commissioned captain, and which became first a part of Likens' Battalion, afterward A. W. Spaight's Texas Regiment. Captain O'Brien soon secured recognition as one of the bravest and most skillful company commanders in his regiment. He was a participant in several important military events, one of which was the capture of two Federal gunboats at the time of the breaking of the blockade at Sabine Pass in 1862. He took part in the battle of Fordoche, La., and served in the trans-Mississippi department to the end of the war. When peace was declared Captain O'Brien was on detached service at Beaumont. He immediately embarked in a vigorous prosecution of the law, and an excellent knowledge of legal matters, coupled with forensic ability of a high order, soon placed him among the foremost lawyers of the state—a position he has ever since maintained. While a Democrat in politics, as well as in all things to which the name applies, Captain O'Brien has frequently refused political preferment (once serving, by election, four years as district attorney), believing it was to his best interest to confine his attention exclusively to a large and constantly increasing clientelle. He has been a member of various conventions, national and local, the more important being the one at Baltimore in 1872 that nominated Horace Greeley for the Presidency. He was opposed to the nomination, but under the unit rule the vote of the Texas delegation was cast by the majority for Greeley. Captain O'Brien is conscientious and tenacious in his views, and his abilities make him a man of extended influence. While this is true, he is ever ready to adopt other opinions when he is clearly convinced that his position is erroneous. When he is unquestionably in the right he courageously advocates it, regardless of public or other opinion. This was demonstrated in a most marked manner when he, as member of a committee on resolutions, refused to subscribe to the resolutions of secession at Beaumont, in 1860, which were identical with those passed by South Carolina. He further refused to vote for the resolution. He is no believer in a depreciated currency, as advocated by many, but on the contrary is an advocate of a currency that is worth one hundred cents on the dollar, and that will pass at par anywhere. In his domestic life, Captain

O'Brien has been especially fortunate and in the home circle he experiences the highest degree of enjoyment. July 21, 1854, he wedded Miss Sarah E., daughter of Timothy T. Rowley, a pioneer of Jefferson County. Mrs. O'Brien was a native of East Feliciana Parish, La., and since eight years of age has been a resident of Texas. To the Captain and her were born these children: Minnie G., the wife of Neal Stark of Dallas; Lillie E., now Mrs. T. L. Townsend of Dallas; George C., now practicing law in partnership with his father; Emma E., Mrs. Harvey B. Smith of Dallas (died April 28, 1895), and Kaleta B., who is the wife of William James of Cleburne. Mrs. Sarah E. O'Brien died July 28, 1873. In 1874 Miss Ellen P. Chenault became the second wife of Captain O'Brien, and to this union two children have been born, viz.: Chenault and Robert P. Captain O'Brien is a Past Master of the Masonic fraternity, belongs to the Knights of Honor, and he and wife are members of the Methodist Episcopal Church. No man in all Jefferson County stands higher in the hearts of his fellow-men than does Captain G. W. O'Brien.

GENERAL ALBERT SIDNEY JOHNSTON.

Perhaps no name is more revered by the Confederate soldiery than Albert Sidney Johnston. Born February 3, 1803, in Washington, Ky., he was the youngest son of Dr. John Johnston, who was a native of Connecticut. His youth was passed in attending select schools; and, later, securing an appointment in the United States Military Academy, he graduated therefrom when twenty-three years old. He served as adjutant of the Second Infantry until his resignation in April, 1834, and during this time was Chief of Staff to General Henry Atkinson through the Black Hawk War. His first wife, Henrietta Preston, to whom he was married in 1829, died in 1835, and for a season after this he farmed near St. Louis, Mo. His military spirit

was aroused by the efforts of the Texans in endeavoring to gain their independence from Mexico, and in 1836 he joined those patriots and threw himself, heart and soul, into their cause, and where he was not long in securing recognition to which his brilliant intellect and undaunted courage demanded. From the ranks he arose, step by step, to the command of the Texan army, although before attaining this position he was compelled to meet General Felix Houston in a duel, in which he was severely wounded. As Secretary of War, appointed by President Mirabeau Lamar in 1838, he completed a line of defense against the invasion of the Mexicans, and after two battles with the Indians, who were committing depredations along the northern border, succeeded in driving them from the country. In 1843 he was engaged in farming in Brazoria County, and it was in this year that he wedded Eliza Griffin. The war between the United States and Mexico enlisted his aid in behalf of his native country, but, although he was strongly urged for a brigade command, this was refused him for political reasons. From 1849 to 1855 he served as paymaster in the United States army, and in the latter year was appointed colonel of the Second Cavalry by President Pierce. He remained in command of his regiment in the Department of Texas until 1857, when he was given the command of the expedition to bring to proper subjection the rebellious Mormons of Utah, which he did most successfully, solely by the exercise of moral suasion, remaining there until February, 1860. The summer of this year he resided in Kentucky, but in December sailed for California to assume command of the Department of the Pacific. This he resigned April 9, 1861, and two months later began an overland march for the states. In September he was placed in command of all west of the Atlantic states and north of the Gulf states. His career from this time on the world knows. His splendid presence and dashing bravery were no less inspiriting to his troops than was the confidence inspired by the knowledge that his mind was planning for the success of his army. At the battle of Shiloh, on Sunday, April 6, at about half past two o'clock, while leading his men in an assault, he fell from his horse mortally wounded. Such ended the life of General Albert Sidney Johnston, one of America's greatest soldiers. His remains lie at Austin, Tex., the state of his adoption.

SAMUEL M. WARD.

The atmosphere of Marion County, Tex., seems fitted for the pro-
duction of a cultivated and progressive class of men, and among them,
taking a leading place in all enterprises of moment, is Samuel M.
Ward, a prominent real estate dealer of that county. His native
home was Memphis, Tenn., his birth occurring there in 1835, and he
was next to the eldest of four children born to William and Sallie
(Blythe) Ward, natives respectively of Georgia and Tennessee.
Mathias Ward, the paternal grandfather, was born in Ireland and left
Dublin for this country about the close of the Revolutionary War.
He had a son known as Colonel Mat. Ward, and at an early date came
to Texas. Here he was elected to Congress of the Republic of Texas
and represented the Lone Star State in the United States Senate
for some time. He died in Raleigh, N. C., while on his way home from
Richmond, where he had been for his health. During the early days
of Jefferson he had followed merchandising for a time. The maternal
grandfather, Samuel K. Blythe, was born in North Carolina, but left
that state for Tennessee in pioneer days. He was a licentiate in the
Cumberland Presbyterian Church, which he assisted in organizing in
Tennessee. In the fall of 1835 he moved to Texas Bowie County,
and there died about 1840. He was of Scotch-Irish origin. The
father of our subject was educated in his native state and graduated
in medicine. Later he moved to Memphis, Tenn., and practiced there
until 1835, when he came to Texas, settling in Bowie County. Here,
in connection with his practice, he followed farming. He was the
first physician at Dalby Springs, and the first camp meeting held in
Eastern Texas was in 1840, and was organized by Blythe, Ward and
Weaver, pioneers of that section. The father of our subject was converted during this camp meeting. About 1842 or '43 he moved to
Clarksville and kept the Star Hotel, one of the first and finest houses
in the state. This he conducted for two years and then moved to

Henderson, Rusk County, where he resumed his practice, and where he resided until 1850. From there he moved to Gilmer, Upshur County, and thence to Dangerfield, where he remained until the opening of the Civil War. His next move was to Van Zandt County, and he there practiced his profession until his death, February 19, 1863. He was a Mason. His wife died in 1871. They were honest, industrious and well-respected citizens. Samuel M. Ward was but a small child when his parents moved to Texas and the principal part of his early education was received at Dangerfield. Later he entered Chapel Hill College and after that Trinity University, under the direction of the Cumberland Presbyterian Church. After graduating from the college he began teaching in the same, and in 1859 was elected professor of mathematics. In 1861 he resigned from college and enlisted in Company D, Ninth Texas Infantry, under Colonel S. B. Maxey, as first lieutenant. Almost immediately his health commenced failing and later he was compelled to resign, in 1862. He returned to Chapel Hill, resumed his place in the college and continued there until 1867, when he moved to Jefferson. The same year he organized Paradise Academy, near Jefferson, and soon built up a flourishing school, which he carried on until August, 1885, when he moved to Jefferson. At the present time he owns several farms and gives his time and attention to those interests and to real estate. During the first year of the war he married Miss Woodie E. Brown, a native of Virginia, and daughter of Hon. John G. Brown, who came to Texas in 1850, located in Rusk County and followed farming there. Later he represented Rusk County in the Legislature and was an influential and popular citizen. Later, moving to Longview, he died there in 1890. He was of Scotch-English origin. His wife's maiden name was Frances Rhodes, a native of Virginia. Mr. Ward and wife are the parents of six children: Fannie Garland, wife of Dr. Walter Dake of Nashville; Sarah Blythe, wife of John C. Harrison of Fort Worth; William Blythe, a merchant of Fort Worth; Woodie May, Zue Aiken, Sammie Theodocia. The members of this family hold membership in the Cumberland Presbyterian Church, and Mr. Ward has been an elder in the same for thirty years. Socially he is a Mason.

HON. ALBERT C. HORTON.

Hon. Albert C. Horton was a native of Georgia, born in 1798. His father was a man of position and affluence, but died while young Horton was yet a boy. The care of the estates fell upon his son's shoulders, the subject of our sketch, who had received from nature a strong understanding and a hardy constitution, and early in life developed those traits of character which in after time made him one of our grandest patriots. He moved from his native state to La Grange, Franklin County, Ala. There he met and married the handsome Eliza Holliday, of the family long prominent in the annals of that state, at the residence of her brother-in-law and guardian, W. J. Croom, father of Colonel John L. Croom of Matagorda. This was in about the year 1823. There he was initiated into the secrets of Masonry, and continued a member throughout his long life. Later he made his home in Greensboro, where he was elected and served one term in the State Senate, about the year 1832. It was at this juncture that he resolved to come to Texas. Giving up position, honor and fame, he turned his face westward, and cast his wealth and fortunes with the young empire. He chose Matagorda County as his home. This was in 1835. After purchasing several leagues of land and making provision for his family's comfort, he offered the patriots his purse and services for the good of the just and holy struggle that liberty was making against the oppressor, Santa Anna, then at the head of the Mexican Government. Santa Anna, seeing the necessity of early action on his part if he expected his policy to be dominant in Texas, in October, 1835, sent General Cos, his brother-in-law, with a well-equipped force to Texas to subdue the revolutionary spirit. How they were met and routed at Gonzales by the patriots, under gallant Moore, driven and forced to take refuge within the walls of the Alamo, at San Antonio; how later his concentrated forces surrendered to the Texans and were allowed to depart for Mexico, are among the brightest achievements of the patriots, and are parts of Texan history narrated elsewhere in this volume. Santa

Anna, after the defeat of his general, set about with his usual celerity to come in person at the head of an army that would crush the revolution out of existence. Early in the year of 1836 he was in Texas with 8,000 men, furnished and provisioned for his campaign of destruction. And now Mr. Horton comes out prominently, and ever after was one of Texas' leading men. He raised, mounted and armed a cavalry force at his own expense, and joined the brave, but afterward the ill-fated, Fannin, then stationed as colonel commanding the Southern army at the fort at La Bahia (Goliad). Fannin's force was made up of volunteers from Georgia and Alabama, many of whom Horton had known in their homes. After some slight fighting, in which Horton and his troops succeeded in beating off the Mexican advance forces sent to attack the fort, the news of the fall of the Alamo and the treacherous butchery of its brave defenders fell like a clap of thunder upon the hearts of the Texan patriots. The certain knowledge of what they had to expect if beaten drew them together and nerved each heart for a struggle to conquer or die. It was then that Fannin received positive orders from Houston, as commander-in-chief, to retreat, fall back and form a junction with the main army somewhere in the East. Here the clear-sightedness of Horton was displayed. He urged Fannin to immediately obey the order, seeing that with the small force then at his disposal what would inevitably follow; but alas, Fannin, rash, reckless and brave to a fault in his daring, with but 350 effective men, imagined himself secure and counted upon his ability to carry his army and supplies safely through, without loss, back East. In vain did Horton urge and plead against his commander's waste of time, until too late. In a few days Urrea and his forces were upon them, when Fannin began his retreat. He dispatched Horton and his cavalry to skirmish in front, and with his forces moved on in the direction of Victoria. When about ten miles on his journey his progress was interrupted by the approach of the Mexican forces, numbering in all about 1,000. Upon Horton's return he found them surrounded and cut off, and with his troops he was fortunate in making good his escape to Victoria. Their subsequent fate, how in violation of a treaty and formal guarantee that their lives and liberty would be spared them, they were taken back to Goliad and by the orders of the tyrant, Santa Anna, murdered, is part of the history of this state. It is only sufficient to say, had Horton's advice been followed this noble band would have been saved to Texas. The subject of our sketch, after the disaster, arrived safely and joined the army in the East. The battle of San Jacinto followed soon after, and in the fearful onslaught on that glorious day, ended with the annihilation of Santa Anna's power in Texas. This victory gave birth to the liberty for which the patriots had expended treasures, and which they consecrated by the blood of the heroes of the Alamo and La Bahia. With the rout of Santa Anna's army, his capture following, hostilities ceased, peace and quiet for a time were restored to the people of the country. Now came the real labor of the patriots, that of bringing order and good government out of chaos and ruin from the demoralized condition of affairs following the splendid victories won by the colonists. To quiet contending factions and inaugurate a unison of thought and feeling between the settlers, taxed the wisdom of the leading men of the day to the utmost. Colonel Horton had retired to his home, but as he had served the people in the field, he was called to lend his talents to her councils. He was elected to the first Congress and served as one of its best members, and helped frame the constitution of the Republic. He was afterward appointed by President Lamar one of the Commissioners to select and locate the city of Austin. When the question of annexation came about he was one of its warmest advocates and served as one of the annexation committee. When Texas assumed state government he was elected Lieutenant-Governor; J. Pinckney Henderson being the first Chief Executive. War against the United States being declared by Mexico consequent to Texas' admission into the Union, Henderson taking the field at the head of the Texas troops, Colonel Horton was called to the executive chair, and acquitted himself in the discharge of the onerous duties to the satisfaction of the entire people. His term of office over, he followed his inclinations and returned to devote his energies to the management of his vast estates. Some time in the early '40s he had moved into the upper part of Matagorda County, but when this county was organized in 1846, became a part of Wharton. Here he went into planting on a scale never before witnessed in this portion of the Union. Considering the sparsely settled condition of the country then, and lack of transportation, the output of his farms was on a vast scale. He would send to market 650 to 700 bales of cotton, but it was the product of sugar and molasses which engrossed his time—450 to 500 hogsheads of sugar and 1,600 barrels of syrup was considered a fair estimate of the yearly output of his cane crop. He had always been a faithful member of the Baptist Church, and was first a trustee and afterward president of the Baylor University, making that institution a present of $5,000 and a magnificent bell, and it was his intention ultimately to endow a professorship of not less than $50,000. But the specter of war loomed up above the horizon and changed the outlook and hopes of a people. The war wrecked his once princely fortune, and the failure of the Southern cause told heavily upon Governor Horton, and he did but survive it. He passed away peacefully at his summer home on Matagorda coast in October, 1865, with the love and esteem of a people and state whom he had helped make great and prosperous.

WILLIAM F. JONES.

The gentleman whose name is mentioned above is the capable and efficient county clerk of Marion County, Tex. His public services have been characterized by a noticeable devotion to the welfare of his county, and his ability and fidelity in his present position have been seen and appreciated by all, irrespective of party. He is a native of this county and one of twelve children born to John M. and Mariah E. (Wood) Jones, natives of North Carolina and Maryland respectively. The father followed the occupation of a farmer through life and, though residing in Georgia and Louisiana for some time, finally came to Marion County (then Cass) and resided near Jefferson until his death in 1884. His wife had passed away in 1876. Our subject was born in 1841 and, in addition to a common school education, finished in New Orleans, where he received excellent training. In the year 1862 he enlisted in Company H, Seventh Texas Infantry, joined the regiment at Marshall and at once went with the same to Tennessee, where he participated in the battle of Donelson and siege of Port Hudson. Later he was at Jackson and Vicksburg, but soon after was taken ill and sent home on sick leave. After recovering he returned to his regiment and was assigned to duty west of the Mississippi in the Third Texas Cavalry. In March, 1864, he was promoted to the rank of lieutenant and attached to General Bee's staff, with which he remained until after the battle of Red River and Yellow Bayou. Following this he was attached to a frontier command, served in the Upper Red River, Texas, but was in the Indian Territory at the time of the surrender. After returning to Jefferson he was bookkeeper for G. A. Kelley, in Kelley Iron Works, near Jefferson, and continued in that capacity for sixteen years. Desiring to embark in business for himself, he engaged as bookkeeper in sawmilling at Atlanta, Cass County, Tex. In 1884 he was elected county clerk and so well did he discharge every duty of this office that he has been re-elected ever since. Miss Sallie E. Nash, who became his wife in 1869, was a native of Louisiana, and daughter of Milton B. Nash, one of the first settlers here. Two children have been given them, Mattie and William Wood. Mr. Jones is a member of the Masonic fraternity, also a member of the Chapter, and has been Secretary of the Blue Lodge since 1890. He and Mrs. Jones are members of the Cumberland Presbyterian Church, and no family is more popular with all.

WILLIAM UMBDENSTOCK.

Among those who have fought the battle of life bravely and are now enjoying the comforts and conveniences that wealth brings, is William Umbdenstock, who, although a native of other climes, has won fame and fortune on this side of the Atlantic. He was born in Alsace, France, in 1826, to the marriage of John and Sallie (Barta) Umbdenstock, also natives of that country. In the year 1854 our subject decided to try his fortune in America and, after reaching this country, made his home in New York for a year and a half. Follow-

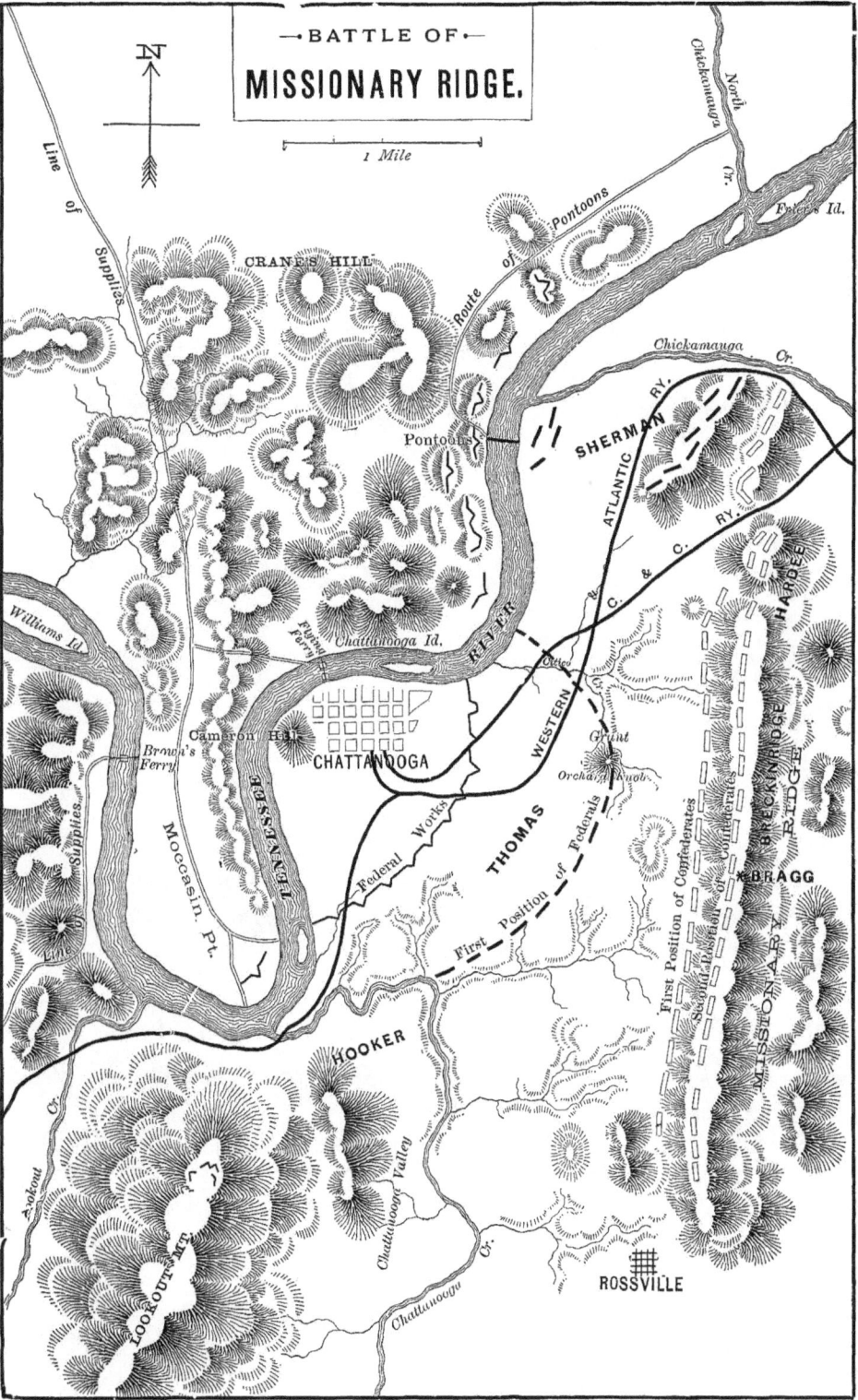

→ BATTLE OF ←
MISSIONARY RIDGE.

1 Mile

N

Line of Supplies

Chickamauga Cr.

North

Friar's Id.

CRANE'S HILL

Route of Pontoons

Pontoons

Chickamauga Cr.

SHERMAN

ATLANTIC RY.

C. & C. RY.

HARDEE

BRECKINRIDGE

RIVER

Williams Id.

Fort Ferry

Chattanooga Id.

Cameron Hill

Brown's Ferry

Moccasin Pt.

TENNESSEE

Giles

Grant

Orchard Knob

CHATTANOOGA

Federal Works

THOMAS

WESTERN

First Position of Federals

Second Position of Confederates

First Position of Confederates

× BRAGG

MISSIONARY RIDGE

Line of Supplies

HOOKER

Chattanooga Valley

Lookout Cr.

Chattanooga Cr.

ROSSVILLE

LOOKOUT Mtn.

ing this, he went on a whaling voyage in the Arctic seas and, meeting with unusual success, was gone a year and a half. Returning, he settled in Connecticut, but only remained there a short time, when he returned to the Empire State. A few months later he went to Iowa City, Iowa, thence to St. Louis and from there to New Orleans a short time afterward. In 1860 he came to Marshall, Tex., and liking the outlook here, decided to settle. Here he has since made his home and by years of good management and industry has gathered around him much that renders life enjoyable. Soon after locating here he engaged in railroad work and built twenty-five miles of the first railroad from Marshall. During the years of the war he followed railroad constructing, then became road master on the completed road. His intelligence and ability in every walk of life brought him into public notice and in 1870 he was elected to the responsible position of county treasurer, an office he filled most acceptably for eight years. In 1880 he was appointed collector of internal revenue, held that position for three years and since then has been living retired. He has one of the finest homes in the city, all made by the honest sweat of his brow, for he is practically self-made. All public enterprises engage his deepest attention and all worthy ones obtain his support and countenance. Mr. Umbdenstock was married in New York in 1856 to Miss Mary Tribold, who has been his earnest helper through life.

GENERAL HENRY EUSTACE M'CULLOCH.

General Henry Eustace McCulloch was born in Rutherford County, Tenn., December 6, 1816, and first came to Texas in the autumn of 1835, accompanied by his brother, Ben McCulloch, five years older. Arriving at Nacogdoches, they had an argument as to the propriety of Henry's coming on. Ben tried almost every way to persuade him to return home, but in vain, until he hit upon the argument that he should take care of his parents in their old age. Selling their horses,

fine saddle animals, they separated, starting off on foot, one east
and the other west. In the fall of 1837 Henry came again to Texas
and stopped at Washington, then the capital of the state and passed
the winter there, hewing house-logs, splitting red oak boards and
building board houses. In the spring he joined a party in the ex-
ploration of the upper Brazos. While out hunting one day, in company with another member of the party, they chanced upon a company of five Indians, whom they attacked, killed two and chased the
other three away. In the summer of 1838 he joined his brother
Ben at Gonzales and formed a partnership with him in surveying and
locating lands, and this partnership lasted until the death of the
brother in 1862. During the pioneer times both the brothers engaged
in much ranger service, with skill and good fortune, the particulars
of which we have not space for here. During a battle with the
Comanches in 1840 Henry saved the life of Dr. Sweitzer, a bitter
enemy of his brother, by driving away the Indians who were about to
take the life of the doctor. Henry had dismounted and taken his
position behind a small sapling in advance of the main Texan force
and was pouring hot shots in the ranks of the enemy, who, in return
had completely scaled the bark of the little tree behind which he
stood. Arch Gipson and Alsey Miller had come up and were sitting
on their horses near Henry, who was standing on the ground beside
his horse, when suddenly Gipson or Miller cried out, "They'll catch
him, they'll catch him!" McCulloch asked, "Catch who?" The reply
was, "Sweitzer." Glancing over his horse's head the gallant young
McCulloch saw a party of eight or ten Indians closely pursuing the
bitterest enemy of his brother, but the life of a human being was
involved, and prompted by that magnanimity of heart which ever
characterized his life, he did not stop to calculate the consequences,
but in a second was in his saddle going at full speed at the risk of his
own life to save that of Sweitzer. His companions followed, and
they reached Sweitzer just in time to save him. August 20, 1840,
soon after the above occurrence, Mr. McCulloch married Miss Jane
Isabella Ashley, and directly settled on the place improved by his
brother Ben, four miles from Gonzales. In September, 1842, General Wolf, at the head of a thousand Mexican infantry and 500 or
600 cavalry, captured San Antonio, but just before the retreat of the

Mexican forces Captain Matthew Caldwell, with 200 men, engaged
the enemy about five or six miles from town and defeated them.
While this fight was progressing Dawson's men were massacred in
the rear of the Mexican army while trying to make their way to
Caldwell, and in this engagement McCulloch was a lieutenant under
Colonel Jack Hays. He was also in Somervell's expedition so far as
it remained in Texas. Becoming a resident of Gonzales County in
1844, he entered mercantile business there. In 1846 he was elected
captain of a volunteer company for the Mexican War and the next
year was elected sheriff of the county. Occasionally he was engaged
in an expedition with the Indians with success. In 1853, on the
Democratic ticket for the Legislature, he was elected over Colonel
French Smith, a Whig, and in 1855 he was again elected, defeating
Thomas H. Duggan. In 1858 he was appointed United States marshal for the eastern district of Texas, which position he held until
the breaking out of the Civil War, and in this mighty struggle he
had a brilliant career. He was promoted from the rank of colonel to that of brigadier-general. March 1, 1876, Governor Coke
appointed him superintendent of the deaf and dumb asylum, which
place he held until dismissed by Governor Roberts September 1, 1879.
In 1885 he was employed by the State Land Board as an agent to
manage the public school, university and asylum lands.

JAMES GRAHAM LOWDON.

James Graham Lowdon, of Abilene, Tex., son of William L. and
Elizabeth (Graham) Lowdon, was born in New York city on December 10, 1856. His father was a well-known and successful business
man of New York, and his mother enjoyed an enviable reputation
as a mathematician, which gift has descended in no small measure
to her son. He acquired his education in the common and high
schools, and immediately after his graduation from the latter he

embarked in business, preferring mercantile to professional life. He first engaged with Haviland & Co. in the importing business, but in 1885 removed to Texas, and there engaged in the banking business. He there enjoys the highest esteem of his fellow-citizens, and has several times served his party (the Republican) in office. He has been twice elected treasurer of Abilene, Tex., once mayor, and once as a member of the Board of Aldermen. He has been from his earliest years connected with the Presbyterian church, and is active in all church and charitable work. He is a Mason and is treasurer of the Royal Arch Masons' chapter of Abilene, and also treasurer and member of Abilene Commandery, Knights Templar, and has also held the position of state representative of the Abilene lodge, Knights of Pythias. On May 20, 1879, Mr. Lowdon was married to Miss Alice Crane, daughter of Benjamin F. Crane, who at one time held the responsible position of superintendent of the parks of New York city. Mr. Lowdon is a man of medium height, and personally is very popular, both in business circles and in society. His popularity is also shared by his charming wife, who is a great favorite of the young people, and is frequently called upon to assist and lead them in their pleasures.

CAPTAIN B. F. HOUSTON.

B. F. Houston, McKinney, Tex., son of Major A. and Esther (Walker) Houston, was born on his father's farm, sixteen miles southwest of Charlotte, N. C., on January 7, 1830. His mother was a daughter of Captain Andrew Walker, of Revolutionary fame, and was born and reared at the old and well-known Walker homestead. In 1840 Major Houston left North Carolina and moved to his lands lying on the Tallahatchie River, northeast of Oxford, Miss. Here young Houston obtained the first rudiments of his education in a little log schoolhouse, improving upon his limited opportunities for five years, when the death of his father occurred, and he, being the eldest son then at home, had to leave school and work the farm. Though but a lad of fifteen years he, aided by his mother's counsel, made an

unqualified success of his work, but five years later he obtained his mother's consent to go back and live with his brother, a merchant in North Carolina, where he completed his rather limited education. In this he succeeded far beyond his expectations, becoming proficient in mathematics, bookkeeping, and business training. His brother finally proposed that he should return to Mississippi, where he was to be supplied with all the necessary stock to start a store, and to share equally in the profits. This offer he accepted, but after returning from a business tour through Texas he was notified of his brother's death and asked to return to North Carolina and take charge of the business. This offer he declined, preferring to return to farming, and in 1853 he bought a farm two miles from his mother's place and began to accumulate land, negroes and other property. This he continued to do until 1861, when he entered the Thirty-fourth Regiment Mississippi Volunteers as a private. He was advanced from time to time until he was severely wounded while leading his company in a charge upon the Federal breastworks at Jonesboro, Ga., and was sent to the hospital camps, where he remained until the final surrender in 1865. After the surrender he returned to his home in Mississippi, a cripple, to find that he had dependent upon him a crippled wife and four helpless children. His negroes were freed, his mules had been taken by the Federals, and his wife was trying to raise as much on the farm as she could with one superannuated mule, having to contend with many other difficulties caused by dilapidated fences and a lack of ready money. Notwithstanding the bad outlook, he determined to restore his estate to its former position, and by hard work raised enough corn to last over until the next season, besides three bales of cotton. In November, 1865, some of his friends, knowing of his business ability, proposed that he abandon farming and become a partner in a mercantile business, he to attend to the buying and look after the finances. This offer he accepted, and in the spring of 1866 bought a stock which he hauled home in wagons and handled with great success. From that time his success has been remarkable. He started another store in October, 1866, at Abbeville, Miss., which was a railroad station, and commenced to trade in lands. He built a storehouse and a cotton gin at Abbeville, and besides his other business, kept the hotel, bought and sold mules, and furnished wood and ties to the railroad company. His business assumed enormous proportions, and every dollar that he could spare from it he invested in lands. In 1876 he exchanged fourteen lots that he owned in South St. Louis for Texas farm lands, which he immediately began to cultivate and improve. He kept adding to his possessions until their extent required his personal supervision, and he removed his family to McKinney, Tex., where they have since resided. In 1853, when he purchased his first farm, Captain Houston was united in marriage to Miss Martha Driver, a daughter of Colonel G. L. Driver, of Mississippi. The union has been a happy one, and to Mrs. Houston's helpful advice, careful management and cheerful self-sacrifice in the gloomy days of the war, is due much of the prosperity that has since been realized. They have reared six children, three sons and three daughters, and well may they be proud of their family, for the sons are all careful, conscientious business men, highly respected by all; while the daughters are highly accomplished women, being equally well versed in the mysteries of successful housekeeping, keeping a set of books, or discussing current literature and music. Captain Houston has always been a democrat, but though often solicited to accept public office, or to allow his name to be placed upon party tickets, has as often declined the honor, excepting such as local public school interests demanded of him. He has ever been a liberal contributor to public and private charities, and to the cause of Christianity, never closing his ears or his purse to those who are worthy and deserving of aid, though having but little toleration for pretense of any kind. He has now retired from active business life, having turned over the care of his interests to his children, who attend to the management and only require their father's advice in matters of special importance. He is now taking life easily and enjoying the fruits of his labor of other years. He enjoys the honor and respect of the entire community where he resides, and none envy him the prominent position to which he has mounted notwithstanding the almost hopeless chaos into which his affairs were plunged by the war, which left him not only poor, but a cripple. His example may well be emulated, for though he may have made some mistakes he never made a failure, and his dealings with his fellow-men have always been marked by fairness and strict business integrity.

BENJAMIN R. MILAM.

Benjamin R. Milam was a native of Kentucky, born of humble parents and having but little education. He distinguished himself in the War of 1812, and was afterward engaged in trade with the Indians at the headwaters of Texan rivers. Later he joined Mina in his disastrous expedition in aid of the revolutionary cause in Mexico, and being one of those who escaped death, rendered valuable services. When Iturbide proclaimed himself emperor, Milam was among the first to join the party to oppose him. For this he was cast into prison, where he languished until Iturbide's dethronement, when he was released. For his services in the republican cause he received, in 1828, a grant of eleven square leagues of land in Texas, but he located it by mistake in Arkansas, and obtained from the government of the State of Coahuilla and Texas an empresario grant. He was in Monclova at the time of Viesca's deposal, and was captured in company with him. Milam escaped from prison near Monterey by winning the confidence of the jailor, and, being supplied with a fleet horse and a little food from a friend he traveled alone for 600 miles, journeying by night and concealing himself by day, till he reached the vicinity of Goliad, almost exhausted. After the capture of that place he enlisted in the ranks, and was soon afterward killed by a rifle ball from the enemy, when he was about forty-five years of age.

DR. THOMAS M. MARKS.

Dr. Thomas M. Marks is a successful follower of Aesculapias at Marshall, Tex., and through ability and well-merited success has built up a practice that is eminently satisfactory. The father of our subject, Nicholas M. Marks, was born in Georgia, and when a

young man went to Alabama, where he met and married Miss Rebecca L. Wright, a native of South Carolina. Like his father, John
H. Marks, who was of English descent and a native of Georgia, Nicholas followed farming and continued this all his life. By his marriage he became the father of fourteen children, all of whom were
born in Alabama or Louisiana, whither the father moved in 1848.
His death occurred in Bossier Parish in 1866. The mother died in
Marshall, Tex., recently. Her father, Joseph Wright, was a product
of South Carolina, but made his home in Alabama, to which state he
moved when first married. Dr. Thomas M. Marks was next to the
eldest of the large family born to his parents. His birth occurred
in Montgomery County, Ala., in 1832, and he there remained until
sixteen years of age, when he went with his parents to Louisiana.
In both states he received good educational advantages and in 1853
he entered Cumberland University at Lebanon, Tenn., where he
took a thorough course in civil engineering. Teaching school for
some time in Louisiana and at the same time studying medicine, he
was prepared to attend lectures at Tulane University and graduated
from that institution in 1860. In the fall of that year he began practicing in Bossier Parish, La., and continued there until the breaking
out of war. In 1862 he enlisted in Company D, Ninth Louisiana
regulars, "Bossier Boys," and at once went to the army of Virginia.
He took an active part in the battles of Malvern Hill, Cedar Mountain, Fredricksburg and soon after was placed on the medical staff
and assigned to duty with the Thirty-ninth battery of Virginia cavalry. He was at the battle of Gettysburg, also Wilderness and in
other battles succeeding the siege of Petersburg and the surrender
of General Lee. Upon his return to Louisiana Dr. Marks resumed
his practice and remained there until 1868, when he came to Texas,
settling in Marshall. This has been his home ever since and he
has been in continuous practice with but few interruptions. For
two months he attended a post-graduate school in New York, where
he made a specialty of diseases of women and children, but since
then he has attended to his large practice in and around Marshall.
He was a president of the Harrison County Medical Association, was
one of its originators, and has been a member of the state and of the
Northeast Texas Association. The year 1865 saw him married to

Miss Robertson, who died in May, 1879, leaving two children: Fannie, wife of C. R. Calvert of Louisville, Ky., and Willie, wife of Rev. L. A. Webb of Wills Point, Tex. Dr. Marks was married to his second wife, Miss Carrie A. Perry, a native of Kentucky, and daughter of William A. Perry, now of Sherman, in the year 1881. One daughter, Eleanor, has been born to this marriage. The doctor is a royal arch Mason, chapter and blue lodge here, and is past master of the latter. In 1894 he was scribe of the chapter, but this year (1895) he is king. He is also a member of the K. of H., the K. and L. of H. and the A. O. U. W. The family hold membership in the M. E. church south. During the latter part of the seventies he was active in the organization of the citizen's party, and for a time chairman of that organization.

THOMAS N. LOCKETT.

Mr. Lockett is a man whose career is a decidedly interesting one, showing what a man with energy, perseverance and strict attention to business can accomplish. He is a native of Georgia, born in 1840, and eighth in order of birth of eleven children born to his parents, Royal and Martha (Smith) Lockett, natives of Virginia and Maryland. Our subject's paternal grandfather, Jacob Lockett, was a native Virginian and a soldier all through the Revolutionary War. All his life was passed in his native state, where he was engaged in farming. This family was of Welsh origin and came to America many years prior to the above mentioned war. The maternal grandfather, Marshal Smith, was also a Virginian by birth and also a soldier in the Revolution. He was captured by the tories in Virginia and was hung by them, but before long the tories were frightened away and he was rescued, more dead than alive. He carried the scars of this adventure until his death. Mr. Smith held the rank of captain under General Marion and served with that famous leader till the close of hostilities. Following the war he moved to Georgia and there his death occurred. He was married five times. Royal Lockett grew to manhood in his native state and when but a boy served a short time in the Revolutionary War, participating in the battle of Cowpens. Later in life he moved to Georgia and was there married to Miss Smith, whose death occurred in 1866. One year later he too passed away. Farming was his lifelong occupation. In 1856 he moved to Texas and settled in Cass (now Marion) County, where he bought 4,000 acres of choice land nine miles north of Jefferson. He made many improvements and his was the first frame house in that section. There his last days were spent. The original of this notice attended school in Georgia until coming to the Lone Star State in 1856, and remained under the parental roof until 1861. He then enlisted in Company B, Langs' regiment, Partisan Rangers, and served in Missouri, Arkansas and Louisiana. He participated in the battles of Mansfield, Pleasant Hill and Yellow Bayou, and was with General Price in his Missouri campaign. His command was disbanded in Western Texas in 1865. Returning home Mr. Lockett turned his attention to farming, but in connection was also engaged in merchandising in Jefferson, and in the real estate business there. He is now the owner of 800 acres in this county, good farming land, and has 500 acres under cultivation. His marriage occurred in 1868 to Miss Laura Moore, a native of Georgia, and of the four children born to this union, Thomas, Albert, Sallie and ————, only Sallie is now living. Mr. Lockett's second marriage was with Miss Laura Pruit, who bore him five children: Emmet, Anna, Opal, Pruit and Royal. Mr. Lockett and wife hold membership in the M. E. church south. Politically Mr. Lockett is a conservative democrat. Our subject had seven brothers in the war, all of whom served until the close with the exception of one, Hamilton, who died in Tennessee. Mr. Lockett takes a prominent part in all public matters and has been active in all enterprises to advance the good of the community. He aided greatly in securing the location of the Lone Star Foundry at Jefferson and bought most of the land for that concern.

DAVID G. BURNETT.

David G. Burnett is first known in the state as an "empresario," who, December 22, 1826, contracted to colonize 300 families in Texas. After the annulment of Edwards' contract his grant was divided between Burnett and Joseph Vehlein. He was a member of the second state convention, which met April 1, 1833, at San Felipe; was selected the first president of the Republic of Texas in 1836; had a stormy time during an engagement with the Mexicans, being accused of treason; resigned his presidency October 22, 1836; was elected vice-president in 1838, but in 1841, as a candidate for the presidency, was defeated by General Houston.

CAPTAIN MILTON MAST.

As a discriminating and competent man of affairs and as an efficient and fearless official Captain Milton Mast stands foremost among Nacogdoches County's most esteemed citizens. He resides on a farm about a mile east of Melrose and the wide-awake manner in which he has taken advantage of every method and idea tending to the enhanced value of his property, has had considerable to do with his success in life. A native son of Texas, born in Nacogdoches County on the farm where he now lives in 1834, he is known far and wide and the people have had every opportunity to judge of his character and qualifications. His father, Jacob Mast, was born in North Carolina, and grew to manhood there. About 1826, when a single man, he came to Texas and settled in Nacogdoches County, on the farm where the captain now resides and has all of his life, and now is sixty years old, and took up about 1,800 acres of land in the home place. Later he located several thousand acres elsewhere, became the owner of a number of slaves, and was one of the prosperous, wealthy, and well respected citizens of the county. In this county he was married to Mrs. Nancy Fulcker, a widow, who died when her son, our subject, was but a child. Another child, Leona, wife of William Teutsch, resides in Oregon. The father passed the last years of his life on this farm in Nacogdoches County, dying in March, 1878. Captain Mast received but little schooling in his boyhood days, but was early trained to the duties of the farm. In 1854 he joined an expedition against the Indians and for twelve months was with Captain John S. Walker's Rangers, participated in one or two skirmishes and captured one or two herds of horses and a few Indians. In August, 1861, he enlisted in Company A, ———— infantry regiment under Colonel O. M. Roberts, and was made captain of the company. He was offered promotion, but refused, preferring to keep with the boys of his company and regiment. He served until the army was disbanded, only being out of service for a few months on account of a wound received in the hand at Saline, Ark. He was also in the battles of Pleasant Hill, Mansfield, etc. At the same time he received the wound in the hand he also had one of the bones of the fore-arm fractured, and was furloughed home. Later he joined his regiment again at Minden, La., and remained with the same the remainder of the war. Returning to his native county he resumed agricultural pursuits and continued this until 1873, when he was elected to the office of sheriff. So ably and well did he fill this position that he was re-elected at the expiration of his term, and yet again, serving in all about eight consecutive years. During that time he made many important arrests, among them being the arrest of the noted and desperate character, Wilson, who was connected with one or more murders in Dallas, Tex., and who, although arrested by others, always managed to make his escape. Captain Mast arrested him without difficulty in Louisiana and returned him to this state. This was considered a daring feat by all who knew Wilson. Another desperate character, Bill Longley of Lee County, had committed numerous murders and although often arrested, always succeeded in making his escape, sometimes by killing an officer and sometimes by killing several of them. Captain Mast captured him in Louisiana and brought him back to Lee County, where he was-

tried and executed. There are numerous other instances of the coolness and courage of Captain Mast. Since leaving that office the
captain has served as collector of the county for six years and has
served as a delegate to numerous state and county conventions. In
whatever position the people of the county have seen fit to place him
he has made a most faithful and efficient officer, and is a representative man of the county. For a number of years now he has been
carrying on his extensive farming interests, about 300 acres, and
is thrifty and prosperous. In October, 1860, he married Miss Nancy
A. Mast, a native of North Carolina, and the daughter of Reuben
Mast, also of North Carolina, but who came here in 1858. The captain and wife are the parents of seven children, as follows: Mollie,
wife of J. W. Mast, a farmer of this county; Cora, wife of C. B. Patton
of this county; Guy, single, is a farmer of McClellan County, Tex.;
Blanche of McClellan County; Oscar, a young man at home; Baxter,
farming on the home place, and Leona, at home.

DR. STEPHEN T. BEASLEY.

The professional career of a skillful and devoted physician ever
furnishes material of great interest to all readers, and the life narrative of Dr. Stephen T. Beasley is no exception to this general statement. He must assuredly have inherited his taste for medicine
for there were prominent physicians on both sides of the house. The
doctor was born at La Grange, Ga., March 11, 1840, and was second
in a family of five sons born to Dr. William P. and Louisa (Edwards)
Beasley, both natives of Georgia. The paternal grandfather, Jarrell
Beasley, was born in Virginia, but later moved to Georgia. His
father was a native of Ireland. Dr. Andrew Edwards, the maternal
grandfather, was born in Georgia and became one of that state's
most eminent physicians. Dr. William P. Beasley was a physician

of Georgia and a prominent whig politician. He was in the State Senate in 1858 and 1860, and was in the secession convention in the latter year. When war broke out he entered the Confederate army, after first assisting in raising a regiment of which he was made lieutenant-colonel, with which he remained until the close of hostilities. After that he followed farming until his death in 1895. He was active in political matters—a democrat. Socially he was a Mason. His wife died in 1886. Dr. Stephen T. Beasley was educated in the University of Georgia and graduated in 1858. After that he entered the law office of Ben Hill for a short time at La Grange, and subsequently taught school for ten months, reading medicine in the meantime. In the fall of 1859 he entered Jefferson Medical College, Philadelphia, and was among the seceding students, caused by John Brown's raid at Harper's Ferry. Returning home he continued his course at Augusta, Ga., and graduated the following fall at Atlanta, where he delivered the valedictory. From there he went to New Orleans and became a private student with Drs. Schopin and Schupert, and at the same time was a student at the N. O. school of medicine, graduating in 1861. Immediately afterward he entered the Confederate army as assistant surgeon of the Thirteenth Georgia Regiment, and was in a campaign in West Virginia with Generals Floyd and Wise and General Lee. On April 1, 1862, he was wounded at Whit Marsh Island, near Savannah, Ga., and was afterward detailed for light duties, serving thus until cessation of hostilities. In 1865 Dr. Beasley came to Texas, settled at Marshall for a year, and then moved to Porter's Springs, Houston County, where he carried on a successful practice until 1884, when he came to Crockett. The doctor was married first in 1862 to Miss Bettie Crook, who died in 1864. In 1867 he wedded Miss Grace Smith, a native of Texas, who died in 1872, leaving two children: Ada Lou, wife of W. H. Denny of Crockett, and Stephen T., Jr. Dr. Beasley's third union was with Miss Kate Smith in 1874. She was born in Macon, Miss., and was brought to Texas by her parents when an infant. To this union six children were born: Bessie, Harold, Lucile, Hugh Lawson, John B. Gordon and Nell. All are members of the M. E. church.

WILLIAM E. SINGLETON.

Mr. Singleton, who is the present clerk of the United States District Court, deputy in charge of the United States Circuit Court, also circuit court commissioner and custodian of the United States courthouse and post-office at Jefferson, Tex., is a man whose intelligence and sound judgment have placed him in the front ranks of the best men of the state. He was born in Marion County, Mo., in 1835, but comes of an old Virginia family, the history of which is well-known in that state. The family came originally from England and was first represented in this country by two brothers who landed in South Carolina about 16—. One subsequently went to Virginia and from this branch our subject is descended. The great grandfather was an officer in the Revolutionary War. Our subject's grandfather, Minor W. Singleton, was born in the Blue Ridge Mountains of Virginia. He married Miss Anna Barbee and about 1833 moved to Missouri, where he was among the first settlers. His son, Samuel Singleton (father of subject), was born and reared in the "Old Dominion," and moved with his father to Missouri; afterward married Miss Sarah Ann Darr, a native of Kentucky; he was a tiller of the soil for many years. He is a prominent man of his section, has held many responsible positions, but is now retired from the active duties of life and resides quietly in Shelby County. His wife died in January, 1894. Her father, William A. Darr, was a Virginian by birth and bringing up, but when a young man went to Kentucky, where he married a Miss Sarah Brown and moved to Missouri in 1829, settled in Hannibal and resided in Marion County until his death. His wife's brother, Anderson Brown, was captured by the Indians, taken north of the Ohio River, and forced to run the gauntlet. He escaped, and later moved to Missouri, where he became county judge of Marion County, and where he lived, honored and respected, for years. The Brown family was of English origin, but came to America in colonial days. William E. Singleton, the eldest child born to his parents, grew to manhood in Missouri, and lived on a farm until nineteen years of age, when he realized that more schooling was what he needed. He then attended school for two years, teaching during vacations to pay his way, and later went to Howard County, where he taught the higher branches in an academy and in the meantime studied law. Civil War then breaking out, he enlisted in the second company organized in the state, for seven years' state service. He participated in the battles of Booneville, Carthage and Wilson Creek. Mr. Singleton went out as lieutenant, but was soon promoted to the rank of captain of his company. He was captured in the last-named engagement and taken to St. Louis, where he soon escaped and for some time afterward lived in Northeastern Missouri. In 1862 he joined General Clark, crossed the Missouri River on the ice and was soon with his command on Osage River. From there he went to Northeastern Arkansas, and soon participated in the battle of Pea Ridge and after that was with the army in Northern Mississippi. At that time the state troops disbanded and re-organized in the Confederate service. Our subject was commissioned to assist in organizing a regiment in Northeastern Missouri, by General Price; first went to Fort Smith, Ark., and then to Missouri, where he organized three companies in his county (Howard). Following this he became attached to General Poindexter's command and participated in the fights under that commander in Northeastern Missouri. This command was disbanded and in October, 1862, Captain Singleton crossed the Missouri River, going south with 125 men to Yellville, Ark., and traveling night and day. He was taken sick and sent to Shreveport, La., where he was subsequently attached to the ordnance department, in which he remained until the close of the war. Afterward he embarked in merchandising at Marshall, Tex., was elected a member of the first Board of Aldermen of that place after the war, and assisted in organizing the city government. In 1867 he went to Missouri, farmed there for two years, and then returned to Marshall, where he was in business until 1872. At that date he was appointed deputy district clerk and in 1873 took charge of the sheriff's office. Two years later he was elected sheriff, held that position until 1879, and was then elected county commissioner. Previous to that, in 1878, he was appointed deputy United States marshal and served until 1883, when he was appointed to his present

position. In 1890 he was made custodian of public buildings at Jefferson. Captain Singleton has been a member of all republican state conventions for twenty years; has been chairman of this congressional district (fourth) for ten years, and is now chairman of this senatorial district. In the month of September, 1865, he was married by Bishop Marvin to Miss Eliza J. Harris, a native of Tennessee, who came with her father, Dr. T. A. Harris, to Texas when but two years old. This was in 1844 and the doctor settled at Marshall, where he at once engaged in practice. He edited the first paper published in Marshall and became well-known throughout all this country. He had two sons in the Confederate army, and one died in the prison in Chicago. The doctor's death occurred in 1873. Captain and Mrs. Singleton became the parents of seven children, six sons and one daughter: William E., Jr.; Hal; Ellie, wife of F. R. Largent; Earl and Ernest (twins), the latter dying in infancy; Robert and Marvin. Mr. Singleton has been a member of the A. O. U. W. since 1876, an Odd Fellow since 1866 and has filled all the offices. While a resident of Marshall in 1873 during the yellow fever panic epidemic, he was a member of the Howard Association and superintendent of same. He remained in the field through it all. He assisted in organizing the first fire company at Marshall, Tex., was president of the old Salamander company for seven years, organized the fire department of that city, and assisted in organizing the Firemen's Association of the state; has been a continual delegate to that association and one of the vice-presidents for several terms.

THOMAS HENRY MATHIS.

No one who has been at all conversant with the southern coast of Texas for the past twenty-five years can have failed to hear the name of Thomas Henry Mathis. His manly form, well-chiseled features and vigorous step form a fitting index to the volume of his

good deeds. Under any circumstances he must have been prominent, and, indeed, the sequel to this narrative will show that he has
developed a fine character, not under the favor of plain sailing, but
despite the buffetings of Dame Fortune. Such a success as he has
achieved could not have been accidental. Accidents do not occur on
such a colossal scale. He was born in Stewart County, Tenn., July
14, 1834. His parents were James and Isabella Mathis, the former
of whom died in 1864, and the latter in 1876. They were both highly
esteemed for their sterling religious character. Thomas received
his early education in the country schools of Tennessee and Kentucky, and, being reared on a farm, he was taught the value of a
dollar by digging for it early and late. As a boy he was proud to
"hoe his own row," and as a youth to swing his scythe with the foremost. At the age of nineteen he resolved to strive for a higher education, and this marks a turning point in his life, as he was thence-
forth thrown entirely on his own resources. Ardently as his father
longed to encourage his aspirations, he could not do so in justice to
his other children. But nothing daunted, Thomas left the paternal
roof to enter the school of Dr. J. T. Mathis in Southern Arkansas. At
the end of the second session here he negotiated a loan of $1,000
from his father, to be paid back by him, or deducted from the estate
on final settlement of the same. With this aid he continued another session at school. At the expiration of this time he took a
school at Warren, Bradley County, Ark. In conjunction with a lady
teacher, he conducted his school successfully one year, and then went
to Bethel College, where he finished his education in 1857. In 1858
he removed to Murray, Ky., where he assisted Dr. J. T. Mathis in
teaching one session. In 1859 he went to Southwest Texas, where his
career as a business man commenced. His very first enterprise was
fraught with extreme peril, from which men of less courage shrink.
It was on February 3, 1859, that he left Gonzales, Tex., with a party
of eighteen, to make a trading tour into Mexico. Any one familiar
with border troubles and border characters, even at this late day,
can have some conception of the hazards of this trip in the next decade after the Mexican War. On reaching Rio Grande City the
party was informed that it was out of the question to think of crossing over into Mexico, as the country was full of robbers and brigands.

Of the party of eighteen only T. H. Mathis and his cousin, J. M. Mathis, had the nerve to cross the Rio Grande. Two young Alabamians, who were not of the original party, also crossed with them into the kingdom of the Montezumas, together with a Mexican guide. As they lay in camp on San Juan River, at China, the first night after reaching Mexico, the customhouse officer demanded of them a duty of 6 per cent of all their money on the penalty of being imprisoned and having all they had confiscated. They sent their interpreter to tell the officer that they were buying stock in his country, and would leave all their money there; but that if he persisted in demanding the 6 per cent he might come and get it, that there were four of them well armed with shotguns and six-shooters, and that many of the Mexicans would bite the dust in the attempted robbery. It is needless to say that Mathis and his party were left unmolested. They remained in the country six weeks, camping at night and throwing out pickets like a regular army. But for this, they would doubtless have been robbed or murdered. Though this trip was quite successful, it was never deemed prudent to repeat it. After making another business trip to the Texas side of the Rio Grande, Mathis temporarily left the stock business and opened a five-months' school in Gonzales County in the spring of 1861. In the summer of that year he removed to Victoria and extended the scope of his business transactions, but was compelled to close his business in the fall of that year on account of the closing of the gulf ports at the outbreak of the great Civil War. He then went to Kentucky and Tennessee and bought a large lot of tobacco, the price of which was rapidly rising in Texas. He barely succeeded in getting out with his commodity from Paris, Tenn., before the town fell into the hands of the Federal troops. He shipped this tobacco to Alexandria, La., and to it added another lot purchased in New Orleans. Meantime he sold the whole in Texas for $1 a pound, in Confederate money. In the spring and summer of 1862 he was busily engaged in forwarding supplies from Texas to the Confederate soldiers of the Trans-Mississippi department. In the fall of the same year he joined Duff's regiment, Company E, and fought for the Confederacy until the close of the war. He is not ashamed of the cause he espoused, nor of the part he played in it. Yet when the flag of the Confederacy was furled he realized that the war was over indeed. The same magnanimous spirit with which he now treats the "boys who wore the blue" enabled him to speedily forget the bitterness of the struggle, and though with reduced resources to recommence his business career. He again engaged in the tobacco trade between Tennessee and Texas, in which he continued a year. In February, 1867, he settled on Aransas Bay, and selected the site on which the thriving little city of Rockport now stands. The firm of J. M. & T. H. Mathis built the first wharf which was established there, and chartered the first steamship, The Prince Albert, that ever entered Aransas Bay for commercial purposes. After this was lost at sea, they induced the Morgan Line to run their ships to Rockport, and became their agents. This part of our narrative deserves to be emphasized. The subject of this sketch was the founder of Rockport in a sense in which no one else can claim that honor. In 1869 the Mathis firm expended $5,500 for the improvement of the Aransas bar, thus blazing the way, like hardy pioneers, of the future highway of commerce. It was about the same time that they built the Orleans Hotel, and erected a number of other good buildings in Rockport. They also built bridges, made good county roads and aided in securing many other public improvements. Later on, T. H. Mathis contributed liberally toward bringing the Union Telegraph to Rockport, and to the building of the first telephone line to that part of the state. He was also a liberal contributor to the establishment of the first cold storage meat refrigerating plant in Texas. He was also one of the first men in the state to introduce blooded cattle and horses into Southwest Texas, and he is said to possess the banner ranch of his portion of the state, with regard to the quality of his stock. When the Aransas Pass Railroad was built into Rockport in 1888 he was one of the principal promoters of the enterprise, and it is one of the best additions to the city which bears his name. When, in 1872, the firm of J. M. & T. H. Mathis was enlarged to that of Colerman, Mathis & Fulton, again the progressive spirit of the subject of this narrative was felt when the firm of which he was from the beginning a member, built the first large pasture that was ever established in the state. In 1879 this firm was dissolved, and J. M. & T. H. Mathis were the following year again associated in business by themselves. Since that time T. H. Mathis has been doing business on his own account, with the exception of the purchase of a one-half interest in about 24,000 acres of land in Wharton County, which he subsequently sold. He now owns about 24,000 acres of fine agricultural land in San Patricio County, on the Nueces River, well fenced and stocked with fine horses and cattle. On the same estate are several farms, orchards and vineyards. The town of "Mathis" is named for him, and is a portion of his original ranch. The growth of a town so near the body of his ranch cannot fail to appreciate the value of every acre of it. Even at the present low prices of land, this is a princely estate, while its prospective value is very considerable indeed. Mr. Mathis possesses an ordinary fortune, entirely aside from these fine lands. He owns one of the best homes in Rockport, besides thousands of dollars worth of realty in different portions of that city. He is liberally insured, to the amount of $60,000 in old line companies. He is a principal stockholder in the First National Bank of Rockport, of which institution he is also president. Such is an imperfect statement of the material results attending a successful business career. But no correct inventory of Mr. Mathis' wealth can be made that does not include his character as the main part. He has not achieved financial success at the expense of character, as is too often done. He was well-equipped for his career, both by nature and acquirements, and hence had no occasion to resort to dishonest methods. His experience in the school room made an indelible impression on his life. Possibly he would have made as much money without it, but he would not otherwise have held money in as strict subjection to higher ends as he now does. Without such culture he might have been made the slave instead of the master of his large possessions. He impresses one as being a man who was not shut up to run in a narrow groove. There are jets of wit, coruscations of humor, and keen logical observations in his ordinary conversation which show that he would have been a successful literary or professional character had he turned his attention in that direction. His public utterances are as rare as they are weighty. The writer remembers an occasion when hundreds of people from all parts of Texas, and beyond its borders, were assembled at Rockport, to consider matters of great public

weal. Naturally, there was a good deal of "orating," and that too
by professional speakers. Mr. Mathis was called on for a speech
with a unanimity that was irresistible. He arose, and his well
chosen words sped like arrows from a strong bow. There was no
resisting his logic. He made the best speech of the day, though he
sat down entirely unconscious of it. No one ever doubted his convictions. An instance will suffice to show that he is not a man to
count the number of his opponents. A few years since an effort was
made to change "Rockport" to "Aransas Pass." In fact, the name
of the post-office was so changed. This Mr. Mathis resented. There
was no good reason for it, he thought. He threw himself into the
breach, and his influence with the Legislature prevented the change
of the name of the city. Later on, the same influence, exerted in a
different direction, caused the post-office name to be changed back
to "Rockport." This was not a mere triumph of opinion, but it prevented endless confusion among the half-dozen places around the
bay that have appropriated the name "Aransas" in some connection
or other. He is a democrat of the Jefferson-Cleveland type. He is
a ruling elder in the Presbyterian church. Religiously, as otherwise,
his professions are not loud, and need not be. Instead of them, he
presents the broad front of a consistent life, and deeds of constant
benefaction. It would be hard to find a beneficent institution near
him that has not been helped by him or that might not have been
for the mere asking. He was married twice. In 1869 to Mrs. Cora
C. Caldwell of Gonzales County, Tex., who died two months afterward, and in 1875 to his present wife (nee Miss Mary J. Nold), in
Murray, Ky. She was born in Goliad, Tex., July 15, 1856, and educated in Kentucky. Her parents were Henry and Mrs. E. M. Nold.
Her father, an eminent educator, died at Murray, Ky., November 2,
1886. Her mother is still living in Murray. Mr. Mathis is the father
of eight children: Walter N., Henry, May, Thomas E., Edgar, Arthur,
Lizzie Belle and Allie. Until a few months since it was an unbroken
family, when little Allie, aged seventeen months and thirteen days,
was taken from the bosom of the family, demonstrating that "our
life is even a vapor, that appeareth for a little time, and then vanish-
eth away."

JOHN J. HAYTER.

Among the sons of Texas whose energy and thrift have brought him substantial returns and who is now one of the wealthiest and most influential citizens of Nacogdoches County, is John J. Hayter. He was born in this county June 4, 1852, and has resided here all his life. He owns and operates numerous farms in this and adjoining counties, but his duties as a citizen are not neglected and he contributes liberally to all worthy enterprises. The father, Samuel Hayter, was born in Tennessee, and after growing up was married in that state to Miss Elizabeth Finch, who was also a native of Tennessee. William Hayter, grandfather of our subject, together with his son Samuel, moved to Texas as early as 1844, and settled in Nacogdoches County, where he bought large tracts of land, several thousand acres in this and adjoining counties. He and his son located about eight miles from the village of Nacogdoches and there opened up a large farm. Owning a large number of slaves he engaged quite extensively in agricultural pursuits and added greatly to his wealth as the years passed by. On this farm, where he had resided for many years, he received his final summons. Samuel Hayter is the only survivor of his father's family. He succeeded to the estate and possessing much of his father's excellent management, became one of the largest land-owners and successful planters of the state, as well as one of the best known men in Eastern Texas. He is now retired from active business and resides with his son in Nacogdoches. Although seventy-nine years old he is well preserved, both mentally and physically, and is enjoying a happy, contented old age. His wife died in 1876. Like his father our subject is the only son born to his parents, but unlike his father, he has two sisters. One of them married H. H. Rainbolt of Weatherford, Tex., and the other became the wife of Dr. S. H. Barham of this state. In his native county our subject reached mature years and was educated in Clarksville and Gilmer, this state. Like his father and grandfather, he displayed a decided aptitude for agricultural pursuits, and when quite young branched out in that line in Rusk County. Later he took charge of his father's extensive farming interests and has since been at the head of it. As before mentioned he owns a large number of farms in Nacogdoches, Rusk and Angelina counties, and is no doubt the largest land-owner in this county. In the month of October, 1878, Mr. Hayter married Miss Mary Buford Hall, a native of Texas, born, reared and educated in Rusk County, and the daughter of Dr. R. W. Hall, a prominent business man of that county. To Mr. and Mrs. Hayter's union have been born three children: Samuel B., Susie Fay and Robert Hall. For many years Mr. Hayter has been identified with the democratic party and supports the measures and men of that party, but has never aspired for office. In his social relation a Mason and a Knight of Pythias. A lifelong resident of this county, its interests have ever received his closest attention and he has assisted in many ways toward its advancement. He and his most estimable wife are highly esteemed in the community and are foremost in all good work.

COLONEL J. D. BUIE.

The subject of this sketch was born on a farm in Moore County, N. C., October 16, 1834, and his father, Daniel Buie, was also a native of that county and state. The latter reached manhood in that county and was married to Miss Laney Dixon, a native of Franklin County, N. C. Later he began tilling the soil there and became a substantial and prominent citizen. His death occurred in 1880, when about ninety-five years old, and his wife followed him three years later, dying when eighty-three years old. They were the parents of five sons and four daughters, all of whom reached mature years, but only our subject, one brother and two sisters now survive. J. D. Buie passed his youthful days like the average country boy, assisting on the farm and attending the country schools, where he received a fair education, and later in life learned the trade of cooper, carpenter, joiner and millwright. These trades he followed in Moore

County for several years, and was thus engaged when the war broke out. In the year 1864 he enlisted in Company E, Fifth North Carolina Infantry as a private, but served as orderly sergeant most of the time until cessation of hostilities. He participated in the battle of Petersburg, was in the last brigade that left the city, and fired the bridge. In the spring of 1865 he returned to Moore County and followed his trade there up to 1870. In December of that year he moved to Texas, settled in Upshur County and plied his trade there and in adjoining counties for twelve years. His marriage with Miss Fannie Bruner occurred in July, 1882. She was born in Alabama, Butler County, and is the daughter of C. L. Bruner, who settled in Texas about 1874. After his marriage Mr. Buie bought his present farm, 196 acres, to which he soon added twenty-five acres, and he now has seventy-five acres under cultivation. He also owns 320 acres on the east line of the county and of this has about sixty acres under cultivation. He rents his farm and tills the other himself. The colonel commenced life for himself with limited means and all his property is the work of his own honest industry. He has ever been thrifty and persevering and is now classed among the substantial men of the county. In politics he has been identified with the Democratic party for years, but has never cared for office. Mrs. Buie is a member of the ——————— church of Gilmer. Their children, four in number, are named in the order of their births: Laney Belle, John Dixon, Jr., Della Lizzie and Lee Clifton.

SOLOMAN A. SPELLINGS.

The livery trade in Jefferson is well and faithfully represented by the well-known citizen, Soloman A. Spellings, who has secured a secure footing and whose livery stable is most profitably patronized. He has resided in this county since the war and his name is a familiar one throughout this section. His parents, Benjamin Fisher and Louisa (Guest) Spellings, were natives of South Carolina and Tennessee, respectively. The father was reared in Gibson County, Tenn., and following his marriage in that state, moved to Mississippi in 1840, and thence to Texas in 1841. He first settled in Panola County, but later moved to Red River County (now Marion), and settled on a headright twenty miles east of Jefferson, which farm still goes by his name. In 1850 he moved four miles north of Jefferson and died there in February, 1875. He owned a valuable tract of land and was considered a most successful tiller of the soil. When he first came to Texas he was accompanied by his brother, Fred Spellings, and his brother-in-law, Elias Guest, both of whom settled headrights in what is now Marion County. Mrs. Spellings died on February 4, 1895, when seventy-four years old. The original of this notice was born in Tallahatchie County, Miss., in January, 1841, and he was next to the eldest in a family of eleven children. He attended the country schools of Marion County, but left school in January, 1862, and enlisted in Company G, Third Texas Cavalry. Soon after he participated in the battle of Elkhorn, or Pea Ridge, and went from there to Corinth, Miss., after which he operated in Northern Mississippi under Van Dorn. He was then ordered to Vicksburg as body guard for General Maury, but was subsequently captured near that city. This was on December 3, 1863, and he remained a prisoner of war at Rock Island, Ill., until June 22, 1865. July 7th of the same year he came to Jefferson, much to the surprise and joy of his relatives, who thought that he was dead. He soon after engaged in the livery business and has thus been occupied up to the present. He has also been active in real estate transactions. His stable, now the Rink Stable, is one of the best equipped in the state. Mr. Spellings also runs the transfer business and is the owner of much real estate. He was married first in February, 1870, to Miss Carrie Thomas, a native of Texas or Mississippi, who died July, 1876, leaving four children, only two now living: Herbert and Leslie Hartwell. On March 19, 1880, Mr. Spellings married Miss Maud Frazor, a native of Texas, and daughter of George Frazor, who settled here at an early date. One living child has been born to this union, Roy Earle. Mr. Spellings is vice-president of the National Bank of this place and for a time was president of the Mabry Grocery Co. of Jefferson. Mrs. Spellings is an earnest member of the Methodist church.

HON. HERMAN KNITTLE.

It was in the Province of Silesia, of Prussia, in Germany, on the 4th of December, 1835, that the subject of this sketch first saw the light of day, and it was there he resided until seventeen years of age, during which time he secured a good practical education under the compulsory school laws of his native land. With the primary object of making the mercantile trade his vocation, he served a three and one-half years' apprenticeship in a store, thus thoroughly, in his youth, equipping himself with a solid business training. This youthful application, no doubt, is one of the chief causes of his splendid success in later years. Meager opportunities for advancement in his native land led to numerous family discussions as to the advisability of seeking a wider and more favorable field, and these culminated in 1852, when, in company with his mother, he crossed the Atlantic Ocean and came direct to Washington County, Tex. After one year spent with a half brother, who had preceded him to America, Mr. Knittle was induced to purchase a team of oxen and begin teaming and freighting goods to and from the city of Houston, which business he continued uninterruptedly and with a fair degree of success until the breaking out of our great Civil War in 1861. His sympathies being with the seceding states, he disposed of his team, volunteered his services to the Confederate army and was elected lieutenant of a company in the famous legion commanded by General Waul, which did such valiant services for the Southern cause. He was an active participant in the battles of Holly Springs, Grenada, siege of Vicksburg and Yazoo City, at the last named place being captured by the Federal troops and by them taken to Johnson's Island, where he was confined a prisoner of war for a period of eighteen months. Then, being paroled, he returned home and shortly after the close of the war opened a general country store at Berlin, Tex., which he conducted with a fair degree of success until 1871, when he moved to Burton, which has since been his place of residence. He erected at this place a large and commodious business building, stocked it with an excellent selection of merchandise and for some years conducted an extensive retail trade. Then disposing of his store, he spent the succeeding three years in caring for his various farms and in agricultural pursuits and stock raising. He then built a substantial two-story brick structure in Burton and has since conducted one of the largest retail mercantile trades in Washington County. He occupies three rooms on the ground floor of his business house, in one of which is a carefully selected stock of dry goods and clothing; groceries, provisions, glass and queensware fill a second room, while the third room is filled with shelf and heavy hardware. The upper floor of this large house is filled with a large and varied assortment of furniture. The village of Burton, in which this business is conducted, may be small as compared with some of the more populous cities of Texas, but it is surrounded by a fertile country, peopled with intelligent, well-to-do and appreciative residents. It is from this source that Mr. Knittle derives an immense trade. Without question, he is the soul and life of commercial Burton. Besides his mercantile interests, he owns extensive tracts of land, divided up into valuable farms in Washington County, particularly near Burton. Mr. Knittle possesses the methodical manner and close application to business generally a characteristic feature of the German people. His close observation furnishes him the knowledge of the requirements of the public, his careful business training and his keen perception cause him to be a cautious buyer and his honorable and upright business methods with both his customers and those from whom he buys, render to him the universal respect of his fellow men. A poor boy in a foreign land and among strangers, he began his career at the lowest rung of the ladder of life under adverse circumstances. The splendid success he has achieved is particularly noticeable on this account and is not only deserving of the highest praise, but is well worthy of imitation by the rising youth even though he may, at the beginning, be much more fortunately situated. While fortune has smiled so kindly upon the efforts of Mr. Knittle, he has been, by no means, either unthankful or unappreciative. No longer is he a German, but, instead, in every sense of the word, he is an American. As such he is identified with American institutions and is imbued with American ideas. He contributes liberally from his means to the support of the churches, schools, benevolent and charitable enterprises and to all matters tending toward the public weal. As a Democrat in politics, he was appointed by Governor Ross as one of the commissioners to the exposition at Paris, in which capacity he served with credit. As the nominee of his party, he was elected to the State Senate in 1884, and so acceptably did he fill the requirements of this position that he was honored by a renomination and a re-election at the expiration of his first term. Mr. Knittle took rank among the ablest legislators of the state, was a member of various committees, including that on finance, and was chairman of the committee of retrenchment and reform, and of contingent expenses. Both as a public official and as a private citizen, Mr. Knittle's record is without stain or blemish. August 28, 1856, he was married to Miss Jane Henecke, who came to the United States when a child of eight years. To this marriage ten children have been given, viz.: Mrs. Ida Hous, a widow, residing in Burton; Emma, now the wife of Thomas Watson, a well-known merchant of Burton; Herman, Jr., a prosperous farmer of Washington County; Ernest, who is associated in business with his father; Lula, died after attaining womanhood; Rachel, died from an accident after reaching mature years; Alvina, Charles and George, the three last named living at home. Socially, Mr. Knittle was actively identified with the Odd Fellows until the surrender of the charter of the lodge at Burton. In the Masonic fraternity he has been raised to the sublime degree of a Master Mason and exalted to the degree of the Royal Arch; he is a Past Master of the Blue Lodge and a Past High Priest of the Chapter. For nearly half a century he has resided in Washington County, where he is universally known, as well as universally liked.

GENERAL WEBSTER FLANAGHAN.

This distinguished citizen, soldier and statesman was born in Cloverport, Breckinridge County, Ky., January 9, 1832. He is the descendant of a prominent ancestry and the inheritor of a great fam-

ily renown, but beyond this, impelled by his own eminent ability and
high character, and influenced by a most praiseworthy ambition, he
has carved his own statue of fame from the marble of passing years.
His father, James Winright Flanaghan, was a native of Gordonsville,
Albemarle County, Va., where he was born September 5, 1805. In
1815 he was taken by his parents to Boonsboro, Ky., where he grew to
manhood and was meagerly educated. By sheer strength of intellect
and force of will he rose above his surroundings and in time became
one of the most prominent men in that section of the state. He first
engaged in mercantile pursuits and for twelve years served as justice
of the peace. He studied law and was admitted to the bar, and in
1825, at the age of twenty years, moved to Cloverport, Breckinridge
County, where he began the practice of his profession. He at once
took front rank among the lawyers of that district and from 1833 to
1843 practiced with great success, following which, after a short stay
in Harrison County, Ky., he moved to Texas and settled in Henderson,
Rusk County. At that time the town had one grocery and one blacksmith shop. Mr. Flanaghan opened a store of merchandise and soon
became interested in cotton planting. In the new country he was
obliged to do a variety of things. He practiced law and appeared in
the first court held in the county, in 1843, ten miles from Henderson,
in the shade of a large oak. He was sent to the lower house of the
General Assembly in 1851-52 and to the Senate in 1855-56. He was
presidential elector in 1857, delegate to the peace congress in 1861,
member of the constitutional conventions of 1866 and 1868, elected
to Congress in 1869 and the same year elected Lieutenant-Governor.
He was elected as a Republican to the United States Senate in 1870
and served in that capacity until 1875, and was a member of the
committees on postoffices and mines and mining, and chairman of the
committee on education and labor. After the expiration of his term
as United States Senator he retired from active labor, except an
occasional appearance in court, and finally passed away in 1887, having left the imprint of his sturdy qualities, his sound sense and his
great genius written indelibly on the history of his state. He was
an old-line Whig before the formation of the Republican party—one
of that class which, in the South, made the name famous in the great
partisan struggles before the war.

Webster Flanaghan, like his father, is mainly self-educated. Reared amid the self-denials of the border, compelled to forego his thirst for education, forced into the wild and rough practices of a frontier community, he early exercised his courage, hardihood and great natural ability far beyond the confines of his own county. He studied law and was admitted to practice before he had attained his majority, in company with Roger Q. Mills, though it required a special act of the Legislature to accomplish this result. He immediately engaged in the practice of his profession and a little later was appointed district judge by Governor Hamilton, and, though young in years and in the practice, served acceptably as such for two years. After the war had broken out, and after Texas had passed its ordinance of secession, he determined, like many other old-line Whigs of the South, to go with his state, and accordingly announced his adherence to the Confederate cause and was promptly commissioned a brigadier-general. He served with distinction and retired to civil life when the Confederacy collapsed.

In 1865 he was appointed judge of the Fifth Judicial District of Texas. He was a delegate to the constitutional convention of 1868 and was elected to the State Senate in 1869, and served as chairman of the internal improvement committee and as member of other important committees. In 1871 he was elected Lieutenant-Governor of Texas to succeed his father, but resigned in 1873 to take his place again in the State Senate, to which position he had been elected. He was re-elected and was one of the ablest and most influential members of the General Assembly of that period. Soon after this he was appointed internal revenue collector of his district, but was removed by President Cleveland in 1885. During all this time he had been a pronounced Republican in a state and district so heavily Democratic that it is doubtful if any other man of his party could have received a majority of the suffrages. His great ability, eminent character and wonderful popularity carried him through. He was also appointed collector of customs at El Paso, but was again removed by President Cleveland in 1893.

Governor Flanaghan is known to politicians throughout the United States as one of the most adroit political leaders of his party in Texas. He has served his party as a delegate of the state to the Republican national conventions from 1872 to the present time. He was a great admirer of General Grant and his firm supporter for a third term in 1880, when, at the Chicago convention he made his famous speech asking the historic question, "What are we here for?" In 1884 he supported General Arthur at the national convention and by him was appointed collector of internal revenue as above stated. He has in his possession his commission as brigadier-general of Texas militia, signed by Governor Sam Houston, and is justly proud of the document. From 1876 to 1880 he officiated as president of the Henderson & Overton Railroad. He is now much interested in the raising of fine horses and Jersey cattle. He owns about 15,000 acres in Rusk County, divided into twenty farms. He resides in his comfortable home in Henderson.

He has been twice married, first December 20, 1855, to Miss Elizabeth Graham, daughter of Major Graham. She died in 1872, having borne him three sons and three daughters, one of the sons, Dr. Emmet Flanaghan, being a prominent physician of Bethany, Tex. Governor Flanaghan was married again in 1873 to Miss Sallie Ware, daughter of Dr. Levi H. Ware, a lady of brilliant mind and many graceful accomplishments, and a graduate of Holland's Collegiate Institute of Virginia. To this marriage four children have resulted— two sons and two daughters.

Governor Flanaghan is a Knights Templar Mason; a member of the Knights of Honor, of which order he served for two years as Grand Dictator; a member of the Knights of Pythias, of which he served as Supreme Deputy; a member of the Independent Order of Odd Fellows, and himself and wife are active members of the Baptist Church. He is a man of strong and attractive personality, a fine and brilliant conversationalist, an eloquent speaker and a charming companion.

A. S. FIELD.

The gentleman whose name heads this sketch is a good example of the public servant, for he is faithful to every duty, is accurate, painstaking and honorable, and is also genial and accommodating. He

→BATTLE OF←

MURFREESBORO.

SCALE

1   ¾   ½   ¼   0   1 M.

has not only rendered this county valuable service as a public official, but as an industrious farmer and law-abiding citizen. Like many of the prominent men of this section, Mr. Field is a native of Tennessee, born in the year 1833, and the youngest of three children born to Robert and Fannie (Jones) Field, both natives of Virginia. The paternal grandfather, Dr. Aléxander S. Fields, was born in Virginia and was of Scotch parentage. He received his medical education in Scotland, where he resided for fourteen years, and was married on a British man-of-war on the Virginia Coast. For years he was quite active in political matters and became high sheriff of his county. The maternal grandparents were of Welsh descent and this family settled in America in colonial days. Robert Field grew to mature years in Virginia, married there, and then, at an early day, removed to Tennessee at a time when Indians were plentiful. In the year 1838 he crossed the Mississippi River into Texas and, settling on a location in Shelby County (now Harrison), sent for his family the following year. He became an extensive land and slave owner and became very comfortably situated. Although a very active Whig in politics, he was no office-seeker. He and his wife both passed away in 1840. They were members of the Presbyterian Church, and Mr. Field was a member of the Masonic fraternity. Our subject grew to manhood in Texas, and, in addition to a fair education received in Marshall, that state, entered the school at Princeton, N. J., from which he graduated in 1852. Afterward he began life as a farmer in Harrison County and continued this faithfully until April, 1861, when he enlisted as a scout and went to Arkansas. His brother was quartermaster of the regiment and promoted to brigadier quartermaster, after which our subject took the position of quartermaster. Still later the latter was detailed as purchasing agent for the Confederacy, buying supplies and cotton, and was thus occupied when the war closed. Since then Mr. Field has been engaged for the most part in looking after his large farm, but in 1879 he was elected to the position of city collector and held that until 1880. In 1881 he was elected to his present office. He and wife are members of the Baptist Church, and he is a member of the A. O. U. W. and K. of H. and has held office in both. In the year 1855 he married Miss Laura Lewis, daughter of Dr. Lewis of Georgia, and five children have been given them, four sons and a daughter.

MAJOR ELIJAH PENNINGTON.

After many years of practical and successful industry, and after a long life spent in the discharge of honorable duty to society and the commonwealth, Major Pennington is passing the evening of his life in the peace of retirement. The state and county first knew him in 1838. He was then a young man, aged nineteen years, and had come to the West from his Indiana home (where he was born in Crawford County June 1, 1819) to seek his fortune in the wilds of the Texan Republic and to assist her in maintaining her independence already secured through the medium of the rifle ball and bloody sword. His father was Riggs Pennington, a native of Kentucky, and his mother, formerly Joanna Osborn, was a native of North Carolina, and both were people of more than ordinary worth and prominence. In 1819 they moved to Franklin County, Ill., and were among the earliest settlers of that portion of the state. Four years later they moved to Schuyler County, two years later to McDonough County and two years later to Knox County, where they made their home for ten years. At the end of this time he had 1,300 acres and considerable personal property. He sold all and in 1837 moved to Texas and a year later located in Washington County, where he bought 1,350 acres and at once began farming on an extensive and profitable scale. He amassed considerable wealth, made life a triumph of honor and industry, and finally died in 1870 at the advanced age of eighty-four years, respected by an immense circle of friends, many of whom had shared with him the hardships of the pioneers and witnessed his growth in the esteem of his fellow citizens. Early in life he was a participant in the Black Hawk War while a resident of Illinois. He also served as commissioner of Knox County, Ill., the first after the creation of that office, and assisted to lay out and plat the county seat at Knoxville. His wife survived him about two years, passing from life in 1872. They were the parents of eight sons and four daughters, of whom the subject of this sketch was the fifth in order of birth. All the members of this large family grew to maturity, though three brothers and two sisters are now (1895) the only survivors. Major Elijah Pennington grew to the age of eighteen years in Illinois, receiving a fair education in the common schools, and in 1837 came to Texas with his father and assisted him to open up the old homestead. He participated in the closing scenes of the war between Texas and Mexico, notably the Summerville and other campaigns, and has in store many interesting reminiscences of those troublous times. He located on a place near the old homestead and engaged in farming and stock raising and soon had around him several hundred head of cattle, sheep and horses, and carried on farming very extensively. He continued to grow in wealth and prominence, leading a busy, useful and creditable life, and rearing his family to be exemplary citizens until, finally, the great Civil War came on to ruin prosperity and antagonize friends and neighbors. In August, 1861, he joined the militia of the state and was soon serving the Confederacy with his usual ardor, fidelity and effectiveness. He thus continued until the war ended and then came back to the farm and once more to peaceful pursuits. He operated the farm until 1876, when he moved to Brenham and conducted a hotel for several years, still continuing to operate the farm. Later he bought a private residence in the city, where he lived a few years, and in 1893 bought his present property, which he has greatly improved. In 1845 Major Pennington was united in marriage to Miss Ellen McCallister, a native of Arkansas, the nuptials being celebrated at Hot Springs, that state. Mrs. Pennington is the daughter of Richard McCallister, a native of Kentucky, and there are now living by this union five sons, as follows: Riggs, a farmer of Johnson County; Asa, conducting a hotel in Brenham; John, a farmer of this county; Joseph, resides at home, engaged in farming and stock raising, and R. E., a prominent lawyer of Brenham. Three daughters were also born to this marriage: Matilda, who grew up, married, and died early in life; Julia, deceased at eight years of age, and Lydia, who died when in her ninth year. The parents, now well advanced in years, are pleasantly passing their time, often visiting one of the many health resorts of the United States, notably among which is the one at Hot Springs, Ark. Major Pennington is a Democrat, a firm friend and advocate of temperance, and is universally respected for his sterling qualities and his blameless life. Mrs. Pennington is a member of the Baptist Church. The family is one of the best in Texas.

C. G. BURNETT.

The business of the merchant is not only one that may be the road to success, but, what is better, in this country certainly, it is one of the most honorable of avocations and those engaged in it are, as a class, composed of the very ablest and brightest of the land. In the list of worthy and honorable business men of Henderson, Tex., that of C. G. Burnett appears as one in every way entitled to the confidence and esteem of his fellow-citizens. Since the year 1856 he has been a resident of this county and for twenty-five years has been engaged in merchandising in Henderson. He affords in his life and its success another evidence that industry, economy and integrity constitute the keynote to honorable competency. A native of Kentucky, born in Cloverport, Breckinridge County, March 14, 1831, Mr. Burnett is a son of James and Louisa Ann (Flanagan) Burnett. The father was born in Virginia, and after reaching manhood went to Kentucky and located at Frankfort, where he was an early settler. He was married in this state to Miss Flanagan, a daughter of Charles Flanagan, and a sister of Major J. W. Flanagan, who was one of the colonial settlers of Rusk County, Tex. Mr. Burnett had learned the tanner's trade during his youth and after his marriage followed it for years. About the year 1845 he moved to Illinois and followed his trade in Fulton County for a number of years. In 1858 he moved to Texas and located in Rusk County. Here he started a tannery in Henderson and was actively engaged in this business for many years. During the latter part of his life he retired from its active duties, and died when seventy-eight years old. His wife had died in 1859, soon after locating in Rusk County. C. G. Burnett was the only son in a family of five children born to his parents, and only two of these besides our subject are living at the present time. He received his schooling in Kentucky and Fulton County, Ill., but is mainly self-educated, having by his own exertions acquired a wide range of knowledge and a polish that would have done credit to a graduate of any university. In 1856 Mr. Burnett came to Henderson, Tex., and engaged in business here, where he was one of the oldest settlers. While a resident of Illinois he had learned the carpenter's trade and after locating in Henderson he followed contracting and building for years. In 1859 he erected a planing mill, put in machinery, and manufactured doors, sashes, blinds, etc., and carried on an extensive business. In February, 1862, he enlisted in the Confederate army, Seventeenth Texas Mounted Regiment, and this was later re-organized into the Seventeenth, under Colonel Taylor. He served until discharged for disability in 1864, and returned home broken in health and unable to work. It was three years before he could resume his business interests, and during that time, in 1864, his property was destroyed by fire and as he had no insurance it was a complete loss. Immediately afterward he rebuilt and resumed his former business up to 1866. At that time he embarked in mercantile pursuits and was thus engaged up to 1879, when he closed out and afterward was engaged in the furniture and undertaking business. He erected the business house that he now occupies, and has been carrying on business in it for twenty-five years. He has a good stock of furniture, undertaking goods, etc., and also deals in sash, doors, blinds, carpenter's tools, glass, etc. Mr. Burnett has built up a good trade and has established an enviable reputation for reliable goods and fair dealing. Few men have lived more quietly or unostentatiously than he, and yet few have exerted a more salutary influence upon the immediate society in which they move, or impressed a community with a more profound reliance on their honor, ability and sterling worth. Politically Mr. Burnet is independent and casts his vote for the man irrespective of party. He was appointed postmaster at Henderson in 1873 and served in that position up to February, 1886, fourteen consecutive years. On May 15, 1860, Mr. Burnett married Miss Sarah Jane Johnston, a daughter of Jacob N. Johnston and a native of Mississippi Two children blessed this union: Eleanor, wife of J. W. Kerr, a prominent business man of St. Louis, Mo., and Katie, wife of E. W. Vinson of Henderson.   Mr. Burnett lost his wife November 2, 1893.   He is an active member of the M. E. church.   For many years he has been a member of the I. O. O. F., is Past Grand, and has represented his lodge in the Grand Lodge of the state, first in 1873, again in 1894.   He is also a member of the A. O. U. W. and Chosen Friends.

ALBERT H. ROWELL.

A descendant of good old Virginia stock, Albert H. Rowell inherited the fundamental principles of industry, integrity and determination which became the attributes of his whole after life.   His ancestors came from England to Virginia in colonial times and his grandfather, George Rowell, was a native of that state.   The latter's son, Howell Rowell, was born in Greenville County, that state, and grew to manhood there.   About 1820 he married Elizabeth Walton, also a native of Greenville County, Va., and the daughter of Isaac Walton, who was of English origin, but a native of Virginia.   Three months after the birth of our subject, which occurred in Virginia in 1821 to the marriage of Howell and Elizabeth Rowell, this young couple moved to Alabama, and settled on the present site of the city of Montgomery, in Montgomery County.   This family was one of several from Virginia that settled in the then new and sparsely settled state, and Mr. Rowell as well as the others made a complete success of farming this new land.   About 1838 he moved with his family to Tallapoosa County, Ala., and there he and his wife both passed away.   Albert H. Rowell was reared and educated in Montgomery County, Ala., and in 1842 moved to Tallapoosa County, where he served as sheriff of that county for three years.   In 1845 he married Miss Tobitha Driskell of Macon County, and afterwards settled near Tuskegee, Ala., where he followed farming until 1865.   During the war he was detailed as county commissioner, to care for the soldiers' widows and orphans, and acted in that capacity all through that trying period and one year longer under General Moore, Federal officer. In 1866 he came to the Lone Star State and first settled in Harrison County, but the following year came to Jefferson, where he has since resided. He is an active Democrat in politics, but is not an office-seeker. For years he has been one of the largest cotton buyers on the market and is a man of unusual good judgment and business acumen. He had nine children: Robert, Mary, widow of Jasper Lawrence; P. H., a lawyer of Ennis; Ella, wife of A. M. Grambling of Dallas; Emma, deceased; Eugenie; Mattie, wife of Mr. Grigsby; Albert, and Willie I. (a daughter). Prior to the war Mr. Rowell was an ardent Whig in politics, and opposed secession, but later when he found that of no use, gave his heart and means to further the Southern cause. His first presidential vote was for Henry Clay. Mr. Rowell was made a Mason in 1848, and the members of the family are active workers in the M. E. church.

CHARLES COBB, JR.

Ability, when backed by enterprising business measures and progressive ideas, will accomplish more than any other professional requirement. An illustration of this is found in the career of Charles Cobb, Jr., the capable secretary and treasurer of the Marshall Car Wheel and Foundry Co. of Marshall, Tex. He was born in the year 1867, in Louisville, Ky., a state in which his parents, Charles and Ellen (Monks) Cobb, first saw the light of day also. His paternal grandfather was a very prominent man and physician and for many years was president of the Louisville Medical College. The maternal grandfather, Joseph Monks, was a native of Louisville, Ky., and one of the foremost business men of that place. He was president of the Louisville Insurance Company and was well-known throughout the state. His father was a relative of Daniel Boone. During his youth our subject attended the public schools of Louisville and fin-

ished his education at the Brooklyn Polytechnic Institute. Soon
after he secured an appointment in the United States Signal Service
in Brooklyn and served' one year on the engineer corps. He then
resigned and came to Marshall, Tex., where he has since been engaged
in the foundry business. The institution with which he is now connected as secretary and treasurer is the largest in the Southwest
and manufactures car wheels mainly. The products are shipped all
through the West and South and over 100 men are employed. Mr.
Cobb is the principal stockholder in the Marshall Building and Loan
Association, and he is also interested in other associations. He was
one of the projectors and builders of the Marshall Street Railway
Company during 1886 and 1888, and has ever been among the first
to advance and advocate measures relating to the progress and development of Marshall and Harrison County. One of the leading
business men, as well as one of the youngest, he is rated as a gentleman of untrammeled honor and in all of his transactions is looked
upon with the utmost popular regard. Mr. Cobb married Miss Sophia
Fry in 1890, and they have two children: Helen Louisa and Charles
Cobb, Jr. Mrs. Cobb's father is E. J. Fry, one of the leading merchants and bankers of Marshall. She is the great-great-granddaugh-
ter of Colonel Fry of Revolutionary fame, and who commanded a
regiment in which George Washington was major.

JAMES L. FORD

This able attorney has his office at Jefferson, Tex., and in every
branch of his profession he is meeting with marked success. He
has a decided veneration for the law, and this, combined with the
accuracy of his legal knowledge, lucidity of statement and felicity of
illustration, has given him the confidence of all his patrons. He is
a native son of Marion County, born in the sixties, and a son of
John V. and Eliza J. (White) Ford, both natives of Alabama. The
paternal grandfather, Dr. William H. Ford, was born in Old Vir-

ginia, but was educated and studied medicine in Europe as well as the United States. He began practicing at Richmond, Va., but subsequently moved to Alabama, where he was one of the leading physicians of his time, and where he spent the remainder of his days. Our subject's maternal grandfather, James S. White, was born in Georgia. In early life he moved to Texas and settled in Morris County, where he remained until 1861, after which he made his home in Marion County until his death in 1879. The Ford family is of English and the Whites of Welsh origin. The father of our subject came to Texas in 1857 and settled in Marion County, where he bought large tracts of land to keep employed the negroes he had brought from Alabama. He married Miss White at about the beginning of the war and although he did not take part in that struggle, he contributed largely to the Confederate cause. Later he erected a fine home in Jefferson and there died in 1878. Mrs. Ford is still living. Of their three children, our subject is the second in order of birth. The eldest son, William H., resides at Fairland, Indian Territory, and is a successful physician. Our subject was educated at Vanderbilt University, Nashville, Tenn., and after taking his degree in 1889, immediately entered upon his practice at Jefferson. He has been connected with some important cases and has conducted them with dignity, ability and discretion. He has a good general practice and is a man of unquestioned integrity. The youngest son, John V. Ford, also resides at Fairland, Indian Territory, and is a druggist.

WILLIAM M'FADDEN.

Of the early pioneers of Texas who braved the perils and hardships of frontier life, and who laid the foundation for the blessings the present generation enjoys, but few are now remaining. Occasionally one of these old frontiersmen is met who has survived the storms and ravages of Time, but his silvery locks and his faltering footsteps tells us that ere long he will lie down "within that tent whose curtain never outward swings." In no way can the present generation honor so well these heroes of the olden time as by imitating their virtues and preserving inviolate the blessings guaranteed unto us in the civil, religious and educational institutions founded and fostered by their wisdom and self-sacrifice. Early in the year 1833 but four white men resided within the present boundaries of what is now Jefferson County. At that time Indians were far more prevalent than white men; domestic animals were much less numerous than were the deer, bear, wild turkey and panther, while farming, at the best, could only be conducted under adverse circumstances. William McFadden, the subject of this sketch, was one of these four white men, and it was under such conditions that he established his present home which, at this time, adjoins the corporate limits of the city of Beaumont. Mr. McFadden dates the time of his residence in Texas since the year 1823—a period of nearly three-quarters of a century—seventy-two years. Born June 8, 1819, at Lake Charles, La., he is a son of James and Elizabeth (Mackey) McFadden, who were natives of Tennessee and South Carolina respectively. The father was a soldier of the War of 1815 and a participant in the battle of New Orleans. At a very early date he settled at Lake Charles, La., but in 1823 moved to Texas and opened up a farm in Liberty County, where he resided a number of years. He died an honored and respected man, at Natchitoches, La., in 1846. The mother, a pioneer with her husband, survived his death a number of years. When a lad of but four years William McFadden came with his parents to Texas and here participated in much of the toil and privation incident to frontier life. Beginning life's battle at the age of fourteen he followed various callings, mostly farming, until the struggle for Texan independence. His spirit of patriotism was aroused and, offering his services to General Sam Houston, was accepted and with a company of about 900 served on detached duty, guarding the sick and supplies at Harrisburg. For his faithful services he was rewarded by two tracts of land, one containing 320 acres, the other 640 acres. Naturally industrious, Mr. McFadden found no time to idle. His motto seemed to be hard work and unswerving honesty. He turned his attention to stock-raising. So successful was he in the avocation of this industry that he now owns 50,000 acres in Jefferson County, 950 acres in Liberty County and enough in other localities to make his landed interests amount to over 50,000 acres. His property was not accumulated all at one time, but is the result of gradual increase from time to time. In every sense of the word Mr. McFadden is a self-made man. Not only is he one of the wealthy men of the state, but his conduct through life has been of such exemplary character that he commands universal respect. Now in the evening of his life, at the age of seventy-six years, he is as hale and hearty as most of men a score of years younger. This no doubt is a direct result of his temperate life and the many hours spent in outdoor work. It is a rare occurrence when he is not on a horse looking after some of his interests by 7 o'clock in the morning. A great lover of the chase his advanced age in no wise prevents his embarking on hunting expeditions. It was on August 24, 1837, that he married Miss Rachel Williams, the daughter of another Texan pioneer, Hezekiah Williams. There are six living children the result of this union, viz.: James A. of Victoria County; Sarah A., wife of M. C. Alexander of Beaumont; David H. of Victoria County; Di, the wife of W. C. Averell; W. P. H. of Beaumont, and C.W., who resides on the old homestead. All are married and have families except David H. Three children have died: Drusilla, who married A. D. Kent; Andrew, killed during the great Civil War, and Elizabeth, the wife of Mr. Coward. Mr. McFadden is one of the conspicuous figures of the Lone Star State. He located within its borders when it was yet a part of Mexico, he fought for her independence, and he has lived to see it one of the most prosperous states in the Union. He fitly represents one of the true gentlemen of the South. Courteous in his bearing, sympathetic in his association with mankind, a generous contributor to all laudable public enterprises, his friends are legion. He appears to the best advantage at his home, where he and his estimable wife dispense hospitality of the most acceptable kind. Mr. McFadden will be remembered for his many kindnesses and acts of charity long after he has obeyed the final summons: "Well done, thou good and faithful servant."

DR. THOMAS H. STALLCUP.

He whose name heads this sketch has built up a large practice
by steady devotion to duty and the constant exercise of energy and
judgment, and, though he belongs to the younger class of physicians,
he has already made an excellent reputation for himself in this most
honorable, if laborious, line of human endeavor. The doctor was
born in Marion County, Tex., in 1851, and was the third in order of
birth of four children born, to William and Betsey (McAdor) Stallcup,
both natives of Tennessee. Isaac Stallcup, the paternal grandfather,
was born in North Carolina, but at an early date moved to Tennessee. In the latter state the doctor's maternal grandfather, Evans
McAdor, lived for many years, but went from there to Texas and
thence to Louisiana, where he died. He was a lifelong farmer. William Stallcup, father of our subject, moved to Texas in 1837, and first
located at Clarksville, where he soon, with other early settlers, engaged in expeditions against the Indians. In those days the early
settlers lived for the most part on game brought in from the forest,
clothing was made from skins, and few luxuries were to be had.
Later Mr. Stallcup engaged in overseeing on Red River, continued
this for about twenty years and then located on a farm in Marion
County, where the closing scenes of his life were passed. His death
occurred in 1889. He served for a term in the Confederate army,
and was in active service in Louisiana until discharged on account
of ill health. The mother is still living. Dr. Thomas H. Stallcup
was educated in Gilmer, Tex., and Fayetteville, Ark., and subsequently began studying medicine with Dr. W. L. Wynne. Going to
Louisville, Ky., he entered Hospital Medical College, from which
institution he was graduated in March, 1877. Following this he immediately began practicing at his old home in Marion County and
in 1890 moved to Jefferson, where his reputation as a first-class
physician was already well known. During 1893 he attended a post-
graduate course in New Orleans. The doctor is a member of the

Northeastern Texas Medical Society, the Texas State Medical Association, and also a member of the examining board of the fifth judicial district. He frequently contributes important articles on medical subjects to the papers, and is well-posted on all that relates to his profession. He selected his wife in Miss Sallie Gray Durrum, a native of Texas, and their marriage took place in 1879. Her parents, Dr. J. C. and Sarah H. Durram, were early settlers of Marion County. To the doctor's union have been born three children: Mary Gray, Sallie Irby, and Tommie Hardin (a daughter). Our subject was made a Mason at Monterey, La., and is now a member of Jefferson Lodge. The family hold membership in the Cumberland Presbyterian Church.

HON. NATHAN E. DEVER.

A native of the Lone Star State and of Washington County, the subject of this sketch was born August 2, 1841, and is one of the prominent and representative farmers and stock-raisers of this portion of the state. William Dever, his father, was born in Tennessee in 1804, and when a young man of seventeen years came to Texas and first settled at San Felipe, where he resided a number of years, then came to Washington County in October, 1834, opened up a large farm and engaged in agricultural pursuits. He was not only one of the early Texan pioneers, but was one of the first to settle within the present confines of Washington County. Here he reared his family and passed the remainder of his days, his death occurring in 1871. He was a man admirably fitted for the trials of pioneer life, had an indomitable spirit and the true grit of the frontiersman, and was one of the brave men who fought for Texan independence against Mexico. Captain Nathan E. Dever is the second in order of birth in a family of two sons and three daughters, all of whom are living and all of whom grew to mature years. Washington County was his birthplace and Washington County has always been his home. His educational advantages were limited to the common schools. When war was declared against the seceding states in 1861, Captain Dever tendered his services to the Confederacy and becoming a member of the Twenty-first Cavalry, served faithfully in Texas, Louisiana and Missouri until peace was declared. Returning to his home he located on a tract of land near Brenham, which he began improving and raising and trading stock. In May, 1870, he was united in marriage with Miss R. H. Foster, a native of Wharton County, Tex., and a daughter of John Foster, one of the honored first settlers of this state who fought for freedom under General Sam Houston. Family tradition is authority for the statement that Mrs. Dever's two uncles, Cyrus and Hiram Campbell, forged the manacles that bound General Santa Anna, the noted Mexican, after his capture. After his marriage Captain N. E. Dever purchased a tract of over 300 acres of land, where he now resides, two miles south of Brenham, and this he has improved until he has one of the best farms in the county. Aside from his farming interests Captain Dever is extensively engaged in raising and trading stock, at which he has been unusually successful. Beginning life a poor man, empty-handed and with no assistance, he has, by his own efforts and enterprise, accumulated a comfortable home and a valuable estate. A Democrat in politics, Captain Dever has been active in promoting the best interests of his party. In 1884 he was elected to the office of sheriff of Washington County, and so satisfactorily did he fill the requirements of this office that he was twice re-elected, serving three terms in all. In 1892 he was the nominee of his party to represent his county in the lower house of the State Legislature, and in the fall of that year was duly elected, serving with honorable distinction and acting as a member of some of the most important committees. To Captain and Mrs. Dever five children have been born, only two of whom, Frank and Mary, attending the city schools of Brenham, are now living. The oldest child, John, died when eighteen months old, and the other two, Walter and Nathan, died in 1886, aged sixteen and fourteen years respectively. The parents are members of the Methodist Episcopal church, and are among the foremost citizens of Texas.

WILLIAM WATSON.

This gentleman is one of the most prominent and successful horticulturists in the state and resides about two miles southeast of Brenham, where he is extensively engaged in propagating all kinds of nursery stock such as fruit trees, ornamental trees and shrubbery, roses, small plants, etc. On his 200 acres of choice land are grown on an extensive scale all the varieties that flourish in this climate. When it is considered that his entire farm of 200 acres is devoted to this business, the extent of his labors and trade will be better understood. His busy life here, filled with activity and industry, his steady advancement from small beginnings to a large and profitable trade, his pure life and refined and hospitable manners—all bear food for useful reflection. He came here to live in 1859 and first located in Brenham when the place was a small village. He soon bought a few acres and began his present business, which he soon carried to profitable results. As his trade thrived and larger demands were made upon him, he bought additional land and increased his stock. From year to year tracts of adjoining land were added until his farm reached its present large size. He removed from Brenham to this place in 1869, and here he has since resided. His farm is under a high degree of cultivation and for its size is one of the most valuable in Washington County. On this place he built a large two-story frame residence, besides the necessary outbuildings for the care and storage of his stock and tenement houses, etc. His large and profitable trade is due almost wholly to his energetic and enterprising business methods and extends all over the state and over much of Louisiana. Mr. Watson was born in Ireland March 21, 1831, of English parents, his father being William Watson, Sr., who was a native of England, where he was reared and fitted for life with a good education. The father established himself in Ireland and engaged extensively in the raising of stock and became prominent in his locality for his industry and usefulness. There the last years of his life were spent. The subject of this sketch, when a lad of twelve years, left home and went to sea on a ship of which his cousin was the captain. On this vessel he remained two years, and later visited all the great cities and capitals of Europe, from Copenhagen to Constantinople, and gaining a great insight into its varied civilization. He often visited the United States and crossed the Atlantic Ocean twenty-one times. He has resided in New York city, Wheeling, W. Va.; Louisville, Ky.; St. Louis, Mo., and a short time in Minnesota. He finally located in Brenham in 1859. He has been twice married—first in England, by which union he has four children living. Sometime after the death of his first wife he married an Alabama lady, who has presented him with seven children. These six sons are all living: The eldest, William Edward Watson, resides in San Antonio, Tex.; D. H. Watson, another son, is an extensive fruit and truck grower of this county; another son, A. W. Watson, is a merchant, farmer and ginner of this county; Arthur O., a prominent architect, resides in Austin; John P. Watson, another son, is a graduate of the State University, and is in partnership with his father in the nursery business; Stanley Watson is a young man living at home. They are all honest and deserving, and a credit to their sturdy progenitor. The parents are active members of the Episcopal church. Mr. Watson is largely self-educated, takes great interest in educational matters and gave all his children superior schooling advantages. He surrounded them with moral influences and educational facilities and at the present time is the possessor of one of the largest and most select private libraries in the state, consisting of about 4,000 volumes. No family under such influences could grow up in either ignorance or depravity. The shelves of good books from the burning pens of the world's greatest authors spoke constantly, not only to the parents, but to the active and developing minds of the children. The result was scholarship, refinement, morality and usefulness. Mr. Watson himself is a great reader and a sound reasoner. During the Civil War he assisted the Confederacy, joining in 1862 the Sixteenth Texas Infantry, and during the greater part of the period of his enlistment served on detached duty. He is one of Washington County's best citizens.

LOUIS WEBSTER.

Industry, sobriety and economy are the words that present themselves to the conservative mind when the question is propounded as to what essentials are necessary to a man's success in any ordinary undertaking. These essentials, together with others equally as important, are found in the person of our subject, Louis Webster, who is the most efficient clerk of the district court of Marion County. His parents, J. B. and Mary (Steele) Webster, were natives of Alabama and Virginia respectively. The paternal grandfather, J. J. Webster, was a Virginian by birth and an early settler of Texas, locating in the eastern part of Harrison County in the thirties. He followed farming there among the Indians, and was an influential man. The maternal grandfather, William Steele, was an early settler of Louisiana, and located on land that a later survey threw into the state of Texas. J. B. Webster, father of our subject, came to Texas with his parents in 1837, and subsequently engaged in farming and merchandising at Port Caddo. His death occurred in 1862 and he was followed to the grave by his wife in 1873. Their family consisted of nine children, of whom our subject, who was born in 1858, was sixth in order of birth. Young Webster secured a fair share of knowledge in the schools of Knoxville, Tenn., and then, following in the footsteps of his father, began tilling the soil. In 1888 he moved to Marion County, settled in Jefferson, and was the originator and builder of the Jefferson Woolen Mills, which he conducted successfully for a year and a half. He then organized it into a stock company as the Jefferson Woolen Mills Company, and became manager of the same. Mr. Webster was connected with this until it closed. For two years he served as city secretary and treasurer, and in 1894 was elected to his present position, which he has filled in a very satisfactory manner since. He has ever taken a deep interest in political matters, has been a delegate to conventions and has often served on committees. In the year 1880 he wedded Miss Tralucia Rives, a native of Marion County, Tex., and daughter of William Rives, of Alabama. Two children have been given them: Louis, Jr., and Lyda May. Mr. Webster is a Mason, and a prominent member of the Cumberland Presbyterian Church.

RISON D. GRIBBLE.

Risdon D. Gribble, son of Joseph B. and Margaret (James) Gribble, was born on a farm near Pittsburgh, Pa., on April 26, 1836. His parents were natives of Devonshire, England, and came to America with their family in 1831, and settling in Pennsylvania remained until 1848, when they went to New Orleans. Young Gribble received his earlier education in the district schools of the Keystone State, but as the school terms were of but about three months' duration each year his advantages did not amount to much until after the family located in New Orleans, where he took advantage of its excellent school system and completed his education. In the summer of 1849 he secured employment in a cotton factor's office and began to earn his own livelihood. He afterward held positions with other firms, each time bettering his condition, until 1853, when he secured a good position with a large commission house, with whom he remained in different capacities until 1870. The firm then established him in the banking business in Jefferson, Tex., where he had gone to represent them. In 1873 he was elected president of the Citizens Bank of Jefferson, from which position he resigned in 1879, owing to the restriction of business caused by the building of railroads. After leaving Jefferson he located in Gainesville, Tex., where, with Captain O. T. Lyon, he entered the lumber business under the firm name of Lyon & Gribble, and under which title the business is still carried on. It has increased to an enormous extent, with branch offices in many of the better towns of the Lone Star State, as well as the large sash and door factory at Houston, conducted under the firm name of R. D. Gribble & Co. Besides his lumber business, Mr. Gribble has been and is connected with many enterprises of both public and private character. He has been in both Jefferson and Gainesville president of different building and loan associations, which have done much toward helping people to own their own homes. At the present time he is the president of the Hesperian Building and Loan Association at Gainesville, Tex., and president of the Texas Lumberman's Association, having held this office for six consecutive years.

In June, 1890, when the United Association of Lumbermen was organized in Chicago, Mr. Gribble was elected president of the association, was re-elected in 1891, and was offered another re-election in 1892, but declined the honor and named as his successor Mr. Joseph Weaver of Ohio.

DR. T. O. HYNES.

In all the realm of business there has been no happier development than in that department which deals with the sick. For hundreds of years it was so much a terra incognita that, from a scientific view-point, the profession was supposed to be given over to all sorts of hippogriffs and hobgoblins and the poor victim was set aside to be practiced upon by necromancers and charlatans from whom he often suffered untold tortures to drive out the evil spirit, and nearly as often death in place of intelligent care and scientific treatment. Fortunately for later generations this condition attracted the attention of some of the ablest men of the time, and from these by gradations, the present practice and care of the ill has evolved. Among those who have taken rank among the ablest and most skillful physicians of Texas is Dr. T. O. Hynes of Brenham. This gentleman is a native of Bladen County, N. C., his birth occurring September 7, 1828, a son of Thomas and Amy (Swindall) Hynes. The father followed the carriage-maker's trade and planting, moved to Catahoula Parish, La., in 1848, there embarked in mercantile pursuits and there died in 1863. His widow afterward moved to Texas and died in Burton in 1871. Dr. Hynes is one of two sons and five daughters, all living to years of maturity and of whom one son and four daughters still live. Although receiving but little educational opportunities, he took advantage of such as were presented until he not only acquired an excellent knowledge of the commoner branches of learning, but some of the higher ones as well. Selecting pathology as his vocation he read medicine under able tutors, took his first course of

lectures at the University of Louisiana in 1856-57, was appointed
interne at the hospital during the summer vacation and graduated
with honors in the class of 1858. Beginning the practice of his profession at Harrisonburg, La., he succeeded in building up a good
practice when grim war enshrouded our land in her sable folds. In
1861 he enlisted as a private in the Seventeenth Louisiana Infantry,
was elected lieutenant upon the organization of his company, and
participated in all the movements of his command up to and including
the battle of Shiloh. In the thick of this sanguinary conflict Dr.
Hynes received such a severe wound in the left arm as to necessitate
amputation on the field of battle. This occurred during the middle
of the afternoon on April 6th, immediately following the fall of the
gallant General Albert Sidney Johnston, while Dr. Hynes was leading his company in a desperate charge on a battery of the enemy.
From the result of this wound the disciple of Esculapius no longer
became a devotee of Mars, and of necessity Dr. Hynes was compelled
to remain idle during the remainder of the war, although his heart
was still with the army of the Confederacy. An incident in his military career which culminated nearly thirty years after the ending
of the great fratricidal strife, is well worthy of being related: When
the amputation of his arm was decided upon, his scabbard, attached
to his belt and containing a valuable sword on which his name was
engraved, was removed and in so doing the sword and scabbard all
were lost. Thirty-one years later the doctor read an account of the
finding of this sword, in the Atlanta "Constitution," on the battlefield by a Federal soldier, who had retained it as a souvenir. Dr.
Hynes opened a correspondence with the finder, S. F. Blythe of Hood
River, Ore., which resulted in the restoration of the weapon and
scabbard to the original owner thirty-one years after its loss, and
mutual expressions of good will and friendship between the loser
and the finder. Returning to his home after being discharged from
the hospital, Dr. Hynes resumed the practice of his profession as
soon as able, continuing the same in Catahoula Parish until 1868. In
January of that year he removed to Brenham, Tex., which has since
been his home, and here he has not only enjoyed a large and lucrative practice, but has been actively identified with the prosperity of
this portion of the state. At the present time he is health physician

for both Washington County and the city of Brenham. While in Harrisonburg, La., in 1860, he married Mrs. Mary E. Slater, daughter of Thomas I. Matthews, who died in Belton in 1884, leaving two daughters: Tannie, the wife of L. F. Ammons of Brenham, and Lee, a young lady of fine accomplishments, a teacher in the Art Conservatory of Belton, Tex., who is residing at Belton with a half-sister, Mrs. Bowman. Dr. Hynes is a Democrat in politics, is honorably connected with the Masonic and Odd Fellows fraternities, the state and local medical associations, and occupies a prominent place among the leading men of Washington County and the State of Texas.

DR. W. D. NORTHCUTT.

Recently published statistical information relative to the progress and advancement made in the various professions of this country reveal the fact that in no calling have such improvements been made as in medicine. Dr. W. D. Northcutt is one of the young physicians of Gregg County and has already built up a practice that is exceptionally large. He is very conscientious in the discharge of his professional duties, is well up with the times in medical lore, and has the ability to apply his knowledge at the proper time and in the proper place. He was born in Marietta, Ga., in November, 1861, and his parents, W. G. and Julia (Moore) Northcutt, were natives of that state also. The paternal grandfather was a pioneer of Marietta, and lived to be an aged man. The Moore family moved from South Carolina to Georgia at an early date. W. G. Northcutt was reared in Georgia and there married Miss Moore. In 1870 he moved to the Lone Star State, and settled in Longview, where he is now engaged in merchandising. He is a wide-awake, live business man and is in comfortable circumstances. To this marriage were born seven children. Our subject received the rudiments of an education in his native state and when nine years of age came with his parents to Texas. He here continued his scholastic training and later evinced a strong desire for the study of medicine. He entered the medical college at Louisville, Ky., and remained there until February, 1884, when he began practicing in Longview. Later he returned to Louisville and graduated in 1890. He has a good general practice and is physician for three railroad companies at Longview. In choosing a wife he selected Miss Eda E. Mautha, a native of Missouri, and their union was celebrated in 1886. Three children have been given them: Dollie, Leon and Emma. Both he and wife are members of the Baptist church and he is an Odd Fellow in his social relations. Mr. Northcutt has a fine orchard of pears, peaches and apples.

JUDGE JAMES M. MAXEY.

One of the most popular of the many worthy men elevated to the bench in the history of Houston County jurisprudence is Judge James M. Maxey, who is now retired from the active duties of his profession and has a comfortable home in Huntsville. Judge Maxey was born in Montgomery, Ala., September 3, 1819, and was second in order of birth of three children born to the marriage of William and Rebecca (Haynes) Maxey, natives respectively of Virginia and Georgia. The paternal grandfather, Walter Maxey, who was born in Virginia, was of French Huguenot stock, his ancestors coming to Virginia in colonial days. He was a farmer all his life. The maternal grandfather, Thomas H. Haynes, was also a native Virginian, and a farmer by occupation. He was of English origin and his ancestors came here prior to the Revolution. William Maxey was educated in Virginia, principally by his own efforts and later moved to Georgia, where he followed merchandising for some time. After the Indian wars he moved to Montgomery County, Ala., where he was engaged in merchandising and planting up to 1833, when he moved to Noxubee County, Miss. There he became one of the most prosperous and successful planters. In 1841 he came to Texas and spent two years in Washington County, where he bought a valuable place on Trinity River, now San Jacinto County, and where he improved a fine estate. There he resided until his death in 1849 or '50. The mother, who was a worthy member of the Baptist church, died in 1848. Judge James M. Maxey was reared in Alabama and Mississippi and received his education at home and in the common schools during his boyhood days. Later he entered the University of Alabama and was graduated from that institution in 1840. He then began the study of law at Mason, Miss., with Colonel Ruff, and was admitted in 1843, immediately after which he began practicing there. While studying he served two years as circuit clerk. In 1842 he volunteered with others and a battalion of young men came to Texas, offering services to the Texas republic. The Mexicans then having withdrawn, our subject, with others, returned to Mississippi. On December 26, 1843, he was married to Miss Virginia Mosely, a native of Alabama. In the fall of 1845 he was elected to the State Legislature of Mississippi, and after serving one term resigned and moved to Texas, arriving at Huntsville in January, 1847. He immediately began practicing. In 1856 he bought a large estate in San Jacinto County and the same year was elected district judge of a district comprising the southeast part of the state. He served in that capacity until 1861, when he resigned and was appointed one of the Confederate State Court officials, serving in that capacity until the close of the war. Returning to Huntsville he resumed his practice and was the leader of the bar here for years, retiring in 1892. Although a political leader he was no office-seeker. In 1872 he was a presidential elector. In 1893 Judge Maxey bought his present place near town and has one of the finest fruit farms in this section. His marriage resulted in the birth of these children: Finnie, entered Wharton's Cavalry Regiment, Confederate army, and died in Tennessee; Manly, died in 1893, when twenty-four years old; Rebecca, wife of Captain Mat. Ross; Annie (deceased); Walter, wife of J. M. Collier; John, graduate of the Naval Academy, and is now at Austin, and Virgil. Our subject's brother, Walter, came to Texas with his parents in 1841, and became an extensive planter. He assisted in raising a company and became first lieutenant, joining the Fifth Texas Regiment, the first infantry regiment to go to Virginia from this section. He was soon taken sick and died. The judge's sister, Lucinda, married Professor Gillette, who now resides on Galveston Bay and who is a noted educator. He was the first instructor in Baylor University at Independence. Albert G. Haynes, brother of Mrs. Maxey, came to Texas about 1841 and became a large planter in Washington County. He became a prominent man and was one of the main supporters of the Baylor University. He served in the Legislature several terms and died after the war.

CAPTAIN BOLLING ELDRIDGE.

This well-known and public-spirited, enterprising gentleman has been a resident of the litle city of Brenham and engaged in business there since May, 1867, during which time he has identified himself with all the movements conducive to the public good and formed a large circle of steadfast friends by reason of his sterling qualities. He was brought to the county in 1849 from Virginia, where he was born in Halifax County. His father, John C. Eldridge, was also a native of Virginia, born in the same county February 18, 1811. He grew to manhood in his native county, receiving in youth a fair education. Upon reaching manhood he married in Northampton County, N. C., Miss Amanda F. Turner, a native of the same county, where she was also reared. After his marriage he engaged in merchandising in Brooklyn, Va., and so continued for the period of twenty years, conducting during the latter part a large and profitable business and building up an enviable reputation for purity of motives and sincerity of conduct. In 1849 he moved to Texas, locating in Washington County, where he bought several hundred acres of land and began planting. He was the owner of a number of slaves and soon became one of the most prominent agriculturists in this part of the state. Although now eighty-four years old he still actively oversees his plantation interests and still takes keen enjoyment in re-

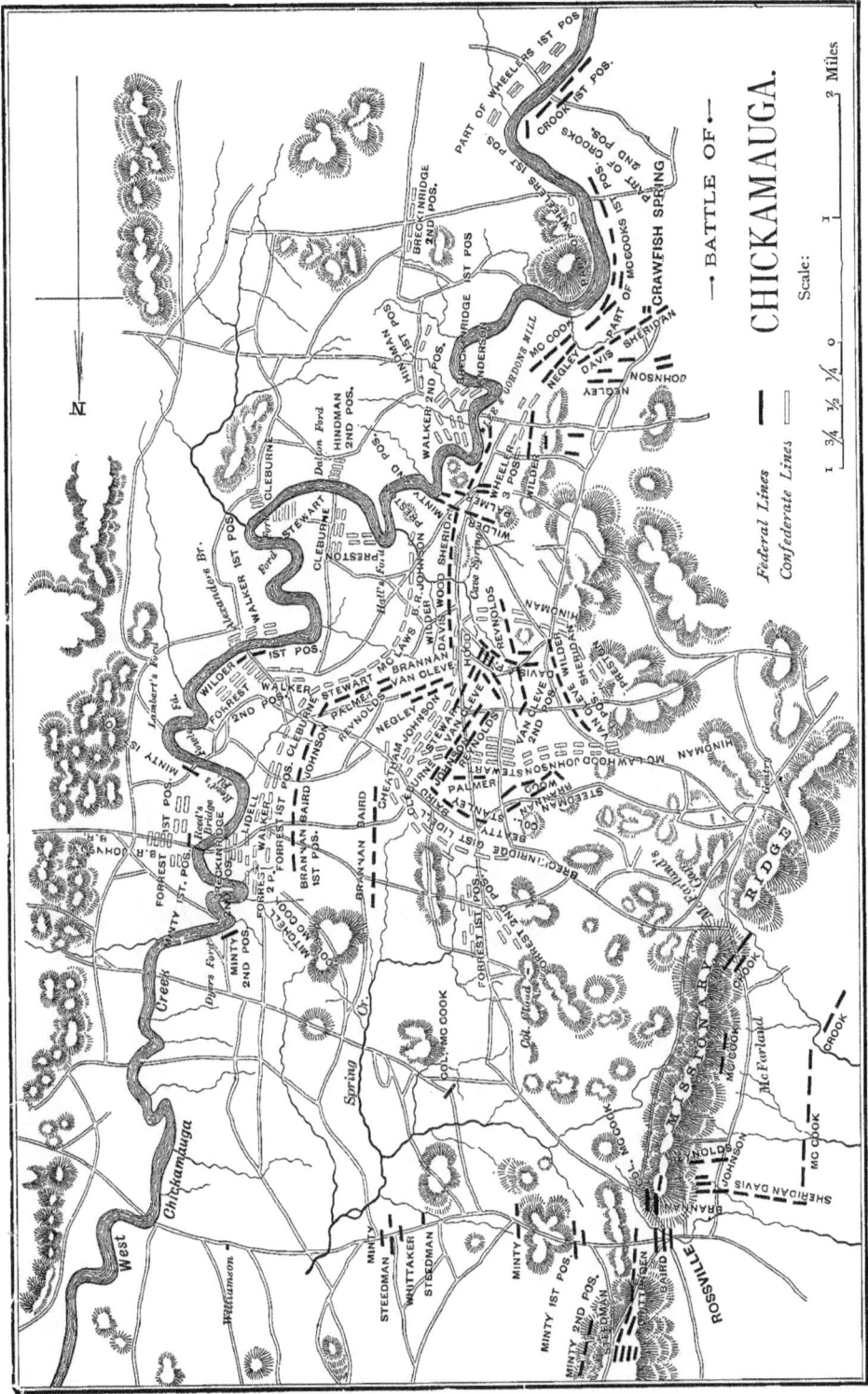

BATTLE OF

CHICKAMAUGA.

Scale:

Federal Lines
Confederate Lines

viewing his long and honorable life. The immediate subject of this sketch, Captain Bolling Eldridge, is one of a family of four sons and three daughters that grew to mature years, though at the present date only three sons and two daughters are living. The eldest of these is a doctor of Southampton County, Va.; Captain Eldridge is the second; F. A., the present postmaster of Brenham is the third; Thomas H., who died of yellow fever; Mrs. V. A. Williams; Mrs. O'Ridan of Austin and one daughter, deceased. Captain Eldridge was brought to Texas when a small boy and grew to mature years in Washington County, receiving here his education and his first experience in the great battle of commercial life. He finished his schooling at Independence, this county, and at an early age joined the Fifth Texas Infantry, Company E, Confederate army, going out at a private, but in 1863 was elected from a private to the rank of lieutenant and serving in this responsible position until the close of the war. His regiment was a part of Hood's Texas Brigade and in all of its bloody battles he was a brave and valiant participant, fighting in all except Sharpsburg and Fredericksburg. Among the battles in which he participated were West Point, Seven Pines, Gaines' Mill, Second Manassas, Gettysburg, Chickamauga, Knoxville, the Wilderness, Spottsylvania Courthouse, Cold Harbor, Fort Harrison, Darbytown Road and many others of lesser note—twenty-eight in all. At Gaines' Mill he received a gunshot wound in the stomach which disabled him for a short time. At Chickamauga he sustained a slight wound, and at the Wilderness was wounded in the left shoulder. At Appomattox Courthouse his regiment was surrounded with the balance of the splendid army of General Lee and at this time Captain Eldridge was the only commissioned officer left and surrendered his company. They were duly paroled and Captain Eldridge returned home, and in 1866 engaged in merchandising as a clerk in Galveston, and in this manner received a thorough business training. In 1867 he came to Brenham, embarking in mercantile pursuits, which he continued with much success and is thus engaged at the present time. Captain Eldridge is now one of the oldest and most prominent business men of the place. He does a retail and jobbing grocery business and is well and favorably known throughout this portion of the state. He was first married in

New Orleans December 1, 1869, to Miss Kate Hurley, a native of Virginia, but reared and educated in the Lone Star State. This lady died in August, 1870. He was married in 1874 to Miss Mary E. Sheppard, a native of Alabama, but who was reared and educated in Texas. They have one son and three daughters. The son, Bolling Eldridge, Jr., is now receiving his education at Asheville (North Carolina) Military Academy. The daughters are Kate Hurley, Maggie Mildred and Anna Belle. Captain Eldridge is a Democrat in politics. He was a charter member of the Knights of Pythias in 1874 in Brenham, in which organization he has held all the principal offices. Captain Eldridge is possessed of superior business qualifications, is active in the promotion of all enterprises that tend toward the advancement of his county and state, and commands the respect and confidence of a wide circle of friends and acquaintances.

DR. A. D. STROND.

It was Mirabeau who said: "When a man is in earnest and knows what he is about, his work is half done." According to this assertion of the famous French statesman, Dr. A. D. Strond, who is well known throughout Eastern Texas, began his career with his work half accomplished, for he is endowed by nature with an earnestness which, while tempered with flexibility, is yet unalterably persistent, and with the clear discrimination and calmness of temperament which enables him under all circumstances to know precisely what he is about. It was in Chambers County, Ala., March 29, 1839, that Dr. Strond was born. His father, Hon. Mark Strond, was a native of Georgia, but when a young man turned his footsteps toward Alabama, where he met and married Miss Sarah Trammell, also of Georgia. His occupation in life was farming and he followed this in Alabama until the winter of 1839-40, when he moved to Texas, locating in what is now Robinson County. For four years he was actively engaged in cultivating the soil there and then moved to Nacogdoches County, where he still continued his former occupation for several years. His next move was to Rusk County, where he located in the southern part and opened up a large farm. Later he sold this and bought again in the northeast part of the county, but only farmed there a few years. Selling out again he bought a farm near Henderson and there died in December, 1888. His wife survived him but a few months, passing away in February of the same year. Mr. Strond was one of the leading men of Rusk County and held many positions of trust and honor. He was elected to the Legislature, served two terms with distinction, and for years was a delegate to the state and county conventions. He was also a delegate to the constitutional convention after the war. He was a man who had the confidence and affection of all. Dr. A. D. Strond was one of two sons and three daughters, the other son now deceased. He was liberally educated in youth, first in the common schools, then in the schools of Lafayette, Ala., and subsequently began the study of medicine in Lafayette under the supervision of an uncle, Dr. F. A. Trammell, one of the leading physicians of that part of the state. Young Strond took his first course of lectures in New Orleans during the winter of 1859-60, and the following year returned and completed the course, graduating in the class of 1861. He soon after enlisted and joined first the Tenth Texas Cavalry as assistant surgeon, and served in that capacity in the Confederate army until the close of the war, receiving no furlough during his service, and was faithful to his duties until cessation of hostilities. Upon coming home Dr. Strond resumed the practice of medicine in Henderson and for about thirty years now has been engaged most successfully in his noble calling. He has built up a very large practice and is well known all over Eastern Texas. For some time Dr. Strond was engaged in the drug business, but gave this up in order to attend more closely to his large practice. On June 14, 1865, the doctor was married to Miss Fannie G. Rogers, a native of Georgia, but who was reared and educated in Rusk County, Tex. Her father, John Rogers, moved to this state and county from Georgia in about 1856 or 1857. Dr. and Mrs. Strond are the parents of six children, the eldest, a daughter, being the wife of E. C. Hearne, a business man of Longwood, La.

The next child, Mattie, is at home; Work, a young business man, is at home; John P. is now in business in Henderson; Albert Sidney is in a drug store in Henderson, and Fannie C. Dr. Strond lost his first wife in 1884, and was again married in December, 1891, to Miss Pattie Forman, a native of Mississippi, and a most estimable lady, the daughter of Charles Forman, now deceased. There has been born one son to this union, Alpheus D. Strond, Jr. In politics the doctor is an earnest Democrat, and socially he is a Royal Arch Mason, a member of Henderson Blue Lodge and Chapter. He is also a member of the Knights of Honor and was for a few years examining physician for the order. He has been a resident of Rusk County for nearly half a century and of Henderson for about thirty years, and is a physician of profound learning and wide reputation.

REV. SAMUEL M. RUSSELL.

This earnest and effective worker in the cause of Christianity is a minister of the Baptist Church. In the study of every man's life we find some mainspring of action, something he lives for. In Rev. Samuel M. Russell it was an ambition to develop in himself a true manhood and minister to the spiritual welfare of his fellowmen. He came originally from South Carolina, born in 1829, and the second of ten children resulting from the marriage of Rev. W. I. F. and Annie H. (Benton) Russell, both natives of South Carolina. This family is of English origin, and the first representatives of the same in this country settled in South Carolina during colonial times. The Bentons were a prominent South Carolina family also. After his marriage the father of our subject moved to Alabama and there followed farming for some time. Later he began preaching in the Baptist Church and became well and favorably known throughout his community. He was an ardent adherent to the Confederate cause during the war and in 1865 was shot near his home by Federal soldiers after the surrender. He left a widow and seven children. Our subject received his education in Alabama, and when starting out to fight life's battles for himself selected farming as his occupation in life. In 1852 he married Miss Louisa Grimes of Alabama, William Grimes, her father, being one of the best men and of the first families of Alabama. In 1859 he came to Texas, where he followed blacksmithing in Harrison County during the entire Civil War. Many horses he shod for the soldiers without recompense, never charging a soldier for entertainment. After the war he moved to Marshall and continued his former occupation one year. In 1866 he bought an interest in the mill of Field & Brown, then a grist mill and planing mill, but in 1868 bought out his partners and soon became an extensive operator. He erected his present mill and also has a planing and saw mill in connection. This is the oldest mill in Marshall and is well equipped in every particular. In 1868 Mr. Russell began preaching in the Baptist Church, was licensed the same year and ordained in 1869. He organized a church near his home at Friendship, twelve miles south of Marshall, with three members, and preached there until it had forty-five members. He then organized a church at Cane Springs and preached there for several years with much success. Hebron Church, near Marshall, was organized by Mr. Russell, and another church five miles west of that town was organized by him. For twelve months after this he preached in Van Zandt County and at four other places with good success, and has continued his ministerial duties up to the present time, having done much mission work in Soda Lake Association and East Texas conventions prior to the last appointment. In March, 1895, he was appointed missionary by the Board of Soda Lake Association and is now extending his good work throughout this county. He has turned his powers into the channel of an honorable and holy purpose and excellent results are the natural consequence. Mr. Russell lost his wife in 1877. She left seven children: William, Annie, Mary, Maggie, Simeon (deceased), Louella and Allen. All are married except the last named. In the fall of 1879 Mr. Russell married Miss Ellen C. Carter, who came to Texas in 1877, and who is the daughter of John Carter of Georgia, one of the first families. They have four children: Mossie, Rosser, Spurgeon (deceased) and Lady Helen Marr.

GEORGE W. PETTEY.

This well known agriculturist has been a resident of Washington County, Tex., for a period of fifty-seven years, during which time he has accumulated a competency and acquired a name of honor second to that of no other man in this portion of the state. He is one of the few remaining honored first settlers left to tell the tale of pioneer self-denial and privation endured in early years. He is far advanced along the pathway of life, but bears the weight of extreme age with great elasticity and fortitude. His life has been a busy one, often filled with trying and thrilling experiences, but through it all he has ever sustained his health and his good name. He was born near the city of Murfreesboro, in Rutherford County, Tenn., April 7, 1812, and is the son of John Pettey, a native of North Carolina, born in Randolph County. The father of John Pettey was Ambrose Pettey, who was of Scotch descent, and moved to Tennessee at an early period in the history of that state. One of his sons, Alexander, was a soldier under General Jackson in the war of 1812. John Pettey was married in North Carolina to Miss Delia Thrift, a native of that state, and soon after that event moved to Tennessee, where his children, twelve in number, were born and reared. He followed the occupation of farmer in Rutherford County, and his sons and daughters grew up familiar with the labors of the agriculturist. All the children of this large family lived to years of maturity and all, except one, married, the one excepted dying upon reaching manhood. In time they scattered and now their descendents live in many states of the Union. In time, too, the parents died and both lie buried in the cemetery at Murfreesboro, Tenn. George W. Pettey is the only survivor of this large family. He grew to manhood in Rutherford County and received a fair education. In 1835, at the age of twenty-three years, he went West to Texas and located in Washington County October 10, 1835, sixty years ago, and first established himself at Independence. A year later, or in the fall of 1836, he moved to another point near Brenham, and the following spring, May 30, 1837, was united in marriage to Miss Marian Wood, a native of Maury County, Tenn., who came to Texas with her father in 1833. After this, for about four years, he lived with his father-in-law, engaged in farming. He then purchased a farm of 762 acres, of which 115 acres were under cultivation, and with his slaves began to farm and improve the place and soon had 550 acres under cultivation. He thus continued until the war, when all his slaves were freed, whereupon he sold the old place and bought the one upon which he now resides. On the 12th of March, 1865, his wife died, having borne him a family of four sons and two daughters, as follows: John A., who resides at Hempstead, engaged in farming and stock raising; Sophia, the wife of John Mills, residing near Hempstead; Isham T., who died at Colorado City, Tex.; Ambros, who resides at Colorado City, engaged in sheep raising; Reuben, who lives in Louisiana, and Virginia, the wife of Lynn Murray. January 31, 1872, Mr. Pettey married Mrs. Lizzie White. daughter of Mansfield Hamm of Tennessee. This lady was reared in Lowndes County, Miss., and her first marriage occurred in that state. To her union with Mr. Pettey two daughters were born, as follows: Ida Lee, wife of Robert Burch, deputy sheriff of Washington County, and Maggie I., a young lady at home. Mr. Pettey is a staunch Democrat in politics and an earnest Baptist in religion, his wife being a member of the Presbyterian church. He has lived to see the wilderness of Washington County transformed into cultivated farms, thriving towns and happy homes. Where now stands the beautiful little city of Brenham he has chased and killed deer, antelope and other wild animals. He is a man of strong physical powers and has lived a long, honorable and useful life. He served the Texan cause in their struggle for Independence and was under General Sam Houston at the battle of San Jacinto, and received land warrants for his services.

JOHN W. ADDIS.

This gentleman is regarded as one of the most influential and worthy citizens of Harrison County, Tex., and it is a pleasure to chronicle here the events that mark his life as one of usefulness. He is at present superintendent of motive power and rolling stock of the

Texas & Pacific Railroad Co. of Marshall, Tex. He was born at East Liberty, Fayette County, Pa., March 13, 1851, and is of German and Scotch ancestry. His parents, Samuel and Permelia (Randolph) Addis, had born to their marriage ten children, who were named in order of their births, as follows: Canada C., Annie, Mary, David, John, Emma, Robert, Samuel, Ida, Maud and Edna. The father followed the occupation of a farmer most of his life, but in connection was also engaged in merchandising. In the common schools of his native county John W. Addis received his education, but as his youth and early manhood were marked by ill health, he at last took the advice of Horace Greeley and made his way toward the setting sun, settling in Magnolia, Iowa, but a few years later moved to Missouri Valley, where he secured a position in the mechanical department of the Sioux City & Pacific Railroad Co., to learn the trade of machinist, in which he soon displayed unusual natural talent and adaptability. Here he remained four years, as a valuable employe, and as he gradually recovered his health, he took the advice of physicians and sought the mild and genial climate of the Lone Star State. He secured a good position in the shops of the International & Great Northern road at Palestine and his strict attention to the duties assigned him, together with his proficiency, attracted the attention of his superior officers and soon afterward he was promoted to the foremanship. While located in Missouri Valley he was married in the month of December, 1873, to Miss Clara Morse, an estimable young lady of Homer, Iowa. To this union was born a daughter, Maud, who is still living. In the spring of 1879 Mr. Addis moved to Marshall, Tex., and was employed by the Texas & Pacific Railroad Co. While here he received an offer to take charge of the Texas & St. Louis shops at Tyler, to which point he soon after moved. While residing there he had the misfortune to lose his wife by death. In June, 1883, the Little Rock, Mississippi & Texas road, now consolidated with the Iron Mountain system, secured his valuable services as manager of their shops at Arkansas City, Ark. In August, 1884, he assumed charge of the Iron Mountain & Texas Pacific shops at Texarkana and nine months afterward was transferred to the same company's shops at Longview Junction, and from there to Bonham, Tex. Still later he moved to Pine Bluff, where he was master mechanic of the Cotton

Belt road. After remaining there a year he moved to Gouldsboro, where he filled the position of master mechanic, having charge of the New Orleans division of the Texas & Pacific road. March 15, 1893, he accepted his present position and removed to Marshall. He is one of the most successful and best known railroad men in Texas and is very popular among all classes. In the month of December, 1891, he married Miss Minnie Kearns of Bunker Hill, Ill. Mr. Addis is a member of the American Railway Master Mechanics' Association.

MRS. KATE WOOD.

The prominence of women in the various lines of industry in this city has become well known. The advance of time, civilization and intelligence has opened the eyes of the public to the fact that in the higher walks of life, women fill positions of prominence and exercise their professional duties with as much success as men. Thus it has been with Mrs. Kate Wood, the present proprietress of the Excelsior House of Jefferson. There is nothing which adds so much to the prestige of a city, in the estimation of the public, as first-class hotel accommodations, and this Mrs. Wood must realize, for she has one of the neatest, most home-like hotels in the county. This hotel is favorably known all over Texas by the "Knights of the Grip" and has an established reputation, for it has been conducted most successfully by Mrs. Wood for twenty years. She thoroughly understands every wish and requirement of her guest and does not spare herself in making them comfortable and contented. She was born across the ocean, in Hesse Darmstadt, Germany, her father, Justus Held, being of a very prominent family of that section. Our subject came to America at an early age and went immediately to St. Louis, Mo., where she made her home for a number of years. Her husband, Benjamin Wood, was a native of Knoxville, Tenn., and during the war was engaged in the livery business in Jefferson. His death occurred in 1864 and since then Mrs. Wood has depended on her own exertions for a livelihood. She is possessed of unusual business acumen, sound judgment and progressive ideas, and has been quite successful in a financial way. Her only living child, a daughter, is the the wife of S. A. McNeeley, who is one of the prominent railroad men of the state, and is now identified with the Gulf, Beaumont & Kansas City railroad, as superintendent of construction. He is a practical and successful railroad builder and is well known in connection with this work. Mrs. Wood has ever taken a deep interest in the welfare and upbuilding of Jefferson and has contributed much toward its advancement. When the United States Government decided to erect a postoffice building here she came forward and offered to donate, free of charge, the ground upon which it was to be erected. Her offer was accepted and Jefferson has to-day one of the finest postoffice buildings in the state. To such citizens is due the prosperity of the place.

JUDGE JAMES T. MARONEY.

The bar of Lufkin, Angelina County, Tex., has won an enviable reputation all over the country for the erudition, success and courtesy of its members, many of whom have achieved a national reputation for their ability and a correct apprehension of what pertains to the profession. Judge James T. Maroney, who stands deservedly high with his brother lawyers and with the courts, has always been a close student in his profession and has won the respect and confidence of all. He is a product of Monroeville, Monroe County, Ala., born January 27, 1853, and the son of John W. M. and Nancy (Pollard) Maroney, natives respectively of New York and South Carolina. The parents were married in Monroeville in 1840 and there the father followed farming until his death, which occurred when he was a comparatively young man. He was of Scotch-Irish origin. The mother also died young. Their children were named as follows: William W., Florence, James T., Benjamin, John, Richard P. and Daniel W. James T., the third in order of birth, early became familiar with the duties of the farm and when not thus occupied was attending the common schools. He suffered the misfortune of losing his parents at an early age and was thrown upon his own resources. After the death of his mother, which occurred when he was fifteen years old, he followed farming and also attended school, thus securing a good foundation on which to build in later years. Afterward he began teaching school in Alabama and followed this in his native state until 1875, when he came to Texas and located on a farm near Homer. He diligently applied himself to the study of law and soon after was admitted to practice. In 1882 the Democrats elected him district clerk and he filled that position most acceptably for one term. In 1884 he was chosen county Judge and was an incumbent of that office for three consecutive terms. In 1892 he was again the unanimous choice of the people for Judge, to which his education and ability eminently fit him. As a jurist he stands in the front rank in a bar which embraces in its list many of the ablest lawyers in this part of the state, and as a public-spirited and liberal citizen he has no superior. Broadgauged, liberally educated and of pleasing manners, he is very popular with the masses. Socially, he is a Mason, having joined them in 1883, and a member of the Methodist church. He was married in 1878 to Miss Tennie Chatham, daughter of William and Belle Chatham, well known and much respected citizens of this county. Mrs. Maroney died in 1880. One child, Grace, was the fruit of this union. In 1887 Judge Maroney wedded Miss Parilee Cochran, daughter of Mr. and Mrs. ELIAS K. Cochran, and these children were given them: Hester (deceased), Ruby, J. T., Fanny and Travis. Mrs. Maroney and the children are active in church work.

JOHN J. HOFFMAN.

The science of farming is one of the primary occupations of man and is absolutely necessary to his existence. It is not only a necessary pursuit, but it is a pleasurable one as well, when not accompanied by a too prolonged or violent exertion. The subject of this sketch has made farming a pursuit, both for business and pleasure. He carries on extensively the farming and ginning business and has accumulated a goodly portion of this world's goods. He came to Texas in 1846 and to Washington County in 1852, and is thus one of the old settlers of this portion of the state. He was born in Hesse Darmstadt, Germany, August 23, 1832, and when fourteen years of age was brought to America by his parents, who located in this county, where the father passed from life in 1872, at the age of seventy-two years. The mother is still living with the subject of this sketch and has reached the advanced age of ninety-one years. The first money earned in the new world by John J. was obtained by blacking boots at Goliad, Galveston and elsewhere, and in doing other small services that came to his hand, as, for instance, serving as waiter at the Washington Hotel for three years. Succeeding this for three years, he kept bar and then, in 1852, came to Washington County and engaged in hauling freight with ox teams from Houston. He continued this, farming to some extent as well, until 1862, when he enlisted in the Confederate army in Company E, Colonel Green's Regiment, and served the Southern cause faithfully until the close of the war, mainly on detached duty, a portion of the time as regimental musician. After the war he returned to this county and engaged in farming. In 1867 he bought seventy-five acres, with some improvements, where he now resides, and here he has since employed his time in farming and ginning. He built a steam corn and grist mill and operated the same. Since his first purchase of land he has added to the farm, until now he owns about 190 acres, all fairly well improved. He has made life a success, in fact, it is very difficult to find a German who, in the end, does not accumulate a competency and acquire a good name. He deserves much credit for his industrious and honorable life, and certainly the county has no better citizen and the residents a no better neighbor. He began life single-handed, working at the first job that presented itself, and has the satisfaction of knowing that he is absolutely self-made. On the 14th of February, 1861, he was united in marriage to Miss Elizabeth Imhoff, a native of Germany, where she was reared, and they have nine children, all grown to maturity, seven being married and two at home. Mr. Hoffman is a Democrat, and a member of the United Workmen and of the Lutheran church. He is one of the most highly respected citizens of the county.

A. M. CLAY.

For nearly half a century—more than forty-nine years to December, 1895—this well-known farmer and stock raiser of Washington County has been a resident here, coming to the state and county in 1846. This long residence here, his active participation in all the movements to build up the community, his industrious and upright life, his friendship for all forms of morality, his advocacy of social, industrial and political reforms, have placed him among the leading citizens of this portion of the state. Farming, as he does, nearly 6,000 acres of the finest land in Texas, he is independent of the fluctuations in wealth which worry and perplex the man who possesses that amount in cash or bonds, because Texas land is a safe and permanent investment that to the proper attention will pay a large percentage of profit. When he was two years old, or, in 1846, his father brought him to Texas, coming from Kentucky, where A. M. was born, March 17, 1844. In Texas he grew to manhood, receiving merely limited educational advantages; but since reaching mature years, self-educating himself. When the great war broke out he enlisted in August, 1861, in the Fifth Texas Infantry Regiment, Company E, Confederate army, being then only in his seventeenth year. His regiment was soon attached to Hood's Brigade and remained with the same, with one year's exception, until the end of the struggle. Mr. Clay participated in many of the most noted and bloodiest engagements of the war, particularly at Athen's Landing, Wilderness, Gettysburg, Sharpsburg, seven days' fight around Richmond and many others, and in all the stern requirements of his position and duty, acquitted himself with conspicuous gallantry and to the highest satisfaction of his superior officers. The last year of the war he served with the Eighth Texas Regiment of Cavalry in active campaigns as rangers until the surrender of General Lee. He then returned home and for six months clerked in his father's store at Brenham, but he tired of this and returned to the farm, where he remained until 1872, when he went West to New Mexico and California and remained there three years, engaged in mining. In 1875 he returned to Independence and engaged in farming. He obtained 1,100 acres of his father, upon which were slight improvements. He went to work with hearty will and soon had his farm under a high degree of cultivation, with good and substantial buildings, and with additions made to the same from time to time until his farm now consists of 4,000 acres in one tract, 800 in another and several smaller places. He has about 1,300 acres under the plow, and is thus one of the largest farmers, stock-raisers and land-owners of the county. He is a man of much personal worth, a genial, hospitable gentleman, whose prominence and prosperity are recognized and merited. He is a Democrat and as such has served his neighbors in both county and state conventions. In 1875, at Independence, he was united in marriage to Miss Paulina Thornhill, a native of Louisiana, and daughter of Dr. Thornhill. Mrs. Clay was reared and educated in Mississippi and Texas, and has presented Mr. Clay with seven children, as follows: Lela, a graduate of the Waco Female College; Alice, now receiving her education in the convent at Galveston; Thomas H., now attending the A. and M. College near Bryan, Tex., and Kate, Nestor, Anna Belle and Tacitus, all at home. Mrs. Clay, a lady of many accomplishments, is an active member of the Episcopal church. The family is intelligent, alive to the progress of the world, lovers of learning, and charming in the daily life of its members. Mr. Clay has much to be proud of, and the county owes him its homage for his staunch and sturdy citizenship.

His father was Tacitus Clay, a native of Virginia, who was taken to Kentucky in childhood, and was a near relative of Henry Clay, the great statesman and orator. He went to Texas when a young man and there bought a tract of land and then returned to Kentucky, where he married Miss V. McCrary, a native of Kentucky. In 1846 he moved permanently to Texas and settled on his land near Independence. He owned one league of land and a number of slaves and was soon engaged in farming on an extensive scale. Here his family were born and reared and here he passed from life in 1878, aged about seventy-four years. His widow survived him many years, finally dying August 1, 1895, at the age of eighty-two years. Both lie sleeping in the cemetery at Independence. They were the parents of two sons and three daughters, all of whom grew to mature years. Thetis married Charles Powers, both of whom are now deceased; Lelia married Thomas Hoxie and is now a widow and resides at Austin; Thomas C., deceased; Teula, married William T. Dever, and A. M., subject of this sketch.

THOMAS H. LANGHAM.

Of those whose active lives are coeval with Jefferson County, Tex., and whose trials and triumphs are interwoven with her history, is Thomas H. Langham. His career illustrates most forcibly the possibilities that are open in this country to earnest, persevering young men, who have the courage of their convictions, and the determination to be the architects of their own fortunes. It proves that neither wealth nor social position, nor influential friends, are the essentials to the attainment of eminent usefulness, honorable distinction and true success. Perhaps there is not a man in the county who stands higher in the estimation of the people than our subject, who has served faithfully as sheriff of the county for a period of twenty consecutive years. He has, by earnest, honest effort, earned the favorable result that has come as his reward, and whatever special trusts have been imposed on him he has proved true to them. Mr. Langham is a native son of the "Lone Star State," his birth occurring in Jefferson County August 3, 1846, and it is but natural perhaps that he takes an active interest in whatever pertains to her material prosperity and good name. His father, James B. Langham, was born in Alabama October 9, 1820. When a child the latter moved with his father, Thomas Langham, to Tennessee and settled in Fayette County. There he grew up and received his education. When a young man he came to Texas with his parents and settled in San Augustine County. This was in 1836 and five years later James made his first appearance in Jefferson County, settling on a farm near the present flourishing little city of Beaumont. Here he was married in 1845 to Miss Sarah Jane Nattles, a native of Louisiana. Mr. Langham prospered in his farming interests and is the owner of two fine, well improved farms near the town of Beaumont. In 1886 he moved to that place and is now retired from the active duties of life. Although seventy-six years old, Father Time has dealt leniently with him, and he appears much younger. He is an honored old settler of the county, having been an actor here when the state was in a formative condition, and he now can enjoy the fruits of a useful and well-spent life. In 1838 he enlisted in the Texas army and served for three months in Mexico under Captain Brooks. All his life he has been an ardent Jackson Democrat and has favored the measures and men of that party. To his marriage were born five sons and five daughters, four sons and four daughters now living. His wife passed away in the year 1875. The youth of our subject was passed in duties on the home place and in attending the common schools, in which he received a limited education. Later, being of a studious and thoughtful turn of mind, he applied himself to his books, and by his individual efforts made up, in a great measure, for the lack of educational advantages in youth. At the breaking out of the Civil War he was too young to enlist, but in 1863, when seventeen years old, he joined the Twenty-sixth Texas Cavalry and was in active service until the close of hostilities, participating in the skirmishes of his regiment in Louisiana and Mississippi. Returning home after the war, he began farming near Beaumont, and followed this very successfully for ten years. In 1875 he was elected sheriff of Jefferson County, and on the 18th of April of the following year took charge of the office. So ably and efficiently did he discharge the duties of that office that he was re-elected and again re-elected, serving in all twenty years in that capacity, and longer than any other sheriff in Texas. At each succeeding election he carried the county by a nice majority, thus showing his popularity with the people. He has conscientiously and intelligently performed his duties, honoring those whom he represented, benefiting the public and doing credit to himself. While holding the office of sheriff he captured some of the worst characters in the state, but never had a prisoner escape while in his personal charge. Mr. Langham was married in Beaumont December 22, 1869 to Miss Mary E. French, a native of this state and county, with whom he had been acquainted all his life. Their three children were named as follows: Lula, wife of Guy W. Junker of Beaumont; H. C., a young man of good habits and character, holds a position with the ———— Lumber Co. of Beaumont, and Sadie, a young lady at home. Like his father, Mr. Langham has ever been identified with the Democratic party and has served as a delegate to numerous county, state and congressional conventions. His life has been one continuous scene of activity and his achievements justify a study of the man, his character, his qualities, his methods of action and acknowledged ability to grapple with the higher forces of life around him, and to govern the agencies of nature and humanity that are so essential to the attainment of eminence and success.

J. M. MARSHALL.

Success in any calling is an indication of close application, industry and faithfulness. There are few industries more honorable or few which offer better opportunities than does that of merchandising. Success in life is something to be proud of, and the world is better for the life of every successful man. The subject of this sketch lays claim to no particular honor for having fulfilled the obligations of his business, and for having become a successful business man and a prominent citizen. J. M. Marshall was born in Chambers County, Ala., November 8, 1846, to the union of Jesse S. and Catherine (Shaw) Marshall, both natives of Georgia. The father was a planter in his native state until after his marriage, when he moved to Alabama, and for many years was engaged in agricultural pursuits in Chambers

County. In 1852 he moved to Texas and settled in Upshur County, where he was among the early pioneers. He opened up a large farm and tilled the soil here for a number of years. After the death of his wife he moved to Gilmer and found a comfortable home with his son until his death in 1869, when seventy-seven years old. He was a prominent man of Upshur County and served as treasurer of the same for two terms. Of the nine children born to this estimable couple, only two sons and three daughters are now living. The son, Edward P. Marshall, is the auditor in the Treasury Department at Washington, D. C., appointed from Dallas, Tex., by Mr. Cleveland. J. M. Marshall attended the common schools of his neighborhood when not assisting on the farm, and when grown began tilling the soil as a livelihood. On the 12th of October, 1871, he married Miss Vina Boyd, who was born, reared and educated in this county, and a daughter of Walter Boyd, one of the prominent business men of Gilmer (see sketch). For five years after marriage Mr. Marshall followed farming and was then elected county clerk and re-elected, serving two terms. Later he was elected county treasurer and served one term. In 1881 he embarked in merchandising in Gilmer, in partnership with W. Boyd, and continued with this for about four years. After that he formed another partnership, which continued for almost seven years, and since that time he has been in business for himself. Mr. Marshall owns a large and select stock of general merchandise and has built up a good trade. He is noted for his fair dealings and honorable business methods. Politically, he is a Democrat, has served as a delegate to state and county conventions, and has held a number of positions of honor and trust. He is a Master Mason, was first treasurer of the Lodge, and he is also a member of the Knights of Honor. He and Mrs. Marshall are members of the Baptist church. Their children were named as follows: Frank W., a young man of education, now holds a responsible position, appointed by Governor Culberson; William H., attending school at Peoria, Ill., will complete his course this year (1895); James Walter, at home; Anna, Edward Aubrey, Archie and Harry. Mr. Marshall has resided in this state for forty-three years, has witnessed the vast improvements that have been made, and has taken a prominent part in all movements of any importance.

THEODORE A. LOW, SR.

The percentage of men who make life a success is infinitesimally small when compared with the millions of people inhabiting our land, and many who do succeed often acquire their financial standing by questionable methods. Therefore, when a man begins life's battle with little or no means at his command, and who, by strict honesty and good management acquires a competency, that man commands the respect of his fellow man and deserves and justly receives the plaudits of all right-thinking people. Such a man is Theodore A. Low, who, for the past twenty-three years has been prominently connected with the business prosperity of the city of Brenham. A native of East Tennessee, he was born in Knox County May 20, 1849, one of seven sons and three daughters that grew to mature years, born to Gen. A. D. W. and Amanda (Matlock) Low, the father having been a General of State Militia, and prominent in Tennessee politics, his death occurring in that state when seventy-two years of age. He was a native of Tennessee, there married, and by occupation was a farmer. Theodore A. Low grew to manhood in his native country, supplementing a good common schooling, with a thorough English course, at the Ewing and Jefferson College, and a business course in Knoxville. In 1872 he started for the Great West and located in Brenham, where, for about three years he was engaged in handling sewing machines and agricultural machinery. Then forming a partnership with W. A. Wood, under the firm name of Wood & Low, in the lumber and agricultural implement business in 1876, Mr. Low and partner did an extensive business for eleven years and thoroughly entrenched their names among the foremost merchants of Central and Southern Texas. In 1887 the partnership was dissolved and two years later Mr. Low established himself in business at his present location. He carries a complete line of agricultural implements, buggies, lumber, doors, dealing justly with his customers, never misrepresenting his ware sashes, blinds, paints, oils, etc., and annually transacts an immense volume of business. His success as a merchant is the result of his and invariably conducting himself with that consideration and courtesy which becomes the true gentleman. He is one of the public-spirited men of Brenham, enterprising, contributes liberally from his means to the support of all laudable public enterprises, is a stock-holder in the First National Bank, as well as one of its directors, and is also an owner of stock in the Brenham Oil and Compress Company. In fact, owing to his well known public spirit, his enterprise, his in-telligence, his advocacy of all proper reforms and his high character, he has been identified with nearly every public enterprise advanced in Brenham for the general good. In politics he is a believer in the prin-ciples of Democracy and supports the men and measures of that party. While he has never been an aspirant for high political pre-ferment, he has held several local honorable positions, and is now alderman from the Third Ward. March 20, 1873, Mr. Low was united in marriage with Miss Cecelia T. Baine, whose father, Moses Baine, was among the earliest of Texan pioneers, coming to what is now the state in 1833, before it had received its independence from Mexico. Four children have been born to their union, as follows: Samuel D. W., a young man of fair education and exemplary habits, now in part-nership with his father; Theodore A., Jr., a young man, now attend-ing the Waco Business College; Cornelia A., an accomplished young lady, still at home, and an infant daughter, as yet unnamed. Mr. and Mrs. Low stand among the best families, socially, in Texas, and their friends equal the number of their acquaintances. Mr. Low is one of the most active, reputable and successful business men of the county and has had not a little to do with the great advancement which has made Washington County one of the most noted in the state. His capacity for business has been enormous and his power of doing great service to the community has often been called into ser-vice by his fellow citizens. The family is one of the most respectable in the county, all the members possessing high moral and intellectual qualities and exhibiting a most praiseworthy ambition. Mr. Low's brothers are Arthur, William G., Robert M., all business men of Brownwood, and Asa A. of Vernon.

DR. H. F. FORD.

One of the old and honored medicine men and citizens of Upshur County, retired from the arduous duties of life, is Dr. H. F. Ford, who came here as early as 1853. He was one of the pioneer physicians of this county and his name was a familiar one in the home of the sick and afflicted. His birth occurred in Madison County, Ala., October 6, 1825, and he received a good education for his time and day. His father, Richard Ford, was born in Madison County, Ala., and was a farmer all his life. Some time after his marriage, which occurred in Virginia, he moved to Hinds County, Miss., and thence to Vicksburg, where the remaining years of his life were passed. His wife had died in Alabama a number of years previous. Their family consisted of ten children, five sons and five daughters, all of whom grew to mature years. One son, George Ford, was a physician of Alabama for a number of years and then came to Texas, locating in Gilmer, where he practiced medicine until his death; John Ford was an editor of "Ripley Advertiser" and resided for some time in West Virginia, and then moved to Mississippi, where he died; Thomas Ford and Richard were both farmers, the former in Mississippi and the latter in Arkansas. Both are now deceased. The others are residents of Louisiana. Dr. H. F. Ford was about thirteen or fourteen years old when he moved with his parents to Hinds County, Miss. He secured his literary education and then began the study of medicine with Dr. B. J. Hich, a noted physician of Vicksburg. In 1846 he joined the First Mississippi Regiment of Jeff Davis and was in the Mexican War for twelve months, participating in the battle of Buena Vista and other engagements. Later he took lectures at the Louisville Medical College and in 1849 began practicing at Vicksburg. In 1853 he located in this county and was one of the pioneers here. Some time afterward he moved to Shady Grove, practiced there until 1861 and then located at ———— Spring. About 1870 he came to Gilmer and practiced his profession until about a year ago (1895), when he retired. He enjoyed a profitable and constantly widening professional popularity, and his rounds of duty carried him over much territory. In 1861 he joined the Confederate army, under Colonel Kemp, but was sent to Upshur County by the Colonel to care for the families in the neighborhood. He was one of the most successful physicians of the day and had the confidence of all, being careful and conscientious. The Doctor was married, first, in Vicksburg, to Miss Ella Foster, a daughter of Dr. Foster of Vicksburg. She died about two years later. The Doctor then selected his second wife in the person of Miss Emily A. Darden, a native of Georgia, and their union was celebrated at Shady Grove, Tex., June 8, 1859. Mrs. Ford was born in Heard County, where her father, George Darden, was a wealthy planter. The Doctor has ever been an ardent Democrat, but has never cared to hold office, preferring to give his entire time to his profession, and to the drug business, which he continued up to 1894. Since then he has been taking life easy, as he deserves, after the arduous duties of past life. For years Dr. Ford has been a member of the Masonic fraternity, is a Royal Arch Mason and a member of Gilmer Chapter. He and Mrs. Ford are members of the Methodist Episcopal Church. For forty-two years he has been a resident of Upshur County, and no man is better known in this and adjoining counties.

MAJOR W. H. PITTS.

The civilization of the day, the enlightenment of the age and the duty that men of the present time owe to their ancestors, to themselves and to their posterity, demand that a record of their lives and deeds should be made. Any worthy history of Camp County, Tex., would be incomplete without mention of Major W. H. Pitts, one of the old settlers and best known men of the same. Since 1854 he has been a resident of this county and during all that time his career has been most honorable and upright. He was born in Warren County, Ga., August 25, 1815, and now, after a long and active career, is retired from the arduous duties of life and enjoys the fruits of his early labors. His father, Hardy Pitts, was a native of North Carolina, and there, after reaching mature years, married Miss Drusilla O'Neal, daughter of Thomas O'Neal, who came from the Emerald Isle. After marriage Mr. Pitts became a prominent planter of North Carolina, but subsequently moved from that state to Georgia, where he was an early settler of Warren County. In that county he reared his family and spent the best years of his life, dying there when quite aged. After his death his widow resided on the home place for some time, but later moved to Texas and there died. Mr. Pitts did not serve in the war of 1812, but furnished a substitute. He was a prominent man in his day and held many positions of trust and honor. He served as sheriff in his county and held other local offices. Major W. H. Pitts, who was one of nine children, secured a fair education for his day in the common schools of Warren County, and on the 18th of December, 1838, married Miss Harriet Ann Hightower, a native of Georgia. After this he served as overseer on his father's plantation for one year and then bought a farm and began tilling it, in connection with merchandising. Thirteen years later, or in 1853, he sold out and the following year moved to Texas, near Belleville, where he rented a farm. One year afterward he moved to Upshur County (now Camp County) and bought about 200 acres of raw land, where he now resides. After that he and his brother bought 3,000 acres about three miles north of the present town of Pittsburg, cleared and improved it, and when the town of Pittsburg was laid off, about 1858 or '59, he gave about fifty acres to start the place. The town was named in his honor. Since then Mr. Pitts has sold off a large portion of his place. He was a soldier in the Creek War of 1836, under General W. Scott, first as a private, but later as sergeant, and served until the close. He is now an honorable pensioner of that war. After starting Pittsburg he engaged in merchandising and was the second man in the place to build a business house and embark in business there. For

They are therefore better adapted to succeed here than a stranger

two or three years he weighed and stored cotton, but after that
turned his attention strictly to merchandising. Mrs. Pitts took sick
and died while on a visit to her mother's in Upshur County. She left
one son, Thomas M. Pitts, a prominent physician of Pittsburg, Tex.
Mr. Pitts' second wife was Miss Lou Hanson, who died about five
years later in Stewart County. On the 18th of December, 1848, Mr.
Pitts married Mrs. Sarah F. Harvey, a native of Thompson County,
Ga., who died in Pittsburg in 1863, leaving one daughter, Elizabeth,
wife of Captain Lewis Flaitau, one of the prominent business men of
Pittsburg. In 1866 the Major married Mrs. Julia F. Carlock, a native
of Alabama, and daughter of T. J. Reynolds, who moved with his
family to Arkansas and settled in Hempstead County. Later Mr.
Reynolds moved to Texas and located at Pittsburg, where his death
occurred. His wife, too, passed away in that city. Mrs. Pitts was
reared in Hempstead County, Ark., and was married there to Samuel
G. Carlock. Afterward they located in Hempstead County. Mr.
Carlock was a soldier in the Confederate army and died during the
war. Mrs. Pitts had two children by her first marriage, DeWitt Carlock, a lawyer of prominence at Winnsborough, Wood County, and
Thomas G. Carlock, a farmer and merchant at the same place, and one
of the representative men of the county. Mrs. Pitts holds membership in the Pittsburg Methodist Episcopal Church and Mr. Pitts, although not a member of any church, is a regular attendant at the
Methodist. For thirty years Mrs. Pitts has taught in the Sunday
School and never missed a Sunday unless in case of sickness. She is
president of the Ladies' Aid Society and has been a member of that
organization for nearly a quarter of a century. Socially, Mr. Pitts is
a Mason, having joined that body in Georgia, and is a charter member
of Pittsburg Lodge. He served as Treasurer of the same for a number of years. In politics he is identified with the Democratic party
and no efforts on the part of his many friends has caused him to seek
official position. He attends, or always has, until retired, strictly to
his business interests. For forty years this estimable citizen has resided in what is now Camp County, and is well known in this and
adjoining counties. He and his excellent wife are highly esteemed
in the community and are identified with all movements of moment.

ELMORE D. MAYES.

Many of the active residents of Wilson County are natives of the same and have here spent the most of their lives. In them we find men of true loyalty to the interests of this part of the state, who understand as it were by intuition the needs, social and industrial, of this vicinity, and who have a thorough knowledge of its resources. could be and are probably without exception warmly devoted to the prosperity of their native place. Prominent in all public movements and a most efficient and capable official is Elmore D. Mayes, county clerk of Wilson County. His birth occurred in this county in 1855, and of the nine children born to his parents, William D. and Mary Ann (Cotton) Mayes, he was sixth in order of birth. The parents were natives of Tennessee, but as early as 1848 they came to Texas, and located in San Antonio. The following year Mr. Mayes had a bad attack of the gold fever and with a party started overland for the Pacific Coast. This trip was attended with many dangers, trials and privations, but he reached California in safety. After a short stay there he returned and purchased land near Sutherland Springs, then in Bexar County, where he made his home until after the war. He was exempted from duty on account of his age, but he had one son, Alverado, in the army. In 1866 he moved to San Antonio, where he remained until his death, in 1872. The mother died on the old home place in Wilson County in 1879. In addition to a good practical education, received in the schools of San Antonio, our subject spent four years finishing his education in Lebanon, Tenn., after which he returned to the farm. Agricultural pursuits and ranching continued to be his principal occupation for about eight years and in this he met with substantial results. In 1883 he came to the county seat and engaged as deputy clerk, holding that position until the fall of 1890, when, the old clerk retiring, Mr. Mayes was elected. He is now serving his second term, to the entire satisfaction of all. In the year 1887 he was married to Miss Mary H. Houston, a native of Texas, and the daughter of John P. Houston, who was one of the early settlers of this state, he and his wife dying at Waco. Mr. and Mrs. Mayes are the parents of two children: Lizzie V. and John H. Mr.

Mayes is a member of the Methodist Episcopal Church South, but his wife is a Baptist in her views. Socially Mr. Mayes is a K. of P. and a Mason, a member of Floresville Lodge No. 515. He is a trustworthy and capable county official and a social, pleasant gentleman.

DR. C. B. PHILLIPS.

Dr. C. B. Phillips of the medical fraternity in DeWitt County enjoys a most extensive practice and is widely known throughout this populous and fertile section of the state. He has built up a large practice by steady devotion to duty and the constant exercise of energy and judgment. Like many of the representative citizens of the county, he came from the East, his birth occurring in Hagarstown, Md., in 1842, and he was third in order of birth of seven children born to David and Sarah (Scott) Phillips, natives of that grand old mother of states, Virginia. The parental grandfather, Samuel Phillips, was born in England and came to Virginia during the Revolutionary War, participating in that war and taking sides with the colonists. He settled in Washington County, Md., where he was a pioneer, and followed farming for many years. His death occurred in Hagarstown. The maternal grandfather, William E. Scott, was also a native of England, and on coming to this country settled in the Old Dominion, where he died. He was a flour-broker and miller. The parents of our subject met and were married in Hagarstown, Md. The father afterward engaged in milling and farming, and when the Civil War broke out he enlisted in the Confederate army from Augusta County, Va., in the Washington Artillery. He participated in many battles, and was killed in the battle of Gordonsville in 1863. His wife, too, passed away during the war. Two of their sons, David and John, served in the Federal army. The former assisted in raising a company, and became captain of a company in the Seventh Illinois Regiment. He was captured, and probably died in prison. John was killed in battle. Dr. C. B. Phillips grew to mature years in Maryland, and received his education in Mount St. Mary's College, Maryland. On account of his health he was obliged to leave school, and he began the study of medicine in 1858 with Dr. R. N. Wright of

Baltimore. In 1860 he attended Jefferson Medical College, and was graduated from Washington University, Baltimore, Md., 1868. About August 1, 1861, he entered the Confederate army as private, Third Virginia Cavalry, and in October he was called before the medical examining board at Richmond, was passed, and made assistant surgeon of the Confederate States Volunteers. He served in various hospitals and camps during the war, and was in the Army of Virginia until the close. In 1865 he went to New Orleans, intending to locate. During the yellow fever epidemic of 1867 he was employed by the Howard Association as surgeon, with which he remained until danger was over. From there he went to Mexico, first to Durango, and then to the City of Mexico, but in the latter part of 1868 he came back to Texas and located in Live Oak County, at Oakville, where he practiced until 1870. He then went to Victoria, Lavaca and DeWitt counties, but finally settled at Burns Station in 1873, and has been practicing in that section since. In January, 1894, he partially withdrew from general practice, and is now treating specially the morphine, liquor and kindred habits by the bi-chloride of gold method. He has an office in Cuero, but is often called in consultation in adjoining counties. Dr. Phillips was married in 1872 to Miss Fannie E. Alkinson, a native of Tennessee, who came to Texas when a child. One son has been born to this union, Calvin B. Phillips.

THOMAS J. PEEL.

This intelligent gentleman is the district clerk of Hays County, Tex., and was born in Montgomery County, Ala., where he first saw the light of day in 1844, the youngest of ten children born to the marriage of David B. Peel and Rebecca Holloway, both of whom were natives of the State of Georgia. The father removed to Alabama at an early day, where he tilled the soil, but died in an adjoining county in Mississippi in 1880. His first wife died in 1848 or 1849, and he afterward married again, and by his second wife became the father of five children. Thomas J. Peel was reared and educated in his native state, his educational advantages being confined to the common schools. Up to 1863 his attention was given to farming, but he then enlisted in the Confederate army, in Company I, Sixty-first Alabama Regiment, and served in the Army of Northern Virginia, participating in the battles of the Wilderness, Spottsylvania Court House and others. He was so severely wounded at Cold Harbor in 1864 that he was entirely disabled for further service and was also unfitted for work for several years afterward. He went home and attended school for some time, then began clerking in a store, although he still suffered a good deal from his wound. Later he became a railroad express clerk, and followed this and clerking in different mercantile establishments until 1875, when he came to Robertson County, Tex., and for three years was engaged in farming on the Brazos River, after which he resumed clerking. In 1881 he came to San Marcos, clerked for four years, then became assistant postmaster of San Marcos, holding that position two years. In November, 1888, he was elected to his present office, and has been re-elected each expiring term since that time without opposition. Socially, Mr. Peel is a member of Hays Lodge of the Knights of Honor, of which he has been Reporter twelve years, and Deputy Grand Dictator; is Secretary of Live Oak Camp of the Woodmen of the World, and is Secretary of Clan Marcos Lodge No. 119 of the Knights of Pythias. He is the oldest in years and in point of membership of the Fire Company of San Marcos, and is secretary of Elect Hose Company No. 1, which office he has held since the organization of the company. In 1875 he led to the altar Miss Mattie E., daughter of P. P. Jones of Hearne, Tex., an early settler of the state, and a brother of Rev. Gifford Jones of Memphis, Tenn. To the union of Mr. and Mrs. Peel the following children were born: Nellie, David, Mary, Coy and Raymond. Mr. Peel and his family are members of the Methodist church, and are highly esteemed members of the best social circles of San Marcos.

REV. FATHER L. WYER.

Rev. Father L. Wyer is a product of the famous Isle of Erin, where he first saw the light of day in 1846, he being the fourth child born to Laurence and Mary Bridget (McAleny) Wyer, and was almost from the time of his birth intended by them for the priesthood. He was given excellent educational advantages and, after thorough preparation, was ordained a priest of the Catholic church in 1868, after which he was made assistant of the parish of Tubbar, which position he retained several years. In 1879 he emigrated to the New World and was assigned to work in the diocese of San Antonio, but gave this up in 1880 and was placed in charge of the Catholic church at Victoria. He entered heart and soul into his pastoral duties, and almost immediately began the work of reorganizing St. Joseph's College, which had before been founded in Victoria and which had, for various reasons, declined until it had in all things but a name become extinct. No better man could have been found for the work than Father Wyer, for he is the soul of enterprise, energy and determination, and under his capable generalship the present commodious buildings were erected and the school was at once started on its present prosperous course. The furniture and appliances are sufficient for all requirements, and a regular collegiate course is given, comprising eight years. In the lay department there is an attendance of two hundred pupils, over which it has been found necessary to place a corps of eight competent instructors, music lessons being given by an extra teacher. There are twelve pupils in the department of divinity; in fact, the school is established on a sound basis and is already patronized by the best people of the South. He became parish priest of this ward in 1892 and in his priestly labors has been no less active than in his labors for St. Joseph's College. He has built up the Catholic church of Victoria and as pastor and friend is dearly loved by his flock, as well as those who differ from him in religious faith.

HON. THOMAS CALHOUN GREENWOOD.

It is a pleasure to review the career of a man whose efforts have been crowned with distinction, and whose life has been honorable and praiseworthy. We all have strivings after a high ideal, but an

ideal alone is of little value if not reinforced by the example of those
who, like ourselves, have human frailties, yet have been enabled to
so overcome them as to lead lives of usefulness and honor. Thomas
C. Greenwood was born in Monroe County, Miss., April 14, 1823, the
sixth of eight children born to Thomas Greenwood and Lydia (Moore)
Greenwood, who were natives of Virginia and North Carolina respectively. The former was a planter by occupation, and died in 1854,
his wife's death occurring two years later, both of whom had been
members of the Baptist church for about sixty years. The subject
of this sketch was reared in the northeast part of Mississippi, and
was educated in LaGrange College, Alabama, from which well known
institution he graduated in 1843. Soon after leaving this institution
he began the study of law, was admitted to practice in 1844, and
soon after opened an office at Greensborough, Choctaw County, Miss.
He was the valedictorian of his class, and the following extract is
quoted from the "North Alabamian" of June 9, 1843:

"Mr. Greenwood's address was characterized by sound reasoning,
and bore the impress of a strong mind, habituated to deep thought,
and well versed in the history of the day and country."

It was not long before his intelligence, native ability and knowledge of his profession began to be recognized, and his faithfulness to
the interests of his clients, whose cases he usually won, was soon the
means of winning him a very large practice. In 1848 he moved to
Chickasaw County, Miss., where, for a short time, he edited a Democratic paper—"The Patriot"—in partnership with Judge T. N. Martin.
After locating in this section he again soon found himself in the
midst of a successful practice, and there he remained and became
widely and favorably known until 1852. Declining health then
compelled him to make a change. He removed to Seguin,
Tex., and during the most of the four years that he resided there he was in partnership with the distinguished judge,
John Ireland. Following his usual habits of faithfulness, industry and attention to his profession, he was very successful
in his practice. In a few years his health again failed, and,
quitting the law, he went to the country and settled on his farm

in Caldwell County, where his home has since continued to be. His estate comprises 800 acres of excellent land, of which 200 acres are under cultivation, and all the improvements instituted thereon have been made by himself, and are of a character to add greatly to the value of the property. On this farm he has made his home for forty years, and during this time his walk through life has been characterized by prudence and circumspection, by many deeds of benevolence and kindness, and by his desire to live an upright and useful life. He is held in high esteem by the citizens of the county, and has prospered financially in the conduct of his affairs. During the war, although ill health debarred him from entering the service, he served the county as commissioner, and did much to assist those families whose fathers, husbands and brothers were fighting their battles at the front. Without doubt, had his health permitted, he would have risen to a high place in his profession and in the offices of the state. In 1844 he was married to Miss Juliet Crocker, a native of South Carolina, and he attributes much of his success in life to her unfailing good judgment and helpful spirit. To their union eight children were born: Thomas, who was drowned in the San Marcos River in 1879, was a noble man and highly respected. He entered the Confederate army when seventeen years of age, and served with distinguished ability in General Green's Brigade. Calphurnia became the wife of W. J. Grubbs; James is county judge of Guadalupe County; Carrie is the wife of A. M. Benner, and resides in Gillespie County; Emmett yet resides with his parents on the farm; Paul Jones is a lawyer at Luling, and Eugenia graduated from Waco University, and died three days afterward, in 1881. One child died in infancy. Mr. Greenwood was ordained a minister of the Baptist church in 1858, and has served as pastor of several churches in his vicinity, mainly at Prairie Lea and Seguin. He and his faithful wife are now in their seventy-second year. They hope to celebrate the fiftieth anniversary of their marriage during this year, 1894. He ascribes his length of days to temperate habits, and a cheerful, abiding faith in God, who "watches the sparrow's fall and feeds the young ravens when they cry."

JUDGE R. H. COLEMAN.

It is a real pleasure to review the career of a man whose efforts
have been crowned with success, and whose life has been honorable
in every particular, as has that of Judge R. H. Coleman. He was a
member of one of the F. F. V's. and first saw light in the Old Dominion in 1820, being the eldest child born to John J. and Catherine
(Hawes) Coleman, who were of English descent, but Virginians by
birth. The father was an extensive planter, and followed this occupation during the five years that the family resided in Kentucky.
At the end of that time they returned to Virginia, and there the
parents spent the rest of their lives. Judge Coleman received a better education than the majority of youths of his day and was an attendant of Virginia College. When starting out in life for himself,
he took up the occupation to which he had been reared, and with
which he was most familiar, and for some time gave his attention to
farming. At the age of twenty years he was appointed sheriff of
Nelson County and filled the office very acceptably for two years. In
1858 he came to Texas and upon locating in Victoria engaged in various speculative enterprises, such as dealing in stock, land, etc.
During the Civil War he was principally engaged in furnishing supplies for the Confederate Government, but was for a time a member
of the State Militia. At the close of the great conflict between the
North and South, Judge Coleman began carrying the United States
mail under Government contract, and as he, at this time, was the
proprietor of a large livery stable in Victoria, he did an immense
business, carrying passengers to all adjoining counties. With shrewd
forethought he caused a position bridge to be erected across the
river at Victoria and this brought him in a large revenue. He has at
all times shown the best of judgment in his business ventures, and,
as a result, is the owner of much valuable city property and good
ranch property. During all these years he has also been engaged in
mercantile pursuits in Victoria, his partner in this branch of human
endeavor being William Shrieve. In 1878 he was elected county

judge of Victoria County and for twelve years was elected successively, which speaks for itself as to his popularity as a citizen and politician.

J. D. ANDERSON.

Few men have lived more quietly and unostentatiously than J. D. Anderson, and yet few have exerted a more salutary influence upon the immediate society in which they move, or impressed a community with a more profound reliance on their honor and ability of sterling worth. His life has not been illustrious with startling or striking contrasts; but it has shown how a laudable ambition may be gratified when accompanied by pure motives, perseverance, industry and steadfastness of purpose. Mr. Anderson is now the owner of a large and excellent farm, and as a stock-raiser stands second to none in the county. He is a native of the Palmetto State, as were also his parents, James and Margaret (Dorrah) Anderson. The paternal grandfather, D. Anderson, was a native of Virginia, while the maternal grandfather, James Dorrah, was born in Scotland or Ireland. William Anderson and wife, who was a Miss Denny, with two sons, David and John, came from Ireland and settled in Pennsylvania, but afterward moved to Charleston, S. C., and thence to Laurens County, S. C., just below the court house. After they had moved to Laurens County, they had four more children: Rebecca, Sallie, one, name unknown, and Denny. They afterward moved to Spartanburg County, on Enoree River, and thence to Tiger River, where William Anderson, at an advanced age, was killed by the Tories and Indians. John Anderson married and settled in York County. David married a Miss Mason and settled on Tiger River, in Spartanburg County. Rebecca never married. Sallie married a man by the name of Brakin, in Charleston, S. C., where they lived. She had one son, who moved to Missouri. Denny married a Miss Elizabeth Massey and settled on Enoree River, S. C., Spartanburg County. They raised a family of eleven children; Rebecca, William, David, John, Denny, Mary, James, Samuel, Martha, Henry and Elizabeth. Elizabeth

Massey Anderson, wife of Denny Anderson on the maternal side, was descended from the Smiths of Halifax County, N. C. The father of our subject was a successful agriculturist and tilled the soil in his native state until his death in 1883. The mother passed away in 1851. Both belonged to the Presbyterian church, and were active workers in the same. Our subject was born in the year 1832, educated in the old field schools and was prevented from entering college by the death of the mother and the subsequent illness of the father. For some time he managed his father's estate, and, when twenty-eight years of age, was married to Miss Ianthe J. Wallace, a daughter of Hon. Alexander Wallace, a well known South Carolinian, who was prominent in state and national affairs, and who was a member of Congress for some time. In 1859 our subject came to the Lone Star State, located in DeWitt County, and in 1862 he enlisted in Company B, Twentieth Texas Regiment, Infantry, serving on the coast in Texas principally and holding the rank of lieutenant. He was in service until the close of hostilities. In 1865 Mr. Anderson bought a portion of his present farm, located near the village of Thomaston, 489 acres in the river track, highly improved, and 200 acres under cultivation. He also owns other tracts, containing 3,000 acres, with 200 acres under cultivation, and he has one of the handsomest homes in the whole section. His fine residence is on a natural building site, a ridge overlooking the beautiful Guadalupe Valley, and he is surrounded by all the comforts of life. His marriage has been blessed by the birth of nine children, three being deceased. They are named as follows: Robert W., N. Bertie, wife of C. E. Kaapke; George S., Mary Ianthe, wife of Rev. A. H. P. McCurdy; William Irvin and three died in childhood. The family holds membership in the Presbyterian church.

MAJOR SAMUEL B. BALES.

Few have lived as quietly as Major Samuel B. Bales, and few have exerted a more salutary influence upon the immediate society in which they move, or impressed a community with a more profound reliance on their honor, ability or sterling worth. His life has not been illustrious with startling incidents or striking contrasts, but it has shown how a laudable ambition may be gratified when accompanied by pure motives, persevering industry and steadfastness of purpose. He was born in South Carolina in 1817, the eldest of seven children born to John and Mary (Blue) Bales, who were also natives of the Palmetto State, where the father followed farming and blacksmithing throughout life, and eventually passed from life. The paternal grandfather, John Bales, was born in the Isle of Erin, and just before the opening of the Revolutionary War in this country had emigrated thither, located in South Carolina, and from that state enlisted in the Colonial army. The maternal grandfather was also a Revolutionary soldier from South Carolina. In the state of his birth the subject of this sketch was reared and he began life for himself as a tiller of the soil. In 1849 he came to Austin, Tex., with a colony of nine families, and he very soon after became superintendent of the erection of the Capitol Building in Austin, which occupied his time and attention for about one year. Following this, he was engaged in building mills and gins until 1856, when he married, and until 1859 was engaged in farming in Travis County, since which time he has been a resident of Hays County, and for many years devoted his attention to agriculture. His wife was Elizabeth Henry, a native of Tennessee, and a daughter of John Henry, who became a resident of Texas in 1851, and took up his abode at Austin. In 1863 Mr. Bales entered the Confederate army, soon became attached to Green's Brigade as ordnance officer, and was in the battle of Mansfield, where General Green was killed. He was detailed to return to Austin with the General's remains, and after that sad duty had been performed was detailed for post duty in that city, where he served until the war closed. For about eighteen months following he was in the service of the United States, in charge of stock and forage, then returned to his farm and once more began tilling the soil. In the fall of 1868 he moved to San Marcos and established the first livery stable of this place, and after conducting it very successfully for a long time he sold out and now owns and conducts a grain and feed store and boarding stable. His farm, which comprises 360 acres, is an exceptionally fertile and valuable one, and seventy-five acres are

in an excellent state of cultivation. Major Bales was elected alderman of San Marcos in 1890, was re-elected at the end of his first
term, and is now president of the Board of Aldermen. During this
time many improvements in the town have been made, and there
are now seven miles of macadamized roads. The Major is a Mason
of long standing, and he and his wife are members of the Cumberland Presbyterian church, in which he is one of the elders. They
have two living children, John H. and Mary, wife of John Cape.
Another child died in infancy, unnamed. Major Bales saw much of
early Texas life in the rough, and was on several expeditions against
the Indians, and was thoroughly familiar with life on the frontier.

JACK SUTHERLAND.

This prominent citizen is a descendant of one of the pioneer families of Wharton County, Tex., where he was born in January, 1838,
and he inherits many of the worthy and sterling traits of his Scottish ancestors. His grandfather, John Sutherland, or Sutherlin, as
the name was originally spelled, came to this country from Scotland
in the early half of the eighteenth century and settled on Dan River,
where be began the cultivation of tobacco. In 1800 he moved to
Clinch River, Tenn., and engaged in farming, residing there until his
children had all married. He then went to Alabama and made his
home with his son John until his death. He was a pioneer in every
sense of the word, and a man whose upright, honorable career endeared him to all. John Sutherland, father of our subject, was born
in Virginia in 1792, on the site of the present city of Danville, and
began life as a merchant at Knoxville, Tenn. While a resident of
Knoxville he was married to Diana Kennedy of that city, by whom
he had three children, David, Sarah Agnes and James. About 1825
he moved to Decatur and thence to Tuscumbia, Ala. While residing
in Decatur he was president of a bank, and while in Tuscumbia a

merchant. His first wife, having died, he selected his second wife in the person of Miss Ann Bryan Lane, a native of Alabama, and our subject was one of the younger children born to this union. In 1835 John Sutherland came to Texas prospecting and looking for a location, and was in San Antonio in 1836, when the Mexicans besieged the Alamo. He was within the walls of that place and was sent out by General Travis with dispatches to Gonzales. By the time he returned the Alamo had fallen and the force had been slain. Returning to Gonzales, he joined the forces of General Houston, who had arrived at that place, and was sent by that officer with dispatches to President Burnet—with whom he served as aide-de-camp and private secretary until the close of hostilities. Returning to Alabama he moved his family to Texas in 1838, settling on the west side of the Colorado River, where he established a ferry which goes by the name of Sutherland's Ferry to this day. In the year 1840 his second wife died, having borne him three sons: George Q., Levin L. and Jack. In 1841 he married a third wife, Ann M. Dickson, widow of Abisha Dickson, killed with Fannin at Goliad. In March, 1849, he moved to a place on the Cibolo Creek, where a small town was laid out and named Sutherland Springs, and a postoffice established, of which he was the first postmaster. This county was mainly organized by his influence, and Sutherland Springs became the first county seat. There his death occurred in May, 1867, at the age of seventy-four years and eleven months. In this county our subject was mainly reared, but his education was received in Knoxville, Tenn. In the year 1861 he enlisted in Company F, Fourth Texas Infantry, a part of Hood's Texas Brigade. It will be remembered that this regiment was the first to break General Potter's line at Gaines' Mill, June 27, 1862, and turn the tide of battle in favor of the Confederates. Mr. Sutherland is quite proud of his honorable record as a member of Hood's Immortal Brigade—is well posted on the history of the war, and, though a good loyal citizen of "Our Own Common Government," as Uncle Abe would put it, says he is as unreconstructed as ever. He went to Virginia, and was organized at Richmond. Mr. Sutherland participated in all the campaigns, and in all the battles of that section, missing but a few engagements. He was severely wounded at Darbytown Road in October, 1864, and was retired on account of disability. He came home just as the war ended. He was promoted from the ranks to lieutenant and adjutant. After the war Mr. Sutherland engaged in surveying and farming for some time, and after the death of the father was administrator of the estate. Until 1885 he lived at Sutherland Springs, when he moved to Floresville to educate his children. He is the owner of 500 acres near the Springs, and is one of the ranchers of the county. Upon the organization of Wilson County in 1860, he was elected district clerk, holding that office when he went to the war, and leaving his father as deputy. In the year 1870 he was married to Miss Mary E. Sutherland of Victoria, daughter of Dr. William Sutherland, a native of Kentucky. Her father came to Texas in 1852, was an early physician of this section, and died in Victoria in 1891. To our subject and wife eleven children were born, ten of whom are now living: Mamie, Annie, Jack, Jr., Agnes, Winnifred, Walter, Frederick, John, Levin, Lucy and Lizzie, who died in infancy. Mrs. Sutherland is a worthy member of the Baptist church.

JUDGE ED R. KONE.

One of the well known attorneys of Hays County, Tex., who commands the respect, as well as the admiration of his brother practitioners, is Judge Ed R. Kone, who is an experienced, shrewd and keen-witted lawyer, whose labors for his clients are herculean, and whose efforts to bring the guilty to justice and to right the wrongs of his fellow-citizens have done much to bring about law and order in Hays County. He is a product of Montgomery County, Tex., born in 1848, the eldest of ten children born to Samuel R. and Rebecca S. (Pitts) Kone, natives respectively of South Carolina and Georgia. In 1839 the former came to Texas at the age of fourteen years, and at once engaged in farm work in Grimes County, and for some time had charge of a force of negroes belonging to his uncle, Louis Depree. He remained in Grimes County until 1850, then bought a farm in

Montgomery County, on which he located and which he greatly improved. He came to Hays County in 1851, bought a tract of land at "Stringtown," and was very successful in tilling the soil and in raising stock. After serving in the Confederate army for about one year he was discharged on account of ill health, returned home and resumed farming, which he continued up to the time of his death, in 1873. He was an active Methodist, and a steward in that church. His father, Samuel Kone, was a carpenter and builder by occupation, and did some important state work in South Carolina. The maternal grandfather of the subject of this sketch, General John D. Pitts, was born in either Virginia or Georgia, which is not definitely known. He was married in Georgia, followed planting there, and represented the section in which he lived in the Georgia State Legislature, serving twice in that capacity. He came to Grimes County, Tex., in 1846, engaged in planting and stock-raising, but his vigorous intellect and many requirements soon brought him into prominent notice, and he was elected clerk of the lower house of the State Legislature, in which capacity he served several sessions, and he was then elected state comptroller, a position he ably filled for one or two terms. He had taken up his residence in Austin in 1848, but in 1849 or 1850 he came to Hays County, and was the first settler of what is now locally called "Stringtown." After a remarkably well-spent life, he breathed his last in 1861 at that place. The immediate subject of this sketch was educated in the schools of San Marcos and at Bastrop, under Colonel R. P. Allen. He began life for himself as a clerk at San Marcos, but at the end of one year began the study of law under Major W. O. Hutchinson, and upon attaining his majority was admitted to the bar. He then formed a partnership with the Major, and after remaining thus associated for three years, was appointed to fill a vacancy in the sheriff's office, and held that position for eight months. After practicing his profession one year the next general election came around, and he was elected presiding justice of this county, and held the office until it was made vacant by the present constitution. He then declined to run for county judge, although strongly urged to do so, and soon after formed a partnership with Captain H. B. Coffield, which he held about one and one-half years, at the end of which time he was elected county judge, and ably discharged the duties of this office for twelve years in succession. During this time he was instrumental in building the present court house and jail. At the time he was elected presiding justice the county was in debt about $30,000, and script was so low that the county was being greatly injured. He went to Austin and was instrumental in having a special act passed, authorizing the funding of the floating debt at 8 per cent. This act enabled the county to proceed on a cash basis, so that in three years the total debt was canceled. He, as ex-officio school superintendent, built up the schools of this county greatly, for when he entered the office there were but thirteen schools in operation, and when he left the office fifty were in fine working order, which admirable state of affairs had been brought about through his own good management and persistent efforts. After twelve years of service, he declined further election to the judgeship, and once more resumed the practice of his profession, and after a time formed a partnership with L. H. Browne, which continued for two years, but since that time he has practiced alone. He has always been active in political matters, and is now a member of the State Democratic Executive Committee, in which capacity he also served several years ago. He has been a delegate to the state conventions every year since he attained his majority, with one exception, and for years has been at the head of the county Democratic organization. His official life was characterized by a desire to benefit his section, and he labored faithfully with that object in view, and success crowned his efforts in almost every instance. He is familiar with all branches of his profession, is a thoroughly posted, keen and far-seeing lawyer, and those who place their interests in his hands may rest assured that they will be carefully guarded. Judge Kone was married in November, 1872, to Miss Lula H. Martin, a native of Texas, and a daughter of Archie Martin, who was killed during the Civil War while serving in the Confederate army, and she was left motherless when an infant. Her union with Judge Kone has resulted in the birth of four children: Julia R., Carrie, Eula Lee and Edna Woods. The Judge and his wife are members of the Methodist church, and socially he is a member of the A. F. and A. M., the I. O. O. F., the K. of P. and the K. of H.

GEORGE W. WATSON.

The subject of this sketch is a gentleman of ripe intelligence and experience, and one of the oldest newspaper men in the "Lone Star State," where he has resided since six years of age. He is at present on the staff of the "Jefferson Jimplecute," a daily, and for two years edited and managed a paper at Schulenburg, this state. He was born in Alabama in 1841 and when but six years old came to Jefferson with his parents, William P. and Mary B. (Taylor) Watson. The father was a man of great force of character, and when a young man edited a paper at Mobile, Ala., in the interests of the Whig party, with which he was in full accord. He published the third newspaper of Jefferson. Mr. Watson was of sturdy Scotch origin and his great-grandfather, coming from that country to this and dying here, was buried on an ancestral estate of 10,000 acres, known as "Pineville Farm," near Raleigh, N. C. Mr. Watson's father was a plumber by trade, and a large slaveowner. Mrs. Watson's father was a large mail contractor, was well known, and was at one time the richest man in the South. When seven years of age George W. Watson began learning the trade of printer with his father, and when the Civil War broke out he was among the very first to enlist, joining Captain S. J. Richardson's company, which was gathered at Marshall, where it was permanently organized for service April 19, 1861. This company was sent to San Antonio, where it was attached to the Second Texas Cavalry, and from there ordered to the western part of the state to fight Indians. One year later this regiment was sent to Arkansas Post, and at the surrender of that place forty-four of the company were captured and sent to Camp Butler, Ill., near Springfield, our subject being among the number. While held prisoners, nineteen of this number died. Our subject was exchanged at City Point with the remainder of those of his regiment and was sent to join the Army of Tennessee under General Bragg. He was in this army for two years, or until almost the close of the war, and at this time only seven of the original forty-four captured were alive and these were transferred back to the Trans-Mississippi army to their old command and comrades. Mr. Watson participated in the batle of Arkansas Post, Missionary Ridge, Chickamauga and Ringgold Gap. At the battle of Chickamauga our subject's brigade held a strategic point when two other brigades had failed. He belonged to Granbury's Brigade, and at the battle of Chickamauga he went ahead of the line to reconnoiter and came back to the line, where men were falling on all sides, and said: "Boys, we are going to have h—l here directly." The reply was: "We think we are getting it now." Mr. Watson's command was camped at Tunnel Hill for six or seven months and was in the memorable retreat with Hood's army. His company was disbanded near Houston, Tex., at the close of the war, and, after returning home, he followed farming for three or four years. In the year 1867 he was married to Miss Marietta Mathews of Marion County. She died in 1891, leaving one child, a daughter, who died in 1894 at the promising age of eighteen. Another child, a son, died when three years old.

CAPTAIN R. D. CHAPMAN.

An active and progressive system in any profession or line of business, when based upon principles of honor, is sure to bring success, and an illustration of prominence gained through these means is seen in the record of Captain R. D. Chapman, who has been a resident of Nacogdoches, Tex., since 1888, and whose career has been above reproach. He is thorough-going and progressive in all business enterprises, is well-liked as a citizen, and is now a popular commercial traveler of Eastern Texas. Captain Chapman was born in Houston County, Ga., December 8, 1839, and is a son of William H. J. Chapman, who was a native of Georgia. His grandfather, William D. Chapman, was a South Carolinian by birth, and of Scotch-Irish parentage. He was a soldier in the Revolutionary War and was a worker in fine metals and rendered valuable services in making edge tools and swords for the officers of the Revolution. He served under General Greene and was three times captured, but each time succeeded in making his escape. After the war he located in Middle Georgia, where his death occurred November 13, 1815. William H. J. Chapman was reared in Middle Georgia and was married in that state to Miss Temperance Cowan, a native of the same. He was the youngest orphan son of a Revolutionary soldier and had limited educational advantages in early life. After his marriage he settled in Central Georgia and there reared his family. In 1840 he moved to Muscogee County, Ga., and from thence to Cuthbert, Randolph County, Ga., in 1844, where he lived until he died September 10, 1884. He married Miss Temperance Jordan, who died in 1860 and they both are interred in Cuthbert Cemetery. He married his second wife, Miss Rosa Bell, in 1864, and this lady survives him. Their children were named as follows: Dr. William P., a physician of Woodville, Tex.; Captain R. D. (subject); Dr. James H. of Lufkin, Tex.; Mary E., Catherine and Eliza. In Cuthbert, Randolph County, Ga., the original of this notice grew to manhood and when but a lad of thirteen entered commercial life as his choice avocation, thus at an early age receiving a thorough training in business methods. Early in 1861 he formed a business partnership with an older brother and was engaged in merchandising at Colquitt, Miller County, Ga., for a few months. He then volunteered his services to the Confederate army in August, 1861, and assisted in raising a company for the Confederate army. But the Confederate authorities refused to accept the services of this company at that time, being destitute of arms and munitions of war. Therefore they joined the First Regiment, Georgia State Troops, for a term of six months, and R. D. Chapman was promoted from private to sergeant-major of the regiment as a reward for his merit and patriotism thus far exhibited in the Confederate cause. At the expiration of this term of service the company was reorganized into the Fifty-fifth Georgia Infantry. Our subject was made first lieutenant of Company E, and was promoted to the rank of captain of the same September 12, 1862, serving as such until the war closed. He took part in the battle of

Richmond, Ky., and then, September 30, 1863, was in the fight at
Cumberland Gap, where the Fifty-fifth Georgia was captured by
Burnside and the officers taken to Johnson Island prison in Lake
Erie. Our subject remained a prisoner up to February 9, 1864, and
then he with a number of others were ordered to be transferred to
Point Lookout, Md. While being conveyed across Pennsylvania in
prison cars on the Pennsylvania Central Railroad Captain Chapman
sprang from the car while in rapid motion and made his escape.
This was at York on the night of February 12, 1864. After three
days and nights of thrilling adventure, traveling by night only, and
with the greatest caution, he managed to escape recapture. He
had but one meal during the three days and nights. · Making himself known to an Irish lady near Westminster, Md., he received much
kindness and assistance from her and gradually made his way to
Emmettsburg, Md., and was assisted into the Confederate lines.
Later he joined his old command, under Lieutenant-Colonel Pierson,
and was appointed adjutant of the post at Andersonville, and was
in service there for several months until the prisoners increased to
32,000. Then General Winder from Richmond, Va., was placed in
charge of the post and Captain Chapman served under him for a
time. He then assumed command of a detachment of the Fifty-
fifth Georgia Regiment for the service of transporting prisoners to
Florence, S. C., being thus occupied for several months. He and
his detachment then went to Savannah to assist the Confederates
against General Sherman's raid through Georgia and when the city
was evacuated Captain Chapman brought up the rear guard and
was among the last to leave the city. After that he participated
in the battle of Bentonville, N. C., March 19, 20 and 21, 1865, the last
fight of the war. Soon after his return to Randolph County, Ga.,
Captain Chapman put up a tent near the old home and resided in
that for six months and taught a three months' term of school. Returning to Colquitt, Miller County, he again engaged in merchandising. In 1867 he withdrew from the firm and on November 21 of
the same year was married to Miss Eugenia Alice McNeil, daughter
of William McNeil of Cuthbert, Ga. In 1868 Captain Chapman engaged in railroad contracting and building, and followed this business for four years in Southwestern Georgia. In 1872 he moved to

LEROY W. COOPER.

Texas and first located in Tyler County, on the Neches River, where he followed farming for five years. During this time he took a contract for clearing out a portion of the Neches River and received for the work about 50,000 acres of Texas wild land. This land the captain subsequently traded for a plantation in Tyler County, about 300 acres of well-improved land, and he tilled this for several years. Following this he was occupied in contracting and transporting timber down the Neches River to Beaumont and continued in this business with varied success for two years. Captain Chapman next went on the road as a commercial salesman in 1881 for W. D. Cleveland of Houston, and sold groceries for this firm one year. After that he contracted with the old firm, Wallace, Lands & Co., grocers of Galveston, and has traveled for that firm in East Texas for about thirteen years, and is an excellent salesman. In 1888 or 1889 Captain Chapman moved to Nacogdoches and bought a neat residence on North Street. There he has since resided and has traveled from this town since that time. He is an ardent supporter of Democratic principles and is active in his support of that party. He and wife have three children: Osgood McNeil Chapman has been well-educated and is a young man of superior business ability, now holds a responsible position with Meyer & Schmidts, the leading mercantile house in Nacogdoches; Mattie C., wife of Rev. Leon Sanfield, a minister of the M. E. church, located at Beaumont, Tex., and Lollie D., a young lady at home. The latter is a graduate of Nacogdoches High School and a bright young lady. ~The captain and family are active members in the M. E. church and the former is steward in the same. Socially Captain Chapman is a Mason and a Knight of Pythias. He is a very popular man, has a host of warm friends and is an excellent citizen.

JUDGE LEROY W. COOPER.

There are many lawyers in Houston County, but there are few left who were members of the bar of this county over a quarter of a century ago. One such is the old and highly honored gentleman

whose name appears above. He is a product of Georgia, born in
October, 1822, and the son of Lewis and Anna (Abbott) Cooper, natives respectively of Virginia and South Carolina. The American
family of Cooper is of English origin as is also the Abbott family.
The paternal grandfather, Leion Cooper, was born in Old Virginia
and was captain in the Colonial army, participating in the battle of
Cowpens. He died in South Carolina at the advanced age of ninety
years. The maternal grandfather, Matthew Abbott, was a South
Carolinian by birth and he also fought for independence. The father
of our subject followed the occupation of a farmer during life and
resided in South Carolina for many years. Later he moved to Georgia and there died in 1858, following his wife who had died in 1856.
They were the parents of nine children, and both held membership
in the Baptist church. During his youth, which was spent in Georgia, our subject attended the common school when not assisting
on the farm, but is mainly self-educated. He assisted on the home
place until he had attained his majority and then began the study
of law, soon after being admitted to the bar. The following year
(1846) he began practicing and the same year was married to Miss
R. A. Brazier, a native of Georgia. In 1849 Judge Cooper and family moved to Griffin, and in 1856 came to Crockett, Tex. In 1862 he
became enrolling officer of the county, and later was made colonel
of the militia and still later brigadier-general. In the fall of 1862
he was elected to the State Senate from this district and served one
term. In 1865 he was appointed judge of the judicial district
(ninth) and served in that capacity until 1866. In 1869 he was
elected to the State Legislature and while this was in session he was
appointed judge of the Third Judicial District, filling that position
for six years. ,He served nine years on the bench altogether, and
there is not another judge in this section in whose rulings and opinions more implicit confidence is placed than in his. In 1876 he was
the candidate for Congress of the Republican party and also a delegate to the national convention that nominated Mr. Hayes for the
presidency. In 1884 he was an elector from his district for Blaine,
and has been and is a leader of the Republican party. The old saying to the effect that it is the man who makes the office honorable,
not the office which dignifies the man, has been exemplified in Judge

Cooper's career. He has added dignity and respect to all the important places he has been called upon to fill. Judge Cooper continued in practice until seventy years of age and then retired from his practice and mainly from politics. He is the owner of large farming interests and is interested in the breeding of fine Durham cattle. In 1858 he erected a fine residence, which is still one of the handsomest in the vicinity, and in this he still resides. To his marriage were born four children: Nettie, wife of Judge W. B. Wall; Georgia, wife of Rev. H. W. Moore of Crockett; Louis N., a graduate of Cornell University, read law, was admitted and became a prominent attorney, went to Fort Worth, Tex., was elected judge of the criminal court, but later retired from the bar and became a minister in the M. E. church, and James L., educated in the University of Virginia, studied medicine at Baltimore and is now doing a large practice at Fort Worth. Both of Judge Cooper's daughters are finely educated, being graduates of a female college. Judge Cooper is a member of the I. O. O. F., and he and his family hold membership in the M. E. church.

FREDERICK A. PIPER.

Frederick A. Piper was born on the third day of May, 1851, in Muehlhausen, in the province of Waldeck, Prussia. His father was Frederick William Piper, and his mother Johanne Waldeck. His parents were married in Muehlhausen in the year 1840. The family came to the United States in 1853 and located in San Antonio, where his father obtained remunerative employment as a carpenter and builder. The family consisted of young Piper and two elder brothers. Young Frederick received a common school education from 1858 to 1864, that being the only kind of education that his parents at that time were able to give him, and that was interrupted by the War of the Rebellion. On this account, in 1864, he was compelled, on account of the closing of the schools, to study at home,

which he did assiduously and diligently for several months and until
he entered the employ of the firm of Webb, Arbuckle & Co., wholesale dry goods dealers, with whom he remained until the failure of
the firm, which occurred in 1866. During this time he received
from $5 to $15 per month, entering their service at the former figure
and leaving it when given the latter sum. In the spring of the following year young Piper entered the service of the hardware firm of
Norton & Deutz, whom he served faithfully for ten years, entering
it at the bottom of the ladder and retiring from it when he was the
trusted and accredited representative of that company, and enjoying
their thorough confidence and regard. The last five years that he
spent with them he was engaged in the onerous and hazardous pursuit of traveling for them over the southwestern and frontier portion of Texas and in the northern portion of Mexico. All of this
territory was then infested with the Mescalero and Apache Indian
tribes, who were constantly committing barbarous depredations,
and this same country was also overrun with desperadoes and
bandits who never hesitated at murder and robbery, the common
calling of both. Some idea may be formed of the constant danger
and privation that young Piper was constantly subjected to when
we state that he was not only charged with the taking of orders
for goods for his employers, in which he was eminently successful,
but had also to make all collections from the customers. He was
compelled to travel with his own conveyance, as then it was impossible to obtain the hire of either horses or a vehicle in the territory over which he traveled. He was also burdened with all the
way from $5,000 to $10,000 in coin, as at that time it was the universal custom to liquidate all indebtedness in silver, and the Mexican
silver dollar was the current circulating medium. Its bulk, therefore, handicapped both Piper and his team, especially as the latter
was frequently driven over long distances of that arid area without
water or food, rendering escape, when attacked by either Indians or
outlaws, very difficult, and he therefore had many hairbreadth escapes. These trips, which lasted from sixty to two hundred days,
necessitated a continuous absence for such long periods of time that
they subjected his wife and family to almost constant alarm. At
the earnest solicitation of Mrs. Piper he was therefore induced to

forego this hazardous pursuit, and on March 1, 1877, resigned his position with the company and moved to Uvalde, a village of 1,200 inhabitants then, and the county seat of the county of the same name. Here he engaged in a general merchandising business on his own account, with a small stock of goods, costing but $2,000, and which he purchased on credit. This stock and establishment he handled so judiciously that he prospered, and continued to do so to such an extent that within less than five years his business had so increased that he handled a quarter of a million of dollars worth of business and stock annually and with success. In addition to this line, in 1881, Mr. Piper embarked in the cattle business, associating with him Mr. V. M. West, under the firm style of Piper & West, their ranch embracing over 36,000 acres of land under fence, and over 4,000 head of cattle, horses and other live stock. In 1889 he returned to San Antonio with his family for the purpose of educating his children. During the latter year he associated with him in the general merchandising and banking business, at Ulvalde, Gus Mueller and G. T. Nunn. In this enterprise $100,000 are invested, thus affording himself more time to oversee his various ventures and interests. In 1891 Mr. Piper also engaged in the hardware business at Uvalde, the firm style being Piper & Hormer, and the capital $15,000. During the same year he also entered into another partnership in the cattle and ranch business, then associating with him in the enterprise Messrs. V. and O. Ellis, the capital invested being over $75,000. In 1892 he organized the Merchants' Transfer Company of San Antonio, which was incorporated under the laws of the State of Texas, and had a paid-up capital of $10,000. During the same year he also engaged in the wool commission business, forming a co-partnership with Mr. Casper G. Feldtmann, a well-known and highly successful handler of wool, the firm being Piper & Feldtmann, and the capital of the firm, also paid up, being $15,000. Mr. Piper was married on November 26, 1874, to Miss Minna Horner, the daughter of the late Hon. George Horner, ex-alderman of San Antonio, she being one of fourteen children of that family. Mr. and Mrs. Piper have been blessed with six children, four boys and two girls, their ages ranging from seven to eighteen years. Mr. Piper has never taken any very active part in politics, but has always been a Democrat. He never sought nor cared to hold any office, but was induced by his constituency to accept the position of alderman of Uvalde, to which position they elected him in 1887, and re-elected him in 1889. He served creditably and satisfactorily until the latter year, when he resigned, upon his removal with his family to San Antonio. He is a man of fine personal appearance, having a magnificent frame and a pleasing address; his habits are steady and exemplary; he possesses excellent executive ability and remarkably good judgment, and is universally recognized as an able financier. In demeanor he is modest and unassuming, and his tastes are refined and tending to domesticity, as he has always preferred the quiet and society of his home and family to any other. He is a member of local lodge 216 of the Benevolent and Protective Order of Elks, having joined that order in September, 1892; also of the San Antonio Turn Verein, and of the Beethoven Maennerchor. While not a member of any particular church he has always been a liberal supporter of churches, and is well-known as one who never refuses an appeal for charity. He is one of the best known and popular men in his section of Texas, being public-spirited, progressive and enterprising. He owes his present prosperity to his own efforts, being in every sense of the word a self-made man. While being connected with many of the best enterprises that have been consummated in Southwest Texas during the past ten or fifteen years, he is one of the last to make display of his wealth and standing, and always conceals, as much as possible, his well-known liberality.

HENRY EXALL.

The subject of this sketch was born at Richmond, Va., August 30, 1848. His father is Rev. George G. Exall, a Baptist minister, well-known in Virginia and the South, who moved from England when but a child. His paternal grandfather was an English astronomer and divine of considerable renown. His mother is Angy E. (Pierce)

Exall, daughter of Joseph Pierce, who was a shipbuilder of Philadelphia, and the representative of a family long prominent in naval construction in this country. Both branches of his family have an ancient and honorable lineage that extends to a very early period in American and English history. Mr. Exall's early education, interrupted when he was thirteen years of age by the Civil War, was acquired at his father's academy. Two years later his strong Southern sympathies made him a soldier in the cause. He was the boy of his brigade, but his brave and brilliant soldiership marked him even then as the child of destined success. At the battle of Ream's Station his brigade commander presented him with a sword in recognition of his gallant services. At the close of the war he studied law, but very soon abandoned it for the wider and more active field of commercial life. In 1867 he moved from Virginia to Kentucky, where he engaged in merchandising and the manufacture of woolen goods. In 1869 he was married to Miss Emma Warner of Owensboro, Ky. Three children were born to them, all of whom died when quite young, and in 1875 his wife also died. In 1877 business affairs brought him on a visit to Texas. When he surveyed the great possibilities of the grand state, for whose industrial development he was to do so much, he determined to sever his ties of residence with old Kentucky and become a Texan. He has represented the State of Texas at conventions of cattlemen, bankers' associations, commercial congresses and expositions and political conventions at many and various times. In 1884 he was one of the representatives of the state in the convention that nominated Mr. Cleveland for the presidency. This same year he was a delegate to the cattlemen's convention which met at St. Louis. He was appointed vice-president for Texas of the Cotton Centennial held at New Orleans in 1885, and this year was also appointed colonel and quartermaster-general of the Texas Volunteer Troops. In 1887 he was elected vice-president for Texas of the American Bankers' Association, held at Pittsburgh, Pa. This year he assisted in the organization of the North Texas National Bank of Dallas, of which he is vice-president. He was chairman of the State Democratic Executive Committee during the stormy time when prohibition promised to split the Democratic party in twain. In

1889 he was president of the Texas State Fair and Dallas Exposition, one of the most successful institutions of its character in the country. In all these places he has reflected credit on himself and on his state, and whether in a state or national convention his conspicuous superiority as a man of force, fearlessness and character has made him a figure of attraction and given him a place as the equal of the best of his fellows. In the discharge of his duties as a representative he displays the enthusiastic interest of a personal champion of a personal friend, and always, whether acting for himself or for others, his task commands his best ability. He is a faithful believer in the future of his state. He has told the story of her undeveloped greatness to the moneyed men of the East and to the traveler from all sections, and has been the means of developing this greatness above and beyond any other. In that development his personal accumulations have approximated a million dollars, a purse that is touched with no sparing hand when the enterprises of his state need encouragement. It may be said with truth, that every dollar of all that fortune that he has made for himself is represented by $10 made for the people among whom he lives. Mr. Exall has just finished the construction of one of the most majestic and costly buildings in -the South. During its construction he might have been seen on any day in light conversation with the men who drove the nails and laid the brick, and attending to the details of the work. His mind is so comprehensive that even the smallest particulars do not escape its notice. This mental scope has made Mr. Exall a successful exponent of all the industrial enterprises that he has originated and promoted. In the city of Dallas, where he lives, everybody is his friend. Here, in 1887, he married his second wife (nee Miss May Dickson), a most attractive and accomplished lady, who makes their home a veritable haven of rest from the many cares of his busy life. His public expressions are always the embodiment of earnest consideration for the betterment of all alike, and when they contain advice as to a line of action every word is tinged with a heart's sincerity. Omission of the mention of the tenderness that characterizes the domestic relations of the subject of this sketch, and the filial regard shown his aged parents, would render it incomplete. Incidents in illustration without number might be given by the writer, but it is sufficient to say that it has been, and still is one of his chief pleasures to minister to the every want of the venerable couple who nurtured him in infancy and inspired his youthful heart with high principles and aspirations which have been realized by the force of his own efforts. He is not known as the donor of any conspicuous gift in charity, but he is the quiet distributor of more alms to worthy objects than the average man of twice his wealth. And while in his modesty he prefers to remain the sole repository of the secrets of his own benevolence, it is known to all that no man ever disclosed to him a worthy cause with a request for help that he did not receive a prompt and liberal response. He has been repeatedly urged by both press and people to allow himself to become a candidate for governor, but he has always declined. As a Democratic commissioner-at-large for the United States (appointed by President Harrison) to the World's Columbian Exposition, he will bring to bear upon its organization and development rare business abilities, and such as cannot fail to be of great value and assistance to his fellow-commissioners, the people of the United States at large and to the people of Texas in particular

JOSEPH CROCKETT HART.

One of the most prominent and useful citizens of Marion County, Tex., is Joseph Crockett Hart, the present able tax collector of the county. He was born in Mount Sterling, Ky., in 1836, and the eldest of twelve children born to William F. T. and Nancy W. (Talman) Hart, both natives of the old Kentucky State. The paternal grandfather, Benjamin F. Hart, was born in Virginia, but moved to Kentucky at an early day, and became a very successful tiller of the soil. He was self-made and reared his large family to be useful men and women. William F. T. Hart studied medicine during his youth and a few years after his marriage, or in 1837, he moved to Missouri. Two years later he moved to Texas and located at Clarksville, where he followed merchandising until his death. In politics he was a Whig before the war. During that eventful period he served as county treasurer. Joseph Crockett Hart was but six months old when his parents moved to Missouri, and but four years old when they came to Texas. He attended the schools of Clarksville and began his career as a merchant in 1857. When Civil War broke out he enlisted in the Confederate army, Company E, Ninth Texas Cavalry, and subsequently became captain of the company. He took part in the battle of Elkhorn, where his colonel was wounded, and resigned to bring him home. In 1863 he was placed in the quartermaster department of the Twenty-ninth Texas Cavalry and served in Indian Territory. He remained in that regiment until cessation of hostilities. After reaching home he began clerking in a store, but later turned his attention to farming in Red River County. In January, 1870, he came to Jefferson and clerked in various stores of that place until 1886, when he was elected to the office of tax collector of Marion County. He has been re-elected at the end of each term since and is a most capable official. In the month of January, 1865, he married Miss Mamie E. Duke, a daughter of Rev. William Duke, who was an early M. E. preacher of this section and one who accomplished much good here. Seven children have blessed this union, as follows: William O., Lulu (died in youth), Lessie Lee, Russell Duke, Joe C. D. (a daughter), and two died in infancy.

S. P. SIMPSON.

S. P. Simpson was born in Belmont County, Ohio, January 11, 1838, the son of Sidney and Mary (Dorsey) Simpson, his mother being a descendant of General Dorsey, an officer in the American army during the Revolutionary War, whose sword is still one of the most treasured heirlooms of the Dorsey family. His mother's brother,

Michael Dorsey, is the oldest man living in Belmont County, Ohio, at this writing being eighty-eight years of age, and is still in business, as hale and hearty as many men of half his age. Mr. Simpson's education was acquired in the public schools and at Marietta College in Ohio, from which institution he graduated in January, 1859. After graduation he secured the position of second clerk on the steamer "Silver Star," an Ohio River packet, and after he had acquired experience as to his duties, was promoted to the position of first clerk on the "Boston," and held the same position afterward on other large packets engaged in the Cincinnati trade. When the war broke out, the boats were laid up, and Mr. Simpson became junior partner of the wholesale grocery house of W. W. Hanly & Co. at Cincinnati. While a member of the firm he was entrusted with much of its business, which was in the main with that portion of the South that remained loyal to the Union. After the close of the war the firm was dissolved and Mr. Simpson went into business at Lexington, Ky., where he remained for several years, when he went to North Platte, Neb., where he operated a cattle ranch until 1879. He then moved to Texas and located at Eagle Pass, where he established the first bank in Texas west of San Antonio. The business of the bank has since increased year by year, until now the banking house of S. P. Simpson & Co. is one of the best known in the Southwest. The business of this house in Southwest Texas and in Mexico is easily the largest done by any in the state. Mr. Simpson is Democratic both in politics and in relation with his fellow-men, believing that a low tariff is preferable to too much protection, and that one man is just as good as another as long as he behaves himself and fulfills his duties as a man in society and as a citizen in the community. He has no complicated views on religious subjects, granting freely to all men the right to their own opinions. He believes that he is doing all that is required who follows the Golden Rule. He was married in May, 1866, to Miss Mary Reed, daughter of Henry W. and Martha Reed, both of Lexington, Ky. Mr. Simpson is a man of medium height, with expressive grey eyes and is of an active, nervous temperament and exceedingly open and frank in manner, making many friends, who are led to admire him more as their friendship lengthens. His position in life is largely due to his own unaided efforts and he may well be proud of his success. It is to him and others of like character and enterprise that Western Texas owes her wonderful development, and while such spirits rule she will continue to prosper. Altogether he is of the sort of men who help any community to develop its best points in every way.

ERASTUS SMITH.

Erastus Smith, who, on account of his being "hard of hearing," was generally known as "Deaf Smith," was born in New York in 1787, moved to Mississippi in 1798, and to Texas in 1817. He was a most indefatigable observer of the movements of the Mexican army during the war, and his perfect knowledge of the country and astonishing coolness and bravery made him an invaluable scout for the Texan army. He married a Mexican lady in San Antonio, and had several children. He died at Fort Bend in 1839, and is buried at Richmond. A county named in his honor is "Deaf Smith."

GEN. THOMAS NEVILLE WAUL.

General Thomas Neville Waul, whose ancestors on both sides took part in the Revolutionary struggle, was born in South Carolina in 1813. After receiving his education at one of the best colleges in that state, he studied law at Vicksburg, Miss., and was admitted to practice in the Supreme Court of that state in 1835, and was soon afterward appointed district attorney. Removing later to New Orleans, he took an active part in politics, being a thorough Democrat of the state right's school, and he won a high reputation. After the war broke out he organized what was known as Waul's Legion, which he commanded in many hotly-contested engagements. At its close he settled in Galveston, where he resumed his profession, and was elected president of the bar association. In 1837 the general married Miss Mary Simmons, a native of Georgia, and in November, 1887, celebrated his golden wedding.

JOSIAH WILBARGER.

Josiah Wilbarger, brother of the author of the work entitled "Indian Depredations in Texas," was one of the earliest settlers in that state, coming here from Missouri in 1828, locating first in Matagorda County for a year. Early in the spring of 1830 he removed to a beautiful location he had selected at the mouth of the creek, named in his honor, ten miles above the point now occupied by the town of Bastrop. At that time his nearest neighbor was about seventy-five miles down the Colorado, and he was not only the first but also the outside settler of Austin's colony until July, 1832, when Reuben Hornsby went up from Bastrop, where he had been living a year or two. He located about nine miles below the present city of Austin. Early in August, 1833, Mr. Wilbarger went to Hornsby and, in company with Messrs. Christian, Strother, Standifer and Haynie, rode out in a northwestern direction to look at the country. On Walnut Creek, five or six miles below Austin, they discovered an Indian, who ran away and disappeared. The white party gave chase, but after a while abandoned it. While eating their dinner, however, after returning from the chase, they were suddenly fired upon by the Indians. Strother was mortally wounded, Christian's thigh bone was broken and Wilbarger sprang to the side of the latter to set him up against a tree, when the latter received an arrow in the

leg and another in the hip. Soon he was wounded in the other leg
also. Three of the Wilbarger party ran to their horses, which had
been tied out for feeding and began to flee. Wilbarger, though
wounded as he was ran after them, begging for an opportunity to ride
behind one of them, but before reaching them he was hit in the neck
by a ball. He fell, apparently dead, though unable to move or
speak he remained conscious. He knew when the Indians came
around him, stripped him naked and tore the scalp from his head. The
character of the wound in the neck probably made the Indians believe that it was broken and that Wilbarger was dead, or at least
could not survive, and they left him. They cut the throats of
Strother and Christian. Late in the evening Mr. Wilbarger so far
recovered as to drag himself to a pool of water, lay in it for an hour,
and then, benumbed with cold, he crawled upon dry ground and
fell into a profound sleep. When awakened the blood had ceased
to flow from his wounds, but he was still consumed with hunger
and again suffering intensely from thirst. Green flies had blown
his scalp while asleep and the larvae began to work, which created
a new alarm. Undertaking to go to Mr. Hornsby's, about six miles
distance, he had only proceeded about 600 yards when he sank exhausted. Remaining all night upon the ground he suffered intensely
from cold, but during the next day he was found by his friends who
had been urged by Mrs. Hornsby to look for him, despite the report
by Haynie and Standifer that he was dead. She was influenced
by a dream, so the story goes, to say that Wilbarger was still alive,
and consequently urged the men to go and hunt for him. It is
stated also that Wilbarger had a dream, or vision, of the spirit of a
sister who had died only the day before in Missouri, which said that
help would come that day. The relief party consisted of Joseph
Rogers, Reuben Hornsby, Webber, John Walters and others. As
they approached the tree under which Wilbarger was lying and
had passed the night, they saw first the blood-red scalp and thought
they had come upon an Indian. Even his body was almost as red
all over with blood, and he presented a ghastly sight. Rogers, mis-
taking him for an Indian, exclaimed, "Here they are, boys." Wilbarger arose and said, "Don't shoot; it is Wilbarger." The poor
sufferer was taken to Hornsby's residence, where he was cared for.

When he had somewhat recruited he was placed in a sled, as he could not endure the jolts of a wagon, and taken down the river to his own cabin. He lived eleven years afterward, but the scalp never grew to entirely cover the bone. The latter, where most exposed, became diseased and exfoliated, finally exposing the brain. By his death he left a wife and five children. The eldest son, John, was killed many years afterward by the Indians in West Texas; Harvey, another son, lived to raise a number of children. The circumstances above related is the first instance of white blood shed at the hands of the red savage within the present limits of Travis County.

GEN. JAMES HAMILTON.

General James Hamilton was a native of South Carolina, of which state he was Governor. Coming to Texas he boldly advocated her independence and contributed both time and means to the cause. Even in South Carolina, as a member of the Senate, he upheld in eloquent phrase the purity of the motives of the revolutionists of Texas, and actively devoted himself to the interests of the new republic. He secured the treaty with Great Britain, and negotiated one with the Kingdom of the Netherlands. In recognition of his services he was invested with rights of Texas citizenship by a special act of its Congress. But while he was a diplomatic agent for Texas in Europe he became involved in embarrassments which eventually ruined him. In 1857 he sailed from New Orleans for Galveston in the steamship Opelousas with the hope of obtaining an indemnification for the losses and of retrieving his fortune in the country for which he had borne so much. The vessel was wrecked on her passage by a collision with the steamer Galveston and Hamilton was one of the victims of the disaster. The State Congress went into mourning out of respect to his memory.

JOHN C. HAYS.

John C. Hays, generally known as Colonel "Jack" Hays, was a
native, it is believed, of Tennessee, and came to Texas when a young
man, bringing with him letters of recommendation from prominent
people to President Houston. The latter soon gave him a commission to raise a ranging company for the protection of the western
frontier. This company is supposed to be the first regularly organized one in the service so far in the West. With this small company—for it never numbered more than three-score men—Colonel
Hays effectually protected a vast scope of the frontier, reaching
from Corpus Christi on the Gulf to the headwaters of the Frio and
Neuces rivers. With the newly-introduced five-shooting revolvers
each of his men was equal to about five or six Mexicans or Indians.
Although the colonel was rather under the medium size, he was
wiry and active, well calculated to withstand the hardships of
frontier life. He was frequently seen sitting before his camp fire in
a cold storm, apparently as unconcerned as if in a hotel, and that
too when perhaps he had nothing for supper but a piece of hard-
tack or a few pecans. Although he was extremely cautious when the
safety of his men was concerned, he was extremely careless when
only his own welfare was in jeopardy. He was elected colonel of a
regiment of mounted volunteers at the breaking out of the Mexican War, and they did valiant service at the storming of Monterey.
Some time after the war he moved to California, where he finally
died a number of years ago. As an example of Hays' heroism we
cite the following anecdote from Mr. Wilbarger's work: "In the fall
of 1840 a party of Comanche Indians numbering about 200 came
into the vicinity of San Antonio, stole a great many horses and
started off in the direction of the Gaudalupe River. Hays, with
about twenty of his men, followed in pursuit, overtaking them at that
river. Riding in front, as was his custom, the colonel was the first
to discover the red rascals, and riding back to his men he said,
'Yonder are the Indians, boys, and yonder are our horses. The
Indians are pretty strong, but we can whip them and recapture our

horses. What do you say?' 'Go ahead,' the boys replied, 'and we'll follow if there is a thousand of them.' 'Come on, then, boys,' said Hays, and, putting spurs to their horses, this little band of only twenty men boldly charged upon the 200 warriors who were waiting for them drawn up in battle array. Seeing the small number of their assailants the Indians were sure of victory, but Hays' men poured shot among them so rapidly and directly as to cut down their ranks at a fearful rate, killing their chief, and the Indians, frightened at what appeared to them a power superior to man, fled in confusion. Hays and his men followed for several miles, killing even more of them and recovering most of the stolen horses. About a year afterward he was one of a party of fifteen or twenty men employed to survey land near what the Indians called 'The Enchanted Rock,' in which, high up, was a cavity large enough to contain several men. Being attacked by Indians in this vicinity, Colonel Hays, who was at some distance from his party, ran up the hill and took a position in this little hollow place, determined to 'sell his life at the dearest price.' He was well known to the Indians, and they were anxious if possible to get his scalp. Mounting the hill they surrounded the rock and prepared to charge upon him. Hays was aware that his life depended more upon strategy than courage, and reserved his fire until it would do the most good. He lay behind a projection of the rock with the muzzle of his gun exposed to their vision and waited the most opportune moment. The savages meantime suspected that the noted white warrior had a revolver besides, and indeed he had two. The Indians yelled with all their might, but our hero was too well acquainted with that style of warfare to be very badly frightened by it. The red men, being ashamed of permitting themselves to be beaten by one man, made a desperate assault, and when the chief in front approached sufficiently near the colonel downed him with the first shot of his rifle. In the next charge he did effective work with a revolver, and soon the remainder of his own men, who had been engaging the main body of the Indians, suspected that their commander was hemmed in there, and turned upon the Indians nearby, immediately routing them." A remarkable example of Colonel Hays' generalship was exhibited in a little skirmish in 1844, when, with fifteen of his company on a

scouting expedition about eighty miles from San Antonio he came
in sight of fifteen Comanches, who were mounted on good horses and
apparently eager for battle.   As the colonel and his men approached
the Indians slowly retreated in the direction of an immense thicket,
which convinced Hays that the Indians they saw were but a part of
a larger number.   He therefore restrained the ardor of his men,
who were anxious to charge upon the Indians they saw, and took
a circuitous route around the thicket and drew up his little force
upon a bridge beyond a deep ravine in order to take advantage of
some position not looked for by the Indians.   The latter seeing they
had failed to draw the white party into the trap they had laid for
them showed themselves to the number of seventy-five.   Directly
the rangers assailed them on an unexpected side, made a furious
charge with revolvers, etc.   The battle lasted nearly an hour, ex-
hausting the ammunition of the whites.   The Comanche chief, per-
ceiving this, rallied his warriors for final effort.   As they were advancing Colonel Hays discovered the rifle of one of the rangers was
still loaded.   He ordered him to dismount and shoot the chief, and
the man did so successfully.   This so discouraged the Indians that
they gave up the day.   In the battle above referred to with the main
body of the Indians the rangers lost only two killed and five
wounded, while thirty Indians were left dead on the field.   For
good generalship as well as cool, unflinching bravery, Colonel Hays
and his men deserve the highest credit.   The above fight is certainly one of the most remarkable in all Indian warfare.   In 1845,
in encountering a large party of Indians, Colonel Hays mounted a
horse which had more "heroism" and "foolhardiness" than he anticipated, as it carried him in spite of all the rider could do, right
through the enemy, the main body of the Comanches.   This so astonished the Indians that they actually gave way for him and another man accompaning him, and the rest of the white party rallied
forward with a yell and with their revolvers actually put the savages to flight.   Not long after the above occurrence Hays with only
fifteen men encountered and totally defeated the famous Comanche
chief, Yellow Wolf, who was at the head of eighty warriors; the
chief himself was slain.   This battle occurred at the Pinta crossing
of the Guadalupe River, between San Antonio and Fredricksburg.

CAPTAIN JAMES G. SWISHER.

Captain James G. Swisher, in whose honor a county in this state is named, was born in Knoxville, Tenn., November 6, 1794. Joining John Donelson's company, under General Jackson, he participated in the battles of New Orleans on the night of December 23, 1814, and on January 8, 1815. He came from near Franklin, Williamson County, Tenn., to Texas in 1833, and during the following January he settled at the town of Tenoxtitlan on the Brazos River, not now in existence, but which up to the year 1832 had been garrisoned by 200 Mexican troops. Swisher commenced life here with his family apparently under the finest auspices, but in a few months two Comanches stole most of his horses, which, however, he recovered after a long journey in pursuit. Captain Swisher was the father of James M. Swisher and John M. Swisher of Travis County. The latter, known as Colonel "Milt" Swisher, was in the employ of the Republic from 1839 up to the time of annexation, and from that time to 1856 in the employ of the state. In 1841 he was chief clerk and acting secretary of the treasury of the Republic, and in 1847 was appointed auditor to settle up the debts of the late Republic.

JOHN L. WILBARGER.

John L. Wilbarger, brother of the author of the "Indian Depredations in Texas," was born in Matagorda County, Tex., November 29, 1829, and grew up in his parents' family in Austin colony, inured to the roughness of pioneer life. Having considerable talent he became well qualified to manage the interests of those exposed on the frontier, but before he had an opportunity to exercise his talent to a considerable degree he joined an expedition which eventually proved disastrous to him. August 20, 1850, he and two other young men were quietly pursuing their way back to the command in Bastrop County, which they had left, when Indians attacked them, shooting down the two other young men at the first fire, and then Wilbarger, after a chase of about two miles. One of the young men (Neal), however, was not killed, and succeeded in getting back home to tell the tale.

COLONEL GEORGE G. ALFORD.

Colonel George G. Alford, prominent in the early history of the state, was born in Cayuga, Seneca County, N. Y., June 19, 1793, reared on Lake Champlain and Cayuga, that state, and served as lieutenant of artillery under General Winfield Scott during the second war with Great Britain in 1811-13, participating in the battles of Queenstown Heights, Lundy's Lane, etc. His father, who was a cousin of General Ethan Allen of Revolutionary fame, had twelve children. In 1815 the family moved to Detroit, Mich., then an obscure and remote frontier Indian village, making the trip in a small sail vessel, which was wrecked at what is now the great city of Cleveland. In 1819 he moved to New Madrid, Mo., the former capital of the Spanish province of Louisiana, and there engaged in mercantile pursuits. In 1821 he married Miss Jeannette Lesieur, a sister of Hon. Godfrey Lesieur, one of the oldest and wealthiest French settlers of that section, who died, leaving him one daughter, Jeannette. About 1829 Colonel Alford married Miss Ann Barfield of Murfreesborough, Tenn., born May 9, 1807, a descendant of Governor Badger of North Carolina. By this marriage there was born Judge George Frederick Alford, now of Dallas. While a resident of Missouri the colonel prospered and became wealthy, and served with satisfaction to his constituents a term in the State Legislature. He came to Texas during the exciting times of the Revolution in 1835, and still inspired with the martial spirit of 1812, he

entered zealously into the cause of Texan independence. He joined
the immortal band under General Houston and participated in the
heroic struggles which culminated in the battle of San Jacinto,
which was so glorious a victory for the Texans, securing for them
what they had unanimously so long sought for—independence.
Soon after this battle Colonel Alford was sent by the provisional
government of the embryo republic to New Orleans for military supplies for the famishing soldiery of Texas. Here he loaded two vessels and returned on one of them, the brig "Julius Caesar"; he was
captured by the Mexican blockading fleet under command of Captain Jose V. Matios of the Mexican brig of war, "General Teran," off
Galveston harbor; the two vessels and cargoes were confiscated
and the captives incarcerated in a loathsome dungeon in Matamoras,
Mex., and Colonel Alford and his brother, Major Johnston H. Alford
(who was returning to Texas with him), were condemned to be shot,
but they were liberated through the intercession of Andrew Jackson, President of the United States. Colonel Alford returned to
Missouri, settled up his business and in April, 1837, moved his family and slaves to Texas, first settling in the old Spanish pueblo of
Nacogdoches and later in Crockett, the capital of Houston County,
and there engaged in planting, in mercantile pursuits and as judge,
until his death April 1, 1847, his wife having preceded him February
10, same year. His death was deplored throughout the young
state which he had served with Spartan heroism.

HON. CHARLES STEWART.

The subject of this sketch was born in the city of Memphis, Tenn.,
on May 30, 1836. Nine years later, in 1845, his parents moved to
Texas and settled in Galveston. In that city his boyhood and youth
were passed. Such educational advantages as the local schools at
that time afforded were his, and he enjoyed in addition to this some
discipline and direction in his reading at the hands of his father, who

was a man of more than average intelligence, and who possessed a large fund of information on historical subjects and concerning practical politics. It was probably from this source that the son received his first promptings for the law, and under his father's guidance formed a fixed resolution to devote himself to its practice. He began the study of law in 1852 under James W. Henderson of Houston, and completed his preparation in the office of Jones & Bollinger, receiving his certificate of admission to the bar in the supreme court in 1854 when in his eighteenth year. For the practice he located at Marlin in Falls County, where his rise at the bar was rapid and substantial. In 1856 he was elected prosecuting attorney for what was then the Thirteenth Judicial District, composed of the counties of Falls, Hill, Navarro, Limestone, Freestone, Leon, Brazos, Madison and Robertson, and was re-elected to the same office in 1858. He had just closed the fourth year of his service in this position at the opening of the war. In the public discussion which preceded the first formal acts of hostility between the sections he was somewhat conspicuous, and this, with his pronounced Southern views and personal popularity, caused him to be selected as a delegate to the convention of 1861 which passed the ordinance of secession. He voted for the ordinance and returning home, at once entered the Confederate army, enlisting in the Tenth Texas Infantry, afterward Baylor's Cavalry, with which he served throughout the war. In 1866 he moved to Houston, where he resumed the practice of his profession and where he has since resided, giving his attention actively and earnestly to law when not engaged in official duties. In 1874 he was elected city attorney of Houston, which position he held for two years. In 1878 he was chosen to represent his district in the State Senate and served as a member of the Sixteenth and Seventeenth Legislatures. In 1882 he was elected to Congress, and was a member of that body by successive re-elections for ten years, voluntarily retiring with the close of the fifty-second session for the purpose of devoting himself more exclusively to his law business and other private interests. In the time that Colonel Stewart has been engaged in the practice of law and in public life, he has met with a larger measure of success than falls to the lot of the average lawyer and public official, not indeed in the matter of money-getting, but in the more desired form of achieved reputation. He has acquired distinction in both the civil and criminal branches of the law and established his name in politics as one of the first men in Texas. It is hardly possible, and probably not desirable, to attempt here a review of his professional and official career. The ground to be gone over in either case covering, as it does, a period of forty years, is so vast and there is so much learning of a special and technical nature that would have to be gone into, that only a brief allusion to this record can be made. He has taken part in many cases involving interesting and important questions of law and fact, some of which he has followed from the trial courts to the courts of last resort, while in his public career he has had more or less to do with all questions which have been before the people, or the various bodies of which he has been a member. The manner in which he has met his obligations is best attested by the esteem in which he is held by those among whom he has lived and labored so long. It is due him to say that his chosen profession has been the ambition of his life, and that he has laid aside its duties only when necessary for the more faithful discharge of those of a public nature placed upon him by his fellow-citizens. He is a logical thinker, an eloquent speaker, ripe lawyer, able legislator, good citizen, kind neighbor, earnest, liberal, progressive and charitable. In 1860, at Marlin, he married Miss Rachel Barry, daughter of Bryan Barry, and a member of one of Texas' old and prominent families. Of this union one son survives, John S., junior member of the law firm of Stewart & Stewart, and present city attorney of Houston.

DR. J. F. ROSBOROUGH.

In a comparatively short period Dr. Rosborough has met with unusual success in the practice of that most noble of callings—medicine—and has gained a substantial reputation as a general practitioner with the profession and the public. He comes of a prominent old South Carolina family, but his grandfather, James F. Rosborough,

who was a native of that state, left there in 1837 and, after spending
two years on the road, settled in the "Lone Star State." He first located at Bastrop, but finally moved to Harrison County, where he
became one of the leading men. At that time there were but a few
log houses in Marshall and Mr. Rosborough located on a large plantation three miles north of that place. Some time later he sold that
to W. A. Adair and located permanently seven miles south of town.
There his death occurred. He was of Scotch-English origin. He was
an old Indian fighter, and had many thrilling adventures. His son,
Wyatt James Rosborough, was born in South Carolina and was but
five years old when he came with his parents to Texas. In this state
he grew to manhood and here married Miss Ibby Yancy Craig, a
native of Tennessee, and the daughter of Eli T. Craig, also a native
of Tennessee. Great-grandfather Craig was a native of the Emerald
Isle and a pioneer of Tennessee. His wife, Nancy Craig Collin, left
England for America two hundred years ago (1695). Eli T. Craig
moved to Texas in 1847, settled in Harrison County, and began tilling the soil. He soon became active in politics and represented his
county in the State Legislature several terms. His death occurred
about 1870. The original of this notice was born in Harrison County,
Tex., in 1855, and was the eldest of six children. He attended the
common schools of Harrison County and then entered Trinity University, Tehuacana, Tex., where he remained three years. After
leaving school he engaged in merchandising at Marshall, remained
there two years, and the following six years was at Easton, Tex., engaged in the same business. About this time he began the study of
medicine and after attending lectures at Tulane University, New
Orleans, graduated in 1893. He at once began practicing in Marshall, and, although he has been here but a short time, he has already
won an enviable reputation as a skilled practitioner. In the year
1887 he married Miss Anna Waldron, a native of Texas, and the
daughter of Frank Waldron, who came to this section after the war.
Mrs. Rosborough died one year after marriage, leaving two children,
twins, Thomas and Eli. Dr. Rosborough is a member of the K. of
P. and the A. O. U. W. In connection with his practice he is engaged in farming to some extent, being the owner of a fine tract of
land, and is also engaged in stock-raising.

SAMUEL THURMAN.

This prominent and influential citizen of Jefferson, Tex., came originally from Virginia, his birth occurring in Lynchburg prior to the time the state was divided, March 6, 1847. This was also the birthplace of Allen G. Thurman, who was a near relative of our subject's father, Samuel B. Thurman. The latter married Miss Mary Cox, and he and wife passed the remainder of their days in old Virginia. In that state our subject grew to manhood and resided there until 1871, when he went to New Orleans, thence up the Mississippi and Red rivers to Shreveport, from there by rail to Marshall and thence to Jefferson by stage, the trip lasting about thirty-one days. At that time Jefferson had a population of from 18,000 to 20,000, was the distributing point for all Northeast Texas and was one of the main trading points in the State of Texas. It had a trade radius of 500 miles and the merchants and tradesmen of Dallas and Fort Worth received the greater part of their supplies from this city. At that time Texarkana, Queen City and Atlanta had not been thought of, but it was not long before the railroads had penetrated this region, and Jefferson furnished the men and money to establish these large towns. Most of the leading bankers and merchants took their goods and money to Fort Worth and Texarkana, and the completion of the East Line & Red River Railroad gave such an impetus to this emigration that Jefferson to-day has only about 4,000 inhabitants. The latter city has had some trouble regarding its indebtedness, but as it is a debt incurred during old reconstruction times, it is thought that it will be refunded. Mr. Thurman is not in favor of repudiation, as a rule, but he knows that this debt, like many others, is not just, and that it has done much to retard Jefferson's growth. As a reminder that Jefferson is still a good business center, our subject states that he sells monthly about 3,000 dozen spools of thread and pays $1,500 monthly for Garrett snuff. The northeast section of Texas has always responded to every call made upon her resources. Mr. Thurman still further states that to points located within a radius of 100 miles from Jefferson the freight rate is but 26 cents on merchandise, while from outside points into the same section the rates are: From St. Louis, 92 cents; New Orleans, 82 cents; Shreveport, 70 cents; Philadelphia, $1.32; New York, $1.32; Chicago, $1.27; Houston, 86 cents, and from Galveston, $1.17. This fact makes it a great trade center. Jefferson has a fine blast furnace and is surrounded by saw mills, abundance of timber is to be found on all sides, principally pine, cypress, hickory, ash, cottonwood and water oak. One of Mr. Thurman's customers, in experimenting with fertilizers, raised one and a fourth bales of cotton per acre and 104 bushels of corn on land treated the same way. During Jefferson's prosperity the store room now occupied by Mr. Thurman rented at $150 per month, but to-day its entire value is not $12,000. Recently the best stone building in the city sold for $600, when its original cost was $22,500. Mr. Thurman thinks this the best country on earth for a poor man to locate, for everything is cheap, taxes are paid only on $1,000, and the Texas, Pacific & Southern Railway Co. is just now pushing the building of the road from Jefferson to Shreveport. This section has very fine fishing and hunting grounds and the general health is very good. Mr. Thurman has resided here for twenty-four years, and, with the exception of a few years at first when he had chills and fever, he has enjoyed excellent health. The soil of Marion County will produce cotton, corn, oats and all kinds of vegetables and fruit, with the exception of apples, producing only the Shockley apple to any great extent. The peaches grown in this county are unsurpassed, and Mr. Thurman saw one that weighed a pound and a half. Sweet potatoes are also raised in abundance. Land is worth from to $2.00 to $5.00 per acre, and a third of a bale of cotton can easily be raised on land that cost the former price. Our subject was married October 29, 1874, to Miss C. M. Nichols of Jefferson, who is a native of Eufaula, Ala. Three bright, promising children have been born to them: Zan, Theo. and Galdie. Mr. and Mrs. Thurman hold membership in the Methodist Episcopal church of Jefferson and are active workers in the same. During the Civil War Mr. Thurman enlisted in the Confederate army—Army of Virginia— under General Walker, Company A, Third Regiment of Virginia Reserve Force, and was made orderly sergeant. He served until the surrender of Lee at Appomattox C. H., April 9, 1865, and was present on that memorable day. He left Lynchburg after Hunt made his raid on that place, June 21, 1864. Our subject says that there was a fort on the turnpike in the suburbs of Lynchburg, to protect the road. At one point near which he was stationed were a number of large boulders, behind which many Union soldiers were hidden. A shot from the Confederates struck the stones and killed twenty-four men. Seventeen years later Mr. Thurman visited this spot and there met an old Union soldier named John Worthington, who immediately mentioned that he had had a very narrow escape there during the war, as he was one of the many who took shelter behind the boulders. Although enemies during the war, Mr. Thurman and Mr Worthington became fast friends. Our subject has held a number of local offices in the county and is at present a member of the Board of Aldermen. Socially he is an Odd Fellow. The Odd Fellow order, organized in America at Baltimore, Md., by Thomas Wildey and associates, and which is now in its seventy-seventh year, was joined by him twenty-four years ago. He says that this order to-day has more members than any other organization in the United States, 800,000 in all, and the expenses of the order in 1874 were $600,000. Mr. Thurman is Noble Grand of the local lodge at Jefferson, known as Jefferson Lodge No. 362. He has two brothers in Washville, Tenn., one, Ed. R. Thurman, being a prominent lawyer, and General Charles Thurman, who was adjutant-general of the state under Governor Bates. Another brother, Alexander Thurman, resides in Lynchburg, and is chief of the Lynchburg Fire Department and vice-president of the National Firemen's Association of America.

A. H. SCHLUTER.

It will be a matter of interest to many of the readers of this volume to learn something regarding the leaders in mercantile circles in Northeastern Texas. There is no section of this grand state that possesses more flourishing cities or brighter business men. It has ever been a pleasure and a privilege to record the character and enterprise of these men, who, on account of their long tenure and extensive operations, comprise almost a history of the business in which they are engaged. Of such men it is unnecessary to speak in words of colored praise. "By their acts ye shall know them." Their very existence is emphatic evidence of the honorable position they occupy and the long course of just dealing that they have pursued. A gentleman in mind is Augustus H. Schluter, whose career as a business man, as well as citizen, has been above reproach. Mr. Schluter is a product of Marion County, Tex., born about three miles west of Jefferson, March 2, 1854, on a farm owned by his father. His early scholastic training was received in Jefferson, but he later attended the Clarksburg school and then took a collegiate course in Looney College at Gilmer, where he remained for two years. When seventeen years of age he left school and embarked in his business career, first as clerk for his father and later, when twenty-one years of age, in business for himself. Being a man of sterling ability, fine artistic taste and a faculty for making staunch friends and supporters in his business, he soon became well and favorably known, not only in Jefferson and Marion County, but in adjoining counties as well. Although a comparatively young man, he has pushed his way to the front and his trade is constantly growing larger. He has ever been an active worker for his city, and much of Jefferson's popularity as a shipping and distributing point may be directly attributed to him. For some time he was engaged in the wholesale and retail mercantile business, but for the past eight years he had carried on an exclusive wholesale trade on an immense scale. Some little idea of the extent of Jefferson's outside business may be gained from the fact that Mr. Schluter's business alone amounts to about a quarter of a million annually. Mr. Schluter's father, F. A. Schluter, came to Jefferson, Tex., as early as 1842, and was engaged in merchandising in that city for a quarter of a century. He was one of the best known business men in Northeast Texas, was thoroughly reliable, and never failed to meet an obligation when it was due. From him our subject no doubt inherited his excellent business acumen. The elder Schluter died June 10, 1882.

JOHN A. FIEDLER.

That Germany has contributed her full share toward the population of Texas is a fact well understood. John A. Fiedler, who came to this country about 1852, was born near Coburg Gotha, Saxony, Germany, July 22, 1835, and he possesses all the estimable qualities of the thrifty, enterprising German. He was but seventeen years of age when he decided to cross the ocean and seek his fortune in America, and as he had learned the tanner trade in the old country, he soon found work in a tannery at Wheeling, Va., where he remained eight months. From there he went to Paducah, Ky., remained there one winter and then migrated to St. Louis to engage in steamboating on the Mississippi River. Four years later he went to New Orleans, where he remained two years, and then came to Jefferson, Tex., first in 1857. From that time until 1860 he spent on the river between this point and New Orleans, steamboating, but in the latter year he gave up this work and engaged in the grocery business, which he continued until March, 1861. He then went to New Orleans, where he remained one year and then, on the 7th day of March, 1862, he enlisted in the army in what was known as the Crescent Regiment. Immediately afterward he started with his regiment for Corinth, Miss. His first battle was at Shiloh, April 6 and 7, 1862, and after that bloody engagement he was made assistant regimental commissary. Still later he was made commissary of General Walker's Brigade. From Corinth Mr. Fiedler's command was ordered to Tupola, Ala., and from there to Ballard, that state, to guard Montgomery, Ky. In the fore part of October, 1862, his command was ordered from Ballard to Berwick's Bay, La. (now Morgan City), but after remaining there a short time was ordered to La Fouche, La., and thence to the fight at ———— in which battle his regiment lost its lieutenant-colonel, G. P. McPheeters. While his command was stationed at Berwick's Bay Mr. Fiedler was commissary of the post. At ———— all his regiment was captured, except about ninety men, and taken to New Orleans as prisoners.

Our subject was among those not captured. On the 12th and 13th of
April, 1863, he was in a battle at Camp Bisland and retreated from
there to Alexandria. His command then went back and captured
Berwick's Bay and the One Hundred and Seventy-sixth New York
Regiment, with commissary and medical supplies of Banks' army.
They retreated then to Alexandria and thence to Monroe, La., where
they went into winter quarters. The following spring the command
was ordered up near Mansfield and fought a battle there on the 8th
of April, defeating General Banks' First Army Corps. In this battle Mr. Fiedler was hit in the face by a minie ball, which was afterward cut out of his back. The regiment to which he belonged entered the engagement with 345 men and at its close only 110 were
left. Mr. Fiedler was sergeant of Company C, this regiment, and
forty-five of the fifty-four men in the company came out alive. After
being wounded Mr. Fiedler was taken to Mansfield and thence to
Shreveport, La. After partially recovering he came to Jefferson
and remained there until entirely well. Soon after he rejoined his
regiment and went with it to New Orleans, where he remained until
the close of the war. In that city he remained from April until September 9, 1865, when he was married to Miss Caroline Nagle of that
place. On the 9th of October, one month later, he and wife came to
Jefferson, where Mr. Fiedler engaged in merchandising, which he
has continued since. He is an importer of fancy groceries and has a
large trade. Of eight children born to his marriage, only two are
now living, John H. and Mamie. In 1872 Mr. Fiedler was elected
alderman of the place, and has ever been an influential citizen.

EARLE ADAMS.

It is an indisputable fact that the United States stands alone in
the pre-eminence of having an array of citizens, who, without adven-
titious aid or accident of birth, have attained to wealth and distinction in public affairs. This is the glory of the country, and every

man who has it in him can prove himself a man. Earle Adams, who was born on his father's plantation in South Carolina in 1848, is now one of the popular and well known attorneys of Houston County, Tex. He is the youngest of four sons born to Thomas and Margaret (Doniphan) Adams, natives of South Carolina, and descendants of old and prominent families of that state. The Adams family is of English-Scotch origin and came to this country before the Revolution. The Earles came originally from Ireland and became noted in the history of South Carolina and Florida. In 1853 the parents of our subject moved to Louisiana and settled in Texarkana Parish, where, in connection with his ministerial duties in the Baptist church, the father was actively engaged as a planter. He died in 1859 and his wife in 1886. Our subject reached the age of fourteen years in the Palmetto State and then entered the Confederate army, serving until the close, and surrendering with Forest at Gainesville, Ala. A part of the time he served on the Mississippi River from Vicksburg to New Orleans, and participated in the battles of Baton Rouge, Jackson and many engagements about Mobile. In June, 1865, he returned home and in September, 1866, entered Centenary College, where he pursued his studies for eighteen months. After that he began the study of law and was admitted in March, 1870. Previous to this, in 1868, he married Miss Emma Miller, a native of Ohio, who came to Louisiana in her youth with her parents. Her father was a minister in the Lutheran church. In 1875 Mr. Adams moved to Texas and settled in Crockett, where he has since had a good practice in all courts and in all departments. He has always taken a decided interest in political affairs, and for a period of six years served as prosecuting attorney of the old Twelfth District. For two years he was also in the county attorneys' office. His activity in the field of politics has caused him to be selected as a delegate to various county and state conventions, and in whatever field or capacity he served, Mr. Adams has acquitted himself creditably and with satisfaction to his constituents. Although beginning life's battle entirely upon his own resources, Mr. Adams has made the financial end of the struggle a success, and, besides being the possessor of a lucrative practice, is the owner of several fine farms, on one of which, where his ideal home is situated, is an excellent orchard, abundantly sup-

plied with the various fruits suitable to the locality. This is located one and one-half miles from Crockett. While a hard worker
in his profession, Mr. Adams by no means neglects the social privileges of life. Studious in habits, with an intense liking for literary
pursuits, much of his time is passed in the home circle, reading and
in the enjoyment of the companionship of wife and children. He is a
member of both Masonic and Odd Fellow orders. Eight children
have been born to Mr. and Mrs. Adams, as follows: Joseph, educated at Crockett, studied law, admitted to the bar when only nineteen years of age, is now district attorney, and is one of the youngest
Worshipful Masters of the Masonic fraternity in the United States;
Earl, educated in Crockett, admitted to practice law in 1894 when
twenty years old; Henrietta, Emma, Densy, and two daughters who
died in infancy. Mr. and Mrs. Adams worship at the Baptist church
and stand deservedly high, socially, morally and intellectually.

W. B. WARD.

Since 1868 this gentleman has been a resident of Marion County,
Tex., and it is largely through his efforts that it has prospered and
become one of the leading counties of the state. Mr. Ward has ever
been foremost in all enterprises for the public good, and it is quite
probable that there is not a man better known in the county than he.
His parents, William and Sally Saunders Blythe Ward, were natives
of Georgia and Tennessee respectively, and were residing at Myrtle
Springs, Bowie County, Tex., at the time of our subject's birth, May 8,
1837. They subsequently moved to Clarksville, Tex., where they
made their home for three years. From there they removed to Henderson, Tex., but after a short residence there of only one year they
took up their quarters at Gilmore, also this state. In 1862 they
moved from Daingerfield to a farm in Red River County, where the
remainder of their days were passed. The early education of our
subject was received at Daingerfield, where he remained until fifteen

GEORGE LORD.

years of age, and then attended school at Clarksville, where he secured a good practical education. In the year 1857 he was married to Miss Zue Aiken of near Daingerfield. Her death occurred in 1880. During the war Mr. Ward enlisted in the Confederate army and was out eighteen months. He then re-enlisted and was in active service until cessation of hostilities. As before stated, it was in the year 1868 that Mr. Ward first came to Marion County, and he took up his residence in Jefferson, then a flourishing place. He first turned his attention to merchandising, but later became interested in the Jefferson National Bank, which was the fourth National bank organized in the state and the first in this section—Northeast Texas. Ever since then he has been connected with it officially, and for the past ten years has been its president. This bank is one of the sound, firmly established institutions of the country and has withstood all panics. Mr. Ward was one of the projectors and incorporators of the East Line & Red River Railway (now known as the Sherman, Shreveport & Southern). He has been identified with many other enterprises originated for the benefit of Jefferson, and, in fact, he is a worthy man and a useful citizen. Had it not been for his perseverance and activity, together with the means advanced by him to forward the enterprise, the East Line & Red River Railway would have been unfinished at the present time.

GEORGE LORD.

Cordial in his manner, apt in expression and full of the knowledge gathered in many years of intelligent observation, one seldom meets a more interesting man than Mr. George Lord, who is now seventy-eight years of age. He was born in County Essex, England, April 12, 1816, and is a son of Felstead and Anna (Siggs) Lord, both natives of England. The father was a bricklayer and by an accident, while repairing a hot brick oven, lost his life. This was when our subject was an but an infant. The mother married again and died in London when eighty-two years of age. George Lord was educated in his native country and there continued to make his home until June, 1834, when he took passage for America. Landing in Canada, he remained there two years, and then removed to New Orleans, where, for a few months, he ran on the Mississippi River steamers. December 27, 1836, he joined a company of seventy-five men, under Captain Lyons, for the war with Mexico, and landed at Galveston February 14, 1837, when there was but one frame building there. On February 14, 1837, he was mustered into service at Camp Independence, on the Lavaca River, in John Holliday's (who escaped from the Fannin massacre) Company of Second Regimental Volunteers, under Colonel Wigginton. In June, 1837, his company was consolidated with Captain Jordan's Company and sent to San Antonio in October, 1837. The following year Mr. Lord was discharged. For his services he was granted 1,280 acres of bounty land. The same year he was at the Cibilo, at the ranch of Colonel Patton, when about fifty Comanches came to hold a consultation. On their return from the lower country they killed a man named Tolbert. After Colonel Burleson's fight with Cordova on the Guadalupe, near Sequin, Mr. Lord joined Captain Dawson's Company in San Antonio, to intercept those who escaped, and they captured two or three. About September 1, 1839, he joined the forces under General Canalis, on Nueces River, and during the first campaign was at the taking of Guerro, in Mexico, and participated in the following battles: Alcantre, Matamoras and Monterey. During the second campaign he was at the taking of Laredo, and in the battle of Saltillo with Colonel Jordan. The men were fighting for the Mexican constitution of 1824, and were led by Molano and Lopez, who treacherously bargained to sell their men to the enemy for a doubloon a head, but failed to deliver the goods. In June, 1842, Mr. Lord joined Captain Cameron's Company at Corpus Christi and was with him at the battle of Lipantitlan, July 7, though during that battle he was engaged in scouting duties, at Salado, and was near San Antonio in September of that year and in the battle of and surrender of Mier, which led to the most dramatic incident recorded of any war, the bean drawing. After the surrender, Mr. Lord and his comrades made several attempts to escape, first at San Juan River and next at Rinconade, both failures because of treachery in their own ranks. The third attempt was made at Salado, Mexico, where they were imprisoned, and was successful through a piece of marvelous daring. Mr. Lord described it as follows: "When all was ready Captain Cameron said in a distinct tone, 'Well, boys, we will go it.' and, suiting the action to the word, he seized one of the sentinels while S. H. Walker seized the other. It was the work of an instant to disarm the guard and get possession of the outer court, where the arms and cartridge boxes were guarded by 150 men. They then charged the enemy outside the building, including the 'Red Caps,' and whipped them in less than two minutes. We had three killed, two mortally and five or six slightly wounded. The enemy lost eight or ten. To sum up: Got up on the 11th inst., ate breakfast, whipped the guard, and traveled sixty-three miles before stopping. A good day's work." After escaping, these brave men retreated toward Texas through a weary, barren land, without the shadow of a great rock to refresh and sustain. They went three days without water and were forced to kill their horses for food. Finally, on the eighth day, famished and exhausted, they were easily recaptured by the pursuing Mexicans, and were marched to Salado, where, on the 25th of March, the bean drawing took place. The following is Mr. Lord's account of it: "Soon after our arrival at Salado we received the melancholy intelligence that we were to be decimated, and every tenth man shot. It was now too late to resist this horrible order. We were closely handcuffed and drawn up in front of our guards, who, with arms, were in readiness to fire. Could we have known it previously we would have again charged the guards and made them dearly pay for this breach of national faith. It was now too late. A manly gloom and proud defiance pervaded all countenances. We had but one alternative, and that was to invoke our country's vengeance upon our murderers, consign our souls to God, and die like men. The decimator, Colonel Domingo Huerta, who was especially nominated to do this black deed after Governor Mexier had refused, arrived at Salado ahead of our men. The 'Red Cap' Company were to be the executioners—those men who had been so humanely spared by us at this place the 11th of February. The decimation took place by the drawing of black and white beans from a small earthen mug, the white beans signifying exemption and the black death. One hundred and fifty-nine white beans were placed in the bottom of the mug and seventeen black ones were placed on top of them. The beans were not stirred, and had so slight a shake that it was perfectly clear that they had not been mixed together, thus showing that they were anxious to catch Captain Cameron and other officers, who had to draw first. Captain Cameron, with his usual coolness, said: 'Well, boys, we have to draw, let's be at it," thrust his hand into the mug and drew a white bean. Captain Eastland was the first to draw a black bean. They all drew their beans with a manly dignity and firmness, which showed them superior to their condition. Some of the lighter temper jested over the horrible tragedy. One said, 'Boys this beats raffling all to pieces;' another said, 'This is the tallest gambling scrape I ever was in.' Those who drew black beans showed no emotion, not even changing color, but, on the contrary, those who drew white beans seemed completely overcome. They wept and appeared completely unmanned. Poor Robert Beard, who lay upon the ground near by, ill and exhausted from his forced marches, called his brother William, who was bringing him a cup of water, and said: 'Brother, if you get a black bean, I'll take your place, I want to die.' The brother with anguish replied: 'No, I will keep my own place, I am strong and better able to die than you.' These noble youths both drew white beans, but both soon after died, leaving this heroic legacy to their venerable parents in Texas. Several of the Mexican officers who officiated in this cruel violation of their country's faith, expressed much regret thereat, and some wept bitterly. Soon after the fated men were placed in a separate court yard and later executed. Several of us were permitted to visit and receive their dying requests. Poor Cocke, when he drew his fatal bean, held it up between his forefinger and thumb, and with a contemptuous smile said: 'Boys, I told you so. I never failed in my life to draw a prize,' and turning to Judge Gibson said: 'Well, Judge, say to my friends that I died in grace.' Cocke further remarked: 'They only rob me of forty years,' and then sat down and wrote a dignified letter of remonstrance to General Waddy Thompson, American Minister to Mexico. Knowing that his remains would be robbed of his clothes, he drew off his pantaloons and handed them to his comrades, dying in his underclothes. Poor Henry Whaling, one of Cameron's best fighters, as he drew his black bean, said, with as bright a smile as ever brightened a man's face: 'Well, they don't make much off of me, anyhow, for I know I have killed twenty-five of the yellow bellies,' then in a firm voice demanded his dinner, saying: 'They shall not cheat me out of it.' He ate heartily, smoked a cigar, and in twenty minutes was launched into eternity. The Mexicans said he had the largest heart they had ever seen. They shot him fifteen times before he expired. Poor Torrey, quite a youth, but in spirit a giant, said he was perfectly willing to meet his fate; that for the glory of his country he had fought, and for her glory was willing to die, and turning to the officer said: 'After the battle of San Jacinto my family took one of your youths prisoner, raised and educated him, and this is our requital.' Captain Cameron, on taking leave of these brave men, and particularly of Turnbull, a brother Scotchman, with whom he had braved many dangers, wept bitterly, and implored the officers to execute him and spare his men. Just previous to this they were bound with cords, with bandaged eyes, and were seated on logs with their backs to their executioners. They all begged the officers to shoot them in front and at a short distance, and said that they were not afraid to look death in the face. This he refused to do, and to make the cruelty as refined as possible, fired at several places, and continued the firing from ten to twelve minutes, lacerating and mangling these heroes in a manner too horrible for description. Such was the effect of the horrible massacre upon their own soldiers who were stationed as guards upon the wall above, that one of them fainted and came near falling over. During the martyrdom of these noble spirits we were separated from them by a stone wall fifteen feet high, and heard their last agonizing groans. J. L. Shepherd, one of the unfortunates, was not killed by the executioners it seems, for the next morning only sixteen bodies were found and we heard afterward that he was recognized on the streets of Saltillo by a Mexican soldier and shot down. When the Mexicans missed him they came to us and demanded another man in his stead. To this we demurred and they finally agreed to let the matter rest. The next morning they marched us out, and halted us before the mangled bodies of our comrades." Their names were as follows: L. L. Cash of Pennsylvania, J. D. Cocke

of Virginia, Robert Dunham of Tennessee, Captain William N. Eastland, Tennessee; Edmond Esta, New Jersey; Robert Harris, Mississippi; Thomas L. Jones, Kentucky; Patrick Mahan, Ireland; James
Ogden, Virginia; Charles Roberts, Tennessee; William Rowan,
Georgia; J. L. Shepherd, Alabama; J. M. M. Thompson, Tennessee;
J. M. Torrey, Connecticut; James Turnbull, Scotland; Henry Whaling, Indiana, and M. C. Wing, New York. An heroic episode touch-
ing these martyrs is related by Mr. Lord. "Walter M. Lane, who,
during the Mexican War, was major of Hays' Regiment of Texas
Rangers, under J. E. Wool, was dispatched by the latter with a small
body of men to go south in the direction of San Luis Potosi, to discover all that was possible in relation to the movements of the Mexican army. There were two roads to that place, one by Matchuala, a
large town, the other by the great ———————— of Salado, where the
seventeen Mier prisoners drew beans in 1843. The two roads were
divided by a range of mountains. Lane took the left hand or eastern road, and actually penetrated to and entered the city of Matchuala, with its twenty thousand people and garrison of several hundred
men. He ordered and obtained dinner at a 'meson' (a compromise
between an hotel and a wagon yard), announced that a large American army was near by, and feasted his men to their satisfaction.
Then remounting, he retired across the mountain to the other road,
and struck the hacienda of Salado. Seizing the Alcalde, he ordered
the resurrection of the bones of the sixteen martyrs, and demanded
mules, sacks, saddles and all things necessary to bear them away.
All were furnished and the remains of the dead duly placed on mules.
Lane tipped his beaver to the Alcalde and assembled villagers, and
bore these relics to General Taylor's headquarters. They were taken
to LaGrange, on the Colorado River, Tex., by John Dusenberry of
New York, one of the Mier prisoners, and there, with all solemnity,
in the presence of thousands, interred on Monument Hill, overlooking the country for miles around. Few know, even to this day, that
to General Walter P. Lane, Texas is indebted for the possession of
these mementoes of heroism never surpassed."

After the death of these noble men Mr. Lord and his fellow prisoners were marched to near Huchuctoca, within seven leagues of the

City of Mexico. Captain Cameron, on entering his quarters for the night, remarked prophetically, "Boys, we all know who goes in, but God knows who'll come out." About eight o'clock that night, April 25, orders came from that tyrant, Santa Anna, to shoot the beloved Captain Cameron, and after the others had started to march for the City of Mexico, he was taken to the rear of the village to the place of execution. A priest was in waiting, and asked him if he wished to confess. He promptly replied, "No, throughout life I believe I have been an honest man, and if I have to confess, it shall be to my Maker." As the guard advanced to bandage his eyes, he said to his interpreter: "Tell them no, Ewen Cameron can now, as he has often done before for the liberty of Texas, look death in the face without winking." So saying he opened the bosom of his hunting shirt, presented his naked breast, and gave the word "fire." Mr. Lord was imprisoned in Tacubaya from May 1 to September 16, 1843, and was employed in making streets. He was then removed to Perote Castle and liberated in 1844. Returning to Texas, he received a letter patent to 1,280 acres of land, which he selected in the beautiful Cheapside country, and has since increased it by purchase to 3,442 acres. His devotion to the Republic in war and prison covered four years and seven months; to the Mexican Confederation one year and one month. When the Civil War broke out he joined the home guards and served two years, although he was exempt from service to his state on account of age.

Previous to this, in 1849, he went to California and dug gold three years, after which he returned to Texas with $7,000 in gold dust, which he presented and had coined at the New Orleans mint. This was the basis of his fortune. In politics he is independent and in religion an Episcopalian. He has served as school trustee and has held other positions. On December 30, 1849, he was married to Miss Kate Myers, who was born in New Orleans, October 15, 1832, and they have had eleven children, nine of whom are still living: Cinthelia Ann, wife of John Johnson; George T., Robert F., Emily Agnes, wife of H. N. Smith; William P., Minnie May (deceased), Sidney Johnston, Henry Lee, Kate A., James E. and Pomona B. (deceased). Mr. and Mrs. Lord have twenty-nine interesting grandchildren.

CHARLES A. LEUSCHNER.

Charles A. Leuschner is a native of that country which has given to the United States some of her most honorable, industrious and prominent citizens—Germany—his birth occurring in the Kingdom of Prussia in 1845. He was the elder of two sons born to G. A. and Emily (Keller) Leuschner, the other member of the family being Augustus Frederick. In 1855 the parents decided to seek a home on American soil, and, after reaching this country, settled in Victoria, Tex., where the father at once engaged in the occupation of carpentering, which he followed successfully until his death, which occurred in 1859. His widow still survives him, and resides in Victoria with her sons. The subject of this sketch laid the foundation of a good education in his native land, and it was fortunate that he did, for after coming to this country he attended the English schools only two months, but being an eager reader he remedied this in a great measure. As a youth he followed farming, or any occupation to which he could profitably turn his attention, and when scarcely sixteen years of age he marched to the war in the ranks of the "old bloody Sixth" Texas Infantry, which regiment proudly bore on its battle-scarred flag the names of "Arkansas Post," "Chickamauga," "Resaca," "Mission Ridge," "New Hope Church," "Atlanta," "Franklin" and "Nashville," in all of which, and wherever the indomitable General Pat Cleburne or dashing Granberry led, no "gray jacket" performed his duty with more bravery than did Mr. Leuschner. He was captured at Arkansas Post and kept a prisoner at Camp Butler, Springfield, Ill., for about three months, when he was exchanged at City Point, Va. Following this he became a member of the Army of the Tennessee, under General Bragg, and was a participant in the engagements around Dalton. He was captured at Franklin, Tenn., and was taken to Camp Douglas, Chicago, but was exchanged four months later at Shreveport, La., and was there also discharged. For some time after his return home he was engaged in stock driving and other occupations, and by the exercise of the utmost diligence eventually found himself in possession of a comfortable competency. At the present time he owns 350 acres of fine farming land, and has a very comfortable, commodious and pleasant home. He has always taken an active interest in the political affairs of his section, and it was mainly through his influence that Democratic supremacy was secured in 1869-70, when it gave a Democratic majority of about seven votes. His services in this connection were recognized by all, and he was generally regarded as legitimately standing in the way of the legislative succession as immediate representative of Victoria County, but his sensitive nature led him to distrust his fitness for this position, and he remained in private life. In 1874-75 he served as alderman of Victoria and in November, 1882, he was elected treasurer of the county by a handsome majority, though opposed by two of the most popular and worthy business men of the county, and has filled the position very acceptably by re-election ever since. In 1870 he was united in marriage with Miss Sophia Bischoff, a native of Victoria County, and daughter of Anton Bischoff. The latter came to the county in 1844, and now lives on a fine farm fifteen miles from the town, being eighty-two years of age. To Mr. and Mrs. Leuschner nine children have been given: Louisa L., born in 1871; Ida, born in 1873; William C., born in 1875; Adelia S., born in 1877; Leopold A., born in 1879; Victor A., born in 1882; Lizetta, Meta and Regina. The family are members of the Lutheran church, and Mr. Leuschner is a member of the Sons of Herman. He is a natural musician, and is a member of the city band and orchestra. He is just in the prime of life, and with his robust health, vigorous mind, correct principles, and deserved popularity, can make his future almost anything he elects.

DR. ROBERT TAGGART KNOX.

The profession of the physician and surgeon is one that has drawn to it the brightest and most honorable of men; for none but an intelligent man could be a physician at all, and no physician not a man of honor could long retain a profitable practice. Dr. Robert T. Knox is the oldest practitioner of Gonzales, was born at Danville, Ky., in 1832, the second in a family of three children born to Andrew W. and Mary (Daviess) Knox, who were born in Pennsylvania and Kentucky respectively. The paternal grandfather, Abner Knox, was likewise born in the Keystone State and his wife, Miss Elizabeth Taggart, was also of an old Pennsylvania family. At an early day he removed to Kentucky with his family, when his son, Andrew W., was but five years old, and in a small way engaged in farming in the vicinity of Danville, his house being built on the block-house plan, to protect himself and family from Indian attacks, and was used by them as a residence for many years, various additions and improvements in the same having been made. The grandfather died in 1790. Andrew W. Knox was reared in Kentucky, and, although a self-educated man, possessed a brilliant intellect. He became a student of law, for his own improvement, but never practiced that profession, and he had a good knowledge of nearly all branches of learning. He devoted his attention to farming and stock-raising, at which he acquired a competency, and in 1863 was called from this life. His widow died in 1870, and both were earnest members of the Presbyterian church. The maternal grandfather, James Daviess, was a Virginian, of Scotch-Irish descent, and the family first became known in this country during colonial times. James Daviess was a minister of the Presbyterian church and was among the pioneer settlers of Kentucky, to which state he was accompanied by two brothers, Robert and Samuel, who became farmers. Another brother, Joseph (the famed "Joe Daviess"), was killed in the battle of Tippecanoe. Captain Samuel Daviess became a prominent lawyer of Harrodsburg, Ky., and in the vicinity of that place Robert devoted his attention to tilling the soil. James Daviess was also a farmer, in addition to his ministerial duties, and his wife was Miss Mary Wrisk, a Virginian by birth, who removed with her people to Kentucky and located on Silver Creek, near Richmond. Her family were greatly troubled by Indians for years, and at one time, in trying to make their escape from them, they ran under a clothes line, which was not seen by the Indians, who were caught by it and thrown to the ground. One child was captured and nearly killed before it was rescued. Dr Robert

Taggart Knox was reared on Blue Grass soil and was educated in the private school taught by Rev. John L. McKee, who is still a resident preacher at Danville, Ky. He began the study of medicine in January, 1851, under the tutorship of Dr. J. M. Meyer of Danville, and graduated from the University of Louisville in 1854. He began the practice of his profession in Central Kentucky, but in 1856 came to Gonzales, Tex., of which place he has since been a permanent resident. He is and has been a member of the Presbyterian church for many years. At the beginning of the war he was offered the position of surgeon of various regiments, but in 1862 went out with Terry's Rangers and was with them in camp at Bowling Green, Ky., for some time, but was finally compelled to leave the service on account of ill health. He returned to Gonzales and was appointed physician in charge of the hospital there, for the workmen who were erecting a fort in the vicinity of the place. In 1878 he became a member of the Texas State Medical Association, of which he has since been a very active member, and in 1878 he was elected and served as its first vice president. He is now and has been for the past ten years a member of the "Medical Examining Board" of the Twenty-fifth Judicial District, most of the time as president. He has been a frequent contributor to journals on subjects relating to his profession, and as he never writes unless he has something new and original to say, his articles are very interesting. He is of an inventive turn of mind also, and has invented a uterine dilater, which is being manufactured by George Tieman & Co. of New York, and is acknowledged by the profession to be the best instrument for this purpose known, and its sales are large and constantly on the increase. Dr. Knox was a commissioner to the World's Fair at New Orleans from this district. The Doctor was married in 1860 to Miss Catherine T. Blake of Chester, S. C., and daughter of Joshua and Martha (Eckles) Blake. To their union five children were given: Thomas Roger, who graduated in medicine in 1886 from the Ohio Medical College of Cincinnati, took his first course of lectures in the Louisville University, and for one year was a practitioner of Sabina, Mexico, and for the Southern Pacific Railroad. He afterward went to Hallettsville, Tex., and is now in partnership with Dr. Ledbetter in a large drug store, and has a large general practice. He was married to the daughter of

Dr. R. H. Harrison of Columbus, Tex., and has three children: May is the wife of Henry Remschel, a merchant of Kerrville, Tex.; they have four children: James Atwood is a merchant of Kerrville and is a Knight Templar Mason; Robert Bailey is studying medicine in St. Louis, Mo., and Katie Blake still lives with her parents. Dr. Knox became a Mason at Gonzales in 1857 and is now a Knight Templar and a member of Gonzales Commandery No. 11. The Doctor is the owner of 200 acres or more of fine farming land, nearly all of which is under cultivation, also a fine family residence in Gonzales, Tex., and he is quite extensively engaged in the raising of Jersey stock. His home has always been a happy and hospitable one, and, being an amiable and courteous gentleman and an earnest student of his profession, his friends and patrons are legion.

JAMES W. DICKEY.

James W. Dickey of the Floresville Chronicle, which is a newsy, spicy sheet, published in the general interests of the locality, came originally from Choctaw County, Miss., born July 8, 1842. His parents, John Milton and Priscilla Johns (Gillespie) Dickey, were natives of Alabama, where the father followed farming. About 1845 the parents moved to Louisiana and located on Red River, occupying a farm on which the battle of Mansfield was fought during the Rebellion. In 1846 they moved to the Lone Star State and settled in Walker County, remaining there until 1851, when they came to Baxter District, a portion of which now constitutes Wilson County, at that time almost a wilderness, and the father followed stock-raising there until his death April 1, 1857. The mother is still living and makes her home at Runge, Karnes County. James W. Dickey had but such educational advantages as were possible at that early day, and his youthful years, when not in the school room, were spent in assisting his father on the farm. In 1861, when the threatening war cloud hung darkly over the Nation, young Dickey enlisted in Company E, Third Regiment, Texas Infantry, and served the first year on the Texas border. Later he was in the Trans-Mississippi Department in Louisiana and Arkansas, Walker's Division, and was a brave and faithful soldier. In March, 1865, he came home on a furlough, and on the 9th of April of the same year was married to Miss Martha J. Gillett, daughter of Rev. R. Gillett of West Texas Conference Methodist Episcopal church South. Returning to the army, he met the command coming home; reported to the colonel and was discharged. He then came back to Wilson County and engaged in farming, purchasing land upon which he lived until January 1, 1880, when he came to Floresville. He was appointed county assessor in 1878 and was elected to that position in 1880, serving four years. Previous to this, in 1868, he was elected justice of the peace and county commissioner, holding both positions six years, being three times elected to the same. In the month of August, 1882, he bought his paper and has been conducting it since. It is published in the interests of the Democratic party of this county, its crisp and trenchant editorials commanding an ever widening area of circulation, while carrying with them that weight and authority which a calm and intelligent judgment must always secure. Mrs. Dickey died July 1, 1880, leaving six children, one of whom, an infant, died soon after: Eugene W., Zella A., Marion W., Leonard M. and Clio E. On the 15th of January, 1882, Mr. Dickey was married to Miss Alice Hobbs, a native of Texas, and daughter of Job Hobbs, a pioneer of Kentucky. Five children have been born to the second union: L. Elmore, R. Lilly, Alma B., Maurice and an infant son, as yet unnamed. The family hold membership in the Methodist Episcopal church South, with which our subject has been connected since the age of fifteen years. When twenty-one years of age he joined the Masonic order, becoming a member of S. G. Newon Lodge, under dispensation attached to the Southern army. After hostilities ceased he attached himself to Union Valley Lodge at Union, Wilson County, of which he was Secretary for a time, and is now a member of Floresville Lodge No. 515.

DR. JOSEPH M. REUSS.

The usefulness of a professional man is not marked merely by his learning and skill, his proficiency in medical practice; but also by his character, both private and professional, his honorable adherence to medical ethics and his personal integrity and prudent benevolence. When a physician combines these characteristics it is with great pleasure that we record his life work, and such a man do we find in Dr. J. M. Reuss. This physician, of Cuero, Tex., one of the oldest in practice here, is a native of Germany, as were also his parents, Stephen and Mary (Muller) Reuss. The father, an hotelkeeper in his native country, died there in 1831, and the mother in 1824. Our subject, whose birth occurred in 1823, was but one year old when his mother died, and he was reared by his elder sister. He received his education in Muennerstadt, in Bavaria, and studied medicine at the University of Wuerzburg in 1843-45. Then he began practicing, but seeing a better opening for a physician in America, he crossed the ocean and landed at Galveston in November, 1845. From there he went to Indianola and began practicing, continuing there until after the storm of 1875. In 1876 he came to Cuero. He established the first drug store in Indianola in 1849. In 1861 Dr. Reuss raised a company and was elected captain of Company B., Shea's Battalion, which was afterward organized into Hobby's Regiment. He was stationed at Tasslabano and participated in the engagement at Lavaca, but on account of rheumatism he was obliged to resign in the spring of 1864. He had a large practice, and passed through three epidemics of cholera and seven of yellow fever. The Doctor was contract surgeon for the United States Custom House at Indianola, both before and after the war, and was contract surgeon for the Quartermaster Department before that eventful period. Most of the time he was also surgeon of the City Hospital at Indianola. He is a member of the State Pharmaceutical Society. In 1873 he established a business in Cuero, mainly on account of his son, Dr. August J. Reuss. Our subject was married in Galveston, Tex., in 1845, to Miss Gesine Stubbeman, a native of Germany. The following children were the fruits of this union: August J., who was educated at Lee University, Lexington, Va., and studied medicine at the Jefferson University at Charlottesville, Va. Later he entered Tulane University, New Orleans, and graduated in 1870. Following this he entered the Prussian army in the war with France, as assistant surgeon, and after the war studied two years at Wuerzburg and Vienna. Returning to the Lone Star State in the fall of 1872, he practiced medicine at Indianola until the spring of the following year, when he located in Cuero. He was a bright, promising young man, and his death, which occurred in January, 1876, was a sad blow to his parents. The three children following August J. died in infancy. The others are named Oscar J., Bertha, Alfreda and Joseph Henry. Oscar J. is a druggist of Cuero, carrying on the business under the old firm name of J. M. Reuss & Son, and is one of the Board of Pharmaceutical Examiners. Alfreda is the wife of William Frobese, of the firm of H. Runge & Co., and Joseph Henry is a physician in partnership with his father. He was educated in the University of Texas, at Austin, and graduated at the College of Physicians and Surgeons in New York in 1889. He is a member of the State Medical Society, and excels in surgery. The mother of these children died in August, 1893. She was a worthy member of the Lutheran church. Dr. Reuss was one of the organizers of the cotton mill, and he is interested in the oil mill in the city, and in building and loan associations. He takes a deep interest in educational and religious matters, is a valuable citizen, and is a member of the Board of Medical Examiners of the district. His son, who conducts a drug store, carries a stock of goods valued at $8,000, and does an annual business of $16,000.

JUDGE BASLEY G. NEIGHBORS.

The expensive and necessary duty of enacting laws calculated to protect mankind from the doers of evil has always been a serious object of legislation. The office of judge is one of honor and dignity, and it should, without question, be filled by a man who possesses a thorough knowledge of the law, a keen, analytical mind, and one who can, on short notice, correctly judge of men and motives. These requirements are possessed by Judge Neighbors, who, in his efforts to preserve law and order, has shown much wisdom, good judgment, and has balanced the scales of justice with impartial hand. He is a product of the Blue Grass State, and there first opened his eyes on the light of day in 1854, being the third of six children born to Henry B. and Louisa F. (Sewell) Neighbors, who were natives of Kentucky and Virginia respectively. The paternal grandfather, William Neighbors, was a Virginian by birth, and was one of the first settlers of Cumberland County, Ky. The maternal grandfather, James A. Sewell, was born in the Old North State, and at an early day came to Tennessee, later locating in Kentucky, where he was called from life. Henry B. Neighbors devoted his attention to tilling the soil in his native state, and for some time during the Great Civil War he was a member of the Federal army. He died in Kentucky, and his wife also passed from life in that state about 1883. Basley G. Neighbors was educated in the common schools, and finished his literary education at Glasgow. He began life for himself as a school teacher, but this occupation was merely a stepping stone to other and better things, and the money thus earned paid his way through college, and he was graduated in 1879. The same year he came to Texas, and located at Lockhart, and during the few terms that he taught school in the vicinity of that place he also pursued the study of law, and in 1881 was admitted to the bar at Lockhart, and entered upon the practice of his profession in that place. In 1882 he was elected to the office of county attorney, in which capacity he served one term very acceptably. After completing his term he bought out a paper and started the Lockhart Register, the first copy of which was issued by him. After publishing this paper for two years he sold out and moved to Kyle, becoming the owner of the Hays County Times, but while conducting this paper also practiced his profession. In 1887 he came to San Marcos, was at once appointed city attorney of the place, and at the expiration of his term was re-elected to the office, but soon resigned. In 1890 he was a popular candidate for county judge, to which position he was elected, and he was re-elected to the same office in 1892. Judge Neighbors has always been quite active in politics, and has been a delegate to various conventions. He has also been quite active in school work, and by virtue of his office is ex-officio superintendent, and to him belongs the honor of holding the first trustees' convention ever held in the state, at Kyle, in September, 1893. He organized the present institute of Hays County, and by strenuous exertion has brought it to a high state of perfection. In his office as county judge he has been laboring to improve the public roads, and owing to his efforts Hays can boast of some of the best highways in the state. He has also called an overseers' convention, which will be the first ever held in the United States. Judge Neighbors is self-made and self-educated, and has made his own way in life from early manhood, and has every reason to be proud of the success which has attended his efforts. He was married September 6, 1888, to Miss Mollie Moore Hubbard, a native of Texas, and a daughter of Miller Hubbard, an early settler of Bastrop County, Tex., from Georgia, and a relative of Governor Hubbard. To Judge and Mrs. Neighbors two daughters have been given: Bessie and Adaline Fairchild. The Neighbors are of Welsh descent, while Mrs. Hubbard's ancestors are of pure English descent. The Judge and his family are attendants of the Baptist church, and are popular in the social circles of San Marcos.

DAVID S. H. DARST.

David S. H. Darst, a pioneer settler of Gonzales, was born in the Territory of Missouri, above St. Louis, in 1821, being the only child born to the marriage of Jacob C. Darst and Margaret C. Hughes, who were born in Kentucky, and on the Holston River in East Tennessee respectively. The paternal grandfather, David Darst, came from Pennsylvania to Kentucky, thence to Missouri, at an early day, at about the time that the famous hunter and Indian fighter, Daniel Boone, went to that section, and there he made his home until his

death. During the early manhood of Jacob C. Darst he participated
in many Indian wars of the Missouri frontier, serving in the capacity
of scout, and while out on one of his expeditions ran out of provisions, and not liking to draw attention to himself by firing on game,
went for a long time without food. In August, 1830, he started from
Missouri for Gonzales, Tex., with his family, but did not reach his
destination until January of the following year, for the long journey
was made with an ox team. They settled on a farm near the town,
but about 1832 moved to a farm about eighteen miles above Gonzales,
but Indians were so numerous and hostile that he was compelled to
return to Gonzales two years later. In the spring of 1835, when the
trouble began with Mexico, he at once began assisting the citizens of
Gonzales in their efforts for home protection, and when the Mexicans
across the river were charged, Mr. Darst fired the first shot from the
only cannon, which was also the cause of contention. He afterward
went with a company to San Antonio, and was in the battles about
there, but was honorably discharged and came home before the final
surrender of that place. In February, 1836, he made a trip to the
coast for a load of salt, being accompanied by his son, David S. H.,
but as it had not arrived he took a load of ammunition and provisions
to Colonel Fannin at Goliad, then returned to the Gulf, got his salt
and returned home. At this time Colonel Travis and his men were
besieged in the Alamo, and a messenger had been sent to Gonzales
for reinforcements. A company was at once made up, consisting of
thirty-two men, of which Mr. Darst was one, and they finally reached
San Antonio and entered the Alamo, but all fell in that battle on the
6th of March. On the 12th of March, Mr. Darst's widow and her son,
David S. H., started on the "run away," and got as far as Trinity
River, where they were at the time the battle of San Jacinto was
fought. They then went to Columbia, where they remained that
winter, then lived in Matagorda one year, after which they returned
to Gonzales, where the mother died in 1846. Mr. Darst had previously been married, and was accompanied to this state by his
daughter, Nancy, who was visiting relatives at the time of the bloody
battle of the Alamo. She afterward married Cyrus Crosby, and was
living one mile south of Victoria when the Comanche Indians made

a raid on that section and burned Linville. She was captured, with one child, by the Indians, and was killed by her captors at the time of the Plum Creek battle, her infant having been previously killed.

CAPTAIN WILLIAM LONDON FOSTER.

Captain William London Foster, an early settler of Gonzales County, and now a resident of Luling, Caldwell County, was born in Calloway County, Ky., in 1828, the eldest child born to John E. and Mary (Moore) Foster, who were natives of the state of Alabama. The grandparents on both sides were early settlers of that state, but soon after the birth of the subject of this sketch his parents moved to Tennessee, thence to Alabama, and then to Mississippi. From Monroe County, of the last mentioned state, they came to Texas in 1838, and in June of the following year settled in Gonzales County, where John E. Foster located a headright of 640 acres in the fork of the San Marcos and Guadalupe rivers. He also bought other land, which he improved and resided on. His first wife, the mother of the subject of this sketch, died in Mississippi about 1836, after which he married Mrs. Dilworth (nee Elizabeth Parchman), a sister of the wife of Colonel John G. King. John E. Foster died in 1840, while on a trip to Mississippi with a drove of horses and mules, and his property was appropriated by a man who was working for him. His widow resided on the farm in Texas for a number of years, and being a courageous and strong-minded woman, she improved the farm and managed it successfully. She later married Dr. Hardeman, and eventually passed from life in Guadalupe County. The first wife of John E. Foster bore him two children, and on coming to Texas he was accompanied by them, the three children which his second wife bore him, and the two children born to his third wife by her former husband. From 1840 to 1846 the subject of this sketch assisted on the home farm, but in the last mentioned year enlisted in Captain Henry

McCullough's Company, Jack Hays' Regiment, for the Mexican war, and started for that country, but was recalled to the frontier of Texas, and during that year was Indian scouting. His company was mustered out of service in 1847, after which he joined Captain Crump's company, Col. P. H. Bell's Regiment, who afterward became Governor of Texas, and for some time he was a Texas Ranger. In 1848 he joined another company of the same regiment and was engaged fighting Indians for some time. In 1849 he was out with a surveying company for a German colony; in fact, was a very useful citizen in the early history of the state. In July, 1850, he was married to Mrs. Eliza Ann Rutledge, nee King, a daughter of Colonel John G. King, after which he located on his farm and ranch on the Guadalupe River, where he made his home for many years. In 1861 he assisted in raising a company for the Confederate army, of which he was made first lieutenant of Terry's Rangers. He was sent east of the Mississippi River with his regiment, and in December of the same year he withdrew and came home on a leave of absence for sixty days, and at once recruited another company, which was mustered into the Confederate service within thirty days from the time he left Kentucky, and he was made its captain. It became Company D of Wood's Regiment and operated in the trans-Mississippi department, participating in the battles in Louisiana in the Banks campaign up the Red River, and was operating on the Brazos River when the war closed. He at once returned home and engaged in farming and stock raising, and lived on his farm above Gonzales until 1889, which consists of about 350 acres under cultivation and 1,000 acres in ranch and pasture. All the improvements on this place were made by himself, and are the result of much thoughtful consideration, for when he became the owner of the place it was totally unimproved. He is a thrifty and painstaking tiller of the soil, and raises, on an average, forty bushels of corn and three-fourths of a bale of cotton to the acre. About 1870 he raised the first crop of wheat in all that section, and at the same time, also, was the first to raise oats. Since that time he has cultivated both crops successfully, and some years the yield has been exceptionally large. Since 1889 Captain Foster has resided in Luling, and is not actively engaged in any employment. He was left a widower in 1883, his wife having borne him nine children, four of whom passed from life prior to their mother. The names of his children are as follows: Mary, who died in childhood; Elizabeth, who died in childhood also; John King, who is a dentist at Eagle Pass; Thomas Pinckney, who died in childhood; James Chism, who lives on his father's farm; Philip Houston, a dentist of Marion; William Lee, who resides on the old home and manages the farm; Minnie Alice, who is the wife of N. Morrison of Leesville, and one child that died in infancy. Mr. Foster's second marriage was consummated in August, 1884, and was to Mrs. Martha Ann (Morrison) King, daughter of Wesley Morrison, an early Texan from Mississippi, and an extensive farmer. Mr. Foster is a member of the Baptist Church, while his wife is a Methodist. Out of the kindness and generosity of his heart Mr. Foster has reared eighteen orphans, several of whom were his relatives. He is an honorable man and an excellent citizen, and is universally esteemed.

JAMES H. MOORE.

Few families in Texas have a higher standing for character and enterprise than the one represented by the name at the head of this paragraph and in its various members it is eminently worthy of the respect which is universally conceded to it. James H. Moore, who was one of the first settlers of the village of Thomaston, Tex., came originally from Mississippi, his birth occurring in Monroe, now Lamar, County in 1844. He is fourth in a family of eight children born to Hon. Thomas C. and Martha (Hollis) Moore, the former a native of South Carolina and the latter of Alabama. The paternal grandfather, James Moore, was born in the Palmetto State and there followed farming for many years. At an early day he moved from there to Mississippi and became a wealthy and extensive planter. There he passed the remainder of his life. The Moore family is of

Scotch-Irish origin and the ancestors came to this country in colonial times. They traced their ancestors back to Sir Walter Raleigh. Our subject's maternal grandfather, John Hollis, was born
in Alabama, where he became a wealthy planter and where he
passed his entire life. The mother of our subject with other members of the family moved to Mississippi and in that state she was
married to Mr. Moore. The latter, after his marriage, followed
planting in Mississippi, and while a resident of that state became
quite active in politics, serving in the Legislature of that state and
holding other prominent positions. In 1853 he came to the Lone
Star State and settled in Bastrop County, where he bought land and
engaged in farming. His superior abilities were soon recognized
and he was solicited to run for the Legislature and for the office of
Governor of State. In 1860 he was a member of the secession convention. During the war he continued farming, but devoted most of
his attention to the Confederate cause, assisting the widows and
orphans at home and doing much good. From there he moved to
Fayette County, where he now resides, engaged in farming. He lost
his sight in 1862, but is now one of the best posted men of the state,
although having to depend on others to do his reading. In whatever field of action Mr. Moore has been called, he has shown his superior qualities and high character. He and Mrs. Moore are earnest
and consistent members of the Methodist Church, and most worthy
and esteemed citizens of the county. The original of this notice was
but a boy when he was brought by his parents to Texas, and he was
reared mainly in Fayette County, where he was attending school
when the war broke out. Abandoning his studies he enlisted in
Company I, Sixteenth Texas Regiment, and served in Henry E. Mc-
Collough's Brigade, participating in the engagements on the Mississippi River, Milligan's Bend, Mansfield and Pleasant Hill. In the
last named battle he was wounded and was discharged for disability. Previous to that, however, he was in numerous minor engagements in Arkansas and Louisiana. After returning home he attended school for a time and then branched out as an agriculturist
in Fayette County. There he was married to Miss Lou V. Thomas,
a native of Fayette County and daughter of Nathan Thomas, who

was born in Tennessee. At an early day her father came to Texas and first settled in Washington, but afterward Fayette County. He was a prominent man, served in the Legislature and held other prominent offices. He was thrown from his buggy and died shortly afterward. When he first settled in Texas he bought a tract of 1,190 acres in DeWitt County for thirty-five cents per acre. The railroad passing through DeWitt County crossed this land and a station located on it was named Thomaston in his honor. Soon after our subject's marriage he moved to Mr. Thomas' land in DeWitt County and erected the first house in what soon became Thomaston. The town was laid out in lots by Henry E. McCollough, who was surveyor for the railroad. Mr. Thomas donated each alternate lot to the railroad, and the town now has a population of 500, four stores, a gin and mill, two churches, two blacksmith shops, and is surrounded by an excellent farming country. Mr. Moore is the owner of 653 acres of the original tract, with 350 acres under cultivation. His land is rich and productive, often raising fifty bushels of corn and one bale of cotton per acre. Our subject has been somewhat active politically, has been a delegate to Democratic conventions and is now justice of the peace of the Seventh Precinct, which has been newly created. He is active in church work, organizing a Sunday school here twenty-five years ago and has been its superintendent constantly since. There is an enrolled school of about 100 scholars. To Mr. and Mrs. Moore have been born seven children: Hattie, wife of M. S. Magee of Thomaston; Sallie; Annie, wife of Dr. W. Shropshire of Houston; Thomas; Susie; Willie, died in infancy, and Hollis—an interesting and most intelligent family. Besides still owning the entire town of Thomaston and his fine farm there, Mr. Moore also owns a most valuable farm in Fayette County. This farm is improved and highly productive, and all his property is rapidly advancing in value. The town of Thomaston is yearly becoming a more active trading and shipping point, and increasing in population. All the surrounding country is fertile and productive. Mr. Moore is a pleasant, courteous and hospitable gentleman and is confident in, and constantly striving for, the advancement of his town and county.

DR. PETER C. WOODS.

Before the Good Samaritan dressed the wounds of the man on the
Jericho road, the healer of diseases was known for his humanity and
kindness. Whatever the skill of the physician and surgeon, he can
never be truly great unless he is touched with the spirit of man's
infirmities, and moved by a heartfelt purpose to relieve suffering
for the sake of the race. In the list of the successful physicians of
Hays County, Tex., stands the name of Dr. Peter C. Woods, who has
long been a practitioner of San Marcos. He owes his nativity to
Tennessee, where he was born in 1820, the second and youngest
child born to Peter and Sarah W. (Davidson) Woods, who were natives of Tennessee and North Carolina respectively. The paternal
grandfather, Peter Woods, was born in Georgia, and was one of the
very first to locate in Tennessee. He eventually died in Missouri,
to which state he had removed at an early day. The maternal grandfather, George Davidson, was a North Carolinian by birth and was
a soldier in the Revolutionary War, under General William Davidson, an older brother, and saw the most of his service in the Southern
States. He in time moved to Tennessee and passed from life in that
state. Peter Woods, the father of the subject of this sketch, spent
his life in Tennessee, became the sheriff of Franklin County, and was
killed while making an arrest, about 1819, a short time before the
birth of the doctor. The latter was reared on Tennessee soil and received the greater part of his literary education at Shelbyville. He
then began the study of medicine at Coffeyville, Miss., under Dr.
Walker, and graduated at the Louisville (Ky.) Medical Institute in
1842, and at once began the practice of his profession in Water
Valley, Miss. In 1853 he came to San Marcos, Tex., and was about
the second physician to locate in the place. He continued the practice of his profession up to 1861, then recruited a company here, of
which he was made captain, Company A, Thirty-second Texas Cavalry, and soon after the organization of this regiment he was elected
its colonel. After serving in Texas for a time, his command was attached to De Bray's Brigade and served on the frontier and coast

of Texas and in the campaign against General Banks in Louisiana, on the Red River. He was in many engagements, among which was the fight at Yellow Bayou, where he was severely wounded and retired from the service. He has since been a very successful medical practitioner of San Marcos, and is professionally well known in this and surrounding counties. He was first married in Mississippi to Miss Georgia Lawshe in 1846, and she died in Texas leaving seven children. His second marriage occurred in 1874, and was to Miss Ella R. Ogletree, a native of South Carolina, by whom he has had five children. The doctor and his family are members of the Methodist Episcopal Church, and he has been connected with the same for over half a century, and now holds the office of trustee. He has been a Mason since his twenty-first year and is a member of San Marcos Chapter, has served as master of his lodge here for twenty years, and held the same position in Mississippi. He is active in his advocacy of Democratic principles, and is a public-spirited citizen. In 1866 he served in the constitutional convention convened to frame the present Constitution of the state, since which time he has taken little part in politics, though he is still as firm a believer in state's rights as he was at the close of the war. He is the owner of a fine tract of land of 640 acres and is making a specialty of the raising of Poland China swine, and he also has a good grade of Durham cattle. He is no less successful in his farming operations than as a medical practitioner, and his friends are both numerous and devoted. He was a brave and able military officer, lent valuable aid to the Southern cause, and is a thorough Christian gentleman.

JOHN HALLET.

(Deceased.)

It is a pleasure to speak of those worthy citizens whose active lives have ceased on earth, but whose influence extends still, and will continue to extend among all who knew them. This truth is doubly true when such a man has established for himself and children a reputation for integrity, character and ability. Such is the case with John Hallet, the original settler of Lavaca County, Tex. He was born in Worcestershire, England, and was the younger son of an English nobleman. When but a lad he was commissioned in the British navy, but served only a short time. Being threatened with punishment by one of the officers of the ship he climbed overboard in the night time and swam to an American vessel in the harbor. The captain of this vessel brought him to the United States and adopted him. He was then in his twelfth year. He followed the sea with his adopted father for years, and was a volunteer in an engagement in Chesapeake Bay against the British. Later he sailed as captain from both the ports of New York and Baltimore for several years. About the year 1808 he married, in Virginia, Miss Margaret P. Leatherbury, a native of the Old Dominion and of an old and prominent family of that state. While sailing on the ocean he lost a ship at Key West, Fla., and with the insurance money he started in business at Goliad, Tex. Soon after the Mexican government confiscated his stock, and later he retired from that business. In 1833 he became a member of the Austin colony and came to Texas, securing his league of land, on which the present town bearing his name was built. He made but few improvements, erecting but a small cabin, and died at Old Goliad in October of the same year. Three children were born to this marriage: John, was killed by the Indians in San Antonio in 1837. He was a soldier in the Texas army and was in the battle of San Jacinto. He had settled near San Antonio and was about twenty-three years of age at the time of his death; William Henry was reared in Matamoras, Mex., from his eleventh to his twenty-first year, and then came here to his mother. Later he was sent by General Johnson and Felix Houston to buy land claims in Matamoras, was arrested as a spy and confined for some time, but was finally paroled. After that nothing further was heard of him by his family; Benjamin, died in 1836, when ten years of age, and Mary Jane, the only daughter. Mrs. Hallet resided on her farm until her death in 1863, when seventy-six years of age. In 1836 a town was laid out on her place, she donated one-half the land for a town site, and it was named in her honor Hallettsville. During these early days she had the genuine pioneer spirit, and deserved great credit for her fortitude and energy. She was justly called the mother of Hallettsville. A most intelligent lady, a great reader and well posted, though in a measure self-educated. She retained her property until death and it then went to her grandchildren. Mary Jane, her youngest child, was educated at home, and when in her fifteenth year was married to Collatinus Ballard, who was born in Virginia, and who came to Texas in 1840. He started a store in Mrs. Hallet's house, and this was the first store in the whole country. In 1843 he married Miss Hallet, as stated, and became an extensive merchant. He also followed farming and stock raising to some extent. This worthy citizen was a member of the Baptist church and died in 1867. To his marriage were born twelve children, eight of whom grew up and five are now living: James; Mary A., died when seventeen years of age; Margaret P., married W. P. Ballard, and died, leaving seven children: Fredonia Jane, now the wife of Mr. Roue; Frances B., wife of M. B. Woodall; Collatinus; John L.; Ezbell, died when in her twentieth year, and two others died in infancy. Mrs. Ballard now resides with her children and has forty-five grandchildren and six great-grandchildren. She has lived in Texas under the Mexican rule, through all the career of the Lone Star Republic, and has seen it become one of the most prosperous states of the Union. She has heard the Indian war whoops, the cry of the panther about her door, but has survived all, and now resides, respected and esteemed, in a city that has grown on her ancestors' estates. Her eldest son, James Ballard, was born in Lavaca County in 1844 and was educated at Baylor University, Independence, and later at Waco. When the war broke out he left school and entered the Confederate army, at first in Shay's Battalion, when he served on the coast, and later in Company K, Thirty-third Texas Cavalry, when he served mainly on the coast. On his twenty-first birthday he was married to Miss Alice Ione Russell, a native of Louisiana, and a daughter of Robert C. Russell, who was an early settler in this part of the Lone Star State. Soon after marriage he began teaching, followed that for about fourteen years, mainly in Hallettsville, and then served as county surveyor from 1888 to 1892. For some time now he has been engaged in surveying. Mr. Ballard has a fine place, partly in the town, and on it he has laid out an addition to the town. He is a member of I. O. O. F. and the A. F. & A. M. His wife is a member of the Baptist church. To their marriage were born ten children, six of whom are living: Susan A., wife of Rev. J. W. Daniels; Beulah, wife of W. C. Baird; Mary E., Addison, Schiller, Eunice H., and four died in infancy.

JUDGE JOHN O'NEIL.

Judge John O'Neil, ex-judge of Calhoun County, Tex., and one of the sound, substantial and popular men of the county, has fully borne out the reputation of that class of energetic and far-seeing men of Irish origin who have risen to prominence in different portions of this country. Mr. O'Neil is a native of Calhoun County, Tex., and the fourth of seven children born to Thomas and Mary (Gallagher) O'Neil, natives of the green Isle of Erin. The parents were married in their native country, and seeing a prospect for bettering their condition in the "land of the free," emigrated to the states in 1845, and first settled in the city of New York. From there they went to Philadelphia, resided there for several years, and then went to Alabama, where they resided in Montgomery and Mobile for several years. They then came to the Lone Star State and the father engaged in stock-raising, which he continued until his death in 1858. He became quite wealthy and owned large stock interests. His wife followed him to the grave in 1867. In the town of Port Lavaca our subject was reared and educated, and on July 12, 1863, he enlisted in Company E, Waller's Battalion, Green's Brigade, and was in all the battles of Banks' campaign on Red River. After that he served in Arkansas on scout duty, but subsequently returned to Texas, where his regiment was disbanded early in 1865. Following this he at once engaged in the cattle business and soon had a large herd of stock on hand. About 1876 he bought land around Port Lavaca and soon became the owner of a fine ranch there. In

BATTLE OF

FORT DONELSON,

Feb. 13-16, 1862.

0   ¼   ½   1 Mile

1888 he erected the Seaside Hotel, a fine house. Judge O'Neil has ever been alive to matters of public importance, is an active politician, and in 1887 he was elected sheriff, serving one term. After that he was elected county judge and served in a very satisfactory manner for two terms. He has often served as delegate to conventions and has always been an active worker for his party. In 1890 he sold his ranch business. Judge O'Neil's happy domestic life began in 1872, when he led to the altar Miss Janie Robinson, a native of Louisiana, and the daughter of William Robinson, who died when a comparatively young man. Eight children, all of whom are living, were born to this marriage: James D., Estella, Annie, Edgar, Jueldine, Louie, John and Florine. Judge and Mrs. O'Neil are members of the Catholic church, and he is a Mason. Both are highly esteemed in the section.

MAJOR ISRAEL B. DONALSON.

The oldest citizen of Hays County, Tex., and whose career is of the greatest historical interest, is Major Israel B. Donalson, who, at this writing, resides in San Marcos, and although ninety-eight years of age is well preserved, physically and mentally. Full of the knowledge of men and events, gathered in many years of intelligent observation, one seldom meets a more interesting gentleman, and it is not often, certainly, that one has the privilege of chronicling the life of a man of that age. In 1892 quite a full memoir of Major Donalson was prepared and published by Isaac H. Julian, the veteran journalist of San Marcos and now the editor of "The People's Era and Free Press." Its unusual historic interest was recognized by the Kansas Historical Society, which solicited from Mr. Julian a copy of the memoir and a photograph of the major, to be embodied in their publications. And that eminent and excellent lady, Mrs. John

A. Logan, with whom, and her father and husband, he was associated during his service in the Mexican War, and to whom the
author sent a copy, responded in the following handsome terms:

"Washington, D. C., July 25, 1892.

"My Dear Mr. Julian—I thank you most sincerely for the copy of
the sketch of dear old Major Donalson. I remember him as if I had
seen him only yesterday, and know so well how fond my husband
and my father were of him. He is one of Nature's noblemen, and in
his long and useful life has done much for mankind. I was so glad
to hear from him once more, though father and the general have
both preceded him to the unknown land, where we hope we shall
meet by and by. I shall write Major Donalson, and will take great
pleasure in giving notice of your article, and of him.

"Very Sincerely Yours,
"MRS. JOHN A. LOGAN."

Mrs. Logan is editor of the "Home Magazine" at Washington. It
will thus be seen that the major is verifying to a considerable extent
the Scripture, which declares that "a prophet is not without honor
save in his own country." So much by way of preface. Now to a
biographical outline compiled from the memoir: Major Donalson
is a native of Bourbon County, Ky., born January 12, 1797. He was
baptized by Elder Barton W. Stone, the famous apostle, who at that
time was an old school Presbyterian, afterward of the old Christian or Newlight movement. His father was of English and his
mother of Irish ancestry. His father, John Donalson, served under
Washington as lieutenant through the Revolutionary War. He was
a pioneer to Kentucky, and his first wife was a sister of the celebrated Tom Ewing, Senator from Ohio. She became the mother
of five children. His second wife, Elizabeth Donnell, was the mother
of our subject, who came upon the scene when people were living
in blockhouses. The latter was about five years of age when his
father died, and not many years older when his mother passed away.
When sixteen years old he began building boats and for some time
was engaged in boating on the Mississippi River to New Orleans.
In the year 1819 he married Miss Lucy Lee Calvert of Kentucky and

five children were born to them. After her death, or in 1821, the major married Miss Lucy Ann Lee, a remote cousin of Robert E. Lee, and eleven children were the result of this union, seven of whom are now living: Lucy, wife of A. B. Cherewith; Benjamin Franklin, contractor; Chauncey B., a farmer at Blanco; George W., banker; Elizabeth, wife of Edward Northcraft; Laura, wife of Dr. Price of Blanco City, and Vernetha, widow of Dr. McGee. In 1835 Major Donalson was tendered the Democratic nomination for the Legislature and elected, serving with Tom Marshall, Cassius M. Clay and other noted men. In 1839 Mr. Donalson removed to Pike County, Ill., where he was elected probate judge, and had a brief service in the Mormon War. In 1847 he raised a company of volunteers for the Mexican War. He was elected major and placed in command of five companies. He served through the war in New Mexico. Later he was voted a handsome sword by the Illinois Legislature for his services. He next joined the '49-ers in their overland march to California, where he engaged in mining and storekeeping. After an absence of two years and four months and the accumulation of about $15,000, he returned home. In 1854 he was tendered by President Pierce the position of United States marshal for Kansas Territory and accepted. His term ran through the terrible period of civil commotion in that territory, and was a most trying experience. He got out by resignation, not removal, which was the fate of so many other officials in Kansas at that time. Having business at Washington he was present at the execution of John Brown, of which his recollections are among the most interesting which have appeared. He remained in retirement during the war at his home in Canton, Mo. In 1865 he removed by wagon, there being no railroads, to Hays County, Tex., where he has ever since resided. The above is the merest outline of the career of Major Donalson of what is set forth with considerable detail in the memoir prepared and published by Mr. Julian, of which we copy below the three closing paragraphs: Not the least remarkable of his characteristics has been his protracted physical force. At the age of seventy-two he did the work of a vigorous man in the harvest field, and ten years later he showed no decline of body or mind, walking erect, alert and vigorous. He attributes his lengthened years to his practice of "temperance in all things," his disinclination to "worry" and his disposition to look on the bright side of life. Major Donalson was born under the administration of President Washington and has voted at every presidential election from Monroe down. In his birth he was contemporary with a host of other Americans of note, who passed away so long since that the remembrance of their names has become dim. James K. Polk, only two years his senior, has been dead over forty years; William Cullen Bryant, whose venerable head and face are so familiar through his portraits, born three years before Major Donalson, died fourteen years ago, at the age of eighty-four, while our more aged fellow-citizen still lives. At the birth of Jefferson Davis he was eleven, and at the birth of Abraham Lincoln, twelve years old. Robert Burns died only the year before he was born. At his birth Sir Walter Scott was a young man unknown to fame, Lord Byron a lad of nine years, and Napoleon Bonaparte had just entered upon his career of transcendent military renown at the head of the French army in Italy. These facts, which might be largely extended, may cause us to realize more vividly what a veteran we have yet lingering in our midst. In him we are permitted to behold one whose life is coincident with that of our great Republic, almost from its beginning. Such a man should be greeted with affectionate reverence by all, more especially by the rising generation, as a link binding them to all the past of their native land.

CARNOT BELLINGER.

Edmund Bellinger, the father of Carnot Bellinger of Luling, was born in Beaufort, S. C., March 4, 1802, received a classical education and completed a full collegiate course of study at Columbia College, South Carolina. He was prevented from graduating, but received a certificate of high standing in all his classes by the faculty. In 1826 he married Miss Ann Le Gare Roach, a native of Charleston,

S. C., a daughter of William Roach of Bristol, England. Through her mother she was a descendant of the "Huguenots" through the Le Gare family, and through her grandfather her family reaches back to the McGregor clan, in Scotland, to the year 700 A. D. Hugh Swinton Le Gare, her first cousin, was Attorney-General of the United States. By marriage she was connected with William Gilmore Simms. Mr. Bellinger was directly descended from the "Landgraves" of South Carolina, a title hereditary conferred by one of the Georges of England on Edmund Bellinger of Westmoreland County, England, who married Elizabeth Cartwright, and emigrated to America about the year 1688, at which time he was created first Landgrave. His son Edmund was second Landgrave. He married Elizabeth Butler; their son Edmund became third Landgrave. He in turn married Mary Lucia Bull; their son Edmund was fourth Landgrave. William Bellinger, the youngest brother of the fourth Landgrave, was the father of this Edmund Bellinger, who, with his wife, soon after his marriage moved to Illinois. He remained there six years and came to Texas in 1839 and assisted in the early development of this country, then "The Republic of Texas." He took part in the Indian troubles, and participated in the battle of Plum Creek and others. The hardest of these struggles fell upon his wife, a woman reared amongst all the luxury and refinement of the most aristocratic society of Charleston, S. C. It is a wonder she passed through those perilous times and lived to enter and almost complete her four-score years. A few of her perils will give an idea of the life she endured in those days. One night she was left alone in her little cabin with her babe and two small children. Mr. Bellinger had gone as an express on horseback to warn some settlers fifty miles distant of their danger from an invading party of Indians, estimated to consist of 500 warriors. He was to collect what men and boys he could to pursue the enemy. At midnight came a gentle tapping on the door with these words: "Mrs. Bellinger, get up very quietly; we are in great danger. Don't speak or strike a light. Fifty Indian warriors are within 100 yards of this house." To use her own words, she came out in a few moments "more dead than alive," with her baby wrapped in her cloak, the two small children in their night clothes. They made their way with the neighbor who came to warn them to a house where all the women and children were assembled, under the protection of four men who were left to guard them. Every other man and boy who was able to handle a gun had gone in pursuit of the Indians under Captain Caldwell (better known in Texas history as Old Paint). The names of those four men who stood guard that night will always be remembered by the descendants of those women who sat up all night to hush and keep their babies quiet—Pleasant Barnet, Adam Zumwalt, Ezekiel Williams and John Patrick. That terrible night of suspense passed with no further alarm. The next day it was considered safe for all to go to their homes. That night Mrs. Bellinger was again aroused with the whispered words: "The Indians are burning and killing as they go; come quick, we are going to the woods (or river bottom) for safety." The news of the burning and massacre at Linnville reached town that night. Whilst they were crouched in the thicket, the mothers keeping watch over their little children, the well-known voice of Captain (afterwards General) Ben McCollough was heard, hallooing at the house he was accustomed to stop at, as saying, "All is well; come, get us something to eat." All emerged from their hiding places. The balance of the night was employed by the women in baking corn bread and molding bullets, the men in getting their saddles, bridles and guns in order for the next day's battle with the Comanches, which took place at Plum Creek, near where the town of Lockhart now stands. Edmund Bellinger owned a ranch in Gonzales County, paid much attention to raising horses and cattle, for many years was county judge and was a man of established reputation. During the Civil War he was a Union man and opposed to the war, as were Sam Houston and others. However, three of his sons were in the Confederate service, and one of them gave his life to the cause. While residing near Springfield, Ill., he came to know and admire Abraham Lincoln, and at a time when it was almost treason to speak his name in kindness Mr. Bellinger had the courage to express his admiration for that great man. Mr. Edmund Bellinger died in Luling in 1878 at the residence of his son, our subject. His widow died in San Antonio in 1885. Carnot Bellinger was born in Gonzales, Tex., June 23, 1850, the youngest of ten children born to the above-mentioned couple. He was reared in that town. The war coming on interrupted his education to some extent. This he has greatly remedied by reading and contact with the world. When eighteen years of age he entered a drug store, and after clerking for a number of years became a thorough pharmacist. He opened a drug store in Prairie Lea in 1869. In 1874 he removed to Luling, was appointed its first postmaster and held the office twelve years. In 1889 he associated himself with the Luling Lumber Company. Later he purchased a dairy farm, and has now a herd of fifty Jersey cows. About the same time he bought a controlling interest in the Luling Water Works, which he still holds. In 1894 he engaged in the grocery business with Mr. W. G. Weaver, under the firm name of Bellinger & Weaver, and is doing a good business. He is a Democrat and a member of the K. of P. In the year 1878 he married Miss Mary E. Keith, at Beaumont, Tex., daughter of Cortez and Sarah (Le Port) Keith, residents of Eastern Texas. Six children have blessed their union: William, Franklin, Bessie, May, Addie and Marguerite.

RICHARD J. BURGES.

Richard J. Burges, who is the able and most efficient county collector of Guadalupe County, Tex., was born in Jackson, Tenn., in 1840. While a man of no great wealth he is the possessor of that which is far more valuable—an honorable name and the confidence and friendship of those who know him best. His great-grandfather, Rev. Henry John Burges, was a native of Devonshire, England, and came to Virginia in colonial times. He was rector of an Episcopal church and was one of the first professors in William and Mary College at Williamsburg, Va. When the Revolutionary War broke out he sided with the colonists, and on many occasions preached to the troops. He was arrested by Colonel Tarlton, who threatened to hang him. Colonel William Washington learned this and sent

word to the Royalist leader that if he hanged his prisoner he would
hang an English officer for every hair on his head. This secured
Mr. Burges' release. After the war he continued in the ministry
until his death. Our subject's grandfather, Dr. A. S. H. Burges,
was born in the Old Dominion, and was quite a prominent man there,
being a member of one of the constitutional conventions. He died
full of years and since the Civil War. The maternal grandfather
of our subject, Dr. Richard Fenner, was born in North Carolina, and
is of Irish origin. His father, Captain Richard Fenner, was one of
twenty sons and one daughter, he the youngest and only one born
in America, the family coming to this country and settling in North
Carolina in colonial times. He was a captain in the colonial army
during the Revolutionary War and afterward resided in North Carolina and Tennessee, dying in the latter state when quite aged. He
was a member of the Order of Cincinnatus, which was started by
Washington for the officers of his army. One of the early members
of this family fought with Drake against the Spanish Armada. W.
H. Burges, the father of our subject, was born in North Carolina,
began life as a midshipman in the United States Navy, and served
on the old seventy-four frigate Guerrier from twelve to nineteen
years of age. He then resigned and married Miss Eugenia A. Fenner, with whom he moved to West Tennessee about 1837. There
he resided until his death in 1851. He was a man of much intelligence and was well read and well posted on all public affairs, but
could not be induced to enter public life. His wife is still living,
and finds a pleasant home with her son, Richard J., in Seguin. He
was and she is a member of the Episcopal church. Socially he was
a Royal Arch Mason, and was greatly devoted to that order. Richard
J. Burges was reared and mainly educated in Tennessee. When he
was fifteen years of age the family moved to Texas and spent one
year in Navarro County. On January 1, 1856, they came to Seguin
and there our subject attended school for over a year. From there
he went to New Orleans, engaged in business there and was there
at the outbreak of the war. In the month of August, 1861, he enlisted in the Confederate army, joining Company D of the Fourth
Texas Infantry, Hood's Brigade, and served one year in Virginia.

He was in five engagements, and at the battle of Manassas was shot through the body. After this he was in the hospital for a long time and was a cripple for four years. In 1864 he was elected county clerk, served a short time and was removed by Federal authority in 1865. The following year he went back to New Orleans, was engaged in business there until 1872, and then returned to Seguin, where he carried on business enterprises for three years. In 1878 he was appointed deputy sheriff and placed in charge of the tax collections in this office for two years. In 1880 the office of tax collector was separated from the sheriff's office, and Mr. Burges was elected its first collector, and has been re-elected at the expiration of each term since. He was married in 1874 to Miss Gray Smith, a native of this county and daughter of George P. Smith, who was one of the early settlers to Texas from Missouri. Seven children were born to this union: Richard J., Jr., William H., Ellis G., Mary G., Bettie M., Eugenia F. and George P., who died in infancy. Mr. Burges is a member of the Episcopal church and his wife a member of the Baptist church. He is a Mason—a member of Guadalupe Lodge No. 109, and has held nearly all the offices from master down. He is also a member of the Alamo Lodge, San Antonio, A. O. U. W. He has served as mayor of Seguin four terms, having been elected each time unanimously.

JUDGE FELIX J. HART.

Judge Felix J. Hart, the present judge of Bee County, is justly recognized as a man of superior ability, force of character and determination. He is a native of this county, his birth occurring in December, 1862, and the fourth child born to the union of Luke and Ann (Hart) Hart, natives respectively of New York and Texas. The maternal grandfather, Felix J. Hart, came to Texas at a period antedating the Revolutionary War and engaged in stock-raising. He was murdered in San Patricio County by the Mexicans. The paternal grandfather, John Hart, was born in Ireland and came to Texas with the McGlowan and McMullen colony. He was also murdered in San Patricio County by the Mexicans at about the same time. Luke Hart, father of our subject, followed in the footsteps of his ancestors and engaged in the stock business principally. During the Civil War he served in Colonel Hobby's Regiment and served in Texas. While a resident of San Patricio County he held a number of local positions and was county and district clerk for a long time prior to the war. In 1861 he moved to Bee County and was county commissioner and justice of the peace for about fifteen years. A few years prior to his death, which occurred in Papalote, Bee County, in 1883, he resigned the above mentioned positions. Mr. Hart was a man of unquestioned ability, a deep thinker and a close reasoner. The original of this notice was educated in the public schools of Bee County, and after his father's death he took charge of the ranch, conducting it successfully until 1890, when he came to Beeville and engaged in merchandising. He has filled a number of local offices, having been a member of the second Board of Aldermen, and in November, 1892, he was elected to his present position. He is a man of straightforward character and genial disposition. These, coupled with indomitable energy, formed the keystone to his success in life. In the year 1892 he was married to Miss Edith Mussett of Corpus Christi, and a native of Texas. Her father, Elias T. Mussett, came to Corpus Christi when a child, and became one of the most prominent residents. He was marshal of the city, and was murdered there on the night of May 5, 1892, by John Parker. Our subject is a member of the Catholic, and Mrs. Hart of the Baptist church. Socially he is a Knight of Honor. While his father was commissioner our subject did much of the work, and in 1886 he was appointed to fill that position, serving until 1888. The Judge's brothers and sisters were named as follows: Mary J.; Catherine, deceased, was the wife of Joseph Ryan; John; Bridget, wife of O. F. West; Luke; Timothy, and Maggie, wife of H. F. Otto, and Albert Hart.

FRANK R. PRIDHAM.

In the whole range of commercial enterprise no interest is of more importance than that respecting the sale of hardware, and among the most notable dealers in this line of goods is Frank R. Pridham, who was born in the town in which he is now doing business, in 1841, a son of the marriage of P. U. and Malinda (Roberts) Pridham, the former of whom was born on the Isle of Guernsey in 1812. He was taken to the vicinity of London, England, when quite young, married there before attaining his majority, and immigrated to Montreal, Canada, in 1832. From this place he moved to Texas with his wife and one child, a son, and settled near Lynchburg, in 1834, near where the battle of San Jacinto was afterward fought, in which engagement he took an active part in the ranks of the Texan Volunteers. He continued to reside in that section until he lost his wife and a little daughter by malarial fever, then moved with his surviving son to Victoria in 1839. During the terrible Indian raid of 1840 Mr. Pridham volunteered to make the perilous journey to Gonzales for assistance, and, keeping near the timber along the river, he succeeded in passing the Comanche camp on Spring Creek and reached his destination in safety. After his return home he assisted in an attack on the Indians at Placido Creek, and later engaged them in battle on Peach Creek, where the savages were defeated. In 1841 Mr. Pridham was married to Miss Malinda Roberts, by whom he became the father of one son, Frank R., the subject of this sketch. Mr. Pridham held the office of chief justice for some time, and soon after became assessor and collector of the county, an office which he efficiently and successfully filled until 1853, at the same time discharging the duties of a merchant. In 1848 he moved to the country, about five miles from Victoria, to the now well known fishing resort, Pridham Lake, and about this time, with a man by the name of William Gamble, started the first cotton gin in this section of the country. He was a worthy member of the A. F. & A. M., and was buried by that order. In 1858 Frank R. Pridham, after receiving a thorough education, went to San Antonio and engaged in newspaper work on the San Antonio "Herald," having charge of the office from the time of entering it until 1861. He lost both his parents while he was still a mere child, and was cared for by his uncle, Judge G. W. Palmer, proprietor of the "Advocate," and it was while under his care that he learned the printer's trade. When his uncle became associated with Colonel Logan in the proprietorship of the "Herald" at the Alamo City, he remained with him until the opening of the Civil War. He became a Knight of the Golden Circle and was active in advancing the cause of the impending Confederate Government, and assisted in securing the Federal arms at San Antonio. With other chivalrous and brave young men of Victoria he joined G. J. Hampton's Company, Sibley's Brigade, later known as Green's Brigade, and was in the severe campaign in New Mexico, taking part in the battles of Val Verde and Glorietta. Upon the reorganization of the Southern forces he was sent to Louisiana, and was in several engagements there, and almost daily skirmishes. He was in Galveston when that city was recaptured, then returned to Louisiana and was in all the engagements of Banks' expedition on the Red River, from Mansfield to Yellow Bayou. He was then for some time engaged in scouting duty in Arkansas, and in May, 1865, was mustered out of the service in Burleson County, Tex. After leaving the service he became a salesman in the large mercantile establishment of R. Owens, and subsequently became associated with Victor M. Rose in the management of the Victoria "Advocate." Mr. Pridham soon became its sole proprietor, and continued its publication until the year 1874. Two years later he was elected assessor of taxes for the county, which position he held continuously for twelve years, a fact which speaks eloquently as to his efficiency and popularity. In 1883 he was appointed receiver of the Texas Continental Meat Company, under bonds of $400,000, and in 1888 was in the custom house service at Eagle Pass, in each and every one of which capacities he acquitted himself very creditably. In 1891 he started in his present business with Mr. L. G. Kreisle, the firm being known as Pridham & Kreisle, and they carry a stock of general hardware valued at $10,000, and do an annual business of some $20,000 or more. These gentlemen are shrewd and practical business men, and Mr. Pridham is well known for his high sense of honor. He is a most worthy citizen in every respect, and is a decided addition to the business circles of Victoria. In 1881 he was married to Miss Minnie, the accomplished daughter of R. Owens, and to their union one son has been given, who has been named Richard Owens, in honor of his maternal grandfather. Mr. Pridham and his wife are members and attendants of the Catholic church.

JOSEPH M. BICKFORD.

As has often been quoted, the finger of time is one of the most satisfactory and reliable endorsers of a man's business career. Many people may, with justification, halt and refuse to listen to the solicitation of a beginner, but the voice of the old, established house always carries with it attention and respect. Joseph M. Bickford, an old time merchant and the oldest citizen of Port Lavaca, Tex., was born in the Granite State in 1827. His parents, Thomas and Ammis (Morse) Bickford, were natives of that state also, and both were of English origin. The ancestors on both sides came to America in colonial days. Joseph M. Bickford received his education at several preparatory schools at Newbury, and in 1851 entered Dartsmouth College, from which institution he graduated four years later, taking a full classical course. After this he taught an academy for over a year in Lisbon, N. H., and then began the study of law. On account of his health he was advised by his physicians to come South and he first settled in Jackson, Miss., where he remained about six months. From there he went to the Lone Star State, and settled in Calhoun County, where, notwithstanding his poor health, he started to school on Matagorda Island. He met with the best of success and was a very prominent and popular educator. When the war broke out he intended entering the army, but was prostrated with a severe fever, and was in bed for six months. Afterward he was in feeble health for some time. From there he came to Port Lavaca and started the Lavaca Institute, which soon became one of the most promising schools in Southwest Texas. This continued until 1869, pupils coming from quite distant points, and most of the time he had an attendance of 125. In 1869 Mr. Bickford engaged in merchandising and has continued in business since that time. He carries a large stock of general merchandise, groceries, notions, glass and crockery ware, boots and shoes, etc., in the same house that he has occupied since 1886. Aside from this he has also been engaged to some extent in the stock business, but has sold much of his ranch property, although he still owns 600 acres of excellent land near the town. In the year 1867 he was married to Miss Mary Hensley, a native of Port Lavaca, and daughter of William R. and Mary P. Hensley, natives of Kentucky, and among the earliest settlers here. Mr. Hensley was a merchant and surveyor, and surveyed much of this and adjoining counties. He was a prominent man, and died in 1849. His wife died in 1872. To the marriage of Mr. and Mrs. Bickford were born four children, all living: Mabel A., Mary L., Florence O., and Joseph Harry. Mr. Bickford is a prominent Mason, a member of Port Lavaca Lodge, the chapter that was located at Indianola, and the San Felipe De Austin Commandery at Galveston. He has held all the offices in the Blue Lodge and the Chapter, and has been an active worker. For years Mr. Bickford has been school examiner, and he has also served a term and a half as county treasurer.

CAPTAIN JOHN LAFAYETTE LANE.

Among the men of Caldwell County, Tex., who have been active and efficient in the work of building up the agricultural and stock-raising interests of this section, Captain John LaFayette Lane takes a prominent position. Born in Jefferson County, Tenn., January 3,

1830, he was fourth in order of birth of nine children born to Pleasant W. and Mary (Colthorpe) Lane. On the paternal side he comes of a prominent old Virginia family, who trace their lineage directly back to the Captain Lane who was left in charge of the first English settlement on the James River. This man turned his attention largely to mining, and the authorities censured him for not devoting every energy to agriculture. Our subject's paternal grandmother was a Fitzgerald and a member of the famous family of that name that came to America in an early day. Pleasant W. Lane was born in Tennessee, and was a physician and farmer. In 1847 he emigrated to Caldwell County, Tex., and the following year settled near Lockhart, and until 1868 practiced over a wide scope of country. While he was on his way to Texas he lingered behind his family and friends to attend to some business, and while riding horseback near the present city of Waco was surrounded by Indians. They examined his saddle bags, pulled the stoppers out of his bottles, inhaled their contents, and then neatly rearranging everything, bade him "go." Their reverence for "medicine men" probably saved the Doctor's life. Mrs. Lane died in Arkansas in 1844 while on the way to Texas, and the family lingered for two years in that state after her death. Captain LaFayette Lane was partially reared in Tennessee, and was in his seventeenth year when he accompanied his parents to Texas. He had received but a limited education, and in 1852 he went to California and mined for gold six years, being quite successful. Returning to Texas in 1858 he engaged in the stock business, and was in Arizona gold mining when the war opened. Again he returned to Texas, and enlisted as first lieutenant in Captain Meyers' company. He was in the trans-Mississippi department, and served through the entire Louisiana campaign, taking part in the battles of Mansfield, Pleasant Hill, Yellow Bayou, etc. He was in the cavalry, and while at Galveston, Meyers was promoted, and our subject became captain of his old company, serving as such the remainder of the war. The last charge at Mansfield was made by the cavalry commanded by Captain Lane, and all the men were armed with six-shooters. 'Twas known as the "Peach Orchard Charge." After cessation of hostilities Captain Lane returned to Lockhart, and with the exception of four years spent in the sheriff's office has devoted all his time to farming and stock raising. He owns a valuable ranch of 600 acres, which averages one-half bale of cotton and forty bushels of corn to the acre. In his political views he has always affiliated with the Democratic party, and fraternally he is a Royal Arch Mason. In the year 1872 he was married to Miss Laura Jane Ferris, who died within ten months without issue. In 1873 the Captain married Miss Minerva Ann McMahan, a native of Alabama, whose parents were John and Rebecca McMahan. The mother died in Alabama, but the father came to Caldwell County, Tex., in 1855, and is still living. Captain Lane's second union resulted in the birth of five children: Annie Laurie, John LaFayette, Queen, George Franklin and Samuel Tipton.

WALTER LITTLE.

This retired farmer and worthy citizen of Fayette County, Tex., was born in Fort Bend County (that county being then a portion of Mexico), Tex., October 31, 1828, son of William Little, a native of the Keystone State, and Jane (Edwards) Little, who was born in Tennessee. When a young man Mr. Little went from his native state to what is now Missouri, and was for a time a resident of St. Louis, which was then a frontier post. Leaving St. Louis in 1821 he came to Texas with Stephen F. Austin and assisted in the erection of a fort, this being the first settlement of whites aside from a small settlement made at St. Augustine, near the Louisiana line, in the state. The company that first settled at Fort Bend consisted of five men, though seventeen came with Austin. However, twelve returned to the states. Those remaining and completing the fort for the protection of future settlers, as well as for themselves, were James or Charles Beard, William Smithers, Joseph Polly, William Little and another not remembered. In 1822 a number of families arrived from the states, among them that of William Morton, the grandfather of our subject. These early settlers had very little trouble with the Indians during 1824, and as new settlers came pouring in the Indians moved farther out. In 1836 Texas had a population of 20,000, though a large number were slaves. Very little farming was done, most of the land being used for pasturage, and large droves of horses and cattle covered the immense prairies. As early as 1828 considerable trouble occurred with the Indians, who began to grow jealous of the many settlers now pouring in. Mr. Little, father of our subject, was never in but one Indian fight previous to 1836, and that was at Jones Creek. In the fall of 1835 Mr. Little was serving in the Texan army, and consequently was not in the battle of San Jacinto. Having been sent by General Sam Houston to remove his family with others, Mr. Little took them into the bottoms of the Brazos River, among the immense canebrakes, and as the river was very high at that time he could not get them across the bayous. Later, when the trouble was over, they returned to their homes. Mr. Little remained on his farm until his death in 1841, when fifty years old. He left seven children: John, William, Walter, Martha, James, Robert and George, all deceased except our subject and the last named, who resides in Columbus, Colorado County, this state. The Edwards and Morton families came to Texas about 1822, and Mrs. Little was the step-daughter of William Morton. The latter was the first white man who ever navigated the Brazos River, as he came with his family from the mouth up to where the town of Richmond now stands, in Fort Bend County. Mr. and Mrs. Little were the first white couple married west of Trinity River, their union taking place April 2, 1824, and although not Catholics, they were married by a priest, on account of the laws of Mexico, which made marriage not legal nor children lawful unless the ceremony was performed by one. John Little, the paternal grandfather of our subject, came from Pennsylvania in 1823 with his wife and when quite an old man served in several Indian wars in the East. He was also in the Revolutionary War. William Little was his only child. The latter's wife, and the mother of our subject, was the step-daughter of William Morton, as before stated. Mr. Morton made the first brick in the state, and was one of the wealthiest men in this section of the state. He died in 1833, leaving a family of four children: John, Louisa, Mary and William. Walter had but little chance for an education. In 1836 a young man came from

Kentucky and taught school in the neighborhood, and young Little
and his brothers attended for six months. This was all the schooling he ever received, but being of an inquiring and investigating
turn of mind, with a thirst for knowledge, he secured a very good
business education and became a competent surveyor. Having
been reared to farming and stock raising he chose that as his life's
occupation, and followed it successfully from 1848 to 1860, being
the owner of a number of slaves when the Civil War broke out. Mr.
Little served in the quartermaster department during those troublesome times, and afterward speculated in land until 1879, when he
returned to his former occupation of farming, and continued this
until 1890. He then sold out, and in 1893 moved to town. He was
married first in 1858 to Miss Sarah Wilson, daughter of Dr. Hugh
Wilson of Rock Bridge County, Va., and by that union became the
father of two children: Hugh of Winchester and Mary, wife of
Edward McRee, of Colorado County. Mrs. Little died in January,
1870, and in November of that year Mr. Little married Miss Maggie
Laird, daughter of Thomas and Ann (Carter) Laird, natives of Pennsylvania and Virginia respectively. Mr. Little's second union resulted in the birth of three children: Nellie, Walter and Sam. On
February 1, 1861, Mr. Little moved to Fayette County, this state,
and here served four years as county commissioner. He was never
an office seeker, takes but very little interest in politics and is independent in his views. Socially he is a member of the A. F. & A. M.
—Morton Lodge No. 72, and is also a K. of H. of this place.

VIRGIL S. RABB.

The life of any man is of great benefit to the community in which
he resides when all his efforts are directed toward its advancement,
and when he is honest, upright and progressive. Such a man is
Virgil S. Rabb, a native of Fayette County, Tex., born February 15,
1839, the son of John and Mary (Crownover) Rabb, and the grandson

of William and Mary (Smalley) Rabb, and John and Mary (Chesney) Crownover. William Rabb was born in the Keystone State, in Fayette County. At an early date he moved with his family to near St. Louis, Mo., on the Illinois side of the river, where he erected a water mill for grinding flour, ran it successfully, sold out and moved to Washington, Ark., and there resided until 1819. He then came to Texas, but did not bring his family until 1822, coming with Austin's colony. However, he himself was here in 1821 and raised his first crop on Rabb's Prairie that year. This was the first crop made by an American in this section. His son, Captain Thomas J. Rabb, accompanied him on both his early trips, and they assisted in building one of the first forts, or block-houses, of Austin's settlement. Early in 1822 William Rabb crossed the Colorado River where La Grange now stands, and one of the first block-houses in the county was erected four miles east of West Point and close to the Colorado River, at a bluff called Indian Hill, the entire neighborhood taking part in the building. William Rabb first located on the west side of the river. In 1831 he built a water mill on the Colorado River, or Rabb's Prairie, getting the stones from Scotland, but the rest of the material from New Orleans. This was the first mill built in the county. In getting the stones from the coast Mr. Rabb made a wooden axle and used the stones for wheels, attaching the tongue to them, wagons not having come into fashion in Texas. In that way he brought them from Matagorda, a distance of over 200 miles. For this Mr. Rabb received from the Mexican Government three leagues of land, which he selected on Rabb's Prairie. In 1833 occurred the big over-flow of the Colorado River and the mill was destroyed, this being the second overflow of the river after the settlement. Previous to this, in 1823, an Indian scare occurred, but the settlers had gathered in the fort, and, although kept there for three days by the Indians, they escaped with no loss greater than having some of their stock killed. After the Indians had left, Mr. Rabb and his friends moved to Wharton County, where his sons, Thomas and Andrew, had previously located, and resided there until 1829. He then returned to this county and settled for the first time on Rabb's Prairie, where he was actively and extensively engaged in raising stock. During the building of the mill before mentioned, or in 1832, he passed away when about sixty years of age. For some time during his life he resided in Illinois, and became the owner of fifty or sixty negroes, but later he lost them all when that state passed a law freeing them, except one called Frank, who came with him to Texas. Mr. and Mrs. Rabb reared a family of five children: Rachel, wife of A. M. Newman; Andrew, John, Thomas (called Captain Rabb) and Ulysses. John Rabb, father of our subject, came to Texas in 1822, and located on the west side of the Colorado River, nine miles north of La Grange. He immediately went in the Colorado bottom and commenced to clear land, but subsequently, on account of Indians stealing his stock, moved to Fort Bend County. From there he moved to Wharton County, Tex., where he improved a good farm and where he resided until 1829, when he located on Rabb's Prairie, this county, on the place now known as the Dr. McKinney place. On the mill mentioned as being built by William Rabb, John Rabb did most of the work and took charge of it until it was washed away. After this he turned his attention to farming and stock-raising and continued this until 1848. Previous to this, in 1835, he joined the Texas army and was in the fight at Gonzales, Conception and others, and when the army had fallen back to Burnham's block-house on Colorado River and began again to retreat, Mr. Rabb came home and took his family, with others, as far as Robin's Ferry on the Trinity. He then returned to the army, but was not in the battle of San Jacinto. Returning home afterward he devoted his energies to building up his fallen fortune, for he was a heavy loser during the war. Later he was in many Indian fights, but did not take part in the war of 1848, but was represented by his son Montgomery, who was a member of Hays' Regiment. In that year Mr. Rabb built the first steam saw mill in the county, located on Rabb's Creek in the northern portion of this county, and he operated this mill until 1859. He then sold to Alexander McDow for $45,000, this being the largest transaction made in the county up to that time, and bought Barton's Springs, near the city of Austin, which embraced a tract of land of thirty acres. The remainder of his days were passed in retirement and he died June 5, 1861, after spending one of the most active lives of the early settlers. His wife survived him until October 13, 1882, dying when in her seventy-seventh year. Both were earnest members of the Methodist Episcopal church, and the first Methodist sermon ever preached west of the Brazos River was preached in his house. The nine children born to this worthy couple were named as follows: Montgomery, George W., Melissa, Marion, J. W., L. D., V. S., Mary, wife of David Croft of this county, and G. T. of Austin. All these children are deceased except our subject, Mary and G. T. Our subject's maternal grandfather, John Crownover, was a native of one of the Carolinas. V. S. Rabb was educated at Rutersville, and branched out for himself in 1862 by joining the Confederate army, Company I, Sixteenth Texas Infantry. He was made third lieutenant and served in the Trans-Mississippi Department, and was in all the battles of Louisiana, except those that occurred while on "leave of absence." Later he was made captain of his company by general promotion, and was honorably discharged from the army at Hempstead, Tex. After his return home he erected a saw mill, but only followed this for six years, when he engaged in farming, continuing this until 1884. He then moved to La Grange to educate his children, and while there was in the lumber business. In 1891 he moved to West Point, this county, and in connection with the lumber business here has been engaged in merchandising since 1890. In the latter occupation he has been successful, and has opened stores at Winchester and Smithville. Mr. Rabb was married in 1869 to Miss Dulcie Kenedy, a daughter of A. S. and Mary (Earthman) Kenedy. Mr. Kenedy came to Texas in 1837 from Alabama, his native state. Mr. and Mrs. Rabb are the parents of six living children: V. S., Jr., Gussie. David P., Dulcie, Jr., George F. and Sallie L. Two children are deceased. Mrs. Rabb is a member of the Christian church. Like his father, Mr. Rabb is a strong Democrat in politics, and takes a deep interest in the welfare of his party. He is a prominent and influential citizen and a man who has done his share toward the county's advancement. His brother, J. W. Rabb, was a member of Captain Jarmon's Company of the Terry Rangers, known as the Eighth Texas Cavalry, and served through Tennessee, Kentucky, Mississippi and Georgia, and participated in all the battles fought by that noted regiment, except during a short period, when he was disabled by a wound, from which he never fully recovered. His death occurred in 1885.

LOUIS TURNER.

This well-known pioneer, who is everywhere respected for his sterling worth, is now retired from the active duties of life and enjoys the ease secured by a well-spent and active career. He was born in Prussia, Germany, November 26, 1834, and of the nine children born to his parents, Christian and Mary (Butterman) Turner, he was seventh in order of birth. The parents were both natives of the old country, and there the father died when our subject was about eight years of age. The latter remained in his native country until grown, received a fair education, and served an apprenticeship at the locksmith and gunsmith trades. He then took passage for the United States, landed at Baltimore, and went from there to Cincinnati, O., where he joined an elder brother. He then worked in a machine shop for several months, after which he traveled for a time, looking for a location. After this he was on a steamboat on the Mississippi River a few months, and then located in New Orleans, where he worked in a gunsmith shop for nearly two years. On account of his health he came to Texas, and spent one year in Victoria, after which, in 1856, he located in Hallettsville, where he engaged with a gunsmith. After remaining with him eleven months, Mr. Turner bought the business out, and carried it on successfully until the spring of 1862. He then enlisted in the Confederate army, Whitfield Legion, and left Hallettsville with Company A, as chief bugler of the legion. He first went to Arkansas, was afterward sent to Mississippi, thence to Corinth, where he was in the battle fought at that place in October, and then went to Iuka. While in the battle at the latter place, and when he had the bugle at his mouth to blow a charge, a bullet from the enemy struck the bugle and made a hole through it, but he kept on blowing until the charge was made. In this battle he was slightly wounded in the side, and five bullets perforated his coat. He was captured on the Hatchie River at the second battle of Corinth and taken to Bolivar, Tenn. The second day in prison some of the boys asked him to play the reveille, and being always full of sport, he complied, and afterward blew a charge. Soon after an officer came and asked for the man who blew the calls. Mr. Turner came forward, and after a little conversation the bugle was taken by the officer and never returned. Mr. Turner was kept in confinement for ten days, after which he was paroled and came to Texas. After being exchanged, he joined Hardeman's Regiment and at once went to Arkansas, where he was in the battle of Poison Springs, etc. His command made a raid on Fort Smith, Ark., and he was one of 300 volunteers to attack a regiment of Federals on the prairie of Des Arc, Ark., six miles from Fort Smith. Before the line was fully formed he was shot in the leg, the bone broken, and the horse on which he was riding killed. From the time he was wounded, 9 o'clock in the morning, until 5 o'clock p. m., he remained on the battlefield, and while lying there wounded, two Indians came on the field and shot a wounded man. Mr. Turner only preserved his life by feigning death. A little later two men came on the field and robbed him of money and all valuables, and then a guard came, who remained until an ambulance made its appearance. In this three dead men were placed, with our subject on top of them, and in this manner rode to Fort Smith, a distance of six miles. Mr. Turner became feverish in the hospital, and got so bad that he was placed in the dead ward, where he remained over a week, after which he began to improve. He was then returned to the hospital, where he remained a long time, and was then sent to Little Rock. There he remained an invalid until the war closed. After leaving prison, and when he began to get a little better, he made rings from buttons, and, selling these, got sufficient money to buy a mule and saddle and bridle. Thus equipped, he made his way to Hallettsville, Tex., from Little Rock, and arrived there July 27, 1865. When he fell from his horse on the battlefield near Fort Smith a friend saw him fall and wrote home to his people that he had been killed. Now, when he made his appearance at home, a most exciting and pathetic scene ensued, for his friends thought he had been dead for a year. After recovering, Mr. Turner resumed business as a gunsmith in Hallettsville, and continued this until 1874. Being a superior workman, he had more work than he could do, and trade came from a long distance. About the year 1872 he began to erect an hotel, and two years later this was completed, and was the first stone building in the town, as well as the best one at that time. Mr. Turner conducted this hotel until about 1884, and it was most popular and well patronized. He is now retired from active pursuits and is enjoying a comfortable and happy existence. He has been quite active in political matters, has served as alderman and mayor, and was deputy sheriff under Smothers. Mr. Turner has also been trustee of the school board, and has held other local positions. In 1861, previous to entering the army, our subject was married to Mrs. Josephine (Bragger) Dubois, a daughter of Jasper Bragger, a native of Germany. Mr. Bragger came to the United States and settled in Texas in 1846. There he died the next year. Miss Josephine was first married to John Dubois, by whom she had two children: Leola, wife of Dr. Shelley, and Mary, who died when thirteen years of age. Her union to our subject resulted in the birth of three children: Ida, wife of Dr. Eidson of Shiner; Louis, died when about fourteen years of age, and Lena. Aside from his property in this city, Mr. Turner has a fine tract of 200 acres adjoining the town. He is a natural musician, and has done much toward maintaining a band in Hallettsville. He joined the band before the war, soon became its leader, and after reorganizing it after the war, was at its head for many years. He was the main organizer of the Hallettsville Shooting Club, and for years its president and main director, building it up to a noted association. He is one of the most prominent men of the county and is well liked.

JAMES C. ODOM.

This leading stockman of Austin County, Tex., was born in De Witt County, this state, February 9, 1854, a son of Albert and Louisa (Cole) Odom, natives of the State of Louisiana. The parents came to this state prior to their marriage, in the early '40s, settling in Harris County, when Houston was a trading village. They married soon after coming to Texas, after which removed to De Witt County, thence to Atascosa County, and in 1862 returned to De Witt County, where he entered the Confederate army as a private. He died shortly after enlisting, in Wharton County, of fever. While residing in Atascosa County the Indians were very troublesome, and on one occasion, while tending his herd of horses, Mr. Odom discovered in the vicinity of his home and stock some twenty-five or thirty Indians of hostile intent, but he got between them and his house and stock and managed to keep them at bay until his man went to Pleasanton for assistance. During this time the family were barricaded in the house, but when reinforcements arrived the Indians retired. On nearly every moonlight night the redskins were to be seen prowling about the homes of the settlers, stealing horses and cattles and sometimes exterminating whole families whose homes were at all isolated. At that time, Mr. Odom states, that Big Foot Wallis was in the country and the settlers felt comparatively secure, for his knowledge of Indian nature was thorough and he knew not the meaning of fear, and consequently was a great protection. Mr. Odom was successfully engaged in the stock business for many years, but confined his attention chiefly to the raising of horses, which were of an excellent breed of Texas stock. At his death he left a wife and five sons, all of whom were too small to look after the stock properly, and by the time the war had closed the stock was scattered over four or five counties and numbers of them had become wild. Of the sons left, Oliver was the eldest, and he was killed in Wilson County in 1884; James C., Milam M., Frank D. and A. M. In 1868 Mrs. Odom was married to A. C. White, and now resides in San Antonio. Her second union resulted in the birth of the following children: Raymond G., J. H., William and Maggie. James C. Odom was left fatherless at the age of seven years, and thus his opportunities for acquiring an education were exceedingly limited, but by attending school for two or three months out of the year, obtained a fair education. He commenced life for himself at the age of fifteen years as a herder and continued this work until 1875. From 1869 to that time he was in the saddle and in camp, and in 1871 took a herd of 800 big steers from near Fort Mason, Tex., to Solomon City, Kan., and made the entire trip on horseback. During this time he says he was thirty-six hours in the saddle without anything to eat or drink and without

changing horses. During 1866 he was employed by some ex-Con-
federate soldiers, who were desirous of keeping out of the hands of
the Federal soldiers, and after he had shielded them on several occasions, Uncle Sam's boys became suspicious of him and young Odom
was arrested, and after they had made him believe that his days on
earth were numbered, they finally let him go, and this episode finished his scouting days. Mr. Odom was in De Witt County in 1870,
when that section was stirred up by civil strife, or a vendetta between the Peace and Jacobs families. He was in the employ of the
Peace brothers, and on one occasion, while herding their horses, some
fifteen men rode up and forced him, at the muzzle of their guns, to
lead them where the Peace brothers were supposed to be stopping,
but fortunately they were not at that place, and thus bloodshed was
averted. Mr. Odom says that he felt decidedly queer, and no doubt
looked even worse than he felt. This vendetta grew to an immense
magnitude, in which some forty men eventually lost their lives. In
1875 Mr. Odom was married in Wharton County to Mrs. Mary (Beeks)
Copeland, a daughter of William and Jane V. (Cavanaugh) Beeks,
who were early Texans, the Cavanaughs experiencing considerable
trouble with the Indians, Mrs. Beeks being at one time quite severely
wounded by them. At that time her father was from home, and the
savages made a raid on three families that lived outside the settlement, and, although Mrs. Cavanaugh tried to make her escape with
her children, she was overtaken by the Indians and all the family
were killed except Mrs. Beeks, who was shot in the left breast and
left for dead. An old Indian placed his foot on her body and pulled
out the arrow with which he had shot her, and she, realizing that
her only chance of escape lay in making them believe she was
really dead, she lay very still and never flinched as he rudely drew
out his murderous weapon. She was twelve or thirteen years of age
at this time, and suffered from this wound all her life. She was in
this country before the war of 1836, and was in what was called the
"run-away." When Mr. Odom was married he was quite a poor boy,
but his wife had some cattle and he continued in this business. In
1873 they came to Austin County, and since that time have lived in
this and Wharton counties. He owns a fine farm of 330 acres, with
115 under cultivation, and he has a beautiful and well-appointed

home in Wallis. He is a member of the cattle syndicate, composed of J. S. Dobney, J. A. Stone, J. S. Jarrol and J. C. Odom, owning some four or five thousand head of cattle in this andWharton counties. He and his wife are the parents of one child, Hettie H. They are members of the Christian church, and the K. and L. of H., and politically he has always been a Democrat.

MAJOR EDWARD BURLESON.

This distinguished old Texas ranger came of a numerous and distinguished family, many members of which became prominent in the sections in which they resided and a number of whom were early settlers of the Lone Star State. His father, Edward Burleson, became an early resident of Hays County, and was a leader of the pioneers who settled on and near the Colorado River, while Texas was a part of Mexico. He was recognized as a man of great bravery and coolness in times of danger, and, although a man of ordinary education, he possessed a naturally good mind and was well posted and up with the times. He was of a social disposition, was an accommodating and kind neighbor, was a faithful and devoted friend, was peaceable in disposition, and seldom had any quarrels. It was said of him that if goaded to a certain point his rule was to fight, unless the other party apologized. After the acceptance of a mission to the United States by General Stephen F. Austin, Edward Burleson was made general of the Texas army, then besieging San Antonio. The party which went to that city under the celebrated Milam, and after he fell were led by Colonel Frank Johnson, were really under Edward Burleson's orders. The town of San Antonio was surrendered to General Burleson December 10, 1835. He then raised a regiment and joined General Sam Houston's army, and bore a distinguished part in the battle of San Jacinto. He was afterward a member of the Senate of the Republic of Texas, and was later elected vice-president of that Republic. On December 26, 1851, General Burleson

died in the city of Austin, at which time he was a member of the
Senate of the State of Texas, and was buried on the plat of ground
which had been set apart as the final resting place of distinguished
Texans. He was one of the naturally great men of the state, and was
distinguished by the clearness of his views, his adaptability to the
interests and welfare of the land of his adoption, for his practical
bent of mind and for the excellence and wisdom of his councils,
which when given could always be relied upon. He could never advocate any measure, which, in his opinion, was a violation of the law,
or which might be injurious to the future well-being of the country;
in fact, he made a model citizen. He was born in Buncombe County,
North Carolina, in 1798, and his wife, who was Miss Sarah G. Owens,
was born in 1796 in Kentucky. The children born to them were:
John, April 6, 1824; Edward (subject), November 30, 1826; Grace B.,
July 4, 1832; Joseph R., David Crocket, September 6, 1837; Elizabeth
T., October 14, 1841, and several that died in infancy. General Burleson became a resident of the municipality of Bastrop, now Bastrop
County, and became the owner of the fine old plantation known as
Baron de Bastrop's, on the Colorado River. At that time the settlers
were frequently subjected to hostile invasions from the Indians, and
security against their outrages was scarcely obtainable in any part of
Texas. General Burleson was possessed of the qualifications to lead
the people in their defense of their firesides and families, and in the
course of time the Toncahuas Indians became the allies of the Texans.
On one Sunday a Toncahua Indian went to the home of General
Burleson to consult him. The general was attending divine services
in a school house near, and on reaching the place of worship the Indian called out "Burleson!" The General looked at the Indian and
shook his head. This was repeated several times. The Indian then
lost patience, and called out distinctly: "Burleson, white man talk
heap, must lie some." General Burleson was a farmer and taught
his sons to work. When quite young they were permitted to accompany their father on his scouting expeditions. Edward Burleson, the immediate subject of this sketch, was sent to school when
opportunity permitted, and he was known to be a rather precocious
youth in many respects, yet he never appeared to appreciate books.

He had a decided taste for out-door sports, and was fond of hunting. Fortune favored him, and when the question of annexing Texas to the United States arose, he entered the service of the United States Government, and was under the command of Major Benjamin Mc-Culloch, with whom he was in the battle of Monterey, his father, General Burleson, being also a participant in that engagement. He was also at Buena Vista, and his company performed able and efficient service on that memorable occasion. He is also entitled to a share of the credit attached to a company, acting the part of spies for General Taylor's army. They penetrated the lines of General Santa Anna's army and carried to their general a correct estimate of the enemy's numbers. Major Burleson was married to Miss Emma Kyle, a native of Mississippi, and daughter of Colonel Claiborne Kyle of Hays County, Tex. They were well suited, and it was a match based on mutual love and esteem. He settled a mile from San Marcos, became a model farmer, acquired property and become very popular with all. He appeared not to covet office, yet he could have been elected to any position within the gift of the people of the State. He was, to a great extent, absorbed by his devotion to his family, and was a kind and indulgent father to his children, who were named as follows: Edward C., John William, James G., Ford McCulloch, Albert Sidney, Kyle, who died in 1856; Edward, Jr., was drowned while bathing in the Rio Blanco in 1873; Emma K., Lily K., Mary K. Mrs. Burleson died March 12, 1877. Ford Burleson became a prominent physician of San Marcos, but died in the prime of life, May 21, 1887, leaving a widow, who was formerly Miss Northcraft, and a young daughter. James G. Burleson, son of Major Edward Burleson, is one of the most prominent business men of Caldwell County, and is the efficient president of the First National Bank of Lockhart. He was born in Hays County, Tex., August 1, 1859. His maternal ancestors, the Kyles, came to Texas during its early history and settled on the Blanco River. Colonel Claiborne Kyle, the maternal grandfather of James G. Burleson, was a very popular man in Mississippi, and at one time was a prominent candidate for Governor of that state. James' father, Edward Burleson, in addition to his other affairs, was a member of the constitutional convention of Texas in 1879, and was also a member of the committee to locate the state penitentiary at Rusk.

The early education of James G. Burleson was acquired in the Coronal Institute at San Marcos, and in 1876-77 he entered Georgetown College, D. C., but, owing to the death of his father in 1877, he left school shortly after, and entered the county clerk's office of Hays County as deputy, and there remained until 1880, when he was elected clerk of the District and County Court, and was successively re-elected to that office for six years. Retiring from office in 1886, he came to Lockhart and organized the banking house of James G. Burleson & Co., which establishment existed and prospered until 1889, when it was succeeded by the First National Bank of Lockhart, which was organized May 20, 1889, with a capital of $50,000, and Mr. Burleson was made its president. The bank has now a surplus and undivided profits of $13,000, and is in a very prosperous condition. It occupies a handsome building on the public square, and is fitted and furnished with all modern appliances and conveniences in the way of fire and burglar proof safe and vaults. The present officials are among the strong financial men of this section: James G. Burleson, president; L. J. Story, vice-president; Ed. J. L. Green, second vice-president; J. M. Jolly, cashier, and A. R. Chew, assistant cashier. Mr. Burleson still owns the old family homestead near San Marcos, which comprises 1,000 acres of fine farming land, of which 250 are under cultivation. He is also a stockholder and one of the directors in the First National Bank of San Marcos, and was one of the organizers of that institution. He also assisted in organizing the Lockhart Oil Mill and Power Company, a valuable corporation of Lockhart. He has always been an active worker for the Democratic party, and has been a delegate to several state conventions. He was married February 15, 1883, to Miss Mary D. Green, a native of Texas, and daughter of Ed. J. L. Green of San Marcos, by Rev. Thomas A. Lancaster, the same divine who, on February 15, 1854, officiated at the marriage of his father and mother. They have four children: Mary, Edward, James G., Jr. and Eliza. Mrs. Burleson is a member of the Christian church. Mr. Burleson devotes his entire time and attention to the interests of his bank and his other financial interests, and has but little time to give to political matters, although he is a staunch Democrat. While at college at Georgetown, D. C., he was appointed to the United States Naval Academy at

Annapolis, Md. It was a life he had for some time been anxious to adopt, but at the same time his elder brother, J. W. Burleson, was appointed to the Military Academy at West Point, and as two members of the same family could not enter the service, James G. withdrew. He is a pleasant and courteous gentleman, an exceedingly shrewd and practical business man, and is in every way worthy the honored ancestry from which he sprung. He is a member of San Marcos Lodge No. 342 and of San Marcos Chapter No. 129, Royal Arch Masons, also a member of Lockhart Lodge No. 115, K. of P., and, while not a member of any church, he is a firm believer in the Roman Catholic religion.

CRAWFORD BURNETT.

This gentleman has been a resident of Gonzales County, Tex., for the past forty-one years, and during that time he has identified himself with the interests of his section, has won numerous friends, and has built up a reputation for honesty, enterprise and fair dealing that is in every way merited. Gonzales County is an Eden of fine farms and agricultural tracts, and there are comparatively few small places. Mr. Burnett is one of the most extensive agriculturists of the county, is the owner of a fine ranch of 10,000 acres, of which 1,000 are under cultivation, and nearly all the rest is susceptible of cultivation. He raises a good grade of stock, his cattle being part Durham, and much attention is also given to raising horses. He has one of the finest horses in the state, registered on both sides, and is a thoroughbred Hambletonian named "Al. S." Mr. Burnett has done much to improve the grade of stock in the county, and this excellent example has been followed by others. Although he has always been keenly alive to his own interests, yet he is noted for his fair and honorable business methods, and for his ready adoption of new and improved methods connected with his calling. He is a native of Harris County, Tex., where he was born April 10, 1835, the youngest of four chil-

dren born to Crawford and Anna (Simons) Burnett, who were born in
the Blue Grass regions of Kentucky, from which state they moved to
Illinois, thence to Missouri, from there to Louisiana, and finally came
to Texas in 1827, locating on Spring Creek, thirty miles north of the
present city of Houston, coming thither as members of Austin's colony. Mr. Burnett took his headright in Brazos County. He was
accompanied to this state by two brothers, Matthew and William,
both of whom participated in the Texas Revolution. William was a
participant in the battle of San Jacinto, and afterward became prominent in public affairs. He was in the Confederate army during the
Civil War, although quite well along in years, and was in the battles
of the Red River campaign under General Banks. He died soon
after the war closed. Matthew died in 1843 or 1844. Crawford Burnett's father died before he was born, and he was also left motherless
before he was old enough to realize his loss or remember her. He
was reared by his Uncle Matthew and wife, and was engaged in the
stock business in Harris County until 1853, when he came to Gonzales
County and purchased a farm about nineteen miles east of the town
of Gonzales. Here he continued to raise stock, but his operations
were for a time interrupted by the opening of the war, for he at once
joined a company for the Confederate service. Very soon after joining he was detailed to return home and raise stock for the Confederacy, and this he successfully did until the war closed. He is one of
the most substantial men of which the county can boast, is a practical
and extensive stockman and farmer, and one of the most influential
and active promoters of the San Antonio & Velasco Railroad, which
runs through over ten miles of his estate. In 1857 he led to the altar
Miss Sarah E. Dillard, who was born in Washington County, Tex.,
in 1838, to Abraham Dillard, a Missourian, who came to Texas in an
early day and was a participant in the battle of San Jacinto. Her
maternal grandfather, Andrew J. Kent, was a Pennsylvanian, was an
early settler of the Lone Star State, and was killed in the bloody engagement at the Alamo. Nine children have been born to Mr. and
Mrs. Burnett, eight of whom survive: Elizabeth, wife of a Mr. Robinson; Sarah Ann, wife of a Mr. Livingston; Frances, who was married and is now deceased; Henrietta is the widow of John A. Clark;
James C., Otho, Lone, Sam Houston and Jesse. Mr. Burnett has

long been a member of the A. F. and A. M., and, although he has always been active in the political affairs of his section, he has by no means been an office-seeker, as his time has been fully occupied in looking after his extensive agricultural and farming interests.

JOHN WILLIAMS.

It is ever a grateful task to the biographer to answer the call to give the life story of a man who has served on the field of battle, and has also done his duty as a private citizen in the ordinary walks of life. This double career exhibits virtues of various scope, but they are after all in union, as they are based upon integrity, conscientiousness and devotion to duty. Such a life do we find in the gentleman whose name we here give. This former member of the Confederate army came originally from Tennessee, where his birth occurred on the 1st of June, 1831, and he is now one of the prominent and substantial farmers of Lavaca County. His parents, William D. and Mary A. (Phillips) Williams, were natives of North Carolina and Tennessee respectively, and his maternal grandfather, Massy Phillips, was one of the first settlers of Middle Tennessee, and a pioneer in every sense of the word. He died in Bedford County, that state. The paternal grandfather spent his life in North Carolina. The father of our subject moved to Tennessee when a young man, was married there to Miss Phillips, and there passed the remainder of his days, engaged in farming. John Williams remained in his native state until twenty years of age, and then came to Texas with his brother and family. He first stopped in Titus County, where he married Miss Catherine Coffee, who came from Alabama to Texas with her father in 1844. The father moved to Lavaca County in 1856 and died in his son-in-law's house a few years later. After his marriage, or in 1854, Mr. Williams came to Lavaca County and bought 100 acres, ten miles north of Hallettsville, to which he has added from time to time until he now owns 800 acres, with nearly 400 acres under cultivation. He has made nearly all the improvements and has a fine place. In 1862 he enlisted in the Confederate army, Company M, of Whitfield's Legion, under General Ross, and afterward crossed the Mississippi River to Corinth, where the company was reorganized. In a battle at Davis' Bridge on Hatchie River in the fall of 1862 Mr. Williams was captured and taken to Boliver, Tenn., where he was paroled. Returning home, he was exchanged and subsequently joined his command in Middle Tennessee. He was in all the battles of the Atlanta campaign and returned with General Hood to Nashville. After the retreat from Nashville he went to Mississippi and from there was furloughed and came to Texas. While in this state the war ended. Since then he has made all his property and is now one of the influential and wealthy men of this section. To his marriage were born four children, only one, James, now living. Mr. Williams and his wife are consistent church members.

JUDGE JOSEPH O'CONNOR.

The bar of Gonzales County, Tex., has won an enviable name throughout the state for the erudition, success and courtesy of its members, many of whom have achieved a wide reputation for their ability and a correct apprehension of what pertains to the profession. Among those who stand deservedly high as a member of this bar, with his brother lawyers and with the courts, is Judge Joseph O'Connor, who has been successfully engaged in the practice of his profession since 1847. He has always been a close student of law and has won the confidence and esteem of the community and the profession as a careful and efficient laywer. He is a Virginian by birth, born in 1823 to Dennis and Elizabeth (Hesser) O'Conner, who were born in the Isle of Erin and the State of Pennsylvania respectively. In his youth Dennis O'Connor came to the United States with his father, and with him located in the Old Dominion, where he followed the calling of a mechanic throughout the remainder of his life. He died there in 1837, and his widow in Missouri in 1860, whither she had moved in the fall of 1837, after the father's death. Up to 1837 Judge O'Connor had been a regular attendant of the schools of Virginia, and he also attended the district schools of Missouri for some time after his removal to that state. Later he entered Marion College, Mo., and in 1844 the Miami University of Oxford, O., from which he was graduated in 1845. Immediately following this he began the study of law in Palmyra in the office of Stanton Buckner, and in 1847 was admitted to the Palmyra bar. In 1852 he came to the Lone Star State and for five years practiced his profession at Bastrop, after which he moved to Corpus Christi and there remained until the opening of the Civil War. In the spring of 1863 he was appointed clerk of the District Court of the Confederate States of Brownsville, later at Corpus Christi, and upon that place being threatened by the enemy, the place of justice was removed to Gonzales. As soon as the courts were reopened in 1867 Mr. O'Connor resumed the practice of his profession, and in a short time had built up a clientele which spoke eloquently as to his standing as a lawyer and his popularity with the masses. In 1860 he had been elected district judge of the Twelfth Judicial District, from Corpus Christi, but soon thereafter the Civil War closed the courts in the state, thus verifying the adage, Non silent leges inter arma. In 1875 he erected a pleasant and commodious residence on the outskirts of Gonzales, where he lives in semi-retirement, his practice now being confined mostly to land cases, in which he has shown remarkable foresight and judgment. In 1864 he was married to Miss Sarah Buchanan, a native of Texas, and a granddaughter of Arthur Burns, who was a member of De Witt's colony, that settled Gonzales. The union of Mr. and Mrs. O'Connor has been blessed in the birth of four children: Birdie, wife of W. L. Clark; Lillie, wife of William Campbell of San Antonio; Etta and Fred J.

CAPTAIN FERG. KYLE.

This gentleman, the founder of the town of Kyle, Tex., owes his nativity to the State of Mississippi, where his eyes first opened on the light of day in 1833. He was the third of eight children born to Claiborne and Lucy (Bugg) Kyle, who were Tennesseeans by birth. The father came to Texas in the winter of 1844, made his home for one year at Gonzales, then moved to Austin, where he remained until 1849. He then settled on the Blanco River, two miles west of the present site of Kyle, and became one of the early settlers of this section. He became very prominent while residing in Mississippi, was active in political matters, served his section as a member of the State Senate, and made an able and incorruptible legislator. At one time he was prominently spoken of for Governor of that state. After coming to the Lone Star State he served as a member of the State Senate one term, and for three terms was a member of the House, and while a member of the Legislative body did some effective work for his section and for the state in general. He became a political leader in this part of Texas and was widely and very favorably known as a shrewd politician, a man of excellent morals, a useful and worthy citizen and a prosperous business man. He was the owner of a very large and valuable farm at the opening of the Civil War. After a useful and well-spent life, he was called upon to pay the last debt of Nature in 1868, and his death was a source of much regret to all who knew him. He was a member of the A. F. and A. M. His wife died in 1863. He was a son of John Kyle, who was of Scotch-Irish descent and one of the early settlers of Tennessee. The Buggs were prominent Tennesseans and one of Mrs. Kyle's uncles was a member of Congress from that state during President Pierce's administration. Captain Ferg. Kyle accompanied his parents to this state, received a practical education in the schools of Austin, and remained under the shelter of the paternal roof until the opening of the great Civil War, when he donned a suit of gray and became a private in the Eighth Texas Cavalry, Terry's Rangers, and was at once sent east of the Mississippi River, and after the first battle in which they participated he was made first lieutenant of his company. After the battle of Shiloh he was advanced to a captaincy and was in all the engagements in the Army of the Tennessee, and acted as volunteer aide to General Cheatham on the 22nd of July, 1864. After the fall of Atlanta an order came from Richmond to send two officers from each regiment from the Trans-Mississippi to return and collect absentees, and Captain Kyle was one of the officers chosen. He collected a number in Texas, and reported to General Hays on the day that they heard of Lee's surrender. He was then ordered back to Austin by General Hays, and by the time he had reached that city the war had ended. His brothers, William, Polk, Curran and Andrew Jackson, were all privates in his company. After his return home, Captain Kyle engaged in farming and stock-raising, and was following this occupation very successfully when he was elected to the Twelfth General Assembly of the state, and while a member of that body served on several committees. He was sergeant-at-arms of the Seventeenth and Eighteenth General Assemblies, and he has always been quite active in politics. In 1860 he was married to Miss Anna Moore, a native of Alabama, and a daughter of Judge David E. Moore, who came to Texas in the early '50s. He eventually became a resident of Hays County, and was county judge of Hays County at one time. He died in the '70s. In 1867 Captain Kyle moved to his present farm, which was formerly the old Moore homestead, and on this the town of Kyle was founded and named in honor of the captain in 1882. The union of Captain and Mrs. Kyle has resulted in the birth of nine children, the eldest of whom died in infancy. The others are: Mary, Sidney Johnson, Albert Johnson, Ailene, Josephine, Edward Johnson, Rosa and Ellen. Captain and Mrs. Kyle are members of the Baptist church and are widely known and have many warm personal friends throughout Hays County.

HON. EDWARD H. RAGAN.

He whose name heads this sketch is regarded as one of the leading lawyers of his section of the state, and commands the respect, as well as the admiration, of his brother practitioners, and is a living refutation of the popular idea that "there is no honest lawyer." He was born in Grainger County, Tenn., February 4, 1834, the eldest of nine children born to Daniel and Catherine (Webb) Ragan, the former

of whom was born in Virginia, and the latter in Tennessee. The paternal grandfather, Daniel Ragan, was born in Ireland, and upon
coming to the United States, located in Virginia, where he followed
the calling of a merchant, and later, but at a still early period, located
in Sullivan County, Tenn., and was eventually called from life at
Kingsport. The maternal grandfather, John Webb, was one of the
very early settlers of Knoxville, Tenn., and there his home continued
to be until his death in 1843. He was a leather manufacturer on a
large scale for that day, and in this branch of human endeavor became wealthy. Daniel Ragan, the father of the subject of this sketch,
was a minister of the Presbyterian church, and spent his life in Sullivan County, Tenn., dying in 1869. Until eighteen years of age Edward H. Ragan spent his life in his native state, and his literary education was obtained in the schools of Knoxville, and at Bakersfield,
Vt. In 1852 he took up his residence in Texas, at Lockhart, Caldwell County, and brought with him a daguerreotype outfit, and finished the first picture ever taken in the town. He soon after sold out,
however, and engaged in teaching school, and at the same time
studied law, and in 1854 was admitted to the bar, and at once entered upon the practice of his profession at Lockhart. Unlike many
who first enter professional life, it did not take him long to obtain his
first brief, and so ably did he handle the cases that were placed in
his charge, that he soon had all the legal work that he could attend
to. In 1856 he was married to Miss Sarah N. Barrow, a native of
Mississippi, who was brought to Texas when a child by her father,
Samuel Barrow, who was for a long time sheriff of Gonzales County.
In 1859 Mr. Ragan was elected to the office of justice of the peace,
and was holding that office when the great Civil War opened. He
at once resigned and enlisted in Company K, Seventeenth Texas Infantry, which command operated in Louisiana and Arkansas, and
he was a participant in the battles of Milliken's Bend, Mansfield,
Pleasant Hill and Jenkins' Ferry. He then returned to Louisiana,
thence to Texas, and was in this state when the war closed. He soon
after went to Galveston and was salesman in a large clothing store
there for one year, at the end of which time he returned to Lockhart
and resumed the practice of law, and also became connected with
newspaper work once more. In 1855 he started the "Watchman,"

which was the second paper of Lockhart, and he continued its publication until he entered the army in 1861, when he stored his material and machinery away, but it was all destroyed during that
period. In 1869, in connection with N. C. Raymond of Austin, he
began the publication of the "Texas Plowboy," for there had been no
paper published in Lockhart since the "Watchman," but he sold his
interest in this paper in 1871 to Mr. Raymond, who removed it to
Austin, but on his way to that city died very suddenly. In the same
year, 1871, Mr. Ragan established the "News Echo," which he conducted for about one year, when the office was destroyed by fire. The
"Plowboy" was devoted to agricultural matters, and the others were
published in the interests of the Democratic party. At one time Mr.
Ragan was appointed to the office of county clerk to fill a vacancy,
was later elected county attorney, a position he held four years, and,
after being out of office for two years, was elected to the same position for another two years. In 1875 he was elected county judge, the
first under the new constitution of 1875, and held the office for three
years. In 1890 he was again honored by his party by being elected
to the Twenty-second General Assembly from the Ninety-first District, composed of Guadalupe, Caldwell and Hays counties, was re-
elected in 1892 from the Fifty-first District, composed of the county
of Caldwell. During his first term he served on judiciary committee
No. 2, agricultural affairs, insurance statistics and history, and constitutional amendments. He introduced the following bills: One for
extending the time in holding the District Court of Caldwell County,
one for amending the attachment laws of the state, and a bill relating to official business, all of which became laws. He was also
the author of an amendment to the constitution, reducing the rate
of interest of the state to 6 and 8 per cent. While a member of the
Twenty-third Assembly he introduced a bill to amend the law in regard to taking depositions in civil suits, which was the first bill
passed and signed by the Governor. A bill establishing a special
road law for Caldwell County; and in connection with Harry Golden
of Dallas, he was the author of a bill to establish a State Board of
Arbitration to settle difficulties between employes and employers.
The bill passed the House, but did not get through the Senate. Another bill which he introduced was for making an appropriation for

the maintenance of the Confederate Home. He served on the follow-ing committees: As second on judiciary committee No. 1, chairman of the committee on judicial districts, committee on international af-fairs, committee on privileges and elections and was a member of the special committee which preferred impeachment charges against Land Commissioner McGaughey, and was appointed speaker of the committee to conduct the trial before the Senate. In his practice he has made criminal law a specialty, and has been very successful. Possessing decided literary taste, he has written much on many sub-jects, and composed a beautiful poem on the death of Jefferson Davis, which was read in his speech in the House of Representatives on that occasion. His first wife died in 1870, having borne him five children, two of whom died before their mother. In 1874 he was married to Mrs. Martha (Rickenbaugh) Gutheridge of Fulton, Mo., who only lived about a year after marriage. He married his present wife in 1877—Miss Ellen Runkle, a native of Missouri, and to them four children have been born, three of whom are living. Mr. and Mrs. Ragan are members of the Presbyterian church, he is superin-tendent of the Sunday School, and socially he is a member of the I. O. O. F.

REV. WILLIAM JASPER JOYCE.

This gentleman is one of the pioneer circuit riders of the Lone Star State, and during the long term of years that he has labored in the vineyard of the Master his efforts have been well rewarded. He is a product of Georgia, born in 1828, the eldest child born to Henry and Sarah (Posey) Joyce, who were born in Georgia and South Caro-lina respectively, the former being a farmer and stock-raiser of con-siderable prominence. The paternal grandfather, Henry Joyce, was a Virginian, while his father was a native of Ireland, and came to America in colonial times. The grandfather was a soldier of the

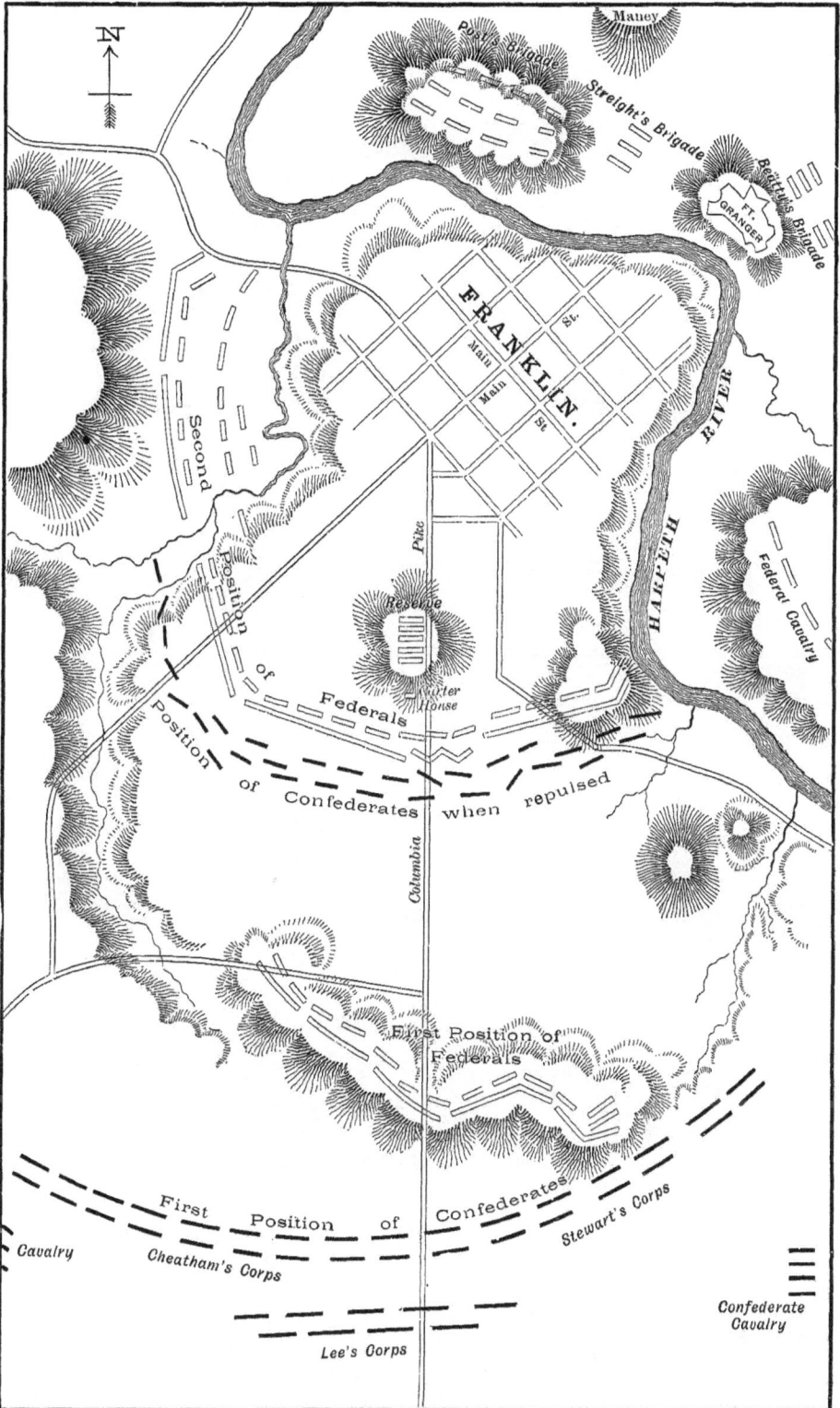

Revolution, and fought principally in the Southern states. In 1836 Henry and Sarah Joyce moved to Alabama, thence to Texas in 1849, and in Red River County the father was called from life in 1855, his widow surviving him until 1893, when she, too, passed away at the age of ninety-three years. In the State of Alabama the subject of this sketch was reared, but he unfortunately received a limited education, although he possessed a naturally fine mind. He came with his parents to Texas in 1849, and when he had attained his majority he left home, and for one year thereafter was engaged in farming in Arkansas. He then went to Ouachita County, same state, and for some time served as deputy clerk of the courts. In the fall of 1852 he again came to Texas, and in 1857 began his labors as a minister of the Methodist Episcopal church south, and has continued in that work ever since. He was ordained a deacon in Tyler and an elder in Jefferson, Tex. He began his work in Harrison County, and for four years remained in the eastern part of the state doing station and circuit work. In 1861 he was stationed at Palestine, but when the war opened he joined the Confederate army, Company A of the Second Texas Mounted Rifles, and served ten months as a private in New Mexico, and was a participant in the battle of Cottonwoods, in which his horse was shot near where he stood. He was then made chaplain of his regiment, but at the end of 1863 resigned this position and resumed his ministerial labors in the West Texas Conference, and was following this occupation on the frontier when he had to carry firearms to protect himself against the Indians. At one time his horse was stolen by them when he was eighty miles from home, and he was often exposed to hostile and marauding bands of savages. After preaching for twenty-eight years in Western Texas, he is now superannuated. About 1874 he came to San Marcos and has since made his home here. He was presiding elder for ten years, eight of which in the San Marcos district. He has been agent for the American Bible Society, but since being superannuated in 1893 he has been associated with Mr. Steele in the real estate business, as a member of the firm of Steel & Joyce, and has done comparatively well financially. He has had some success as a revivalist, has done some effective work at camp meetings, and his experiences on his way to fill appointments on the frontier were many times thrilling. He was married in 1863 to Miss Laura Mitchell of San Antonio, a daughter of Asa Mitchell, a native of Pennsylvania, who came to Texas about 1824. Nine children have been born to Mr. and Mrs. Joyce: Emily, wife of Professor S. W. Stanfield of Coronal Institute; May, wife of Judge W. Kelso of Eagle Pass; William H., special fire insurance agent at Dallas; Harvey W., bookkeeper American National Bank, Dallas; Albert G., financial clerk in the postoffice at Dallas; Martin O., cashier of the Mexican International Railroad at Pedris Negris, Mexico; Laura Lee, Robert D. and Dora A. Mr. Joyce is a Mason, and he and his family are well known and highly honored citizens of the Lone Star State.

MRS. SARAH ANN BRACHES.

Sarah Ann Ashby, now the Widow Braches, was born in Shelby County, Ky., in the town of Shelbyville, March 12, 1811, the daughter of John M. and Mary (Garnett) Ashby, the former of whom removed to Kentucky from Ashby's Gap, Va. In 1831 he located at Old Petersburg, Lavaca County, Tex., and while returning to his home in this state, after a visit to Kentucky, died at Matagorda, Tex., his wife's death having occurred a few years earlier. In 1829 Sarah Ann Ashby was married to Bartholomew A. McClure of Kentucky, with whom she came to Texas in 1831 as one of De Witt's colonists, and located on a large tract of land on Peach Creek, in Gonzales County, nine miles from the town of Gonzales. Mr. McClure became very prominent in the affairs of this section, and was a participant in the Texas Revolution of 1835-36, but was not a participant in the battle of San Jacinto, owing to the fact that he had been sent as a special messenger for General Houston to Eastern Texas for recruits. Upon the retreat of General Houston from Gonzales in 1836, he camped one night at the McClure homestead, and in the morning he made a speech to the people beneath a live oak tree, that is still standing in front of the house, warning the citizens of the danger of remaining in the locality, which eventually resulted in the "runaway" before the army of Santa Anna. Mrs. McClure (now Mrs. Braches) started in an ox cart, with two young sons, and followed the army so that she was within hearing of the guns in the battle of San Jacinto, at a place called Grigby's Bluff. She and some other women visited the battle-field a few days after the battle, and found all the Mexicans who had been slain still lying on the ground unburied. Mr. McClure was with General Sid Johnston for about one year after this before he rejoined his family, who were then living near the present city of Houston. Mrs. McClure saw the site of that place surveyed, at which time it consisted of one house—a mere hut—and many tents. In the spring of 1838 they returned to their home, and when the county of Gonzales was organized Mr. McClure became the first county judge, an office he held four years. During this time he had begun the arduous work of improving his place, but died in 1841, before he had made much headway in this respect. He was in what was called the Blanco Valley Indian fight, a number of years before his death, and it is to such men as him that the present state of advanced civilization was made possible. He and his wife became the parents of three sons, but two of them died while they were residing in the eastern part of the state. In 1843 Mrs. McClure and her son returned to Kentucky, where she inherited seven negro slaves, with whom she returned to Texas and began farming and stock-raising. After remaining a widow for two years she married Charles Braches, who came to Texas from Mississippi about four years prior. He was a participant in the Mexican War, and was also in several bloody Indian battles. After his marriage he turned his attention to agricultural pursuits, became an extensive stock-raiser, and also became prominent in political affairs of Gonzales County. Prior to his marriage he had been elected to the State Legislature, and he was always interested in and had a comprehensive knowledge of the current issues of the day. His career was closed by death in 1889, after a useful and well-spent life. He left one child, Mrs. H. K. Jones, of Dilworth, who has one daughter who is married and resides in Gonzales—Mrs. J. B. Kennard—and had three children that died in infancy. Joel B. McClure, Mrs. Braches' eldest child, was a soldier of the Civil War, and was

one of Terry's Rangers. He was wounded at the battle of Shiloh,
which compelled him to leave the service, and he returned home very
much broken in health, and never fully recovered, and died a few
years later. John M. Ashby, Mrs. Braches' father, had six children,
who came to Texas, and one daughter, who was born in Gonzales.
There are now four daughters living, of whom Mrs. Braches is the
eldest. The others are: Isabella, wife of General Henry E. McCulloch of Seguin; Fannie, wife of Major Roderick Gellhorn of Big Hill.
Gonzales County, and Euphemia, wife of Major William King of
Seguin, all prominent and esteemed people. Mrs. Braches has a
pleasant and comfortable home, which was erected forty years ago,
of material brought overland from Port Lavaca and other places.
She owns about two leagues of land, and the most of her fine farm
is under cultivation. This farm is located on the old stage road from
Columbus to San Antonio, and for over twenty years she kept a stage
stand. In 1839, while she and Mr. McClure were returning home
from Columbus on horseback, and had reached a point a few miles
from home, they encountered a band of hostile Indians, and they at
once began a race for their lives, the better speed of their horses
alone saving them. While Mrs. McClure was attempting to make a
short cut to the timber she encountered a gully which seemed almost
an impassable barrier, but her noble horse made the leap safely and
carried its mistress to safety. When the Indians arrived at the gully
they all halted and looked with wonder on such a feat, which none
of them dared attempt. Mrs. McClure halted at a hill beyond and
hurled back a shout of triumph at the Comanches. In all the country no one has seen more of frontier life than has she, and her reminiscences of old-time incidents are of thrilling interest. She has managed her large estate successfully, and is known for miles and miles
around, not only for her many charities, but for her knowledge of
frontier life and the bravery she displayed during many trying periods. Although somewhat feeble from her many years of toil, she still
takes a great interest in current affairs, and being a great reader, is
well posted on nearly all topics. Her friends are legion, and she is a
noble example of those women who braved dangers, hardships and
privations that she might secure a home and the comforts and blessings of civilization for her descendants.

JOEL W. ROBISON.

(Deceased.)

One of the earliest settlers of Fayette County, Tex., as well as one of the first of the state, was Joel W. Robison, who was born in Washington County, Ga., October 5, 1815. He came to Texas with his parents and one sister in 1832, and settled first in Brazoria County. He found the country new and most of the people Mexicans there. The political condition of the country was in a turmoil, there being two factions of Mexicans struggling for supremacy. Santa Anna, the leader of the government faction, had declared in favor of the constitutional government. Mr. Robison and his father, J. G. Robison, enlisted in Captain Henry S. Brown's Company, and under the command of Captain John Austin, marched to Velasco, June 26, 1832, and engaged in that desperate struggle, which, after eleven hours' conflict, resulted in the surrender of the garrison to the Texan army. In 1883 Mr. Robison, with his father and the remainder of the family, moved up to the border settlements between the Colorado and Brazos rivers. He, as a boy soldier, joined Captain York's Company in an expedition against the Indians in the territory, and continued to do service in defense of the advancing frontier settlements. In 1835 he joined the expedition against the Indians on the Upper Trinity, and soon after his return from the last-named expedition, the Texans assembled in consultation at San Felipe. They proclaimed a declaration of rights and advocated measures of resistance to the quartering of Mexican troops in the state, in violation of the colonization contract, when it was decided to raise an army for this resistance. Young Robison was among the first to respond. He went at once to San Antonio, engaged under Colonel Bowie, and was in that splendid victory, the battle of Concepcion, October 28, 1835. In November of the same year he was one of the number under Colonel Bowie in the Grass fight before San Antonio, where another splendid victory for the Texan army was achieved. Mr. Robison continued with the army as a private until the battle of San Jacinto, April 21,

1836, and he was one of a party of six with Sylvester when Santa
Anna was captured. They surrounded him in a small tract of timber, and Sylvester, not knowing who he was, proposed shooting him.
Mr. Robison opposed doing so. The soldiers started Santa Anna
toward the headquarters of General Sam Houston, on foot, and as his
feet were sore he said he could not walk, and that the soldiers might
kill him if they wished to. They prodded him with their guns, but it
had no effect. Santa Anna had made up his mind not to walk. Mr.
Robison took compassion on him and had him mount behind himself,
and they thus proceeded to General Houston's tent. There for the
first time Sylvester and his men found out the true value of their
prisoner. No doubt had they found it out before, the "Little Napoleon" would never have reached camp. After returning home (at
the close of the war), Mr. Robison's father, J. G. Robison, was elected
from a county to the first Texas Congress, which assembled at Columbia. In the latter part of 1836, immediately after the adjournment of Congress, the father returned home, his family then residing in the territory of which this county was afterward composed,
between Round Top and Warrenton, within one mile of the latter
place. Afterward Mr. Robison, together with his brother, Walter,
and a faithful old negro servant, took an ox team and went to Columbus for a sack of salt (twenty miles). On their return home at the
close of the second day, and when within a half mile of that place,
they were surrounded, captured, killed and scalped by the Indians.
Joel W. Robison, his son, and the subject of this sketch, looking over
the trail leading toward Columbus next day, saw at no great distance his father's oxen with the wagon, and at once went to investi-
gate. His horror can be imagined. He carried his father and uncle,
as well as the negro, to a place of safety from the wolves, etc., until
he could get help to give them Christian burial. In 1837 Joel W.
Robison married Miss E. A. Alexander, a native of Kentucky. From
1837 to 1845 he was in nearly all the expeditions against the Comanches and other Indians in Texas. He was a private while in the
army, although appointed lieutenant by General Houston. His wife
was born in Kentucky, June 25, 1821, and emigrated with her father,
Samuel Alexander, to this county in 1832, settling in what is known
as the Block House Settlement, five years before the organization of

Fayette County, making her one of the earliest settlers in the county —a period of fifty-four years—from 1832 to 1887. While Colonel Rcbison performed his duties as a soldier for his country, Mrs. Robison was ever mindful of hers, faithfully discharging the onerous duties of pioneer life with a cheerfulness that was remarkable. She had but one brother, Jerome Alexander, who fell with Dawson on the Salado, near San Antonio, in 1842. In 1858 Mrs. Robison professed religion and joined the Methodist church, with which she remained until her death in 1887. Mr. and Mrs. Robison were the parents of seven children, three sons and four daughters, five of whom survive: Almeida, wife of T. A. Ledbetter; Samuel A. (deceased); Neal of this city, Lucy, wife of J. F. McClatchy; Fannie, wife of Dr. J. W. Smith; J. G. of Williamson County, and one died young. Mr. Robison chose the occupation of farming as his life's work and became a wealthy citizen. He represented Fayette County in the State Legislature from 1860 to 1862, and advocated secession. Mr. Robison was always a very pronounced Democrat, and was a leader of his party in the county, attending all the state and county conventions, and was chairman of the County Democratic Committee for several years. For many years prior to his death Joel W. Robison was one of the leading men in his section, or in the state. In 1874 he was a member of the convetion that formed the present constitution of Texas. Prominent men of Texas, in passing through his section, always made his house their home. He was an old-school gentleman, courteous, kind and pleasant to all, and was much honored and respected throughout the county and state. His son, Neal W. Robison, the present county collector, was born in Fayette County, Tex., July 16, 1848, and was educated in this county during 1867, '68 and '69, when he attended the University of Virginia. There he made law a specialty, but never entered into the practice of the profession. In 1870 he formed a partnership with his father in the mercantile business in the village of Warrenton, and was thus engaged until 1879. At that date he was married to Miss Halley P. Carter, a native of Texas, and daughter of John H. and Nunly Carter, natives of Virginia, where their ancestors were among the pioneers. Mr. Carter came to the Lone Star State in 1845 and engaged in merchandising, in which occupation he met with substantial results. His death occurred in 1894, when seventy-eight years old, regretted by many friends. Of the nine children born to his marriage seven now survive: Bettie, now Mrs. Davis of Houston; America, married S. C. Olive of Waco; Judith, now Mrs. Horwell of this city; John B. of this place; F. C. of this county; Mrs. James Farquhar of this city, and Hallie P., wife of subject. Directly after his marriage Mr. Robison engaged in the cotton brokerage business for a number of years, or until 1882. He was then elected tax collector of this county, an office which he has filled up to the present time—twelve years—to the entire satisfaction of all concerned. He is a member of the A. F. & A. M., and his father was a Royal Arch Mason of Fayette. Like his father he has been a lifelong Democrat, and is a public spirited and progressive citizen. This family is one of the best known and most highly respected in the county, and the male members have taken a deep interest in the welfare and upbuilding of the same.

MRS. TOBITHA KILLOUGH.

This estimable lady, the widow of I. G. Killough, and daughter of Colonel John H. and Eliza (Cummins) Moore, is a lady of much more than ordinary ability, as she received a moderate education in her youth and has since, year by year, added to her stock of knowledge. Her maternal grandfather, James Cummins, was a member of Austin's first colony, coming here in 1821 or '22. He followed farming the first year, but, while he went back East for his family, the Indians destroyed his crop of corn, and for three months after returning the family lived without bread. His home was on the opposite side of the river from where Columbus now stands, in Colorado County, and his great-granddaughter now owns the farm. A few years later he moved on what was later known as Cummins Creek, and began tilling the soil there. He was the first man to settle on that creek and it received his name. While living there he held the position of judge of what is now Colorado County, and was a prominent man in his time and day. He was too old to take part in the war with Mexico and died in 1849, leaving five children: Eliza, mother of subject; Nancy, married Jesse Burnham; Sarah, widow of a Mr. Strong; Harriet, wife of Abram Bairer, and Wiley. Several of Mr. Cummins' children died young, but one of them, Mariah, was the wife of a Mr. Cook. Colonel John H. Moore came from Tennessee to Fayette County, Tex., in 1819, when about nineteen years of age, with a trading party by way of Santa Fe, N. M. He followed trading through the states for two years, and in 1826 was married to Miss Cummins, with whom he settled on Cummins Creek. He was married by bond by the Alcalde or political chief, and this was afterward sanctioned by the priest in order to be lawful. About 1828 Colonel Moore received his headright from the Mexican Government, and located where the town of La Grange is now standing. He built the first house in that place, a blockhouse, close to where the magnificent courthouse now stands. Indians were troublesome in those days, but the residents of La Grange were not molested, although about six miles north of that place many citizens were massacred. Colonel Moore was in nearly all the wars with the Indians and took part in nearly all the principal engagements. At the battle of Red Fork, on Colorado river, he followed the Indians to their homes, destroyed their wigwams and took prisoners their women and children, holding them at La Grange and Austin until they could exchange them for whites. Captain Moore kept an Indian boy for two or three years. The latter was but seven years old when captured, and when ten years of age he could talk the English language quite fluently. He became much attached to Colonel Moore and family, and did not wish to be exchanged, as his mother and father had been killed during the fight. Colonel Moore commanded a company of men in the war with Mexico in 1835 and '36, and fought at San Antonio and other engagements, but was not in the battle of San Jacinto, but was in hearing distance of it, being on the other side of the bayou, which was past fording or swimming. He was not in the war with Mexico in 1848. When not scouting for Indians he was engaged in farming and stock raising and occasionally went out on hunting expeditions. He always kept a pack of hounds for bear hunting, a sport of which he was particularly fond, and not infrequently had narrow escapes, often being obliged to carry his disabled dogs home. About 1832 Colonel Moore presented the city of La Grange with the land on which it is situated. This place and Austin were competing points for the capitol and Austin secured it by one vote. Mr. Moore was quite an active politician, and he was public spirited and progressive. His death occurred in 1883, April 12th. Mrs. Moore died in 1875. They left six children: William, deceased; Tobitha; Eliza, deceased, was the wife of R. V. Cook of Columbus; John H., deceased; Robert, deceased, and Mary, wife of Mr. Hunt. Mrs. Killough was educated in Rutersville, Tex., and after finishing went to Tennessee to visit her relations, going by way of New Orleans and returning with two of her uncles, who brought their families and slaves by the overland route. They were about six weeks in making the trip. Mrs. Killough was married in 1854 to I. G. Killough, a native of Tennessee, of the town of Bolivar. He came to Texas in 1851 and engaged in farming and stock raising, and also speculated in real estate. A strong Democrat, he took an active interest in political matters, and was elected to the Thirteenth General Assembly, serving one year. About this time he moved to Austin, resided there for a number of years, and then returned to La Grange, where his interests were centered. He was a farmer, and at the time of his death, which occurred October 2, 1878, was one of its most popular ones. He left a family of eight children: Eliza M., wife of R. O. Foris of Flatonia; Lucy, wife of W. H. Saunders of La Grange; Maggie E., wife of W. T. Burns of Houston; Annie, wife of J. M. Moon of this state; David M., of this county; John H.; Robert E. Lee, at home, and Ira G., at home. Mr. Killough was a member of the A. F. & A. M., and was an elder in the Cumberland Presbyterian Church for a number of years, and an active worker in the same. He was a man of generous impulses and a warm heart, and was noted for his liberality to the friendless and forsaken. In 1861 Mr. Killough raised a company known as Company I, Green's Brigade, and first went to New Mexico, where he participated in three fights. Later he was in the battle of Galveston, and went from there to Louisiana, where he was in the fight with General Banks from the 13th of April to the close of the campaign, Mansfield, Yellow Bayou and all the other engagements of that campaign. Mr. Killough was noted for bravery, and at the taking of Fort Donelson was hit on the head with a brick-bat, being in too close quarters for a gun to be used. He continued in the army until cessation of hostilities and then surrendered. He was home but three times from 1861 to 1865, and was in active service all the time.

COLONEL JOHN JACOB MYERS.

(Deceased.)

The life narrative of the head of a family is interesting, not only to posterity, but also to the citizens of the section in which he has resided, and this truth is doubly true when such a man has established for himself and his children a reputation for integrity, character and ability, and has been of value in the development of that portion of the country which has been his home. Such a narrative do we have in this sketch of the life of Colonel John Jacob Myers, who was born in Lincoln County, Mo., October 25, 1821, a son of Elijah Myers, who was an early settler of that state from Kentucky. In the State of Missouri the subject of this sketch was reared on a farm, and much of his education was obtained at home, under the instruction of his father. He was with General John C. Fremont in his expedition across the plains to the Pacific coast, and thence to Mexico with the famous pathfinder. After the close of the Mexican War, Mr. Myers returned to Missouri, and married Miss Sarah E. Hudspeth of Jackson County, Mo., October 3, 1848. The only child of this union, Samuel Myers, aged ten months, died in 1850. He was engaged in gold mining in California, 1849 to 1851. He then returned by water to New York city, then by rail to Missouri. After a short stay at his old home he came to Texas, where his wife died, March 14, 1852. He purchased lands, began farming and stock raising in Caldwell County. November 6, 1856, he was married to Miss Eliza Jane Skaggs of Warren County, Ky., a daughter of Abram

Moredock and Rhoda Boone (Smith) Skaggs, who were also Ken-
tuckians by birth, their parents being among the very first settlers
of the Blue Grass State from Virginia. The mother was a relative
of Daniel Boone, and the father was a soldier of the War of 1812,
and fought on the frontier with General W. H. Harrison, being one
of the famous "Hunters of Kentucky," of which poem the opening
verse reads as follows:

> "Ye gentlemen and ladies fair
>   Who grace this famous city;
> Just listen while you've time to spare,
>   While I repeat a ditty.
> And for this opportunity
>   Just think yourselves quite lucky,
> For 'tis not often that you hear
>   A hunter from Kentucky."

Mr. and Mrs. Skaggs removed to Caldwell County, Tex., in 1851,
and the mother was called from life in the following year. In 1856
the father returned to Kentucky, and died in that state in the fall
of 1861. He was a Master Mason. He was always interested in
military affairs, mustered a company, and was captain of the local
militia. After the marriage of Mr. Myers, he and his family resided
on a farm near Lockhart until the opening of the Civil War, and when
a company was raised in June, 1861, Mr. Myers was at once chosen
its captain, and his commission as captain of the Lone Star Mounted
Rifles is dated July 1, 1861. He was ordered to report to Colonel
Moore at Galveston and started with his company September 6, 1861,
and was mustered into the Confederate States army September,
1861, for during the war. He was advanced in rank from captain
to major, then to lieutenant-colonel, while at Galveston. He was in
many engagements at the head of his company, and later while serv-
in Louisiana was promoted to the rank of colonel. He was in the
Red River campaign in Louisiana against Banks' army and at the
battle of Mansfield on April 8, 1867, was promoted to colonel of his
regiment, the Twenty-sixth Texas Cavalry, and commanded the same
until the close of the war. He was in many severe encounters in
the swamps of Louisiana, and saw some hard service, but faithfully,
ably and bravely performed every duty as a Confederate soldier. He

was home on a short furlough just before the close of the war, and was on his way to join his command when met by the news that the Confederates were overpowered and the war ended. He at once returned home, resumed farming and stock-raising, also buying and driving stock, and, in the latter occupation soon became one of the most extensive in that section of the country. He was one of the first to drive cattle to the northern states and later he drove large herds to Kansas and Utah. He was taken sick in Kansas while on a trip there with cattle and returned home and died December 10, 1874. He left a widow and seven children: Hettie Virginia, wife of James F. Cahill, an attorney-at-law of San Antonio; George, married, and living at Batesville, Tex.; John Jacob; Abram Elijah; Robert E. Lee; Eliza; Jane, married J. H. Williams, a stockman, and lives at Marfa, Presidio County, Tex.; Eva Boone; Carrie Ellen, and Lafayette, who died in infancy, preceding their father to the better land. Colonel Myers was an enthusiastic member of the A. F. & A. M. (was a Royal Arch Mason), was a member of the I. O. O. F., and he and his wife were worthy and consistent members of the Presbyterian church. He removed with his family to Lockhart in 1870, and there, before death claimed him, he made numerous friends, and his life was one of usefulness and honor. He was a member of the United States army in California and throughout the Mexican War till 1847, and was advanced from a private to a lieutenant in rank, which fact speaks highly of his military ability and popularity, because advancement then in the United States service to a commission was rarely granted to other than trained soldiers, and even then only to those of high courage and military power. He left a goodly property, as well as the heritage of an honest name to his children, and on the old homestead the widow still resides.

JUDGE JOHN P. BELL.

It seems to have been the ambition of Mr. Bell, one of the foremost lawyers of this county, to make the best use of his native and acquired powers, and to develop in himself a true manhood, and the large

clientage he has gathered around him, as well as the large circle of
friends he has won, abundantly testifies as to the success of his
efforts. He was born in Austin County, December 22, 1844, whither
his parents, Andrew J. and Calpernia (Shellbourne) Bell, came in
1832 or 1833. They were natives respectively of Tennessee and Alabama, and were married in the State of Texas. After coming to this
county they located near where New Ulm now stands, in this county,
and Mr. Bell's first service for Texas was in the Blue Grass fight
with the Indians west of this place. He was also a member of the
Texas army against Mexico in 1846-48, and participated in many engagements with the Mexicans and Indians. His career was a remarkable one. A fine specimen of the frontiersman, Mr. Bell was
ever ready to serve his country, and, enjoying excellent health, no
one ever found him missing when duty called. The first office he
held in the county was that of sheriff, to which he was elected in
1850. As this office did not pay him he resigned at the close of the
first year, and in 1853 was elected to represent Austin County in
the Legislature, with but slight opposition. So satisfied were his
constituents at the close of the term that he was re-elected in 1855.
He favored the "Know Nothing" wing of the Democratic party. Mr.
Bell was a true and chivalrous son of the South, and during the Civil
War devoted his energies to the Southern cause. At the election for
President in 1860 he supported Breckinridge of Kentucky and although when the war broke out, his health would not permit his
serving on the field, he became provost in his county and rendered
essential aid to his cause. When the cause was lost he submitted
with heroic fortitude, but remained unchanged in faith and principle until the day of his death, dying a true Jeffersonian Democrat.
It may be truly said that perhaps no individual has ever resided in
Austin County, whose career has been more indelibly stamped upon
its history, and whose memory has been more revered by his numerous friends and associates than that of Andrew J. Bell. His love for
his friends was one of his ruling passions, and his great fidelity,
reliability, sincerity and devotion to them were well known. He
came to this country when a boy, and as a boy he trod the broad

plains of the Lone Star State when deer, buffalo and other animals were to be seen in vast numbers. His wife survived until April, 1887. They reared four children, viz.: Mrs. R. Minturn of this place; John P.; George C., also of Austin County and Mrs. C. H. Bethany of this county. John P. Bell, ex-county judge and generally known as Judge Bell, received the rudiments of an education in the common schools of this county, and later attended Williams' Academy at Fayetteville, Fayette County, for a short time. When but sixteen years of age, he joined Captain Hargroves' company of scouts, which afterward became a part of Colonel Reuben Brown's regiment of cavalry. Serving in the trans-Mississippi department for some time, he was then promoted to sergeant, and participated in a few skirmishes. After the war he engaged in farming, and followed this with varying success until 1868, when he began the study of law, being admitted to the bar in January, 1869, Judge McFarland presiding. The same year he was elected presiding justice of the county, and held that position until 1876, and was then elected county judge, which office he held until 1881. Since that time he has held no office, but devotes his time to his profession, and has all the legal work he can possibly attend to. In 1881 he formed a partnership with James H. Shellbourne under the title of Bell & Shellbourne, and this firm is one of the best known in the county and enjoys an enviable reputation. Judge Bell was married in 1872 to Miss L. A. Bethany, daughter of J. W. and M. A. (Woods) Bethany, who were married in Alabama in 1843, and came to Texas in 1847. In this state Mr. Bethany passed away, leaving a wife and nine children. He was a prominent Mason and a successful farmer. Mr. and Mrs. Bell became the parents of four children: Lucy, James J., Anna, and Bessie. The judge is a member of the A. F. & A. M. Bellville Lodge No. 223, of which he is past master, and he is a member of Bellville Chapter, R. A. M. No. 151, of which he is a high priest and past high priest. He is a charter member of the chapter and is the past grand high priest of the R. A. M. of Texas. He is also a member of the Knights Templar Lodge of Brenham No. 15. Both he and wife are consistent members of the M. E. church.

WILLIAM ARMSTRONG.

This gentleman is one of the early settlers of Texas and a veteran of the Mexican War, but is a product of the Buckeye State, his birth occurring in the vicinity of Cincinnati in 1823. His parents, George and Theresa (Rice) Armstrong, were worthy people, and he was well reared, but he left home when very young and with a friend, Jim Luka, went to the headwaters of the Mississippi River, and there hunted, trapped and traded in furs and skins on Lake Pippin for one winter. They dealt principally with the Indians, trading them whisky for furs and skins, but this was dangerous business, for at one time, after imbibing too much "fire water," they took possession of the place and Mr. Armstrong and his companion were glad to escape with their lives. They made their way to the mouth of the Saint Croix River by water, and during this voyage Mr. Armstrong lost overboard a fine silver-mounted gun. Worn out and without a dollar, all his winter's work in the hands of the Indians, he worked his way down four hundred miles to Dubuque, Iowa, in the mining region, where he met with another loss—his fine watch and his friend disappeared simultaneously. Being still of an adventurous spirit, he and five companions started overland for California, and with the expectation of joining a wagon train went to Independence, Mo., but the train had passed several days before, and he and his companions decided to come to Texas. During this journey of more than two thousand miles he rode a horse, "Iowa Jim," which he afterward sold in Austin, Tex., for $120. There he joined the ranging service, becoming a member of Captain Katy's Company, and served three months, at the end of which time he joined Captain Ross' Company for six months. While stationed at Waco a treaty was made with the Indians, in which the whites were to take charge and destroy all whisky. Mr. Armstrong was put in command of fifty men to perform this duty, and, as Mr. Armstrong says, "of course our canteens were full all the time in those days." A short time afterward the Mexican War broke out and all the rangers of each company of Texas volunteers enlisted, except ten men in each company. Mr. Armstrong was put under command of General Harney, and started for Mexico. In crossing the Rio Grande River several men were drowned. Pushing on through Carmargo a part of the command of 800 men was left in that vicinity and the remainder went on to Monterey, where Mr. Armstrong had his horse shot from under him in the storming of the city. Afterward he was sent back on the Rio Grande, and made a few raids up and down that river. He was finally retired and paid off at San Marcos, after which he lived in different parts of the state. From that time on, as no settlers were on the frontier but the rangers for many years, he met with many thrilling adventures and narrow escapes. In 1848 he married in Burleson County Miss Zaruah Fulcher, a native of Arkansas, after which he removed to Lavaca County and engaged in farming and stock raising to a considerable extent, annually driving large herds of animals inland. While in the ranging service he took out a land warrant for pay, and had he held it would at this time have been one of the largest land owners of the state, as he had the offer of many acres of land where Waco now stands for 10 cents per acre. In 1864 Mr. Armstrong's wife died, leaving him with five sons and one daughter, and in the fall of that year he was married to Miss Nancy Ryan, also from Arkansas. In 1868 he moved to Bee County and bought a large ranch below Beeville, in the conduct of which he was very successful and on which he resided until he came to Frio County in 1882. He made a specialty of raising good horses, and had some of the finest animals in the state at that time. Upon coming to Frio County he purchased a ranch on McGill Creek, twelve miles from Pearsall, and has 6,000 acres under fence. This is the best ranch of its size in the county, and over its broad acres roam a large herd of good graded cattle, horses, mules, etc. Mr. Armstrong's home is in Pearsall, and is commodious and comfortable. He has seen much of Texas, but thinks that Frio County is destined to be the most desirable portion of this great state, and here expects to spend the remainder of his days. He has many friends and is a very desirable and useful citizen.

JACOB HILL.

This old settler and worthy citizen, now living at San Felipe, Tex., has been a resident of this state since his thirteenth year, and during all that time his career has been above reproach, and by judicious and honorable management his affairs have developed to a gratifying magnitude. Mr. Hill owes his nativity to St. Francis County, Ark., born September 15, 1827, and his parents, John and Mary M. (Bollinger) Hill, are natives of Kentucky and Missouri respectively. When a young man John Hill went to Arkansas and was married in St. Francis County of that state in 1825. There his death occurred in 1841, at which time he was living in Pope County. The Bollinger family came from Pope County, Ark., to Texas in 1833, and settled in Jefferson County, remaining there until after the war with Mexico. This family furnished its full quota of men for Texas service, and two of them, our subject's uncles, served in the battle of San Jacinto, Ephriam and Peter, both of whom were privates. Afterward the family moved to Austin County, and there John Bollinger, grandfather of subject, died full of years and honors. He and wife reared a family of eleven children: Ephriam was killed by the Mexicans or Indians about 1839; Conrad, died in this county; Elizabeth, died in Fort Bend County, was the wife of William I. Allbright; Mary M. (mother of subject); Peter, deceased; Sarah, wife of H. B. Littlefield, died in Fort Bend County; Hiram, died in this county; Caroline, married Benjamin Allen and died in this county; Catherine, deceased, was the wife of Mr. Hillyard, who was county clerk of the county for many years; John, Jr., died in this state, and Louie, died in this county. Mrs. Hill left Arkansas and came to Texas in 1842, and, as she found most of her relatives located in this county, decided to settle here too. She made the trip from Pope County, Ark., in wagons, brought her family with her, also her household effects, and although the trip was fraught with danger, she arrived in safety. Here her death occurred in this county in 1855. She was the mother of five children, four of whom reached mature years: Jacob, John of this county; Elizabeth, deceased, was the wife of William Pitts of this county, and George W. died in the Confederate service. Jacob Hill received only a limited education, and most of that after he became a man, and came with his mother to Texas in 1842. When twenty-one years of age he started out for himself as a stockman, and at this made a decided success. During the Civil War he served for a short time in the Confederate army, but hired a substitute and gave his time and attention to stock-raising. Since the war, however, he has given much of his attention to farming, and in 1881 sold off his cattle, 1,800 head, and put the proceeds in land. He now owns 250 acres of land, after giving each of his children a 400-acre tract. Mr. Hill was married in 1854 to Miss Sarah A. Allbright, a native of Arkansas, and daughter of William I. Allbright. Seven children were born to this marriage, one of whom died in infancy: Annie, deceased, was the wife of Arthur Gray; James H.; Georgie E., wife of R. S. Hinsly of this county; George B.; William I; Jacob W., and John, deceased. Mrs. Hill died in 1889. For many years she was an earnest member of the Methodist Episcopal church. In 1893 Mr. Hill married Miss Lorena Davidson of Belton, Tex., and daughter of W. T. and Callie (Smith) Davidson, early settlers of Bell County. She is a member of the Methodist Episcopal church. Mr. Hill takes very little interest in political matters, but votes with the Democratic party. When Mr. Hill first came to the Lone Star State game abounded, and he was in many exciting bear hunts, and had many narrow escapes. He still keeps a relic of those exciting times—the old smooth bore rifle with which he did all his hunting. He has killed hundreds of deer and other animals, bear, panthers, etc., and many of them at where the town of Sealy now stands.

THOMAS STERNE.

In recounting the forces that have combined to make Victoria County, Tex., what it is, more than a passing reference must be made to the life and labors of Thomas Sterne, of whom it may be

truthfully said that no one has done more to lay the foundations of
the county's prosperity deep, and to build upon them surely and
well. He is a product of Bedford, Pa., born February, 1817, and
was the son of Thomas and Jane (Guthrie) Sterne, the father a native of England, and the mother of Scotch descent, but born in
Pennsylvania. The father was sheriff of the county in which he
lived in Pennsylvania for some time, also followed teaching, and
there died in 1817, when our subject was but two weeks old. The
mother received her final summons in Pennsylvania in 1867. Owing
to circumstances over which he had no control, our subject received
but a limited education in youth, and when fourteen years of age he
entered a printing office, serving as an apprentice for seven years
in "the art preservative of arts," in the office of the Bedford "Gazette," where, while learning a trade which might secure for him
a living in the future, he stocked his mind with much and varied
informantion. A bright young man attends a pretty good school
when he works in a newspaper office at the case. This, we think,
Mr. Sterne will admit is true. In 1840, young, in excellent health
and willing to work for the fruition of his hopes, Mr. Sterne removed
to the city of Louisville, Ky., where he worked as a journeyman
printer on the Louisville "City Gazette." Previous to that he was in
the Buckeye State for some time. From Kentucky he went to Arkansas in 1842, and established the "Arkansaw Intelligencer" in the
town of Van Buren, this being the first paper of the town. He was
near Indian Territory, and his paper had a large circulation among
the Indians. In 1845 he made a trip on horseback throughout
Texas, and was over most of the southwestern part of the state. He
passed from San Antonio through the then desert to the gulf, at
Corpus Christi, and over much of the intervening country. Visiting
Victoria he thought it the best place to launch a new enterprise, and
soon had the press, cases, type and other fixtures of his office moved
to that city. There the first number of the "Texan Advocate" was
issued May 2, 1846, and it was the first paper published west of the
Colorado River. Mr. Sterne published this paper until 1853, when,
on account of failing health, he sold out and engaged in stock-raising. The paper is still published here. He bought the present
place, three miles from Victoria, in 1859, and now has a very lovely

home. Mr. Sterne is the owner of about 3,000 acres of good land, all capable of cultivation. He has about 200 acres under cultivation, and can raise thirty-five bushels of corn to the acre. Since 1860 he has only known one failure of crops in this section. He has graded stock, Durham, Holstein, and Hereford cattle, and good blooded hogs. He has held a number of prominent positions in the county—county commissioner, alderman of Victoria, etc., and is prominently identified with every enterprise of note. In the year 1841 he was married to Miss Mary E. Jones of Louisville, Ky., who accompanied him to Texas, and here died in 1853. His second marriage occurred in 1854, to Miss Araminta Cunningham, a daughter of Judge John A. Cunningham. To this union eight children were born, all living: Thomas J., resides in Victoria; May, became the wife of H. D. Sullivan, sheriff of the county, and makes her home in Victoria; Ida, became the wife of F. E. Sibley of Victoria; Wilson C. of Port Lavaca; Minnie, married Eugene Sibley, banker of Victoria; Andrew G., lawyer, living in Rio Grande City, Tex.; Sadie and Ford, still living with the parents. In the year 1839 Mr. Sterne was made a Mason at Flemmingburg, Ky., and in 1846 he was made an Odd Fellow at Newport, Ky. He was one of the charter members of the first Masonic lodge established in Southwest Texas, founded in 1846, Victoria Lodge No. 9, and from this lodge all the lodges of the surrounding counties were founded. Mr. Sterne commenced his apprenticeship in 1831, and is probably the oldest printer in the Lone Star State, and is enjoying the sunset of life surrounded by a loving family and many warm personal friends. The members of this family hold membership in the Presbyterian church.

JUDGE CHARLES RILEY.

This prominent man and able judge of Colorado County, Tex., was born in Princeton, Ky., July 14, 1849, and is a son of Philip Riley, who was born and reared in Madison County, Miss. The father,

Professor Phillip Riley, from his native county went to Princeton, Ky., and entered Cumberland College, and after graduating from this institution, he filled a professorship in his alma mater for some time, then went to Bethel College, Tennessee, where he remained for about six years. In 1856 he came to Texas and located at Columbus, and took charge of what was known as Columbus Female Academy, which school he conducted with marked ability up to the first year of the war, when he entered the Confederate service. For two years he was on detailed duty at Columbus, Tex., as clerk and book-keeper in the commissary department, but after hostilities had ceased he again turned his attention to teaching, first in Colorado College and then in Columbus. Following this he became bookkeeper for the firm of Young & Allen, and continued to fill this position up to the day of his death, in November, 1872, when about fifty-four or fifty-five years of age. He was married to Rose Frazier, who bore him six children and is still living. The immediate subject of this sketch is the eldest of the five now living. Lucy, wife of Robert Ennis, manager of the Aransas Pass Railroad, lives in San Antonio; Ida, wife of Robert Wolters, resides in Columbus, Tex.; Edward E. is secretary and treasurer of the Keith & Perry Coal Co. of Kansas City, Mo.; Philip M. is in Jefferson, Tex., and is a Cumberland Presbyterian minister, and Estelle died in Columbus, the wife of George Atkinson. Judge Charles Riley received his education in the high school of Columbus and in Colorado College, and he also went to school a short time after the war had closed. He then entered the printing office of the Columbus "Times" and later of the "Colorado Citizen," continuing thus occupied for four or five years, or until 1871, at which time he entered the office of the district clerk, and after a time became deputy district clerk of the county. He continued as deputy until February, 1874, when the clerk resigned his office and Mr. Riley was appointed to his place, and continued thus to serve until the present State Constitution was adopted, when he made the race for the office, but was defeated by a small majority. Following this he was deputy in the county clerk's office for two years, and in November, 1878, was elected to the office of county judge, and has held this position ever since, with the exception of the years 1891-92, being again elected to the office in 1892. He has worn the judicial ermine with dignity and ability, has shown the utmost fairness and intelligence in his decisions, and has proven a popular and very efficient officer. In May, 1872, he was married to Miss Sallie M. Grigsby, who was born in Wharton County, Tex., a daughter of William Grigsby, who became a very extensive planter of that county. She died June 18, 1894, having become the mother of three sons and one daughter: Cora, who is a prominent and talented music teacher in Columbus, Tex.; Marion E., Charles ,and Joseph. Judge Riley is a member of the I. O. O. F., Columbus Lodge No. 51; politically is a stanch Democrat, and in his religious views in a Methodist.

JUDGE DON EGBERT ERASTUS BRAMAN.

Nearly eighty years have passed over the head of the venerable man who is the subject of this sketch, leaving their impress in the whitening hair and lined features, but while the outward garments of the soul show the wear and tear of years, the man himself is richer, and nobler, and grander for the experience that each successive decade has brought him. He is an early settler of Matagorda County, Tex., ex-county judge of the same, and is now a resident of Victoria. His birth occurred September 21, 1814, at Norton, Bristol County, Mass., and he is the son of Andrews and Nancy (Hawes) Braman. In tracing the genealogy of the family we find that he is the grandson of Sylvanus and Sarah (Andrews) Braman, great-grandson of Sylvanus and Experience (Blanchard) Braman, great-great-grandson of Daniel and Rachel (Campbel), and great-great-great-grandson of Thomas Braman, who came from England about 1635 and settled in Northern Massachusetts. Andrew Braman, father of our subject, graduated from one of the New England colleges, and although he studied for the bar, did not practice. Instead, he followed agricultural pursuits, and subsequently moved to Providence, R. I., where his death occurred about 1833. The mother followed him to the grave about two years later. The ancestors on both sides were among the Pilgrims. Judge Braman was educated in Providence, R. I., and in 1833 went to Georgia, where he remained until 1835. He then went to what is now Eufaula and participated in a raid against the Cherokee Indians. In 1836 he went to New Orleans and the following year came to Texas with a lot of volunteers for the Texan army. Landing at Matagorda, he soon went out and joined the army at Camp Johnson, in Jackson County, and was in service twelve months. From there he went to Matagorda and became a custom officer for about a year. In 1847 he was appointed clerk of the First Judicial District Court, and, studying law while he held that office, was admitted to the bar of that court in 1853. Afterward he practiced his profession for years. For several years he was mayor of Matagorda, and was appointed county judge by Governor Pease. He was greatly opposed to the war, and wrote articles against it during the time. Judge Braman is the owner of large tracts of land in the county, thousands of acres of the most fertile portions, and to some extent has been engaged in stock raising. On the 28th of April, 1841, he was married to Miss Mary Elizabeth, daughter of George Burkhart, a native of Philadelphia, who came to Texas in 1839. The following children were born to this union: Nancy, died in childhood; Erastus, died in manhood; George, died in 1852; Daniel Hawes, died in 1861; Alexander, educated and became a lawyer; William Cheever, resides in Matagorda, was educated at Andover and at home, studied law with his father, was admitted to the bar in 1877, and owns land in Matagorda County, and a large number of cattle; Mary Elizabeth; Nancy Hawes; Catherine Burkhart, died in 1892; Daniel Hawes, and Julia. Daniel Hawes was educated at Victoria and New Orleans, studied medicine at Tulane University, New Orleans, and is now practicing in Victoria. Our subject is a member of the Catholic church, but Mrs. Braman and most of the children hold membership in the Episcopal church. Formerly Judge Braman had a large law practice, but he has now retired from the active duties of life, and makes his home partly in Victoria, where he has a handsome residence, and partly in Matagorda.

BISHOP ALEXANDER GREGG.

(Deceased.)

Alexander Gregg, first Episcopal bishop of Texas, was born in the Darlington District of South Carolina, October 8, 1819, at Society Hill. He was a descendant of the famous Highland clan, the Mc-Gregors, whose heroic deeds have been told in song and story. Not long after the time of Cromwell a fragment of this clan moved from the North of Scotland to Londonderry, Ireland, whence the immigration to America took place. The name underwent a gradual and easy transformation from McGregor to Gregg, and in 1752 the name under this last form first appeared on the Pedee River. From the brothers, John and Joseph, descended the large connection of the name. From Joseph came David, the father of our subject. The Greggs of that early day in America were men of force and enterprise, and became locally famous in the Indian wars, and in the War of the Revolution. Rev. B. A. Rogers knew Bishop Gregg long and closely, and from the memorial sermon delivered by him we gather the following facts, best told in his graceful and gracious words: "At the age of nineteen the young Alexander, a stalwart youngster, straight as an arrow, without the taint of a single bad habit and inheriting in a marked degree much of the mental, moral and physical structure peculiar to his Scotch ancestors, graduated with first honors at South Carolina College, was soon after admitted to the bar, and commenced the study of law at Cheraw. As a lawyer his practice was not long, but said to have been successful. Up to the age of twenty-four years he seemed to have no special religious tendencies, but at that time, while upon a visit to relatives, his attention being unexpectedly and pointedly called to the claims of both religion and church, he returned home, gave himself for some days to solitude, thought, prayer and study, and then announced his determination to renounce the profession of law and enter the ministry. This was in 1843, and the same year he was baptized and confirmed, and at once became a candidate for holy orders. In 1846,

at St. David's Church, Cheraw, he was ordained deacon, and at St.
Phillip's Church, Charleston, on the 10th of December, 1847, he was
ordained to the priesthood, both by Bishop Gadsden of South Carolina.   During the convention of 1859, though he was personally unknown to any member of that body, upon the high recommendation
of Bishops Elliott of Georgia and Davis of South Carolina, Mr.
Gregg was put in nomination, and upon the first ballot every clerical
vote but two was given to him, and he was unanimously confirmed
by that body.   Yet he himself knew nothing of such an effort being in contemplation until after his election, and then, according
to the bishop of Tennessee, first learned from the lips of one who
was sitting behind him in the convention of the Diocese of South
Carolina that was then in session, who whispered over his shoulder
the news just received, that to him was so bewildering and so fateful.
With those who knew him best there was no question as to what
he would do.   It was not his first trial.   Though his parish was the
oldest field of legal labor, it was the seat of his early friendships, the
home of his friends.   His family was around him there, and always
with him, and his heart was in Cheraw.   Texas was far away, almost boundless, almost trackless; with little to offer but endless
work, limitless fatigue and constant separation from his wife and
children.   And he came, having been consecrated in Memorial
Church, Richmond, during the session of the general convention
there in 1859.   The election of a stranger, utterly unknown to any-
body in the diocese had naturally given occasion to some little adverse comment, and it is not strange that his arrival should have
been anticipated with some anxiety.   But when he came his very
appearance set all hearts at rest.   Of good size and fine form, erect,
open-browed, clear-eyed, of manly and dignified bearing, speaking
according to his own convictions, yet guarded in form and manner
of expression; cool and collected, but decided and self-confident;
claiming no infallibility, but tenacious of the right and dignity of
his position, he was everywhere accepted at his true value, as every
inch a man, every ounce a Bishop.   Before the meeting of the dio-
cesan convention in 1860, the Bishop, with his family, had settled
in Austin, and began his work by the publication of a pastoral letter
in the newspapers, in which he invited correspondence with every

member of the church throughout the state. And in reply to the great number of answers received, he sent back letters filling each particular case, and all written with his own hand, and eventually he visited every place and nearly every family from which those letters had been received. And what he did then was but the beginning of a work that ended only with his life, and up to 1874, when the diocese was divided, with no curtailment of limits either in territory or hardships, for, though railroads and stage lines had multiplied, so had country parishes, missions and families. So that still his visitations were made by every type of conveyance known to our frontier life, and a large proportion of the nights, as well as the days, of each year were spent upon the road. During his whole official life his visitations were not simply from parish to parish, but literally from house to house. He was not content to know the leading persons of the church, but he knew them all, could call them by name, and was familiar with their personal affairs, hopes and anxieties. In every family his coming was a pleasure, the father honored, the mother revered and the children loved him. Even his Sunday school catechisms were so seasoned with something unexpected and pleasurable that the children looked forward to them from year to year as times of especial enjoyment. Of the outcome of his long labors here I can do no better than to compare the beginning with the end. At the convention of 1860 (his first) the statistical showing of the diocese was: Number of communicants, so gathered as to be capable of tabulation, 456; clergy, 14. At that convention, in his first address, the Bishop showed a clear comprehension of the work he had undertaken. He adverted to the salient points of duty, put himself into the van, sounded a bugle call for advance, and unfalteringly led the missionary work for the thirty-three years. When at last literally worn out in the work, he fell by the way, and from the middle of his last visitation, he went home to die, he could count within the limits of his old diocese more than sixty clergymen. In preaching Christ he never forgot his church, and his giant shoulders carried such weight as no other man in the American church ever bore. But there was no shrinking or turning back, no repinings, no regrets for the choice that had placed them upon him. His heart was larger than his load, and he loved every ounce of its weight and rejoiced in every effort that it demanded. At his home in Austin, surrounded by his children, he passed away July 10 1898." Bishop Gregg married Miss Charlotte Wilson, daughter of Oliver H. and Sarah (Wilson) Kollock. Oliver H. Kollock was a native of Massachusetts, who in his young manhood emigrated to South Carolina. In early life he was a lawyer, but later a farmer. His ancestors came over on the Mayflower. Of ten children born to Bishop Gregg, only five survive him: David, a prosperous merchant of Luling; Wilson, a lawyer of Fort Worth; two widowed daughters, Mrs. Wilmerding and Mrs. Cochran, residing at Sewanee, and Oliver Hawes Gregg, a farmer and stock raiser of Guadalupe County, who was born in Cheraw, S. C., September 12, 1845, where his boyhood was spent and his education received. At the age of seventeen (after removal to Texas a short time prior to the breaking out of Civil War) the last named entered the Confederate service as first lieutenant, with a recruiting commission. He was soon transferred to Baylor's Texas Rangers, and saw duty on the frontier. He was in the last battle of the war at Brownsville. At that time he was serving in Carrington's Company, Ford's Regiment. After the war he clerked in San Antonio some time, and in December, 1866, he was placed in charge of a branch house at Prairie Lea, established by his San Antonio house. In 1871 he bought the place upon which he now resides, and with an interval of seven years, during which time he was associated with his brother, David, in the mercantile business in Luling, has led the life of a planter. He married November 7, 1867, Miss Margaret Amelia Rector, a daughter of Pendleton Rector, a native of Alabama, who emigrated to Brazoria County in 1831, and was conspicuous in all the Mexican and Indian troubles during the Confederation and the Republic. He was at the battle of San Jacinto, and served as courier to Sam Houston, when the duties of the position were equivalent to running the gauntlet. He was the owner of a letter patent from his government for services rendered, and was a man of great bravery. He died in Guadalupe County in March, 1888. Two gentle and cultured daughters and a promising son grace the hospitable home of Mr. and Mrs. O. H. Gregg: Mary E., Charlotte W., and Alexander Pendleton.

ISAAC H. JULIAN.

Among the earlier Western poets the name of Isaac H. Julian
was once familiar and is still remembered. He began writing in boyhood, and his productions appeared in various publications, notably
the Ladies' Repository, Cincinnati, and the National Era, Washington, D. C. Of the latter John G. Whittier was corresponding editor,
and in it Mrs. Stowe's "Uncle Tom's Cabin" first appeared as a serial.
Other contributors were the Cary sisters, "Grace Greenwood," etc.,
with whose names that of the subject of this sketch was honorably
associated. The Julian family is of French extraction in the paternal
line, and dates 200 years in America. Prior to the Revolution, the
progenitors resided in Maryland, Virginia and North Carolina. Isaac
Julian, father of the poet and the third of that name in regular succession, was a native of the state last named, and removed in 1808 to
that part of Indiana Territory known as Wayne County. The year
following he married Rebecca, a daughter of Andrew Hoover, a
member of the Society of Friends, also from North Carolina. Isaac
and Rebecca Julian settled on a farm near Centerville, the county
seat, and endured all the privations of pioneer life during the war of
1812, when Indians and wild beasts were among their frequent visitors. In 1822 Mr. Julian was a member of the Indiana Legislature,
which then convened at Corydon. The subject of this sketch was
born June 19, 1823. In the fall of that year the father removed his
family to what is now the county of Tippecanoe, where he died in the
December following, and his widow and young family returned to
their relatives in Wayne County. In consequence of this disaster,
their subsequent lot was a hard one. The opportunities for obtaining an education were limited to the log school houses, and a few
sessions in these comprised the school attendance of Isaac Julian, Jr.
But this was fairly supplemented by self education. In the intervals

from farm labor he early accomplished quite an extensive course of reading in the departments of history and general literature. Mr. Julian resided in Iowa from the spring of 1846 to the fall of 1850. Heretofore his poetic effusions had been casual and desultory. But in 1848 he became deeply interested in the political and social upheavals of that period, more especially in the anti-slavery cause. These gave inspiration to many of his subsequent poems. Later he studied law and in 1851 was admitted to the bar, but found the practice so distasteful that he did not long engage in it. In 1854 he went to Fort Wayne, and for a short time edited the Standard of that city. In 1857 he prepared and published an interesting pamphlet of the "Early History of the Whitewater Valley." In 1858 he bought the "True Republican" newspaper, at Centerville, and removed it to Richmond in 1865, afterward changing the name to the "Radical," and continuing its publication to the fall of 1872. He was postmaster at Centerville during Lincoln's first term, and at Richmond from May, 1869, to July, 1871. He was married in 1859 to Miss Virginia M. Spillard of College Hill, O., by whom he had five children, three of whom survive. Because of his wife's failing health, he removed in the summer of 1873 to San Marcos, Tex., and began the publication of the "Free Press," from which he retired in August, 1890. His wife died a few months after his arrival in Texas, leaving a family of young children to his care. Thus engrossed with an exacting business and severe domestic cares and trials, Mr. Julian for many years had very small opportunity for the gratification of his literary taste.

The above biographical sketch appeared in the Magazine of Poetry of Buffalo, N. Y., for January, 1892, in connection with selections from the poems of Mr. Julian. To render it more complete, it should be added that in 1872 he allied himself with the Liberal movement for national reconciliation, led by Horace Greeley as its candidate for president, and thereafter acted with the Democratic party down to 1892, when he identified himself with the People's party, the leading principles of which had received his life-long advocacy, and began the publication at San Marcos of the "People's Era," in which he is still engaged. In 1893 he was again married, the lady of his choice being Mrs. Belle McCoy Harvey of Minnesota.

ROBERT WILLIAM PIERCE.

In tilling the soil and in raising stock he whose name heads this sketch has shown excellent judgment, and being also persevering and progressive he has made the most of every opportunity that has presented itself, which tended to benefit him financially, the result being that he has accumulated a good property. He was born in Tuscaloosa, Ala., January 25, 1827, the fourth of nine children born to John King and Sarah Oldham (Finch) Peirce, the former of whom was born in Cork, Ireland. He came to America in his young manhood. In 1821 he settled in Tuscaloosa, Ala., where he conducted an oyster saloon and restaurant. After accumulating sufficient funds he opened a confectionary and notion store. In 1838 he removed to Columbus, Miss., where he continued the same business until reverses in fortune overtook him. His friends elected him magistrate, and he obtained prominence in this capacity. He was a member of the I. O. O. F. and of the A. F. & A. M. In the former order he was a member of the Encampment. He was very active and prominent in Masonic circles. He was reared a Roman Catholic, but while in Columbus, under the preaching of Dr. Daniel Baker, he was converted, and joined the Cumberland Presbyterian Church. He died in March, 1855, and was buried by the Masons and Odd Fellows in Columbus. His wife was born in Newport, R. I., but she met Mr. Peirce in Baltimore, and married him there. She died in 1869, and was buried by her husband's side. The boyhood days of Robert William Peirce were chiefly spent in Columbus, and his education was received principally at the old Franklin Academy there. After leaving school he entered the printing office in Columbus; after three years he went into the drug business. In the fall of 1848 he removed to Mobile, Ala., where he continued in the same business, pursuing it with reasonable financial results until the spring of 1853, when he came to Texas, landing in Galveston. From thence, after a short stay there, to Indianola; thence to Lavaca, Petersburg, Gonzales, and up the beautiful San Marcos River to Prairie Lea, to Lock-

hart, and finally settling in Austin. His brother, John K., a daguer-
reotypist, accompanied him to Texas. At the places above named
they took pictures with good success. His object in thus traveling was to find a suitable location and enter the drug business again,
but becoming convinced that it was his duty to preach the gospel he
applied to the Quarterly Conference of Austin Station, Texas Conference, March, 1855, and was licensed, Rev. Daniel Morse, presiding elder, and Rev. James Wesson, preacher in charge, as secretary,
signing the license. In the interim, before the session of the Texas
Annual Conference in December of the same year, he was employed
to preach on the Fayetteville circuit by Rev. Homer S. Thrall, D. D.
He made his home with Dr. Thrall and his estimable lady. Besides
the study of theology, he studied moral and intellectual philosophy,
rhetoric, and composition; reciting lessons in these last to the wife
of Dr. Halsey at Rutersville College. She was a most accomplished
teacher. Mr. Peirce had received instructions from her twenty years
before this in Tuscaloosa, Ala. Before the meeting of the annual
conference at Galveston in December, same year, his quarterly conference recommended him as a suitable candidate for membership.
He was received. His first appointment was on both sides of Galveston Bay; second, Kerrville circuit; third, Perdinales circuit;
fourth, Oakville circuit; a part of this last year, 1859, he had charge
of Corpus Christi Station. Although not an eminent preacher, he
was a good pastor, and revivals resulted from his zeal for the salvation of souls. The two years that he traveled in the mountains
—1857 and 1858—he had not only to put his trust in God, but "keep
his powder dry." It was an Indian country. Roving bands of
them made frequent forays on the frontier settlements for the purpose of theft. Coming down their wonted trails during the full of
the moon they would carry off the horses of the settlers, sometimes
sneaking up very near the house where a horse had been tethered,
cutting the rope, thus securing him for their own use. They were
very cunning. It is customary on the frontier for the "cowboys"
to take with them on their hunt for stock a number of cow ponies.
When in camp these are generally herded, and if discovered by these
diablos—as the Mexicans call them—they tie to the tail of one of
their horses a dry cow's hide and dash through the herd, stamped-

ing them. Then they are almost sure to get some of them Exposed as he was among them, it was prudent that he should be prepared to defend himself. One good man, a Methodist local preacher, on his circuit in 1858, thought he ought not to carry a gun, but put his "trust in God." In a few months after this advice was given this same good man, Rev. Jonas Dancer, was killed by the Indians. They are cowardly. If they are discovered while on their forays they invariably try to kill the person; if not, they do not molest them. This conduct is for the purpose of evading pursuit. He did not get sight of an Indian during the two years, but on several occasions saw fresh signs of them. In 1857 he was on two scouts after them; once with Mr. Alonzo Reese, who had been out early in the morning to look for his oxen. About one mile from his home—where Mr. Peirce had spent the night—he discovered moccasin tracks. He came back hurriedly. Mr. Peirce, being the only man at hand, went back with him. They discovered the tracks, which led toward a high mountain, and they climbed it, where they saw the two moccasin tracks, one very large, the other very small. These were noted tracks; had often been seen on the frontier, but could never be overtaken. Another time he accompanied a party of eight others to the headwaters of the Guadalupe. The main object was to find the bones of two young men who had been killed by the Indians, a few months before, in order to give them decent sepulture. At the same time they kept a close watch for Indians. They did not see any recent signs, nor did they find the bones of the unfortunate young men. At the time of this sad affair above spoken of Mr. Spencer Goss, who was one of the party, was severely wounded, his thigh being broken by the Indian's bullet, and thought by his family and friends to be dead; but after nineteen days, crawling through the Cedar Mountains, he reached Kerrville, twenty-five miles from the scene of conflict. He subsisted during this time on wild grapes. This party of young men had become careless, and had placed most of their guns out of reach. While eating their breakfast the Indians crawled up and secured their guns and opened fire on them. Mr. Goss met with one thrilling adventure while on his arduous trip. He was confronted by a large black bear, and for some time the menacing attitude of bruin was such that he despaired of life, but he was unharmed, and left to pursue his painful journey. On an occasion that Mr. Peirce accompanied his presiding elder, Dr. H. S. Thrall, to a quarterly and camp meeting near San Saba, the wife of Dr. Thrall, who was with him, thought she discovered an Indian dodge into a cedar thicket, about one hundred yards ahead of them. They halted and consulted what was best to do. The conclusion was, as they had only one six-shooter between them, to return a few miles to get a gun, which they did, and returning, Mr. Peirce suggested, and they placed a long stick having the appearance of a gun in the front part of the vehicle, while he carried the borrowed gun on his horse. They reached their destination without molestation. Mrs. Thrall seemed as little frightened as either of the trio. Once, as Mr. Peirce was going to Bandera to preach, near by the Bandera Pass, he thought he discovered an Indian attempting to cut him off; the person was too far off to be distinguished. His first impulse was to put spurs to his fine mare and make his escape; a second thought, there is only one, and having a Sharp's rifle, he could make a good fight. It was only a cowboy wishing to make inquiries. Only a short time before this Indians had attacked a citizen in the suburbs of Bandera, killing a man with a spear. At the annual conference held in Goliad in the latter part of 1859 Mr. Peirce located with the intention of returning on a visit to his mother in Columbus, Miss., but on account of the Goliad "Messenger" being left without printers (they having volunteered to go to the Rio Grande to join Colonel John S. Ford's command to help subdue Cortinas, the notorious Mexican bandit), the proprietor, Rev. A. F. Fox, prevailed on Rev. H. S. Horton and Mr. R. W. Peirce, to remain a short time with him till he could procure printers. It was almost impossible to get them, and he made a reasonable offer to sell a half interest to Mr. Peirce, which he accepted, deferring the contemplated visit till the fall of 1860. His connection with the paper as publisher, then editor, continued till 1866. He then itinerated three years more, and taught school two years. When the great Civil War opened, he entered the Confederate service as chaplain in Colonel Tom Green's Regiment, Sibley Brigade. On their way to Arizona, near the Rio Grande River, it was reported to Colonel Green that Indians were seen on a mountain to the left. The Colonel sent a scout of men under command of St. Clough to attend to them. This was a false alarm. Before reaching Fort Thorn, he was preaching to the soldiers one night, and when about half through the sermon, tattoo was sounded for roll-call, when he dismissed them with the benediction. Next morning he informed the Colonel that he would resign his office as chaplain as soon as the expected fight at Fort Thorn took place. Colonel Green was a kind, genial, generous hearted man, and why he permitted Divine service to be interrupted has always been a mystery to Mr. Peirce. The Colonel thought that he ought to remain with them, but Mr. Peirce thought it too personal. After the fight at Val Verde—one mile above Fort Thorn—in which Mr. Peirce connected himself with Captain Campbell's Company to participate in the battle, he returned to Texas. A short time after this General H. A. McCulloch left with a body guard for Arkansas, where he took command of a division of troops. Jesse Boring, M. D. and D. D., was appointed chief surgeon of the division. Mr. Peirce was employed to purchase medicine, and act as druggist for Dr. Boring temporarily, expecting to get a chaplaincy when there was a vacancy. When encamped on the waters of White River, in Arkansas, the death rate was large in the division. Mr. Peirce contracted rheumatism, and was failing in health, when Dr Boring advised him to return to Texas. The Doctor and Mr. Peirce were intimate friends, and he assured him that men were dying in camps, whose pulse indicated no disease. Mr. Peirce himself felt that he would die if he remained in Arkansas; and he says that the atmosphere at times during his stay there had to him a putrid odor. He returned to Goliad, Tex., where in a short time a company of cadets was formed. These were youths from sixteen to eighteen years of age, the commanding officers being older men. Some of the parents of these youths were solicitous for Mr. Peirce to accompany them, to look after their morals, etc. Lieutenant Colonel Fulcrod was anxious for his presence with them. He went and acted as chaplain for the battalion without a commission. But it was not long, victory perching on the banner of the Stars and Stripes, they were disbanded to return home. These young soldiers were called "the seed corn of the Confederacy." Mr. Peirce became a member of the Masonic fraternity at the age of twenty-one in Columbus, Miss.,

and is now a member of Hardeman Lodge No. 179, Luling, Tex.
He also joined the "Temple of Honor" at the age of seventeen in
Columbus, Miss., and is yet a teetotaler. Politically he is a Popu-
list, believing that a reform in our government is essential to its
prosperity. He was married December 18, 1871, to Mrs. Fannie
Appling, widow of Mr. Frank M. Appling, daughter of Mastin and
Sarah Gane (Martin) Ussery. She is a native of Tennessee. They
emigrated to Texas in 1852. The father died in 1883, but the mother
still survives. Mrs. Peirce became the mother of one child by her
first husband, whom she named Collie Frank. Her last union has
resulted in the birth of four children: John Mastin, Sarah Fannie,
Mary Roberta, and Annie Louisa Finch. He still preaches as a local preacher when his health permits. His home is in Guadalupe
County, five miles west of Luling, Tex. His wife, by her frugality
and industry, assisted much in his prosperity.

GENERAL WILLIAM HUGH YOUNG.

One of the professions of life which seems to require a particular
adaptability and natural gift is that of the lawyer. It is one of the
most highly honored as well as most exacting ones. It requires an
abundance of legal lore to gain the plane of success, but when that
plane is once reached, the reward of patient study and work is a
goodly and honorable one. A gentleman particularly gifted in this
way, who has chosen San Antonio, Tex., as the favored place wherein
to practice his profession, is General William H. Young, an old soldier and a prominent real estate man. He is a native of Missouri,
born January 1, 1838, to the union of Hugh F. and Fannie Hampton
(Gibson) Young, both natives of Virginia, the former born in Augusta
and the latter in Montague County. Hugh F. Young followed merchandising and farming in his native state until 1834, and then

moved to Yazoo County, Miss. There he married Miss Gibson and subsequently went to Missouri, but only remained there a short time, when he came to Texas via Arkansas, and in 1841 settled at Clarksville, Red River County. There he followed farming and business enterprises, and became a prominent politician, holding the office of chief justice of Red River County. In 1853 he moved to Grayson County, where he held the same position, and was one of the representative men. When the Civil War broke out he was commissioned brigadier-general of the reserved force by the Governor. In 1863 he moved to Palestine, and from there to San Antonio in the fall of 1864, making his home there until his death in 1888. His wife, the mother of our subject, died in 1842, and his second union was with Miss Electa Alexander, who bore him one child, Newton Alexander, and who died at the time of this child's birth. Mr. Young's third union occurred in 1849 with Miss Sarah E. Rainey. One son was born to this union, Frank E., who is now deceased. The original of this notice was educated in Texas and at Nashville, Washington College, being in the latter three years. For two years after this he was in Mackenzie College, Clarksville, Tex., and then entered the University of Virginia for a five years' course. However, two years later he was compelled to leave on account of the Civil War, and he returned to Texas, where he enlisted on the first call of the government for infantry troops. He was at once elected captain of Company C, Ninth Texas Infantry, and started for Bowling Green, Ky. At Memphis he received orders to go to North Mississippi, where he participated in the battle of Shiloh. Immediately after this terrible engagement he was elected colonel of the regiment, and participated in the battle of Chickamauga, and was afterward in all the battles of that campaign. During the battle of Murfreesboro the regiment joined the army of Jos. E. Johnston, in Mississippi, where he was wounded. For a time he was in the hospital at Columbus, but joined his regiment before the battle of Chickamauga, where he was badly wounded in the chest. After this he was unfit for duty until the middle of December, when he joined the army at Meridian, Miss. In March, 1864, he went to Richmond on military business, but later rejoined the army and was all through the Atlanta campaign in all the battles. At Atlanta, Ga., General M. D. Etor, in command of our subject's brigade, was wounded and Colonel Young was promoted to brigadier-general August 15, 1864, and was in command of the brigade until the surrender of Atlanta. He was with General Hood in his campaign northward, and was with General French in his battle at Altoona Heights on the Georgia Railroad, on October 5 and 6. At that place he was wounded and left on the battlefield for some time. Two days later he was captured and placed in a hospital, and still later sent to Johnson's Island, where he was released July 25, 1865. He then came to Texas and joined his father at San Antonio. Immediately he began the study of law and was admitted to the bar April, 1866, soon after beginning to practice with his father-in-law. They were also engaged in the real estate business, and have shown themselves gentlemen of prime ability, honor and conservatism. On the 3d of November, 1869, he was married to Miss Fannie M. Kemper of Virginia, and one son, Hugh Hampton, has been born to this union. This son is now a student of the University, where he ranks high.

JESSE J. HARRISON.

Prominent among the people of Colorado County, Tex., who have made for themselves honorable names, and who have acquired a competency of this world's goods largely through their own unaided efforts, is the gentleman whose name forms the heading of this sketch. He has always interested himself in the political affairs of this section, and has for some time ably filled the office of district clerk of the county. He was born in Obion County, Tenn., September 7, 1850, and is a son of Dr. Jesse Harrison, for a sketch of whom see the biography of Dr. R. H. Harrison. Jesse J. Harrison spent his school days in his native county and in Leake County, Miss., and at the age of twenty years became a salesman in a general store in Dunklin County, Mo., and was there married to Miss Abbie Sheets, and as a wedding trip started from Southeast Missouri for Texas in a

E. MULLEN.

wagon. After reaching the Lone Star State he farmed in Grayson County for four years, then came to Columbus, Colorado County, and, after remaining in his father's office for some time, was elected to the position of city marshal, and filled this position with marked ability for six years, at the end of which time he was elected district clerk, and since then has attended to the duties of that office with efficiency and to the entire satisfaction of all concerned. Mr. Harrison is personally very popular, for he is not only cordial and sincere in manners, but he endeavors to do his duty at all times; is an honorable, upright gentleman and a true and devoted friend. Mrs. Harrison's people were residing in Clarkson, Mo., at the time of her birth. To her marriage with Mr. Harrison five children have been given: Maggie, Robert H., William and Ed., living, and Lily, who died when quite young. Mrs. Harrison and her daughter Maggie are earnest and active members of the Baptist church, and the entire family move in the best social circles of the place, and their home is a pretty and hospitable one. Mr. Harrison has always been noted for his social disposition, and socially is a member of the I. O. O. F. and the K. of P.

E. MULLEN.

He whose name heads this sketch has charge of the interests of "Uncle Sam" at Yoakum, Tex., and has proved himself in every way worthy the trust reposed in him. He was born on the Isle of Erin, and, like his countrymen, he possesses much natural mother wit and versatility, and that he is a substantial and useful citizen is a self-evident fact. In 1849, when he was but one year old, he was brought by his parents, Barney and Mary (Murray) Mullen, to the United States, and in the "Hoosier State" they settled and engaged in farming in Martin County. There the father died in 1867 and the mother in 1856. E. Mullen was reared to the honorable and useful calling of the farmer, and while pursuing his laborious duties he learned many useful lessons, chief among which was energy and perseverance, but, unfortunately, was denied the privilege of obtaining a scholastic education, with the exception of about twelve months. He was engaged in farm labor until he was about twenty-eight years of age, when he turned his attention to coal mining in Indiana, a calling which occupied his attention for about two years. He was very anxious to give his services to the Union cause in 1862, enlisted in the service and went to Indianapolis, but owing to his extreme youth he was rejected by the officials. In 1868 he began the study of telegraphy, and soon after secured work on the Cairo & Vincennes Railroad, with which he was connected for eight years at station and telegraph work. He was then for some time stationed at Columbia, Ill., as employe on the Cairo & St. Louis Railroad, but after a short time returned to the Cairo & Vincennes Railroad, with which he remained two years more. In 1882 he came to Austin, Tex., as operator for the Texas & Great Northern Railroad for four months, was then located at San Diego for six months, was twelve months with the Mexican National Railroad at Santa Catarina, Mexico, was then at Lampazos, Mexico, with the same road two years, was with the F. C. I. M. R. R. twelve months at Sabinas, Mexico, at the end of which time he went to San Antonio, Tex. He was the agent, operator and train dispatcher for the S. A. & A. P. there, the first agent that road had at any point. For the same road he went to Kennedy Junction as agent and operator, but after a short time returned to Mexico, and for four months was the operator at Monterey. He was next connected with the G. C. & S. F. R. R. at Ballinger, Tex., for about a year and a half, and in 1889 went to Lexington, Tex., and was for some time with the S. A. & A. P. again, where he filled the position of station agent and operator. While there, and during the administration of President Harrison, he was appointed postmaster of Yoakum, receiving his commission July 1, 1890. He has greatly advanced the revenue of the office by placing boxes on the street to secure the mail that was usually posted on the train, and in six months' time the office was raised in grade to a presidential office, and in other ways has greatly advanced in importance, owing to Mr. Mullen's labor and push. Mr. Mullen has been quite active in political matters, and in 1892 was a delegate to the Fort Worth Republican convention. He was a candidate for mayor of Yoakum and received a majority of votes, but by a typographical error in the printing of four tickets lost the office. He has shown the greatest interest in the prosperity of Yoakum, owns considerable real estate in and about the place, and is one of the most substantial and highly respected citizens of the town. He is an efficient postmaster, and higher honors await him in the way of political preferment. He has made an enviable reputation for himself in all locations where his lot has been cast, and as a railroad man was efficient, trustworthy and intelligent, and a favorite with the officials of the different roads with which he was connected. He was married to Miss Mary Fonkhauser of Illinois in 1880, and by her became the father of four children, all of whom are deceased. Mr. Mullen is a member of the Catholic church, while his wife is a Lutheran. Socially Mr. Mullen is a member of the A. F. and A. M., and is a charter member of Yoakum Lodge No. 348 of the I. O. O. F.

CLARENCE W. M'NEIL.

The Daily News of Laredo, Webb County, Tex., is ably edited and successfully managed by Clarence W. McNeil, and the paper finds a warm welcome in all the best homes of this section. Mr. McNeil owes his nativity to Woodville, Tyler County, Tex., where he first saw the light on the 31st of December, 1859, the youngest of four children born to Dr. William L. and Victoria (McNeil) McNeil, natives of Ohio and Florida respectively. The father was a graduate of the Medical Department of Yale University, and began the practice of his noble and useful calling in the state of his birth, but in 1853 left his old home to come to Texas, and took up his residence in Colorado County. Here he was eventually united in marriage with Miss McNeil, who had come to this state with her parents in 1846.

Later they removed to Wharton County, and after residing there for
some time, came to Tyler County, and here Dr. McNeil successfully
practiced his profession, and also conducted a drug and commercial
business in the town of Tyler, his career in these lines being closed
only by the hand of death in 1873. During the great struggle between the North and South he served in the Confederate army as a
surgeon, and was always a strong Southern sympathizer, although
Northern born. His wife was called from life February, 1860, when
the subject of this sketch was but six weeks old, after which Dr. Mc-
Neil married a second time, his wife being a Miss Moir. When the
subject of this sketch was one year old he was placed in charge of his
maternal grandmother at St. Mary's, Refugio County, but shortly
after the family removed to San Antonio, and there resided until
1865, at which time Live Oak County became their home, and continued such up to 1868, when they once more made a change, this
time taking up their abode in Rockport, the county seat of Aransas
County. After Clarence McNeil had attended school for about
eight years he was sent to Gonzales and became an apprentice on the
Gonzales Enquirer, under Editor S. W. Smith, but about one year
later he went to Galveston and worked on the Galveston News for
several years. He then returned to Live Oak County and established
the Lagarto Echo, which he sold out after conducting it for one year,
and since 1883 has resided in Laredo. He worked on the Times as a
printer for some time, and subsequently as editor. From 1885 to
1887 he was engaged in "teaching the young idea" in Webb County,
after which he engaged in merchandising in Laredo, which occupation he successfully followed for five years. Following this he became the editor of the Laredo News, which position he has since very
acceptably, faithfully and ably filled. He has been constantly in the
newspaper business, as editor, reporter or correspondent, since his
early boyhood, and at various times has represented the New York
Herald, the St. Louis Globe-Democrat and Republic, the Chicago
Times, the New Orleans Picayune, the Galveston News, the Houston
Post and San Antonio Express. He is an honorary member of the
San Antonio International Typographical Association. In his political views he has always been a staunch Democrat, an active
worker for the party, and has been delegate to many conventions. On

the 4th of March, 1888, he was married to Miss Pinkie Taylor of Laredo, to which union three children have been given: Edna Victoria, Clarence Wallace and Brewer Taylor. Mrs. McNeil is a member of the Episcopal church.

JUDGE WILLIAM J. PHILLIPS.

Judge William J. Phillips is one of Wharton County's most respected citizens; his private character is one to be admired and loved, his public record is without a blemish. Throughout his career he has been actuated by pure motives and manly principles, and by following a fixed purpose to make the most and best of himself he has overcome many difficulties and risen step by step to a place of influence and honor among public-spirited and high-minded men. He came to Texas in 1837 with Lieutenant-Governor Albert C. Horton, and this state has continued to be his home up to the present. Judge Phillips is a native Virginian, born in Fredericksburg in 1828, and when but a child was left fatherless, his father, William J. Phillips, dying in Alabama, whither he had moved to get a start after losing all his means on security debts. Young Phillips received the principal part of his education in Alabama, and after his parents died was adopted by Governor Horton, who subsequently moved to Texas, accompanied by our subject. Here the latter attended school as opportunity offered, first at Columbia and later at Matagorda. He was associated with Governor Horton in all his expeditions against the Indians and Mexicans on the frontier during the Mexican War, and went with the latter to Austin, where he was in the attorney-general's office; later he joined the company of spies and scouts in the army of Ben McCulloch, under General Taylor, and in that capacity furnished the army much valuable information. Bold and determined, with a courage that never failed, he entered upon his career

as a spy, and although placed in many trying and hair-raising positions, knew no such word as fail. He and General Ben McCulloch,
with much coolness, entered General Santa Anna's lines and became
possessed of such information that General Taylor was enabled to
conquer the enemy. This was a very dangerous undertaking for Mr.
Phillips, for certain death awaited him if captured, and at one time
he was chased by the Mexicans, but succeeded in getting back in
time to notify General Taylor that the whole army was coming. Mr.
Phillips was orderly sergeant of McCulloch's spy company, and as
he had for many years been fighting Mexicans and Indians, he was
used to their ways and wonderfully successful as a spy. This all
happened before our subject was of age, and he is the only member
of the company now living. At one time, while riding along, he had
his saddle perforated with bullets, but he himself escaped uninjured.
Mr. Phillips received his discharge in 1847, and soon after, when
General Taylor was elected President of the United States, our subject was appointed collector of customs at the port of Matagorda,
which position he held during Taylor's and Fillmore's administra-
tions, and was re-appointed by Pierce. Later he began his career as
a merchant at Matagorda, on a very extensive scale, shipping sugar
and cotton to New York City. After the storm of 1854, when Matagorda was destroyed, Mr. Phillips moved to Wharton, where he was
about the first merchant. He received the contract from the state
to clean Colorado River from the mouth, and this he did, making it
navigable to Wharton. Next he received the contract to grade a
railroad, with Colonel D. Hardeman, to Columbia, and finished that
contract just before the war, but the rails were not laid on account of
the war. During this trying time Mr. Phillips opposed secession. He
held the office of county judge for a time, and when the war cloud
was the darkest he went to Matamoras, Mexico, and remained there
until peace was declared. He and Governor Horton differed in but
two particulars—secession and the railroad. Mr. Phillips, not favor-
ing disunion, voted against secession, but as his was the only vote
of the kind it was not counted, those having charge of the election
wanting theirs to be the banner county of the state. After the war
Judge Phillips went to Washington City, and, after remaining there
a short time, returned to Texas, where he was appointed assessor

of internal revenue'of his district. He took the qualified oath (not the iron-clad oath, as he had held office during the war),.and served eighteen months. The Senate would not confirm him, because he had failed to take the oath, and he afterward went to Washington, where, by hard work, he had a bill passed for the purpose of paying himself and other officials in the same condition. In the year 1876 General Grant appointed him United States marshal for the East District of Texas, with headquarters at Galveston, without solicitation, and he held that position three terms, under Grant, Hayes and Garfield. He was burned out during the big fire at Galveston, but soon retrieved his fortune. Planting has been his principal occupation in life—cotton exclusively, and he has met with substantial returns. In the month of December, 1858, he was married to Miss Sarah A. Boone of La Grange, La., and she died in Galveston in 1882. Three sons born to this union are also deceased: David S. was thrown from a horse and killed when thirteen years of age, June, 1872; William J. died in 1866 when four years of age, and Ben McCulloch, named for Mr. Phillips' old comrade, was born in June, 1861, and died in 1887. He was with his father in the marshal's office. On the 23d of October, 1889, Mr. Phillips married Miss Evans of a well-connected family of Texas, and daughter of Joseph L. Evans, who died in San Antonio. Judge Phillips has been a member of the Baptist church since 1852, but he is not associated with any secret organization.

WILLIAM H. WHEELER.

William H. Wheeler, liveryman, who ranks among the leading business men of Flatonia, is a native of the "Old North State," born in Wilkes County, August 16, 1840. His parents, Richard and Katie (Church) Wheeler, were also born in North Carolina, and there resided for many years. From there they moved to Georgia, where the mother died in Gilmore County, and then, when our subject was still

but a small boy, he was brought by his father to Alabama. There the
father died in Jackson County soon after. The family consisted of
eight children, as follows: James of Randolph County, Ark.; Sarah
A., widow of Robert Garen of Texas; Martha of North Carolina, A.
L. of Benningham, Ala., William H., John of Jackson County, Ala.,
Amanda, deceased, and Bethel of Jackson County. His parents dying when he was but a small boy prevented our subject from getting anything but a limited education, and he was thrown on his
own resources at an early age. When sixteen years of age he began
the struggle of life for himself, and in 1857 came to Texas by way of
New Orleans and Galveston, the latter being a small place at that
time. From Galveston he went to San Saba County, engaged in
wagoning for J. H. Gay during the winter season, and in summer attended school. In 1861 he joined Company D, Second Texas Cavalry,
was in service in New Mexico, where he engaged in the battle of Valverde. From there he returned to San Antonio, thence to Galveston,
and was engaged in the recapture of that city. From there he went
to his command in Louisiana, and was engaged in but one battle, La
Fouche Crossing. Following this his command was at various points
in Texas and was stationed at Corpus Christi at the close of the war.
He was discharged in June, 1865, and came at once to Hallettsville,
Lavaca County, where he remained for ten years. During the first
three years he was engaged in clerking in a general store, but in 1868
he established a general mercantile business there and for seven
years conducted this business. However, during the years 1869 and
1871 he traveled for J. B. Woodyard & Co., from Galveston, and in
1876 or '77 he moved to that place. There he embarked in the hotel
and livery business, and this he has since followed with more than
ordinary success. After the war he started out with limited means,
and after coming to Flatonia, met with good success and is now the
owner of a nice property in town. He also owns some fine farming
land and a large interest in a stone quarry which, when properly developed, will be a fortune in itself. On the 8th of January, 1873, Mr.
Wheeler married Miss Emma A. Arnim, a native of Texas, and
daughter of Albert and Louisa Arnim, who were born in Germany.
Mr. and Mrs. Arnim came to America in 1851, and were one of the
early German families of Texas. Mr. Arnim was a prosperous mer-

chant for many years, but, feeling the infirmities of age coming on him, retired from business recently. He makes his home at Hallettsville. Mr. and Mrs. Wheeler have six children: Ella, Richard, Katie, William, Leslie and Margaret. Mrs. Wheeler is a member of the Methodist Episcopal church, and, with her husband, is a member of the Royal Society of Goodfellows of Flatonia, Lodge No. 333. Mr. Wheeler joined the Odd Fellows Lodge at Galveston in 1868 and is a member of Clark Lodge No. 336 of Flatonia. Politically he is a strong supporter of Democratic principles.

ABNUS B. KERR.

A noted writer has said: "The present is the child of all the past, the mother of all the future." If this be true, where will the generations of the future find a more impressive lesson or faithful guide than in the study of the lives of those men who have achieved a successful prominence in the busy walks of life? There is in the intensified energy of the business man, fighting the everyday battle of life, but little to attract the attention of the idle observer; but to the mind fully awake to the stern realities of life there are noble and immortal lessons in the life of the man who, without other aid than a clear head, a strong arm and a true heart, conquers adversity and wins for himself honors and distinction among his fellow men. Among such men we may mention Abnus B. Kerr, who is one of the leading business men of the county. He was born March 4, 1832, in Augusta County, Va., of which state his parents, Robert G. and Cassandra C. (McCutchen) Kerr were also natives. Robert G. Kerr was born in 1803 and died in Fayette County in 1893, at the ripe old age of ninety years. His father, William Kerr, was one of the first settlers of Virginia, and was in the war for independence. He came from either Scotland or Ireland, and his wife was a native of Holland. William Kerr and wife reared a family of eight children:

David Samuel X., William, Jr., Robert G., Betsie, wife of John Wallace; Sallie, married Peter C. Hogue, an eminent Baptist minister; Peggie, married Elijah Hogshead of Virginia, and Jane, who married Dr. William T. Anderson, a prominent surgeon of White Sulphur Springs for many years, is still living. Our subject's maternal grandparents, Downey McCutchen, commonly known as Captain McCutchen, was also in the Revolutionary War and held the rank of captain in the Army of Patriots of Virginia. Both the Kerrs and McCutchens were large property owners and very influential families. Mr. McCutchen reared a family of seven children: Robert, Chapman, Cyrus, a physician; Amanda, married Colonel Emonson of Lexington, Va., and became the mother of three daughters: Cassandra C., Rebecca and Temperance, who married William Suddeth and became the mother of one son, James, who is now an eminent physician of Washington, D. C. Robert G. Kerr, a farmer and planter, was the son of wealthy parents, and remained in Virginia until 1874. He met with many reverses on account of security debts, and our subject cared for him and the remainder of the family until the death of both parents, the mother dying in 1880, when seventy-five years of age. This worthy couple reared four children: A. B., Mary C. A., Jerusha E., wife of J. E. Gillespie, and Robert O. of Bell County. Abnus B. Kerr, the oldest of the above mentioned children, secured a fair education in the common schools of Augusta County, Va., and in 1852, when twenty years of age, he started out to fight the battle of life for himself. He went to Charleston, W. Va., and from there down the Ohio and Mississippi rivers to New Orleans. Many were taken sick with cholera on the boat, and died at the rate of five a day, and of the eighteen who started with our subject, two died of that dread disease. Boats were not allowed to stop in the towns, but would land at wood yards, and other places, and dig pits in the sand for the corpses of their unfortunate comrades. About fifty persons were thus buried. On this boat was a lady who was going South with her little child to join her husband, who was a merchant in Louisiana. The lady promenaded the deck with Mr. Kerr, seemingly in the best of health, but before morning she was a corpse. Her body was placed in a casket and conveyed to New Orleans. The child clung to Mr. Kerr, and would not go with any of the ladies, and he took charge of the forlorn little creature until it reached its father in New Orleans. From New Orleans Mr. Kerr went to Indianola, and thence made his way to Gonzales by ox team, landing in that town with little money November 1, 1852. He at once succeeded in getting work, and was bookkeeper for a Mr. Gishard, a Frenchman, with a salary of $51 per month. He remained with that gentleman but one month, for he had to keep the books and clerk as well. As he could not do both at once, he was obliged to take care of the books at night, in a little house open to the weather. There Mr. Kerr contracted pleurisy, came very near dying, and when he recovered paid all his money to the doctor. He was without money, out of a position, had no friends, and was too proud to write home for money. As he could not get work at his business—bookkeeping—he decided to turn his hand at anything; and as the first brick house of Gonzales was under construction at that time, he accepted a position as hod-carrier for the masons, at seventy cents a day and board himself, paying forty cents per day for board. This building was known as the Kiser Hotel, and on it our subject worked as hod-carrier until March, 1853. At that time Major Neighbors was raising a company of rangers to guard the surveyors going north to survey land in Peters Colony. This land was to be surveyed from where Dallas now stands, north. Mr. Kerr wished very much to go, but had no horse or outfit, which all rangers were required to furnish. He had shown such spirit and grit after his sickness, in taking up the hod, that he won the respect and esteem of all, and one citizen, a Mr. R. Saddler, said he would furnish the saddle, a countryman furnished the horse, another a gun and thus Mr. Kerr was equipped, with the understanding that he was to pay for the outfit should he ever get able. The company was organized at Austin and started in March, with a company of surveyors, under Colonel Hitchcock. This land was to be surveyed for the Texas Emigration and Land Company of Peters Colony. Seventeen hundred square miles were surveyed in nine months, and many very interesting experiences had our subject during that time. At one time a chief of the Wichita tribe had stolen a number of Government horses from Fort Crogan, or near Burnett, and Major Sibley, who was in command, followed with horses and men, and overtook him and wife and followers near the Indian agency, on the Clear Fork of the Brazos, where the company of rangers were camped. The latter assisted in capturing the chief and his wife, and he was kept closely confined in a tent. While there he stabbed his wife and started for Major Sibley's tent to assassinate him, but was stopped by a guard, whom he shot. Other guards came up and the chief was shot through the breast. Finding the wound mortal, the latter plunged the knife in his own breast. On the 2d of July, 1853, Mr. Kerr and a friend, Mr. Gibbons of Arkansas, decided to go to Fort Belknap, a distance of twenty-five miles from the camp of the rangers, to get their guns repaired. While hunting a suitable place to cross the Brazos River, they came suddenly on a camp of 150 Indians on the warpath. Mr. Kerr and his friend lost no time in getting away from there, but were pursued by Indians on foot and on horseback. The friend was on a fine mare, and this left our subject's little pony far in the rear. Mr. Kerr called to his companion to wait, but the latter seemed to be deaf. The race continued until within sight of Fort Belknap, and the horses of the boys were almost exhausted. They reached that place in safety, and a party of soldiers started back after the Indians, but did not succeed in capturing any. After remaining a week at the fort the boys returned by a different route, and with an escort of dragoons. On the 31st of November Mr. Kerr was transferred from the ranger service to the surveying corps, where he received $60 per month, $30 more than he had received previously. Still later he was transferred to the transcribing department, where he received $75.50 per month. In that capacity he served until he reached Austin, November 1, 1853. He then clerked for some time, and was offered a salary of $75 per month to work in the land office. About this time Mr. Kerr and his companions were paid off for their trip with the surveyors, and Mr. Kerr received $440. Returning to Gonzales, he paid off his debts, spent a short time with his friends, and on the last of January, 1854, he went to Cibolo, near Selma, Bexar County, and purchased a small herd of cattle and a tract of land from J. M. Hill. He made considerable money out of this. During the fall of 1854 he met his first wife, Miss May Murcer, and while she was attending school, they were married, August 2, 1855. Mrs. Kerr was the daughter of Levi and Sarah (Munifee) Murcer, the father, a large sugar merchant and a wealthy and influential citizen at Egypt. During the fall of 1855 Mr. and Mrs. Kerr loaded their household goods in an ox wagon and moved to Fayette County, on a tract of 200 acres of land that her grandfather, Judge Munifee, had given her. This land was unimproved, and Mr. Kerr built his own house with lumber brought from Higgins' mill at Bastrop. He also fenced in some land and engaged in farming and improving his place up to the outbreak of war. During that eventful period he took charge of his father-in-law's stock, and, together with his own, moved them to Colorado County, where he remained for two years. Returning to Fayette County in 1866, he began surveying, and soon became familiar with the land of the county. He engaged largely in land speculations, buying and selling large tracts of land, and accumulated considerable property. Since then he has been engaged for the most part in farming, stock-raising and merchandising. By his first union Mr. Kerr became the father of four children, as follows: Thomas O., a merchant of Muldoon; James L., manager of a rock quarry; William B. of San Antonio, manager of the coal and wood business at that place; and R. L. Kerr (deceased). Mrs. Kerr, who was a most estimable lady, and an earnest member of the Baptist church, died in 1868. In 1870 Mr. Kerr married Miss Bettie Ragsdale, a native of Texas, and daughter of Charles C. and Sarah (Sealorn) Ragsdale, early settlers of Texas. Four children were born to his second union; John A., a graduate of the Law School of Texas, at Austin, prior to his twenty-first year (something that had never happened in Texas before), is now practicing his profession in Fayette; Mary, died in 1882; Charles G., a student, and Alice L. Mr. Kerr and sons own a large business in Muldoon, this county, and a large stone quarry at that place, the finest in the state. He has a $300,000 contract with the city of Galveston to furnish rock for the city, and sends out from thirty-five to forty car loads per day. Mr. Kerr also owns one-half interest in coal mines at Rockdale, Milam County, shipping twelve car loads per day. The company has leased this mine to the Brickett & Egget Plant Co., and on this they get a royalty of thirty cents per ton. The company with which Mr. Kerr is connected have other mines they will open soon, and sell in the crude state as now. The mercantile business is in charge of one of his sons, and is the most successful enterprise of the kind in the county. Mr. Kerr owns in Texas 50,000 acres of land, and has under cultivation about 4,000 acres, which makes about seventy-five farms, occupied by about seventy-five renters. Mr. Kerr also owns 50,000 acres of land in Mexico, on which there is quite a village. This ranch is worth at least $300,000. The Southern Pacific is planning a road through it, and Mr. Kerr has given the right-of-way. Our subject has taken little interest in political matters for a number of years, but during middle life he served fourteen years as justice of the peace, tax collector, school director, notary public and county commissioner. Finding nothing in politics, he quit. He was sent by the county to Denver, Col., to devise a means of getting deep water at Galveston. This was the convention that gave that enterprise a start. He is a strong advocate for deep water on the Texas Coast. Socially he is a member of the A. F. and A. M., a Royal Arch and demitted member. Few men in the state are at the head of as many enterprises as Mr. Kerr. Charitable and generous, he gives freely to all worthy enterprises, and takes the lead in all good work. From the year 1870 to 1880 Mr. Kerr was prominently identified with the organization of the Texas State Grange, and for eight years was a member of the first executive committee. He undoubtedly possesses a mind the equal of which few men can boast. He controls to-day more different financial enterprises than any other man in the state, and is known and recognized far and near as the "Millionaire Rock King of Texas."

HON. JAMES HARVEY M'LEARY.

In order to become distinguished at the bar it is necessary that a man should possess excellent judgment, a thorough education, an intimate knowledge of his profession, and a decided liking for its arduous labors. Such a man is Judge J. H. McLeary, a prominent lawyer of San Antonio, Tex., where he has resided for more than twenty-four years. Judge McLeary is of Scotch-Irish extraction;

his ancestors having come to America from the north of Ireland in the early years of the seventeenth century. One of the family, who then spelled their name "McCleary," was killed at the battle of Bunker Hill, and his name was mentioned by Daniel Webster in his great oration at the laying of the corner-stone of the Bunker Hill Monument. Himself a soldier of the Civil War, in the army of the Confederacy, he is descended from Revolutionary sires by more than one branch of his family. His father's maternal grandfather, Samuel Moore, was a captain in Morgan's Riflemen; and his maternal grandmother's grandfather, Michael Hogg, belonged to Morgan's Riflemen, and participated in the battles of Cowpens and Ryefield. The first member of the family in this country was called Thomas Mc-Cleary. His son, Michael, settled in Pennsylvania, where his son, John, was born in 1765. John McCleary was the great grandfather of the subject of this sketch. His eldest son, James Allen McCleary, was born on the 28th of April, 1788, in Virginia, where his father resided until he was four years old. John McCleary then removed to Oglethorpe County, Ga., where he resided until about the breaking out of the war of 1812, in which his son, James Allen, participated. James Allen McLeary was married to Miss Eliza Allen Moore, daughter of Captain Samuel Moore, in Lincoln County, Ky., on the 6th of August, 1809, and shortly after removed with his father, John Mc-Leary, and his father-in-law, Captain Moore, to Middle Tennessee. Here, in Bedford County, Samuel Davies McLeary was born, on the 9th of February, 1816. He was one of a large family of children. Samuel D. McLeary, after acquiring a classical education in the common schools of West Tennessee, where his father had removed while he was yet a boy, graduated with the degree of M. D., at Transylvania University, at Lexington, Ky., in 1841, and shortly thereafter married Sarah Ann Weller, at Randolph, Tenn., and began the practice of his profession in the neighborhood of Randolph. His health failing, he moved to Middle Tennessee, and settled in Smith County, near Carthage, where James Harvey McLeary was born on the 27th of July, 1845. Dr. Samuel D. McLeary lived for several years at La Fayette, Macon County, and in 1854 removed to Tipton County, where he resided for two years, and in January, 1856, he, with his father, James Allen McLeary, immigrated to Texas, bringing his family,

which consisted of his wife, his son and a daughter, and settled in
Colorado County near Weimar, on Harvey's Creek, where his son
Harvey was partially educated in the county schools. In 1859 Harvey was sent to Soule University at Chapel Hill, Tex., where he
remained until June, 1861, when he joined the Confederate army, and
was mustered into the service of the Confederate states at San Antonio, Tex., on the 28th of August, 1861, becoming a member of Company A of the Fifth Texas Cavalry, a regiment at that time commanded by Colonel Tom Green, afterwards so famous as a cavalry
leader in the campaigns of the Trans-Mississippi Department. The
lad served as a private soldier for four years, participating in numerous battles and skirmishes, and receiving four wounds, two of them
very serious, which left him at the close of the war a cripple, hob-
bling around on crutches. His discharge states all this and adds:
"None deserve more credit than the above soldier." He returned
from the war, and in September, 1865, resumed his studies at Soule
University. In September, 1866, he went to Lexington, Va., to attend the Washington College—now Washington and Lee University—then presided over by General Robert E. Lee. He remained at
Washington College for three years, graduating in June, 1868, with
the degree of Bachelor of Arts, and in June, 1869, with the degree of
Bachelor of Laws. During the last year of his college course he was
assistant professor of History and English Literature; the professor
of the above branches being Colonel William Preston Johnston, son
of General Albert Sidney Johnston, now president of the Tulane University of Louisiana. While in the intermediate class at college he
received the gold medal of the "Graham Philanthropic Society" for
oratory; the medal was presented to him by the Hon. George B. Peters, then the president of the society, who was afterward attorney-
general of Shelby County, Tenn. General Peters, from that day to
the present, has been a staunch friend of McLeary; and during the
celebrated trial of H. Clay King, Peters was for the prosecution,
while McLeary was for the defense. On his graduation, in June,
1868, he stood first in his class, and received the highest honor in the
gift of the college, which was the Cincinnati Oration, "Awarded to
that student who attains the highest standard of general scholar-

ship." At this time there were over four hundred young men at the Washington College, many of them over twenty-one years of age, who had been officers in the Confederate army from the rank of brigadier-general down. With such honors as these, why should not this Texas boy feel proud, after competing with young men much older than himself, and many who had received the advantages of good schools in their younger days. In June, 1869, he returned to Texas, and in the District Court of Colorado County, at Columbus, was admitted to the bar, and at once began the practice of law. During these years at college, he was engaged to be married to Miss Emily Mitchell of San Antonio, Tex., and in December, 1869, they were married and shortly afterward settled in San Antonio. Three years after his young wife died, leaving him two children, one of whom survived her mother only a few weeks. In August, 1875, he married Miss Mary King, his present wife, daughter of Hon. V. O. King, afterward the Commissioner of Insurance, Statistics and History for the state. Immediately on his arrival in San Antonio, he formed a law partnership with Judge C. L. Wurzbach, with whom he continued in business for five years. In 1873 he was elected to the lower branch of the Texas Legislature, and served in that capacity until he was elected to the State Senate two years later. In 1880 he was elected attorney-general of the state, and served in that capacity for two years, declining the nomination for the same office two years later.

While in the Legislature Judge McLeary served in the House as chairman of the committee on education, and in the Senate as chairman of the committee on privileges and elections and state affairs. From his position he took a leading part in shaping legislation, and was the author of the law giving to towns and cities the right to control their own public schools. He also had the honor of being godfather to the fifty-six new counties, comprising the Panhandle of Texas, since he named each one of them after some prominent historical character, among others, the heroes who perished at the Alamo. It was the prominent part he took in legislative affairs which brought him forward as a candidate for attorney-general. While attorney-general he recovered from the International & Great Northern Railroad Company, 4,680 square miles of land, which that company claimed for that portion of its line constructed between Austin and Laredo.

During all these years McLeary has been an ardent and devout Mason, having taken his first degree the night of his twenty-first birthday. He was promoted step by step until he was elected Grand Master of Masons in Texas, and served in that exalted position during the year 1881. To the literature of Masonry he has contributed a little work upon which he might be satisfied to rest his reputation as a scholar in this branch of learning. The publication embraces 156 pages of closely printed correspondence, with domestic and foreign representatives of the order, and contains an instructive review of the progress and achievements of Masonry in every part of the civilized world.

After retiring from the office of attorney-general he returned to private life, and resumed the practice of law in San Antonio. In 1884 he was elected an elector from the state at large on the Cleveland ticket, and had the honor of casting an electoral vote for President for the first winning Democrat in twenty-five years. In May, 1886, without any solicitation whatever on his part, he was appointed associate justice of the Supreme Court of Montana, being the first Democrat ever appointed to that bench. He held this office until March, 1888, when he resigned on account of the severity of the climate and deficient salary. He then returned to Texas and formed a partnership with Judge W. W. King in the practice of law. Their partnership was particularly agreeable and profitable, and was only dissolved when Judge King was appointed to the district bench in 1889. In 1888 he was again an elector on the Democratic ticket, and for the second time had the honor of casting an electoral vote for Grover Cleveland for President. This time he was chairman of the Electoral College. From his course in politics it can readily be inferred that Judge McLeary is, and always has been, a staunch friend of Grover Cleveland. Everyone in Texas has always known where to find him politically—a staunch and true Democrat, "without variableness or shadow of turning."

When the trial of H. Clay King came off at Memphis, Tenn., Judge W. W. King, McLeary's former partner—being Colonel H. Clay King's half-brother—requested him to go to Memphis and assist in the defense of the case. Judge McLeary readily consented, and reached Memphis shortly after the trial had begun, and made an argument before the jury which took up three days and consumed eight hours in actual delivery. The court-room was crowded during the entire time of McLeary's speech, many men and women being moved to tears. 'Twas said by many of the old people present that the speech was the grandest and most eloquent ever delivered in Memphis since the days of Sargeant S. Prentiss. In June, 1890, he formed a law partnership with Hon. J. R. Fleming, under the firm name of McLeary & Fleming. This partnership continued for over three years, Judge Fleming retiring in September, 1893. On the invitation of Judge McLeary, Colonel R. W. Stayton then assumed the place in the firm made vacant by the retirement of Judge Fleming, and since that time the partnership has been continued under the name of McLeary & Stayton. It is considered the ablest law firm in the city of San Antonio, and the peer of any in the state. Its members are so well known and popular that when any important question arises in Southwest Texas they are always consulted. Although devoted to his profession, Judge McLeary deems it the duty of every patriot to take a becoming interest in politics. He attended the state convention in Lampasas in 1892, and was sent as delegate to Chicago. As might have been expected, he was an enthusiastic supporter of Mr. Cleveland, and being personally acquainted with the nominee, he was appointed on the committee of notification to inform the candidates of the action of the convention. Chairman Wilson, recognizing the sound judgment and literary culture of Judge McLeary, made him a member of the sub-committee to prepare the address to Cleveland and Stevenson, which duty he performed to the entire satisfaction of all concerned. After the grand ceremonies of notification at Madison Square Garden, in New York City, on the 20th day of July, in which Judge McLeary took a prominent part, he spent a month or two with his wife and son on the New England Coast, from which pleasant recreation he returned to resume his arduous labors at the bar. Since his retirement from the Supreme Bench in Montana, Judge McLeary has devoted himself unremittingly to the duties of his profession. For the last few years he has been quite in demand as an orator, delivering addresses at the reunion of Green's Brigade, and before the faculty and students of Tulane University of Louisiana, before the University of Texas, the Italian Society of San Antonio, and other addresses, which may be considered models of correct style and elegant oratory. Doubtless, if the demands of his profession would permit, he could become quite a successful man in purely literary pursuits, and some of his friends venture the prediction that when he retires from the duties of his profession on the laurels and the fortune already acquired, and hereafter to be achieved by him, that he will devote his later years to the pleasures and profits of authorship.

James Harvey McLeary is a man of fine physique, having a well-shaped, massive head, with broad forehead, indicating well-developed intellectual powers, depth of learning, firmness and zeal; those requisites so necessary to make a brilliant, talented and successful lawyer. He is now in the height of his prosperity, with such a law practice that he is often compelled to refer clients to other firms. He is blessed with a comfortable home, made happy by an accomplished and Christian woman for a wife; his eldest daughter, Mary, having been recently married to a wealthy young planter, Noah R. Cotton of Louisiana; and three other beautiful daughters, Helen, Sarah and Bonnie, and one son, Samuel, to comfort him as he grows older. A good and true husband, a kind and affectionate father, a devoted friend, a staunch Democrat, an able lawyer and unflinching patriot, are words most fit to describe James Harvey McLeary, who is already known as a worthy son of Texas throughout the limits of the Nation.

"Statesman, yet friend to truth; of soul sincere,
In action faithful, and in honor clear;
Who broke no promise, served no private end,
Who gained no title, and who lost no friend;
Ennobled by himself, by all approved,
And praised unenvied by the men he lov'd."

COLONEL FRANCIS MARION HICKS.

This prominent old settler of Texas was born in Georgia, November 16, 1826, being the fourth of five children born to William A. and Margaret (Moon) Hicks, who were married near Raleigh, N. C., and were born in Tennessee and North Carolina respectively. The paternal grandfather, John Hicks, was born in Virginia, and was a soldier of the Revolution. After that great strife was over he moved to Tennessee, of which state he was among the first settlers. He came of English ancestors, who settled in Virginia during colonial days. William A. Hicks settled in Georgia when a young man and engaged in planting and trading, but afterwards moved to Alabama and then to Mississippi, thence to Arkansas, and finally to Texas in 1849. Here he settled in Cherokee County, and became one of the settlers of Rusk. He was an old line Whig politically, and was elected to the Legislature from Cherokee County, which was strongly Democratic. He was also a county clerk in Georgia, and was quite a party leader of the Whigs there, and a strong Henry Clay man. He became a prominent planter of Cherokee County, and there made his home until death closed his career. His wife died when the subject of this sketch was a boy, in Hickstown, Ga., which place was named in his honor. It was a gold mining town, and his early days were spent as a miner. He was a Royal Arch Mason, and was an active and enterprising citizen. Francis M. Hicks was educated in Mississippi, was married at Paulding, Jasper County, and began life as a merchant. In 1852 he came to Cherokee County, Tex., but shortly after removed to Corsicana, Navarro County, Tex., and began business as one of the early merchants of the place. Shortly after he sold out and returned to Rusk, where he was engaged in business until the outbreak of the war. In 1861 he entered a company and went to Galveston, where he was detailed to act as commissary at Rusk, and served in that capacity about one year. He was then detailed by General Kirby Smith as the financial agent of the Government iron works at Rusk, and served in that capacity until the war closed, his

assistance being most invaluable to the Government. The war left
Mr. Hicks almost destitute, but he at once embarked in business at
Rusk, where he continued until 1868, when he went to Shreveport
and opened a commission house, which is known as the Hicks Company, Limited. In 1872 he associated with him Mr. Robert H. Howell, under the firm name of Hicks & Howell, dealers in groceries and
the cotton factorage business. They were very fortunate in their
operations and prospered from the very beginning, and on the solid
foundation which was then laid there had been builded the staunch-
est commercial organization in the state of Louisiana, outside of the
city of New Orleans. After sixteen years of lucrative business, the
firm of Hicks & Howell was dissolved, and Mr. Howell took from the
establishment a fortune without the least affecting its standing or
credit. Mr. Hicks then took into partnership his son, S. B. Hicks, a
young gentleman whose education, training and natural business
ability peculiarly fitted him for the responsible position to which he
was called. The firm name was then changed to F. M. & S. B. Hicks,
and continued in existence for four years, during which time the
failing condition of Colonel Hicks' health caused him to throw the
burden of the extensive business, in all its multitudinous details, on
the shoulders of his son, who proved equal to the occasion, and won
his spurs in an arena where many older and more experienced had
failed. In 1892 the present incorporation was formed under the name
of the Hicks Company, Limited, whose business is exclusively wholesale grocers and cotton factors. Their place of business is admirably
located where the house has for many years been established. Colonel
Hicks' name is justly at the head of this establishment, though he
is no longer able, on account of his health, to take an active part in its
affairs. He was compelled to seek a change of climate, came to San
Antonio, and has been greatly benefited thereby. The active management of the business now devolves upon his son, S. B. Hicks, vice
president, who is ably assisted by Captain W. T. Crawford, secretary
and treasurer. Mr. W. F. Chase is the cashier and bookkeeper, T H.
Scovell is head salesman, and F. H. Gosman has charge of the cotton department All these gentlemen have been long connected with
the business, and are by experience and special adaptability thor-

oughly equipped for their several responsible and exacting positions. To give an idea of the immense business transacted by this house, it is but necessary to state that its store-room, merchandise and cotton warehouses have a floor space, under roof, exceeding by 16,000 square feet, an acre of floor space, and the annual sales aggregate considerably over a million dollars. Colonel Hicks' kindly face and genial manners endear him to all with whom he comes in contact, and socially or otherwise make him popular with all classes. He is a man of rare business qualifications and indomitable energy, and to him is due full credit for the decided success achieved by the firm, whose name will always adorn the best pages of Shreveport's commercial history. He was made a Mason in Mississippi, and in April, 1851, was married to Miss Ann E. McDugald, a daughter of James McDugald of Scotland, who became a prominent lawyer of Mississippi at Paulding, where he was an active citizen and served as State Senator. To Colonel Hicks and his wife four sons and four daughters were given: Emma L., Lelia, wife of Dr. Lawrence of Longview, Tex.; Francis Marion, Jr., Clara, wife of Callie McArthur Walke, who is a business man of Shreveport; Samuel B., who was educated at Shreveport and graduated at Soule College, New Orleans, in which educational institution he won a medal. He is now general manager and vice president of the Hicks Company of Shreveport; Marshall was educated at Shreveport and graduated at the Southwestern University of Clarksville, Tenn. He studied law for two years at the State University, Austin, Tex., from which he graduated and began practicing at Minneola, Tex., with Captain Giles, a prominent lawyer. He came to San Antonio and was appointed district attorney of Laredo District by Governor Hogg, after which he was elected to that office and served four years. He is now a practitioner of San Antonio, but was married in Clarksville. Richard Yale is also a lawyer of San Antonio. Annie McD., and one that died early. Francis Marion was educated at Rusk and Shreveport, La., studying medicine in the latter place also, after which he attended lectures at Bellevue College Hospital, New York, from which he graduated. He began practicing at Rusk, but in a short time went to Tyler, Tex., where he built up a large practice, but labored so incessantly that he injured his health, to improve which he went to California, and in 1890 returned to San Antonio, where he has built up a large practice. His attention is given to all branches of his profession, but he makes something of a specialty of surgery and surgical cases, and is a member of the Texas State Medical Society; and is also a member and first vice president of the Southwest Texas Medical Association. He is surgeon of the International & Great Northern Railway at San Antonio, and while at Tyler he was chief, and later consulting surgeon of the Cotton Belt Railroad, but resigned from the former office on account of ill health. While at Tyler he was medical examiner for nearly all the old line life insurance companies. The doctor is a student in his profession, and in 1882 spent six months studying at the Jefferson Medical College, and the medical department of the University of Pennsylvania at Philadelphia. In 1885 he went to New York and took a post graduate course at the New York Polyclinic Medical College, and made a special study of surgery and diseases of the eye, ear and nose, to aid him in his office of chief surgeon of the Cotton Belt Railroad. In 1887 he made a trip to California in search of health, but since coming to San Antonio he has enjoyed comparatively good health. He was married in 1887 to Miss Margaret R. Spence, a native of Texas, and a daughter of John Spence, one of the early settlers of the Lone Star State from Maryland. He belongs to an old Scotch family that came to this country during colonial times, that assisted in founding and became members of the first Presbyterian church in America, at Snow Hill, Md., and from that time down to the present day some member of the family has been an elder in that historic church. Mrs. Hicks is a highly educated lady, of decided literary and musical taste and talent. She graduated from the Augusta Female Institute at Staunton, Va., the finest young ladies' college in the South. There she won a medal for scholarship and music. Her union with Dr. Hicks has resulted in the birth of two children. The doctor and his wife are members of the First Presbyterian church, and he is an elder in the same. Politically he has always been in sympathy with the Democratic party, and has served as delegate to various conventions.

COLONEL STEPHEN W. BLOUNT.

This historic name will live while Texas has a history as one of the signers of the Texas Declaration of Independence. In 1888 he was the oldest surviving one of the signers. He was born in Georgia, February 13, 1808, and became prominent there as an official, and especially in connection with military affairs. He was colonel of the Eighth Regiment of Georgia Militia, and was aide-de-camp to military generals in 1832-34. In 1835 he emigrated to Texas, and there conceived a warm personal friendship for General Houston. In 1836 he was elected a member of the convention that declared the independence of Texas and nominated General Houston for commander-in-chief of the Texan forces. In 1837 he was elected clerk of San Augustine County, and held that position four years. His life was a most active one, and he never ceased to recall with pride the part he took in the achievement of independence for Texas, or to regard Houston as one of the grandest of men.

ABERNATHY, B. 87
ABBOTT, Anna (Cooper) 296
    Mathew 296
ADAIR, W. A. 318
ADAMS, Densy 326
    Earle 324, 325, 326
    Emma 326
    Emma (Miller) 325
    Henriatta 326
    Margaret (Doniphan)
        325
    Thomas 325
ADDIS, Annie 258
    Canada C. 258
    Clara Morse 258
    David 258
    Edna 258
    Emma 258
    Ida 258
    John 258
    John W. 258
    Mary 258
    Maud 258
    Minnie (Kearns) 259
    Permelia (Randolph)
        258
    Robert 258
    Samuel 258
ADRIANCE, D. E. Nash 80
    Duncan 80
    George C. 77, 79
    John Hon 77, 79
    Lydia A. 80
AIKEN, Zue (Ward) 327
ALAMAN, Lucas 25
ALBRIGHT, Elizabeth
        (Bollinger) 420, 421
    William I. 420, 421
ALEXANDER, Miss E. A.
        (Robinson) 408
    Electa (Young) 439
    Jerome 409
    M. C. 237
    Samuel 408
    Sarah A. (McFadden) 237
ALFORD, Ann (Barfield) 314
    George Fredrick, Judge
        314
    George G. 314, 315, 316
    Johnston H. Major 315
ALKINSON, Fannie E.
        (Phillips) 277
ALLEN, Miss 62
    Benjamine 420
    Caroline (Bollinger)
        420
    Ebenezer 54
    Elizabeth 130
    Ethan, General 314
    R. P. 289
ALMONTE, General 41
ALSTON, Ariela 88
    Wellis 88
ALTO, Palo 23
AMMONS, Fannie (Hynes)
        247
    L. F. 247
AMPUDIA, General 40
ANASTACE, Pe're 20
ANDERSON, Elizabeth
        (Massey) 283, 284
    David 283
    Denny 283, 284
    George S. 284
    Henry 283
    Ianthe J. (Wallace)
        284
    Jane (Kerr) 450

ANDERSON (cont.)
    James 283
    John 283
    J. D. 283, 284
    Kenneth L. 45
    Martha 283
    Margaret (Dorrah) 283
    Mary 283
    Mary (Atkins) 108
    Mary Ianthe (McCurdy)
        284
    Miss Mason 283
    N. Bertie (Kaapke)
        284
    Rebecca 283
    Robert W. 284
    Sallie (Brakin) 283
    Samuel 283
    William 283
    William Irwing 284
    Dr. William T. 450
ANDREWS, Col. H. B. 97
    Richard 30
    Sarah (Braman) 425
ANGELINE, Abram 149
    Adeline 149
    Catherine Duty 149
    Elisha 147, 148
    John 149
    Margaret Moody 149
    Mary Bates 149
    Nancy (Faulkenberry)
        149
    Opha (James) 149
    Rebecca Catherine 149
    Rachel (Wilson) 149
    Sarah (Chaffin nee
        Crist) 149
    William 149
ANTHONY, D. W. 53
APPLING, Fannie (Ussery)
        Pierce 438
    Frank M. 438
ARCHER, Branch T. 27, 30
ARISTA, General 39
ARMSTRONG, George 418
    Nancy (Ryan) 419
    Thresa (Rice) 418
    William 418, 419
    Zaruauh (Fulcher) 419
ARNIM, Albert 448
    Emma A. (Wheeler) 448
    Louisa 448
ARNOLD, John 140
    Virginia 140
ARTHUR, General 226
ASHBY, Euphemia (King)
        404
    Fannie (Gellhorn) 404
    Isabella (McCulloch)
        404
    Jane Isabella 194
    John M. 400, 404
    Mary (Garnett) 400
    Sarah Ann (Branches)
        400
ATKINS, Mary Anderson 108
    Mattie Ward 108
    Mattie A. (Murphy) 108
    S. Crawford 108
    Samuel J. 108
    William T. 107, 108,
        109
ATKINSON, Estello (Riley)
        424
    George 424
    General Henry 180
ATTAWAY, Dr. 140

AUGUSTIN, Major 38
AURY, Commodore 24
AUSTIN, -- 39
    James Brown 139
    John 26
    John, Capt. 407
    Moses 21, 138
    Stephen Fuller 21, 22,
        25, 26, 27, 28, 29,
        30, 43, 44, 138,
        310, 381
AVERELL, Di (McFadden)
        237
    W. C. 237
BADGE, Governor 314
BAIRER, Abram 411
    Harriet (Cummins) 411
BAIRD, Beulah (Ballard)
        354
    W. C. 354
BAINE, Cecelia T. (Low)
        270
    Moses 270
BAKER, Rev. Dr. Daniel
        433
    Joseph 53
    Moseley 28
BALDWIN, Dr. Charles 163
    Miss Clara 163
    Dr. F. 157
    Mildred F. (Hilliard)
        157
BALES, Elizabeth (Henry)
        285
    John 285
    John H. 286
    Mary (Blue) 285
    Mary (Cape) 286
    Samuel B. Major 284,
        285, 286
BALL, George 115
    Miss J. E. 115
BALLARD, Addison 354
    Alice Ione (Russell)
        353
    Beulah (Baird) 354
    Collatinus 353, 354
    Eunice H. 354
    Ezbell 353
    Frances B. (Woodall)
        353
    Fredonia Jane (Rosie)
        353
    James 353
    John L. 353
    Margaret P. (Ballard)
        353
    Mary 353
    Mary E. 354
    Mary Jane (Hallett)
        353
    Schiller 354
    Susan A. (Daniel) 354
    W. P. 353
BANKS, -- 42, 324, 386,
        413
    Brigade 366, 413, 414
    General 65, 351, 386
BARBEE, Anna (Singleton)
        209
BARFIELD, Ann (Alford)
        314
BARHAM, Emily F. (Hamlett)
        139
    Emmett 141
    George 141
    Dr. J. H. 139, 140
BARHAM, Joel H., Jr. 141

BARHAM (cont.)
John 139, 140
R. J. 139
Dr. S. H. 217
S. H. 140
Ruth (Garrison) 82,
141
Virdiam 141
Virginia 140
BARNES, Colonel 115
BARNET, Pleasant 360
BARROW, Sarah N. (Ragan)
396
Samuel 396
BARRY, Bryan 317
Rachel (Stewart) 317
BARTA, Sallie (Umbden-
stock) 192
BARRETT, -- 29
BASTERRA, Prudencia 46
BATES, Gov. -- 321
Mary Angline 149
Silas H. 149
Mr. -- 148
BAUTISTA, Juan 46
BAYLOR's Calvery 316, 430
BEAN, Ellis 23
Ellis P. 91, 92, 93
BEARD, Charles 370
James 370
Robert 330
William 330
BEARDSLEE, C. 79
BEASLEY, Ada Lou (Denny)
208
Bessie 208
Bettie Crook 208
Grace (Smith) 208
Harold 205
Hugh Lawson 208
Jarrell 207
John B. Gordon 208
Kate Smith 208
Louisa (Edwards) 207
Lucile 208
Nell 208
Stephen T. 207, 208
Stephen T., Jr. 208
Dr. William P. 207
BEE, Bernard 639
General 192
BEEKS, Mary (Copeland-
Odom) 380
Jane V. (Cavanaugh)
380
William 380
BELL, Andrew J. 416
Anna 417
Bessie 417
Calpernia (Shellborn)
416
C. H. (Bethany) 417
George C. 417
James, J. 417
John 64
John P. 417
Judge John P. 415, 416,
417
L. A. (Bethany) 417
Lucy 417
P. H. 47, 346
Mrs. R. (Minturn) 417
Rosa (Chapman) 293
BELLINGER, Addie 361
Ann Le Gare (Roach) 358
Bessie 361
Carnot 358, 359, 360,
361
Edmund 358, 359, 360
Edmund, Jr. 359
Elizabeth (Butler) 359
Elizabeth (Cartwright)
359

BELLINGER (cont.)
Franklin 361
Marguarita 361
Mary 361
Mary E. (Keith) 361
Mary Lucia (Bull) 359
William 359, 361
BENTON, Annie H. (Russell)
254
BENNER, A. M. 281
Carrie (Grunwood) 281
BETHANY, C. H., Mrs.
(Bell) 417
J. W. 417
L. A. (Bell) 417
M. A. (Woods) 417
BICKFORD, Ammis (Morse)
367
Florence O. 368
Joseph Harry 368
Joseph M. 367, 368
Mabel A. 368
Mary (Hensley) 368
Mary L. 368
Thomas 367
BIGELOW, Horatio 53
BISCHOFF, Anton 335
Sophia (Leuschner) 335
BISHOP, Delia 145
BLACKBURN, Ephraim 23
BLAIN, Miss Margaret 77
BLAKE, Abigail Lee 70
Addie L. 72
Bennett (Judge) 69,
70, 71, 72
Bennett, Jr. 72
Catherine T. (Knox)
337
Ella (Harris) 72
Joshua 337
Keziah (Harrison) 72
Levina 70
Martha (Eckles) 337
Myrta S. 72
Samuel D. 70
BLANCO, Victor 47
BLANCHARD, Experience
(Braman) 425
BLOCKER, Eads T. 177
E. B., Dr. 176, 177
Eugene E. 177
Fannie 177
James Henry 177
Jessie General 176
John 176
John W. 177
Mary 177
Mattie 177
Michael 176
William Frank 177
William J. 176
BLOUNT, Eudora (Power)
154
E. Y., Dr. 154
Stephen C., Col. 115,
116, 465
BLUE, Mary (Bales) 285
BLYTHE, Sally (Ward) 184
Sally Ward (Saunders)
326
Samuel K. 184
S. F. 246
BOLLINGER, Caroline
(Allen) 420
Catherine (Hillyard)
420
Conrad 420
Elizabeth (Allbright)
420
Ephriam 420
Hiram 420
John 420
John, Jr. 420

BOLLINGER (cont.)
Louie 420
Mary M. (Hill) 420
Peter 420
Sarah (Littlefield)
420
BONAPARTE, Napoleon 258
BONCO, Justo 46
BONNER, Abigail 81
BOON, Mr. 123
Nellie (Futrell) 123
BOONE, Daniel 233, 343,
414
Rhoda (Smith-Skaggs)
414
Sarah A. (Phillips)
447
BORDEN, Gail 53
Thomas H. 53
BORING, Jesse, Dr. 437
BOSSIER, -- 202
BOWIE, -- 30, 35
Colonel 407
James 110
John 110
Regin 110
Veramendi, Mrs. 110
BOWLER, Addie L. 72
Carrie L. 72
Ella A. 72
Lizzie A. 72
Myrta A. 72
Samuel A. 72
Willie May 72
BOWLES, -- 38
Chief Cherokee 71
BOWMAN, Mrs. 247
BOYD, Anna T. 165
Bessie 165
Dempsey 165
J. W. 165
Levina P. 165
Lititia (Bussey) 164,
165
Margaret 165
Mary V. 165
Margaret E. (Mosby)
165
Mattie 165
Sarah L. 165
Verna (Marshall) 268
W. 123
Walter 164, 165, 268
Walter, Sr. 164, 165,
166
BRADBURN, -- 26, 27
BRAGG, -- 69, 171
General 291, 334
BRAGGER, Jasper 378
Josephine (Dubois-
Turner) 378
BRAKIN, Sallie (Anderson)
283
BRAMAN, Alexander 426
Andrews 425
Catherine (Burkhart)
426
Daniel 425
Daniel Hawes 426
Don Egbert, Judge 425,
426
Erastus 426
Experience (Blanchard)
425
George 426
Julia 426
Nancy (Hawes) 425, 426
Mary Elizabeth 426
Mary Elizabeth (Burkhart)
426
Rachel (Campbell) 425
Sarah (Andrews) 425
Sylvanus 425

2

BRAMAN (cont.)
  William Cleever 426
  Thomas 425
BRANCHES, Charles 403
  Mrs. H. K. (Jones) 403
  Sarah Ann (Ashby) 400,
    401, 402, 403
  Sarah Ann (McClure)
    400, 403, 404
BRAZIER, Miss R. A.
  (Cooper) 296
BRECKINRIDGE, -- 416
BREMOND, -- 97
BRIDGES, Miss M. E. 69
  Miss Sarah E. 69
BRINKERHOFF, -- 77
BRODIE, Virginia (Hawkins)
  89
BROOKS, Capt. 266
BROWN, Ada 137
  Anderson 209
  Annie 138
  Benjamine B. 127
  Charles T. 137
  Della G. 137
  Fannie (Rodes) 137
  Frances (Rhodes) 185
  Flora (Crutcher) 137,
    138
  Frank B. 137
  Hallie 138
  Henry S. 407
  John C. 138
  John G., Hon. 137, 185
  John W. 137
  L. H. 290
  Lula Frances 137
  Mary E. 137
  Maggie L. 138
  Nettie (Flewellen) 137
  John Raiders 208, 357
  Robert G. 138
  R. G. 136
  Ruben, Col. 417
  Sarah E. 137
  Sarah (Darr) 209
  Sidney 137
  Victoria A. 137
  Virginia J. 137
  William, Capt. 46
  Woodie E. (Ward) 185
BRUNER, C. L. 219
  Fannie 219
BRYAN, K., Capt. 178
  Eliza A. (O'Brian) 178
BRYANT, William Cullen
  358
BUCKANAN, Sarah (O'Conner)
  391
BUCKNER, Stanton 391
BUGG, Lucy (Kyle) 392
BUIE, Daniel 218
  Della Lizzie 219
  Fannie (Bruner) 218
  J. D., Colonel 218, 219
  John Dixon 219
  Laney (Bell) 219
  Laney (Dixon) 218
  Lee Clifton 219
BULL, Mary Lucia
  (Bellinger) 359
BURCH, Ida Lee (Petty)
  257
  Robert
BURHAM, Jesse 411
  Nancy (Cummins) 411
BURKHART, George 426
  Mary Elizabeth (Braman)
  426
BURLESON, -- 31, 37, 65
  Davy Crocket 64, 65,
    66, 382
  Edward, Gen. 30, 45,

BURLESON (cont.)
  Edward, Gen. (cont.)
    64, 66, 381, 382
  Edward, Major 65, 381,
    382, 384, 385
  Edward C. 383
  Elizabeth T. 283
  Eliza 383
  Emma 383
  Ford McCullock 383
  Grace 382
  Colonel 328
  James G. 383, 385
  John 382
  John Williams 383, 385
  Joseph R. 382
  Lily (Kyle) 382
  Louisa (Ware) 65
  Mary 383
  Mary D. (Green) 383
  Mary K. 383
  Miss Northcraft 383
  Sarah G. (Owens) 64,
    382
BURG, Eliza 101, 102
BURGES, A. S. H., Dr. 361
  Bettie M. 363
  Ellis G. 363
  Eugenia A. (Fenner)
    362, 363
  George P. 363
  Gray Smith 363
  Henry John, Rev. 361,
    362
  Mary 363
  Richard J. 361, 362,
    363
  William H. 362, 363
BURNETT, Anna (Simmons)
  386
  C. G. 230, 231, 232
  Crawford 385, 386, 387
  David G. 24, 27, 31,
    43, 44, 47, 205
  Eleanor (Kerr) 232
  Elizabeth (Robinson)
    386
  Frances 386
  Henrietta (Clark) 386
  James 230
  James C. 386
  Jessie 386
  Katie (Vinson) 232
  Lone 386
  Louisa Ann (Flannagan)
    230
  Mathew 386
  Otho 386
  President 287
  Sam Houston 386
  Sarah Ann (Livingston)
    386
  Sarah E. (Dillard) 386
  Sarah Jane (Johnston)
    231
  William 386
BURNS, Arthur 391
  Maggie E. (Killough)
    412
  Robert 358
  W. T. 412
BURR, Aaron 23
  Robert 44
BURTON, Isaac W. 46
BUSTAMANTE, -- 25, 26
BUSTILLOS, Juan Antonio
  46
BUSSEY, J. W. 165
  Lititia (Boyd) 164
  Margaret (Boyd) 165
BUTTER, Elizabeth
  (Bellinger) 359
  Jessie 176

BUTTER (cont.)
  Mary 176
BUTTERMAN, Mary (Turner)
  376
BYRON, Lord 358
CABELLO, Domingo 46
CAHILL, Hettie Virginia
  (Meyers) 415
  James F. 415
CALDWELL, Capt. 360
  Cora C., Mrs. 216
  Matthew 40, 195
CALHOUN, John C. 147
CALLIHAN, James H.,
  Capt. 65
CALVERT, C. R. 203
  Fannie (Marks) 203
  Lucy Lee (Donaldson)
    365
CAMERON, Capt. 328, 329,
    330, 331, 333
CAMPBELL, Capt. 437
  Mr. 146
  Cyrus 240
  Hiram 240
  J. 46
  Laura L. (Van Ness)
    146
  Lillie (O'Conner) 391
  Rachel (Braman) 425
  William 391
CAMP, Virginia (Futrell)
  122
CANALIS, Colonel 328
CANBY, (Federal) 42, 43
CAPE, John 286
  Mary (Bales) 286
CARLOCK, De Witt 274
  Julia (Pitts) 274
  Samuel G. 274
  Thomas 274
CARRINGTON's Co. 430
CARSON, Samuel P. 44
CARTER, Ann (Laird) 372
  Ellen C. (Russell)
    255
  Holly P. (Robison) 409
  John 255
  John N. 409
  Nunly 409
CARTWRIGHT, Elizabeth
  (Bellinger) 359
CARRAVAHAL, J. M. 28
CARVER, Emeline 145
CARY, Sisters 430
CASH, L. L. 331
CASAS, Juan Bautista 23
CASTENADO, Capt. 29
CASTLEMAN, S. 138
CATES, Fannie 129
CAVANAUGH, Jane V. (Becks)
  380
CHAFFIN, Sarah (Crist)
  149
CHAISON, Brandon 164
  Charles 164
  Clara (Baldwin) 163,
    164
  Elizabeth 164
  Eliza McFadden 162
  Jeff, Judge 162, 163
  Jimmie 164
  Harriet (Russell) 164
  McGuire 162
  William 164
CHAPLIN, -- 24
  Catherine 293
  Eliza 293
  Eugenia Alice (McNeil)
    294
  James H., Dr. 293
  Lollie D. 295
  Mary E. 293

3

CHAPLIN (cont.)
  Mattie C. (Sanfield)
    295
CHAPMAN, Osgood McNeil
    294
  R. D., Capt. 292, 293,
    294, 295
  R. M. 53
  Rosa (Bell) 293
  Temperance (Cowan) 293
  Temperance (Jordan) 293
  William D. 292
  William P. 293
  William H. J. 292, 293
CHASE, W. F. 462
CHATHAM, Belle 261
  Tennie (Maroney) 261
  William 261
CHEATHAM, General 392
CHEREWITH, A. B. 357
  Lucy (Donalson) 357
CHENAULT, Ellen P. 180
CHESNEY, Mary (Crownover)
    373
CHEW, A. R. 383
CHRISTIAN, Mr. 307
CHURCH, Katie (Wheeler)
    447
CLARDY, Martha 75
CLAIBORNE, Delia Hayes
    174
  Fannie 176
  Herbert 174
  Howard 176
  Lucy Lee 176
CLAIBORNE, Lucy (Perry)
    175, 176
  Perry 176
  V. H., Capt. 174, 175,
    176
CLARK, Adolphus 106
  Amelia (Taylor) 106
  Anna 106
  Birdie (O'Conner) 391
  Charles Taylor 106
  Colonel 107
  Edward 47
  Henrietta (Burnett)
    386
  Irion 106
  John A. 386
  Julia 106
  Laurence 106
  Leonard 106
  Martha 106
  Mary 106
  William 106
  William, Hon. 90, 105
  W. L. 391
CLAY, Alice 264
  Anna Belle 264
  A. M. 263, 264, 265
  Cassus M. 357
  Henry 233, 461, 264
  Kate 264
  Lelia (Hoxie) 264, 265
  Nestor 264
  Pauline (Thornkill)
    264
  Tacitus 264
  Teula (Denver) 265
  Thomas C. 265
  Thomas H. 264
  Thetis (Powers) 265
  Miss V. (McCrary) 264,
    265
CLEBURNE, Pat General 334
CLEVELAND, Colonel 147
  President 301, 225
  W. D. 295
  Grover, President 458,
    459
COAHUILA, -- 43

COATS, Franklin 149
  Rebecca Catherine
    (Angline) 149
COBB, Charles 233
  Charles, Jr. 233, 234
  Ellen (Monks) 233
  Helen Louisa 234
  Sophia Fry 234
COCKE, J. D. 330, 331
COCHRAN, Mr. and Mrs.
    Elias K. 261
  Mrs. (Gregg) 430
  Parilee (Mahoney) 261
COFFEE, Catherine
    (Williams) 387
COFFIELD, H. B., Capt.
    289
COKE, Governor 195
  Richard 47
COLE, Louisa (Odom) 378
COLEMAN, Catherine
    (Hawes) 282
  John J. 282
  Octavia 135
  R. H., Judge 282
COLLIER, J. M. 249
COLLIN, Nancy (Craig) 318
COLLINGSWORTH, George,
    Capt. 29
  James 44
COLTHORPE, Mary (Lane)
    369
COOK, -- 24
  Dr. 80
  Mrs. (Coleman) 133
  Lewis P. 46
  Lydia A. 80
  Mariah (Moore) 411
  R. V. 412
COOPER, Ann (Abbot) 296
  Charles Hudson 144
  Dora 144
  Dora (Hudson) 144
  Georgia (Moore) 297
  James L. 297
  J. C. 143, 144
  Leion 296
  Leroy, W. Judge 295,
    296, 297
  Lewis 296
  Louis N. 297
  Lucy Catharine 144
  Lucy (Harris) 143, 144
  Nettie (Wall) 297
  Miss R. A. (Brazier)
    296
  St. Cloud, Dr. 143,
    144
CORDERO, Antonio 46
CORDOVA, Vincenta 38
CORTINA, -- 43
COS, General 29, 30, 31,
    37, 186
COSTRELLON, -- 35
COSPER, Mary Ann 83
COTTON, Bonnie 460
  Godwin B. 53
  Helen 460
  Mary (McLeary) 460
  Mary Ann (Mayes) 275
  Matilda G. (Taylor)
    132
  Noah R. 460
  Samuel 460
  Sarah 460
COWAN, Temperance
    (Chapman) 293
COWARD, Elizabeth
    (McFadden) 237
  Mr. 237
COX, Mary (Thurman) 319
CRAIG, Ann (Waldron) 318
  Eli. T. 318

CRAIG (cont.)
  Ibby Yancy (Rosborough)
    318
  Nancy 318
CRANE, Alice (Lowdon) 196
  Benjamin F. 196
CRAWFORD, S. 108
  W. T., Capt. 462
CRESENT REGIMENT 323
CROCKETT, Bill 125, 35
  David 111, 112, 125
  John 111
CROCKER, Juliet (Greenwood)
    381
CROFT, David 375
  Mary (Rabb) 375
CROMWELL, -- 427
CROOK, Bettie (Beasley)
    208
CROOM, John L. Col. 186
  W. J. 186
CROSBY, Mattie Boyd 165
  W. F. 165
CROW, James F. 135, 136
  Lewis F. 136
  Louise (Terry) 136
  Martha Wadsworth 136
  Mary 136
  Philps Terry 136
  W. H. 136
CROWNOVER, Mary (Chesney)
    372
  Mary (Rabb) 272
  John 373, 375
CRUTCHER, Flora 137
  J. G. 137
  Mrs. J. G. 137
CULBERSON, Governor 268
  Charles 66
  David B. 66, 124
  James H. 66, 69
  Mrs. M. E. (Bridges)
    69
  Mr. S. E. (Bridges) 69
  S. J. 69
  -- Mrs. (Wilkinson) 66
CUMMINS, Eliza (Moore)
    410
  James 410
  Mariah (Cook) 411
  Wiley 411
CUNNINGHAM, Araminta
    (Sterne) 423
  John A., Judge 423
DANA, Napoleon, Gen. 42
DANCER, James, Rev. 435
DANIELS, J. W., Rev. 354
  Susan A. (Ballard) 354
DARDEN, Emily A. (Ford)
    272
  George 272
DARR, Sarah Ann (Singleton)
    209
  Sarah (Brown) 209
  William A. 209
DARST, Cyres Crosby 344
  David 343, 344
  David S. H. 343, 344
  Jacob C. 343, 344
  Margaret C. (Hughes)
    343
  Nancy 344
DAVIESS, James 336
  Joseph 336
  Mary (Knox) 336
  Mary (Wrisk) 336
  Robert 336
  Samuel 336
DAVIDSON, Callie (Smith)
    421
  George 350
  Lorena (Hill) 421
  Sarah W. (Woods) 350

4

DAVIDSON (cont.)
William, General 350
W. T. 421
DAVIS, -- 40, 42
Bettie (Robinson) 410
Bishop 428
Catherine (McLennon)
119
E. J. 47
Jefferson 126, 271,
358, 398
Governor 134
Harvey 77
L. E. R. 119
Virginia 77
W. H. 77
DAVENPORT, Samuel 24
DAWSON, -- 195, 228, 409
Annie (Flint) 142
S. W. L., Col. 141,
142
James 141
Lucy (Hammond) 141
Nicholas 40
Sarah R. 46
DE AGUAYO, Marquis 46
DE ALARCONNE, Don Martin
46
DE ALMAZAN, Fernando 46
DE ANAYA, Don Gaspardo 46
DE BLAREJEANS, -- 20
DE BRAYS, Brigade 350
DE BARRISS, Jacinto 46
DE BEJAR, San Antonio 39
DE FRANQUIS, Carlos 46
DE GAVALO, Lorenzo 111
DE HERRERA, Jose Manuel
24
DE LARA, Gutierrez
Bernardo 23
DE LA SALLE, Robert
Cavalier 17, 20
DE LEON 19, 25
Martin 25
DE MADIAVILLA, Melchoir
46
DE MARTOS, Antonio 46
DE MORSE, Charles, Col.
150
DENNY, Ada Lou (Beasley)
208
Anderson 283
David 283
John 283
W. H. 208
DENTON, Matilda 143
DEPART, -- Mr. 115
DEPREE, Louis 288
DE RIPERDA, Brown 46
DE SALCEDO, Manuel 46
DE SANDOVAL, Manuel 46
DE SOTO, -- 17
DEVER, Frank 240
John 240
Mary 240
Nathan E. 239, 240
R. H. (Foster) 240
Teula (Clay) 265
Walter 240
William 239
William T. 265
DE WITT, -- 25
DE ZAVALA, Lorenzo 28,
31, 43
DICKERSON, Miss 109
DICKEY, Alice Hobbs 339
Alma B. 339
Clio E. 339
Eugene W. 339
James W. 338, 339
John Milton 338
L. Elmore 339
Leonard M. 339

DICKEY (cont.)
Marion W. 339
Martha J. (Gillett)
339
Maurice 339
Priscilla (Johns-
Gillispie) 338
R. Lilly 339
Zella A. 339
DICKINSON, Lt. 35
Abisha 287
Ann M. (Sutherland)
287
Mary (Exall) 302
DILLARD, Abraham 386
Sarah E. (Burnett)
386
DILWORTH, Mrs. Foster
345
DOBNEY, J. S. 381
Dominguez, Christoval
46
DONALSON, Benjamin
Franklin 357
Clauncey B. 357
Elizabeth (Donnell)
356
Elizabeth (Northcraft)
357
-- (Ewing) 356
George W. 357
Israel B., Major 355,
356, 357, 358
John 356
Laura (Price) 357
Lucy Ann (Lee) 357
Lucy (Cherewith) 357
Lucy Lee (Calvert) 356
Vernetha (McGee) 357
DONELSON, John 313
DONIPHAN, Margaret (Adams)
325
DONNELL, Elizabeth
(Donalson) 356
DORRAH, James 283
Margaret (Anderson)
283
DORSEY, Mary (Simpson)
304
Michael 305
DRAKE, -- 362
Fannie Garland (Ward)
185
Walter, Dr. 185
DRISKELL, Tobitha
(Rowell) 232
DRIVER, Martha (Houston)
200
G. L., Col. 200
DUBOIS, Ida 378
John 378
Josephine (Bragger-
Turner) 378
Lena 378
Leola 378
Louis 378
DUFFS REGIMENT 213
DUGGAN, Thomas H. 195
DUKE, Mamie E. (Hart) 304
William, Rev. 304
DUNHAM, Robert 332
DURRAM, J. C., Dr. 239
Sally Gray (Stallcup)
239
DURRAM, Sarah H. 239
DUSENBERRY, John 332
DUTY, Catherine 149
EARTHMAN, Mary (Kenedy)
377
EASTLAND, Wm., Capt. 330,
332
EBERLY, Jacob, Capt. 78
ECKLES, Martha (Blake) 337

ECTOR, General 86
EDISON, Dr. 378
Ida (Turner) 378
EDWARDS, Andrew, Dr. 207
Hayden 24, 25
Jane (Little) 370
Louisa (Beasley) 207
EKWURZEL, M. O. G. 165
Sarah L. (Boyd) 165
ELDRIDGE, Anna Bell 252
Amanda F. (Turner)
250
Bolling, Capt. 250,
251, 252
Bolling, Jr. 252
F. A. 251
John C. 250
Kate Hurley 252
Maggie Mildred 252
Mary (Sheappard) 252
-- Mrs. (O'Ridam) 251
Thomas H. 251
Mrs. V. A. Williams
251
EL GUAZEBEL, Juan Bautista
46
ELLICOTT, -- 24
ELLIOTT, Bishop 428
ELLIS, O. 299
Richard 31
V. 299
EMONSON, Amanda (McCutchen)
450
Cassandra C. 450
Colonel 450
Rebecca 450
Temperance (Suddith)
450
ENGLISH, -- 87
ENNIS, Lucy (Riley) 424
Robert 424
ERATH, George B., Capt.
119
ESTA, Edmund 332
ETOR, M. D. General 439
EVANS, Joseph L. 447
Major 35
Mrs. Phillips 447
EWING, Amanda Melvina 157
Edley 157
Tom 356
EXALL, Angy E. (Pierce)
300
Emma Warner 301
George G., Rev. 300
Henry 300, 301, 302
Mary (Dickson) 302
FALKNER, Mrs. Martha
(Power) 154
W. R. 154
FANNIN, -- 30, 36
Colonel 36, 189, 344
FARIAS, Gomez 27, 28
FARQUHAR, Mrs. James
(Robison) 410
FAULKENBERRY, Daniel 148,
149
Nancy 149
FELDTMANN, Casper G. 299
FENNER, Eugenia A.
(Burges) 362
Richard, Capt. 362
Richard, Dr. 362
FERRIS, Laura Jane (Lane)
370
FIEDLER, Caroline Nagle
324
John A. 323, 324
John H. 324
Mamie 324
FIELD, Alexander, Dr. 227
A. S. 226, 227
Fannie Jones 227

5

FIELD (cont.)
Laura (Lewis) 227
Robert 227
FILISOLA, -- 25, 35
FILLMORE, Millard 64, 446
FINCH, Annie Louisa 438
Elizabeth (Hayter) 217
John Mastin 438
Mary Roberta 438
Sarah (Oldham-Pierce)
433, 438
Sarah Fannie
FISHER, S. (Rhodes) 44
FITZGERALD, -- (Lane) 369
FLAITAU, Elizabeth (Pitts)
274
Lewis, Capt. 274
FLANAGAN, Charles 230
Elizabeth (Graham) 226
Emmet, Dr. 226
James Winright 223
J. W., Major 137, 230
Louisa Ann (Burnett)
230
Sallie (Ware) 226
Webb Hon. 87
Webster, General 223,
225
FLEMING, J. R., Hon. 459
FLEWELLEN, J. J. 137
Nettie 137
FLINT, Annie 142
Eliza 142
Thomas 142
FLOYD, General 208
FONKHAUSER, Mary (Mullen)
443
FORD, Dr. 140
David, Rev. 128, 134
Emily A. (Darden) 272
Eliza J. (White) 234
Evelyn (Thompson) 135
Fannie (Cates) 129
F. C., Dr. 128, 129,
134
George 271
H. F., Dr. 271, 272
James L. 234
Jean 135
John 271
John S., Col. 43, 436
John V. 234, 235
Maria V. (Hamilton)
134
Octavine (Coleman) 135
Regiment 430
Richard 271
Thomas 271
W. H., Judge 133, 134,
135, 235
FORIS, Eliza M. (Killough)
412
R. O. 412
FORMAN, Charles 254
Pattie (Stroud) 254
FOSTER, Dr. 272
Elizabeth 347
Elizabeth (Parchman-
Dilworth) 345
Eliza Ann (Rutledge-
King) 346
Ella (Ford) 272
James Chism 347
John 240
John E. 345
John King 347
L. L. 80
Martha Ann (Morrison-
King) 347
Mary 347
Mary (Moore) 345
Mary (Moore-Hardeman)
345

FOSTER (cont.)
Minnie Alice (Morrison)
347
Philip Houston 347
Miss R. H. (Dever)
240
Thomas Pickney 347
William Lee 347
William London, Capt.
345, 346, 347
FOX, A. F., Rev. 436
FRAZIER, Rose (Riley)
424
FRAZOR, George 220
Maud (Spelling) 220
FREMENT, John C., General
413
FRENCH, General 440
Mary E. 267
FRIEND, C. C. 171
Maud (Heartsill) 171
FROBESE, Alfreda (Reuss)
341
William 341
FRY, Colonel 234
E. F. 234
Sophia (Cobb) 234
FULCKER, Nancy (Mast) 206
Zaruah (Armstrong) 419
FULCORD, Colonel 437
FUTRELL, Anderson 123
Anna (Hoyler) 123
Anna T. (Boyd) 165
Berry 122, 123
C. D. 123
Frankey 123
F. D. 122, 123, 165
J. A. 123
Lucy B. (Lambertson)
123
Lillie 123
Nellie 123
Virginia (Camp) 122
GADSDEN, Bishop 428
GALLAGHER, Mary (O'neil)
354
GAMBLE, William 365
GARCIA, -- 31
GAREN, Robert 448
Sarah A. (Wheeler) 448
GARFIELD, President 447
GARNETT, Mary (Ashby) 400
GARRISON, Abigail (Bonner)
81
Elizabeth 141
Elizabeth H. (Lacey)
82
George F. 85
George M., Judge 83
Henry D. 82
James F. 81, 82 -
James G. 82
James H., Capt. 83,
84, 85
Gay, J. H. 448
John H. 81, 82
John I. 82
Mary Ann (Casper) 83
Mary C. (Young) 85
Rora B. 82
Ruth 82, 141
William Young 85
Z. B., Capt. 80, 82,
83, 84, 141
GELLHORN, Fannie (Ashley)
404
Roderick Major 404
GIBSON, Fannie Hampton
(Young) 438
Judge 330
-- Mr. 452
GIDDINGS, George, Col.
130

GILDER, Jacob 102
Mary A. H. 102
GILIS, Capt. 463
GILLESPIE, J. E. 450
Jerusha E. (Kerr) 450
Priscilla Johns
(Dickey) 338
GILLETTE, Lucinda (Maxey)
250
Martha J. (Dickey) 339
Professor 250
GILLETT, R. Rev. 339
GIPSON, Arch. 194
GISHARD, Mr. 451
GOLDEN, Harry 397
GONZALEZ, Rafael 25, 47
GOSMAN, F. H. 462
GOSS, Spencer 435
GOODBREAD, Joseph 40
GOODLOVE, Capt. 106
GRAHAM, Charles, Gen.
124, 125
C. G., Capt. 124
Elizabeth (Flanaghan)
226
Elizabeth (Lowdon) 195
Jennie 124
Karl 124
Major 124
Texie (Harris) 124
GRAMBLING, A. M. 233
Ella (Rowell) 233
GRANBURY'S BRIGADE
GRANT, Dr. 35
General 84, 226, 447
GRAY, Annie (Hill) 421
Arthur 421
F. C. 53
GRAYSON, Peter W. 44
GREELY, Horace 179, 258,
432
GREGG, Alexander Bishop
427, 428, 429, 430
Alexander Pendleton 430
Charlotte (Wilson) 430
Cochran, Mrs. 430
David 427, 430
John 427
Joseph 425
Oliver Hawes 430
Margaret Amelia
(Rector) 430
Mary E. 430
Wilmerding, Mrs. 430
Wilson 430
GREEN BRIGADE 354, 412,
460
Ed J. L. 383
General 293
Mary D. (Burleson) 383
Thomas, Col. 169, 262,
285, 366, 436, 437,
456
GREENWOOD, Calphurnia
(Grubbs) 281
Carrie (Benner) 281
Emmett 281
Eugenia 281
James 281
Juliet (Crocker) 281
Lydia (Moore) 280
Paul James 281
Thomas 280, 281
Thomas Calhoun 279,
280, 281
GRIBBLE, Joseph B. 244,
245
Margaret (James) 244
Rison D. 244, 245
GRIFFIN, Eliza 183
GRIGSBY, Mattie (Rowell)
233
Mr. 233

6

GRIGSBY (cont.)
　Sallie M. (Riley) 425
　William 425
GRIMES, Louisa (Russell)
　255
　William 255
GRISHAM, William 147
GRITTON, -- 29
GRUBBS, Calphurnia
　(Greenwood) 281
　W. J. 281
GUEST, Elias 220
　Louisa (Spellings) 219
　Guerrero 25
GUTHERIDGE, Martha
　(Rickenbough-Ragan)
　398
GUTHRIE, Jane (Sterne)
　422
GUTIERREZ, -- 24
HAIL, Amanda Melvina
　(Ewing) 157
　Benjamine (Ewing) 158
　Edward E. 158
　James Wilson 158
　Jonas 157
　Mary H. (Smith) 158
　Taylor J. 158
　Wilson E. 157, 158
HALL, R. W., Dr. 218
　Mary Buford (Hayter)
　218
HALLET, Binjamin 352
　John 351, 352, 353
　Margaret P.
　(Leatherbury) 352
　Mary Jane (Ballard)
　352, 353
　William Henry 352
HALSEY, Dr. 434
HAMN, Mansfield 257
HAMILTON, A. J. 47
　James General 39, 309
　Governor 225
　Maria V. 134
HAMLETT, Emily 139
　Stephen 139
HAMMOND, Lucy 141
HAMPTON, G. J. 366
HANCOCK, -- 87
HANLY, W. W. 305
HANSON, Lou (Pitts) 274
HARDEMAN, Bailey 44
　Col. D. 446
　Dr. 345
　Regiment 377
GARGROVE, Capt. 417
HARRIS, Ella 72
　Eliza J. (Singleton)
　211
　Lucy 143
　Robert 332
　Texie (Graham) 124
　T. A., Dr. 211
HARNEY, General 419
HARRISON, Abbie (Sheets)
　440, 441
　Ed 441
　Jessie J. 440, 441
　John C. 185
　Keziah 72
　Lillie 441
　Maggie 441
　President 303, 442
　R. H., Dr. 338, 339,
　340
　Robert H. 441
　Sarah Blythe (Ward)
　185
　W. H., General 414
　William 441
HART, Albert 364
　Ann (Hart) 363

HART (cont.)
　Benjamin F. 303
　Bridget (West) 364
　Catherine (Ryan) 364
　Edith (Mussett) 364
　Felix J., Judge 363,
　364
　Joe C. D. 304
　Joseph Crockett 303,
　304
　John 364
　Leslie Lee 304
　Luke 363, 364
　Lula 304
　Maggie (Otto) 364
　Mamie E. (Duke) 304
　Mary J. 364
　Nancy W. (Telman) 303
　Russell 304
　Timothy 364
　William F. T. 303
　William O. 304
HARVEY, Mrs. Belle
　(McCoy-Julian) 432
　Sarah F. (Pitts) 274
HAVILAND, -- 196
HAWES, Catherine
　(Coleman) 282
　Nancy (Braman) 425
HAWKINS, Ariella (Alston)
　88
　Edgar 89
　Ella 89
　Frank 89
　James 89
　James B., Col. 88
　John D. 89
　Sallie 89
　Virginia
　Willis 89
HAYNES, Albert G. 250
　Rebecca (Maxey) 248
　Thomas H. 248
HAYNIE, -- Mr. 307, 038
HAYS, General 395
　John C. 310, 311, 312,
　332
　Reigment 374
HAYTER, Elizabeth (Finch)
　217
　Mrs. H. H. Rainbolt
　217
　John J. 217, 218
　Mary Buford (Hall) 218
　Samuel 217
　Mrs. S. H. Barham 217
　William 217
HEARNE, Mrs. E. C. Stroud
　253
HEARTSILL, Abraham 170
　Abram 170
　Charles E. 171
　Eliza (Stevens) 171
　Kate 171
　Louisa (Rankin) 170
　Mattie 171
　Maud (Friend) 171
　Minnie 171
　Willie 171
　W. W. 170, 171
HELD, Kate (Wood) 259
　Justus 259
HENDERSON, Governor 41,
　45, 190
　James W. 316
　J. P. (General) 45
　J. Pickney 44, 47
HENECKE, Jane 223
HENRY, Elizabeth (Bales)
　285
　John 285
　John L., Colonel 87
HENSLEY, Mary (Bickford)

HENSLEY (cont.)
　Mary (Bickford) (cont.)
　368
　Mary P. 368
　William R. 368
HESSER, Elizabeth
　(O'Conner) 388
HICH, B. J., Dr. 271
HICKS, Annie E. (McDugald)
　463
　Clara (Walker) 463
　Emma L. 463
　John 461
　Francis Marion, Col.
　461, 462, 463, 464
　Francis Marion, Jr.
　463
　Lelia (Laurence) 463
　Margaret (Moon) 461
　Margaret R. (Spence)
　464
　Marshall 463
　Richard Yale 463
　Samuel 463
　S. B. 462
　William A. 461
HIDALGO, -- 25
HILL, Annie (Gray) 421
　Ben 208
　Elizabeth (Pitts) 420
　Ephriam 420
　George B. 420
　Georgie E. 421
　George W. 421
　Jacob 420, 421
　James H. 421
　J. M. 452
　John 420, 421
　Lorena (Davidson) 421
　Mary M. (Bollinger)
　420
　Peter 420
　Sarah A. (Allbright)
　421
　William I. 421
HILLIARD, Amelia Ann
　(Toole) 156
　Annie 157
　Emma 157
　Etta 157
　Eugene 157
　Henry 157
　H. J. 156, 157
　Irwin 157
　J--- 156
　Mildred F. (Baldwin)
　157
　Myra 157
　Myrtle 157
　Vernon 157
　Walter 157
HILLYARD, Catherine
　(Bollinger) 420
HIGHTOWER, Harriet Ann
　(Pitts) 273
HINDMAN, General 175
HINSLEY, Georgie E. 421
　R. S. 421
HITCHCOCK, Colonel 451
HOBBS, Alice (Dickey)
　337
　Job 339
HOCKLEY, George W., Col.
　37
HOOD, General 440
　-- 177, 287, 387
　Brigade 124, 163, 251,
　263, 362
　John B., Col. 151, 292
HODDE, Albert 156
　Amelia 156
　August 156
　Fred 156

HODDE (cont.)
  Henry 154, 155, 156
  Kate (Wickleman) 156
  Louisa (Kramer) 155
  Louisa 156
  Matilda 156
  William 156
HOFFMAN, Elizabeth
  (Imhoff) 262
  John J. 261, 262
HOGSHEAD, Elijah 450
  Peggie (Kerr) 450
HOGG, Governor 153
  J. S. 47
  Michael 455, 463
HOGUE, Peter C. 450
  Gallie (Kerr) 450
HOLCOMB, Anna 114
HOLMS, General 175
HOLMAN, Nancy B. 113
HOLLIDAY, Eliza (Horton)
  186
  John 328
HOLLINGSWORTH, J. E. 80
HOLLIS, John 348
  Martha (Moore) 347
HOLLOWAY, Rebecca (Peel)
  277
HOOD, -- 177, 287, 387
  General 440
HOOVER, Andrew 431
  Rebecca (Julian) 431
HORNER, George Hon. 299
  Minna (Piper) 299
HORNSBY, Ruba 307, 308
HORTON, -- 36
  Albert C., Gov. 445,
    446
  Albert C., Hon. 46,
    186, 189, 190, 191
  Eliza (Holliday) 186
  H. S., Rev. 436
HORWELL, Judith (Robison)
  410
HOUS, Ida (Knittle) 223
HOUSTON, -- 39, 40, 42,
  48, 62, 63, 64, 189
  Mrs. Allen 62
  B. F. 196, 200
  Esther (Walker) 196
  General 36, 38, 39,
    44, 61, 78, 116,
    126, 183, 205, 240,
    257, 287, 315, 352,
    371, 381, 400, 408,
    430, 465
  John P. 275
  Margaret (Moffette) 63
  Martha (Driver) 200
  Mary H. (Mays) 275
  Major A. 196
  President 38, 40, 44,
    45, 63, 310
  Sam 27, 29, 31, 37,
    47, 71, 226, 236,
    360
HOWARD, Capt. 38
  A. 113
  Mollie A. 113
HOWELL, Robert H. 462
HOXIE, Lelia (Clary) 265
  Thomas 265
HOYLER, Anna 123
HUBBARD, Governor 343
  Hilery, Dr. 173
  Mollie (Moore) 343
  Miller 343
  R. B. 47, 166
HUDGINS, Eliza A. 150
  Thomas D. 150
HUDSON, Dora 144
HUDSPETH, Mr. 413
  Sarah E. (Myers) 413

HUERTA, Domingo, Colonel
  329
HUGHES, Margaret C.
  (Darst) 343
HUNT, Mary (Moore) 412
HURLEY, Kate (Eldridge)
  252
HUTCHINSON, W. L., Major
  289
HYNES, Amy (Swindall)
  245
  Fannie (Ammons) 247
  Lee 247
  Mary E. (Slater) 247
  T. O., Dr. 245, 246,
    247
  Thomas 245
IMHOFF, Elizabeth
  (Hoffman) 262
IRELAND, John 47
  Governor 153
ITURBIDE, -- 201
IVES, Caleb S. 53
JACK, Wm. H., Col. 30
JACKSON, Charles W. 40
  General 61, 93, 112,
    114, 124, 125, 256,
    313
  President 45, 62, 315
JACOB, -- 380
JAMES, Kaleta B. (O'Brien)
  180
  Orpha 149
  William 180
  Margaret (Gribble) 244
JARMON'S CO. 375
JARROL, J. S. 381
JOHNSON, -- 177
  Cinthelia Ann (Lord)
    333
  Frank (Col.) 381
  F. W. 28, 35
  General 352
  John 333
JOHNSTON, Albert Sidney,
  Gen. 180, 183, 246,
    403, 456
  Eliza (Griffin) 183
  Henrietta (Preston)
    180
  Jacob N. 231
  John, Dr. 108
  Joseph E. 439
  Sarah Jane (Burnett)
    231
  William Preston, Col.
    456
JOLLY, J. M. 383
JONES, Anson 40, 45, 47
  Capt. 112
  Christina 119
  Eli 119
  Erastus 108
  Fannie (Field) 227
  George W., Hon. 169
  Gifford, Rev. 278
  Mrs. H. K. (Branches)
    403
  John M. 191
  Mariah (Wood) 191
  Mary E. (Sterne) 423
  Mattie E. (Peel) 192,
    278
  P. P. 278
  President 45
  Sallie E. (Nash) 192
  Thomas L. 332
  William F. 191
  William Wood 192
JORDAN, Capt. 328
  Temperance (Chapman)
    293
JOYCE, Albert G. 400

JOYCE (cont.)
  Dora A. 400
  Emily (Stanfield) 400
  Harvey W. 400
  Henry 398
  Laura Lee (Mitchell)
    400
  Martin O.
  May (Kelso) 400
  Robert D. 400
  Sarah (Posey) 398
  William H. 400
  William Jasper, Rev.
    398, 399, 400
JULIAN, Belle (McCoy-
  Harvey) 432
  Isaac H. 355, 356, 357,
    431, 432
  Isaac H., Jr. 431
  Rebecca (Hover) 431
  Virginia M. (Spillard)
    432
JUNKER, Guy W. 267
  Lula (Langham) 267
KAAPKE, C. E. 284
  N. Bertie (Anderson)
    284
KARNES, Capt. 37
KATIP, Capt. 418
KEARNS, Minnie (Addis)
  259
KEITH, Cortez 361
  Mary E. (Bellinger)
    361
  Sarah (LePort-Ballinger)
    361
KELLER, Emily (Leuschner)
  334
KELLY, G. A. 192
KELSO, May (Joyce) 400
  W., Judge 400
KEMP, Colonel 272
KEMPER, Fannie M. (Young)
  440
KENNARD, J. B. (Mrs.)
  403
KENNEDY, A. S. 375
  Caroline 89
  Diana (Sutherland) 286
  Dulcie (Robb) 375
  J. M. 89
  Mary (Earthman) 375
KENT, A. D. 237
  Andrew J. 386
  Drusilla (McFadden)
    237
KERR, A. B. 456
  Abnus B. 449, 450, 451,
    452, 453, 454
  Alice L. 453
  Betsie (Wallace) 450
KERR, Bettie (Ragsdale)
  453
  Charles G. 453
  Cassandra (McCutchen)
    449
  David Samuel 450
  Eleanor (Burnett) 232
  James L. 453
  Jerusha E. (Gillespie)
    450
  John A. 453
  J. W. 232
  Jane (Anderson) 450
  May (Murcer) 452
  Mary 453
  Mary C. A. 450
  Peggie (Hogshead) 450
  Sallie (Hogue) 450
  Robert G. 449, 450
  Robert O. 450
  R. L. 453
  Thomas O. 453

8

KERR (cont.)
  Wallace B. 453
  William 449
  William, Jr. 450
KILGORE, Capt. 86
  C. B., Colonel 85, 86
KILLOUGH, Annie (Moon)
    412
  David M. 412
  Eliza M. (Foris) 412
  I. G. 410, 412
  Ira G. 412
  John H. 412
  Lucy (Saunders) 412
  Maggie E. (Burns) 412
  Robert E. Lee 412
  Tobitha 410, 411, 412,
    413
KIMBALL, Agusta 122
  Allen, Dr. 122
KIMBROUGH, Capt. 158
KING, Capt. 36
  Elizabeth Ann Rutledge
    (Foster) 346
  Euphemia (Ashley) 404
  H. Clay 456, 458
  Mary (McLeary) 457
  John .G. Colonel 345,
    346
  V. O., Hon. 457
  William, Major 404
  W. H., Colonel 124
  W. W., Judge 458
KLING, F. 120
  Dr. 120
KNITTLE, Alvina 223
  Charles 223
  Emma (Watson) 223
  Ernest 223
  George 223
  Herman, Hon. 221, 222,
    223
  Ida (Hous) 223
  Jane (Henecke) 223
  Lula 223
  Rachel 223
KNOX, Abner 336
  Andrew W. 336
  Catherine T. (Blake)
    336
  Elizabeth (Taggart)
    336
  Mary (Daviess) 336
  May (Remschell) 338
  Robert Taggart, Dr.
    335, 336, 337, 338
  Thomas Roger 337
KOLLOCK, Oliver H. 430
  Sarah (Wilson) 430
KONE, Carrie 290
  Edna (Woods) 290
  Ed. R., Judge 288, 289,
    290
  Eula Lee 290
  Julia R. 290
  Lula H. (Martin) 290
  Rebecca S. (Pitts) 288
  Samuel R. 288, 289
KRAMER, Fredrick 156
  Louisa (Hodde) 156
KREISLE, L. G. 366
KYLE, Ailene 395
  Albert Johnson 395
  Andrew Jackson 395
  Anna (Moore) 395
  Claiborne, Col. 383,
    392
  Curran 395
  Edward Johnson 395
  Ellen 395
  Emma (Burlson) 383
  Ferg, Capt. 391, 392,
    395

KYLE (cont.)
  John 392
  Josephine 395
  Lucy (Bugg) 392
  Mary 395
  Polk 395
  Rosa 395
  Sidney Johnson 395
  William 395
LA BRANCHE, Alcee 44
LACEY, Elizabeth H. 82
LAFITTE, -- 24, 110, 145
LAIRD, Ann (Carter) 372
  Maggie 372
  Thomas 372
LALLEMAND, Gen. 21
LAMER, -- 38, 44, 45, 63
  Lucius Quintus,
    Cincennatus 174
  Mirabeau Buonaparte
    37, 44, 47, 173,
    174, 183, 190
LAMBERTON, Lucy B.
    (Futrell) 123
  W. A. 123
LANCASTER, Thomas A. 383
LANE, Ann Brown
    (Southerland) 287
  Annie Laurie 370
  Fitzgerald 369
  George Franklin 370
  John Lafayette, Capt.
    368, 369, 370
  Laura Jane (Ferris)
    370
  Mary (Colthorpe) 369
  Minerva Ann (McMahan)
    370
  Pleasant 369
  Queen 370
  Regiment 144
  Samuel Tipton 370
  Walter M. 332
  Walter P. 151, 331,
    332
LANGHAM, H. C. 267
  Mary E. (French) 267
  James B. 265
  Lula Junker 267
  Saie 267
  Sarah Jane (Nattles)
    266
  Thomas 265
  Thomas H. 265, 266,
    267
LANGS, D. A. (Barham) 140
  Regiment 204
LARGENT, Ellie
    (Singleton) 211
  F. R. 211
LAURENCE, Dr. 463
  Jasper 233
  Lelia (Hicks) 463
  Mary (Rowell) 233
LAWSHE, Georgia 351
LEAK, Alonzo 102
  E. E., Dr. 102
  Eliza (Burge) 101
  Garlington 101, 102
  James 102
  M. G. 102
  Mary A. H. (Gilder)
    102
  R. A., Dr. 102
  Robert, Dr. 101, 105
  Samuel
LEATHERBURY, Margaret P.
    (Hallett) 352
LEDBETTER, Almeida
    (Robison) 409
  Dr. 337
  T. A. 409
LEE, Abigail 70

LEE (cont.)
  Ebenezer 70
  General 84, 202, 208.
    264, 395, 456
  Lucy Ann (Donalson)
    357
  Robert E. 357
LEFTWICK, Robert 161
LE GARCIA, Don Luciana 47
LE GARE, Hugh Swinton 359
LE NOIR, Frances 125
LE PORT, Sarah (Keith)
    361
LETONA, Jose Maria 47
LEUSCHNER, Adelia S. 335
  Agustus Fredrick 334
  Charles A. 334, 335
  Emily (Keller) 334
  G. A. 334
  Ida 335
  Leopold A. 335
  Lizetta 335
  Louisa L. 335
  Meta 335
  Regina 335
  Sophia (Bescohoff) 335
  Victor A. 335
  William C. 335
LEWIS, Dr. 227
  Laura (Fields) 227
  Mark B., Capt. 40
LIKENS, Battalion 179
LINCOLN, -- 64, 146, 358,
    360, 432
  Abraham, Mrs. 150
LINSCOM, Joseph 146
  Laura L. (Van Ness)
    146
LITTLE, George 371
  Hugh 372
  James 371
  Jane (Edwards) 370,
    371, 372
  John 371
  Maggie (Larid) 372
  Martha 371
  Mary (McRee) 372
  Nellie 372
  Robert 371
  Sarah (Wilson) 372
  Walter 370, 371, 372
  William 370, 371
LITTLEFIELD, H. B. 420
  Sarah (Bollinger) 420
LIVINGSTON, Sarah Ann
    (Burnett) 386
LOCKETT, -- 204
  Albert 204
  Alice (Roberson) 115
  Anna 204
  Emmet 204
  Hamilton 204
  J. 115
  Jacob 203
  Laura (Moore) 204
  Laura (Pruit) 204
  Martha (Smith) 203
  Opal 204
  Pruit 204
  Royal 203, 204
  Sallie 204
  Mrs. Smith 204
  Thomas 204
  Thomas N. 203, 204
LOGAN, Colonel 366
  Mrs. John A. 356
LONG, -- 110
  General 53
  James 24
LONGLEY, Bill 206
LOPEZ, -- 328
LORD, Ann (Siggs) 327
  Cinthelia Ann (Johnson)

9

LORD (cont.)
  Cinthelia Ann (Johnson)
    (cont.) 333
  Emily Agnes (Smith) 333
  Filstead 327
  George 327, 328, 329,
    330, 331, 332, 333
  George T. 333
  Henry Lee 333
  James E. 333
  Kate A. 333
  Kate (Myers) 333
  Minnie May 333
  Pomona B. 333
  Robert F. 333
  Sidney Johnston 333
  William P. 333
LOUGHRIDGE, Prof. 17
LOVELADY, Cyrus 110
  Martha 110
LOW, A. D. W., General
  269
  Arthur 270
  Amanda (Matlock) 269
  Asa A. 270
  Cecelia T. (Baine) 270
  Cornelia A. 270
  Robert M. 270
  Theodore A., Jr. 270
  Theodore A., Sr. 269,
    270
  Samuel D. W. 270
  William G. 270
LOWDEN, Alice (Crane) 196
  Elizabeth (Graham) 195
  James Graham 195, 196
  William L. 195
LUBBOCK, F. R. 47
LUKA, Jim 418
LUSK, Beersheba 131
  Samuel 131
LYNCH, Bridget 109
LYONS, Capt. 327
  O. T., Capt. 244
MACKEY, Elizabeth
  (McFadden) 236
MADDOX, Dr. 110
MAGEE, Augustus 23
  Hattie (Moore) 349
  M. S. 349
MAGRUDER, (Confederate)
  42
MAHAN, Patrick 332
MALLON, Bernard 48
MARK, Mr. 97
MARKS, Carrie A. (Perry)
  203
  Eleanor 203
  Fannie (Calvert) 203
  John H. 202
  Nicholas M. 201, 202
  Rebecca L. (Wright) 202
  Robertson (Mrs.) 202
  Thomas M. 201, 202, 203
  Willie (Webb) 203
MARIA, Juan 46
MARION, General 204
MARONEY, Benjamin 260
  Daniel W. 260
  Fanny 261
  Florence 260
  Grace 261
  Hester 261
  James T., Judge 260,
    261
  John 260
  J. T. 261
  Nancy (Pollard) 260
  Parilee (Cochran) 261
  Richard 260
  Ruby 261
  Tennie (Chatham) 260
  Travis 261

MARONEY (cont.)
  William W. 260
MARR, Lady Helen
  (Russell) 255
MARSHALL, Anna 268
  Archie 268
  Catherine (Shaw) 267
  Edward Aubrey 268
  Edward P. 268
  Frank W. 268
  Jesse S. 267
  J. M. 123, 165, 267,
    268
  Harry 268
  James Walter 268
  Levina Boyd 165
  Tom 357
  Vina Boyd 268
  William H. 268
MARTIN, Archie 290
  Lula H. (Kone) 290
  Sarah Gane (Ussery)
    438
  T. W., Judge 280
MARTINEZ, Antonio 46
MARVIN, Bishop 211
MAST, Baxter 207
  Blanche 207
  Cora (Patton) 207
  Guy 207
  Jacob 205
  J. W. 207
  Leona 206, 207
  Milton, Capt. 205, 206
  Mollie 207
  Nancy A. 207
  Nancy (Fulcker) 206
  Oscar 207
  Reuben 207
MASON, Mrs. David
  (Anderson) 283
MASSEY, Elizabeth
  (Anderson) 283
MATHEWS, Abraham 176
  Ann 172
  Dr. 140
  Marietta (Watson) 292
  Thomas I. 247
MATHIS, Allie 216
  Arthur 216
  Cora C. Caldwell 216
  Edward 216
  Henry 216
  Isabella 212
  James 212
  J. M. 213
  J. T., Dr. 212
  Lizzie Belle 216
  May 216
  Mary J. (Nold) 216
  Thomas E. 216
  Thomas Henry 211, 212,
    213, 214, 215, 216
  Walter N. 216
MATIOS, Jose V., Capt.
  315
MATLOCK, Amanda (Low) 269
MAURY, General 220
MAUTHA, Edna E.
  (Northcutt) 238
MAXEY, Annie 249
  Finnie 249
  James M., Judge 248,
    249, 250
  John 249
  Lucinda (Gillette) 250
  Manly 249
  Matilda (Denton) 143
  Rebecca (Hayes) 248,
    250
  Rebecca (Ross) 249
  Samuel Bell, Hon. 142,
    143

MAXEY (cont.)
  S. B., Colonel 185
  Virginia (Mosley) 249
  Virgil 249
  Walter 248, 249
  William 248
MAYES, Alverado 275
  Almore D. 275, 276
  John H. 275
  Lizzie V. 275
  Mary Ann (Cotton) 275
  Mary H. (Houston) 275
  William D. 275
MC ADOR, Betsey (Stallcup)
  238
  Evans 238
MC ALENY, Mary Bridget
  (Wyer) 278
MC CALLISTER, Ellen
  (Pennington) 229
  Richard 229
MC CHRISTIAN, James 154
  Sarah (Power) 154
MC CLATCHY, J. F. 409
  Lucy (Robison) 409
MC CLEARY, Eliza Allen
  (Moore) 455
  James Allen 455
MC CLELLAND, Birdwell 77
  Charles Edwin 77
  Canfield 77
  Delow 77
  Faye 77
  Gracie 77
  Hugh 75
  John 75
  Jane (Stanley) 75
  Leela (Wilkerson) 77
  Margaret (Blain) 77
  Martha 75
  Martha (Clardy) 75
  Martha (Scaggs) 77
  May 77
  R. H., Dr. 77
  Ruth 77
  W. C., Rev. 75
  W. H., Rev. 75, 76
MC CLURE, Bartholomew A.
  400
  Joel B. 403
  Sarah Ann (Ashby) 400,
    403
MC CONNELL, Bridget
  (Lynch) 109
  Daniel 110
  Dickerson, Mrs. 109
  Esther 110
MC CONNELL, Henry 110
  Jeff 109
  John 109, 110
  Lizzie 109
  Martha (Lovelady) 109
  Patrick 109
  Phillip 110
  Robert E. 110
  Ruth 109
  William 109
MC COY, Belle (Harvey-
  Julian) 432
MC CRARY, Col. 86
  V. (Miss (Clay) 264
MC CULLOCH, Alexander 125
  Ben General 125, 126,
    127, 193, 194, 360,
    383, 445, 446
  Frances (Le Nois) 125
  H. A., Gen. 437
  Henry Eustace 193, 194,
    195
  Isabella (Ashly) 403
  Jane Isabella Ashly
    194
MC CULLOUGHS, Henry, Capt.

MC CULLOUGHS (cont.)
  Henry, Capt. (cont.)
    346, 348, 349
MC CURDY, A. H. P., Rev.
    284
  Mary Ianthe (Anderson)
    284
MC CUTCHEN, Amanda
    (Emonson) 450
  Cassandra (Kerr) 449
  Chapman 450
  Cyrus 450
  Downey 450
  Robert 450
MC DANIEL, Sarah Elizabeth
    173
MC DOW, Alexander 374
MC DUGAL, Ann E. (Hicks)
    463
  James 463
MC FADDEN, Andrew 237
  C. W. 237
  David H. 237
  Di (Averell) 237
  Drusilla (Kent) 237
  Elizabeth (Coward) 237
  Elizabeth (Mackey) 234
  Eliza (Chaison) 162
  James 162, 236
  James A. 237
  Rachel (Williams) 237
  Sarah A. (Alexander)
    237
  William 162, 235, 236,
    237
  W. P. H. 237
MC FARLAND, Judge 417
MC GAUGHEY, -- 398
MC GEE, Dr. 357
  Vernetha (Donaldson)
    357
MC GEEHE, James A., Dr.
    102
MC GLOWAN and MC MULLEN,
    -- 364
MC GREGOR, -- 427
MC KEE, John L., Rev. 337
MC KENZIE, J. W. P., Rev.
    151
MC LEARY, Emily (Mitchell)
    457
  James Harvey, Hon. 454,
    455, 456, 457, 458,
    459, 460
  John 455
  Mary (Cotton) 460
  Mary (King) 457
  Michael 455
  Samuel Davis, Dr. 455
  Sarah Ann (Weller) 455
  Thomas 455
MC LENNAN, Catherine
    (Davis) 119
  Christina (Jones) 119
  Duncan 119
  John 119
  Laughlin 116, 119
  Neil 116
  Neill 116, 119
MC LEOD, Hugh 151
  H. D., General 38
MC MAHAN, John 370
  Minerva Ann (Lane) 370
  Rebecca 370
MC NEIL, Brewer Taylor
    445
  Clarence W. 443, 444,
    445
  Edna Victoria 445
  Eugenia Alice (Chapman)
    294
  Moir, Mrs. 444
  Pinkie (Taylor) 445

MC NEIL (cont.)
  Victoria (McNeil) 443
  William 294
  William L. 443
MC NEELEY, S. A. 260
MC PHEETERS, G. P. 223
MC REE, Edward 372
  Mary (Little) 372
MEJIA, -- 26
MENIFEE, William 46
MEYERS, Capt. 369
  J. M., Dr. 336
MALAM, -- 24
  Benjamin R. 29, 201
  Colonel 31
MILLARD, Henry, Lt. Col.
    37
MILLER, Alsey 194
  A. P. 152
  Emma (Adams) 325
  J. B. 27
  John, Hon. 78
  Judge 86
  Marion B. 152
MILLS, John 257
  Roger Q. 225
  Sophia (Pettey) 257
MINA, -- 201
MINTURN, Mrs. R. (Bell)
    417
MITCHELL, Asa 400
  Emily (McLeary) 457
  Laura (Joyce) 400
MOFFETTE, Margaret 63
MOIR, Mrs. (McNeil) 444
MOLANO, -- 328
MONKS, Ellen (Cobb) 233
  Joseph 233
MONROE, President 145
MONTEZUMA, -- 23, 26
MOODY, John 149
  Margaret Angline 149
MOON, Annie (Killough)
    412
  J. M. 412
  Margaret (Hicks) 461
MOORE, -- 186
  Anna (Kyle) 395
  Annie (Shropshire) 349
  David E., Judge 395
  Eliza Allen (McLeary)
    455
  Eliza (Cook) 412
  Eliza (Cummins) 410
  General 233
  Georgia (Cooper) 297
  Harriet (Bairer) 411
  Hattie (Magee) 349
  H. W., Rev. 297
  Hollie 349
  James 347
  James H. 347, 348, 349
  John H., Col. 28, 38,
    410, 411, 412, 414
  Julia (Northcutt) 247
  Laura 204
  Lou V. (Thomas) 348
  Lydia (Greenwood) 280
  Martha (Hollis) 347
  Mary (Foster) 345
  Mary (Hunt) 412
  Nancy (Burnham) 411
  Robert 412
  Samuel, Capt. 455
  Sallie 349
  Sarah (Strong) 411
  Susie 349
  Thomas 349
  Thomas C. 347
  Tobitha (Killough) 410,
    411, 412
  Wiley 411
  William 412

MOORE (cont.)
  Willie 349
MORRELL, Z. N. 53
MORRIS, Major 35
  T. C. 77
MORRISON, Martha Ann
    (King-Foster) 347
  Minnie Alice (Foster)
    347
  N. 347
  Wesley 347
MORGANS, Rifleman 445
  Regiment 171
MORELOS, General 93
MORSE, Ammis (Bickford)
    367
  Clara (Addis) 258
  Daniel, Rev. 434
MORTON, John 371
  Louisa 371
  Mary 371
  William
MOSLEY, Levina 165
  Margaret E. (Boyd) 165
  Mason 165
  Virginia (Maxey) 249
MULLEN, Barney 441
  E. 441, 442, 443
  Mary (Fonkhauser) 443
  Mary (Murray) 441
MULLER, Gus 299
  Mary (Reuss) 340
MUNSON, George C., Mrs.
    80
MUNOZ, Manuel 46
MURCER, Levi 452
  Sarah (Munifee) 452
  Mary (Kerr) 452
MURRAH, Pendleton 47
MURRAY, Lynn 257
  Mary (Mullen) 441
  Virginia (Pettey) 257
MURPHY, Mattie A. 108
MUSSETT, Elias T. 364
  Edith (Hart) 364
MUGPUIZ, Lt. 23
MYERS, Abram Elijah 415
  Carrie Ellen 415
  Eliza 415
  Elijah 413
  Eliza Jane (Skaggs)
    413
  Eva (Boone) 415
  George 415
  Hettie Virginia (Cahill)
    415
  Jane (Williams) 415
  John Jacob, Col. 413,
    415
  Kate (Lord) 333
  Lafayette 415
  Robert E. Lee 415
  Samuel 413
  Sarah E. (Hudspeth)
    413
NAGLE, Caroline (Fiedler)
    324
NAPOLEON, -- 21
NASH, Mrs. D. E. 80
  Milton B. 192
  Sallie E. (Jones) 192
NATTLES, Jane (Langham)
    266
NAVARRO, Jose Antonio 39,
    166
NEIGHBORS, Adaline
    (Fairchild) 343
  Basley G., Judge 341,
    342, 343
  Bessie 343
  Henry B. 342
  Louisa F. (Sewell) 342
  Major 451

NEIGHBORS (cont.)
    Mollie Moore (Hubbard)
        343
    William 342
NEWMAN, A. M. 374
    Rachael (Rabb) 374
NICHOLS, C. M. Thurman
    320
NOLAN, -- 20, 23
    Philip 23, 91
NOLD, E. M., Mrs. 216
    Henry 216
    Mary J. (Mathis) 216
NORMAN, A. B. 90
    Ophelia 90
NORRIS, Nathaniel 38
    R. C., Major 30
NORTHCRAFT (Mrs. Burleson)
        383
    Edward 357
    Elizabeth (Donalson)
        357
NORTHCUTT, Dollie 248
    Edna E. (Mautha) 247
    Emma 248
    Julia (Moore) 247
    Leon 248
    W. D., Dr. 247, 248
    W. G. 247
NORTON and DEUTZ 298
NUNN, G. T. 299
O'BRIAN, Chenault 180
    Eliza A. (Bryan) 178
    Ellen P. (Chenault)
        180
    Emma E. (Smith) 180
    George Bryan 178
    George C. 180
    G. W., Capt. 177, 178,
        179, 180
    Kaleta B. (James) 180
    Lillie E. (Towsend)
        180
    Minnie G. (Stark) 180
    Robert P. 180
    Sarah E. (Rowley) 180
O'CONNER, Birdie (Clark)
        391
    Dennis 388
    Elizabeth (Hesser) 388
    Etta 391
    Fred J. 391
    Joseph, Judge 388, 391
    Lillie (Campbell) 391
    Sarah (Buckanan) 391
OCHILTREE, -- 122, 124
ODOM, Albert 378
    A. M. 379
    Frank D. 379
    Hettie H. 381
    James C. 378, 379, 380,
        381
    Louisa (Cole) 378
    Mary (Beeks-Copeland)
        380
    Milam M. 379
    Oliver 379
OGDEN, James 332
OGLETREE, Ella R. (Woods)
        351
OLIVE, America (Robison)
        410
    S. C. 410
O'NEAL, Drusella (Pitts)
        273
    Thomas 273
O'NEIL, Annie 355
    Edgar 355
    Estella 355
    Florene 355
    James D. 355
    Janie (Robinson) 355
    John 355

O'NEIL (cont.)
    John, Judge 354, 355
    Jueldine 355
    Louie 355
    Mary (Gallagher) 354
    Thomas 354
O'RIDAN, Mrs. (Eldridge)
        251
OSBORN, Joanna (Penning-
        ton) 228
OTTO, H. F. 364
    Maggie (Hart) 364
OWEN, I. N., Capt. 130
    Minnie (Pridham) 367
    R. 366, 367
    Sarah G. 64
PACHECO, Rafael 46
PALMER, Ann (Van Ness)
        145
    G. W., Judge 366
PARCHMAN, Elizabeth
        Dilworth (Foster)
        345
PARKER, Adeline Angline
        149
    Angelin 148
    Daniel 149
    James 148
    John 364
    Silas 148
    Martha (McClelland) 75
PARKS, W. 75
PARSONS BRIGADE 171
PARTISAN RANGERS 204
PATRICK, John 360
PATTON, Colonel 328
    C. B. 207
    Cora (Mast) 207
PEACE, -- 380
    E. M. 47
    Governor 41, 426
PEEL, Coy 278
    David 278
    David B. 277
    Mary 278
    Mattie E. (Jones) 278
    Nellie 278
    Raymond 278
    Rebecca (Holloway) 227
    Thomas J. 277, 278
PENNINGTON, Asa 229
    Ellen (McCallister)
        229, 230
    Elijah, Major 228,
        229, 230
    Joanna (Osborn) 228
    John 229
    Joseph 229
    Julia 229
    Lydia 229
    Matilda 229
    R. E. 229
    Riggs 228, 229
PEREZ, Colonel 24
PERKINS, James Judge 72
PERRY, -- 23, 24
    Carrie A. (Marks) 203
    H. B., Dr. 177
    James F. 138
    Lucy Claiborne 175
    William 175
    William A. 203
    Miss (Smith) 176
PETERS, George B., Hon.
        456
PETTY, Alexander 256
    Ambrose 256, 257
    Delia (Thrift) 256
    George W. 256, 257
    Ida Lee (Burch) 257
    Isham T. 257
    John A. 257
    John 256

PETTY (cont.)
    Lizzie White (Hamon)
        257
    Maggie I. 257
    Marian (Wood) 256
    Ruben 257
    Sophia (Mills) 257
    Virginia (Murray) 257
PHILLIPS, Ben McCullock
        447
    Calvin B. 276
    C. B., Dr. 276, 277
    David 276
    David S. 447
    Miss Evans 447
    Fannie E. (Alkinson)
        277
    June 447
    Mary A. (Williams)
        387
    Massey 387
·   Samuel 276
    Sarah (Scott) 276
    Sarah A. (Boone) 447
    William J. 445, 446,
        447
PHILLIPS, William J., Jr.
        Judge 445, 446, 447
PIEDRAS, -- 26
PIERCE, Angy E. (Exall)
        300
    Collie Frank 438
    Fannie (Appling-
        Ussery) 438
    Franklin 63, 101, 126,
        183, 357, 446
    John King 433, 434
    Joseph 301
    Robert William 433,
        434, 435, 436, 437,
        438
    Sarah Oldham (Finch)
        433
PIERSON, Lt. Col. 294
PILSBURY, T., Hon. 86
PIPER, Fredrick A. 297,
        298, 299, 300
    Fredrick William 297
    Johanne (Waldeck) 297
    Minna (Horner) 299
PIRTLE, A. J. 89
    Alwyn 90
    Caroline (Kennedy) 89
    Claudie 90
    J. L. M., Judge 89
    John 90
    Ophelia (Norman) 90
    Staten 90
PITTS, Drusilla (O'Neal)
        273, 274
    Elizabeth (Flaitau) 274
    Elizabeth (Hill) 420
    Hardy 273
    Harriet Ann (Hightower)
        273, 274
    John D., General 289
    Julia F. (Carlock) 274
    Leu (Hanson) 274
    Rebecca S. (Kone) 288
    Sarah F. (Harvey) 274
    Thomas M., Dr. 274
    W. H., Major 272, 273
    William 420
POINDEXTER, -- 210
POLK, James K. 358
POLYACKS' BRIGADE 154
POOL, Alfred 165
    Lititia 165
POLLARD, John W. M. 260
    Nancy (Maroney) 260
POLLY, Joseph 370
POPE, -- 46
PORTER, Frances Amanda 146

PORTER (cont.)
  Miss M. M. 146
POSEY, Sarah (Joyce) 398
POTTER, General 287
  Robert 44
POWER, Bille J. (Weatherly)
  154
  Catherine (Willingham)
  154
  Catherine (Samuels)
  154
  Eudora (Blount) 154
  H. L., Rev. 153
  James W. 153, 154
  Julia Ann (Tindall)
  154
  Martha (Falkner) 154
  Mary L. 154
  Sarah (McChristian)
  154
  Strickland 154
POWERS, Charles 265
  Thetis (Clay) 265
PRENTISS, Sargeant S. 459
PRESTON, Henrietta 180
PRICE, Dr. 357
  General 141, 204, 210
  Laura (Donalson) 357
PRIDHAM, Frank R. 365,
  366, 367
  Malinda (Roberts) 365
  Minnie (Owens) 367
  P. U. 365
  Richard Owens 367
PRUIT, Laura 204
RABB, Andrew 373, 374
  David P. 375
  Dulcie (Kennedy) 375
  George F. 375
  George W. 375
  G. T. 375
  Gussie 375
  John 372, 374
  J. W. 375
  L. D. 375
  Marion 375
  Mary (Croft) 375
  Mary (Crownover) 372
  Mary (Smally) 373, 374
  Melissa 375
  Montgomery 374, 375
  Rachel (Newman) 374
  Sallie L. 375
  Thomas 373, 374
  Thomas J., Capt. 373
  Ulysses 374
  Virgil S. 372, 373,
  374, 375
  William 373, 374
RAGAN, Catherine (Webb)
  395
  Daniel, Rev. 395
  Edward H., Hon. 395,
  396, 397, 398
  Ellen (Runkle) 398
  Martha (Rickenbaugh-
  Guthridge) 398
  Sarah N. (Barrow) 396
RAGSDALE, Bettie (Kerr)
  453
  Charles C. 453
  Sarah (Sealorn) 453
RAINBOLT, H. H. 217
RAINEY, Sarah E. (Young)
  439
RALEIGH, Walter Sir 348
RALSTON, Joseph 115
  Louisa (Roberson) 115
RAMON, Capt. 19
RANDOLPH, Permelia (Addis)
  258
RANKIN, John 170
  Louisa 170

RAYBURN, Jennie 124
RAYMOND, N. C. 397
REAMS STATION 301
RECTOR, Margaret Amelia
  (Gregg) 430
  Pendleton 430
REED, Henry W. 305
  Martha 305
  Mary (Simpson) 305
REESE, Alonzo 435
REICHARDT, Bertha
  (Winterfield) 101
  E. 94, 97, 98
  E. W. 101
  Louise 101
  W. E. 101
REMSCHEL, Henry 338
  James Atwood 338
  Katie 338
  May (Knox) 338
  Robert Bailey 338
REUSS, Alfreda (Frobese)
  341
  August J. 341
  Bertha 341
  Gesine (Stubberman)
  340
  Joseph Henry 341
  Joseph M. 340
  Mary (Muller) 340
  Oscar J. 341
  Stephen 340
REYNOLDS, T. J. 274
RICE, Theresa (Armstrong)
  418
RICHARDSON, J. S., Capt.
  171, 291
RICKENBAUGH, Martha
  (Guthridge) 398
RIGAULT, General 21
RILEY, Charles, Judge
  423, 424, 425
  Cora 425
  Edward F. 424
  Estelle (Atkinson) 424
  Ida (Wolters) 424
  Joseph 425
  Lucy (Ennis) 424
  Marion E. 425
  Philip 423, 424
  Rose (Frazier) 424
  Sallie M. (Grigsby)
  424
  Tralucia (Webster) 243
  William 243
ROACH, Ann Le Gare
  (Bellinger) 358
  William 359
ROBERSON, A. J. 114, 115
  Alice Lockett 115
  Anna (Holcomb) 114
  Ella 115
  Eugene 115
  George 115
  Josephine (Depart)
  115
  Mrs. J. E. (Ball) 115
  Julia 115
  Katie (Watson) 115
  Louisa (Ralston) 115
  Ludwick 114
  T. J. 115
ROBERTS, Charles 332
  Malinda (Pridham) 365
  O. M. 47, 206
  Governor 195
ROBERTSON, Miss 202
  Sterling C., Col. 158,
  161
ROBINSON, Andrew, Capt.
  46
  Elizabeth (Burnett)
  386

ROBINSON (cont.)
  James W. 29
  Janie (O'Neil) 355
  Lt. Governor 31, 43
  William 355
ROBISON, Almeida
  (Ledbetter) 409
  America (Olive) 410
  Bettie (Davis) 410
  E. A., Miss (Alexander)
  408, 409
  Fannie (Smith) 409
  F. C. 410
  Halley P. (Carter)
  409, 410
  James Mrs. (Farquhar)
  410
  Joel W. 407, 408, 409,
  410
  J. G. 407, 408, 409
  John B. 410
  Judith (Harwell) 410
  Lucy (McClatchy) 409
  Neil 409
  Samuel A. 409
  Walter 408
RODES, Fannie 137
RODGERS, J. H., Gen. 69
ROGERS, B. A., Rev. 427
  Fannie G. (Stroud)
  253
  John 253
  Joseph 308
ROSE, Victor M. 366
ROSBOROUGH, Eli 318
  Ibby Yancy (Craig) 318
  James F. 317
  J. F., Dr. 317, 318
  Thomas 318
  Wyatt James 318
ROSS'S BRIGADE 135
ROSS, General 378
  Governor 153, 223
  L. S. 47
  Mat., Capt. 249, 418
  Rebecca (Maxey) 249
ROUL, Mr. 353
  Fredonia Jane (Ballard)
  353
ROWAN, William 332
ROWELL, Albert 233
  Albert H. 232, 233
  Agusta (Kimball) 122
  Charles A. 122
  Ella (Grambling) 233
  Elizabeth (Walton) 233
  Emma 233
  Eugenia 233
  George 232
  Gussie 122
  Howell 232
  Lizzie 122
  Mary (Laurence) 233
  Mattie (Grigsby) 233
  Mollie 122
  P. H. 233
  Robert 233
  Robert E., Dr. 121,
  122
  Tobitha (Driskell) 232
  Willie I. 233
  Zula 122
ROWLEY, Sarah E. 180
  Timothy T. 180
RUFF, Colonel 249
RUNKEL, Ellen (Ragan) 398
RUNNELS, H. R. 47
  Harrison B. 64
RUSK, General 38, 71
  T. J., General 147
  Thomas J. 44
RUSSELL, Alice Ione
  (Hallet) 353

13

RUSSELL (cont.)
Allen 255
Annie 255
Annie H. (Benton) 254
Ellen C. (Carter) 255
Harriet (Chaison) 164
Helen Lady (Marr) 255
Louella 255
Louisa (Grimes) 255
Maggie 255
Mary 255
Mossie 255
Robert C. 253
Rosser 255
Samuel M., Rev. 254
Simeon 255
Spurgeon 255
W. I. F., Rev. 254
W. A. 164
William 255
RYAN, Catherine (Hart)
364
Nancy (Armstrong) 419
Joseph 364
SADDLER, R. 451
SALCEDO, Don Nemisio 22
SALTILLO, -- 65
SAMUELS, Catherine
(Power) 154
James 154
SANDOVAL, Colonel 29
SANFIELD, Leon, Rev. 295
Mattie C. (Chapman)
295
SANTA ANNA, -- 26, 27, 28,
29, 31, 32, 35, 37,
39, 41, 43, 78, 148,
166, 186, 189, 190,
240, 333, 383, 403,
407, 408, 446
SAUNDERS, Lucy (Killough)
412
Mary V. (Boyd) 165
W. H. 165, 412
SAYERS, Joseph D., Hon.
169
SCAGGS, Martha 77
SCHOPIN, Dr. 208
SCHLUTER, A. H. 321
Augustus H. 322
F. A. 322
SCHURENBERG, F. W. 101
Bertha (Reichardt) 101
SCHUPERT, Dr. 208
SCOVELL, T. H. 462
SCOTT, David 276
John 276
General 273
Sarah (Phillips) 276
Sir Walter 358
William 276
Winfield, General 314
SEALORN, Sarah (Ragsdale)
453
SEELHORST, Adolph 101
Louise (Reichardt) 101
SEWELL, Louisa F.
(Neighbora) 341
James A. 342
SHEA'S BATTALION 340
SHAW, Catherine (Marshall)
267
SHAY'S BATTALION 353
SHEETS, Abbie (Harrison)
440
SHELLBORNE, Calpernia
(Bell) 416
James H. 417
SHELBY, Leola (Dubois)
378
Dr. 378
SHEPHERD, J. L. 331, 332
Mary E. (Eldridge) 252

SHERMAN, Col. 37
Sidney, General 54,
294
SHIELDS, -- 41
SHRIEVE, William 282
SHROPSHIRE, Annie 349
W., Dr. 349
SIBLEY'S BRIGADE 366, 436
SIBLEY, (Confederate) 42
Eugene 423
F. E. 423
Ida (Sterne) 423
Major 451, 452
Minnie (Sterne) 423
Ann (Lord) 327
SIMMONS, Anna (Burnett)
386
Mary (Waul) 307
SIMMS, William Gilmore
359
SIMPSON, Mary Dorsey 304
Mary (Reed) 305
S. P. 304, 305
Sidney 304
SINGLETON, Anna Barbee
209
Eliza J. (Harris) 211
Earl 211
Earnest 211
Ellie (Largent) 211
Hal. 211
Marvin 211
Minor W. 209
Robert 211
Samuel 209
Sarah Ann (Darr) 209
William E. 209, 210,
211
SKAGGS, Abram 413, 414
Eliza Jane (Myers) 413
SLOUGH, Col. 42
Mary E. (Hynes) 247
SMALLEY, Mary (Rabb) 373
SMITH, Miss 204
Callie (Davidson) 421
Capt. 158
Emily Agnes (Lord) 333
Erastus 306
Fannie (Robison) 409
French (Col.) 195
Grace (Beasley) 208
Gray Miss. (Burges)
363
George P. 363
Governor 31, 43, 175
H. N. 333
Harvey B. (Mrs.)
(O'Brien) 180
Henry 29, 43, 44, 47
James 158
J. W., Dr. 409
Kate (Beasley) 208
Kirby, General 43, 106,
461
Marshal 203
Mary (Smith-Hail) 158
Martha (Lockett) 203
Morgan L., Col. 79
Rhoda (Boone) 414
S. W. 444
Thomas I., Capt. 40
SMITHERS, William 370
SMOTHERS, -- 378
SPAIGHT'S REGIMENT 179
SPENCE, John 464
Margaret R. (Hicks)
464
SPELLING, Carrie (Thomas)
220
Herbert 220
Leslie Hartwell 220
Roy Earl 220
SPELLINGS, Benjamine

SPELLINGS (cont.)
Benjamine Fisher (cont.)
219
Fred 220
Louisa (Guest) 219,
220
Soloman A. 219, 220
SPILLARD, Virginia M.
(Julian) 432
STALLCUP, Betsey (McAdor)
238
Mary Gray 239
Sallie Gray (Durvum)
239
Sallie Irby 239
Thomas H., Dr. 238,
239
Tommie Hardin 239
William 238
STANDIFER, Mr. 307
STANFIELD, Emily (Joyce)
400
S. W., Professor 400
STANLEY, Jacob 75
Jane 75
STANSBERRY, William 62
STARK, Neal 180
STAYTON, R. W., Col. 459
ST. CLOUGH, -- 437
ST. DENIS, -- 20
STEEL, Mr. 399
Mary (Webster) 243
STEELE, William 243
STERNE, Andrew G. 423
Araminta (Cunningham)
423
Ford 423
Ida (Sibley) 423
Jane (Guthrie) 422
Mary E. (Jones) 423
May (Sullivan) 423
Minnie (Sibley) 423
Sadie 423
Thomas 422
Thomas, Jr. 421, 422,
423
Wilson C. 423
STEVENS, Eliza 171
STEWART, Charles, Hon.
315, 316, 317
John S. 317
Rachel (Barry) 317
STITCH, Ferdinand 89
Sallie (Hawkins) 89
STONE, Barton W., Elder
356
J. A. 381
STORY, L. J. 384
STOWES, Mrs. 431
STRONG, Commander 42
Sarah (Cummins) 411
STROTHER, Mr. 307, 308
STROUD, A. D., Dr. 252,
253, 254
Albert Sidney 254
Alpheus D., Jr. 254
E. C., Mrs. (Hearne)
253
Fannie C. 254
Fannie G. (Rogers) 253
John P. 254
Mark, Hon. 252
Mattie 254
Pattie (Forman) 254
Sarah (Trammell) 252
Work 254
STUBBERMAN, Gesine (Reuss)
340
SUDDITH, James 450
Temperance (McCutchen)
450
William 450
SULLIVAN, H. P. 423

14

SULLIVAN (cont.)
  May (Sterne) 423
SUTHERLAND, Agnes 288
  Ann Bryant (Lane) 287
  Ann M. (Dickson) 287
  Annie 288
  Diana (Kennedy) 286
  David 286
  Fredrick 288
  George Q. 287
  Jack Sutherlin 286,
    287, 288
  Jack 287
  Jack Jr. 288
  James 286
  John 286, 287, 288
  Levin L. 287, 288
  Lizzie 288
  Lucy 288
  Mamie 288
  Mary E. (Sutherland)
    288
  Sarah Agnes 286
  Walter 288
  Winnifred 288
  William, Dr. 288
SWEITZER, Dr. 194
SWINDALL, Amy (Hynes) 245
SWISHER, James G., Capt.
    313
  James M. 313
  John M. 313
  "Milt", Col. 313
SYLVESTER, -- 408
TAGGART, Elizabeth (Knox)
    336
TALKINGTON, Margaret 133
TALMAN, Nancy W. (Hart)
    303
TARLTON, Colonel 361
TAYLOR, Amelia 106
  Ann (Mathews) 172
  Charles S. 106
  Christine 113
  Colonel 231
  Cook, Mrs. (nee
    Coleman) 133
  Dick, General 69
  E. W. 173
  F. M. 173
  Frank 173
  H. L. 173
  Holman 113
  James F., Hon. 113
  J. H., Dr. 113
  Job, Dr. 131, 132, 172
  John B. 173
  Mabel 113
  Marion DeKalb, Hon.
    172
  Mary 173
  Mary B. (Holman) 113
  Mary B. (Watson) 291
  Margaret Ann
    (Talkington) 133
  Matilda G. (Cotton) 132
  Matt. 173
  Mollie A. (Howard) 113
  Moses 132
  Mittie 133
  Pinkie (McNeil) 445
  Richard, Gen. 169, 232,
    383, 445, 446
  R. R. 173
  Sarah Elizabeth
    (McDaniel) 173
  Thomas H. 131, 132,
    133
  Ward 172
  Zachary, Gen. 41, 174,
    383
TENORIO, Capt. 28
TERAN, Domingo 46

TERAN (cont.)
  Manuel Mier Y. 25
TERRY, Louise 136
TERRY'S RANGERS 337, 346,
    375, 392, 404
TEUTSCH, Leona (Mast)
    206
  William 206
THOMAS, Carrie (Spelling)
    220
  David 44
  Lou V. 348
  Nathan 348, 349
  P., Dr. 136
THOMPSON, Evelyn 135
  J. M. M. 332
  Waddy, Gen. 330
THRALL, Homer S., Rev.
    434, 436
  Mrs. 436
THRIFT, Delia (Pettey)
    256
THROCKMORTON, James W. 47
THORNHILL, Dr. 264
  Pauline (Clay) 264
THURMAN, Mr. -- 321
  Alexander 321
  Allen G. 319
  C. M. (Nichols) 319
  Gen. Charles 321
  Ed. R. 321
  Galdie 320
  Mary Cox 319
  Samuel 319, 320, 321,
    322
  Theo. 320
  Zan. 320
TIEMAN, George 337
TINDALL, Julia Ann 154
TODD, Alexander Miller
    152
  Charles C. 152
  Eddie (Van Dyke) 152
  Eliza A. (Hudgins)
    150
  Eva 152
  George T. 150
  George Thomas, Capt.
    149, 150, 151, 152
  Lula 152
  Marion B. (Miller)
    152
  May 152
  Van Dyke 152
  William, Judge 150
  William H. 152
TOLBERT, -- 328
TONTI, Lt. 20
TOLLE, Mary Ann (Hilliard)
    156
TORNEL, Senor 32
TORREY, -- 331, 332
TOWNSEND, Mrs. T. L. 180
TRAMMELL, F. A., Dr. 253
  Sarah (Stroud) 252
TRAVIS, -- 26, 32, 35,
    36, 287, 344
  W. B. 28, 112
TRESPALACIOS, -- 24, 46
TRIBOLD, Mary
    (Umbdenstock) 193
TROUTMAN, Miss 46
TURNBULL, James 331, 332
TURNER, Amanda F.
    (Eldridge) 250
  Christian 376
  Lena 378
  Louis 376, 377, 378
  Mary (Butterman) 376
  Ida (Edison) 378
  Josephine (Bragger-
    Dubois) 378
TWIGGS, General 41, 42

UGARTECHEA, Gen. 28, 29,
    30
UMBDENSTOCK, John 192
  Mary (Tribold) 193
  Sallie (Barta) 192
  William 192, 193
URREA, General 32, 35,
    36, 189
USSERY, Mastin 438
  Sarah Gane (Martin)
    438
VAN ALSTINE, -- 97
VAN DORN, -- 177, 220
  General 175
VAN DYKE, Eddie 152
  L. D. 152
VAN NESS, Ann (Palmer)
    145
  Benjamin 145
  Delia (Bishop) 145
  Frances Amanda (Porter)
    146
  Henrietta 146
  Isaac 145
  James A. 146
  John 145
  Julius B. 144, 145,
    146
  Laura L. 146
  Lillie (Futrell) 123
  Llewellyn 146
  Mrs. M. M. (Porter)
    146
  Olin 146
  Theodore E. 146
VANN, William 123
VASQUEZ, Rafael, Gen. 39
VEHLEIN, Burnett 206
  Joseph 24, 206
VERAMENDI, Miss. 110
VIDAURI, Francisco 47
VIESCA, Jose Maria 47,
    201
VINSON, E. W. 232
  Katie (Burnett) 232
WADSWORTH, Martha (Crow)
    136
WALDECK, Johanna (Pipes)
    297
WALDRON, Ann (rosborough)
    318
  Frank 318
WALKER, Andrew, Capt. 196
  Division 339
  Dr. 350
  Esther (Houston) 196
  John S., Capt. 206
  S. H. 329
WALKI, Callie (McArthur)
    463
  Clara (Hicks) 463
WALL, Nettie (Cooper) 297
  W. B., Judge 297
WALLACE, Alexander, Hon.
    284
  Betsie (Kerr) 450
  Ianthe J. (Anderson)
    284
  John 450
WALLER'S BATTALION 354
WALLIS, Big Foot 379
WALTERS, John 308
WALTON, Elizabeth (Rowell)
    232
  Isaac 232
WANGEMAN, Adam 119, 120,
    121
  Arthur 121
  Mrs. F. (Kling) 120,
    121
WARD, Fannie (Garland-
    Drake) 185
  Frances (Rhodes) 185

15

WARD (cont.)
  Lt. Colonel 46
  Mat. Colonel 184, 185
  Mathias 184
  Sarah (Blythe-
    Harrison) 185
  Sally (Blythe) 184
  Sally (Saunders-Blythe)
    326
  Samuel M. 184, 185
  Sammie Theodocia 185
  W. B. 326
  William 184, 326
  William Blythe 185
  Woodie May 185
  Mrs. Woodie E. (Brown)
    185
  Zue (Aiken) 185, 327
WARE, A. G., Col. 65
  Frances A. (Blocker)
    177
  Henry 177
  Levi H., Dr. 226
  Louisa 65
  Sallie (Flanaghan) 226
WARNER, Emma (Exall) 301
WASHINGTON, -- 170, 362
  George 234, 358
  William, Col. 361
WATSON, Archibald 115
  Arthur O. 242
  A. W. 242
  D. H. 242
  Emma (Knittle) 223
  George W. 291, 292
  John P. 242
  Katie (Roberson) 115
  Marietta (Mathews) 292
  Mary B. (Taylor) 291
  Stanley 242
  Thomas 223
  William, Sr. 241, 242
  William Edward 242
  William P. 291
WAUL, General 221
  Mary (Simmons) 307
  Thomas Neville, Gen.
    155, 306
WEATHERLY, Belle J.
    (Power) 154
  William 154
WEAVER, W. G. 361
WEBB, Arbuckle and Co. 298
  Catherine (Regan) 395
  John 396
  L. A., Rev. 203
  Willie (Marks) 203
WEBBER, Mr. 308
WEBSTER, Daniel 455
  J. B. 243
  J. J. 243
  Louis 243
  Louis, Jr. 243
  Lyda Mae 243
  Mary (Steele) 243
  Traclucia (Rives) 243
WELLER, Sarah Ann
    (McLeary) 455
WELLS, Samuel 110
WERNER, -- 155
WEST, Bridget (Hart) 364
  O. F. 364
  V. M. 299
WESSON, James, Rev. 434
WHALING, Henry 331, 332
WHARTON, Wm. H. 27, 30
WHEELER, A. L. 448
  Amanda 448
  Bethel 448
  Ella 449
  Emma A. (Arnim) 448
  Katie 449
  Katie (Church) 447

WHEELER (cont.)
  Leslie 449
  Margaret 449
  Martha 448
  James 448
  John 448
  Richard 447, 448, 449
  Sarah A. (Garen) 448
  William H. 447, 448,
    449
  William, Jr. 449
WHITE, A. C. 379
  Eliza J. (Ford) 234,
    235
  General 62
  James S. 235
  J. H. 379
  Lizzie (Pettey) 257
  Louisa Cole (Odom) 379
  Maggie 379
  Raymond G. 379
  William 379
WHITFIELD'S LEGION 134,
    376
WHITTIER, John G. 431
WIGFALL, Lewis T., Col.
    151
WIGGINTON, Col. 328
WILBARGER, Harvey 309
  John 309
  John L. 313, 314
  Josiah 307, 308, 309,
    310
WILDEY, Thomas 321
WILKEMAN, Katie (Hodde)
    156
  William 156
WILKINS, Beersheba
    (Lusk) 131
  Elizabeth (Allen) 130
  James A., Hon. 129,
    130, 131
  J. B. 130
  Wallace 131
WILKINSON, Leela 66, 77
WILLIAMS, Catherine
    (Coffee) 387
  Ezekiel 360
  Hezekiah 237
  James 387
  Jane (Myers) 415
  J. H. 415
  John 387, 388
  Mary A. (Phillips) 387
  Rachel (McFadden) 237
  Samuel 28
  Mrs. V. A. (Eldridge)
    251
  William D. 387
WILLIAMSON, R. M. 28
WILMERDING, Mrs. (Gregg)
    430
WILLINGHAM, Catherine 154
  Nancy 154
  William 154
WILSON, -- 206
  Charolette (Gregg) 430
  Hugh, Dr. 372
  Rachel 148
  Robert 44
  Sarah (Hollock) 430
  Sarah (Little) 372
WINDER, General 294
WING, M. C. 332
WINTERFELD, Bertha 101
WISE, General 208
WOLF, General 194
  Yellow 312
WOLL, -- General 40
WOLTERS, Ida (Riley) 424
  Robert 424
WORTH, General 41
WOODALL, Frances B.

WOODALL (cont.)
  Frances B. (Hallet)
    (cont.) 353
  M. B. 352
WOODRUFF, Capt. L. T. 107
WOOD, Benjamin 259
  George T. 47
  Kate 259
  Meriah E. (Jones) 191
  Marian (Pettey) 256
  Mrs. S. A. (McNeeley)
    260
  W. A. 269
WOODS, Ella R. (Ogletree)
    351
  Georgia (Lawshe) 351
  M. A. (Bethany) 417
  Peter C., Dr. 350, 351
  Regiment 346
  Sarah W. (Davidson)
    350
WOODYARD, J. B. 448
WOOL, J. E 332
WORTHINGTON, John 321
WRIGHT, Joseph 202
  Mary (Knox) 336
  Norris, Major 110
  Rebecca L. (Marhs) 202
  R. N., Dr. 276
WURZBACH, C. L., Judge
    457
WYER, L. Father, Rev. 278
  Lawrence 278
  Mary Bridget (McAleny)
    278
WYNNE, W. L., Dr. 238
YORK, Capt. 407
YOUNG, Electa (Alexander)
    439
  Fannie (Hampton-
    Gibson) 438, 439
  Fannie M. (Kemper) 440
  Frank E. 439
  Hugh F. 438
  Hugh Hampton 440
  Mary C. 85
  Newton Alexander 439
  Sarah E. (Rainey) 439
  William 85
  William Hugh General
    438, 439, 440
ZACATECAS, -- 31
ZAMBRANO, Juan 23, 28
ZAVALA, -- 44
ZUMWALT, Adam 360